TAKING LAW SERIOUSLY

This book celebrates the scholarship of Peter Cane. The significance and scale of his contributions to the discipline of law over the last half-century cannot be overstated. In an era of increasing specialisation, Cane stands out on account of the unusually broad scope of his interests, which extend to both private and public law in equal measure. This substantive breadth is combined with remarkable doctrinal, historical, comparative and theoretical depth. This book is written by admirers of Cane's work, and the essays probe a wide range of issues, especially in administrative law and tort law. Consistent with the international prominence that Cane's research has enjoyed, the contributors are drawn from across the common law world. The volume will be of value to anyone who is interested in Cane's towering contributions to legal scholarship and administrative law and tort law more generally.

Taking Law Seriously

Essays in Honour of Peter Cane

Edited by
James Goudkamp
Mark Lunney
and
Leighton McDonald

•HART•
OXFORD • LONDON • NEW YORK • NEW DELHI • SYDNEY

HART PUBLISHING

Bloomsbury Publishing Plc

Kemp House, Chawley Park, Cumnor Hill, Oxford, OX2 9PH, UK

1385 Broadway, New York, NY 10018, USA

29 Earlsfort Terrace, Dublin 2, Ireland

First published in Great Britain 2021

A catalogue record for this book is available from the British Library.

Library of Congress Cataloging-in-Publication data

Names: Cane, Peter, 1950- Honouree. | Goudkamp, James, 1980- editor. | Lunney, Mark, editor. | McDonald, Leighton, editor.

Title: Taking law seriously / edited by James Goudkamp, Mark Lunney and Leighton McDonald.

Description: Oxford, UK ; New York, NY : Hart Publishing, an imprint of Bloomsbury Publishing, 2021. | Includes bibliographical references and index.

Identifiers: LCCN 2021042205 (print) | LCCN 2021042206 (ebook) | ISBN 9781509940721 (hardback) | ISBN 9781509956074 (paperback) | ISBN 9781509940745 (pdf) | ISBN 9781509940738 (Epub)

Subjects: LCSH: Law—English-speaking countries. | Torts—English-speaking countries. | Administrative law—English-speaking countries. | Cane, Peter, 1950-

Classification: LCC K561 .T35 2021 (print) | LCC K561 (ebook) | DDC 340—dc23/eng/20211014

LC record available at https://lccn.loc.gov/2021042205

LC ebook record available at https://lccn.loc.gov/2021042206

ISBN: HB: 978-1-50994-072-1
ePDF: 978-1-50994-074-5
ePub: 978-1-50994-073-8

Typeset by Compuscript Ltd, Shannon

FOREWORD

It is a deep pleasure to be able to introduce this fine collection of essays in honour of Peter Cane. The task of assembling a collection suitable to both the range and the quality of Peter's work over the course of his distinguished career must have been a significant challenge; but it is one to which the editors have risen magnificently. Right across the broad terrain of Peter's scholarship: constitutional and administrative law; the law of torts, alongside a range of compensation and insurance schemes with cognate concerns; jurisprudence; the structure, history and impact of legal ideas and institutions: the authors have truly done their subject justice.

The scope of the essays included in the volume makes it difficult to encapsulate their contribution – like that of their subject – in any integrated, thematic way. In this brief introductory appreciation, I will therefore focus my remarks on just a few of the many reasons which make Peter such a worthy recipient of this celebration volume; and on some aspects of his work which have had particular significance for me personally.

It probably makes sense to begin with the academic world of the late 1970s in which Peter's career began. When he took up his Fellowship at Corpus Christi College Oxford in 1978, it was usual for an Oxford law tutor to teach across four or even five of the core subjects in the undergraduate curriculum; and perfectly respectable to make a career focused on teaching, perhaps interspersed with the publication of case notes, reviews and the occasional journal article. From the perspective of the increasingly research-oriented and specialised structure of legal scholarship and indeed teaching today, this world looks extraordinarily remote. I recall an unusually research-minded colleague taking me aside, early in my own academic journey in the mid-1980s, and advising me that if I wanted to build a good career, I must streamline my teaching down to the subjects in which I intended to focus my research. By the early 1990s, this revolution in the UK legal academy was more or less complete, spurred on by the invention of national Research Assessment. The typical Oxford tutor was teaching perhaps one or at most two core subjects and possibly an optional course or two, close to their research interests. Very, very few legal academics continued to work across a range of doctrinal fields; and the number who combined this breadth with the publication of truly original scholarship vanishingly small. Indeed, it is hard to think of anyone other than Peter who was able to pull off this extraordinarily difficult feat; and certainly no one else has done so with such consistency and over such a long period of time. He is, truly, a renaissance scholar of the field.

Doubtless the specialisation of the academy has had some benefits. But Peter's remarkable scholarly output reminds us, I think, of what has been lost in the rush to hone our focus on our specialist fields. Unlike practitioners, who understand very well that legal problems do not organise themselves along the lines of conveniently delineated fields of doctrine, one of the ironies of the legal academy has been that the very period which has seen a diversification of methods and a burgeoning of innovative and even multi-disciplinary approaches to legal scholarship, has also seen an increase in the balkanisation of the terrain of the conventional common law classifications. One of the huge strengths of Peter's work has always been his acute sensibility to the interaction between, for example, the broadly conceived tort and public law fields which have been his principal substantive interest, while also being attentive to the distinctive institutional logics which shape particular fields of law. In a remarkable way, he has been able to combine a vast amount of detailed exposition, systematisation and 'mapping' of the field – for example through his work on a number of textbooks, handbooks and companions – with scholarship which has genuinely pushed forward and redrawn the boundaries of the discipline. Combined also with his quite exemplary contribution to institution-building – notably but of course not exclusively at both the Research School of Social Sciences and the College of Law at the Australian National University and through the Australasian Association for Legal Philosophy – Peter's work reflects not only a singular range of intellectual and communicative talents but also a quite prodigious work ethic.

Peter's work has been of particular significance for me at a number of stages. As a result of the teaching culture already mentioned, I found myself catapulted into teaching second-year administrative law in Oxford: a particular challenge since I had myself studied administrative law only as a small part of a first-year constitutional law course. It was the mid-1980s, and a period in which, as a result of the efforts of a series of ministers in the Thatcher administration, practically every week seemed to throw up a new judicial review case. I remember Peter's marvellously incisive yet economical *An Introduction to Administrative Law* (1986) – the very paradigm of a Clarendon Law Series text as originally conceived by its founder, HLA Hart – as an absolute lifesaver, giving me as well as the students (!) an elegant map of how the field fitted together; a clear and thoughtful account of the key issues and cases; and some critical ideas about the field, all within the compass of a mere 318 pages. As textbooks become ever longer and more elaborate, Peter's book stands in my mind as the model of a book from which to teach gifted undergraduates.

Although we were colleagues in Oxford for more than a decade, it was really at ANU that I had the opportunity to form a close intellectual relationship with Peter, amid the relaxed yet invigorating environment of the RSSS where we were (part-time) colleagues for several years. As good luck would have it, we were both working on projects on responsibility in which, albeit in somewhat different ways, we were questioning the analytical/philosophical paradigm which had dominated treatments of this concept which was so central to a number of legal fields. It was an incredible pleasure and privilege to be able to have lengthy and regular discussions – often on the terrace at the Coombs building – exchanging ideas as our projects developed. Peter's book, *Responsibility in Law and Morality* (2002) bears all the hallmarks of his scholarship; its pellucid clarity of structure and exposition; its innovative range in pushing analysis of responsibility beyond the criminal law and into civil and public law; and, best of all, its boldness of vision. This is reflected in Peter's insistence that once one looks at the issues from an adequately institutional and comparative point of view, one sees not only the different significance of responsibility in different areas of law, but also the interactive and complementary relationship between legal and moral understandings of responsibility in particular fields, as opposed to the common vision of morality as the critical standard against which the law should be judged. It is a book which is seldom far from my desk, and to which I return regularly: it has a very special place in my lexicon of key works in legal scholarship.

Rarely can any university have pulled off such a hiring coup as ANU accomplished in recruiting Peter and Jane (Stapleton) in 1997. But I think it is fair to say that the move gave Peter not only the time but also the research environment in which to develop his ideas in a way which would have been much more difficult in Oxford or any other British university of the time. It was a marvellous thing to watch Peter making the most of the multi-disciplinary environment of the Research School, while steadfastly defending and advancing the interests and reputation of legal scholarship, and providing generous support and mentoring to younger colleagues in both Research School and Faculty (as it then was). *The Political Economy of Personal Injury Law* (2007) and the subsequent development of his (broadly speaking) public law scholarship in both comparative and historical directions, leading inter alia to *Controlling Administrative Power* (2016), are, I think, in part a legacy of that time. I have followed this work, too, with interest and admiration. So, in concluding this brief foreword, I simply thank Peter for his inspiration, friendship and collegiality, and tell him that I look forward to whatever is coming next …

Nicola Lacey
March 2021

PREFACE

It is an enormous privilege for us to be able to commemorate Peter Cane by way of this collection of essays. All three of us have co-authored works with Peter and have had the immense benefit of his advice and mentoring as colleagues and friends. We have been struck throughout this project by how many of the contributors have also been enriched both by Peter's friendship and through his role as a facilitative critic. Like us, some of the contributors have worked with Peter as a co-author or otherwise have participated in projects he managed. All of them have been inspired by the brilliance, creativity and rigour of his scholarship. In whatever way we have come across Peter's work, we have seen how his scholarship reflects his commitment to the importance of law as an academic discipline. For Peter, law matters.

As Nicola Lacey notes in her foreword, one of the most remarkable features of Peter's scholarship is its combination of breadth and depth. Few, if any, scholars have illuminated the traditional territory of both public and private law with such imagination and insight. Even more impressively, that illumination has been shone from doctrinal, comparative, empirical, historical and theoretical perspectives. For this reason, it was never going to be possible to reflect the full range of Peter's scholarly interests and achievements within the covers of a single volume. Accordingly, contributors to this collection were given essentially free rein to decide how they wished to engage with Peter's scholarship. Nevertheless, their essays are a testament to the variety of subject matter and methodological sophistication evident in Peter's oeuvre.

While the book is broken up into several sections for convenience, it will be apparent that the boundaries between the sections are somewhat porous. This is as it should be, for Peter's own work defies neat classification. Consider one of his most important and inspiring books, *Responsibility in Law and Morality*. On one level, the book is theoretical, a critique of agency-centred moral philosophy in light of the law's own responsibility practices. Tony Connolly's contribution deals with this aspect of the book. Yet the unpacking of the law's responsibility practices sheds important light on both public and private law. While his authorship of influential textbooks regarding tort and administrative law shows consummate command of the often dense and confusing details of the law, his overarching purpose in these works was always to provide ways of thinking about the law. Underlying themes are teased out, reasons for rules identified and connections between different areas explored irrespective of whether established doctrine recognises them. And his analysis of the law is routinely and deftly informed by insights from various perspectives. It is unsurprising that these books have provided generations of scholars and students with pathways to developing their own understandings of the law.

In *Controlling Administrative Power: An Historical Comparison*, Peter paints on a large canvas with a broad brush to reveal an innovative and richly suggestive explanatory account of the structure and norms of administrative law. As Jerry Mashaw notes in his essay, Peter's magisterial analysis considers differences in the regimes for the control of administrative power in several common law jurisdictions by reference to divergences in the tendency of 'systems of government' to concentrate or diffuse political power.

From his *Key Ideas in Tort Law*, which forms the subject of Stephen Sugarman's essay, to his taking over the authorship of Patrick Atiyah's *Accidents, Compensation and the Law*, to his editorships (among many collections) of *The New Oxford Companion to Law*, *The Oxford Handbook of Legal Studies*, *The Oxford Handbook of Empirical Legal Studies* and the forthcoming *Cambridge Legal History of Australia*, the pluralism that underpins so much of Peter's scholarship shines through. For Peter, law is a human artefact, constructed as a compromise between many divergent views as to the law's purpose and function. This orientation also explains his preference for non-essentialist approaches to the study of the nature of the law and legal systems more generally.

This collection was conceived in the pre-Covid world and the pandemic significantly affected its development. As editors, we are grateful to contributors who, despite the challenges, have produced a collection of which we hope Peter is proud. We would also like to thank the team at Hart Publishing. In particular, we are grateful to Sasha Jawed, whose sleuth work allowed us to use the cover image of the collection, and whose unfailing patience, good humour and good sense have brought this project to a conclusion with much less stress than might otherwise have been the case. We are also grateful to Sophie Hepburn, Eleni Katsampouka and Peta Lisle who provided us with editorial assistance.

There is always the risk that a Festschrift is seen as the end of the road for its subject, a celebratory but somewhat wistful look backwards to past glories. This collection is certainly a celebration of an extraordinary academic career but, fortunately for all, Peter shows no sign of putting the cue in the rack. We look forward to more of the outstanding work that prompted this collection.

Finally, as anyone who has ever had a conversation with Peter knows – whether that conversation be about one's own work, his work or about the world and life beyond the realm of legal scholarship – one leaves brimming with ideas, energised and with renewed resolve. We offer this collection, then, not only as an appreciation for his remarkable contributions to legal scholarship but also as a celebration of Peter, the complete person. While Peter's work has immeasurably enhanced our stock of ideas about law and its relationship with society, his professional and personal interactions have enriched and inspired all those who have had the very good fortune to work with him or to get to know him.

Peter, on behalf of all the contributors (and many more besides), we salute you!

James Goudkamp
Mark Lunney
Leighton McDonald

CONTENTS

CONTRIBUTORS

TRS Allan FBA is Professor of Jurisprudence and Public Law at the University of Cambridge and a Fellow of Pembroke College, Cambridge.

Christine Beuermann is Senior Lecturer at Newcastle University.

Anthony J Connolly is Professor at the Australian National University College of Law.

James Goudkamp is Professor of the Law of Obligations at the University of Oxford and a Fellow and Tutor in Law at Keble College, Oxford.

Elizabeth Fisher is Professor of Environmental Law at the University of Oxford and a Fellow and Tutor in Law at Corpus Christi College, Oxford.

Carol Harlow QC FBA is Emeritus Professor of Law at the London School of Economics and Political Science.

Nicola Lacey FBA CBE is School Professor of Law, Gender and Social Policy at the London School of Economics and Political Science.

Mark Lunney FAAL is Professor of Tort Law at King's College London and Professor of Law at the University of New England.

Leighton McDonald is Professor at the Australian National University College of Law.

Jerry L Mashaw is Sterling Professor Emeritus of Law and Professorial Lecturer in Law at Yale Law School.

Janet McLean QC FRSNZ is Professor of Law at the University of Auckland.

Donal Nolan is Professor of Private Law at the University of Oxford and Francis Reynolds and Clarendon Fellow and Tutor in Law at Worcester College, Oxford.

Sandy Steel is Associate Professor of Law at the University of Oxford and a Fellow and Tutor in Law at Wadham College, Oxford.

Jenny Steele is Professor of Law, University of York.

Stephen D Sugarman is Roger J Traynor Professor of Law at UC Berkeley School of Law.

TABLE OF CASES

Australia

Canada

European Court of Justice/European Court of Human Rights

New Zealand

United Kingdom

United States

TABLE OF LEGISLATION

Australia

United Kingdom

Statutes

Statutory Instruments

Germany

New Zealand

United States

TABLE OF INTERNATIONAL MATERIALS

PART I

Private Law

1

Tort Law Beyond the Forms of Action: Achieving the Goal of *The Anatomy of Tort Law*

CHRISTINE BEUERMANN

I. Introduction

Peter set himself an enormous challenge in *The Anatomy of Tort Law* (*Anatomy*):[1] to move our understanding of tort law beyond the original formulae that had been used to describe that liability (in some cases, for centuries). Although he failed in this endeavour, he failed magnificently. His many invaluable insights into the law of torts remain at the forefront of both legal theorising and judicial decision making some 20 years after the book's publication.

This chapter will examine why *Anatomy* was unable to shift our thinking about the law of torts beyond the various formulae used to describe those torts. It may seem churlish in the circumstances to focus on *Anatomy's* failures, rather than its successes. The task Peter set himself in writing *Anatomy*, however, was an important one.

Section II of this chapter examines Peter's reasons for trying to move beyond a formulaic to a more systematic understanding of the law of torts. It argues that those reasons remain not only valid, but urgent. Peter reconstructed the law of torts in *Anatomy* in order to promote this more systematic understanding. Section III will explore his key insights into the law of torts, including the distinction between the backward-looking (dispute resolution) and forward-looking (conduct guidance) functions of tort law and the balance struck by judges between the different parties to the dispute. Section IV considers why *Anatomy* failed in its principal goal of moving our understanding of tort law beyond the series of discrete formulae used to describe the torts. Particular attention will be paid to the extent that the forward-looking functions of tort law were prioritised in *Anatomy* over the backward-looking functions. The final section of the chapter contemplates what it might actually take to achieve the goal Peter set himself in *Anatomy*.

[1] P Cane, *The Anatomy of Tort Law* (Oxford, Hart Publishing, 1997).

The answer, it is suggested, lies in adopting a more process-oriented approach to the role of judges and the judicial tools used to strike a balance between the interests of the parties to the dispute.

II. Need for a More Systematic Approach to Tort Law

In addition to the benefits of viewing tort law more holistically as a 'system of ethical rules and principles of personal responsibility for conduct',[2] Peter outlined five distinct reasons in *Anatomy* why it was important to move beyond a formulaic understanding of the law of torts.[3] In summary, those reasons were:[4]

- the potentially misleading nature of negligence as a 'single legal formula' for liability;
- the tendency to conceal important organising categories;
- potential overlap between different torts;
- difficulties in understanding the relationship between the law of torts and other areas of law; and
- difficulties reforming the law.

A brief review of some of the more significant developments in the law of torts since *Anatomy* was published suggests that the courts have been working towards addressing such concerns but have made relatively little progress in so doing.

Consider first the tort of negligence. Peter demonstrated in *Anatomy* that the 'tort of negligence protects various interests differently'.[5] It followed that it was potentially misleading to treat the tort of negligence as a 'single legal formula'.[6] This observation is an important backdrop to the recent series of cases in which the Supreme Court of the United Kingdom has sought to limit the application of the *Caparo*[7] three-stage test for determining the existence of a duty of care to novel cases only. Since the 2018 decision in *Robinson v Chief Constable of West Yorkshire*,[8] the Supreme Court has directed lower courts to develop the law incrementally and by analogy with existing categories of liability.[9] This seems to acknowledge the difficulties of applying a 'single legal formula' to the existence of a duty of care (and in turn, liability in the tort of negligence).

[2] ibid 8–9.
[3] ibid 9–10.
[4] ibid.
[5] ibid 10.
[6] ibid 9.
[7] *Caparo Industries plc v Dickman* [1990] 2 AC 605 (HL).
[8] *Robinson v Chief Constable of West Yorkshire* [2018] UKSC 4, [2018] AC 736.
[9] Lord Reed stated in *Poole Borough Council v GN* [2019] UKSC 25, [2020] AC 780 [64]: '*Caparo* did not impose a universal tripartite test for the existence of a duty of care, but recommended an incremental approach to novel situations, based on the use of established categories of liability as guides, by analogy, to the existence and scope of a duty of care in cases which fall outside them. The question whether the imposition of a duty of care would be fair, just and reasonable forms part of the assessment of whether such an incremental step ought to be taken. It follows that, in the ordinary run of cases, courts should apply established principles of law, rather than basing their decisions on their assessment of the requirements of public policy.'

It also confirms that the reasons for imposing liability might be localised to specific fact patterns rather than generalised across the full range of circumstances in which negligence might arise. This development might be viewed as going someway to address, or at least acknowledge, Peter's concern. It does not, however, remove it. As demonstrated in *Poole Borough Council v GN*,[10] there may be more than one analogy that can be drawn and it is not always clear which analogy is more appropriate in a given circumstance.[11] The claimants in that case were Council tenants who had been harassed and abused by their neighbours. In determining the liability of the Council in failing to relocate the claimants, the various judges found it difficult to determine whether they should draw analogies from cases concerning a failure to control third parties, the misconduct of professionals or omissions more generally.

Another reason Peter gave for moving beyond a formulaic understanding of the law of torts is that such formulae may conceal important organising categories.[12] Consider the recent expansion of vicarious liability. After a series of cases involving the sexual assault of children in schools or halls of residence by carers, vicarious liability was declared by the House of Lords in 2013 to be 'on the move'.[13] First, the traditional Salmond test for determining the scope of vicarious liability was replaced by the 'close connection' test.[14] The test for determining the relevant relationship by reason of which vicarious liability might arise was then replaced by the 'akin to employment' test.[15] These new tests broadened both the nature of the relationship that might attract vicarious liability and the type of torts for which vicarious liability might be imposed (specifically, intentional torts).[16] More recently, however, the Supreme Court suggested in *WM Morrison Supermarkets plc v Various Claimants*[17] that there might have been something specific about the prospect of imposing vicarious liability in the child sexual assault cases; namely, the conferral of authority by the defendant on the carer to supervise the child.[18] The significance of this factor as an organising category had previously eluded detection.[19] In so recognising the factor in *Morrison*, the Supreme Court seemed to indicate that the child sexual assault cases should have been treated differently from cases of vicarious liability more generally.[20] The result is that the scope of vicarious liability may have been unduly widened in order to address a particular category of case.

The potential for overlap between different torts has long been of concern in the law of torts, made worse by a range of jurisdictionally inconsistent responses.

[10] ibid.

[11] Note the differences between the housing and social welfare claims, with the court ultimately relying on the omissions line of authority.

[12] Cane (n 1) 9

[13] Lord Phillips in *Various Claimants v Catholic Child Welfare Society* [2012] UKSC 56, [2013] 2 AC 1 [19].

[14] See generally *Lister v Hesley Hall* [2001] UKHL 22, [2002] 1 AC 215.

[15] *Catholic Child Welfare Society* (n 13).

[16] See generally *Lister* (n 14).

[17] *WM Morrison Supermarkets plc v Various Claimants* [2020] UKSC 12, [2020] AC 989.

[18] ibid [23].

[19] Though see C Beuermann *Reconceptualising Strict Liability for the Tort of Another* (Oxford, Hart Publishing, 2019) ch 4.

[20] *WM Morrison Supermarkets* (n 17) [23].

The possibility of pursuing an action for negligent trespass persists in Australia,[21] for instance, but not in England and Wales.[22] Peter was particularly concerned in *Anatomy* with the overlap between nuisance and negligence, not surprisingly since nuisance is traditionally considered a strict liability tort and negligence fault based.[23] This concern was not ameliorated when the House of Lords subsequently declared in *Transco plc v Stockport Metropolitan Borough Council*[24] that the tort of *Rylands v Fletcher* should be considered part of the law of nuisance, following the decision of the High Court of Australia in *Burnie Port Authority v General Jones Ltd*[25] that it should be part of the law of negligence.

The potential for overlap is partially addressed by accepting the possibility of concurrent liability,[26] but not removed. The conceptual difficulties underpinning the extent of the overlap remain, and it encourages claimants to select the most advantageous cause of action available on the particular facts, often to the defendant's detriment.[27] There is also the possibility that relevant factors might be altogether overlooked depending on the specific formula chosen by a claimant to bring their case. This can be seen in the recent decision of the High Court of Australia in *Binsaris v Northern Territory*.[28]

The specific legal issue in the case was the availability of a defence of statutory authorisation. The majority found that no such defence could be raised, although it is the dissenting judgment of Gageler J which is of most interest for present purposes. The facts of the case were as follows. The plaintiff had been lawfully detained in a Youth Detention Centre operated by the Northern Territory government. One of the other detainees 'escaped from his cell, damaged property and caused a serious disturbance'.[29] In order to regain control over the escaped detainee, the Immediate Action Team employed by the Centre decided to use a form of tear gas. After issuing a warning about the potential use of tear gas, the tear gas was deployed. The plaintiff, who was detained in a neighbouring cell, was affected by the gas.[30]

The claim was brought in battery and counsel for the Northern Territory government conceded that the deployment of tear gas amounted to a battery in respect of the both the plaintiff and the escaped detainee.[31] Justice Gageler was of the view that the defence of statutory authorisation could be relied upon in respect of any claim that might be brought by the escaped detainee. He then had to consider what impact that finding had on the claim brought by the plaintiff. The difficulty for Gageler J was that he clearly thought that there were some circumstances where the

[21] *Williams v Milotin* (1957) 97 CLR 465 (HCA).
[22] *Letang v Cooper* [1965] 1 QB 232 (CA).
[23] Cane (n 1) 9.
[24] *Transco plc v Stockport Metropolitan Borough Council* [2003] UKHL 61, [2004] 2 AC 1.
[25] *Burnie Port Authority v General Jones Ltd* (1994) 179 CLR 520.
[26] *Henderson v Merrett Syndicates Ltd* [1995] 2 AC 145 (HL).
[27] Cane (n 1) 23.
[28] *Binsaris v Northern Territory* [2020] HCA 22, (2020) 94 ALJR 664, heard alongside *Webster v Northern Territory, O'Shea v Northern Territory* and *Austral* v *Northern Territory*.
[29] ibid [1].
[30] Along with the other inmates in the concurrent actions.
[31] *Binsaris* (n 28) [23].

deployment of tear gas might indeed by reasonable in circumstances where a third party might be affected by that deployment (for example, a hostage situation[32]). Reasonableness, however, is not a component of the tort of battery.

Restricted by the formula for battery, Gageler J started by noting that the deployment of tear gas in respect of the plaintiff 'could not be said to have been unintentional',[33] in the sense that it was an inevitable consequence of the deployment of tear gas in respect of the escaped detainee. The potential for negligent trespass in Australia may, though, have affected Gageler J's definition of intention in these circumstances. It could be said that the tear gas was intentionally released but, importantly, the release of the tear gas was not directed at the plaintiff and no harm to the plaintiff was intended. Consider the example of a person lighting a fire which causes a person standing nearby to be affected by smoke.[34] Would Gageler J have said that the intention and/or directness elements were satisfied in such circumstances? His reasoning does little to clarify any potential overlap between the two torts in the specific circumstances.

Having satisfied himself that a battery towards the plaintiff had been committed by the defendant, Gageler J then moved on to the question of whether there was an available defence. One possibility was the availability of some type of common law immunity for the exercise of police power or an analogous development of the defence of necessity. Neither of these approaches gave Gageler J the capacity to consider the reasonableness of the conduct of the Immediate Action Team. The 'all or nothing' nature of either response made them rather blunt instruments. Ultimately, he found neither of them to be satisfied and allowed the plaintiff's claim.

Justice Gageler may not have reached a different conclusion if the action had been brought in negligence, but the nature of his analysis would have been quite different.[35] Justice Gageler would have had at his disposal the more finely honed tools incorporated in the formula for negligence to weigh the respective interests of the parties in the case. A relevant factor in this exercise might have been that the plaintiff was not in a position to take steps to protect his own interests (for example, by running away), given he was lawfully detained by the defendant. That a higher standard of care might be required in these circumstances is confirmed by the duty owed by a goaler to a prisoner generally being described as 'non-delegable'.[36] The potential relevance of such a factor was totally overlooked by the claimant's use of the battery formula and the need to resort to defences such as necessity in the circumstances.

It is not only overlap between the different torts that is of concern but the potential for overlap between the law of torts and other areas of law. As Peter noted, the formulaic nature of tort law can make it very difficult to understand the relationship

[32] ibid [35]. Thank you Professor Donal Nolan who gave a similar example of having to deploy a canister of tear gas at a bear to save children the bear was about to attack.

[33] ibid [34].

[34] Thank you Professor Mark Lunney for this example.

[35] As noted, an action for negligent trespass is still permitted in Australia.

[36] See *Racz v Home Office* [1994] 2 AC 45 (HL). See also *British Columbia v Zastowny* (2008) 290 DLR (4th) 219 (SCC).

between the law of torts and other areas of law.[37] This is the case even where the desired consequences of any overlap appear intuitive. Consider the relationship between the law of torts and contract. Lord Sumption noted in the recent case of *Woodland v Swimming Teachers Association*[38] that it was difficult to justify different treatment in tort for the patient of a private hospital, as opposed to a patient of the NHS; or a student at an independent school, as opposed to a student at a school run by a local authority.[39] To bridge the gap between patients and students in these two circumstances, Lord Sumption employed the concept of an 'assumption of responsibility'. Whether or not a hospital or school owed a 'non-delegable duty of care' to a patient or student was therefore to be determined by whether the hospital or school had assumed 'a positive duty to protect the claimant from harm', not the existence of a contract for the supply of services.[40]

The difficulties with reducing the overlap between the law of torts and contract to an 'assumption of responsibility' are three-fold. First, the courts have failed to use the concept of an 'assumption of responsibility' with any consistency. As Kit Barker has demonstrated, the concept is used in a variety of senses: sometimes it indicates an implied promise by the defendant to take care; sometimes it means the defendant has assumed the legal risk of the consequences of her actions; and on yet other occasions, it means nothing more than that the defendant has voluntarily chosen to act in a particular way.[41] Second, it led the Supreme Court in *Woodland* to conflate the different types of liability that might arise in tort law (as opposed to the single type of liability that arises in contract). The question in *Woodland* was not whether the school (or, on different facts, a hospital) might owe a greater standard of care to a student (or patient), but whether the relationship between the school and a student (or hospital and patient) might give rise to strict liability for the tort of another. An 'assumption of responsibility' was too blunt a tool to make this distinction. Finally, it distracted the court from more closely examining the specific features of the particular relationships and fully assessing whether they should be treated the same way. As noted above, schools have authority to direct the behaviour of their students and can confer this authority on carers who might harm those students. It is very difficult to say that hospitals have a similar authority with respect to patients.[42] It follows that the two relationships might need to be treated differently in respect of different types of tort liability.

The final reason Peter gave for moving beyond a formulaic understanding of the law of torts was the difficulties such formulae presented in efforts to reform the law. The particular reform he had in mind was the failed attempt to create a tort of harassment following the curtailment of the tort of nuisance to claimants with an interest in land.[43] Since the publication of *Anatomy* there have indeed been some successful

[37] Cane (n 1) 9.
[38] *Woodland v Swimming Teachers Association* [2013] UKSC 66, [2014] AC 537.
[39] ibid 573–74.
[40] ibid 583.
[41] K Barker, 'Unreliable Assumptions in the Modern Law of Negligence' (1993) 109 *LQR* 461.
[42] See C Beuermann, 'Do Hospitals Owe a So-Called Duty of Care to Their Patients? (2018) 26 *Medical Law Review* 1.
[43] *Khorasandjian v Bush* [1993] QB 727 (CA); overruled by *Hunter v Canary Wharf* [1997] AC 655 (HL).

attempts to reform tort law. The circumstances of such reforms are, however, telling. Consider the development of the tort of misuse of private information, a tort influenced more by the duty of confidence in equity and the Human Rights Act 1998 than any existing tort.[44] The influence of the Human Rights Act can also be seen in the replacement of the *Bolam* test for determining the standard of care in respect of negligent advice in *Montgomery v Lanarkshire Health Board*.[45] The formulae have not only had a chilling effect on reform of the common law but also on legislative attempts at reform. Lower courts resisted giving full effect to the requirement that a claimant show 'serious harm' in order to commence an action for defamation as required by section 1(1) of the Defamation Act 2013, a state of affairs that persisted until the 2019 decision of the Supreme Court in *Lachaux v Independent Print Ltd*.[46] A similar issue arose in a number of Australian states with the attempt to replace the common law 'reasonable foreseeability' test in determining the breach of a duty of care with a statutory test that requires, at least in some states, the risk to be 'not insignificant'.[47]

It follows that Peter was right. Our formulaic understanding of tort law is a problem. The limited success of the courts in addressing the problem since the publication of *Anatomy* simply confirm the urgency of the task Peter first set himself in writing the book.

III. Key Insights into the Law of Torts

Peter's proposal to move beyond the formulaic understanding of the law of torts was to reconceptualise tort law as a 'system of ethical rules and principles of personal responsibility for conduct'.[48] This idea was based on three key insights into the law of torts:

- tort law has both backward-looking (dispute resolution) and forward-looking (conduct guidance) functions;[49]
- tort law is bilateral, with some elements aimed at the injurer (defendant), and some at the victim (claimant);[50] and
- tort law weighs 'freedom against responsibility' by striking a balance between the defendant's 'freedom to' act and the claimant's 'freedom from' interference.[51]

[44] See 'Comparing Hard Cases' in P O'Callaghan, *Refining Privacy in Tort Law* (Berlin, Springer, 2012) ch 4.

[45] *Montgomery v Lanarkshire Health Board* [2015] UKSC 11, [2015] AC 1430. Although the impact of human rights jurisprudence is much more indirect in *Rogers v Whitaker* (1992) 175 CLR 479.

[46] *Lachaux v Independent Print Ltd* [2019] UKSC 27, [2020] AC 612.

[47] For example, Civil Liability Act 2002 (NSW), s 5B. For a discussion of cases applying this section, see The Hon Justice Peter Garling, 'A Judicial Perspective on the Civil Liability Act 2002 – Ten Years On', Speech given at New South Wales Bar Association Personal Injury Conference 3 March 2012, available at www.austlii.edu.au/au/journals/NSWJSchol/2012/11.pdf. The High Court of Australia also refused to amend the common law test in light of the statutory changes in *New South Wales v Fahy* [2007] HCA 20, (2007) 232 CLR 486.

[48] Cane (n 1) 1.

[49] ibid 5.

[50] ibid 13.

[51] ibid 15.

On the basis of these insights, Peter was able to identify three core components of tort law (beyond the discrete formulae used to describe individual torts):

- sanctioned conduct (the defendant-focused elements of tort law);[52]
- protected interests (the claimant-focused elements of tort law);[53] and
- sanctions ('important in balancing the interests of victims and injurers').[54]

The principal work undertaken by Peter in *Anatomy* was to dismantle those three core components from the various tort formulae and reassemble them as a coherent system of tort law.

That the core components identified by Peter were influenced by his key insights into the law of tort is self-evident. In viewing tort law bilaterally, Peter had to identify separate elements that addressed the interests of both parties to the dispute. The elements aimed at the defendant in turn had to be capable of setting standards of behaviour since it was understood that tort law had both forward-looking (conduct guidance) and backward-looking (dispute resolution) functions. There also had to be a mechanism by which those interests could be weighed or evaluated. The integrity of the core components identified by Peter therefore rests on the veracity of his initial insights into the operation of the law of torts. This section examines those insights and suggests that their power remains undiminished.

The backward-looking functions of tort law are well established. Tort law is invoked by a claimant in order to resolve a dispute with the defendant. A court (if the dispute proceeds that far) will in turn make a determination as to whether the defendant is liable and, if so, determine an appropriate remedy.

That tort law has forward-looking functions is also considered relatively uncontroversial in the current theoretical landscape. Both economic and corrective justice/rights theorists generally acknowledge that tort law guides appropriate human behaviour (either by deterring inefficient conduct or identifying and enforcing legally recognised wrongs). Where the theories differ is the purpose for which that conduct guidance function is exercised and the nature of the content which informs it.

Importantly, Peter did not associate the forward-looking functions of tort law with any pre-existing theoretical position. His starting point was more basic; the doctrine of precedent.[55] In Peter's view, the fact that the doctrine of precedent applied to a tort dispute meant that legal rules and/or principles created in the context of one dispute were not limited to the immediate parties to that dispute and could be applied to future parties. It followed that the courts made law in the process of resolving tort disputes.[56] Because judges made law in the process of resolving tort disputes, it also followed that judges were not limited to considering issues when making that law that only affected the immediate parties; it was sometimes necessary to consider issues that might also affect future parties.[57]

[52] ibid 13.
[53] ibid 14.
[54] ibid 15.
[55] ibid 16.
[56] ibid.
[57] ibid.

This raises an important point about methodology. In writing *Anatomy*, Peter was not looking to confirm or justify a pre-existing theoretical position by reference to the cases. Instead, he looked to develop an understanding of tort law that fitted the cases; specifically, those elements that had precedential value. His focus was explaining what it was that judges did.[58] It follows that when Peter reassembled the various components of tort law into the coherent system found in *Anatomy*, he was able to accommodate more of the cases than either the corrective justice/rights or economic tort theorists had previously been able to do.[59]

What Peter did assume, in line with both corrective justice/rights and economic tort theorists, is that the forward-looking functions of tort law were directed at individuals and their conduct as members of society. He did not countenance any other target for the forward-looking functions of tort law. This fitted, in Peter's view, with the language used by judges to describe rules and principles in tort law; references to the duties and obligations being relatively common.[60] As a result, Peter's list of sanctioned conduct was largely conduct which a defendant should not engage in, the defendant being the object of the forward-looking functions of tort law.

Peter's second key insight into the law of torts was that it was inherently bilateral, with different elements aimed at the claimant (protected interests) and the defendant (sanctioned conduct). Despite obvious overlaps with the concept of 'correlativity' used by corrective justice theorists, Peter explicitly chose the term 'bilateral' to distance his position from the normative conclusions drawn by corrective justice theorists when utilising the concept of 'correlativity'. Peter did not see any necessary correlation between 'rights' and 'obligations' in the law of torts. Nor did he see any necessary correlation between the interference with the protected interest and the ultimate sanction awarded. His observation that the law of torts was bilateral emphasised nothing more than the fact that tort law was relational. Liability in the law of torts is not determined in a vacuum. It involves two parties and the courts have to examine the position of both parties in determining the fact and extent of liability in tort.[61]

The extent to which Peter's second key insight into the law of torts is mirrored by other theorists again makes it relatively uncontroversial. Peter did not draw the same normative conclusions as the other theorists, but nor would those other theorists deny that, to the extent tort law involves both a claimant and a defendant, it is two sided. The significance of the insight is once again methodological. Peter's observation that tort law was bilateral was not based on any pre-existing theoretical position but drawn from the practice of judges when deciding the cases; a practice for which there is evidence throughout the development of tort law. Consider the judicial consideration of the extent to which a claimant should take reasonable care for their own safety

[58] What Jane Stapleton describes as middle theory. See generally, J Stapleton 'Comparative Economic Loss: Lessons from Case-Law-Focussed "Middle Theory"' (2002–2003) 50 *UCLA Law Review* 531.

[59] The selective use of cases being a common criticism aimed at both economic and corrective justice/rights theorists.

[60] Cane (n 1) 24.

[61] ibid 12.

in determining both the existence[62] and extent of liability in negligence,[63] notwithstanding the defendant's own failure to take reasonable care. Also, the prominent role given to the concept of an 'assumption of responsibility' by the defendant to the claimant in determining a range of liability in tort.[64]

The extent to which Peter's first two key insights into the law of torts are reflected in existing theoretical frameworks confirms they have force. Peter's third key insight into the law of torts is different. Both economic and corrective justice/rights theorists have a ready answer when it comes to determining how a court should assess or evaluate the claimant-focused and defendant-focused elements of tort law given the backward-looking (dispute resolution) and forward-looking (law making) functions of tort. That answer is provided by the theory which led to the key insights first being drawn. For economic theorists, judges should evaluate the claimant-focused and defendant-focused elements of tort law with a view to achieving economic efficiency,[65] whereas the object for corrective justice/rights theorists is the attainment of corrective justice. Peter could not draw on any pre-existing theory to inform his view of how the claimant-focused and defendant-focused elements of tort law should be assessed by judges. Instead, he had once again to examine judicial practice to determine what judges actually did when faced with the different claimant-focused and defendant-focused elements of tort law.

Peter observed that when judges determine liability in tort, they do not start with a pre-determined endpoint in mind, but balance the claimant-focused elements of tort law against the defendant-focused elements. Specifically judges weigh 'freedom against responsibility' by balancing the defendant's 'freedom to' act against the claimant's 'freedom from' interference.[66] Peter did not stipulate how the process of balancing was conducted or the intended result of the balancing process being applied. He simply observed that, faced with both claimant- and defendant-focused elements of tort law, judges looked at both and tried to ensure that protecting a claimant from interference did not unduly interfere with the generally accepted freedom of defendants to act autonomously.

This focus on process makes Peter's third key insight into the law of tort distinct. Existing theories assess the appropriateness of decisions in tort against prescribed outcomes (be that economic efficiency, or corrective justice). Peter's insight was that there was no such yard stick. Judges determined liability in tort not by reference to a desired outcome, but by utilising a particular reasoning process as a result of which they considered and weighed both the claimant-focused and defendant-focused elements of tort law against one another. Examples of this balancing process are not difficult to find. Explicit references to balancing are made by judges in respect of a number of a torts. Consider the tort of nuisance where judges weigh a range of factors in order to

[62] See, for example, the decision of the High Court of Australia in *Nagle v Rottnest Island Authority* (1993) 177 CLR 423 where a duty of care was denied because the plaintiff should have taken personal responsibility for their own safety.

[63] The availability of contributory negligence as a defence.

[64] For example, *Woodland* (n 38).

[65] Although admittedly the economic theorists would place considerably more emphasis on the defendant-focused as opposed to the claimant-focused elements of tort law.

[66] Cane (n 1) 15.

determine the point at which neighbours should enable one another to 'live and let live'.[67] The tort of defamation provides another, yet slightly different, example. In this tort, the protection afforded to reputation by the cause of action is then balanced by the protection afforded to free speech by the available defences. In other torts, the use of a balancing process is more implicit, but nonetheless present. Consider the longstanding distinction between acts and omissions in negligence. The Supreme Court recently reaffirmed in *Poole Borough Council v GN* that although liability might readily be imposed on a defendant for 'making things worse', liability for 'not making things better' should not ordinarily be imposed unless something specific between the parties creates such an expectation.[68] The evident concern with imposing such liability is the potential consequences for defendants in making decisions for their own lives.[69]

'Balancing' can be a controversial notion. For some theorists it suggests an instrumental approach to tort law and an overreliance on policy concerns that might be beyond both the experiential and jurisdictional remit of judges.[70] But surely that depends on the nature of the factors being weighed and whether the process of weighing has a particular social objective in mind? Peter was himself clear that he did not view how judges approached the determination of liability in tort law as instrumental:[71]

> … I think that for most of its history the common law of tort has not been viewed instrumentally by the judges and lawyers who were primarily responsible for making it, but on the contrary as a set of principles of personal responsibility.

Peter did not deny that 'tort law can be used as a means to an end',[72] it is just that this was not what judges actually did.[73]

Although controversial, Peter's third key insight into the law of torts has considerable force. The focus on process provides a mechanism by which the claimant-focused and defendant-focused elements of tort law (which most tort theorists readily acknowledge exist) can be assessed or evaluated without the need to resort to a pre-existing theory. It reflects the actual practice of judges and explains why judges can be seen to take into account a broad range of factors as well as occasionally reaching apparently inconsistent judgments when determining liability in tort. It is also methodologically consistent with Peter's other key insights, which were confirmed by existing tort theories.

To be sure, the focus on process does raise important questions about tort law, not the least of which is how do judges know when they have the balance between the claimant-focused elements and defendant-focused elements of tort law right? Even if the idea of process were accepted, it might be possible to envisage other types

[67] *Bamford v Turnley* (1860) 3 B&S 62, 122 ER 25.

[68] *Poole* (n 9) [28].

[69] See Lord Hoffmann in *Stovin v Wise* [1996] AC 923 (HL) 943–44.

[70] See, eg, A Beever *Rediscovering the Law of Negligence* (Oxford, Hart Publishing, 2007).

[71] Cane (n 1) 24.

[72] ibid.

[73] Different views might also be formed on whether framing tort law as a 'system of personal responsibility' is not in and of itself instrumental. The more important point, however, is that this is not how judges do view any balancing they undertake in tort law.

of processes other than balancing that could be utilised by judges to assess both the claimant-focused and defendant-focused elements of torts law. The more mathematical approach of the Learned Hand calculation for determining breach in negligence comes to mind. It is difficult, though, to contemplate any other mechanism that could be utilised with sufficient flexibility throughout the entirety of tort law. It follows that Peter's third key insight has much to commend it.

IV. Why has the Formulaic Approach to Tort Law Persisted?

If Peter's three key insights into the law of torts have the force suggested in the previous section, why then have the courts resisted adopting a more systematic approach to tort law? Why has it proved so difficult for judges to move beyond the original formulae for the various torts, many of which were devised during the operation of the writ system which has long since been abolished?

Considerable assistance in answering this question can be found in Peter's more recent work. On the basis of this work it is suggested that Peter may have unduly prioritised the forward-looking (conduct guidance) function of tort law in *Anatomy* when identifying the core components of the law of torts. As a result, judges may have been left somewhat confused as to the nature and/or extent of the change Peter was suggesting.

In 2019, some 20 years after *Anatomy* was published, Peter wrote the concluding chapter to *Scholars of Tort Law*.[74] The book was a commentary on the contribution of prominent common law scholars to the development of tort law. Peter's chapter, titled 'Law, fact and process and common law tort scholarship', addressed the relationship between the academy and the judiciary by comparing two models of legal scholarship which he called the 'common law model' and the 'civil law model'.[75] The first he described as a 'law of actions' and the second a 'law of the word'.[76] Peter was clear that he intended the models to be more interpretive than descriptive,[77] but nonetheless, the two models were based on broad historical developments in the two legal systems. In comparing the two models, Peter highlighted a number of differences in the role of judges and the relationship between scholars and the judiciary in the two models. Three of those are particularly relevant for present purposes.

First, the role of the judge in the common law model was initially procedural.[78] Historically, there were competing local laws and then competing levels of courts.[79]

[74] J Goudkamp and D Nolan, *Scholars of Tort Law* (Oxford, Hart Publishing, 2019).
[75] ibid 359.
[76] ibid 366.
[77] ibid 360.
[78] ibid 363 ff.
[79] ibid 362.

The role of the judge was to determine whether the matter could be brought before the particular court and how. The judge was not the decision maker.[80] As Peter explained:[81]

> What the parties argued about between themselves and with the judge (and what may be recorded) is whether the claim would be put to judgment, and on what issue, not what the outcome should be. The writs, likewise, told claimants what they had to do to get their claim to judgment, not what they had to do to win. The judgment-giver would decide, without explanation, what the facts were and how the relevant law applied to those facts, declaring the result of consideration of these issues in simple binary form: judgment for C or for D.

The nature of the judgment-giver changed over time in this early period, with a variety of methods, from trials to juries, being used. What was clear was that it was not the role of the judge to determine the substantive issues between the parties. The role of the judge, as dictated by the writ, was to determine the appropriate procedure to be followed.[82]

In contrast, the influence of the Catholic church on the Continent meant that irrational modes of judgment-giving were abandoned much earlier.[83] As a result, the judge in the civil law model was the primary judgment-giver. The judge's role was to both determine the facts of what occurred between the parties and to apply the substantive law to those facts to resolve the dispute.[84]

A second, yet related, distinction between the common law and civil law models that Peter highlighted lies in development of the applicable substantive law. In the civil law model, substantive law emerged from the work of scholars in universities who sought to identify substantive legal principles governing the behaviour of individuals which judges would then apply.[85] As Peter explained:[86]

> The court found the facts, matched the facts to a pattern identified in the texts, and applied the relevant law as expounded by the scholars of the sacred texts.

In the common law model, substantive tort law remained hidden for a significant period in a largely inaccessible and non-transparent 'black box'.[87] Recall that in the common law model the judge was not originally the judgment-giver. After the abolition of the irrational modes of judgment-giving, that role largely fell to the jury. Jury deliberations were not recorded. Nor was there any requirement for a jury to give reasons for its decisions.[88] The jury simply declared who won.

When substantive law did emerge from the 'black box' in the common law model it was used very differently to how it was used in the civil law model, leading to a third distinction identified by Peter between the two models.[89] Fact and law are kept quite

[80] ibid 363.
[81] ibid.
[82] ibid.
[83] ibid 366.
[84] ibid.
[85] ibid 377.
[86] ibid.
[87] ibid 363.
[88] ibid.
[89] ibid 372

distinct in the civil law model. As noted above, it is the judge's role to find the facts and then apply the substantive law as found in the relevant texts to resolve the dispute. In the common law model, fact and law were intertwined in the 'black box' and remained intertwined after the writ system was abolished and use of the jury system fell into demise. The doctrine of precedent meant that any substantive law developed by a judge in a tort case was fact dependent. As Peter explained:[90]

> The judge must find the facts, ascertain the relevant law, state both, and explain the court's decision by reference to the facts and the law, issue by issue. This is the logic of the procedural regime in place since 1875. And notice: according to this logic, just as law and the facts of the case were intertwined inside the black box of God, Fate or the jury, they are still intertwined, but now in the public, observable role of the judge. The common law – judge-made law – is still not a law of the word in the civilian sense, identifiable separately from and prior to consideration of the facts of the case. Rather, the procedural matrix of common law adjudication harnesses law to those facts. This explains why one way of side-lining an authoritative precedent is to say that it 'depends solely on its facts': if the facts are unique, the law they generate is singular.

It was the combination of these various distinguishing features – emphasis on procedure, hidden substantive law principles, integral connection between law and facts – that led Peter to describe the common law model as a 'law of actions'. It was not a 'law of the word' in the same way as the civil law model in that the law existed 'separately from and prior to consideration of the facts of the case' and was then applied by the judge to the facts of a dispute.[91] The common law instead emerged from and was shaped by the procedures employed by the judges for resolving particular disputes on particular facts, with the substantive law principles emerging from the cases themselves.

This observation in terms of the nature of the common law model has significant implications for Peter's thesis in *Anatomy*. Much of what Peter did in *Anatomy* was consistent with this model; including the methodology he adopted (focus on judicial practice, rather than pre-existing theory) and the attention he paid to the process used by judges in resolving disputes (balancing). The concept of sanctioned conduct, however, appears somewhat at odds. By 'sanctioned conduct' Peter meant a range of different types of behaviour that could be engaged in by a defendant which tort law would recognise as potentially giving rising to liability. That behaviour included intentional, reckless, fraudulent and negligent conduct.[92] Such behaviours are necessarily prescribed by tort law in advance of the behaviours being engaged in by a defendant in accordance with the forward-looking (conduct guidance) function of tort law. To be sure, it is an issue to be determined in each and every case whether the *particular* behaviour engaged in by the defendant should be sanctioned on the particular facts. The forward-looking (conduct guidance) aspect of sanctioned conduct, as explained in *Anatomy*, is achieved by the generic descriptions of the type of conduct that has attracted liability previously

[90] ibid.
[91] ibid.
[92] Cane (n 1) ch 2.

and may attract liability in the future.[93] These descriptions of sanctioned conduct are meant to signal to individuals the types of conduct they should not engage in. Peter's concept of sanctioned conduct appears, therefore, to operate as a set of legal principles that exist 'separately from and prior to consideration of the facts of the case'.[94] As Peter's more recent work demonstrates, however, such legal principles are more in keeping with the civil law model as opposed to the common law model.

Peter is not the first common law theorist to fall into error in this way. When the writ system was abolished, judges did not have an established body of substantive legal principles to draw from. Whatever substantive legal principles that had previously been applied by the relevant judgment-givers lay hidden within the 'black box'. Textbooks started to emerge to fill the void. The writers of those textbooks, however, did not start with a blank sheet. They looked to other systems for inspiration, including Roman law and their fellow jurists on the Continent, as Blackstone had done before them.[95] The textbook writers were still restrained by the original formulae which resulted in the development of specific torts. But they were also attracted by the idea that substantive legal principles could be extracted from those torts. The substantive legal principles they chose were not dissimilar to those that existed on the Continent. The focus of those principles was fault or wrongdoing and they were aimed at the conduct of individuals. What resulted was a mismatch of substantive legal principles, not dissimilar to those that already existed in the civil law model, being mapped on to the old forms of action. It was a bond that has proven pervasive and very difficult to break.

In *Anatomy* Peter identified three core components of tort law: sanctioned conduct (defendant-focused elements of tort law), protected interests (claimant-focused elements of tort law) and sanctions ('important in balancing the interests of victims and injurers'[96]). It was evidently Peter's intention that judges could use these three components to slowly reconfigure tort law in a more systematic way and, in so doing, address the problems identified in section II of this chapter. The component of sanctioned conduct, however, sat more easily with the civil law model of substantive legal principles than the procedurally driven common law model. The alternative approach to tort law Peter offered was, therefore, perhaps not quite as in keeping with common law judicial practice as he might have hoped.

V. Change in Approach

If Peter's concept of sanctioned conduct is more in keeping with the civil law model than the common law model, it follows that his focus in *Anatomy* on the forward-looking (conduct guidance) functions of tort law was misplaced. It does not necessarily follow,

[93] This explains why sanctioned conduct is often described in terms of the behaviour of, or towards, a class as opposed to a specific individual.

[94] Cane (n 1) ch 2.

[95] Though note that Peter cites Simpson as saying the connections between the common law of contract with the civil law model is stronger than tort law: Goudkamp and Nolan (n 74) 375.

[96] Cane (n 1) 15.

however, that all hope of achieving Peter's objective in shifting tort law from a formulaic to a more systematic approach is lost. Recall that Peter's insights into the law of torts discussed in section III of this chapter still have considerable force. The question that remains is what might now actually be required to secure a change in approach?

To answer that question it is necessary to return to the common law model Peter outlined in *Scholars of Tort Law* and how that model differed from the civil law model. Three such features were highlighted in the previous section, namely: emphasis on procedure; hidden substantive law principles; and integral connection between law and facts. The necessary implication from those features is that substantive law in the common law model must be drawn from the process adopted by judges when resolving disputes. Those principles must come from within the dispute resolution process and not exist beyond it. The point at which Peter's approach in *Anatomy* came unstuck was pointing the forward-looking functions of tort law at the conduct of individuals. But what if there was another candidate for those forward-looking functions? Specifically, judges themselves?

To be sure, this is a radical notion.[97] The dominance of positive legal theory in the last century has led few to challenge the idea that the concept of law is aimed at individuals (real or artificial, organisational or institutional) and how they behave.[98] It is, though, an idea that could finally lead judges to shift from the traditional formulaic approach to a more systematic understanding of the law of torts in a manner that reflects both Peter's key insights into the law of torts and the distinguishing features of the common law model. The shift entails putting judicial process at the centre of tort law theorising. Rather than discrete torts organised around forms of inappropriate human behaviour, tort law would be organised around the different types of balancing processes used by judges to resolve disputes in light of the particular features of the factual relationships existing between the parties before them.

To unpack this idea further it is necessary to return to Peter's three key insights into the law of torts. Tort law is bilateral. By this Peter meant that tort law had both claimant-focused and defendant-focused elements (and was therefore relational). Furthermore, when considering those elements in the context of a dispute, judges weigh 'freedom against responsibility' by striking a balance between the defendant's 'freedom to' act and the claimant's 'freedom from' interference.[99] Use of a balancing process fulfils the backward-looking (dispute resolution) function of tort law but says little about the forward-looking (conduct guidance) function of tort law unless that forward-looking (conduct guidance) function is primarily directed at judges. As noted in section III of this chapter, one of the problems with judges utilising a process of balancing is that it is difficult to know, without guidance, when the judges have reached an appropriate balance between the claimant-focused and defendant-focused elements of tort law after weighing 'freedom against responsibility'. What is now being suggested is that judges

[97] Though note the work of the short-lived process school started by Henry Hart and Albert Sacks: H Hart and A Sacks, *The Legal Process: Basic Problems in the Making and Application of Law* (Tentative edition, 1958, unpublished). For a recent discussion of the process school, see E Ursin, 'Roger Traynor, the Legal Process School and Enterprise Liability' (2020) 71 *Hastings Law Journal* 1101.

[98] See, generally, HLA Hart, *The Concept of Law* (Oxford, Oxford University Press, 1961).

[99] Cane (n 1) 15.

do indeed have guidance in determining the appropriate balance and that guidance is provided by the substantive law that has been generated by judges in tort law since the abolition of the writ system.

Note that the possibility of tort law having a role in guiding individual behaviour is not denied. Individuals can, of course, plan their behaviour by reference to decisions that might be reached by judges in tort law cases. Judges are also often conscious that tort law might be used in this way and may tailor their judgments accordingly.[100] The point is just that guiding human behaviour is not the *primary* focus of the substantive law in tort. Indeed, it would be difficult for judges to develop substantive legal principles aimed simultaneously at guiding individual behaviour and directing the decision-making process of judges. Substantive legal principles aimed at guiding individual behaviour would necessarily prescribe an end point for that behaviour; that is, identify the particular behaviour that an individual should not engage in. Such substantive legal principles would also need to be sufficiently transparent and clear for individual members of society to digest and act accordingly. In contrast, substantive legal principles aimed at directing the decision-making process of judges would necessarily regulate the process by which judges go about determining the dispute rather than the particular result to be reached as a result of that process. The sophisticated nature of the judicial audience also allows for such substantive legal principles to be crafted in a more nuanced and reflective way.

Consider what most tort lawyers would view as one of the more obvious examples of a substantive legal principle aimed at guiding human behaviour, the tort of battery. It is not uncommon for this tort to be reduced to a directive not to hit or apply force to another person. The requirements to establish liability under the tort itself, however, are not so simple. Much ink has been spilt on what is required to satisfy the defendant-focused elements of directness and intention, particularly in England and Wales where it is not possible to proceed on the basis of a negligent battery.[101] The elusiveness of these elements is difficult to explain to individual members of society. In line with the broader thesis of this chapter, however, it can be argued that the elements of directness and intention in the tort of battery set the parameters for the scope of the balancing exercise to be undertaken by judges in determining liability in such cases. The very nature of the circumstances triggering a battery claim tend to favour the claimant's 'freedom from' interference, but the requirements of directness and intention force the judges to pay appropriate attention to the defendant's 'freedom to' act. The question then is whether it should take more than the simple reducibility of a tort to a potential direction for guiding human behaviour for the conclusion to be reached that the object of the substantial legal principle underpinning the tort is indeed guiding human behaviour? This question is particularly pertinent since, as Peter pointed out in *Scholars in Tort Law*, such substantive legal principles do not sit altogether comfortably with the common law

[100] Particularly when test cases are brought.
[101] See *Letang* (n 22).

model. There is also a very real difference in how the authority exercised by judges in respect of the two types of substantial legal principles would need to be justified. The threshold for establishing the authority of judges to regulate the behaviour of members of society is necessarily much higher than the threshold for establishing the authority of judges to regulate the behaviour of other judges (and the necessary concomitant of issuing orders affecting the particular parties to a dispute).

It is also important to note that just because individuals may plan their behaviour by reference to decisions that might be reached by judges in tort law cases it does not necessarily follow that tort law is reduced to whatever Holmes' notorious 'bad man' might predict a court will do.[102] As has been argued, judges are constrained in how they resolve disputes in tort law. They are constrained by a series of substantive legal principles that dictate what particular balancing process should be utilised in tort to resolve the dispute and how that particular balancing process should be conducted. In this way, certainty and consistency are maintained and judges can ensure that like cases are treated alike when fulfilling their public function of resolving disputes.

Examples of tort law operating in this way are not too difficult to find once the lens through which tort law is examined is adjusted. Recall the problems Peter identified with the courts taking a formulaic approach to tort law which were discussed in section II of this chapter. The first was the potentially misleading nature of negligence as a 'single legal formula' for liability. The difficulties in determining a single test for the imposition of a duty of care in negligence are notorious. Many of those tests were formulated in a way that reflected the defendant's viewpoint: was the risk of harm to the class of claimant reasonably foreseeable? Was the defendant proximate to that class of claimant? More recently, the Supreme Court of the United Kingdom has sought to limit the scope for applying such tests by directing lower courts to instead develop the law incrementally and by analogy with existing categories of case.[103] The guidance is not directed towards individuals and it does not dictate to individuals how they should act. What the guidance dictates is the bounds of the balancing process to be undertaken by a judge when determining the existence of a duty of care, the finding of which has the potential to impose significant constraints on the freedom of a defendant. This shift is a prime example of the idea that the forward-looking (conduct guidance) function of tort law is directed at judges and not individuals.

Another problem Peter identified with the formulaic approach to tort law was the tendency of the existing formulae to conceal important organising categories. The example of this tendency given in section II above was the recent expansion of vicarious liability as a result of the cases involving the sexual assault of children within institutions by individuals charged with their care. It took the Supreme Court almost 20 years to recognise that there was a particular feature of the relationship between the defendant and the claimant in those cases that attracted liability; namely the conferral of authority by the defendant to direct the behaviour of the child on the carer who then went on

[102] OW Holmes Jr, 'The Path of the Law' (1897) 10 *Harvard Law Review* 457, recently considered in the context of private law by Stephen A Smith, *Rights, Wrongs and Injustices: The Structure of Remedial Law* (New York, Oxford University Press, 2019).

[103] See section II above.

to sexually abuse that child.[104] The failure to recognise this feature earlier led the Supreme Court to make various changes to the test for vicarious liability. Those changes broadened the potential circumstances which might fall within the test, and hence the possible occasions where liability might be imposed. The overarching direction to lower court judges when applying those new tests had been to determine what was 'fair and reasonable' or consider whether it was 'right for the employer to be held liable under the principle of social justice'.[105] The High Court of Australia expressly denounced the appropriateness of such guidance in *Prince Alfred College v ADC*.[106] Rather than follow the Supreme Court of the United Kingdom, the High Court of Australia directed lower courts to pay attention to the particular features of the relationship between the defendant and the plaintiff (including: 'authority, power, trust, control and the ability to achieve intimacy with the victim'[107]) and determine liability in accordance with the body of existing cases where such liability has been imposed. In so doing, the High Court of Australia was directing judges to adopt a balancing process more in line with the common law model than the civil law model. The behaviour of individuals was not the focus of the substantive law being developed by the High Court of Australia in respect of vicarious liability; once again, it was the behaviour of judges.

The potential overlap between different torts is yet another area where the forward-looking (conduct guidance) function of tort law can be seen to be directed at judges, particularly the overlap between trespass and negligence. As noted above, the trespass torts are commonly associated with substantive legal principles directed at individuals; namely a rule that an individual should not intentionally interfere with another person, their land or their goods. The considerable debate over what constitutes intention for the purpose of the trespass torts, combined with the advent of the tort of negligence in *Donoghue v Stevenson*,[108] has often made it difficult to determine whether a particular type of conduct fell within one tort or the other. What has resulted is a series of cases offering judges guidance on how to deal with the overlap. The guidance in some of those cases, such as the decision of the English Court of Appeal in *Letang v Cooper*,[109] has been explicit: negligent conduct does not fall within the tort of trespass to the person in England and Wales. In others, it has been more implicit, but nevertheless present. Consider the following examples: the expansion of the 'exigencies of everyday life' exception to trespass to the person claims in *Collins v Wilcock*[110] to exclude situations where a defendant has not been acting unreasonably in the circumstances due to the close physical proximity of other people; limiting the tort of false imprisonment to the *fact* of a prisoner's containment as opposed to the *circumstances* of that containment in *R v Deputy Governor of Parkhurst Prison, ex p Hague* and *Weldon v Home Office*;[111] or the refusal to vitiate consent to medical treatment where the doctor has advised the

[104] *WM Morrison Supermarkets* (n 17) [23].
[105] ibid [45] (Lord Toulson).
[106] *Prince Alfred College v ADC* [2016] HCA 37, (2016) 258 CLR 134.
[107] ibid [81].
[108] *Donoghue v Stevenson* [1932] AC 562 (HL).
[109] *Letang* (n 22).
[110] *Collins v Wilcock* [1984] 1 WLR 1172 (QB).
[111] *R v Deputy Governor of Parkhurst Prison, ex p Hague* and *Weldon v Home Office* [1992] 1 AC 58 (HL).

patient negligently in *Montgomery v Lanarkshire Health Board*.[112] What can be seen in each of these cases is a direction to lower court judges to apply the (arguably more sophisticated) balancing process utilised in negligence cases rather than the balancing process previously utilised in these specific instances of trespass.[113]

Many more examples of the forward-looking (conduct guidance) function of tort law being directed at judges can be given, not the least of which are the torts in which judges are explicitly directed to engage in a balancing process (of which nuisance and defamation are noted examples). The idea that the forward-looking (conduct guidance) function of tort law is directed at judges and not individuals can, however, appear incongruous with the language sometimes used by judges to describe tort liability. Cases are replete with references to duty and obligation which all suggest that the forward-looking (conduct guidance) function of tort law is directed towards individuals. There is, though, another explanation for this. It should be recalled that the common law model and the civil law model, as Peter outlined in *Scholars of Tort Law*, have not always been kept separate. The use of such language was, if not introduced, at least reinforced by legal scholars who sought to emulate substantive legal principles developed by their civil law counterparts. It also continues to be reinforced by modern schools of tort scholarship. Common law judges may have used that language because it was available to them, but they did not change their practices, which – as Peter has pointed out – have remained distinct from the civil law model.

Although radical, this is not the first time it has been suggested that the forward-looking (conduct guidance) function of tort law, at least in part, is directed at judges and not individuals. Stephen Smith has recently published a detailed examination of remedies in private law titled *Rights, Wrongs and Injustices*.[114] In that book Smith argues that remedial law[115] is distinct from substantive law. It is distinct, because the rules of remedial law are directed at guiding judges as to when they should award those remedies (or, in Smith's language, rulings), whereas substantive law is directed at guiding individuals.[116] As Smith explains:[117]

> Of course, the practice of issuing rulings is governed by rules. But these rules are also distinctive. Rules about rulings ('remedial law') govern relations between courts and citizens. They provide citizens with powers to obtain rulings and they tell courts what they should do when citizens come to them seeking rulings … In contrast, substantive-law rules govern individuals' interactions with each other. As the previous paragraph's examples illustrate, substantive rules tell individuals how they should treat one another in day-to-day life or how they can create or alter legal relationships with others. Like all legal rules, substantive rules may be applied by courts. But, unlike remedial rules, the guidance they provide is intended primarily for individuals.

[112] *Montgomery* (n 45).

[113] For broader discussion see the two-part article in the *Tort Law Review* by Christine Beuermann, 'Are The Torts of Trespass to the Person Obsolete?' (2018) 25 *Tort Law Review* 103 and (2018) 26 *Tort Law Review* 6.

[114] Smith (n 102).

[115] A broad term which Smith breaks down into the further categories of rights-threats, wrongs and injustices.

[116] Smith (n 102) preface.

[117] ibid 7.

The obvious question that arises in light of the previous discussion is why Smith drew the line where he did? What is so different between remedial law and substantive law that the target of the forward-looking (conduct guidance) functions differ? The answer he gives is particularly intriguing, not only in light of the distinctions between the civil law and common law models that Peter highlighted, but because Smith appears to classify negligence (and a range of other tort actions) as an 'injustice' (rather than a rights-threat or wrong-responding). The significance of this distinction is that for Smith, judicial practice under the 'injustice' umbrella (in contrast to the 'rights-threat' or 'wrongs' categories) does not respond to substantive rights but is largely remedial. It follows that, in Smith's view, the law of negligence is principally aimed at judges and not individuals.[118] The areas of tort law that Smith would classify as responding to substantive rights are therefore relatively small. Not surprisingly, they are also the torts that have historically been capable of being readily reduced to a directive guiding human behaviour.

VI. Conclusion

Anatomy was a ground-breaking piece of tort scholarship. The emphasis placed on the forward-looking (conduct guidance) functions of tort law was, however, as demonstrated by Peter's later work, misplaced. It followed that Peter was unable to shift our understanding of tort law beyond the original formulae to a more systematic understanding of the law of torts.

It was argued in this chapter that Peter's key insights into the law of torts can still be used to achieve that goal. It requires shifting the target of the forward-looking (conduct guidance) functions of tort law away from the conduct of individuals to the conduct of judges. Under this approach, the different processes utilised by judges to resolve disputes in tort law becomes the basis upon which tort law is organised rather than the sanctioned conduct of the defendant.

Peter did not examine in *Anatomy* the different types of balancing processes utilised by judges in resolving disputes in the law of torts or how those balancing processes were conducted. It is beyond the scope of this chapter to examine those processes or to consider more broadly how tort law might look if reorganised in this way.[119] It is hoped though that the value of undertaking that work is now evident.

In closing, three comments can be made in respect of the advantages that might be secured by this shift in approach. First, recall the difficulty encountered by the various judges asked to resolve the dispute in *Poole Borough Council v GN*.[120] Namely, the lack of clarity as to which of the available analogies that might be drawn on the facts was the more appropriate. Considerable assistance could be provided to judges in these circumstances if the balancing processes adopted in respect of the various factual

[118] ibid ch 8.
[119] For some preliminary thoughts on this see the postscript to Beuermann (n 19).
[120] *Poole* (n 9).

circumstances (or more pertinently, types of relationships) in tort were identified. The judges would then not only be looking for factual similarities with previous cases but have a framework for determining which of those factual similarities were relevant and when.

Secondly, it would negate the somewhat perverse conclusion currently drawn by many tort theorists, including Peter in *Anatomy*, that interests in land are somehow protected more vigorously in tort law than interests in personal security.[121] Land is fundamentally different to people. It does not move. It follows that the balancing process between a defendant's 'freedom to' act and a claimant's 'freedom from' interference where land is involved will be conducted in a slightly different way. This is because the prospect of limiting a defendant's 'freedom to' act is somewhat lessened (although not entirely) given the need for the defendant to bring themselves into the vicinity of the land in the first place. As a result, a different approach may be taken to determining whether the elements of directness or intention have been satisfied. Shifting attention to the nature of the balancing process will reveal the extent to which allowances are made for differences in the nature of the protected interest in question without resulting in a normative value being attributed to the protected interest itself.

Finally, the shift in approach would provide a comprehensive framework for understanding the importance of a pre-existing relationship between the parties to the dispute. There are a number of instances in tort law where courts highlight the existence of a pre-existing relationship between the parties when resolving the dispute. The concept of an assumption of responsibility, although flawed, is a good example of this. As is the recent recognition of the importance of the 'conferral of authority' in a relationship giving rise to strict liability for the tort of another.[122] At present, it is not understood when or why these relationships are significant.[123]

[121] Cane (n 1) 139–49.
[122] See discussion of *WM Morrison Supermarkets* (n 17).
[123] See postscript to Beuermann (n 19).

2

Elements of Torts

JAMES GOUDKAMP*

I. Introduction

In a well-known article, Paul Robinson and Jane Grall traced a revolution that occurred during the twentieth century in understanding regarding the criminal law.[1] They recounted a general shift in scholars' attention from the level of offences to the level of elements of offences. This re-orientation of the prevailing approach to analysis made a major mark on the criminal law. In particular, and as Robinson and Grall emphasised, it revealed that offences often do not have a single *actus reus* or single *mens rea* but are instead commonly constituted by several conduct elements and several fault elements. It also demonstrated that conduct elements sometimes, but do not always, have a corresponding fault element (and vice versa) and that the fault element that is paired with a certain conduct element (if any) may be different from the fault element that relates to another conduct element. These insights may seem banal today but they were anything but at the time.

Glanville Williams was a (if not the) leading figure in this sea change in understanding regarding the criminal law, principally on account of his *Criminal Law: The General Part*.[2] In that pioneering work, Williams partitioned the criminal law into what he labelled the general part and the special part. In outline, the former comprises principles that apply to more than one offence or across the board while the latter concerns rules particular to specific offences. A substantial proportion of the general part is constituted by ingredients that are common to a range of crimes such as intention, causation and non-consent. Accordingly, in large part Williams's book about the general part entailed a search for and elucidation of the fundamental building blocks from which crimes are constructed. It was an exercise in element analysis *par excellence*.

* I am indebted to Roderick Bagshaw, David Campbell, Matthew Dyson, David Foster, Neil Foster, Eleni Katsampouka, Mark Lunney, Ben McFarlane, Charles Mitchell, John Murphy, Jason Neyers, Donal Nolan, Nicholas Sage, Lionel Smith, Stephen Smith, Jane Stapleton, Robert Stevens, Barbara von Tigerstrom and William Twining for their comments on a draft of this chapter.

[1] PH Robinson and JA Grall, 'Element Analysis in Defining Criminal Liability: The Model Penal Code and Beyond' (1983) 35 *Stanford Law Review* 681.

[2] GL Williams, *Criminal Law: The General Part* (London, Stevens & Sons, 1953). For discussion, see P Cane, 'The General/Special Distinction in Criminal Law, Tort Law and Legal Theory' (2007) 26 *Law & Philosophy* 465.

The offence of rape[3] is a good illustration of a crime that cannot be properly understood without descending to the level of its elements. The offence is generally understood as having two conduct requirements, namely, penetration and non-consent. Each of these conduct elements is linked with a fault element. Specifically, the fault element associated with the requirement of penetration is an intention to penetrate whereas that paired with the ingredient of non-consent is the absence of a reasonable belief in consent.[4] It follows that the offence of rape does not have a single *actus reus*. Nor, since it is premised on both intention and the absence of a reasonable belief, does it have a single *mens rea*. The legal complexity of the crime is, therefore, suppressed if one operates only at the level of the offence and speaks simply of its *actus reus* or of its *mens rea*.

Torts, like crimes, are also constituted by elements.[5] Although it has been said that the purpose of a tort textbook is to explain 'the "elements" that must be proved in order to succeed in each kind of tort action',[6] the reality is that tort law has not been studied at the level of elements in anything like the detail that the criminal law has been. This is reflected in the fact that tort textbooks are invariably arranged in terms of torts rather than elements of torts whereas criminal law textbooks often include substantial treatments of commonly occurring ingredients.[7] Analysis of specific crimes is frequently postponed until after the building blocks of criminal liability have been comprehensively addressed.[8]

Operating at the level of torts can lead to a superficial understanding of the subject. Consider the familiar distinction between fault-based torts and strict liability torts.[9] This dichotomy is often used in a manner that obscures the fact that torts, like crimes, are regularly constituted by several conduct elements and that these conduct elements are often coupled with different fault elements or, sometimes, no fault element at all. In other words, branding individual torts as being based on strict liability or fault liability is almost always an oversimplification since most torts are blends of both forms of

[3] Sexual Offences Act 2003 (UK), s 1.

[4] The position at common law was different. Liability would not arise under the common law where the defendant believed, whether or not reasonably, that the intercourse was consensual: *DPP v Morgan* [1976] AC 182 (HL).

[5] Indeed, all causes of action in private law are, or are at least arguably, constituted by elements. As regards contract, see *Atlantic Lottery Corp Inc v Babstock* 2020 SCC 19, (2020) 447 DLR (4th) 543 [91] (Brown J observing that '[t]he elements of a cause of action for breach of contract are the existence of a contract and the breach of a term of that contract'). It is well established that 'four elements … constitute the conceptual structure of a claim in unjust enrichment': A Burrows, *A Restatement of the English Law of Unjust Enrichment* (Oxford, Oxford University Press, 2012) 25. Equitable wrongs are similarly comprised of elements: see, eg, *El Ajou v Dollar Land Holdings plc* [1994] 2 All ER 685 (CA) 700 (knowing receipt); *Coco v AN Clark (Engineers) Ltd* [1969] RPC 41 (Ch D) 47 (breach of confidence); *Burns v Burns* [2021] EWHC 75 (Ch) [28] (dishonest assistance). Regarding the role of elements in relation to equitable wrongs, see PG Turner, 'Fusion and Theories of Equity in Common Law Systems' in JCP Goldberg et al (eds), *Equity and Law: Fusion and Fission* (Cambridge, Cambridge University Press, 2019) 19–21.

[6] C Witting, *Street on Torts*, 15th edn (Oxford, Oxford University Press, 2018) 8.

[7] See, eg, D Ormerod and K Laird, *Smith & Hogan's Criminal Law*, 14th edn (Oxford, Oxford University Press, 2015) chs 4–5.

[8] See, eg, ibid.

[9] 'We operate within the paradigm of the opposition of fault and strict liability and assume that this basic dichotomy lies at the foundation of the system': GP Fletcher, 'The Fault of Not Knowing' (2002) 3 *Theoretical Inquiries in Law* 265, 265–66.

liability. Deceit is a striking example of a tort that defies classification according to the divide between strict liability and fault liability. As Peter Cane incisively observes:[10]

> The elements of liability for deceit are: (1) making a false statement; (2) either knowing it to be false, or not honestly believing it to be true; (3) with the intention that another rely on it to their detriment. Liability for deceit extends to (4) harm caused by the making of the false statement, regardless of whether the harm was intended, foreseen or foreseeable. The elements of the tort of deceit, then, are an amalgam of knowledge, belief, intention, recklessness and cause-based (strict) liability. This shows that the various components of legal responsibility judgments (intention, negligence, knowledge, and so on), are building blocks that can be put together to produce complex and subtly different liability criteria. The example of deceit draws attention to an important legal distinction between conduct and extrinsic consequences. It is by no means uncommon for the criterion of liability for conduct to be different from the criterion of liability for the extrinsic consequences ('outcomes') of that conduct. For example, the criterion of liability for conduct might be intention, while the criterion of liability for the outcomes of that conduct might be foreseeability. … Similarly, a criterion of responsibility regardless of fault in relation to conduct may be combined with a fault-based criterion of responsibility for outcomes.

As this passage demonstrates, it would miss an important part of the truth to pigeon-hole deceit by reference to the dichotomy between strict liability and fault liability. In reality, torts, including that of deceit, are almost always far more complex creatures than these labels suggest, and it is necessary to descend to the domain of elements in order properly to appreciate their nuances.

The purpose of this chapter is not to populate a periodic table of elements of torts. Nor is its objective to investigate individual elements. Rather, this chapter's concern is with the more fundamental issue of the concept of a tort element itself, which appears to be virgin territory. Among other things, the analysis distinguishes elements from certain related concepts, addresses the functions served by elements as a matter of substantive law, catalogues various types of elements and enquires whether torts should be constituted by elements.

At the outset it is necessary to address the meaning of the word 'element'.[11] Although it is and has long been ubiquitous in the case law[12] and literature,[13] no attempt to define it appears to have been made. The word is sometimes invoked to refer to major structural patterns detected in tort law. For example, John Wigmore claimed that all torts have a damage element, a responsibility element, and an excuse or justification element[14] while Thomas Cooley maintained that torts require the conjunction of

[10] P Cane, *Responsibility in Law and Morality* (Oxford, Hart Publishing, 2002) 89.

[11] The term 'ingredient' appears to be used interchangeably with it: see, eg, *OBG Ltd v Allan* [2007] UKHL 21, [2008] 1 AC 1 [191].

[12] See, eg, *Allen v Flood* [1898] AC 1 (HL) 98.

[13] See, eg, the sources referred to in nn 14–15.

[14] 'There are, therefore, three distinct classes of limitations dealt with in the law relating to Torts, which may be conveniently termed the Primary, Secondary, and Tertiary limitations. The first class deals with the sort of harm to be recognized as the basis of the right; this may be called the Damage element. The second class deals with the circumstances fixing the connection of the obligor with this forbidden harm; this we may call the Responsibility element. The third class deals with the circumstances in which, assuming both the Damage and the Responsibility elements to be present, the nexus still has no validity, – in other words, the considerations which allow the harm to be inflicted with impunity; this we may term the Excuse or Justification element': JH Wigmore, 'Tripartite Division of Torts' (1894) 8 *Harvard Law Review* 200, 202–203.

two elements namely, a wrong and damage.[15] Cane employed the idea of an element in the same or a similar way when he contended that:[16]

> [e]very cause of action in tort … has two basic (sets of) elements, one concerned with the position of one party to a bilateral human interaction (the 'victim' of the tortious conduct) and the other concerned with the position of the other party to that interaction (the perpetrator of the tortious conduct, or the 'injurer').

Much more frequently, however, the language of 'elements' is employed to refer to the confluence of particular factual circumstances that the law stipulates needs to exist in order for a tort to have been committed. So understood, an element is a necessary part of a set of conditions that are collectively sufficient to constitute a tort. This is how Lord Hope used the word 'element' in *Three Rivers District Council v Governor and Company of the Bank of England (No 3)*:[17]

> The following are the essential elements of the tort [of misfeasance in a public office] … First, there must be an unlawful act or omission done or made in the exercise of power by the public officer. Second, as the essence of the tort is an abuse of power, the act or omission must have been done or made with the required mental element. Third, for the same reason, the act or omission must have been done or made in bad faith. Fourth, as to standing, the claimants must demonstrate that they have a sufficient interest to sue the defendant. Fifth, as causation is an essential element of the cause of action, the act or omission must have caused the claimants' loss.

It is with this sense of the word 'element' that this chapter is concerned.

II. General Observations Regarding Elements

As a prelude to the analysis that follows, it is convenient to draw attention to several basic characteristics of elements.

A. The Distinctiveness of Elements

Elements of torts can be distinguished from several related concepts. One contrast concerns compounds. Compounds are composites of two or more elements. They are commonly mistaken for elements. The tort of negligence supplies notorious illustrations. To give just one example, it is regularly claimed that causation of damage is an element

[15] Under the heading 'Element of a Tort', Cooley wrote 'It is said by the authorities that it is the conjunction of damage and wrong that creates a tort, and there is no tort if either damage or wrong is wanting. Here the word wrong is used in the sense of a thing amiss; something which for any reason the party ought not to do or to permit, and which does not become the actionable wrong called a tort unless the other element is found in the same case, namely, a damage suffered in consequence of the thing amiss': TM Cooley, *A Treatise on the Law of Torts or the Wrongs Which Arise Independent of Contract* (Chicago, Callaghan & Co, 1879) 62 (footnote omitted).

[16] P Cane, *The Anatomy of Tort Law* (Oxford, Hart Publishing, 1997) 13.

[17] *Three Rivers District Council v Governor and Company of the Bank of England (No 3)* [2001] UKHL 16, [2003] 2 AC 1 [42].

of the tort of negligence.[18] This is incorrect. Causation of damage is a compound rather than an element of the tort since the issue of whether C suffered damage is fundamentally different from that of whether D's breach of duty caused it.[19] Failing to distinguish compounds from elements is fraught with danger. For example, if the courts mistake two elements of a given tort for a single requirement there is a serious risk that they will not properly investigate whether both elements are present. Another obvious problem that can arise from treating two elements as though they were a single ingredient is that rules governing one element may be wrongly extended to the other. Of course, difficult questions will sometimes arise as to whether one is dealing with an element or a compound. The Court of Appeal was concerned with this issue in *Kawasaki Kisen Kaisha Ltd v James Kemball Ltd*.[20] It considered whether Lord Hodge had been correct in *Global Resources Group Ltd v Mackay* to isolate as an element of a claim for inducing a breach of contract the requirement that 'A must induce B to break his contract with C by persuading, encouraging or assisting him to do so'.[21] The parties in *Kawasaki Kisen Kaisha* had treated this requirement as entailing two elements, one of which was based on inducement and the other being concerned with causation. However, Popplewell LJ considered that there was just a single element and wrote:[22]

> As formulated by Lord Hodge the … ingredient, of inducement, encompasses both the conduct which constitutes an inducement and the causative effect it has on B breaching the contract. Before us and the Judge below, these were to some extent treated as separate ingredients, comprising inducement and causation, but I would respectfully agree with Lord Hodge's treatment of them as a single ingredient because, as appears from the discussion below, it is of the essence of conduct by A which can amount to inducement that it should have some causative effect on B breaking the contract.

Another concept that can arguably be differentiated from that of an element is a standing requirement. It is often said that a claimant, in order to be able to sue for certain torts, must have *locus standi*. For example, it is commonly asserted that in order for a claimant to be able to sue for private nuisance he must have standing,[23] in the form of a proprietary interest in the land in issue. It is debatable whether tort law in fact recognises principles that are properly regarded as standing requirements.[24] But if it does, it may be that elements are distinct from them in that elements are constitutive of the wrong in issue whereas standing rules are not.

Liability for some torts is said to depend on an actionability precondition being satisfied, and such preconditions can arguably be contrasted with elements. For instance,

[18] See section III.

[19] Regarding the tendency to conflate the causation and damage elements of the tort of negligence, see D Nolan, 'Rights, Damage and Loss' (2016) 37 *OJLS* 255, 270–72.

[20] *Kawasaki Kisen Kaisha Ltd v James Kemball Ltd* [2021] EWCA Civ 33.

[21] *Global Resources Group Ltd v Mackay* [2008] CSOH 148, 2009 SLT 104 [11].

[22] *Kawasaki Kisen Kaisha* (n 20) [22].

[23] See, eg, *Hunter v Canary Wharf Ltd* [1997] AC 655 (HL) 717.

[24] Consider, for example, Peter Cane's remark that 'Standing is not normally a requirement for bringing a "private law claim" … There are certain private-law concepts that resemble rules of standing: for example, duty of care in the tort of negligence, and the principle that breach of a statutory duty will be actionable in tort only if the duty is owed to the claimant as an individual (as opposed to the public generally) … However, these are not seen as separate from the rules that define the relevant wrong, but as part of the definition of the wrong': P Cane, *Administrative Law*, 5th edn (Oxford, Clarendon Press, 2011) 281–82.

John Murphy contends with reference to the tort of deceit that 'the need to show consequential loss is a mere condition of actionability, but not an element of the tort *strictu sensu*'.[25] In support of this claim Murphy refers to the dictum of Stephenson LJ in *Diamond v The Bank of London and Montreal* that '[i]n deceit … the false representation … has to cause damage to be actionable, but no damage to the plaintiff is necessary for the tort to be committed'.[26] Whether or not this is correct is debatable.[27] However, the important point for present purposes is that if actionability requirements exist they would appear to be distinct from elements in that they are not constitutive of the wrongs to which they relate. Whether or not actionability preconditions are synonymous with standing requirements is unclear.

B. Variability in the Number of Elements

Considerable variability exists regarding the number of ingredients from which individual torts are made. Rightly or wrongly, some torts are said to have just a single element. For example, in *Johnson v Chief Constable of Surrey* Neill LJ claimed that the tort of false imprisonment has just one element, namely, imprisonment.[28] By contrast, most torts are usually understood as having several elements, typically three or four. Some torts, such as the torts of inducing a breach of contract[29] and malicious prosecution,[30] are said to have as many as five. According to Lord Steyn in *Three Rivers*, the tort of misfeasance in public office has six.[31] Whether or not the elements of the foregoing torts have been accurately counted is debatable. However, the point of interest for present purposes is simply that there is considerable divergence in terms of the number of ingredients from which torts are made.

Why are some torts more intricate assemblages than others? One possible explanation is that there is, for one reason or another, a particular concern precisely to locate

[25] J Murphy, 'Misleading Appearances in the Tort of Deceit' (2016) 75 *CLJ* 301, 323.

[26] *Diamond v The Bank of London and Montreal* [1979] QB 333 (CA) 349.

[27] For discussion, see J Neyers, 'Form and Substance in the Tort of Deceit' in A Robertson and J Goudkamp (eds), *Form and Substance in the Law of Obligations* (Oxford, Hart Publishing, 2019).

[28] 'In one sense it is true to say that the tort of false imprisonment has two ingredients; the fact of imprisonment and the absence of lawful authority to justify it … But as I understand the law, the gist of the action of false imprisonment is the mere imprisonment': *Johnson v Chief Constable of Surrey*, The Times, 23 November 1992 (CA).

[29] '[F]irst, there must be a contract, second, there must be a breach of that contract; thirdly, the conduct of the relevant defendant must have been such as to procure or induce that breach; fourthly, the relevant defendant must have known of the existence of the relevant term in the contract or turned a blind eye to the existence of such a term; and fifthly, the relevant defendant must have actually realised that the conduct, which was being induced or procured, would result in a breach of the term': *Aerostar Maintenance International Ltd v Wilson* [2010] EWHC 2032 (Ch) [163] (Morgan J). Some scholars deny the existence of the tort of inducing a breach of contract and argue that the supposed tort is simply a form of accessorial liability: see, eg, PS Davies, *Accessory Liability* (Oxford, Hart Publishing, 2015) 139–40. The merits of this view are beyond the scope of this chapter.

[30] 'The claimant must show: i) He was prosecuted by the defendant. ii) The prosecution was determined in his favour. iii) The prosecution was without reasonable and probable cause. iv) It was malicious. v) He suffered actionable damage': *Rees v Commissioner of Police for the Metropolis* [2018] EWCA Civ 1587 [43] (McCombe LJ referring with approval to the trial judge's description of the elements of the tort).

[31] *Three Rivers* (n 17) 191–96. *cf* Lord Hope's list in the same case: see the text accompanying n 17.

the borders of certain torts, and the inclusion of additional elements reflects an attempt to realise this goal. Another potential reason for the variability may lie in a concern to prevent particular torts from imposing liability too readily. On this view, extra elements are incorporated simply in order to limit liability rather than (as per the previous explanation) to fine-tune a tort's scope. A final possibility is that some torts have simply been the subject of greater scrutiny than others and that this has led to their being dissected into a greater number of components.

C. Minimum Requirements

All torts have at least one conduct element.[32] Thus, the tort of trespass to land entails the defendant entering upon the claimant's land and the tort of conversion consists in the defendant usurping the claimant's rights over a chattel. It follows from the fact that all torts incorporate a conduct element that there are no torts that consist exclusively in a mental element. Accordingly, tort law never attaches liability to a mere mental state.[33] The point can be taken further. Not only are there no torts that consist exclusively in a mental element but there are no torts that require proof of a mental element in connection with a consequence without that mental element being accompanied by a conduct element. Thus, all torts that require proof that the defendant intended to injure the claimant (such as both forms of conspiracy and the unlawful means tort) are committed only if the defendant actually causes the claimant to suffer damage. Because tort law, when liability depends on a mental state in connection with a consequence, always requires that the defendant brought about that consequence before liability will arise, simply attempting to commit a tort is never itself tortious.[34]

D. Interdependence

The elements of torts are often interlinked. Denning LJ drew attention to this in the negligence context in *Roe v Minster of Health* when he said that 'you will find that the three questions, duty, causation and remoteness, run continually into one another'.[35] Consider also the following comments of Lord Pearson in *Home Office v Dorset Yacht Co Ltd*:[36]

> The form of the order [providing for the court to determine as a preliminary issue whether the defendant owed the claimant a duty of care] assumes the familiar analysis of the tort of negligence into its three component elements, viz., the duty of care, the breach of that duty and the resulting damage. The analysis is logically correct and often convenient for purposes of exposition, but it is only an analysis and should not eliminate consideration of the tort of negligence as a whole.

[32] The concept of a conduct element is explored further below in section V. E–F.
[33] 'The mere intent cannot constitute actionable matter': Cooley (n 15) 61–62 (footnote omitted).
[34] See generally JCP Goldberg and BC Zipursky, 'Unrealized Torts' (2002) 88 *Virginia Law Review* 1626.
[35] *Roe v Minster of Health* [1954] 2 QB 66 (CA) 86.
[36] *Home Office v Dorset Yacht Co Ltd* [1970] AC 1004 (HL) 1052.

Interconnections between elements can occur in several different ways. One or more elements of a given tort may draw upon a common concept. For example, in the tort of negligence the idea of foreseeability features in relation to whether a duty of care was owed, whether any duty that was owed was breached and whether the claimant's damage was non-remote.[37] Thus, in order for a duty of care to arise, injury to a person such as the claimant must be foreseeable,[38] before a duty will be breached there must have been a foreseeable risk of injury[39] and the requirement that the damage not be remote will be unsatisfied unless the loss was of a foreseeable kind.[40] Although the concept of foreseeability is not applied in precisely the same way in relation to each of these parts of the tort of negligence, it is nevertheless a common thread running through them.

Elements of torts can also be interconnected in that the process of determining whether one ingredient of a given tort is present may call for consideration of another. The tort of negligence again serves as an excellent illustration.[41] For example, because very different duty rules apply depending on the nature of the claimant's loss it is inadequate to ask whether a defendant owed the claimant a duty of care without first enquiring as to the nature of the claimant's damage.[42] Similarly, the issue of whether a claimant's act of self-harm will prevent causation from being established depends on whether the defendant's duty of care extended to taking reasonable steps to prevent the claimant from injuring himself.[43] One strongly suspects that this interconnectedness is a feature of all torts to at least some degree albeit it is not always as visible or pronounced as in the case of the tort of negligence.

The structure of judgments and textbooks sometimes implies that elements of torts, or at least some torts, should be addressed sequentially.[44] However, the interdependence of elements suggests that this may not always be possible. As just observed, it may be the case that a judge sometimes cannot properly reach a final conclusion regarding the existence of particular elements of certain torts without considering another element. In such situations, a judge may need to reach merely provisional conclusions regarding the presence of a given element and revisit that initial view in the light of the analysis of other ingredients. On this account, the process of ascertaining whether a tort has been committed is not akin to following a recipe[45] or chain.[46]

[37] See J Goudkamp and D Nolan, *Winfield & Jolowicz on Tort*, 20th edn (London, Sweet & Maxwell, 2020) para 5.003.

[38] See, eg, *Robinson v Chief Constable of West Yorkshire* [2018] UKSC 4, [2018] AC 736 [73]–[74].

[39] See, eg, *Jones v Whippey* [2009] EWCA Civ 452 [16]. According to a different line of authority, the need for the risk that materialised to have been foreseeable is not a precondition to the breach element being satisfied but simply a factor to take into account in deciding whether the defendant was negligent. This rival view is addressed in Goudkamp and Nolan (n 37) para 6.017.

[40] See, eg, *The Wagon Mound* [1961] AC 388 (PC) 426.

[41] See further J Stapleton, *Three Essays on Torts* (Oxford, Oxford University Press, 2021) ch 3.

[42] For discussion, see Goudkamp and Nolan (n 37) para 5.005.

[43] *Reeves v Commissioner of Police for the Metropolis* [2000] 1 AC 360 (HL).

[44] Consider, eg, the cases cited in n 66.

[45] Consider Cane (n 16) 3–10.

[46] Consider Turner (n 5) 19–20.

E. Coincidence

One of the first rules to which students of the criminal law are introduced is the coincidence principle. This doctrine stipulates that in order for liability to arise the *mens rea* and *actus reus* of an offence must occur simultaneously. The rule is heavily qualified. For example, it will be satisfied if the *mens rea* is superimposed on an already present *actus reus*. Thus, in *Fagan v Metropolitan Police Commissioner*[47] it was held that D was rightly convicted of battery when, having accidentally driven his car onto the foot of a police constable, he intentionally left it there. It did not matter that the *actus reus* commenced before the required *mens rea* existed in circumstances where the *actus reus* was ongoing. The courts sometimes hold that the coincidence doctrine is satisfied by analysing a series of events as a single transaction. Thus, the coincidence principle was no answer to liability for murder in *Thabo Meli v R*[48] in which the defendants mistakenly thought that they had killed a man by bludgeoning him and throwing him off a cliff whereas he in fact died some while later from exposure. Lord Reid said that 'it is much too refined a ground of judgment to say that, because [the defendants] were under a misapprehension … and thought that their guilty purpose and been achieved before in fact it was achieved, therefore they are to escape the penalties of the law'.[49]

The coincidence principle is not mentioned in torts textbooks, which is odd given that tort law provides for several causes of action that match, in both name and substance, criminal offences. However, it is obvious that tort law also embraces it. For example, it is surely the case that D will not incur liability for deceit unless he intended to defraud C at the time of making the misrepresentation in issue. If D intended to defraud C but no longer held that intention at the time of making the misstatement concerned liability for deceit will not arise. Nor, undoubtedly, will D be liable for conspiring to injure C unless he intended, at the time of entering into the conspiracy, for C to be injured by the conspiracy's implementation. The possession by D at some other point in time of an intention to injure C will not suffice.

It is worth observing that tort law insists on certain elements being simultaneously present in a way that goes beyond the strict requirements of the coincidence principle, which is concerned only with whether conduct elements and fault elements overlap temporally. For example, liability will not arise for the tort of negligence in respect of an injury that D caused to C unless a duty of care arose no later than the time of the careless conduct. Similarly, C must have a proprietary interest in land at the time when D interferes with C's use and enjoyment thereof if C is to have a valid claim for private nuisance.[50] It is obvious that liability will not accrue if C disposed of his interest prior to the interference or acquired it after the interference ceased.

[47] *Fagan v Metropolitan Police Commissioner* [1969] 1 QB 439 (Div Ct).
[48] *Thabo Meli v R* [1954] 1 WLR 228 (PC).
[49] ibid 231.
[50] The discussion here ignores the possibility that the need for a proprietary interest is not an element of the tort of private nuisance but is instead a standing requirement. See the text accompanying n 23.

III. Instability in the Elements of Torts

Whenever it is objected that tort law is uncertain, the target is typically the scope of a particular element of a given cause of action. Often, however, the uncertainty runs far more deeply than is generally appreciated and afflicts not only the parameters of discrete ingredients of torts but the contents of the list of ingredients itself. This is symptomatic of insufficient concern with the elements of torts and hence worth briefly addressing. Consider the tort of negligence.[51] In *Matthews v Ministry of Defence*, Lord Phillips MR said that '[a] cause of action in negligence, as a matter of substantive law, requires duty, breach of duty and entitlement to a remedy'.[52] In *Rothwell v Chemical & Insulating Co Ltd*, Lord Rodger offered a very different formulation. His Lordship wrote that:[53]

> three elements must combine before there is a cause of action for damages for personal injuries caused by a defendant's negligence … There must be (1) a negligent act … by the defendant, which (2) causes an injury to the claimant's body and (3) the claimant must suffer material damage as a result.

Seabrook v Adam[54] supplies yet another variation. In that case, Asplin LJ said that in order for a claim in negligence to succeed 'the defendant must owe the claimant a duty of care, that duty must have been breached and the breach must have caused damage of a kind which is recoverable'.[55] These configurations differ meaningfully from each other. It follows that they cannot all be correct. In fact, none of them is accurate. It is beyond the scope of this chapter to isolate all of the difficulties from which they suffer. It suffices to say that Lord Phillips MR's and Asplin LJ's lists respectively omit and elide the causation and damage elements[56] while Lord Rodger's overlooks the need for a duty of care.

Similar definitional diversity exists in the textbooks. The authors of *Clerk & Lindsell on Torts* claim that the tort of negligence has four elements, namely: (i) a duty of care; (ii) breach; (iii) causation and damage; and (iv) the damage must not be too remote.[57] By contrast, Nicholas McBride and Roderick Bagshaw also perceive the tort as being composed of four elements but their list is as follows: (i) a duty of care; (ii) breach; (iii) causation of 'some kind of loss'; and (iv) the loss suffered must be actionable.[58] The author of *Street on Torts* enumerates the elements of the tort in yet another way, namely: (i) duty of care; (ii) breach of duty; (iii) 'factual causation of damage'; and (iv) neither the damage is too remote nor any defence is applicable.[59] These definitions differ not only from those drawn from the cases identified above but also from each other. Again, none of them is correct. Among other problems, they are all afflicted by the same difficulty as Asplin LJ's, that is, they conflate the question of whether the claimant suffered damage with the issue of whether the defendant caused it.[60]

[51] See further DG Owen, 'The Five Elements of Negligence' (2007) 35 *Hofstra Law Review* 1671 (identifying the diversity of ways in which the elements of the tort of negligence have been propounded in the US).

[52] *Matthews v Ministry of Defence* [2002] EWCA Civ 773, [2002] 1 WLR 2621 [66].

[53] *Rothwell v Chemical & Insulating Co Ltd* [2007] UKHL 39, [2008] 1 AC 281 [87].

[54] *Seabrook v Adam* [2021] EWCA Civ 382, [2021] 4 WLR 54.

[55] ibid [11].

[56] Regarding this error, see Nolan (n 19).

[57] *Clerk & Lindsell on Torts*, 23rd edn (London, Sweet & Maxwell, 2020) para 7.4.

[58] NJ McBride and R Bagshaw, *Tort Law*, 6th edn (Harlow, Pearson, 2018) 72.

[59] Witting (n 6) 25.

[60] See Nolan (n 19).

Related to the problem of definitional instability is the tendency for facts to be treated as pertaining to a given element of a tort when, in actuality, they bear upon a different ingredient. This error, which can result in valid claims being denied or in the success of proceedings that ought to fail, is frequently committed, particularly in the negligence context. A notorious illustration is *Darnley v Croydon Health Services NHS Trust*.[61] In this case, the Court of Appeal considered that the amount of care that the defendant hospital could reasonably be expected to take for a patient bore upon whether it owed the patient a duty of care. This led the Court to conclude that no duty of care arose. Two fundamental difficulties with this reasoning are obvious.[62] First, there was no scope for argument as to the existence of a duty of care because precedent establishes that hospitals owe a duty of care to their patients. Second, the amount of care that the defendant exercised or could reasonably be expected to exercise has, in any event, no bearing on the existence of a duty of care but instead pertains to the breach element of the tort of negligence. The Supreme Court put things right on appeal[63] but there are many other cases in which facts relevant to the breach ingredient were wrongly treated as affecting the existence of a duty of care.[64]

IV. The Functions of Elements

It is conventional for judges hearing tort claims to enumerate the elements of the tort that the claimant contends the defendant committed[65] and then proceed to consider, *seriatim* and often in a highly structured manner, whether each is present.[66] Elements of torts are clearly thought to be important. But why, specifically, is this the case?

A. Substance

Elements are substantively important for the simple reason that liability in tort cannot arise unless all of the elements of the tort for which the claimant sues are present.[67]

[61] *Darnley v Croydon Health Services NHS Trust* [2017] EWCA Civ 151, [2018] QB 783.

[62] For further discussion, see J Goudkamp, 'Breach of Duty: A Disappearing Element of the Action in Negligence?' (2017) 75 *CLJ* 480.

[63] [2018] UKSC 50, [2019] AC 831.

[64] See, eg, *Orange v Chief Constable of West Yorkshire Police* [2001] EWCA Civ 611, [2002] QB 347 [48]; *Fernquest v City & County of Swansea* [2011] EWCA Civ 1712 [20].

[65] See, eg, *Reckitt & Colman Products Ltd v Borden Inc* [1990] 1 WLR 491 (HL) 499 (passing off); *Aerostar* (n 29) [163] (inducing a breach of contract); *Dowson v Chief Constable of Northumbria Police* [2010] EWHC 2612 (QB) [142] (harassment); *Berezovsky v Abramovich* [2011] EWCA Civ 153, [2011] 1 WLR 2290 [5] (intimidation); *Dunnage v Randall* [2015] EWCA Civ 673, [2016] QB 639 [121] (negligence); *O v Rhodes* [2015] UKSC 32, [2016] AC 219 [73] (intentional infliction of physical or psychological harm); *Zurich Insurance Co plc v Hayward* [2016] UKSC 48, [2017] AC 142 [58] (deceit); *Pirtek (UK) Ltd v Jackson* [2017] EWHC 2834 (QB) [54] (malicious falsehood); *FM Capital Partners Ltd v Marino* [2018] EWHC 1768 (Comm) [94] (unlawful means conspiracy); *Rees* (n 30) [43] (malicious prosecution); *Secretary of State for Health v Servier Laboratories Ltd* [2019] EWCA Civ 1160, [2020] Ch 717 [19] (causing loss by unlawful means); *London Borough of Lambeth v AM* [2021] EWHC 186 (QB) [20] (misuse of private information).

[66] Good examples of decisions that adhere to this approach include *Chalfont St Peter Parish Council v Holy Cross Sisters Trustees Incorporated* [2019] EWHC 1128 (QB); *Vald Nielsen Holdings A/S* [2019] EWHC 1926 (Comm).

[67] *cf* Lord Neuberger's curious suggestion in *O* (n 65) [105] regarding the tort of intentional infliction of physical or psychological harm that 'it would be dangerous to say categorically that each ingredient of the tort must always be present'.

Thus, it is often stressed that the ingredients of torts must be 'separately'[68] established before a remedy can be granted, and that a claimant cannot avoid the need to substantiate a given element by proving some other fact, such as that the defendant acted maliciously[69] or was guilty of *crassa negligentia*.[70] Accordingly, if an element of a tort for which the claimant sues is absent, the court cannot award the claimant a remedy,[71] and that is so regardless of whether, according to some conception of justice, the claimant is nevertheless thought to be deserving of relief.[72] *Kaye v Robertson*[73] illustrates the point. In this case, the claimant was convalescing in hospital when journalists working for the defendant newspaper burst into his room and interviewed and photographed him. When the newspaper announced that it intended to publish an article based on the interview, the Court granted an interim injunction restraining it from doing so on the basis that the publication would amount to malicious falsehood. However, Bingham LJ emphasised that had the claimant 'failed to establish any cause of action, we should of course have been powerless to act, however great our sympathy for [him] and however strong our distaste for the defendants' conduct'.[74] Of course, if a court wishes to grant the claimant a remedy, it may abolish a particular element or broaden an element so that it is more easily satisfied or even recognise a new tort.[75] However, none of this affects the points set out above. The fact remains that the claimant must establish the presence of all of the elements of the tort (howsoever they are defined) in which he sues in order for liability to arise.

Just as the absence of any of the elements of the tort for which the claimant sues dictates that the claimant cannot obtain a remedy however worthy the claimant's claim may otherwise be thought to be, where all of the ingredients of a claim in tort are present the court has no choice but to award the claimant at least nominal damages. Thus, the court cannot withhold damages because it considers, despite the claimant having proven all of the elements of a tort, that the claimant is, for one reason or another, undeserving of a remedy. In *Re T & N Ltd* David Richards J put the point as follows in the negligence context: 'There is no element of discretion … If the ingredients of the tort of

[68] See, eg, *Qema v News Group Newspapers Ltd* [2012] EWHC 1146 (QB) [58]; *Mosley v Associated Newspapers Ltd* [2020] EWHC 3545 (QB), [2021] 4 WLR 29 [32].

[69] For instance, in *Mosley* (n 68) [32] Nicklin J wrote that '[e]vidence of malice, of whatever degree, cannot dispense with or diminish the need to establish separately each of the [other] elements of the tort' of malicious prosecution.

[70] 'A man is entitled to be as negligent as he pleases towards the whole world if he owes no duty to them': *Le Lievre v Gould* [1893] 1 QB 491 (CA) 497 (Lord Esher MR).

[71] According to Mitchell McInnes, it is 'trite' that 'regardless of the nature of the remedy sought, every element of a tort must be satisfied': M McInnes, 'Restitution, Disgorgement, and Waiver of Tort in the Supreme Court of Canada' (2021) 137 *LQR* 188, 190.

[72] Instances where the court evidently had sympathy for the claimant but in which a remedy was nevertheless withheld because one or more of the elements of the tort on which the claimant relied was missing are innumerable but see, eg, *Seligman v Docker* [1949] Ch 53 (Ch D) 66–67; *Wilsher v Essex Area Health Authority* [1998] AC 1074 (HL) 1092; *Croft v Broadstairs & St Peter's Town Council* [2003] EWCA Civ 676 [76]; *Hewes v West Hertfordshire Acute Hospitals NHS Trust* [2020] EWCA Civ 1523 [100]; *Brand v No Limits Track Days Ltd* [2020] EWHC 1306 [2]; *HXH v Surrey County Council* [2021] EWHC 250 (QB) [45]–[48].

[73] *Kaye v Robertson* [1991] FSR 62 (CA).

[74] ibid 70.

[75] Classic examples include *Wilkinson v Downton* [1897] 2 QB 57 (QBD); *Willers v Joyce* [2016] UKSC 43, [2018] AC 779.

negligence … are established, the claimants are entitled to damages. [That entitlement does] not depend on an exercise of discretion by the court'.[76]

B. Procedure

The concept of an element is also important procedurally. It is convenient to give three examples. Consider, first, the fact that claimants must plead facts that satisfy all of the elements of a tort known to the law, or the elements of a tort that they plausibly contend that the law ought to recognise, or they risk having summary judgment entered against them or having their claim struck out. *Fowler v Lanning*[77] is a famous illustration. In this case, Diplock J said that '[t]respass to the person does not lie if the injury to the plaintiff, although the direct consequence of the act of the defendant, was caused unintentionally and without negligence on the defendant's part'.[78] Because the claimant had alleged simply that the defendant had shot him, his Lordship struck the claim out.

A second example of the procedural significance of elements relates to the burden of proof. Because the claimant carries the onus of establishing facts that satisfy the elements of the tort in which he sues, the fact that a given issue constitutes an element determines that the claimant must prove it.[79] It is true that claimants sometimes bear the onus of establishing various matters that are not elements of torts. For example, if a defendant raises a limitation defence, the claimant is obliged to show that he issued the claim form before the expiry of the relevant time period.[80] And claimants must prove facts relevant to the availability of the remedy claimed. Thus, if the claimant seeks punitive damages, the claimant must prove facts that bring the claim within the categories established by *Rookes v Barnard*.[81] But this does not alter the fact that if an issue constitutes an element of a tort the claimant carries the onus of proof in respect of it.

A third illustration of the procedural importance of elements concerns the running of time for limitation purposes. As a general rule, time starts running when the cause of action concerned accrues. This occurs when 'the last element constituting it has come into existence'.[82] It follows that one needs to be able to ascertain the elements of any given tort in order to identify when the limitation period commenced.

[76] *Re T & N Ltd* [2005] EWHC 2870 (Ch) [55].
[77] *Fowler v Lanning* [1959] 1 QB 426 (QBD).
[78] ibid 439.
[79] *Kuwait Oil Tanker Co SAK v Al Bader* [2000] 2 All ER (Comm) 271 (CA) [132]; *Hall v Herbert* [1993] 2 SCR 159, 184.
[80] *Lloyds Bank plc v Crosse & Crosse* [2001] EWCA Civ 366, [2001] PNLR 34 [41]; *Fiona Trust & Holding Corp v Privalov* [2010] EWHC 3199 (Comm) [315].
[81] *Rookes v Barnard* [1964] AC 1129 (HL).
[82] A Zuckerman, *Zuckerman on Civil Procedure: Principles of Practice*, 4th edn (London, Sweet & Maxwell, 2021) para 26.15 (footnotes omitted).

V. Types of Elements

Elements come in different types. As we will see, the case law and literature are populated by references to conduct elements, consequence elements, fault elements, primary elements, mental elements and more. This section explores the various species of element.

A. Alternative Elements

Unless the claimant proves all of the elements of the tort for which he sues, liability will not arise. However, some torts can be established by one or more different sets of elements. Such torts incorporate alternative elements.[83] Take, for example, the tort of deceit. In order to succeed in a claim for deceit the claimant must prove, among other things, that the defendant made a false statement and that he did so with a relevant state of mind. Specifically, the claimant must demonstrate that the defendant made the false representation concerned '(i) knowingly, (ii) without belief in its truth, or (iii) recklessly, careless whether it be true or false'.[84] In effect, therefore, the requirement that the defendant make a false statement has linked with it three alternative fault elements. Another example of a tort with alternative elements is that of misfeasance in a public office. This cause of action requires proof, among other things, of either (i) 'targeted malice by a public officer, i.e. conduct specifically intended to injure a person or persons' or (ii) that the public officer concerned acted knowing that he lacked the power to perform the act in question and that it would probably harm the claimant.[85]

B. Negative Elements

Most tort elements require proof of the presence of something, such as a particular state of mind on the part of the defendant or the existence of damage. Sometimes, however, the absence of something must be established. A good illustration of a tort that incorporates a negative element is that of malicious prosecution, which requires the claimant to demonstrate that his prosecution was 'without reasonable and probable cause'.[86] Another example is the tort of battery, which is committed only where the claimant withheld consent to the defendant's contact concerned.[87] Tort law makes use

[83] It is not only tort law that makes use of alternative elements. Perhaps the most striking use of alternative elements is found in the context of unjust enrichment. A claim in unjust enrichment requires an unjust factor, and the law recognises a lengthy catalogue of unjust factors any one of which will supply this element. A different view of the law, perhaps more conventional, is that each unjust factor identifies a separate cause of action in unjust enrichment. Consider, eg, K Barker, 'Unjust Enrichment in Australia: What Is(n't) It? Implications for Legal Reasoning and Practice' (2020) 43 *Melbourne University Law Review* 903, 922–23, 930–31.

[84] *Derry v Peek* (1889) 14 App Case 337 (HL) 376 (Lord Herschell).

[85] *Three Rivers* (n 17) 191 (Lord Steyn). See also at 192.

[86] *Clerk & Lindsell on Torts* (n 57) para 15.13.

[87] Consent is sometimes characterised as a defence to liability in battery as opposed to a negative element. The better view is that non-consent is part of the definition of a battery: see J Goudkamp, *Tort Law Defences* (Oxford, Hart Publishing, 2013) 65–67.

of negative elements rather sparingly. One possible explanation for this situation may lie in the fact that the onus of proving elements falls on the claimant.[88] The significance of this is that it is often supposed, rightly or wrongly, that it is unfairly onerous to require a party to prove a negative.[89]

C. Non-Elements

Non-elements are matters that are not part of the definition of a tort. Accordingly, where the law declares that something is a non-element of a particular tort, the tort concerned is simply insensitive to the issue of whether the thing concerned exists. Consider the defamation context. It is often observed that it is not an element of the torts of libel or slander that the statement in issue be false.[90] Nor is it an element of those torts that the claimant be individually named by the statement concerned or that any particular person otherwise understood the statement to refer to the claimant.[91] To take some examples from different settings, 'negligence is not an essential element in nuisance',[92] 'the elements of liability under the rule in *Rylands v Fletcher* do not include want of reasonable care',[93] 'bad faith' is not an ingredient of the tort of false imprisonment[94] and dishonesty is not an element of the tort of conspiracy.[95]

D. Primary Elements

Reference is often made to the 'primary elements' of torts.[96] Sometimes the word 'primary' is used in such a way that it adds nothing to the word 'element'.[97] When the term 'primary' is so employed, the primary elements of a tort are simply its ingredients. On other occasions, however, the language of primary elements is invoked such that defences to liability in tort are presented not as rules that are external to the definitions

[88] See n 79.

[89] Consider Lord Kerr's remark in *Crawford Adjusters (Cayman) Ltd v Sagicor General Insurance (Cayman) Ltd* [2013] UKPC 17, [2014] AC 366 [109] that '[e]stablishing the various rudiments of the tort of malicious prosecution is no easy task. … It has to be shown that there was no reasonable or probable cause for the launch of the proceedings. This requires the proof of a negative proposition, normally among the most difficult of evidential requirements'.

[90] See, eg, *Barron v Vines* [2015] EWHC 1161 (QB) [15].

[91] *Lachaux v Independent Print Ltd* [2015] EWHC 2242 (QB), [2016] QB 402 [15].

[92] *Overseas Tankship (UK) Ltd v Miller SS Co Pty* [1967] 1 AC 617 (PC) 639 (Lord Reid).

[93] *Margereson v JW Roberts Ltd* [1996] PIQR 154 (QBD) 179 (Holland J).

[94] *R v Governor of Brockhill Prison* [2001] 2 AC 19 (HL) 42.

[95] *ED&F Man Sugar Ltd v T&L Sugars Ltd* [2016] EWHC 272 (Comm) [33].

[96] The courts also refer to 'basic elements' (see, eg, *Clerk & Lindsell on Torts* (n 57) para 21.163), 'core elements' (see, eg, *Planet Art LLC v Photobox Ltd* [2019] EWHC 1688 (Ch) [66]), 'essential elements' (see, eg, *Overseas Tankship* (n 92) 639; *Zurich* (n 65) [58]), 'prima facie elements' (see, eg, *Ware v McAllister* [2015] EWHC 3086 (QB) [27]), 'necessary elements' (see, eg, *Overseas Tankship* (n 92) 640; *Secretary of State for Health v Servier Laboratories Ltd* [2021] UKSC 24, [2021] 3 WLR 370 [2]–[3]) and 'substantive elements' (see, eg, *Ivy Technology v Martin* [2019] EWHC 2510 (Comm) [12]) of torts. It is unclear whether these expressions bear a meaning different from that of 'primary elements'.

[97] Consider *Jones v Environcom Ltd* [2011] EWCA Civ 1152, [2012] PNLR 5 [19].

of torts but as negative elements of torts. For example, the authors of *Clerk & Lindsell on Torts* write:[98]

> When a claimant fails to establish the primary elements of the particular tort of which he complains, his action necessarily fails. He may however succeed in proving that prima facie a tort has been committed, only to be met with a defence by virtue of which the defendant argues that he is exculpated from liability in all the circumstances.

So understood, the primary elements of a tort are matters that, when present, merely lead to the provisional conclusion that a tort was committed (hence the language of 'prima facie'), a conclusion that may turn out to be incorrect when defences are considered. This construes defences as bearing upon whether a tort exists in the first place rather than as, for example, justifications for torts.

Although defences are often conceptualised as negative elements of torts[99] this understanding is controversial. A rival view is that defences are rules that preclude liability from arising despite a tort having been committed. On this account, using the language of primary elements in the way that the editors of *Clerk & Lindsell on Torts* do is misleading. That is because defences are not things that prevent 'prima facie' torts from maturing into actual torts but are things that are external to the elements of torts and which, accordingly, have no bearing on whether a tort exists. This is not the place to debate the merits of these alternative accounts of the nature of defences.[100] My own allegiance lies with the view that defences exist independently of torts. The significant point to note for present purposes is that the language of primary elements, depending on how it is used, raises the issue of whether defences are negative elements of torts.

E. Conduct Elements and Fault Elements

Conduct elements are often distinguished from fault elements.[101] This dichotomy[102] seems loosely to track that which the criminal law recognises between the *actus reus* of an offence and its *mens rea*. Examples of conduct elements include making contact with the body of another person (which is one of the conduct elements of the tort of battery) and entering land in the possession of another (which is one of the conduct elements of the tort of trespass to land). Illustrations of fault elements include the requirement that a person know or ought to know that a given course of conduct amounts to harassment of another (which is one of the fault elements of the tort of harassment[103]) and an intention to strike at the claimant through a third party (which is one of the fault elements of the unlawful means tort).

[98] *Clerk & Lindsell on Torts* (n 57) para 3.01.

[99] See, eg, the position taken in *Street on Torts* quoted at the text accompanying n 59 which expressly defines the tort of negligence as involving the absence of defences.

[100] They are addressed in Goudkamp (n 87) ch 2 in an analysis that owes much to J Gardner, *Offences and Defences: Selected Essays in the Philosophy of Criminal Law* (Oxford, Oxford University Press, 2007) chs 4–5.

[101] See, eg, *Zurich* (n 65) [58] (Lord Toulson referring to the 'conduct element' and 'fault element' of the tort of deceit).

[102] A related distinction is that between conduct elements and mental elements, the latter being a subset of fault elements: see, eg, *O* (n 65) [73] (Lady Hale and Lord Toulson referring to the 'conduct element' and 'mental element' of the tort of intentional infliction of physical or psychological harm).

[103] Protection from Harassment Act 1997 (UK), s 1(1)(b).

Several points are of interest regarding conduct elements and fault elements. First, it is doubtful that the distinction between them is exhaustive. An example of an element that does not appear to be either a conduct element or a fault element is the need for the purposes of the tort of malicious prosecution for the prosecution to have terminated in the claimant's favour. Negligence (in the sense of a falling short of the standard of the reasonable person) does not map easily onto the distinction either. Negligence is a form of conduct rather than a state of mind[104] and so it may be thought that a negligence requirement is a conduct element. Conversely, negligence is a species of fault with the result that a negligence requirement can be (and typically is) identified as a fault element.

Second, conduct elements are sometimes but not always paired with fault elements. When a conduct ingredient is not linked with a fault requirement the tort in question imposes strict liability at least in so far as the conduct ingredient in question is concerned. An illustration of a tort which has conduct elements that are not linked with fault elements and which accordingly, to a degree, makes use of strict liability is that of trespass to land.[105] Thus, the conduct requirement that the defendant enter upon land in the claimant's possession is not matched with a fault element. It is immaterial to liability in trespass to land, for example, whether the defendant reasonably believed that the land was his or that the claimant had consented to the entry.[106]

Third, fault elements are often classified as being subjective or objective. Subjective fault elements are prescribed states of mind. Cane identifies these mental states as '"intention", "recklessness", "knowledge/belief" and "malice"'.[107] By contrast, objective fault elements involve comparing the defendant's conduct with that in which the reasonable person would have engaged. However, the distinction between subjective fault elements and objective fault elements is far from straightforward. In the first place, because mental states are not directly observable and must (exceptions aside[108]) be ascertained indirectly by reference to conduct, all fault elements are, in a sense, objective. Futhermore, recklessness, although it is sometimes classed as a form of subjective fault,[109] is in fact neither a purely subjective nor a purely objective type of fault. Recklessness has two components, namely: (i) D must have been actually aware of a particular risk; and (ii) D must have run that risk despite its being unreasonable to do so. The first half of this definition is subjective while the second half is objective. Finally, the issue of whether the defendant was objectively at fault often does not reduce to comparing the defendant's conduct with that in which the reasonable person would have engaged and the reality is that the defendant's state of mind is often considered. For example, in determining whether a defendant was negligent the courts routinely investigate what

[104] See HLA Hart, *Punishment and Responsibility: Essays in the Philosophy of Law* (Oxford, Oxford University Press, 1968) 147–48.

[105] Consider also the unlawful means tort: see section V.F.

[106] *Conway v George Wimpey & Co Ltd* [1951] 2 KB 266 (CA) 273–74.

[107] Cane (n 10) 78. Tort law generally does not discriminate between intention and recklessness but treats intention as encompassing recklessness. However, there are some exceptions to this position. For example, the tort of deceit is specifically concerned with whether the defendant made the misrepresentation concerned recklessly: see the text accompanying n 84. In the context of the tort of intentional infliction of physical or psychological harm, intention is defined so as to exclude recklessness: *O* (n 65) [87].

[108] Consider, eg, admissions and confessions.

[109] See the text accompanying n 107.

the defendant actually knew about the situation in issue.[110] And where the defendant was aware of some circumstance relevant to the reasonableness of his conduct, that knowledge will be factored into the analysis even if the reasonable person in his position would not have been aware of the matter concerned.[111]

F. Conduct Elements, Circumstance Elements and Consequence Elements

The divide between conduct elements and fault elements has just been discussed. A related classification, often drawn by criminal law scholars[112] but also capable of being applied to tort law, is that between conduct elements, circumstance elements and consequence elements. In this trichotomy, the idea of a conduct element relates to the defendant's acts and omissions. Conduct elements have both physical and fault aspects. For example, the physical dimension of the conduct element of the tort of defamation is publishing a statement to a third party while the accompanying fault requirement is an intention to publish the statement or being negligent with respect to the risk that the statement would reach a third party.[113] Circumstance elements refer to the conditions in which the defendant performed the conduct element. Like conduct elements, they also have both physical and fault dimensions. Thus, the tort of deceit has a physical circumstance element, namely, the statement concerned must be false, while the associated fault requirements are that the defendant must have made the statement in issue knowing that it was false, without belief in its truth or reckless as to whether it is true or false.[114] Consequence elements are concerned with outcomes and they too can be understood in physical and fault terms. Thus, it is a physical consequence requirement of the tort of unlawful means conspiracy that the claimant suffer damage while the associated mental ingredient is an intention to injure the claimant. The elements of some torts can be reasonably neatly arranged according to this threefold classification. An example of such a tort is that of causing loss by unlawful means as per the table below. Arranging the elements of torts in this tabular form shows the extent to which a particular tort makes use of fault liability and strict liability. Thus, the table below reveals that the unlawful means tort, contrary to Lord Hoffmann's claim in *OBG Ltd v Allan* that '[t]he tort is not one of strict liability',[115] simultaneously imposes both fault liability and strict liability. The conduct and consequence elements are governed by a fault standard whereas the circumstance element is not.

[110] See, eg, *Tedstone v Bourne Leisure Ltd (t/a Thoresby Hall Hotel & Spa)* [2008] EWCA Civ 654 [15] (Moore-Bick LJ dismissing an appeal against a judgment absolving the defendant of negligence on the basis that '[t]here was no evidence that the defendant knew that a significant pool of water was likely to appear in the area in which the claimant fell …, and accordingly the evidence called by the claimant did not point to the conclusion that prima facie there was a breach of duty on the part of the defendant').

[111] See, eg, *Baker v Quantum Clothing Group Ltd* [2011] UKSC 17, [2011] 1 WLR 1003 [104].

[112] See, eg, Robinson and Grall (n 1) 706–10.

[113] See Goudkamp and Nolan (n 37) para 13.027; *cf* D Rolph, 'The Concept of Publication in Defamation Law' (2021) 27 *Torts Law Journal* (forthcoming).

[114] See the text accompanying n 84.

[115] In *OBG* (n 11) [141].

Table 1 The elements of the unlawful means tort

	Conduct element	**Circumstance element**	**Consequence element**
Physical	Conduct interfering with the claimant's ability to deal with a third party[116]	The means employed must be unlawful	Damage to the claimant caused by the unlawful means
Fault	Intention to engage in the conduct concerned	None[117]	Intention to injure the claimant

G. Presumed Elements

The claimant carries the onus of proof in respect of all of the elements of the tort in which they sue.[118] In certain circumstances, however, elements will be presumed. Consider, for example, the torts of libel and slander. In the case of libel, once it has been shown that the statement concerned is defamatory, damage will be taken to exist,[119] apparently on the footing that damage is likely to have been suffered. The same rule applies in relation to slander in two situations,[120] namely, where: (i) the defendant disparages the claimant in the course of any profession or trade carried on by him; and (ii) the defamatory imputation is to the effect that the claimant is guilty of a criminal offence punishable by a sentence of imprisonment.[121] On one view, damage is an element of all torts but is presumed to be present in relation to torts that are actionable *per se* upon proof that their other ingredients exist.[122] On this account, the position that has just been described in relation to libel and slander is simply part of a wider pattern.

H. Implicit Elements

Many elements are implicit. For instance, it is strongly arguable that all torts, like all crimes, contain a volition element,[123] that is, an ingredient that requires some type of voluntary action. This is separate from, and more basic than, for example, a requirement that the defendant intend to bring about some result. To give an example of an implicit element particular to a specific tort, it is surely the case that the tort of deceit impliedly requires that C understand D's statement concerned. If C suffers damage because, for

[116] *Secretary of State for Health v Servier Laboratories Ltd* (n 96).

[117] *Racing Partnership Ltd v Sports Information Services Ltd* [2020] EWCA Civ 1300, [2021] 2 WLR 46 (holding that it is irrelevant that the defendant did not know that the means were unlawful).

[118] See n 79.

[119] *Lachaux v Independent Print Ltd* [2019] UKSC 27, [2020] AC 612 [6].

[120] Historically, there were four such situations. The other two were purged by the Defamation Act 2013 (UK), s 14.

[121] See *Gatley on Libel & Slander*, 12th edn (London, Sweet & Maxwell, 2017) ch 4.

[122] This was Cooley's opinion: see Cooley (n 15) 62–64. *cf Brownlie v Four Seasons Holdings Inc* [2017] UKSC 80, [2018] 1 WLR 192 [52] (Lady Hale contending that 'damage is not an essential part of every cause of action in tort').

[123] See Goudkamp and Nolan (n 37) para 3.002.

example, he is frightened by D's statement despite his not having comprehended it, D will not be liable in deceit (although he may be liable for another tort, such as assault).

VI. Should Torts be Element-Based?

Because torts are, as a matter of positive law, constituted by elements, tort law cannot be properly understood without element analysis. But this does not dispose of the issue of whether the law should conceive of torts as being based on elements. The principal objection to structuring torts in terms of elements is that doing so elevates form over substance. On this view, perceiving torts as things that are comprised of ingredients diverts attention from the merits of claims and reduces the enquiry as to whether a given defendant wronged a particular claimant to a mere box-ticking exercise. It is certainly the case that deciding claims in tort by reference to the existence or otherwise of elements precludes tort law from adhering fully to the maxim *ubi jus, ibi remedium*.[124] Unfortunately, however, abandoning an element-based understanding of tort law is no solution. Dispensing with formal prerequisites to liability risks creating a legal vacuum in which judges would impose or withhold liability based on an instinctive sense of whether a wrong had been committed.

In addition to ensuring that tort claims are decided according to rules rather than whims, significant advantages flow from comprehending torts in terms of elements. In the first place, structuring torts in terms of elements increases the precedential value of decisions. Because certain elements, such as intention and damage, are common to numerous torts, decisions regarding the parameters of such ingredients are in, principle, generalisable.[125] By contrast, if judges were to decide whether a defendant was a tortfeasor not by reference to the elements of the tort on which the claimant relies but according to some amorphous conception of justice, decisions in tort cases would have reduced precedential worth.

Second, understanding torts as being constituted in terms of elements permits causes of action in tort to be precisely calibrated with a view to addressing various anxieties. For example, if there is concern that a particular tort may impose overly extensive liability, a more demanding fault element could be selected. The law could insist, for example, that recklessness as to a particular outcome will not suffice and that nothing short of an intention to bring about the consequence concerned will do.[126] Similarly, if a particular tort is defined in a way that unduly favours

[124] Consider Lord Sumption's remark in *Crawford Adjusters (Cayman) Ltd v Sagicor General Insurance (Cayman) Ltd* (n 89) [122] that '[d]efining the legal elements of a tort and the legal limitations on its ambit will commonly involve a large element of policy which may conflict with the simple principle that for every injustice there should be remedy at law'.

[125] *cf* Lord Sumption and Lord Lloyd-Jones's remark in *JSC BTA Bank v Khrapunov* [2018] UKSC 19, [2020] AC 727 [6] that '[s]ome of the elements of the [economic] torts, notably intention and unlawful means are common to more than one of them. But it is dangerous to assume that they have the same content in each context'.

[126] Consider the remarks in *O* (n 65) [87].

one of the parties, it may, for example, be appropriate to rebalance things by jettisoning an element (to make it more claimant favourable) or adding a new ingredient (to improve the position of defendants). No such fine-tuning of the parameters of liability would be possible if wrongs were defined in wholly generalised terms.

Third, breaking torts down into elements tends to promote rationality in decision-making and encourages judges to deal comprehensively with the parties' dispute. For example, isolating discrete requirements reduces the prospect that aspects of the tort for which the claimant sues will be glossed over. It also guards against the possibility of enquiries being duplicated since structuring torts in terms of elements greatly increases the visibility of the issues for determination and thus operates as a check on a particular matter being inadvertently counted twice.

VII. Conclusion

Although cases and textbooks are replete with references to elements of torts, the concept of a tort element has not previously been the subject of sustained consideration. Accordingly, this chapter aimed to unpack it. Among other things, it sought to show precisely why elements matter, to consider whether elements are distinct from various related concepts, to identify the different types of elements that tort law recognises and to consider the case for structuring torts in terms of elements.

3

Culpability and Compensation

SANDY STEEL*

It is almost undeniable that moral culpability is not a necessary condition of liability to compensate in English private law, as the law stands. In so far as we are seeking to articulate general conditions of private law liability to compensate, such liability hinges, at most, on responsibility for an outcome, not moral culpability with respect to it. And yet, moral culpability nonetheless has a significant impact upon the incidence of compensatory liability.[1] Peter Cane's work has greatly illuminated theoretical understanding of both of these facts. In the first section of this chapter, I examine his and other explanations of the fact that moral culpability is not a necessary condition of liability to compensate in private law. I point out a neglected theoretical cost of insisting upon a culpability condition for compensatory liability, and suggest some friendly amendments, or additions, to his account of why compensatory liability is not necessarily contingent upon culpability.

The second, central, section of the chapter turns to consider the role of moral culpability in the current law. Despite the prevalence of culpability-independent liability in private law, I describe various doctrines which nonetheless appear either to require culpability to establish liability or justify an expanded liability by reference to it. The paper offers various explanations of these doctrines. In some cases, they are probably mistaken. In other cases, the appearance that the doctrine makes liability hinge upon culpability is misleading. In still others, culpability justifies an expanded liability in virtue of defeating or diminishing an objection to liability that would otherwise exist. That objection may be one that, as Cane has argued, points to the social interest in conditioning liability upon culpability. But it may also be an objection that an individual defendant could reasonably make to bearing the particular form of liability in the absence of elevated culpability. I conclude with some sceptical observations on views which would elevate moral culpability to a positive sufficient ground of compensatory liability in private law, alongside responsibility.

* With thanks to Tom Adams, Leo Boonzaier, James Edwards, James Goudkamp, Alex Kaiserman, Mark Lunney, Nick McBride, Adam Perry, and Jonathan Turner for helpful comments on a draft. Ben Cartwright provided valuable research assistance.

[1] It clearly impacts non-compensatory liability, too, but my focus here is on compensation, since the role of culpability in relation to at least punitive, non-compensatory liability seems relatively straightforward to explain.

I. Compensatory Liability in the Absence of Moral Culpability

The claim that the culpability-independent nature of private law liability to compensate is 'almost undeniable' may raise an eyebrow.[2] After all, 'fault' is a major determinant of compensatory liability, and fault perhaps raises a connotation of moral culpability. As is well known, however, the law's understanding of 'fault' includes 'objective fault'. The latter permits liability when a person fails to adhere to a standard of conduct, despite that failure not being traceable to a choice to behave impermissibly or otherwise the result of an insensitivity to the moral reasons that ought to govern their conduct.[3] Thus, a learner driver is required to adhere to standard of care of a reasonably experienced driver.[4] There is no reason to believe that every failure to adhere to this standard on the part of the learner is the result of a culpable choice or another insensitivity to the moral reasons that should govern their conduct. Suppose that A, suffering from a delusion as a result of a schizophrenic episode, believes that B will seriously A and harms B in mistaken self-defence. English law is likely to hold such a person liable to compensate in the tort of negligence on the basis of a failure to take reasonable care.[5] In a decision holding a person liable for harm caused during a schizophrenic episode, the Court of Appeal described liability as blocked only when the defendant's 'condition entirely eliminates responsibility'.[6] This suggests that the boundary of liability in negligence is more akin to 'responsibility' in the sense that one's conduct – one's *agency*, even if one's agency is not capable of functioning in other than a highly defective manner – must be a cause of an outcome.[7]

Even before one turns to cases in which liability is conditioned upon objective fault, however, the scope of compensatory liability regardless of objective fault is striking. This type of liability applies under the rule in *Rylands v Fletcher*,[8] vicarious liability for the tort of another, contractual compensatory liability for breach of a duty to secure an outcome, liability in trespass despite a reasonable belief in consent, liability in defamation, compensatory liability for breach of trust, statutory liability for defective products, damages for innocent misrepresentations,[9] liability for loss

[2] For a piece that seems to assume that tort law must be in the business of culpability-tracking and then takes tort law to task for its 'confused' notions of culpability, see L Alexander and K Ferzan, 'Confused Culpability, Contrived Causation, and the Collapse of Tort Theory' in J Oberdiek (ed), *Philosophical Foundations of the Law of Torts* (Oxford, Oxford University Press, 2014).

[3] Throughout, I assume that moral culpability involves acting impermissibly without excuse. I aim to focus on clear examples in which there would be general agreement that there is no moral culpability, whatever one's account of excuses. The formulation in the text aims to capture, very roughly, (some) volitionist and (some) attributivist accounts of culpability.

[4] *Nettleship v Weston* [1971] 2 QB 691 (CA).

[5] Compare the facts of *Dunnage v Randall* [2015] EWCA Civ 673, [2016] QB 639.

[6] ibid [114] (Rafferty LJ).

[7] If the defendant loses consciousness, then he is not liable, absent prior responsibility: ibid [115]. On this, or a closely related, notion of responsibility, see T Honoré, *Responsibility and Fault* (Oxford, Hart Publishing, 1999) ch 2.

[8] *Rylands v Fletcher* (1868) LR 3 HL 330.

[9] When damages are awarded in lieu of rescission under the Misrepresentation Act 1967, s 2(2) in respect of a non-negligent misrepresentation.

suffered in protecting a person or their property in a situation of necessity, and liability for damage caused to another's person or property in circumstances of necessity.[10] It is true that, once account is taken of the various defences to liability which exist in relation to these rules, liability may sometimes ultimately be conditioned upon objective fault. For instance, a manufacturer of products may avoid liability for a risk upon proof that it was not identifiable based on scientific knowledge at the time of distribution.[11] But in many cases, such as vicarious liability, contractual liability for breach of a duty to secure an outcome, liability in trespass despite a reasonable belief in consent, and breach of certain trust duties, there is no significant weakening of the strict position.

Each of these liabilities is arguably still conditioned upon a person's *responsibility* for an outcome in the sense that the rules require their agency to be implicated in its occurrence. For instance, a person is only liable in trespass for *doing something*, and liability for destroying another's property in a situation of necessity is still liability in respect of the effects of one's agency. It is open to doubt, however, whether all of the rules are conditioned upon responsibility in this sense. If A sells goods to B and fails to deliver them due to an unforeseen heart attack that rendered A unconscious, A is still potentially liable in damages to B, if B suffers actionable loss as a result. A's agency was, of course, implicated in the creation of the duty to deliver the goods, but not in the events which constituted a breach of that duty. In that sense, contractual liability may be independent of responsibility. In German law, §829 of the German Civil Code imposes a 'fairness-based' – and apparently responsibility-independent – liability upon a person who causes damage while in an unconscious state.[12] In assessing the fairness of imposing liability, the courts take into account a wider range of considerations than under the responsibility-based tort provisions, such as the relative resources of each party, so it is recognised the responsibility makes a normative difference.[13] It appears not, however, to be a necessary condition of liability.

It follows, then, that if moral culpability is a necessary condition of justified compensatory liability, the current law is seriously askew. That may be so, of course. But the theoretical cost of insisting upon a culpability requirement for compensatory liability would go beyond rejection of much of contemporary practices of

[10] For a similar list, see S Smith, *Rights, Wrongs, and Injustices: The Structure of Remedial Law* (Oxford, Oxford University Press, 2019) 225–26. The position may be different in relation to reasonable belief in facts justifying defensive action, which might relieve from liability: *Ashley v Chief Constable of Sussex Police* [2008] UKHL 25, [2008] 1 AC 962. If so, this seems hard to square with compensatory liability for justified harm imposed for one's benefit: see *Vincent v Lake Erie Transportation Co*, 109 Minn 456, 124 NW 221 (1910).

[11] Consumer Protection Act 1987, s 4(1)(e).

[12] *Bürgerliches Gesetzbuch* (BGB) §829, provides: 'A person who, for reasons cited in sections 827 and 828 [being in a state of unconsciousness, a state of pathological mental disturbance or minority] is not responsible for damage he caused in the instances specified in sections 823 to 826 must nonetheless make compensation for the damage, unless damage compensation can be obtained from a third party with a duty of supervision, to the extent that in the circumstances, including without limitation the circumstances of the parties involved, equity requires indemnification and he is not deprived of the resources needed for reasonable maintenance and to discharge his statutory maintenance duties.'

[13] See further F Jürgen Säcker et al (eds), *Münchener Kommentar zum BGB* §829, 7th edn (Munich, CH Beck, 2017) [10]–[21].

compensatory liability.[14] Consider this argument, made by the German natural law theorist, Thomasius, in the early eighteenth century. Why, he asked, if a person is permitted to damage an innocent, non-culpable (and possibly, non-responsible[15]) person – he gave the example of an insane person or a child – in self-defence, is one not also permitted to take that person's resources *ex post* by way of compensation for the damage caused by the innocent?[16] Thomasius and a number of later writers conceived of the right to extract compensation from another as an entailment of one's right to act in defence of one's rights, governed by the same principles.[17] Since liability to defensive damage does not require culpability (or, possibly, responsibility), neither should liability to give up one's resources to pay compensation.[18] An implicit assumption of Thomasius's argument is that compensatory liability has the same moral grounding as defensive liability. This allows him to argue that if defensive liability is independent of culpability, then so too must be compensatory liability. If this assumption is correct, then a culpability requirement for moral compensatory liability would entail a culpability requirement for moral defensive liability. Absent some other justification for harming an attacker, it would then be impermissible to defend oneself against a responsible, but non-culpable threatener. At the very least, this result will strike many as implausible, and it is inconsistent with legal systems' approaches to self-defence.

One might object to the last argument – that a culpability requirement on compensatory liability entails a culpability requirement on defensive liability – in at least two ways. First, one could reject Thomasius' view that defensive liability and compensatory liability have the same moral basis. Second, one could accept that the two have the same moral basis and nonetheless argue that, when it comes to the legal regulation of compensatory liability, there are reasons for the law to insist upon different principles to those applicable to defensive liability.

Consider the first type of objection. A full defence of the claim that defensive liability and compensatory liability – or at least certain kinds of compensatory liability – have the same or a highly similar moral grounding would take us too far afield.[19] Some of the apparent disanalogies between the two can, however, be dispelled. Most obviously, justified defensive force is aimed at prevention of damage or the infringement of a right, while justified imposition of the cost of compensation is aimed at undoing or

[14] Why is this a theoretical cost at all? One could think that the current law enjoys no presumption of justificatory merit whatsoever. When we find strict liability independently developing in different legal systems, and perhaps even within different compartments of the same legal system, as a result of the reasoned, or intuitive, judgements of officials, it seems to me that there is at least some (defeasible) reason to think that it is not simply a widespread mistake.

[15] It is not entirely clear if Thomasius means to refer to non-responsible, non-culpable threats, or merely non-culpable threats.

[16] C Thomasius (ed M Hewett), *Larva Legis Aquiliae: The Mask of the Lex Aquilia Torn Off the Action for Damage Done*, IX (Oxford, Hart Publishing, 2000) 10–11.

[17] For some of the details, see F Gisawi, *Der Grundsatz der Totalreparation* (Tübingen, Mohr Siebeck, 2015), 69–70; 102–106.

[18] Thomasius used the example of a 'furiosus' – an insane person: '… *furiosus, cum nullum ius habeat, injuriam mihi facit. Igitur cum possim furiosum, etiam cum gravi damno corpori eius illato, repellere, cur non possim petere restitutionem damni dati ex bonis eius?*'.

[19] See G Sela, 'Torts as Self-Defense' (6 August 2019) https://papers.ssrn.com/sol3/papers.cfm?abstract_id=3433223, accessed 1 July 2021. See also S Steel, 'Defensive and Remedial Liability' in P Miller and J Oberdiek (eds) *Oxford Studies in Private Law Theory* (forthcoming, OUP, 2022).

counterbalancing damage. Some forms of compensation, as awarded by courts, however, are either simply preventative in nature or are conceptually similar to prevention. Damages to provide for pain medication to prevent future pain are an example. More generally, damages which aim to cure a breach by providing means to put a person in the materially identical position they would have been in had the breach not occurred can reasonably be described as preventing the persistence of the breach or the effects of the breach. So, in relation to these forms of compensation, the analogy between defence and compensation is a reasonable one. It is not surprising that, in relation to these forms of compensation, considerations of proportionality are directly assessed by the courts in deciding whether to make the award, just as defensive liability is subject to a proportionality condition.[20]

A further apparently significant difference between defensive damage and imposition of compensatory costs is the mode of agency involved. In taking resources in order to compensate for damage, one uses the other person or their resources for some further end, namely, to prevent, negate, or counterbalance damage. In typical defensive damage cases, one merely eliminates the source of the risk of damage. For instance, if B punches A to prevent A from punching B, B does not use A's body as a means to a further end. Sometimes, however, it is permissible to use a person as a mere means in cases of defensive damage. For instance, if the only means by which I can save my life from a boulder that another person has directed towards me with the intention of killing me is by using that person as a shield, that seems permissible. However, intuitively, this kind of use of a person requires special justification. It is this difference which is sometimes invoked to explain why it is impermissible to throw a large person's body from a bridge to prevent a train from hitting five people further down the track, while it seem permissible to do so in other cases.[21] If all cases of compensatory damage involve this kind of use of a person or their resources, then something extra is required to justify compensation above and beyond what is required to justify defensive damage, all else being equal. It might be argued that the *extra* thing is culpability.

This is not fully satisfying, however. First, the mode of agency involved in extracting compensation for damage and that involved in defensive damage are very similar. In both cases the damaging is done in order to make it the case that the risk created by the other person does not render the victim worse off. It is misleading to describe the imposition of compensatory cost as simply one person deriving benefit from the use of another. Second, the imposition of compensatory costs involves the deprivation or use of a person's property, not their body, in order to protect another person's health or property. Setting aside property which has a direct impact upon a person's bodily resources, such as a pace-maker, it is not clear that the special restrictions against using a *person* as a means extend to their external objects that do not directly impact upon their bodily resources.

The second kind of objection is more persuasive. Even if moral liability to defensive damage has the same moral grounding as moral liability to the imposition of

[20] *Ruxley Electronics v Forsyth* [1996] AC 344 (HL).

[21] See, eg, V Tadros, *The Ends of Harm: Moral Foundations of the Criminal Law* (Oxford, Oxford University Press, 2011) ch 6.

compensatory costs, it does not follow that the two should be legally regulated in the same way. Suppose, for example, that we agreed with Thomasius that it is morally permissible defensively to damage a non-culpable person who poses a risk of damage to one's body. It may nonetheless be undesirable, possibly even wrongful, for the law to provide assistance in enforcing this liability. On Cane's view, tort liability involves a *sanction*.[22] It may be that Cane's conception of sanction is simply any judicial order that imposes a burden of some kind. If so, it provides no special objection to liability for non-responsible damage. But if a sanction inherently communicates disapproval or worse about the defendant's conduct, then it is inappropriate to recognise tortious liability in relation to innocent, non-responsible risks, whose conduct is not justifiably censured in this way.[23] It seems true that tort liability *sometimes* involves a sanction in this sense. The clearest example is exemplary damages. But it is less plausible as a claim about all tort liability when we consider cases in which the defendant behaved entirely non-culpably, but with responsibility.[24] At any rate, this is not a *necessary* feature of compensatory legal liability between individuals, even if it is a necessary feature of tort law.

A different argument for a divergence between compensatory and defensive liability begins with the observation that it is possible legally to prohibit compensatory action being taken without leaving the victims of damage materially worse off. Refusing state assistance to pursue compensation claims does not necessarily involve the refusal of all state assistance. The state could, for example, provide compensation in relation to damage caused by bodily risks for which individuals have no agency responsibility. If liability insurance in relation to such risks would be extremely costly, given their highly unpredictable nature, then there would be good reason to establish such a scheme or, more realistically, provide payments through general welfare provision. This would protect the innocent risk imposer and the victim of the innocent risk from unexpected damage which they had no reasonable opportunity to avoid. A humane legal system could reasonably take the view that it ought to protect people from unexpected risks of catastrophic damage – even damage which another person could permissibly impose upon them – especially when it is difficult for the persons involved to protect themselves against such risks. Given the potentially enormous costs of compensation for bodily injuries, each of us has a reason to protect each other from these costs. Unlike situations in which a risk imposer is culpable, or otherwise had a reasonable opportunity to avoid the harm they cause, third parties cannot reasonably object that they are being required to bear costs for which other people are morally responsible. The expressive and deterrent potential of institutionalising a compensation claim are also non-existent in cases of non-responsible, non-culpable risks. So we can see why the law could be justified in protecting defendants from a liability to bear a cost that, as a matter of morality, it would be permissible to impose upon them. However, this is still some distance from

[22] P Cane, *Responsibility in Law and Morality* (Oxford, Hart Publishing, 2002) 43, referring to 'reparative' sanctions.

[23] For an argument in favour of recognition of an insanity defence in tort which relies upon the claims that: (a) tort liability involves a sanction; and (b) sanctions involve a mark of disapproval, see J Goudkamp, 'Insanity as a Tort Defence' (2011) 31 *OJLS* 727, 746–47.

[24] See the examples given above, text at n 10.

an argument that the law should protect all non-morally-culpable inflictors of damage. If, for example, a person chooses to enter into a strict liability contractual arrangement, against a fair background set of entitlements, it is difficult to understand why the law must protect them from strict compensatory liability for breach of contract.

So far we have seen the considerable costs of insisting upon a culpability requirement of liability to compensate: it would require a re-writing of swathes of private law, and it would sit uneasily with basic understandings about the scope of defensive liability. But the culpability-independence of liability still stands in need of an explanation. Cane's account emphasises, in part, the role of victims in tort law, compared to other domains, such as criminal law: 'Mental fault elements play a smaller role in tort law than in criminal law … This is because tort law is more concerned than criminal law with the interests of victims and, consequently, less concerned with degrees of fault'.[25] Strict or stricter forms of liability are 'in some contexts … seen as essential for giving proper weight to the interests of victims'.[26] By contrast, the criminal law is 'essentially agent-oriented'.[27] These observations seem to me correct in important respects. The criminal law is more defendant-oriented in that it is more concerned with the defendant's moral culpability and victims have less normative control over the course of proceedings – the power to enliven or discontinue proceedings is not fully the victim's. But this re-raises the question of *why* this defendant-centredness is such a central feature of criminal law and whether it is justified. Similarly, it only takes us so far to say that tort law is more in the business of protecting victims and so is less concerned with the defendant's culpability. It doesn't follow from the fact that tort law is concerned to protect victims that it should do so in a culpability-insensitive way. Of course, victims will receive more protection the less the insistence on a culpability requirement. But perhaps victims *ought* only to be legally protected – in the private law way – from culpably inflicted damage. Further, comparisons with the criminal law can only deliver a comparative conclusion: there is less reason, say, for tort law to be culpability-sensitive than the criminal law because the consequences for the defendant are *generally* less severe in tort law: compensatory damages versus punishment. But this is consistent with thinking there is still strong reason for culpability requirements in tort.

The observation that private law is a zero-sum game – that every legal protection given to a defendant cuts back from the victim's legal protection – is also potentially misleading here.[28] The fact that a victim is worse off than they would be if the defendant had less legal protection is not, in itself, normatively significant: everything depends upon what one considers to be the appropriate baseline for protecting victims.[29] The idea that private law compensatory liability is zero-sum in nature, provides us with a useful reminder that any distribution of liability has to be rationally acceptable to both affected parties – it stops too short if it merely points to a good that would be achieved for one party if liability were imposed. Although this is a useful reminder, as yet it

[25] Cane (n 22) 86.
[26] ibid 87.
[27] ibid.
[28] This zero-sum feature of private law compensatory liability is put to justificatory work by John Gardner in *Torts and Other Wrongs* (Oxford, Oxford University Press, 2019) ch 6.
[29] Contrast ibid.

does not provide us with much guidance as to which standards of liability satisfy the criterion of being rationally acceptable to both parties.

A different account of the relatively culpability-insensitive nature of compensatory liability in private law can be brought out by thinking first about contractual liability.[30] Some contractual duties are strict: the duty is a duty to φ, not merely a duty to use reasonable endeavours to φ. If a person has a duty to φ, it follows that they have a reason to φ. If they breach their duty, and thus fail to conform to this reason, this reason or the reason that gave rise to the reason, may require a new action, as a means of imperfect conformity to the original reason. If I promise to build you a house by Monday but fail to do so, then, other things being equal, on Tuesday I am still required to complete the house. My promise gives me reason to build by Monday and, failing that, Tuesday. No mention so far of any moral culpability. It may be that I was non-culpably unable to complete by Monday, but, given the continued rational force of my promise, I am now required to complete by Tuesday.[31]

Although this is a contractual example, the point is a general one. A fundamental, general, reason why compensatory liability is relatively culpability-insensitive is a product of two propositions. The first is that reasons for action are generally culpability-independent. I have a (mandatory) reason not to damage you, not merely a reason not to damage you *culpably*. I may also have a special reason not *culpably* to damage you, but that is a separate matter.[32] The second is that compensation is, at least in a central category of cases, required as a means of conforming to one's initial reason not to damage. Compensation is a means of imperfectly conforming to reasons not to worsen others' positions, after one has failed in some measure to conform to this reason. If the original reason not to injure is culpability-independent, then it follows that there is a reason to compensate that is also culpability-independent. The rational case for a person compensating another is thus often already in existence prior to any consideration of culpability. Hence the title of Gardner's essay: 'The Negligence Standard: Political not Metaphysical'.[33] Gardner's point is that a negligence requirement does not itself fall out of the practical reasons that explain compensation. To that extent, it is not a 'metaphysical' requirement.

If one accepts Gardner's view that reasons to succeed are intelligible, and the further claim that one can be responsible for failure to conform to such reasons even despite reasonable efforts or, more precisely, despite due sensitivity toward those reasons – a proposition about responsibility which seems to be shared by Cane[34] – then there is a (defeasible) moral case for a person compensating another independently of culpability.

[30] The next paragraphs invoke John Gardner's continuity thesis explanation of compensatory duties, which holds that the reason(s) which justified the primary duty also justify the compensatory duty. See Gardner (n 28) ch 2. For a clarification and response to some objections to this kind of view, see S Steel, 'Compensation and Continuity' (2020) 26 *Legal Theory* 250.

[31] Gardner illustrates the continuity thesis with the example of a justified breach of a promise: Gardner (n 28) 55–56.

[32] For inconclusive ruminations on this, see below text after n 92.

[33] Gardner (n 28) ch 7.

[34] Cane accepts that one can be morally responsible for an outcome and have a moral duty to repair it, without blame being apt: Cane (n 22) 108–109.

On this view, legal fault standards are typically cut-backs which, for various reasons, protect a person from being legally required to do that which they have at least moral reason to do. Hence Jansen's description of the fault principle as a liability-*limiting* (rather than liability-*generating*) principle.[35]

Gardner's view may be challenged. Gardner's view of duties and reasons is, in some ways, an unusually demanding one.[36] First, on his view, one can have a duty and a reason to φ, even if, relative to the available evidence, one has no reason to believe that the facts which ground one's duty or reason to φ obtain in the circumstances. In this sense, it is epistemically demanding. Second, one can have a duty and reason to φ even if one has no ability to φ.[37] In this sense, it is practically demanding. If one accepts these views, then there is much scope for non-culpable breaches of duty. Notice, however, that even if one rejects these views about duties and reasons, one could still identify cases in which non-culpable failure to conform to a duty or reason gives rise to a duty or reason to compensate. For instance, if A intentionally damages B's car in order to save A's life, A will normally have a distinctive reason, that is, distinctive from that of a bystander, to compensate B. Here, on any view, A has a reason, or *pro tanto* duty, not to damage B's car. This reason also contributes to the explanation of A's distinctive reason to compensate B. This is true despite A's being justified – and so non-culpable – in damaging B's car.

Perhaps Gardner's view, or a modified version of that view which drops the epistemic and practical demandingness elements, is ultimately not so different from one held by Cane. Another line of argument that comes out in his account of the relative culpability-independence of private law liability is that private law is in the business of protection of rights: '[s]trict liability is a necessary corollary of a system of rights'.[38] For Cane, a right is a strong interest.[39] Given that Cane believes that our strong interests – our rights – are what justify the duties in the tort of negligence, it seems that a right can also justify an objective-fault-based rule. This makes it unclear why there is a particular association in his account between rights-as-strong-interests and strict liability. But perhaps the explanation for this association is that our interests generate basically strict reasons of non-interference. Each of us has a reason simply not to interfere with others' basic interests, not merely a reason to take care not to do so.[40] Objective-fault-based liability has, then, to be justified as a departure from this basic position.

[35] N Jansen (translated by S Steel), *The Structure of Tort Law* (Oxford, Oxford University Press, 2021) ch 9. For Jansen, outcome responsibility is strict and generates a *pro tanto* duty to compensate from which a defendant is sometimes protected by the fault principle or another liability-limiting principle.

[36] The following two sentences could also be said to express the worry that, on Gardner's view, reasons and duties do not serve a 'guidance' function. See NJ McBride, *The Humanity of Private Law Part 1: Explanation* (Oxford, Hart Publishing, 2019) 37–39.

[37] See J Gardner, 'The Wrongdoing that Gets Results' (2004) 18 *Philosophical Perspectives* 53.

[38] Cane (n 22) 198.

[39] ibid 197.

[40] Cane would likely reject this explanation, however, as the connection between rights and strict liability seems much closer on his view: it is *in virtue* of something's being a right that it attracts strict liability (ibid). This is not the case on Gardner's view, which locates strict liability ultimately in the nature of practical reasons generally – regardless of whether those reasons relate to *rights*.

Possibly the discussion so far fails to do justice to Cane's (further) thought that the justifiability of strict liability in private law is in part based on the idea of a *fair balance* of interests. In some contexts, a fair balance between the victim's interest in security and the defendant's interest in liberty will generate liability for interference with the former in the absence of objective fault.[41] This idea is suggestive, but it is at a high level of abstraction, and one might aim to concretise the argument so that it provides a theoretical justification for strict liability in particular; after all, there is a sense in which compensatory liability for *culpable* wrongdoing also achieves a fair balance of the parties' interests. Cane refers to necessity cases in which A damages B's property as exemplifying the kind of balancing he has in mind.[42] Consider A's liability to pay compensation for justified damage to B's property, which A intentionally, and necessarily, causes in order to protect A from death resulting from a risk not created by B.[43] One way in which the fairness argument might be made more precise is as follows. Here B has a strong interest in B's property being undamaged. A has a much stronger interest in A's life. If it were all-things-considered *wrongful* for A to damage B's property, then A would be morally required to sacrifice A's life to protect B's property, which is obviously unacceptable. However, another moral arrangement would permit A to damage B's property, but require A to compensate B. This arrangement gives B's strong interest some residual moral force in relation to B, even though it is permissibly infringed upon. This achieves a fair balance, it might be argued, because it gives each parties' claims due weight in distributing entitlements: B's claim to be undamaged is given some residual force alongside A's claim to preserve A's life.[44] The extent to which this fairness account differs from, or is preferable to, the idea that A's reason not to damage B persists and gives A reason to compensate B is an interesting question which merits further examination.

II. Culpability's Influence

Considerations of culpability clearly – as a descriptive matter – play a role in compensatory liability in private law. In the remainder of this central section of the chapter, I describe eight examples of this, some more well-known than others.[45]

[41] ibid 108, 189.

[42] ibid 107–108.

[43] See *Vincent v Lake Erie Transportation Co*, 109 Minn 456, 124 NW 221 (1910).

[44] Sometimes it is said that A's permission to damage is morally 'conditional' upon the actual payment of compensation to B in these necessity cases. This does not seem true, however, in cases in which there is a conflict between a property interest and an interest in retention of life. Even if A knows that A will be unable to compensate B for the property damage caused in saving A's life, it seems permissible, all things considered, for A nonetheless to damage B's property. A may avoid wronging B by payment of compensation, though A's act of damaging may be permissible in the absence of compensation. For further discussion, see S Steel, 'Liability for Permissible Harm' (ms).

[45] For a (largely) different set of examples, see P Cane, 'Retribution, Proportionality, and Moral Luck in Tort Law' in P Cane and J Stapleton (eds), *The Law of Obligations: Essays in Celebration of John Fleming* (Oxford, Clarendon Press, 1998) 159.

My aim is not to provide a comprehensive account of the impact of culpability upon compensatory liability. These examples are chosen partly because some have received relatively little theoretical discussion and partly because they provide useful illustrations of different possible justificatory roles of culpability. Then I turn to whether the influence of culpability upon liability in these ways can be rationally explained. In some cases, I argue that the doctrines may rest upon a mistaken assumption or are not, on closer inspection, truly based upon culpability. In other cases, I suggest that the defendant's culpability defeats or diminishes the weight of reasons against the imposition of liability upon him – these reasons may be defendant-centred, concerned with the impact liability will have on the defendant as an individual, or society-centred, concerned with the impact of stricter forms of liability upon society as a whole. I contrast these explanations with one which understands culpability as evidence of a retributivist impulse within the private law of wrongs. The section concludes with some sceptical observations on theories which understand culpability as an independently sufficient positive ground for compensatory liability.

A. Culpability's Impact Upon Compensatory Liability

(i) Diminishing the Causal Requirement

It is sometimes suggested that high culpability can in certain contexts diminish the causal requirement of liability insisted upon. When A seeks to rescind a contract on the basis of fraud or duress to the person, it has been stated that A is not required to demonstrate on the balance of probabilities that *but for* the duress or fraud, A would not have entered into the contract.[46] As Lord Cranworth put it in relation to fraud: 'Once make out that there has been anything like deception, and no contract resting in any degree on that foundation can stand'.[47] One possible interpretation of this is that it suffices that the fraudulent misrepresentation made a contribution – even an unnecessary and insufficient one – to the entry into the contract for rescission. However, absent fraud or duress to the person, but-for causation is required for rescission or damages.[48] The law does not appear to be fully consistent here, however. In relation to compensatory damages for fraudulent breach of a fiduciary duty, it is clear that but-for causation is required.[49] Further, in some contexts, an unnecessary, insufficient causal contribution is accepted as sufficient to generate liability without any heightened culpability.[50]

[46] *Barton v Armstrong* [1976] AC 104 (PC). The Privy Council relied upon cases concerning deceit to justify, by analogy, the rule in cases of duress to person (118–19).

[47] *Reynell v Sprye* (1852) 1 De GM & G 660 (Ch) 708. This statement seems to be interpreted in *Barton* (n 46) as merely asserting that the representation need not be the *sole* cause, however (118), and this is the case even in relation to non-fraudulent representations.

[48] See *Raiffeisen Zentralbank Osterreich AG v Royal Bank of Scotland plc* [2010] EWHC 1392 (Comm), [2011] 1 Lloyd's Rep 123 [162], but acknowledging that the position might differ in relation to fraud: [198].

[49] *Swindle v Harrison* [1997] 4 All ER 705 (CA).

[50] *Bailey v Ministry of Defence* [2008] EWCA Civ 883, [2009] 1 WLR 1052. For the explanation of this case as admitting this possibility, see J Stapleton and S Steel, 'Causes and Contributions' (2016) 132 *LQR* 363.

(ii) Defeating Counterfactual Arguments about Loss

Normally, compensatory liability is conditioned on the present or future existence of a loss. A person suffers a loss as a result of a wrong if – and normally only if – the wrong is a cause of their being worse off than they would have been had the wrong not occurred. Sometimes the suggestion is made that the wrongdoer cannot argue 'it would have happened anyway' in relation to *loss* when there is a high degree of culpability. Thus in holding A liable to pay the market value of B's shares at the time of conversion when the shares dropped in the value by the time of judgment, Lord Atkin responded to the argument that this was unjust by referring to the fraudulent nature of the conversion.[51] While compensation for breach of trust generally requires a counterfactual loss, in *AIB v Redler* Lord Toulson noted that different considerations may apply in cases of fraud.[52]

(iii) Altering Proof of Causation Requirements

An alternative interpretation of some of the cases mentioned in (i) is that they reverse the burden of the proof on causation when a high level of culpability is shown. For instance, it may be that, in *Barton v Armstrong*, the Privy Council thought that, by virtue of the defendant's high culpability, the *possibility* that the duress may have made a difference sufficed for liability, even though normally this would have to be shown on the balance of probabilities.[53] German law provides a clear instance of this kind of phenomenon. In cases in which *gross* negligence is shown against a medical professional, the legal burden of proof is shifted to the professional to show that their gross negligence was *not* a cause of the claimant's damage.[54]

(iv) Legal Causation and Remoteness

The general remoteness rule in the tort of negligence is that the type of damage must be a reasonably foreseeable consequence of the breach of a duty of care at the time of breach.[55] A broader rule is said to apply in the 'intentional torts'. This broader rule entails the defendant's liability for all *directly* caused losses, even if of an unforeseeable type or extent. 'Intentional torts' is ambiguous between torts committed with a culpable intention and torts in which a voluntary, but not necessarily culpable, act constitutes the tort

[51] *Solloway v Mclaughlin* [1938] AC 247 (PC) 259: 'no injustice is done if the principal benefits, as he occasionally may, by the superior astuteness of an unjust steward in carrying out a fraud'.

[52] *AIB Group (UK) plc v Mark Redler & Co Solicitors* [2014] UKSC 58, [2015] AC 1503 [62]. See also *OMV Petrom SA v Glencore AG* [2016] EWCA Civ 778, [2017] 3 All ER 157, ignoring counterfactual issues in deceit at [57].

[53] *Barton* (n 46). This is suggested by Clarke J in *Raiffeisen* (n 48) at [198]. See also *BHP Billiton Petroleum Ltd & others v Dalmine SpA* [2003] EWCA Civ 170 [36], effectively reversing the burden of proof on 'loss' in deceit.

[54] See S Steel, *Proof of Causation in Tort Law* (Cambridge, Cambridge University Press, 2015) 200–206.

[55] The 'general' rule because the contractual remoteness rules apply in negligence cases in which the duty arises in virtue of a (contractual) assumption of responsibility: *Wellesley Partners LLP v Withers LLP* [2015] EWCA Civ 1146, [2016] Ch 529.

(such as the trespass torts). The broader rule appears to apply to any tort committed with culpability-implying intention – and so it is misleading to describe the rule as applicable to the 'intentional torts': in truth, the rule seems to apply to the non-equivalent category of torts committed with a culpable intention.[56] Although trespass to land requires a voluntary act, it can be committed without any moral culpability due to a reasonable, but mistaken, belief in the permissibility of using another's land. In such a circumstance, a reasonable foreseeability remoteness rule seems to apply. On the broader, directness, rule, if A intentionally destroys B's chair, and B suffers a psychiatric illness because of his unusual emotional attachment to this chair, A is liable to compensate B for this loss.[57]

It is sometimes said that intended consequences are never too remote.[58] If it exists, this is a distinct rule from the one just discussed. The last rule concerns liability for *unforeseeable*, and thus unintended, consequences of an intentionally committed wrong. The rule that intended consequences are never too remote only applies to those consequences that are intended, and so foreseeable at least to the wrongdoer. Suppose A knows that if A negligently injures B, B will be taken to a hospital which has been defectively constructed. A, but no one else, knows of the defective construction of the hospital. A has calculated that the hospital will collapse when B is treated there. It does, and B suffers further severe injuries. It seems that A is liable for those further severe injuries. Although B's injuries in hospital would be considered a coincidence from the epistemic vantage point of anyone else other than A, A is nonetheless liable for them because he intended to produce them.

(v) Culpability-Implying Wrongs

It may seem that certain wrongs, by their nature, cannot be committed without moral culpability. Consider the tort of deceit. This requires a person to make a false statement, knowing it to be false or reckless as to its truth, with the intention of inducing reliance upon it.[59] Whereas the objective standard of care in negligence may often, or at least sometimes, render a person liable without moral culpability, it seems that most persons who satisfy the elements of the tort of deceit will be culpable. Ultimately, though, the connection between deceit and moral culpability is probably contingent: sometimes it is morally justified to deceive and justification defeats moral culpability.[60] Malice-based torts may be different. One cannot justifiably harm another maliciously: if one believes

[56] See *Kuwait Airways Corp v Iraqi Airways Co (Nos 4 and 5)* [2002] UKHL 19, [2002] 2 AC 883 [105] (Lord Nicholls). Note, however, Lord Reed's explanation of the directness rule in *AIB* (n 52) [92]. His explanation is that reasonable foreseeability of harm is not what makes deceit wrongful (unlike in, for example, negligence). If that were the complete explanation, however, it would imply that a directness rule should apply to all trespass torts, regardless of the culpability of tortfeasor.

[57] In French law, the intentionality of the breach is relevant in contract, too: see J Gordley, 'Responsibility in Crime, Tort, and Contract for the Unforeseeable Consequences of an Intentional Wrong: A Once and Future Rule' in Cane and Stapleton (n 45) 202–203. If the English rule is culpability-dependent, rather than wrong-dependent, it is not clear why it should not also apply to breach of contract, unless the view is taken that a certain threshold of wrongfulness is needed, and breach of contract does not meet that threshold.

[58] eg *Reeves v Commissioner of the Police for the Metropolis* [2000] 1 AC 360 (HL) 394 (Lord Hoffmann).

[59] *Pasley v Freeman* (1789) 3 TR 51, 100 ER 450; *Derry v Peek* (1889) 14 App Cas 337 (HL).

[60] It is morally permissible and non-culpable to deceive (and to lie to) Kant's murderer at the door.

that one has a justification for harming, it is difficult to describe one's motive as malicious. Even here, however, we could perhaps imagine defendants acting maliciously due to an excusable lack of self-control, induced by severe, unexpected, mental disturbance.

(vi) Defences

Culpability sometimes blocks the availability of a defence. In relation to justificatory defences, the general trend appears to be that, if the defendant does not act for reasons which legally would justify the conduct, this disapplies the defence.[61] If a parent disciplines their child for the sake of self-gratification, this would fall outside the defence of discipline.[62] Sometimes the non-application of contributory negligence to torts such as deceit has been rationalised on the basis of the defendant's culpable intention to harm, albeit this does not account for the non-application of the defence to other torts even when the defendant has not behaved culpably.[63] Culpability is also relevant to the application of certain defences. For instance, in determining whether the defence of illegality ought to apply, one consideration is whether refusing relief would be 'disproportionate', and the claimant's culpability is relevant to this issue.[64]

(vii) Remedial Rules

Interestingly, the culpability of a breach bears upon the award of remedies, even beyond the obvious context of exemplary damages. Consider, first, injunctive relief, before turning to compensation. A mandatory injunction to take positive steps to cure a breach will generally not be awarded if there is a stark disproportion between the cost of reparative measures to the defendant and the benefit to the right-holder.[65] However, if the defendant has acted wantonly and quite unreasonably … he may be ordered to repair his wanton and unreasonable acts by doing positive work to restore the status quo even if the expense to him is out of all proportion to the advantage thereby accruing to the plaintiff.[66] The disproportionality between the cost to the defendant and benefit to the claimant has diminished force depending on the culpable nature of the breach.

If this is true in relation to mandatory injunctions, it would seem to apply *a fortiori* to monetary awards which are conditional upon the court's assessment of the reasonableness of the award, once it is accepted that proportionality is relevant to the reasonableness of a monetary award.[67] Therefore, if building a wall to protect against

[61] See J Goudkamp, *Tort Law Defences* (Oxford, Hart Publishing, 2016) 99–100.

[62] ibid.

[63] *Standard Chartered Bank v Pakistan National Shipping Corp (No 2)* [2002] UKHL 43, [2003] 1 AC 959 [45] (Lord Rodger). For criticism of this position, see J Murphy, 'Misleading Appearances in the Tort of Deceit' (2016) 75 *CLJ* 301. I agree with Murphy to the extent that contributory negligence could reasonably have application in relation to consequential losses in deceit, but full responsibility for any loss constituted simply by entry in the transaction will virtually always rest with the defendant. For the non-application of the defence to assault and battery, see *Pritchard v Co-operative Group Ltd* [2011] EWCA Civ 329, [2012] QB 320 [32].

[64] *Patel v Mirza* [2016] UKSC 42, [2017] AC 467 [107].

[65] *Redland Bricks v Morris* [1970] AC 652 (HL) 666 (Lord Upjohn).

[66] ibid.

[67] See *Ruxley Electronics v Forsyth* [1996] AC 344 (HL).

further landslides onto the right-holder's land would cost an exorbitant amount and only protect the right-holder from very minor damage, the court may decide not to grant compensation to allow for the wall to be built. However, if the defendant has culpably damaged the land, this may alter the position. Conversely, this consideration of the burdensome nature of a monetary order is likely to carry more weight when the breach is wholly innocent. This is most starkly in evidence in German law. Under §829 BGB, which, as we saw, imposes liability even for non-responsible causation of injury, the extent of the defendant's liability is sensitive to their personal resources.[68]

The *SAAMCO* limitation on compensatory damages is also culpability-dependent. The right-holder cannot recover, in cases of negligent misrepresentation, for loss which would have occurred even if the representation had been true.[69] This limitation does not apply in deceit.[70] This stands in contrast to rules such as mitigation, which apply regardless of the wrongdoer's culpability.

(viii) Apportionment of Liability

Moral culpability is relevant to the apportionment of liability. Comparative moral culpability is said to be one factor in determining the reduction made for contributory negligence.[71] Similarly, in contribution proceedings between persons liable for the same damage, an important factor is their comparative moral culpability.[72] Thus, even if each defendant is liable under a strict liability cause of action, say breach of contract, their relative shares of liability are partly determined by their comparative culpability in contributing to the loss caused by the breach.

B. Explaining the Influence of Culpability

(i) Error

Some of these doctrines may simply be mistaken. Consider the cases which might suggest that culpability diminishes the causal requirement of liability by dispensing with the need to satisfy a but-for test. There is reason to be sceptical. It should not always necessary to satisfy the but-for test even with *innocent* misrepresentations. Suppose that A relies upon two innocent misrepresentations made by B, each of which was sufficient to induce A to enter the transaction with B. Clearly, B cannot successfully argue, in relation to a particular misrepresentation, that A would have entered into the transaction because of the other one. Similarly, if B made three innocent or negligent

[68] See above n 12.

[69] *South Australia Asset Management Corporation v York Montague Ltd* [1997] AC 191 (HL).

[70] *Smith v New Court Securities* [1997] AC 254 (HL).

[71] *Jackson v Murray* [2015] UKSC 5, [2015] 2 All ER 805 [50]. In negligence, the issue of whether the claimant failed to take reasonable care is, however, determined objectively. Hence it is not entirely clear that the law is truly interested in comparative moral culpability, rather than, for instance, comparative responsibility for risk.

[72] Civil Liability (Contribution) Act 1978, s 1. See, eg, *Carillion JM Ltd v Phi Group Ltd* [2011] EWHC 1379 (TCC) [252].

misrepresentations, none of which individually was necessary or sufficient to induce A to enter the contract, but only collectively necessary, rescission should still be possible.[73] Further, at least in relation to certain kinds of transaction, such as a gift, even if A would have entered into the transaction anyway, the value of the transaction as an expression of A's autonomy may be undermined if A entered into the transaction on a false basis – regardless of B's culpability.[74] If the transaction can be unwound without significant hardship to B, then there is a reason for doing so, independently of whether A is worse off by entering into the transaction. In claims for rescission, there is no general reason for *loss* to be a necessary condition of relief – and this is so regardless of B's culpability. The significance of culpability in claims for rescission is probably best re-rationalised as bearing (only) upon the normative significance of *B* suffering a loss as an objection to granting rescission.[75] B could normally object to rescission on the basis that it will impose a hardship on B. But if B has behaved with significant culpability in producing the situation in which unwinding the transaction will cause such a hardship, B's complaint is diminished.

The idea that culpability defeats counterfactual arguments about *loss* is also open to doubt. A person suffers a loss as a result of an event when the event is a cause of their being worse off. In law, this normally entails a counterfactual: the loss is constituted by the person being worse off than had the event not occurred. If the event is a breach of duty, the counterfactual question supposes that the defendant *conformed* to their duty in the circumstances. What amounts to conformity in the circumstances will generally be unaffected by the fact that the breach was *highly culpable*. If a person behaves with gross negligence, just as with ordinary negligence, the loss question is still: what would have occurred if there had been *no negligence*? If the breach was highly culpable, this, if anything, might suggest that the defendant would do the *very minimum* to conform to their duty in the closest possible world in which the breach does not occur. For a highly culpable person, presumably minimal compliance is a closer possible world than supererogatory conformity. Whether a person behaves with a high degree of culpability seems constitutively independent, then, of whether a person is worse off as a result of the breach. And in so far as culpability has an evidential role in determining the closest possible no breach world, it is likely to disadvantage claimants rather than to benefit them.

(ii) Not Really Based on Culpability

The rule that 'intended consequences are never too remote' can be explained without supposing that heightened culpability impacts liability. If a person knows that a consequence will occur, then the risk of that consequence is reasonably foreseeable to that person. It may be that, as in the example above, no one else could reasonably foresee

[73] See generally J Stapleton, 'Unnecessary Causes' (2013) 129 *LQR* 39.

[74] For a justification of rescission that points to the underlying values of the transaction in question, see NJ McBride, 'Rescission' in G Virgo and S Worthington (eds), *Commercial Remedies: Resolving Controversies* (Cambridge, Cambridge University Press, 2017).

[75] This judgment already underlies the fact that s 2(2) of the Misrepresentation Act 1967 does not apply to fraudulent misrepresentations.

the risk. Nonetheless, the basis of the person's liability in the example is that the risk was reasonably foreseeable and not one that should have been taken. If the person had somehow forgotten their knowledge about the fact that the hospital was about to collapse at that time, they should still be liable: in their circumstances, the risk remained reasonably foreseeable.

Consider again the tort of deceit. Here are two doubts as to whether liability really is responsive to culpability as such in this tort. First, the wrongfulness of deceit may be explicable on the basis that it involves one person exercising *intentional* control over another person. There is a special badness about being subject to another's intentional control without one's permission. Consequently, it is not the agent's improper engagement with reason *as such* which explains the wrong, but the fact that this constitutes improper control over the deceived person.[76] Second, suppose that you deceive me into investing in some shares because a third party has threatened to break your arm if you do not. It may be that you are still liable in deceit here, but the deceit is excusable. If that is the case, then liability is not *ultimately* conditioned upon culpability, even in deceit. If duress is not a defence to trespass, it is not clear why it should be to deceit.[77] A third, distinct, point, which relates to the argument in the next section, begins with the observation that it is possible to be negligently deceptive. An advertisement may be deceptive, without the advertiser intending this or being aware of its likelihood. The law also recognises that there is a case for undoing transactions that were entered into because of a false belief induced by a wholly non-culpable misrepresentation. It may then be reasonable to think of *deceit* as an aggravated form of these other cases of causing false beliefs in others. If so, the knowledge of or recklessness as to the falsity of the statement performs a merely ancillary function – it opens up the possibility of a wider range of remedies.[78]

(iii) Culpability and Opportunity to Avoid

A number of authors have drawn attention to the moral significance, in justifying a person's liability to bear a cost, of the quality of a person's opportunity to avoid the act or omission to which that cost is attached.[79] If a person had a reasonable opportunity to avoid the act, their objection to bearing the associated cost is diminished. The ampler the opportunity, the less force the objection. One sense in which it might be thought that a person has a higher quality opportunity to avoid *seriously* culpable wrongs compared to *low* culpability wrongs is that it is, in some sense, easier to avoid committing the former.

[76] See, for this kind of view of deceit, A Beever, *A Theory of Tort Liability* (Oxford, Hart Publishing, 2018) ch 6.

[77] *Gilbert v Stone* (1641) Aleyn 35, 82 ER 902.

[78] The point that intention plays an 'ancillary' role in deceit is made by Cane in '*Mens rea* in Tort Law' (2000) 20 *OJLS* 533, 547–48.

[79] See especially E Voyiakis, *Private Law and the Value of Choice* (Oxford, Hart Publishing, 2017) ch 5; A Slavny, 'Nonreciprocity and the Moral Basis of Liability to Compensate' (2014) 34 *OJLS* 417. The idea is also developed in illuminating ways in M Oliver, 'Liability and Culpability' (DPhil thesis, University of Oxford, 2018) and L Boonzaier, 'Duties in Tort Law and its Theory' (DPhil thesis, University of Oxford, 2020), to which this section is indebted.

Intentional wrongdoing is generally easier to avoid than negligent wrongdoing. Another sense is that the quality of a person's opportunity not to φ is affected by the strength of their reasons against φ-ing. The more powerful the moral reasons against φ-ing, the less that is given up by a person in not φ-ing, and arguably, if it is bad for a person to be a wrongdoer, the more that is gained by the wrongdoer in not φ-ing.

The fact that a person could easily have avoided being a cause of damage (or the conduct constituting the basis of their liability, more generally) seems to have considerable bearing upon liability across private law. The level of protection we can reasonably expect from damage from others intuitively depends, at least in part, upon the extent to which we ourselves could avoid that damage. Indeed, this helps to explain the sense in which a person is partly responsible for their own damage in cases of contributory negligence. It is odd to describe a person who is contributorily negligent as *morally culpable*, because they need not breach any duty to others or to themselves, but to the extent they had good opportunities to avoid the damage, they may be partly responsible for it. Conversely, in rare cases in which the law imposes positive duties upon people to come to others' assistance, when they had no reasonable opportunity to avoid the imposition of the duty, the costs the defendant is expected to bear are more sensitive to the defendant's personal circumstances.[80]

The relevance of the foregoing to the present topic is that when a person behaves with high culpability in φ-ing, they will frequently have had a low-cost opportunity to avoid φ-ing.[81] When liability attaches in such cases, it will be because of the defendant's fully responsible choice. To a defendant's possible complaint that liability is particularly burdensome, a reasonable response is available: you could easily have avoided this situation by not culpably wronging another and (so) are responsible for being in it. Similarly, when a person enters into a contract when they had a range of valuable alternative options, and the contract turns out badly for them, it may not be unfair, up to some limit, to hold the person to the deal.

This helps to justify some of the doctrines above. The clearest example is probably remedies (vii). If a person chooses wrongfully to knock down another's wall, and this exposes them to a considerable liability for cost of repair, the objection they have to bearing it (its burdensomeness) is diminished by the fact that they had ample opportunity to avoid incurring the burden, at least when the size of the burden was reasonably predictable. Of course, there are limits. If paying for the cost of repairing the wall will destroy the defendant's life and give a minimal benefit to the right-holder, then it will still be disproportionate to impose it.[82] The dictum from *Redland Bricks*[83] goes too far

[80] See *Goldman v Hargrave* [1967] 1 AC 645 (PC) 663.

[81] To be clear, the point here is not that the moral significance of the quality of a person's opportunity to avoid a negative outcome is identical to the moral significance of a person's culpability. The fact that a person had an opportunity to avoid the act or activity that grounded their liability has an independent significance. For instance, the fact that a person had adequate options to avoid the activity to which *strict* liability attaches (eg transporting explosives) might have a bearing on the justifiability of the strict liability, but this has nothing to do with culpability. See Gardner (n 28) ch 6.

[82] It may also still be disproportionate in that it would be socially wasteful, even if not disproportionate in relation to the wrongdoer.

[83] Text at n 61 above.

in stating that considerations of proportionality are irrelevant when the defendant is an intentional wrongdoer.

Remoteness is more difficult. Consider again the example of A intentionally destroying B's chair, with the unforeseeable result that B suffers a psychiatric illness. Remoteness is sometimes described as a liability-limiting doctrine.[84] On this view, if taken at its word, a person is responsible even for unforeseeable consequences of their actions in the sense that they have special reason to repair them. The reasonable foreseeability remoteness rule amounts to the law's refusal to require B to compensate A, even though B has a special reason to do so. Why would the law protect defendants in this way?

One answer is that the rule protects defendants from overly burdensome liabilities. If that answer is correct, then, again, we might consider culpability as diminishing the defendant's objection to bearing a higher than usual burden, just as it does in defeating objections to injunctive relief or to a particular mode of compensatory relief. The idea that the reasonable foreseeability remoteness rule protects from overly burdensome liabilities seems only to cover some of the ground of remoteness, however. If the rationale of the rule were only to protect defendants from overly burdensome liabilities, its focus upon the *type* of damage is difficult to understand. Suppose that harm of type C is reasonably foreseeable and would expectably result in a liability of £500, but type D materialises, causing £500 of damage. If the concern is the size of the burden, then B should be liable when a different type of damage occurs, but is no greater in extent than the type reasonably foreseeable. Further, the extent of damage may be enormous, even if the type is reasonably foreseeable.[85]

A different justification is that the reasonable foreseeability rule renders the incidence of liability more predictable by defendants, even if the liability is predictably sizeable. Why is this valuable? Its value is more apparent in the case of strict liabilities which attach to particular activities. Without the assurance which the reasonable foreseeability rule provides, some defendants may decide not to engage in the – potentially valuable – activities to which strict liability attaches because those activities expose them to a wholly unpredictable, and not easily insurable, liability. This case for the rule is less strong in relation to negligence, when the defendant can avoid liability by taking reasonable care. However, given that the objective standard often imposes requirements that many defendants may not be able reliably to meet, the concern is perhaps still present. When the defendant's conduct is clearly wrongful and culpable, as is generally the case in deceit, this concern falls away. There is no valuable activity that the defendant will be deterred from engaging in due to the risk of an unpredictable liability. Furthermore, in so far as the defendant is exposed, in deceit, to the risk of a very extensive liability, this concern is again diminished (though not entirely defeated) by the fact that the defendant can avoid all liability simply by not behaving wrongfully and culpably. So it may be that the pattern of remoteness rules can be partly explained both by the fact that, with highly culpable wrongs, the defendant can easily avoid liability and by the fact that there

[84] A Burrows, *Remedies for Torts, Breach of Contract, and Equitable Wrongs*, 4th edn (Oxford, Oxford University Press, 2019) ch 7, 'Principles limiting compensatory damages', contains discussion of remoteness.

[85] Sometimes, however, the description of the type of damage does seem to be influenced by a concern to avoid disproportionate burdens on a contract-breaker: see *Victoria Laundry (Windsor) Ltd v Newman Industries Ltd* [1949] 2 KB 528 (CA).

is no risk, or a very low risk, of deterring valuable activity. The explanation is still partial, however, as these considerations do not explain the law's insistence, in negligence, upon a matching between the risks which it was unreasonable to impose, and the risk which materialised.[86]

Earlier I offered reasons why the role of heightened culpability in diminishing the causal requirement of liability may be mistaken. However, the idea that 'high' culpability can make up for 'low' causation so as to generate justified liability is one which has been endorsed by some philosophers.[87] Frowe gives the example of a person who is fleeing an attacker, and needs to cross a narrow bridge to reach safety.[88] Unfortunately, but philosophically inevitably, the bridge can only bear the weight of one person. As the person fleeing approaches the bridge, she encounters a selfish pedestrian, who refuses to step aside from the bridge because it will muddy her new shoes. Generally, according to Frowe, the selfish pedestrian could justify not moving out of the way if this involved a significant personal cost. For instance, suppose the only way the pedestrian could move in time to save the fleeing person would be to jump to a lower platform, breaking both legs. This requires too much of her, given her indirect involvement in the situation. But suppose the pedestrian maliciously decides to block the person's path. Now, Frowe says, she is liable to lethal defensive force. The thought is that 'obstructing' is a more indirect form of causal involvement than directly posing a threat and so generally does not generate extensive liability, but things change when obstruction is coupled with high culpability. It seems possible to explain this idea, however, without supposing that culpability is itself the ground of liability. The obstructor's duty of easy rescue (or a similar duty) only requires a relatively minimal burden to be borne (because, perhaps, that duty requires positive use of their resources and is not voluntarily chosen). However the obstructor has less objection, as Frowe points out, to bearing a greater burden *having breached* her duty of easy rescue, because she had an additional opportunity to avoid being subject to *that* greater burden.[89] Nonetheless, the reason for bearing the greater burden is still the same reason as the one that applied prior to the breach: that it will save the life of the pedestrian. It is this reason, in combination with the fact that the burdens of conforming to it have discounted weight in virtue of the culpable breach, which justifies the liability.

Liability in contribution proceedings allots shares of liability in respect of a damage in proportion to each liable person's relative culpability and causal contribution. A comparison between these is said to be a comparison of each person's *responsibility* for the damage.[90] The same factors determine the reduction for contributory negligence. It seems, then, that greater culpability with respect to the damage entails greater responsibility and this greater responsibility justifies the person bearing more of the

[86] See *Tremain v Pike* [1969] 1 WLR 1556 (Exeter Assizes).

[87] S Lazar, *Sparing Civilians* (Oxford, Oxford University Press, 2015) 94; H Frowe, *Defensive Killing* (Oxford, Oxford University Press, 2014) 76. The Austrian legal theorist, Walter Wilburg, endorsed a view of this kind. According to Wilburg, the heightened satisfaction of one element of liability could 'compensate' for the diminished satisfaction of another, at least with respect to some elements. For discussion, see Jansen (n 35) ch 9.

[88] Frowe (n 79) 76.

[89] We need not agree with Frowe that it permits *fatal* damage to accept the basic idea.

[90] Civil Liability (Contribution) Act 1978, s 2(1).

cost of the liability (or, in contributory negligence, in bearing more of the cost of their own loss). A person's outcome-related culpability gives them, then, a positive reason to bear more of the cost, or gives the court a positive reason to allocate more of the cost to that person. Even here, however, it may be that culpability acts so as to diminish the normative weight of the defendant's interest in not bearing a burden, which the defendant has independent reason to bear. By distributing the cost of the liability between the persons liable in proportion to their degree of culpability, the law achieves a morally superior distribution of the burden because it allocates more cost where there is less objection to bearing it. There is some reason to think this is what underpins the law. This is because the basic case for apportionment exists even before any consideration of responsibility or culpability has been made. Suppose each defendant breaches a joint contractual duty entirely non-culpably and without responsibility, and one of the two defendants satisfies the compensatory duty that arises from the breach. The case for that defendant having a claim against the other defendant is a principle of fairness. The principle is this: if a number of persons each has a duty to bear a burden in respect of the same damage, it is, other things being equal, unfair if only one of the duty-bearers bears the burden, when it is possible for more than one of them to do so. It is simply arbitrary for one of two persons who are morally required to bear a burden to be singled out if this can be avoided.[91] This principle of fairness justifies distributing shares of compensatory burden independently of responsibility considerations. Each defendant's culpability is relevant only as a secondary matter, which alters whether 'other things are equal'.

Consider, finally, the German idea that high culpability may justify a reversal of the burden of proof of causation. The basic justification for the orthodox burden of proof is that the disvalue of a false positive and false negative is equal, but since a false positive involves imposing unjust damage rather than failing to alleviate it, the claimant loses when the probabilities are equal or impossible to ascertain. The defendant's *proven* high culpability might be considered to diminish the disvalue of a false positive against the defendant.[92] A false negative would wrongly fail to compensate a person entitled to compensation whereas a false positive would wrongly hold liable a highly culpable person. This alleged justificatory role of the defendant's is slightly different from the role it plays in the earlier examples in this section. The idea there was that a culpable defendant cannot complain too much about bearing a cost which they *in any event* have good reason to bear. In cases in which it is unclear whether the defendant was a cause of the outcome, it is simply unclear whether they have a reason to bear the cost of compensation. If one thought that the defendant was responsible for creating a situation in which proof of causation is uncertain, then perhaps *this* gives the defendant a reason to bear a greater risk of uncertainty in the determination of causation. But this does not correlate with situations in which the defendant behaved with high culpability.

[91] See NJ McBride, *The Humanity of Private Law: Part I: Explanation* (Oxford, Hart Publishing, 2018) 212–13.

[92] In previous work, I prematurely rejected this argument because I associated the lesser disvalue of a false positive with the claim that retributive justice would be done in the event of a false positive.

(iv) Culpability and Protection of Social Interests

As Cane observes, '[w]hen a harm-causing activity has high social value, a requirement of intention for tort liability helps to protect society's interest in the continuance of that activity'.[93] This insight helps to explain the role of malice in some torts.[94] One way in which a normal negligence standard may interfere with the continuance of an activity is its uncertainty. If there were a tort of negligent institution of legal proceedings, this may deter valid, and socially valuable, litigation in part because of uncertainty surrounding the content of what 'reasonableness' will be held to require in the context of bringing litigation. However, a malice-based standard mitigates this problem: an honest prospective litigant only needs to take into account the (likely small) possibility that they will erroneously be found to be dishonest. And this is one way in which the courts have justified the requirement of *malice* in the tort of malicious prosecution – as an answer to the potential chilling effect of liability upon valid claims.[95]

(v) Culpability as a Ground of Liability

In all of the examples discussed so far, the appeal to the defendant's culpability has either (probably) been a mistake, an appeal to something else, constitutive of a form of control over the claimant which is wrongful, or merely operated to defeat or diminish an objection the defendant or society would have to the defendant being held liable. In none of them has culpability been part of the positive case for holding the defendant liable in the first place. In this section, I consider three lines of arguments that would assign a positive role to culpability in generating liability.

(a) Retribution

One might seek to explain some or all of the doctrines on a retributivist basis. Retributivism comes in many forms and the following observations may not apply to all forms. A central strand in retributivist theories of punishment is that there is a reason (or it is apt) to impose a burden upon a person because and to the extent that they *deserve* to bear or suffer this burden. The standard basis for such desert is wrongful and culpable conduct. One might seek to explain the additional burdens the law imposes upon culpable defendants under the doctrines described on the basis that the law considers culpable defendants to deserve to bear those burdens.

A deep difficulty with this view – that desert-as-a-positive reason justifies the additional burdens under these doctrines – is that, looking to this argument alone, there is no rational connection between the defendant's desert and the nature of the additional burden imposed by the law under these doctrines. Consider (iii) – the alteration of the burden of proof on the basis of higher culpability. If a person behaves with gross negligence towards another, it is unclear why their desert provides a reason to impose *this*

[93] Cane (n 71) 554.

[94] ibid; D Nolan, 'Varying the Standard of Care in Negligence' (2013) 72 *CLJ* 651, 686.

[95] *Crawford Adjusters (Cayman) Ltd v Sagicor General Insurance (Cayman) Ltd* [2013] UKPC 17, [2014] AC 366 [72].

particular burden – namely, the alteration of the burden of proof. Similarly, in relation to remoteness (iv), a highly culpable wrongdoer may deserve to suffer a burden, but *why this burden*? One could give the defendant what they deserve by fining them (or simply by leaving such matters to the criminal law). And there is no guarantee or even likelihood that the burden will match the defendant's desert. Furthermore, what a person deserves seems to be in large measure luck-insensitive, even if other parts of morality are luck-sensitive. Many of the doctrines above expose the defendant to considerable luck. Whether a person is held liable under the reversal of the burden of proof for gross fault depends upon the happenstance availability of exculpating evidence.

It might be objected that, even if desert cannot be a standalone justification of the doctrines in question, it can be part of the justification. It might be asserted that it is a person's moral desert which removes their objection to bearing a more extensive cost under some of these doctrines. This seems doubtful in relation, for instance, to a person's contributory fault, which is not necessarily morally culpable. More generally, however, the difficulty with this objection is that moral desert is independent of the person's relationship to the particular outcome to which these doctrines apply. A person could be morally deserving – if one believes in moral desert – in virtue of some previous culpable wrong that the person committed prior to the events to which these doctrines apply; this has no bearing, however, on their private law liability to compensate.[96]

(b) Culpability Sufficientism

Some have argued that culpability itself, independently of causation of damage, is a sufficient ground of both liability to defensive damage and to being required to compensate.[97] Let's call this culpability sufficientism (CS). To illustrate, consider this example:

> *Shooters.* D1 and D2 are independently both about to fire their guns at C, each aiming to kill C. C notices that, unbeknownst to D2, D2's gun has a lock which will prevent D2 firing. C is only able to protect himself from D1's shot by pulling D2 in front of D1.

D1 and D2 are equally culpable. Both aim to kill an innocent person without justification. CS holds that C is permitted to harm D2 in virtue of D2's culpability, despite the fact that D2 is not causally responsible for the risk to C's life. This is supported by an appeal to intuition – some think it is intuitive that C is permitted to kill D2 in *Shooters*. There is also a theoretical argument. It is that D2 has no reasonable complaint against a moral rule which permits C to kill D2 in such circumstances. Such a rule benefits everyone, including D2, in providing each person with more opportunities to avoid undeserved harm. Further, to D2's complaint that D2 is being harmed, an answer is: 'you could easily have avoided being harmed by simply not choosing to try to do serious

[96] Here I am not necessarily in disagreement with Cane's conclusion that retributive justice justifies aspects of tort law: Cane's conception of retributive justice is responsibility-centred, and not exclusively desert-based: see P Cane, 'Retribution, Proportionality, and Moral Luck in Tort Law' in P Cane and J Stapleton (eds) *The Law of Obligations: Essays in Celebration of John Fleming* (Oxford, Clarendon Press, 1998).

[97] See, eg, in the context of defensive harm, L Christie, 'Causation and Liability to Defensive Harm' (2020) 37 *Journal of Applied Philosophy* 378, and V Tadros, *To Do, To Die, To Reason Why* (Oxford, Oxford University Press, 2020) ch 10.

wrong'. Although such a rule widens the circumstances in which D2 is liable to harm, D2 is only liable to the same level of harm as D2 would be in relation to a risk which D2 culpably created: their liability is subject to the same proportionality limit.[98]

One could in principle accept CS without thinking that culpability provides a positive reason for liability. If culpability merely diminishes the normative significance of a person's interest in not suffering a burden, then it still acts merely negatively. The positive justification of liability is benefit that will – or is expected to – occur to another person if the culpable person or their resources are damaged. If so, then the truth of CS (if it is true) is unlikely to have much bearing on tort liability, unlike defensive liability. This is because, in cases like *Shooters*, it is necessary, in the factual circumstances of that case, to damage culpable D2 to protect a particular person, C, from damage. The factual circumstances make it such that it is necessary to single out D2 and C. But these factual circumstances do not obtain in tort liability, unless there is already a reason to single out D2 and C, such as a causal link between D2's culpable risk imposition and C's damage.[99] Although highly culpable people would be normatively open to having their resources taken to compensate others for harms for which they are not causally responsible in tort law, if CS were true, this is only one possible way in which their liability to harm could be realised. Their resources could be used to improve disability welfare schemes or more generous compensation funds than currently exist, if their contributions are necessary to achieve this.[100] It seems arbitrary, without more, for the persons whom they have culpably risked, but not caused harm to, to benefit in particular.

(c) Culpability as an Enhancer

A third possible positive normative role for culpability is that it *enhances* the case for taking compensatory action by adding weight to the reasons for it, but without forming an independent reason itself to compensate a particular individual. To explore this, it may be helpful to consider this example:

> *Drugs*. A drug company, D, creates three batches of drugs. The first batch was distributed when the risk of an extremely serious side-effect S was not reasonably discoverable. The

[98] For what it is worth, my intuitions are somewhat unsettled in *Shooters* and related examples. If we vary the facts of *Shooters*, such that D2 has tried to fire and is now standing near C not posing any danger, or if D2 is trying to harm C2, a different victim, my intuition is against it being permissible to harm D2 to protect C. As the defenders of this type of view realise, it leads to what many would regard as highly counterintuitive implications. If the basis of the idea that culpability grounds liability is that a person's normative protection from harm diminishes in some relation to their culpability with respect to harm, in principle, *any* culpable person is open to being used to protect others from harm – be it wrongful harm or otherwise. If a well-known serial killer, D3, is on the loose nearby in *Shooters*, having just killed his latest victim, then C is apparently permitted to kill D3 too, on this view.

[99] For a similar point, see Gardner (n 28) ch 3, 96–99.

[100] It is also not clear, if *culpability sufficientism* is true, how a culpability basis for compensatory liability interacts with liability to punishment. When a person is liable to punitive and compensatory harm, there are two grounds of liability in play, if CS is true, and responsibility for failure to conform to a strict duty/reason is an independently sufficient basis of liability: a responsibility ground and the CS-provided culpability ground. But if the culpability ground of liability is the only one in play, then it would seem particularly necessary to co-ordinate the criminal law and tort law in relation to that ground. If tort law has imposed compensatory liability upon a person on the culpability ground, then this should have a direct impact on their punitive liability. It is also far from obvious why any particular victim of harm should get the full benefit of the defendant's culpability-based liability.

> second batch was distributed when the risk of S was reasonably knowable, but not known by D. The third batch was distributed when D knew about S, but D continued to distribute the drug because of its profitability. There are five victims of each batch, each of whom suffers the same degree of damage, but D only has sufficient funds to provide effective medical treatment for S to a total of five victims.

If culpability provides an additional reason for compensation, then D ought to provide compensation to the batch 3 victims. Further, if the strength of the reason varies in proportion to the degree of culpability, then there is stronger reason to compensate batch 3 victims than batch 2 victims. D's culpability and degree of culpability provide various new reasons for action and render apt certain responses. It makes blame *pro tanto* apt. It gives D a reason to feel certain emotions – guilt, perhaps – that would not be apt in relation to batch 1, or potentially batch 2. Possibly the batch 3 victims will feel dehumanised because of the attitude shown to them by D's conduct. This might give a reason to favour compensating batch 3: it will do more good because the victims will understand the compensation as a recognition of their moral importance. But suppose that the victims will always remain unaware of the fact that D behaved culpably in relation to batch 2 and batch 3. I'm uncertain here, but it is not clear to me why D's defective attitude towards and engagement with reasons itself gives rise to a new reason to *compensate* or otherwise enhances the case for compensating the batch 2 or 3 victims. This makes sense if we think that culpability's normative effect is primarily to allow a kind of moral discounting of the defendant's objection to bearing a burden. This normative effect gives the defendant less complaint to bearing a burden, but it does not give them a new reason to bear it. The law seems to agree with this: in insolvency, all tort victims of the insolvent will have equal priority, regardless of the culpability with which the tort was committed.[101]

A possible argument is that D has reasons not only not to damage the victims, but reasons of *respect* towards the victims. Respect for others requires correctly taking into account their moral status in one's deliberation. Given that there was no evidence-relative reason against damaging with respect to batch 1, D did not fail to deliberate properly in relation to the batch 1 victims. The damage is not disrespectful. But this is different with batch 2 and batch 3. By compensating batch 2 or batch 3, it may be that D (imperfectly) conforms to those reasons of respect by giving a greater priority to those reasons in his deliberation. In other words, we have reasons to have certain attitudes to our reasons for action. There is something morally problematic, for example, about a person who adopts an intention to conform to their promises only in so far as it serves their self-interest. This is not an appropriate attitude to one's duties. In relation to the batch 2 and 3 victims, D fails to adopt the appropriate attitude to D's duties. What would be the appropriate attitude toward the reason not to damage, now, having undervalued or overlooked the reason in the past? Tentatively, it is not clear (to me) that one's reason to have an appropriate attitude towards one's reasons for action requires *additional* weight to be given to a reason in respect of which one adopted an inappropriate attitude.

[101] The Insolvency Act 1986, s 382, permits tort claims (except claims based on fraud: s 281(3)) to constitute a 'bankruptcy debt'. This permits tort claimants to recover to the same extent as the bankrupt's other creditors.

In the promise example, it would be odd if merely adopting a stance of 'perform one's promise if it is in one's self-interest' could give an additional rational force to one's promise. More plausibly, one ought simply to recognise the force of the reason, now, and to give the reason its proper weight in one's deliberation. If that is right, then we still lack an argument for culpability as an enhancer.

III. Conclusion

To recap, in this chapter I have aimed to explain both why moral culpability is not a necessary condition of private law compensatory liability, and yet why it continues to play a role in determining its scope. The connection between compensatory and defensive liability puts an account of compensatory liability that makes moral culpability a necessary condition on the back foot, and the intelligibility of culpability-independent duties and reasons not to damage explains why fault principles generally operate so as to cut-back, rather than generate, liability. While in some cases I have sought to argue that culpability's role in determining liability is mistaken or only apparent, in other cases, I have defended its value, with Cane, as a protective device, which defeats or diminishes individual or societal objections to liability that would otherwise arise.

4

Peter Cane on Torts

STEPHEN D SUGARMAN

In 2017, Peter Cane published a stimulating little book titled *Key Ideas in Tort Law* as part of the Hart Publishing series *Key Ideas in Law*.[1] While intended in many respects as an introduction to torts for those just coming to the subject, the book provides even the expert reader with a goodly number of provocative insights about tort law in England and more broadly, which I review below.

I. Tort Law is Rarely Enforced

Perhaps most important among Cane's insights is his observation that tort law is rarely enforced.[2] Cane means two things by this. First, he observes that tort law is rarely enforced in the sense that most people behave reasonably not because they fear they will be held liable if they injure someone with their carelessness, but because they are morally responsible; they would avoid socially unacceptable, dangerous conduct regardless of whether or not tort law existed. The behaviour of this vast majority of people is not influenced by tort doctrine. In fact, the vast majority of people are not even familiar with tort law's precise requirements for conduct. It is therefore not sensible to conclude that these requirements guide their actions.

Second, if 'enforcement' refers to the active involvement of public officials in carrying out claims against wrongdoers, tort law is also rarely enforced, at least in comparison with the criminal law. For Cane, the most significant reason for this is that people who file tort claims almost always resolve them informally, typically via a settlement with a liability insurance company rather than through a trial. (As he notes, only about one per cent of claims result in trials.[3]) Furthermore, many people who would qualify as tort victims under the law never file claims and hence do not enforce their rights. Most often this is because the injurer is clearly judgment-proof and it would be a waste of time and money to bring suit against her. Other times, the victim is simply unable to provide

[1] P Cane, *Key Ideas in Tort Law* (Oxford, Hart Publishing, 2017).
[2] ibid 83.
[3] ibid 84.

adequate proof of how his injury occurred – specifically, he cannot demonstrate that he was harmed by someone who should be legally liable for the injury.

Cane acknowledges, however, that lack of enforcement hardly means that few tort claims are made. In England alone, there are more than one million successful road accident tort claims made each year.[4] Indeed, when the act of motoring leads to bodily injury or death, there is a substantial likelihood that a lawsuit will follow. Still, because tort law in the UK and most of the rest of the world is based on 'fault', many auto accidents do not give rise to tort claims, most obviously when a solo driver carelessly crashes her vehicle and is injured. Data from the US suggest that perhaps a quarter of physical injury victims of motoring accidents are not compensated by tort law.[5]

II. Tort's Real-World 'Enforcers' are Liability Insurance Administrators

In any event – and this is Cane's next important insight – the real-world 'enforcers' of tort law are not public officials, but rather those who administer the liability insurance system.[6] This is most evident for auto accidents, which comprise the largest category of tort claims for physical injury. However, it applies as well to the other important categories of accidents that result in physical injury and then legal claims, including medical malpractice, injuries from defective products, physical accidents that occur on the premises of the party claimed against, and other forms of transportation injuries. For a victim of any of these types of accident to have a realistic hope of collecting a substantial award, it is nearly always necessary for the party the victim is suing to have prepared for the possibility of being sued by obtaining liability insurance. (That said, some large enterprises and governmental agencies can and do self-insure a substantial share of their tort liability risk.)

Moreover, as Cane points out, liability insurers do not slavishly apply tort doctrine in dealing with claimants. Since virtually all the claims made will eventually be settled (or perhaps dropped), liability insurers take into account factors beyond the law of torts in deciding whether to make a settlement offer and, if so, for how much.

I add here that settlement negotiation is also informed by insurers' and claimants' respective 'risk aversion' profiles. Insurers on one side and victims' lawyers on the other are aware both that insurers will deal with lots of future claims and that victims hope for a one-time experience with making a claim. This tends to make victims more fearful of taking the case to trial, especially when, under England's 'loser pays' rule, they would be liable for the defendant's legal costs were the case to end in a verdict for the defence.

[4] ibid.

[5] According to a 1991 RAND study, approximately 27% of motoring accident claimants in tort states receive no third-party compensation for their physical injuries: SJ Carroll et al, *No-Fault Approaches to Compensating People Injured in Automobile Accidents* (RAND Corporation, 1991) https://www.rand.org/content/dam/rand/pubs/reports/2006/R4019.pdf, accessed 1 July 2021.

[6] Cane (n 1) 85–87.

In determining what sort of settlement to pursue, both sides speculate about how a case arising from a victim's injury would turn out were it actually tried in court, as well as how much future harm the victim will suffer when the injury is permanent (or at least continues to affect the victim while the claim is being handled). Until a claim is settled, however, the victim may be without funds and pressed to find ways to pay for both routine living expenses and any special costs incurred because of the injury. Meanwhile, insurers earn continuous income on the liability insurance premiums they collect from their clients. Claimants in need of funds may be reluctant to risk pursuing their claims in court and willing to accept even low settlement offers rather than extend negotiation. These factors often push victims to accept less in settlement than their cases might theoretically be worth.

At the same time, and cutting in the opposite direction, insurers are acutely aware of their costs of administering claims, and lawyers representing claimants also realise that the insurers are eager to minimise these costs.[7] For insurers, this means developing simple rules of thumb for their staff to apply in the hope of getting small claims promptly off the books and into the 'resolved' category. Hence, as Cane points out, empirical evidence suggests that victims with relatively small injuries (eg a simple broken limb) are actually often able to recover *more* than they would win were their claim resolved in court.[8] (Indeed, a not insignificant share of these victims would probably lose their cases if they went to trial.) By contrast, those with serious injuries typically receive considerably less than full compensation through the settlement of their tort claims.[9] In short, the administration of tort law by insurers produces results that vary significantly from what the formal, precise rules of tort (and the law of damages governing physical injury torts) would produce.

III. How Tort Law for Personal Injuries and Death Developed

How did we get to this state of affairs? As Cane explains, tort law for personal injuries and death was not a coherently developed area of the law until the nineteenth century.[10] Much earlier on, what we now call the law of 'battery' provided a legal remedy for intentional physical harm. Some trace the early development of this legal remedy to efforts by the Crown to dissuade the King's subjects from responding with further violence when physically attacked by other subjects.[11] By insisting on the payment of money by the initial aggressor in such instances, the Crown hoped to discourage vengeance, ensuring

[7] See, eg, N Engstrom, 'Sunlight and Settlement Mills' (2011) 86 *New York University Law Review* 805, 827–29.

[8] Cane (n 1) 98.

[9] ibid.

[10] ibid 14–15.

[11] See generally G McBain, 'Modernising the Common Law Offences of Assault and Battery' (2015) 4 *International Law Research* 39, 52 (describing the development of the option to sue for damages instead of seeking vengeance in response to 'offences against the person').

the survival of more civilians and soldiers and resulting in a stronger economy from which to extract taxes.

Intentional torts that qualify as batteries occur all too often in the twenty-first century, but they are not commonly the basis of actual tort claims because liability insurance, generally speaking, does not cover intentional torts. And, absent insurance coverage, all too large a share of those who resort to violence against others have no meaningful amounts of wealth or income for the victims to attach. Hence, the world of battery is in practice given over to the criminal law (or divorce law, or juvenile law).

What we think of today as the core of tort law with respect to physical harms largely developed in the middle of the nineteenth century alongside scientific and industrial progress that permitted entrepreneurs to harness energy as never before. Factories, railways, and the exploitation of natural resources created enormous economic advances, but they also created enormous new opportunities for workers, consumers, and strangers to be harmed. These injuries were generally seen as 'accidents' even if enterprise leaders were clearly aware that their activities would cause the very sorts of injuries that they did cause. It was not the enterprise leaders' intention to inflict these harms; they were simply the collateral damage of commercial activity. Sometimes, accidents caused by commercial activity were readily avoidable. For instance, employees had simply failed to take appropriate precautions, or managers had failed appropriately to train employees or adopt sensible safety devices or measures that would have prevented the accidents (or at least many of them). Other times, physical injuries were simply not reasonably avoidable because no safer alternative way of carrying out an enterprise's activity was available.

As accident litigation increased and courts in the UK and elsewhere in the common law world grappled with the scope of enterprise tort liability, the dominant rule that emerged was that victims had to prove that their injurers – or injurers' employees acting within the scope of their employment – had behaved negligently, and that it was this carelessness that had caused the victims' injuries.[12] This meant that predictable but not reasonably avoidable accidents were generally the legal responsibility of victims, not injurers. This 'fault'-based regime has continued to anchor nearly all of tort law with respect to physical injury ever since.

A small exception was carved out for certain activities that actors knew might cause serious harm whether or not they had exercised due care to try to prevent that harm, such as dynamite blasting or building water reservoirs on private land. In those cases, liability was imposed without injurer fault.[13] But by the twenty-first century, this 'strict liability' exception continued to cover only a very narrow range of risks throughout the common law world.

As tort law evolved along with the industrial revolution, so too liability insurance evolved out of the world of casualty insurance, in which pools of premiums were

[12] Cane (n 1) 41, 45.

[13] In *Rylands v Fletcher*, a case from the 1860s, the defendant's reservoir flooded his neighbour's underground mine shafts. The courts held that landowners could be liable for harm flowing from their 'non-natural' activities (such as private reservoir construction) even absent proof that their deliberate or negligent conduct had caused the harm: *Rylands v Fletcher* (1865) 3 Hurl & C 774; 159 ER 737; affd (1868) LR 3 HL 330.

collected to be directed to valid claims resulting from ship accidents, fires, and the like. But, whereas casualty insurance functioned apart from legal responsibility (insureds sought to cover their own property), liability insurance was specifically designed to indemnify buyers from legal risk (insureds sought to cover harm they might do to others).

Liability insurance covered accidents that imposed tort liability (assuming the potential defendant could obtain coverage in the first place), and so it was not the absence of insurance protection that pushed courts to embrace 'fault,' reject 'strict liability', and leave the costs of so-called 'unavoidable' accidents on victims. Rather, as Cane explains, this judicial solution seems more clearly based on a moral determination that it is not fair to make someone liable for harms they caused but could not reasonably have avoided.[14] Of course, when an enterprise escapes tort liability for accidents its activity causes, the costs of these accidents are not internalised into the price of the enterprise's activity (or product). The failure to impose tort liability on accidents thus implicitly subsidises the conduct that produces these accidents (although were strict tort liability to be imposed on such activities, this would implicitly subsidise the *victims*' activities by freeing them from the unavoidable costs of accidents in which they are involved).

Parties often contest whether an injurer has negligently *caused* an accident, and this frequently leads to substantially discounted settlement awards, since neither party finds it worth risking an all-or-nothing resolution by leaving the matter to be determined in court. In this respect as well, tort law in practice becomes far more distant from the precise contours of technical tort doctrine.

As tort law continued to develop in the increasingly industrial setting of the second half of the nineteenth century, it was typically the only measure by which victims could obtain compensation for their physical injuries. The costs of medical care and the income lost because of physical harms would fall on victims (or their survivors) if no tort claim were available. On the other hand, were the injurer liable, tort law would impose on the injurer an obligation to pay not only for these 'pecuniary' (or 'economic' or 'special') damages, but also for what today is often termed 'pain and suffering' (or 'non-economic loss'). As I have noted in past work, in the US, relatively huge sums can be awarded for pain and suffering[15] (although as a practical matter, it is out of this portion of the award that the victim's lawyer is remunerated). For various reasons, some nations award very small sums for pain and suffering (in Europe, such nations include Denmark, Greece, Portugal, and Sweden).[16] England ranks on the more generous side for Western Europe, although victims there still receive far less for pain and suffering than victims in the US stand to obtain for similar injuries; £500,000 awarded in a quadriplegia case in England might be millions of dollars in the US.[17]

[14] Cane (n 1) 54.

[15] SD Sugarman, 'A Comparative Law Look at Pain and Suffering Awards' (2006) 55 *DePaul Law Review* 399.

[16] ibid 410.

[17] SD Sugarman, 'Tort Damages for Non-Economic Losses: Personal Injury' in M Bussani and AJ Sebok (eds), *Comparative Tort Law: Global Perspectives* (Cheltenham, Edward Elgar Publishing Ltd, 2015) 323, 341, 343.

IV. Tort Law is No Longer a Victim's Only Source of Compensation

Over the past decades, central governments in most wealthy nations have built up an array of social insurance (or social security) systems that deal with critical financial needs of their residents. The main focus of these plans has been on disabled people, retirees, and surviving dependants of decedents. Although the scope of these social security measures is much broader than that of tort law, these measures include in their coverage those who might also be tort victims, primarily people who are disabled or killed in accidents.

Cane helpfully gives considerable attention to how these social security schemes mesh with tort law.[18] The need for medical attention is a significant convergence point. Most nations today have some sort of national health insurance system that provides for victims' medical needs, making it unnecessary from the victim's standpoint for tort law to compensate for these already-covered costs. (Nations still vary sharply as to whether these costs should be borne directly by the health care system or whether the tort liability system should reimburse the health care system for its expenditures in this area.) Still, sometimes victims arguably have legitimate medical expenses that are not covered by health insurance, and those with valid tort claims are able to shift these expenses to their injurers.

Cane also examines the role of 'workers' compensation' or 'industrial accident' plans, the first mechanism for replacing the lost income of an injured or killed worker. A little history adds context to his description of how workers' compensation operates today.

When workers' compensation came into effect at the end of the nineteenth century in England and Germany and in the early twentieth century in the US,[19] it garnered political support largely because of tort law's failure to compensate many injured workers and survivors of workers who had been killed. In the US, for example, the so-called 'holy trinity' of defences that employer-injurers could raise undercut a huge share of potential legal claims. These defences included 'contributory negligence' by the injured worker; 'assumption of risk' when a worker had been aware of a work danger, even if that danger could have been readily and cheaply ameliorated by the employer; and the 'fellow servant' rule, which blocked employer liability when the injury had been caused by a careless fellow worker of the victim rather than by an employee higher up in the management chain.[20] (Of course, the typical fellow employee had neither liability insurance nor savings to pay for harms he or she negligently caused.) Although workers' compensation plans rarely issued payments as generous as those tort law might provide, they usually paid victims or their survivors quickly, thereby much reducing their need to sue for uncovered losses.

[18] Cane (n 1) 121.

[19] ML Perlin, 'The German and British Roots of American Workers' Compensation Systems: When Is an Intentional Act Intentional' (1985) 15 *Seton Hall Law Review* 849, 857, 864, 873.

[20] ibid 861–62.

Interestingly enough, in England and most other nations, those suffering work injuries can still both claim benefits under their workers' compensation plan and sue under tort law (but usually not for losses already compensated, or at least any such recovery in tort must be passed back to the plan that already paid for the victim's loss). By contrast, workers' compensation benefits in the US fully substitute for tort claims by employees against employers. Most wealthy nations continue to have special arrangements for work-related injuries, maintaining the early distinction created by workers' compensation plans. Hence, it is important to appreciate that broad social insurance plans do not typically cover future income losses of people who had not entered the workforce at the time of their injury, and that in many places the amount paid even to injured workers is lower if the injury occurred away from work rather than at work.

Workers' compensation plans generally cover both temporary and permanent injuries and the full range from minor to very serious injuries (and deaths). The result is a complex pattern of compensation paid to victims with very different needs. From the perspective of employees, this is somewhat incoherent. Their highest priority tends to be uniform and reasonably generous disability protection regardless of how their disabling injury occurred – whether it happened while they were on the job, driving to their workplace, showering at home while preparing for work, playing a recreational sport at the weekend, or falling off the sofa while watching TV.

In response to work by Lord Beveridge, the UK concluded after World War II that work injury compensation itself was too narrow. It adopted its separate, more comprehensive social insurance scheme to address a broader range of income needs of workers and their dependants, again creating an even larger overlap with potential tort claimants.[21] Such plans exist throughout the Western world.

It is important to appreciate that these broad social insurance schemes tend not to award any sums for pain and suffering. The coverage and award level decisions built into such regimes greatly impact how much uncovered loss is potentially recoverable from a tort claim.

Given the National Health Insurance and other social insurance schemes that have operated in the UK for decades now, it is at least imaginable that tort law for accidental physical injury could be repealed, leaving physical harm victims of torts treated equally with those in need of medical treatment and income replacement for other reasons. But this has not happened. Indeed, only in New Zealand has tort law for accidentally caused personal injury and death been fully replaced by social insurance – and there by a plan that is more generous in its income replacement terms for 'accident' victims than for social insurance claimants compensated for other reasons (eg those seeking benefits due to retirement, birth defects, unemployment, or non-employment-based illness).[22] Many successive governments in New Zealand have tinkered with this regime over the more than four decades of its existence. But the basic principle of substituting loss based social insurance for tort law when people are accidentally injured has remained firmly in place.

[21] WHB Beveridge, *Social Insurance and Allied Services: Report by Sir William Beveridge* (London, HM Stationery Office, 1942).

[22] Accident Compensation Act 2001 (NZ). See also GWR Palmer, *Compensation for Incapacity: A Study of Law and Social Change in New Zealand and Australia* (Oxford, Oxford University Press, 1979).

Although no other jurisdiction has followed the sweeping New Zealand solution, a number of nations (or parts thereof) have replaced tort law for specific categories of injuries. Here, I start with the most prominent of such replacements – auto no-fault compensation plans. A good example is the scheme now in place for several decades in Quebec, Canada.[23] Victims of motoring accidents in Quebec may not sue those who negligently injured them for their personal injury losses. Instead, whether anyone was at fault or not, the victim simply claims from the province-wide compensation plan (to which all motorists contribute). The plan generously covers lost income and pays out what can be considerable sums for general damages (that is, pain and suffering) where the injuries are serious. Medical needs not met by Canada's national health plan are also generally covered by the auto no-fault plan, which also makes a lump sum payment to the national health plan each year meant to approximate the value of the health care it provides to injured motorists.

In short, Quebec's scheme is meant to internalise a reasonable measure of driving's physical injury costs into the activity of driving, and to provide benefits to victims in a timely and administratively inexpensive way. Those with bad driving records (as measured by 'points' accumulated from bad driving infractions) pay more into the auto no-fault plan to 'offset' the heightened risk that they will cause an accident (injuring themselves or others). But once an accident occurs, all victims are treated alike. This means that drivers who hurt themselves in one-car crashes are well-compensated, as are those who are at fault under a system of comparative negligence and who would therefore receive reduced recovery in tort (for example, when both drivers are at fault in a two-car crash).

Additionally, a number of nations have adopted plans designed to compensate victims of vaccines in the rare instances in which a vaccine inoculation results in a serious side effect, or to compensate victims of the side effects of pharmaceutical drugs.[24] Various political explanations justify these plans, but common themes include the goal of keeping product-makers free from the risk of crushing liability in tort (a risk that could lead them to withdraw from the production of important public-health-promoting products) and the goal of caring for unlucky victims (especially those who contribute to the broad social benefit of 'herd immunity' by receiving vaccinations).

While criticisms can be mounted against any of these alternatives or additions to tort law, it is clear from the compensation perspective that any number of regimes can deliver benefits to victims at a lower cost than does tort law. This is largely because compensation regimes tend to involve much lower administrative costs and to award much smaller pain and suffering awards (or none at all). In turn, these savings make it possible to provide benefits to more victims. In Quebec, for example, motorists end up

[23] Société de L'Assurance Automobile du Québec, *Québec's Public Automobile Insurance Plan* (Gouvernement du Québec) https://saaq.gouv.qc.ca/en/traffic-accident/public-automobile-insurance-plan, accessed 1 July 2021.

[24] In the US, the National Vaccine Injury Compensation Program compensates individuals and families of individuals injured by covered childhood vaccines: 42 USC §§300aa-10–17 (2006). Drug injury compensation plans have been enacted in jurisdictions including Germany, Sweden, and Japan: JG Fleming, 'Drug Injury Compensation Plans' (1982) 30 *American Journal of Comparative Law* 297.

making payments into the auto no-fault system that are an estimated one-third lower than the payments made by motorists in Canadian provinces without auto no-fault plans;[25] at the same time, many victims in Quebec who would go uncompensated by tort law (whether in Quebec or elsewhere) can recover from the plan.

Given the superiority of some sort of social insurance as compared with tort as a compensation device, many academics argued some years back that the New Zealand solution (or some variation on it) would take hold throughout the Western world.[26] For example, in the UK, an Oxford-based group proposed an income replacement plan for people disabled not only by accidents but also by sickness.[27] I proposed an even more sweeping expansion of the general social insurance plans of economically advanced countries, designed to improve the financial situations of disabled people as well as unemployed and under-employed people and retirees and their survivors.[28] But this sort of sea change has not taken place. Interestingly enough, as formerly socialist or communist nations have (at least partially) embraced capitalism and legal regimes of private property rights, even they have not generally adopted sweeping New Zealand-like schemes. Instead, even for motoring accidents, they have tended to embrace fault-based tort law combined with private liability insurance.[29] What accounts for this?

V. Tort Law is Thought to Serve Important Functions Beyond Compensation – But it May not be the Best Mechanism for Doing So

The reasons are tied to another insight of Cane's, who suggests that tort law, at least in the minds of some, serves other important social purposes beyond compensating victims – social goals that are perhaps compromised or even fully sacrificed by the New Zealand approach. I now turn to these other supposed positive social functions of tort law.

Perhaps most importantly, tort law is seen by its supporters as serving a crucial regulatory function, what is sometimes termed the 'optimisation' of accident costs.[30] It is widely feared that absent sanctions, some actors (especially profit-seeking enterprises) would carry out their activities in unreasonably dangerous ways, causing more accidents

[25] Data from the Insurance Bureau of Canada indicate that Quebec's auto insurance premiums remain the lowest in Canada; there, the average premium in 2017 was $685, compared with $819 in New Brunswick and $1,445 in Ontario: Insurance Bureau of Canada, *Québec Automobile Insurance Market* https://bac-quebec.qc.ca/en/insurance-issues/quebec-automobile-insurance-market/, accessed 1 July 2021.

[26] See, eg, JG Fleming, 'Is There a Future for Tort?' (1984) 44 *Louisiana Law Review* 1193, 1211.

[27] D Harris et al, *Compensation and Support for Illness and Injury* (Oxford, Oxford University Press, 1984).

[28] SD Sugarman, *Doing Away With Personal Injury Law: New Compensation Mechanisms for Victims, Consumers, and Business* (Westport, Quorum Books, 1989).

[29] In China and Ukraine, for example, the doctrine of fault-based liability continues to dominate: K Wang and D Mendelson, 'An Overview of Liability and Compensation for Personal Injury in China Under the General Principles of Civil Law' (1996) 4 *Torts Law Journal* 1, 21; T Hoffmann, 'Europeanisation of Private Law in Ukraine: Comparisons in the Field of Law of Obligations' (2017) 138 *Problems of Legality* 55, 65.

[30] Cane (n 1) 104.

than are socially acceptable. Notice that the goal here is not completely to eliminate all accidents regardless of the cost; no one seems to be arguing for a five-miles-per-hour speed limit for motor vehicles, for example. But the thinking is that where precautions can efficiently reduce accidents (or their severity), they should be taken. Supporters of tort law therefore stress its capacity to encourage the adoption of such precautions.

Of course, actors can be guided to safer conduct in many ways. As already discussed, a large portion of society behaves responsibly and would continue to do so for personal moral reasons even in the absence of tort law. These personal moral reasons include the belief that it would violate one's sense of self to needlessly harm another, as well as the desire to maintain a reputation among acquaintances as a caring and responsible member of society.

To be sure, some people may regularly or opportunistically subject others to unreasonable risks in the absence of sanctions, out of selfishness or for whatever other reason. But there are yet other ways to encourage safer conduct. For example, in a capitalist economy, the market itself can promote safety when consumers choose to pay more for products that are less likely to injure them or their loved ones. Some people may even be willing to pay more to promote the safety of strangers. Still, often market signals will not be enough to generate socially desirable levels of safety precautions, leading to what might be described as negative externalities. These are not restricted to harms to strangers who do not have an economic relationship with their injurers. Un-internalised social costs that should be avoided might also include harms to consumers and workers who are theoretically able to bargain for more safety but fail to do so because of their bargaining positions relative to their potential injurers, or because information asymmetries have left them under-informed about the risks they are taking.

A conventional response to this problem is the introduction of business regulation through legislation, followed by ongoing regulation of businesses carried out by administrative agencies. Workplace safety, transportation safety, product safety, and the like are common political priorities of Western governments seeking to promote safer societies. But for defenders of tort law, the first line of governmental intervention should be the mere threat to injurers of legal liability to victims.[31]

This outlook is especially appealing to those who are sceptical about the effectiveness and social desirability of big government and the administrative state. What is supposedly magical about tort law is that it is privately implemented, both by the threat of victims suing as well as by the actual lawsuits they bring. The threat of being sued is said to prompt actors to take efficient precautions. This is the basic insight that has driven 'law and economics' thinking about torts: It is cheaper to pay less now for a cost-effective safety precaution than to pay more later when someone is hurt who should not

[31] See generally G Calabresi, *The Costs of Accidents* (New Haven, Yale University Press, 1970) (framing the goal of accident law as the minimisation of accident – and accident avoidance – costs); RA Posner, 'A Theory of Negligence' (1972) 1 *Journal of Legal Studies* 29 (emphasising tort law as a system for identifying the party capable of preventing a loss at the lowest cost rather than as a mechanism for identifying the party who is 'really' responsible for a given harm).

have been. Since negligence law only imposes liability for the failure to take precautions that should have been taken, the financial signal to risk-creators is supposedly clear. If tort law worked perfectly in this respect, it would produce the 'optimal' level of safety for a society, all without victims actually having to sue and without the need for taxpayer-funded agencies working to promote public safety.

VI. Tort Law on the Ground Often Fails to Function as Intended

While the theory is very tidy, whether tort law actually functions in this way is another matter. Explanations related to businesses' organisational structures can help explain why tort falls far short of achieving what societies want in terms of safety, which I offer here. For one, many executives are rewarded (and reward their employees) based on the short-term profits their enterprises generate, and the cost of safety precautions can cut into those profits. At the same time, the longer-term benefits of lowered accident levels and hence reduced legal claims against an enterprise might not appear until well down the road, when today's leadership is already gone. This makes the trade-off between short- and long-term priorities rather different from what the basic law-and-economics tort model envisions.

Furthermore, in large organisations especially, it is not always easy for top executives to get subordinates to discover, spend on, and implement safety improvements when those subordinates have their own financial and upward mobility goals, which may not dovetail with the longer-run financial success of an organisation. Additionally, many business leaders experience tort law in action (or see it in action with respect to competitor firms) as something of an unpredictable roll of the dice and hence become sceptical that, in practice, they will actually be protected when they do the socially appropriate thing and not protected when they do not. Hence, fighting tort claims as they come along may seem a better way to invest firm funds than investing in safer operations. Finally, business leaders often find the decision to recall or stop selling a profitable product because of early indications that it might cause unexpected and serious harms a difficult call to make. Fears of needlessly losing profits or damaging their company's public image may lead them to monitor developments for too long before taking action to pull a dangerous product from the market.

In the end, the fact is that Western nations have not been content to rely on tort to regulate safety. In light of the convincing argument that tort liability is simply not doing enough, governments worldwide have created a huge range of agencies that have safety as at least one of their core missions. Given the wide existence of administrative agencies concerned with safety, it becomes even more uncertain just what tort law achieves when added into the mix of other laws that regulate business. If, for example, a nation has in place a government agency that oversees commercial aviation safety and investigates and publicly reports on any serious airplane crash, is it still the threat of being sued that prompts airlines to better train their pilots and mechanics? Add to this regulatory landscape the moral and financial concerns surrounding the loss of planes and human lives (of both employees and passengers) in the event of deadly crashes – to say nothing of the loss of business following any carrier's air crash – and it is hard to see how tort law does anything additional to promote safer airline conduct.

To be sure, administrative agencies are not immune to their own problems. There is reason for concern that they may become 'captured' by the firms they are supposed to regulate, adopting those firms' viewpoints and therefore developing less onerous regulation than is socially desirable. And agency personnel have their own agendas in terms of money and power, which can distort how they exercise their regulatory authority. Where agencies fail or are likely to fail in their safety-promoting missions, the decentralised, privately initiated tort law system may seem more attractive.

Still, whether tort law as a deterrent of unsafe conduct is worth the cost of its operation is by no means clear. Were tort law truly effective as an optimiser of safety precautions, one would expect to see fewer and fewer valid tort claims for accidental physical injury thanks to the adoption of effective precautions; one would also expect that a larger and larger share of the accidents that did happen would be socially acceptable and not reasonably avoidable. But this does not seem to be the real-world situation.

For one thing, for reasons already explained, some firms are simply not going to invest properly in safety despite the threat of tort liability; and for another, humans employed in risk-creating activities often make mistakes they are not really able to prevent, despite the fact that tort law might view these activities as unreasonable behaviours to which liability should attach. To the extent that 'fault'-based tort litigation stems from inherent human fallibility, as much of it does, what we observe is not tort serving a deterrent function but instead tort imposing what is effectively strict liability under the guise of a fault-based regime.[32]

For some defenders of tort law, the justification for threatening and then, as needed, formally imposing legal liability on wrongdoers is simply a moral one. You harmed me when you should not have; I am entitled to claim against you, bring you to court if need be, and, in any event, hold you financially responsible for the consequences of your misconduct.[33]

Like the deterrence justification for tort law, this argument has traditionally held particular appeal for those with politically conservative outlooks, although for an altogether different reason. While fans of tort law's potential to deter stress their scepticism of big government, the conservative viewpoint underlying the moral argument for tort is that tort is and should be about personal responsibility. Whereas those with a more social-democratic outlook tend to focus on institutions as serving their own and sometimes wider social goals, traditionalists emphasise individual rights and remedies and seek to identify specific actors who have failed to behave as they should – the proverbial bad apples in a barrel of otherwise tasty ones. Indeed, from the individual responsibility perspective, it is important for good apples to identify bad apples not

[32] See, eg, MF Grady, 'A New Positive Economic Theory of Negligence' (1983) 92 *Yale Law Journal* 799 (arguing that conventional negligence theory's formal rules neither minimise costs in conditions of uncertainty nor align with the decision rules courts actually use).

[33] EJ Weinrib, 'Corrective Justice' (1992) 77 *Iowa Law Review* 403, 425 ('[a] judgment of liability simultaneously affirms both the entitlement of the plaintiff and the obligation of the defendant.').

only to impose consequences on them, but to signal that the 'bad apple' label does not apply to them.

Because it imposes tort liability on individual (or enterprise) wrongdoers, tort law then can be seen as simultaneously punishing bad behaviour and providing satisfaction to victims. Not only can tort victims receive the tangible benefit of personal compensation, which hopefully serves, as well as money can, to put them in the position they were before their injuries. Through tort, victims can also receive the symbolic benefit of having won their case.

While this vision may sound appealing in theory, tort law once more seems to fall quite short in practice. As already discussed, very few tort claims result in actual trials where the defendant is held personally liable. Instead, nearly all 'successful' claims are via settlements, with the money coming from insurers rather than the actual wrongdoers. When an employee negligently injures someone, the employee's firm is held vicariously liable. As a formal legal matter, firms held vicariously liable may be able to recoup payouts they or their insurers make from the individual employees who were at fault, but this almost never happens.

Indeed, for a wide range of negligence-caused accidents, the at-fault employee does not even lose his or her job or get demoted. For firms, this may be a matter of convenience as much as anything else. Firms often take the initial position that neither they nor their staff were at fault, making it difficult from an administrative or public relations standpoint for them to turn around and say otherwise by imposing employment consequences on at-fault workers after these firms reach settlements with victims. Ultimately, personal responsibility for misconduct simply does not manifest in tort in the way it does in the criminal law, where those convicted of crimes are subject to individual fines or periods of incarceration.

Furthermore, settlements of tort claims are usually worked out by lawyers for victims on one side and insurers' representatives on the other. What these parties conclude is the best deal a claimant can get is then simply presented to the claimant, who typically just accepts what is recommended. Given their lack of control over the process, claimants may all too rarely have the satisfying personal experience that those who view tort as an enforcer of moral obligations might believe the tort system provides to victims.[34]

To be sure, the imposition of tort liability informs how much insurers charge for liability insurance. Those who are held liable and on whose behalf liability insurers pay settlements may face higher future premiums as a result. In this way, tort law internalises accident costs to certain types of accidents and to specific actors to some degree. Still, the full force of a settlement or judgment is normally not felt by an insured wrongdoer, since the whole point of insurance is to spread costs.

[34] E Lind et al, 'The Perception of Justice: Tort Litigants' Views of Trial, Court-Annexed Arbitration, and Judicial Settlement Conferences' (RAND Corporation, 1989) https://www.rand.org/pubs/reports/R3708.html, accessed 1 July 2021, 61 (finding a high positive correlation between litigants' sense of control over their cases and their satisfaction with the civil court system). See also Engstrom (n 7) 817.

VII. Tort Law is not the Only Mechanism for Internalising Accident Costs, Setting Standards for 'Due Care', Encouraging Whistle-Blowing, or Deterring Retaliation

It is also important to appreciate that tort law is not the only mechanism for internalising accident costs. The Quebec auto no-fault plan described above charges motorists to generate funds that pay for income loss replacement, medical care, and pain and suffering (in serious injury cases) for those harmed by motor vehicles. Individual drivers with bad driving records are asked to contribute more to the plan. It would be hard to say that fault-based tort law regimes in other jurisdictions do a better job of internalising the costs of motoring.

The US offers another example of efficient cost internalisation via a compensation scheme. Funding for the National Vaccine Injury Compensation Program is paid for by a surcharge on each vaccine dose administered,[35] hence internalising accident costs to vaccines. This is analogous to the way that pharmaceutical companies raise prices of their drugs to account for their legal liability to people harmed by those drugs under the tort law system. Furthermore, governmental agencies that regulate drugs, vaccines, and motor vehicles are empowered to impose fines and other penalties on irresponsible actors, serving the deterrence and punishment functions valued by tort law's supporters.

An additional function tort law is said to serve is drawing the line between socially acceptable and unacceptable conduct – in other words, setting the standard as to what constitutes 'due care.' As the ongoing evolution of the common law shows, this standard of due care is adjusted relative to developments in society at large. Technological advances create new kinds of activities that in turn lead to accidental injuries, and as this sequence unfolds, societies must determine whether or not the new activities are being carried out in a safe enough manner (or indeed, whether they are so dangerous that they should be disallowed altogether). And even when injury-causing activities are not themselves new, victims may claim that evolving social norms suggest that new responsibilities should be imposed on those who undertake those activities.

The day-to-day operation of tort law addresses these developments as judges (or juries, in the US) confront real injury situations in which victims claim that the injurers should have acted differently. For example, judges or juries may consider what precautions, if any, alcohol servers must take to prevent their customers from engaging in drunk driving that leads to road accidents; what measures sporting event organisers should implement to protect spectators from injuries without spoiling the pleasure of attendance; or whether electronic cigarettes should be treated as an undesirable gateway for teens on the way to becoming regular cigarette smokers or rather as an effective smoking cessation product for otherwise addicted smokers.

[35] The Vaccine Injury Compensation Trust Fund administers compensation for injuries related to vaccines provided on or after 1 October 1988: 42 USC §300aa-15(i) (2006). This fund is supported by an excise tax incorporated into the cost to the consumer of each dose of a covered vaccine: Health Resources & Services Administration, *About the National Vaccine Injury Compensation Program* https://www.hrsa.gov/vaccine-compensation/about/index.html, accessed 1 July 2021.

While answering these questions is undoubtedly something that tort law does, it is by no means clear that tort produces wise solutions, and it is hardly the only place a jurisdiction might locate the authority to make such socially relevant decisions. Legislative and administrative agencies are capable of deciding what outcomes are socially desirable and who should take responsibility for dangers that are not sensibly resolved by the market. These governmental bodies can have staff study an issue, take public comments, offer potential solutions for public evaluation, and ultimately settle on a path forward. And while they surely make mistakes, such bodies are probably considerably better informed about the matters within their purview than are trial courts or appeals courts.

To be sure, parties to litigation can and do bring in experts to testify and aid judges' and (in the US) juries' decision-making, but common law judges (unlike their civil law counterparts) rarely generate expert advice on their own and tend to be more isolated from public opinion than are the other law-making bodies. Besides, only a tiny share of tort claims raise novel issues about who should be taking what sort of due care. The vast majority of claims arise from well-understood legal settings. These disputes are generally about exactly what happened and how seriously the victim was hurt, and their resource-intensive processing does little or nothing to further the goal of setting new standards of care.

Tort law is sometimes defended on the related ground that it serves the whistle-blowing function of identifying corporate wrongdoing that might otherwise go unreported.[36] Again, while this may be true of a very small share of claims, most are not of this sort. The example of products that injure large numbers of people makes this clear. While the first successful tort claim against an injurious product may further the goal of pinpointing a product that should have carried a better warning or a better safety feature, most of the ensuing claims against the product are then follow-on litigation in which others seek compensation in a copycat way. The cost of dealing with these copycat claims is a high administrative price to pay for whistle-blowing, especially when appropriate administrative agencies themselves could offer rewards to those who come forward to identify unreasonably dangerous activities or products.

Meanwhile, although tort claims for battery might have dissuaded some barons in the Middle Ages from seeking vengeance against those who attacked them and their men, there is good reason to doubt that the opportunity to sue for money damages now works to keep victims and their family members from violently striking those who carelessly injure them. Today, criminal law sanctions go a long way to discourage private retaliation, and those who are not discouraged by the threat of criminal sanctions are unlikely to be persuaded by promises of money.

What all of this means is that, in theory, tort law is a charmed mechanism that simultaneously promotes an amazing array of different social objectives, while in practice, it falls far short of achieving these aspirations. Tort's defenders often seem to imagine that tort is the only way of realising the goals they value; they are generally oblivious to the reality that Western nations have turned to many other mechanisms for influencing behaviour and dealing with unreasonable conduct that continues to occur.

[36] AM Linden, 'Tort Law as Ombudsman' (1973) 51 *Canadian Bar Review* 155, 156 (arguing that tort law fills a 'watchdog role' in which 'every court and lawyer in the land may be called upon to participate').

VIII. The Trouble with Tort Law's Staying Power

Cane argues that at present, despite the strong case for doing away with personal injury law as New Zealand has, tort law seems here to stay.[37] One reason he points to for personal injury law's enduring popularity is that when a tort claim by a seriously injured victim is successful, the benefits are likely to be significantly larger than the benefits promised by basic social insurance schemes. While this may be so as an empirical matter, I point out several troubling realities with this state of affairs.

First, as discussed earlier, seriously injured tort victims tend to recover smaller shares of their losses than do those with minor injuries. While this alone does not make for an argument to go down the New Zealand route, it does suggest that tort law could be dramatically reformed to redistribute how its compensation benefits are handed out. For example, different thresholds (or 'deductibles') could be instated, with general damage awards for pain and suffering made available only to those suffering serious injury (which could be defined in a variety of ways).[38] Meanwhile, an income loss threshold could further shift the focus to victims in greatest need: For example, responsibility for a victim's first week of lost wages could remain with the victim (who would then often have to take 'sick leave' or 'vacation pay' to cover the loss). If these changes were combined with a rule that tort damages would not cover medical care already provided by the national health insurance plan, then a huge share of small tort claims would probably disappear from the system. The funds saved in this way (including the administrative cost savings) could be redirected to those tort victims with more serious injuries.

To promote better treatment of the more severely injured, defendants could also be encouraged to make generous early settlement offers. One way to do this would be to impose a multiplier penalty on defendants who do not make an early offer that is at least reasonably close to what is eventually paid out on a judgment or in a settlement.[39]

Second, one reason why some seriously injured tort victims do much better with litigation than with social insurance is that tort seeks fully to replace lost income, whereas social insurance plans typically provide either modest, flat-rate income replacement for all victims or wage-related benefits subject to a moderate ceiling. While injured high earners may thus find it personally advantageous to pursue their remedy within the tort system, it is not clear that this state of affairs is socially desirable. Tort law is regressive in its income-redistributing function: All of us pay in to the system in the same way, but higher-earning victims get more out of the system. Think of a train crash that injures low-earning, working-class passengers as well passengers who are high-earning

[37] Cane (n 1) 129.

[38] For example, the rule in New South Wales applicable to certain types of case is that a victim may not recover any damages for non-economic loss that is less than 15% as serious as a most extreme case: SD Sugarman, 'Tort Reform through Damages Law Reform: An American Perspective' (2005) 27 *Sydney Law Review* 507, 516.

[39] J O'Connell, 'Expanding No-Fault Beyond Auto Insurance: Some Proposals' (1973) 59 *Virginia Law Review* 749.

professionals. Assuming they all paid the same amounts for their tickets, and assuming they are injured in the same ways to the same degrees, the higher earners will nonetheless be able to obtain far more money in settlement of their claims.

In a few places, legislatures have begun to do something about this aspect of tort law by capping the income replacement award to, for example, three times the average wage in the jurisdiction, thereby blocking extremely high earners from drawing disproportionately large sums from the system.[40] While this leaves them less than fully compensated by the tort system for income loss incurred by serious injury, the highest earners are also those who are most likely to have private disability insurance (or life insurance, if they are killed) that well protects their income loss apart from whatever tort might provide. Indeed, those with generous first-party insurance protection might find themselves more than fully compensated when tort payouts are added on.

Third, most social insurance plans do not make awards for special damages to compensate for victims' pain and suffering (the Quebec auto no-fault plan is exceptional in this regard).[41] It is the seriously injured who obtain the largest of these damages, although as noted earlier, victims with minor injuries are often able to milk what many regard as windfall-level amounts of special damages from insurers who are eager to close out claims. This phenomenon starkly raises the question of what social purposes benefits should serve, whatever their source.

Social insurance plans, as Cane points out, address basic need. Tort law goes beyond basic need, compensating for losses that have no real monetary value but are undeniably real by putting arguably arbitrary prices on those losses. As noted earlier, nations vary enormously on how much they provide via tort to seriously injured victims those who, for example, were blinded, lost a leg, or became paraplegic in an accident that was someone else's fault.

Putting aside the super-generous US system (at least in most states), even within Europe, there is a wide variety.[42] Some of this variation perhaps has to do with national wealth, which may explain why nations like Greece and Portugal are much less generous than are Ireland and Germany. But countries like Denmark and Sweden also award low levels of pain and suffering damages to seriously injured tort victims as compared with England and Italy, which is not explained by national wealth. One reason may be that the Scandinavian countries invest in robust social provision for disabled residents in general and hence feel less of a need to give yet additional money for intangible loss. Indeed, in these countries, the net additional cash benefits individual victims can receive by pursuing tort claims are relatively quite low. Still, interestingly enough, Denmark and Sweden have not gone down the New Zealand route, choosing to maintain tort law recovery for personal injury and death.

[40] New South Wales is one jurisdiction that has limited recovery for income loss to three times the average yearly earnings of full-time adult workers: Civil Liability Act 2002 (NSW), s 12.

[41] But the US National Vaccine Injury Compensation Program does pay up to $250,000 for pain and suffering: 42 USC §§ 300aa-15(a)(2).

[42] Sugarman (n 17) 340.

IX. What Explains Tort Law's Continuing Dominant Role?

This brings me to Cane's conclusion, in which he asserts, 'Tort law is here to stay – live with it!'[43] Why is this true? Politics can shed some light on the answer to the question in the US context. Lawyers who represent tort victims sometimes see and present themselves as 'Davids' taking on 'Goliaths'. Particularly when corporate enterprises are the target of litigation, these 'good guys in the white hats' claim that they are the last line of protection for consumers, employees, and the like in what they view as a grand struggle for power in today's capitalist economies. For such zealots, the idea of relying on the administrative state to protect the public interest seems like a foolish fantasy. And even if they cede that government agencies are doing their jobs properly in some settings, exposing and condemning corporate misconduct and rendering tort largely duplicative on these fronts, they may still insist that tort law should remain undisturbed so that victims can harness the legal system if other branches of government fail.

This outlook epitomises the position taken for years by Ralph Nader, the most prominent crusader in the US consumer movement of the second half of the twentieth century. Given Nader's political visibility and the strength of a range of consumer safety non-profits he helped create, it is perhaps not surprising that in the US, it has largely been a political non-starter to talk of introducing a social insurance plan to replace tort law as the primary response to injuries caused by corporate behaviour.

Moreover, even those on the political right tend to side with Nader to some degree. They generally favour the continued punishment of wrongdoers (even if tort law, as already noted, does a poor job of that in practice). Many conservative leaders also strongly oppose the expansion in government that a deeper social security safety net would require (even if their own voters passionately support government payment of health care costs). Furthermore, tort law in the US is a state-by-state matter, not a nationally uniform set of common law rules as it generally is in the UK and Commonwealth nations. This makes a single national approach to reform politically infeasible.

These points may help explain why visions from years past that the US would adopt something like the New Zealand scheme have gone nowhere. But what about the failure of any of the US states to adopt the Quebec auto no-fault solution? Auto accident claims are not about holding big business responsible; they are mostly about one local resident seeking to hold another responsible. Why stick with such an administratively expensive and cumbersome system? A partial explanation might be, as I have explained in the past,[44] that in the US, embracing the Quebec solution would mean asking tort victims to give up more benefits than Canadian tort victims gave up when Quebec adopted its auto no-fault scheme. Plus, the US has a not insubstantial share of uninsured drivers, who are often poor people with no good access to public transportation. Some on the left fear that a no-fault plan requiring payment from these low-income drivers would mean a tradeoff of more auto insurance for less food on poor families' tables. Furthermore,

[43] Cane (n 1) 129.

[44] SD Sugarman, 'Quebec's Comprehensive Auto No-Fault Scheme and the Failure of Any of the United States to Follow' (1998) 39 *Les Cahiers de Droit* 303.

many US residents actually like the lottery aspect of tort law – the remote possibility that were they badly injured in an auto accident by a very deep pocket defendant (or the defendant's employee), they could recover a fortune from the system. And then there are the professional parties who lose out in the Quebec scheme: lawyers representing tort victims (a very politically powerful group in the US) and private insurers (assuming that a single public administrator were to take over the compensation payout job, as in the Quebec model).

Finally, while the lesson from Quebec is that motorists pay less for what is realistically better coverage than that provided by tort law, it is hard to convince people in the US that this same pattern would carry over across the border. While it does seem to be the case that the US social security system very efficiently delivers retirement and survivor benefits, its delivery of disability benefits is fraught with problems, delays, and perceived injustice.[45] Moreover, its delivery of health insurance via Medicare and Medicaid is rife with fraud and excessive costs.[46] To be sure, a specialised public agency like the one operating the Quebec system could be prompt and effective, but experience with disorganised state-run workers' compensation plans in some places in the US leave many doubtful that auto accident compensation could be carried out more efficiently.

But these are perhaps special US barriers. Why has the UK not followed the Quebec solution? The simple answer seems to be that neither of the two leading parties that have governed over the past many decades has seen auto accident compensation as a problem that deserves their attention. And since legal professionals and insurance companies benefit considerably from the tort system in the UK, as in the US, the inertia of the status quo is very powerful.

Moreover, as far as society prioritises directing additional funds toward those in greatest need, auto accident victims may not be seen as uniquely deserving these days – or at least not viewed as having more urgent claims than those with the bad luck of suffering a disabling illness or a degenerative condition and who also require medical care and income replacement. And with ongoing anguish in the UK about the National Health Service being desperately underfunded, it might be impossible to make the case that saving money on auto insurance premiums and better compensating victims of motoring accidents are timely political priorities.

Furthermore, the global auto industry is moving in the direction of self-driving vehicles. This will take some time fully to implement, of course. But on the horizon is a time when auto accident injury and fatality rates should be dramatically reduced by this technology, and responsibility for harms that still occur on the road will mostly lie with the motor industry rather than with individual at-fault motorists.[47] Even Quebec may have to rethink its approach to deal with that sort of future.

[45] MT Alred, 'Judicial Relief for Delay in the Social Security Administration's Disability Determination Process' (1983) 15 *Loyola University Chicago Law Journal* 61, 61–62.

[46] WJ Rudman et al, 'Healthcare Fraud and Abuse' (2009) 6 *Perspectives in Health Information Management* 1, 1–2.

[47] KS Abraham and RL Rabin, 'Automated Vehicles and Manufacturer Responsibility for Accidents: A New Legal Regime for a New Era' (2019) 105 *Virginia Law Review* 127, 147; KD Logue, 'Should Automakers Be Responsible for Accidents?' (2019) *Regulation* 20, 21.

In Germany today, most accident victims are well protected by first-party insurance arrangements that pay for their medical care and generously replace lost income. Still, German tort law works hard to shift these costs to tortfeasors in pursuit of efficient social cost accounting. This same attitude is likely to accompany the implementation of self-driving vehicles, with vehicle makers held responsible for internalising the cost of accidents in the price of their vehicles; from their perspective, safer vehicles will mean lower costs and hence higher profits.

There is a certain irony here in that today, a substantial share of auto accident costs is not captured in the cost of driving but rather is borne by victims through whatever broad-based first-party insurance protection they have, if any. In this respect, Quebec's plan does a better job of cost-internalising, because it includes among its beneficiaries all those who are unable to win compensation via tort law. While this is yet another argument that could support the enactment of a Quebec-style no-fault plan, the time for implementing such a plan in both the UK and US may have passed.

In the meantime, Cane's realistic perspective is one students of tort law should keep in mind. While tort law on the ground is fascinating to observe, it is very different from tort law on the books. This does not mean that grappling with the logical underpinnings of complex tort doctrines is not worthwhile, but rather that it is equally important to understand how the law is actually operationalised.[48] *Key Ideas in Tort Law* neatly demonstrates the relevance of this dichotomy to the study of tort.

[48] SD Sugarman, 'A Century of Change in Personal Injury Law' (2000) 88 *California Law Review* 2403.

PART II

Public Law

5

Constitutional Rights, Moral Judgement, and the Rule of Law

TRS ALLAN

I. Introduction

The relationship between law and morality, or between legal and moral reasoning, is the focus of Peter Cane's absorbing essay, 'Morality, Law and Conflicting Reasons for Action', based on his Maccabaean Lecture in Jurisprudence at the British Academy.[1] Befitting its author's remarkable range of expertise in private law, public law, and jurisprudence, the essay raises an important challenge to some standard scholarly assumptions. It makes uncomfortable reading for those – whether lawyers or moralists – who suppose that they can work contentedly in one of these spheres while largely ignoring the other. These domains of normative reasoning are, as Professor Cane contends, intertwined and interdependent. In pursuit of this theme, I shall argue that legal reasoning is essentially moral reasoning, adapted or attuned to the social and political context in point.

In questioning the various distinctions between law and morality suggested by HLA Hart, Cane draws attention to the interwoven nature of the legal and moral contributions to practical reasoning. The focus on practical reasoning serves to highlight a characteristic of morality mentioned by Hart but distinct from the formal or structural features on which he mainly concentrated. What is distinctive about morality is 'the part played by morality in the lives of individuals', being conceived as 'the ultimate standard by which human actions … are evaluated'.[2] Insofar as we can distinguish between law and morality in particular circumstances, the role of morality as a source of ultimate standards would explain why it trumps merely legal reasons in the event of conflict. It would also explain our belief that the law is always subject to moral evaluation.[3]

Cane emphasises, nevertheless, that law is an essential supplement to morality and hence ignored by moral philosophers at their peril. The law can provide a degree of determinacy that morality would otherwise lack: it can establish and enforce

[1] P Cane, 'Morality, Law and Conflicting Reasons for Action' (2012) 71 *CLJ* 59.
[2] HLA Hart, *The Concept of Law*, 2nd edn (Oxford, Clarendon Press, 1994) 176, 230.
[3] Cane (n 1) 80–81.

the rules on which morality depends for its practical implementation. The law can also provide reasons to act or to refrain from acting in particular ways in the face of moral disagreement: 'law can promote social good by enabling people to live together successfully and well despite significant and serious differences of moral opinion and outlook'.[4] In conjunction, the indeterminacy of morality, the fact of moral disagreement, and the institutional resources that law can contribute to practical reasoning may result in legal reasons amounting to all-things-considered reasons for action.[5]

From that perspective, however, we may wonder whether any supposed conflict between legal and moral reasons, permitting the latter to trump the former, is finally spurious – the product of a questionable and unhelpful dualism. If law serves to give morality a concrete practical expression in circumstances of uncertainty and disagreement, marking out an appropriate framework for the conduct of social and political life, it cannot surrender to any contrary moral vision without unfairness or injustice. There may, admittedly, be a certain disparity between anyone's private vision of the ideal society and her legal obligations, which depend on the conception of justice embodied in legal practice and tradition. But what warrant could she have for insisting on universal compliance with her own private vision if it has no firm anchorage in the practice of her community? Unless, of course, she repudiates that practice as morally repugnant – an illegitimate system of organised violence – she acquits her responsibility as a citizen, faithful to her community, only by adherence to the law. Or, at least, so I shall argue.

The law is subject to moral appraisal in the sense that official claims about legitimacy or legality are always subject to sceptical scrutiny. It is only when a de facto government is duly respectful of human dignity, honouring the fundamental rights of persons, that it can claim the mantle of legality. Legality depends on legitimacy: it invokes the powers and privileges that only a legitimate government, morally entitled to obedience, can exercise. When 'legal reasons' are only the product of appeal to the bare facts of political power, conceived independently of any plausible appeal to justice or the public good, they are plainly trumped by moral reasons. A wicked regime, serving only private or sectarian interests, must be condemned and opposed: its 'laws' are only a parody of their proper namesake, in which law is the closest approximation to justice that we can attain in respectful collaboration with our fellow citizens.

From an internal, interpretative viewpoint – the perspective appropriate to the loyal adherent of a legitimate legal regime – the law encapsulates the chief demands of political morality. It identifies the rights and duties of the citizen, whose civic virtue is displayed in compliance with the law on which all must rely for the successful pursuit of their various interdependent and interconnecting aims and interests. While the law may fall short of justice in its practical administration, the relevant standards of appraisal are supplied by the legal and constitutional principles that structure the legal

[4] ibid 82.

[5] ibid 82–84. See also P Cane, 'Theory and Values in Public Law' in P Craig and R Rawlings (eds), *Law and Administration in Europe: Essays in Honour of Carol Harlow* (Oxford, Oxford University Press, 2003) 3–21. For critique and analysis, see P Craig, 'Theory and Values in Public Law: A Response', ibid 23–46; TRS Allan, *The Sovereignty of Law: Freedom, Constitution, and Common Law* (Oxford, Oxford University Press, 2013) 333–37.

order and render it a unified governmental scheme. Conceived as a coherent body of legal principle, treating everyone equally according to the criteria that these principles identify, the law displaces conceptions of justice that belong largely to the realm of the private imagination, owing little or nothing to the practice and traditions of the political community.[6]

Roughly corresponding to the relationship between political morality and national law is that between international human rights, on the one hand, and domestic constitutional rights, on the other. Universal rights, articulated or enforced by international courts, express widely accepted dimensions of human dignity that all states should honour. Constitutional rights in national law can be regarded as lending greater determinacy to these abstract standards of justice, adapting the various guarantees to local conditions. If morality is the ultimate standard for evaluation of human actions, we may consider the basic rights enshrined in the Universal Declaration of Human Rights to be ultimate standards for judging the actions of states. If so, however, problems of indeterminacy and disagreement inevitably arise, permitting a range of interpretations responsive, in each domestic jurisdiction, to local experience and legal tradition.[7]

Constitutional rights translate the abstract demands of political morality into legal limits on the state's coercive authority. In securing those limits they ensure the legitimacy of official rules and rulings, preserving the unity of law and morality. Constitutional rights express a vision of the proper relationship between citizen and state: government exists to promote the public good within the constraints of justice, which affirm the equal dignity of all members of the political community. While many constitutional rights concern the law's proper administration, ensuring that the law's requirements can be readily ascertained and fairly applied to particular cases, other rights are more substantive, circumscribing the powers available to further the public interest. Rights to due process are supplemented by rights that give specific content to the abstract ideals of equality and human dignity – especially rights to freedom of thought, speech, conscience and association, which underpin our conception of the independent moral agent whose allegiance to law is finally a matter of interpretative judgement and responsibility.[8]

While securing the boundaries of legitimate government, constitutional rights leave appropriate space for the exercise of political freedom – the freedom to fashion a public good that embraces all aspects of human well-being, as judged by citizens acting together as authors as well as beneficiaries of state law. Law and political

[6] Compare R Dworkin, *Law's Empire* (London, Fontana, 1986). Dworkin's theory of law as 'integrity' requires legal practice to be interpreted, as far as possible, as a coherent body of principles

[7] Dworkin distinguishes helpfully between the right to equal concern and respect, correctly understood, and the more fundamental and abstract right to be treated by government with the appropriate attitude – a 'right to be treated *as* a human being whose dignity fundamentally matters': R Dworkin, *Justice for Hedgehogs* (Cambridge, Mass, Belknap Press, 2011) 335. A government may respect that more fundamental right even when it fails (we may think) to achieve a correct understanding of more concrete political rights.

[8] Dworkin associates these rights with his second principle of dignity. While the first principle requires government to treat all its subjects as equally worthy of concern and respect, the second principle protects each person's ethical independence – the freedom to live her life in accordance with her own ethical convictions, reflecting her responsibility for the shape of her own life. See ibid 336.

morality are appropriately aligned only insofar as a proper balance is maintained between judicially enforceable rights, on the one hand, and the effective pursuit of public policy on the other. Although certain measures are precluded as inherently immoral – flagrant denials of human dignity – basic rights for the most part operate to qualify the pursuit of legitimate public ends, seeking to ensure that people are fairly treated as persons of equal worth. There must be a defensible relationship between burdens imposed and benefits obtained, consistent with equal respect for all.[9]

An insistence on the identification of law with political morality, albeit a morality attuned to political context, will inflame the opponents of liberal constitutionalism who associate judicial review with the suppression of democracy. They prefer a robust republicanism that leaves even questions of rights to majority vote, removing controversial moral issues as far as possible from courts.[10] But that view is associated with a doubtful theory of law. It treats enacted legislation as a largely freestanding source of law, supposing that statutes can normally be applied to particular cases without much reflection on general principles of justice, implicit in legal and constitutional practice. When, however, statutes confer broad discretionary powers on government ministers and officials, they present a clear danger of arbitrary coercion: powers may be exercised with little or no regard for those whose interests must suffer in the single-minded pursuit of public policy. The equal protection of the law can be guaranteed only if statute law is interpreted and applied in the light of the law as a whole – the law as a coherent body of general principles, preserving a balance of fairness between public and private interests.[11]

Even those more sympathetic to liberal constitutionalism, acknowledging the value of judicially enforced rights as shields against the abuse of political power, may fear the danger of an overbearing judiciary, threatening the proper separation of governmental powers. The model of rights adopted by many jurisdictions, exemplified by the content and structure of the Universal Declaration and the European Convention on Human Rights (ECHR), may be thought to undermine democratic decision-making by unduly enlarging judicial discretion. Broadly defined rights, subject in practice to limitation for a wide range of permissible state objectives, appear to engulf questions of public policy better left to ordinary political debate and decision. Adoption of the proportionality test by constitutional and international courts, moreover, invites the weighing and balancing of conflicting interests, more appropriate to securing a desirable state of affairs than protecting specific individual entitlements.

[9] See also TRS Allan, 'Democracy, Legality, and Proportionality' in G Huscroft et al (eds), *Proportionality and the Rule of Law: Rights, Justification, Reasoning* (Cambridge, Cambridge University Press, 2014) 205.

[10] See for example R Bellamy, *Political Constitutionalism: A Republican Defence of the Constitutionality of Democracy* (Cambridge, Cambridge University Press, 2007).

[11] For a telling critique of Bellamy's 'political constitutionalism', see D Dyzenhaus, 'How Hobbes Met the "Hobbes Challenge"' (2009) 72 *MLR* 488. Dyzenhaus observes that Bellamy 'suppresses sovereignty by implausibly supposing that questions about arbitrary power will be settled by making the only checks on power the kinds of checks that can be exercised prior to the enactment of law', leaving legal subjects at the mercy of whatever content 'subordinate public officials or judges choose to give to the law' (506).

As NE Simmonds argues, rights are best understood, not as entitlements to a state of affairs, but rather to the performance of actions (whether the action of the right-holder or the action of another) subject to a corresponding duty.[12] It is in the nature of rights to have peremptory force, reflecting our judgment of their overriding importance; being resistant to balancing, they depend on respect for the rules that define their scope. Simmonds laments the tendency of broadly framed rights, such as those of the Universal Declaration or the ECHR, to absorb large areas of law, thereby reducing all legal rights (even in private law) to a balancing test, defeating the distinctive logic of rights.[13] We may even have serious doubts about the commensurability of the various interests in play, leaving judicial discretion largely unchecked.[14]

We should not, however, treat these legitimate concerns as reasons to countenance a severance of law from morality. Respect for the rules that specify the scope and content of fundamental rights is a requirement of political morality itself, which must negotiate the distinction between rights and goods. The development of legal doctrine is necessary for the law to perform its role as mediator between justice, or political morality at large, and its local or domestic application, sensitive to the needs and traditions of the political community. In the absence of doctrinal guidance, the judicial defence of rights would become inconsistent and unpredictable, undermining the rule of law. As Simmonds observes, even if legal reasoning is always structured and informed by considerations of justice and the common good, proficient lawyers strive to make legal doctrine rule-like, as far as possible, so as to preserve the peremptory force of rights.[15]

The connection between law and morality is secure as long as there is an appropriate interplay between specific rules and more general principles. If legal rules are intended to protect constitutional rights, they must be subject to appraisal and amendment when, in the light of experience, they prove too blunt, failing to distinguish appropriately between different cases. Common law rules provide a fine illustration, promoting an equilibrium between continuity and change. While dependent on the force of its underlying rationale, a rule of common law nonetheless enjoys a provisional independence. The rule stands until its foundations are undermined by subsequent judicial decisions in related areas, implicitly challenging its claim to represent the requirements of justice. That fine balance between settled rule and underlying principle, exhibited in the varying degrees to which courts of different levels of seniority are free to depart from precedent, is critical to the rule of law as a scheme of just governance.[16]

[12] NE Simmonds, 'Constitutional Rights, Civility and Artifice' (2019) 78 *CLJ* 175, 183.
[13] ibid 192–93.
[14] Simmonds observes that the problem is exacerbated if rights are treated as 'optimisation requirements' in line with the view defended in R Alexy, *A Theory of Constitutional Rights*, translated by J Rivers (Oxford, Oxford University Press, 2002). Simmonds is doubtful about the practicality of Alexy's 'Law of Competing Principles', whereby a body of rules should gradually emerge to state the circumstances under which one principle must take precedence over another (Simmonds (n 12) 190).
[15] Simmonds (n 12) 184.
[16] Compare SR Perry, 'Judicial Obligation, Precedent and the Common Law' (1987) 7 *OJLS* 215, especially 234–57.

Even if international human rights law can be seen as a pure expression of justice, encapsulating essential elements of respect for human dignity, it cannot legitimately displace large areas of domestic law. As Simmonds contends, we endanger mutual civility if we make no allowance for reasonable disagreement over justice; and we cannot simply delegate every judgement about the common good to an international or constitutional court. Compliance with basic human rights can certainly be treated as a necessary feature of justice; these rights define the limits of legitimate government and in that sense underpin the rule of law. The general values that these rights embody, however, must obtain their determinate shape and practical implementation largely within the national legal order. Constitutional adjudication must honour the practical experience of grappling with issues of justice in a local context, where choices can properly be made between different ways of furthering the common good.

Insofar as the proportionality test poses a threat to the rule of law, converting law into judicial discretion, it must be reinterpreted as the more modest requirement of reasonableness or rationality. In place of the balancing of interests, sometimes envisaged, there is a reconciliation of the right and the good, attentive to the specific context in point. Properly understood, as a dimension of due process, proportionality requires governmental action to be guided by appropriate reasons. Those reasons must appeal to an account of the public good consistent with the basic ideal of equal respect or dignity, fundamental to the rule of law. The judicial enforcement of constitutional rights is not inimical to democratic government, which requires an appropriate division of authority between legislature, executive and judiciary. That division acknowledges the difference between rights and goods, promoting the development of public policy within the boundaries of equal respect for persons. Law and political morality are thereby conjoined: legality and legitimacy are united by an interpretation of legal practice grounded on the ideal of mutual civility.[17]

II. Law, Morality, and Interpretation

Hart defended the separation thesis, emblematic of legal positivism, insisting that what is lawful may nevertheless be immoral. When law is identified by reference to a 'rule of recognition', consisting of the characteristic conduct of officials, there is plainly no guarantee of justice. Wickedly motivated officials may enforce an evil system of law. From a wholly external perspective, detached from allegiance to a legitimate legal order that commands our respect, the familiar interdependence of law and morality may slip from view.

Hart's 'soft positivism' acknowledged that the rule of recognition may in practice allow for the incorporation of moral principles as criteria of legal validity. The courts may be empowered to strike down legislation for breach of constitutional rights. As Cane explains, Hart's view that morality is a matter of personal conviction plays an

[17] As an ideal of civic friendship, the common good entails respect for rights: it is, at its core, 'an orderly structure of rights and practices grounded in the virtue of citizens': Simmonds (n 12) 187.

important role here. Judges are, in effect, authorised to use their 'best moral judgement' in interpreting such constitutional limitations: 'such provisions do not make the existence and validity of law depend on what moral principles prohibit, require or permit but on what particular legal officials in particular cases believe particular moral principles prohibit, require or permit'.[18] Because we can criticise the beliefs of officials, when we think them mistaken, the distinction between what the law is and what it ought to be is preserved.[19]

The distinction is preserved, however, only from the perspective of the descriptive social theorist. From an internal point of view, characteristic of the legal interpreter, whether citizen or official, the law requires conformity to moral principles. In our legal reasoning and our appraisal of the actions and decisions of others, we invoke the pertinent moral standards. The law is not to be equated with the moral opinions or attitudes of certain officials – even the views of Supreme Court judges, whom we may consider confused or mistaken about what fundamental rights or freedoms entail or demand. In practice, the judges themselves are likely to disagree. If we give weight to the opinions of senior judges or officials about what constitutional rights or principles require, we do so appropriately only when their reasons are found persuasive on careful examination. Our allegiance must be to the law itself, correctly interpreted in accordance with moral principle. It is our responsibility as good citizens to distinguish between rival interpretations, defending the vision of justice or good governance that we believe best illuminates our legal traditions.

In the context of a legitimate regime, political morality dictates adherence to law, correctly interpreted in accordance with principle. Individual rights, rooted in basic ideas about human dignity or equal citizenship, acquire a greater specificity, unique to the jurisdiction concerned. Legal interpretation, involving argument over the implications of general principles for particular cases or contexts, will be disciplined by respect for familiar paradigms.[20] If there were not paradigmatic examples of such rights as freedom of thought, speech or association, legal reasoning would be unable to remedy the deficiencies of abstract moral argument. People would in effect be calling in aid different principles, which merely shared a similar nomenclature.

It does not follow, however, that legal judgement ceases to be moral judgement, or that legal interpreters must set aside their moral convictions. Confronted by the problems of indeterminacy and disagreement, we should honour legitimate legal and constitutional practice as a proper substitute for the alternative arrangements we would have chosen in an ideal world, as we might each privately imagine it. We embrace representative democracy as a reasonable way of settling our differences over large areas of public policy, subject to certain conditions. The principle of equality, or equal dignity, that mandates a truly representative democracy has implications for the limits of majoritarian governance. We must look to our legal and constitutional practice as a guide to such limits, identifying the fundamental rights that guarantee equality. When these

[18] Cane (n 1) 70 (see Hart (n 2) 254).

[19] As Cane observes, this view also enables Hart to remain neutral as between realist and constructivist views about the status of moral judgment (see Hart (n 2) 253–54).

[20] For the role of paradigms in legal argument, see Dworkin (n 6) 72–73, 88–92, 138–39.

basic rights are reliably enforced, preserving the structure of broadly (if imperfectly) just arrangements, we can obey the law in good conscience. Within certain boundaries, over which the individual conscience is finally sovereign, personal morality is satisfied, in the domain of politics, by adherence to the public law.

Interpretation bridges fact and value, connecting social practice with the moral ideals that provide its inspiration and contribute to its justification. As Ronald Dworkin argues, a theory of law, applicable to the jurisdiction currently in view, must be addressed to local practice, building on paradigms that give that practice a determinate shape. But it must also justify that practice in the sense of giving its adherents good reason to pursue and develop it, extending its principles to all areas of social or political life, as the context requires. While Dworkin rightly emphasises the moral responsibility of the 'protestant' interpreter, whose best judgement must discriminate between competing interpretations of legal practice, it is also true that the practice itself is ultimately a collaboration between people who acknowledge the limits of their own experience and understanding.[21] An interpreter's conclusions are addressed to other members of the community, appropriately sensitive to their understanding of a common, collaborative endeavour.[22]

The law mediates between private moral judgement, which embraces the legal order as a reasonable basis for cooperation with others, and public solutions to questions of justice that must be sought in collaboration. But because only those solutions that satisfy the basic conditions of legitimacy are acceptable, in the judgement of any conscientious interpreter, legal reasoning must keep faith with its moral foundations. Fundamental rights, implicit in a view of law as a guide to justice, will exert their influence throughout the legal system. Parliamentary statutes must be interpreted on the assumption that these rights are inviolable, even if their application to varying contexts may be complex and contested. Legal doctrine must be developed in a way that seeks broad moral coherence, its rules being shaped and refined by recourse to principles that safeguard the basic rights and freedoms.

Moral criticism of legal rules and requirements is intrinsic to democracy and the rule of law alike. Coercive state action stands always in need of justification; we must be alert to identify and condemn abuses of power. It is important to emphasise, however, that such moral criticism has itself a necessary legal dimension. It appraises specific rules or rulings in the light of moral standards internal to the legal order – the standing requirements of legitimacy, underpinning the moral obligation of obedience to law. Insofar as the law departs from justice, in the relevant respects, it falls short of the moral standards to which it aspires. Infringements of due process or fundamental equality are departures from legality, rupturing the proper relations between citizen and state. While the detailed implications of these basic principles may depend on local tradition,

[21] Dworkin defends a protestant account of political obligation: 'fidelity to a scheme of principle each citizen has a responsibility to identify, ultimately for himself, as his community's scheme' (*Law's Empire* (n 6) 190).

[22] Compare GJ Postema, '"Protestant" Interpretation and Social Practices' (1987) 6 *Law and Philosophy* 283.

legal practice is steered, nonetheless, by what are conceived to be universally valid conditions of governmental propriety.[23]

While legal positivists, keen to emphasise the separability of law and morality, usually treat legislation as the primary source of law, their natural law opponents can point to the common law tradition by way of counterexample. In common law adjudication judicial precedent is treated as a guide to the demands of justice. There is usually scope for reappraisal, at least in the higher courts, in circumstances where strict adherence to previous rules would do evident injustice, contrary to more fundamental principles of law. As a by-product of the resolution of particular disputes, the law reflects the considerations of justice that have persuaded courts in previous cases. It is inherently provisional and tentative, sensitive to a better appreciation of the moral demands at stake. As Cane observes, judicial efforts to bring precedent and principle into harmony are similar in structure to Rawlsian reflective equilibrium, applicable to moral reasoning.[24] The common law, accordingly, offers a challenge to Hart's suggestion that morality, unlike law, is impervious to deliberate change: 'The common law treats every principle as revisable at the point of application and provides a working model of how change can occur in a normative regime, like morality, that puts high value on stability and in which change is typically gradual and incremental.'[25]

In the common law tradition, each judge (even in a multi-member court) must take responsibility for her own interpretation of the applicable law, giving appropriate reasons. She can, if necessary, give a dissenting judgment, criticising her colleagues' arguments and rejecting their conclusions. The judge's personal integrity is thereby preserved: she offers an account of the law that she believes to be morally correct, upholding the rights and duties that the law, on its true construction, secures. It is ultimately her freedom to insist on her own understanding that enables her to square her judicial duties with her moral and intellectual integrity. She need never bow to an interpretation of law that would threaten its legitimacy in her own eyes. Violations of fundamental rights should therefore be condemned, even if a Supreme Court majority, for its own part, denies such violations on the facts in view. To accede to such infringements, as the judge conceives them, would be to render the law a mere instrument of official power, cancelling any moral obligation of obedience.[26]

It follows, on this view, that there no intelligible gap between personal moral conviction, as regards the requirements of justice in the particular case, and the true content of the law. For all practical purposes, justice means justice according to law, where the law is viewed as a coherent scheme of principle that honours the equal dignity of all. If, as Cane observes, judges doubt whether they can properly give effect to their own moral

[23] A similar view is arguably implicit in Lon Fuller's distinction between the 'internal' and 'external' moralities of law: see LL Fuller, *The Morality of Law*, revised edn (New Haven, Yale University Press, 1969). While the internal morality of law concerns mainly matters of due process, conceived as universally valid moral requirements, external morality encompasses broader, more substantive and contentious matters. But Fuller emphasises the connections between the two moralities as they apply in practice: the former conditions and qualifies the proper regulation of the latter.

[24] See J Rawls, 'Outline of a Decision Procedure for Ethics' (1951) 60 *Phil Rev* 177; see also TRS Allan, 'Principle, Practice, and Precedent: Vindicating Justice, According to Law' (2018) 77 *CLJ* 269, 275–78.

[25] Cane (n 1) 75.

[26] See further Allan (n 5) 154–67.

convictions in determining the law, they adopt too narrow a conception of law. Legal interpretation involves moral judgement, discriminating between different accounts of legal principle. Judges should not worry about the legitimacy of their role when 'the extant legal materials provide no determinate answer to the issue they have to decide.'[27] Even the most clearly drafted statutory provision, taken alone, will prove indeterminate in the face of unforeseen and unusual cases. Determinacy is finally a function of legal and moral principle, connecting specific legal rules or rulings with the broader notions of justice on which their justification depends. There is a seamless continuity between the 'extant legal materials' and the principles of justice or good governance on which they draw. We seek a reflective equilibrium in which legal rules and moral principles form at least a tentative and provisional unity, each set of norms informing or clarifying the other.[28]

Cane gives the wise advice that, in the face of reasonable and intractable disagreement, a judge should follow his or her own best moral judgement.[29] But there is here no departure from the law. Anyone's best judgement of the rights and wrongs in any legal controversy is his best interpretation of the applicable law, informed as necessary by the principles that lend it moral coherence. If adoption of the internal, interpretative posture, characteristic of adjudication, involves moral commitment – the legal order is embraced as a legitimate basis on which to proceed – every determination of the law's content is equally a moral judgement. The law's requirements are those that follow from the most persuasive interpretation of legal practice, understood as a collaborative quest for justice.[30]

A judge who is fearful of resorting to moral judgement, when no determinate answer can apparently be found in positive law, assumes that the law expires in the manner that legal positivism supposes. In the absence of a legal answer, provided by the authoritative sources of law, he must turn instead to morality. It is implicit in this view that morality offers determinate guidance quite independently of law, even if that guidance is often opaque and fiercely contested. Utilitarianism is a prime example of this mode of thought. Utilitarian thinkers such as Austin and Bentham treated law instrumentally, as a means of advancing utility – an ideal independent of positive law and often in conflict with it.[31]

If, by contrast, the law is understood to extend or develop morality, by giving concrete specification to abstract moral principle, the positivist's beloved dichotomy dissolves.

[27] Cane (n 1) 70–71.

[28] See also TRS Allan, 'The Moral Unity of Public Law' (2017) 67 *UTLJ* 1, especially 5–7, 20–22.

[29] Cane (n 1) 71.

[30] Compare Dworkin's initial response to the objection that his ideal judge, Hercules, relies on his own moral convictions. See R Dworkin, *Taking Rights Seriously* (London, Duckworth, 1977) 125: 'Hercules does not find the limits of law and then deploy his own political convictions to supplement what the law requires. He uses his own judgment to determine what legal rights the parties before him have, and when that judgment is made nothing remains to submit to either his own or the public's convictions.' Insofar as Dworkin's later work apparently adopts a different view (see eg *Law's Empire* (n 6) 245–50), the former understanding is much to be preferred.

[31] Compare M Stone, 'Legal Positivism as an Idea about Morality' (2011) 61 *UTLJ* 313, arguing (at 328) that 'what drives Austin and his successors is the thought that, as one pursues the chain of reason-seeking interrogatives that are put to the law, a sharp break must occur: one will have to leave the province of jurisprudence (with its human commands) and enter the domain of critical morality (with its standards of reason, binding on conduct in virtue of their merits)'.

In exercising judgement in a contested legal dispute, the court is engaged in determining, for the facts in view, what morality itself requires – bringing principle and precept to fruition by application to the relevant circumstances. If the law is in this sense a branch of morality, legal interpretation must always be a moral endeavour. Dworkin's interpretative legal theory is best understood in this way, resisting the standard view that the law and political morality are wholly separate sets of norms.[32]

In his account of the 'minimum content of natural law', Hart examines the overlap between law and morality that results from various contingent facts about human beings, set in the context of their shared aim of survival.[33] A system of mutual forbearances is a practical necessity, whether in law or morality. Beyond the minimum content of natural law, Hart observes, there may be a wide disparity between the demands of law and those of morality. As Martin Stone suggests, however, what chiefly separates Hart's legal positivism from the classic natural law view is his instrumentalism: 'morality's dependence on law is merely a matter of various empirical defects or inconveniences of the pre-legal state'.[34]

In his critique of legal positivism, Lon Fuller complained that there was insufficient recognition of the role of legal rules in making possible 'an effective realisation of morality in the actual behaviour of human beings'.[35] Without the assistance of legal standards such moral precepts as that against taking another's property 'could not achieve reality in the conduct of human affairs'.[36] Fuller is best interpreted, as Stone suggests, as connecting positive law to critical morality, not as an instrument for attaining an independent blueprint, but as giving determinate content to morality's more abstract form: 'This goes beyond saying that ownership is made effective through positive law; it says, also, that there is no such thing as rightful possession apart from the judgments of civil authority.'[37] No account of what we owe one another – no determinate distinction between 'mine' and 'thine' – can be given 'except way of judgments in particular types of cases'.[38]

Fuller's response to Hart's jurisprudence can now be better appreciated as a rejection of Hart's instrumentalist outlook. Fuller can be understood as postulating a union of law and morality in the sense that law is itself a segment of morality, where public authority is needed to play a constitutive role. Positive law has, accordingly, a constitutive moral realm, necessary to realise the conditions of rightful possession and reciprocal forbearance. The law's merits are internal to its nature as a segment of morality: the law is in this sense 'its own court of appeal'.[39]

[32] See Dworkin (n 7) ch 19. Legal rights, accordingly, are 'those that people are entitled to enforce on demand, without further legislative intervention, in adjudicative institutions that direct the executive power of sheriff or police' (ibid 406).

[33] Hart (n 2) 191–200.

[34] Stone (n 31) 339.

[35] Fuller (n 23) 205.

[36] ibid.

[37] Stone, (n 31) 337 (citing Kant's observation, 'only in a civil condition can something external be mine or yours': *Metaphysics of Morals* in MJ Gregor (ed), *Practical Philosophy* (Cambridge, Cambridge University Press, 1996) at 6:256).

[38] Stone (n 31) 340.

[39] ibid 337.

III. The Rule of Law and Equality

When we perceive the role of law within morality itself, we can better understand the intimate connection between legality and legitimacy. Fuller sought to articulate the connection in terms of the reciprocity between governors and governed, a reciprocity that underpinned the various requirements of due process that amounted to an 'inner morality' of law.[40] No one could fairly be held responsible for breach of a secret, obscure, contradictory or retrospective law. Not only must legal requirements be made accessible in advance of people's actions, enabling them to act with knowledge of the legal consequences, but the rules must be fairly applied by officials to the relevant facts: there must be congruity between the law as announced and the law as applied.[41]

The underlying idea is that the law cannot be merely a useful instrument in the hands of the ruler for any and every purpose. It is an inherently moral mode of governance, respectful of the humanity and rationality of the law's subjects.[42] Fuller's precepts or desiderata are arguably constitutive of legality, which is itself a certain region of morality: they operate to fulfil the demands of morality in the legislative or administrative context. These principles of legality cannot, accordingly, be dismissed, in Hart's manner, as merely principles of efficacy, by analogy with principles about effectiveness in poisoning.[43]

The instrumentalist conception of law is most clearly displayed in Joseph Raz's account of the rule of law.[44] Raz identifies the rule of law with principles of formal and procedural legality that largely mirror the elements of Fuller's internal morality of law. But he denies that they establish any necessary connection between law and justice. In Raz's hands, Fuller's desiderata become a means for the efficient pursuit of whatever aims the lawgiver intends: the 'rule of law' is the 'specific excellence' of law only in the sense that it makes the law a more efficient tool for the attainment of ends in view. A ruler's compliance with procedural legality will ensure that his instructions are capable of being obeyed. No one can obey a secret, obscure or retrospective law; and a ruler's purposes are frustrated if the rule is misapplied in particular cases. Insofar as the 'rule of law' protects human dignity, limiting the evils of uncertainty and the frustration of expectations that would otherwise arise, it is only a 'negative' value, minimising the harm to freedom and dignity that the law may cause in its pursuit of governmental objectives.[45]

We should reject an account of the rule of law fashioned to fit an instrumentalist conception of law. The rule of law is instead the ideal of governance through law

[40] Fuller (n 23) 39–40, 61–62, 137–40.

[41] ibid 81–91.

[42] 'Every departure from the principles of the law's inner morality is an affront to man's dignity as a responsible agent' (ibid 162).

[43] See Hart's review of *The Morality of Law* (1965) 78 *Harvard Law Review* 1281, reprinted in HLA Hart, *Essays in Jurisprudence and Philosophy* (Oxford, Clarendon Press, 1983) 343–63.

[44] J Raz, 'The Rule of Law and its Virtue' in *The Authority of Law: Essays on Law and Morality* (Oxford, Clarendon Press, 1979) 210.

[45] ibid 224–25. In Raz's view, the law, being an instrument, has a specific virtue which is morally neutral because it can be applied for various ends: 'It is the virtue of efficiency; the virtue of the instrument as an instrument. For the law this virtue is the rule of law' (ibid 226).

by contrast with the subjection to an arbitrary power – power wielded for purposes that may diverge from the demands of justice or the public good, reflecting only the interests of a governing elite.[46] The constraints of formal and procedural legality make up only one part of the rule of law, which requires people to be treated, in all relevant respects, as equal members of the political community. The law reigns supreme only when human dignity is fully honoured in the formulation and application of legal rules. The rule of law is in place when the law provides a moral justification for the incidence of state coercion – in the sense that official action or decision is directed toward the creation or maintenance of a legitimate political order, respectful of fundamental equality.

The rule of law is first and foremost the rule of *private* law, specifying criteria for the just resolution of disputes arising between citizens.[47] The ordinary civil law, together with criminal law, define protected domains of liberty within which persons can pursue their own ends, where possible in cooperation with others. It must be a system of equal liberty, the individual domains structured in such a way as to allow each person the maximum freedom compatible with a similar freedom for others. The opposite of an instrumentalist conception of law is one that treats law as essential for the just and ordered conduct of social life, government being conceived as the guarantor of the scheme of equal freedom. Fuller's distinction between law and 'managerial direction' was critical to his repudiation of legal positivism. If the law were intended primarily to enable a person to conduct his own affairs, subject to reasonable restraints in the public interest, there must be general rules that preserve his basic freedom: 'law furnishes a baseline for self-directed action, not a detailed set of instructions for accomplishing specific objectives'.[48]

From a Kantian perspective, public law is subservient to the basic scheme of civil and criminal law. Constitutional law is intended to secure a rightful civil condition, wherein all enjoy an equal freedom, which is best understood as *independence* – independence of the power of another, each person being able freely to pursue his own ends, subject only to the similar freedom of others.[49] Freedom is not a right intended to achieve a certain state of affairs or to further a specific interest: it is simply 'the right to act independently of the choice of others, consistent with the entitlement of others to do the same'.[50] Public law regulates the exercise of coercive state authority to ensure that it imposes no excessive or arbitrary constraints on freedom, unnecessary to the attainment of a rightful civil condition. The basic civil and political rights are inherent in the scheme of equal liberty, preserving independence; government is entitled to obedience only insofar as it strives to preserve a regime in which these rights are

[46] Compare J Waldron, 'The Concept of Law and the Rule of Law' (2008) 43 *Georgia Law Review* 1, 11, arguing that far from being merely a protection against the abuse of *law*, the rule of law provides a shield against arbitrary power from wherever it appears.

[47] See further TRS Allan, 'The Rule of Law as the Rule of Private Law' in LM Austin and D Klimchuk (eds), *Private Law and the Rule of Law* (Oxford, Oxford University Press, 2014) 67.

[48] Fuller (n 23) 210.

[49] For the Universal Principle of Right, see I Kant, '*The Doctrine of Right (The Metaphysics of Morals, Part I)*' in MJ Gregor (ed), *Practical Philosophy* (Cambridge, Cambridge University Press, 1996).

[50] A Ripstein, *Force and Freedom: Kant's Legal and Political Philosophy* (Cambridge, Mass, Harvard University Press, 2009) 35.

enjoyed. Positive law is needed to translate abstract rights into determinate entitlements, reflecting the judgements of citizens and officials: public law is an expression of political morality as it applies in a local context.[51]

Under conditions of moral uncertainty and disagreement, the rule of law is substituted for perfect justice, as anyone might imagine the latter in an ideal world. Mutual civility is expressed by adherence to the law, correctly interpreted in accordance with legal and constitutional principle. While the general structure of rights can be ascertained abstractly, by reference to the basic ideal of human dignity and equal freedom, the specific content of these rights depends on legal and constitutional practice as it has developed within the domestic legal order. Abstract moral ideals find concrete expression within an argumentative, interpretative practice. Democracy serves the rule of law, bringing political judgement and experience to bear on the requirements of law within both private and public domains of regulation.[52]

Equality is preserved when the law as a whole is morally coherent and faithfully applied to particular cases. The rule of law insists that the distinctions made between persons are morally defensible – compatible with general principles applicable to everyone. While universally acknowledged rights and freedoms may embrace a range of competing conceptions, applicable to divergent legal or political traditions, state law must embody a single, univocal account. A coherent scheme of governance eliminates arbitrary treatment – treatment that violates that unified vision of justice according to law. There is an integration of practice and principle, legal rules and requirements serving to give determinate content to abstract ideals of equality and justice.[53]

Mutual civility, grounded in an acceptance of reasonable moral disagreement, requires compliance with rules that we may consider unjust. But we are entitled, nevertheless, to challenge questionable official interpretations, pointing to relevant considerations of principle and practice. Interpretative debate enables legal practice to move closer, by incremental steps, to the moral unity favoured by the rule of law. When we challenge the justice of a dubious rule or ruling, we are – if our objections are relevant to any practical purpose – insisting on its incompatibility with the wider *corpus juris*. We are juxtaposing an official view of the law's requirements with what we suppose is a superior understanding, more consistent with settled principle and previous practice.

We are entitled, moreover – even obligated – to resist very grave injustice by disobedience to the pertinent official demands. Grave injustice, inflicted in disregard of the basic rights of its victims, abrogates the ordinary duty of obedience to law. As Simmonds observes, 'Our compliance with the law is the primary expression of our civility or civic friendship.'[54] But mutual civility does not require compliance with

[51] See also Allan (n 5) 128–32.

[52] Compare J Weinrib, *Dimensions of Dignity: The Theory and Practice of Modern Constitutional Law* (Cambridge, Cambridge University Press, 2016) 60: 'The ideal of public law is a democratic legal order in which each person contributes to and, in turn, is bound by lawgiving that leaves the independence of each person bound by it undiminished.'

[53] See also Allan (n 24).

[54] Simmonds (n 12) 193.

enacted rules that are themselves a clear breach of that ideal – rules 'so grossly unjust that no reasonable person could possibly consider them to be just; rules that could not plausibly be claimed to be good faith, albeit misguided, attempts to articulate the requirements of justice'.[55] In repudiating gross injustice, we appeal to our fellow citizens and conscientious officials to remember their commitments to the legal and constitutional order: we invoke 'the commonly shared conception of justice that underlies the political order'.[56]

While adherence to the rule of law is the appropriate response to moral uncertainty and disagreement, rendering the law itself a principal forum for moral reflection and dialogue, legal rules provide the necessary degree of certainty for social and economic life to flourish. If, in deference to mutual civility, we must sometimes qualify our preferred conceptions of justice in recognition of legitimate disagreement, the same is true of our favoured interpretation of legal rules. A prevailing consensus about the meaning of rules, within a particular context, may assert a moral claim for conformity, conducive to clarity and efficiency. That consensus, however, will always be vulnerable to challenge in appropriate circumstances: considerations of clarity and efficiency must sometimes yield to persuasive arguments of countervailing principle.

The rule of law, conceived as a coherent scheme of legal principle, provides a response to moral uncertainty; and the enforcement of legal rules supports that ideal by securing a measure of legal certainty. But just as the rule of law operates only in an enlightened regime, properly respectful of human dignity, so legal certainty has value only when the rule of law is upheld, enforcing rules that serve an intelligible account of justice and the public good. Legal certainty is a value premised on the assumption that the legal order is intended to serve the interests of all. It is the assurance necessary for everyone to pursue her own interests within limits that secure a similar freedom for others. Legal certainty is only one element of justice and, hence, only one dimension of the rule of law.[57]

Gustav Radbruch argued that while legal certainty justified the enforcement of rules that fell short of justice, ideally conceived, it could not justify compliance with iniquitous state demands. The denial of basic rights or the imposition of harsh penalties in response to merely minor offences stripped state power of its legitimacy. The deliberate flouting of equality, striking at the very core of justice, deprived statutory demands of their legal character. In the absence of any serious attempt to further the interests of justice and the common good, genuine law was displaced by 'statutory lawlessness'.[58]

[55] ibid 194.

[56] J Rawls, *A Theory of Justice* (Oxford, Oxford University Press, 1972) 365.

[57] By way of analogy, the German Federal Constitutional Court rejected complaints that East German border guards, convicted of homicide after German reunification, were improperly subjected to retrospective punishment. East German law, even if applicable, could not give rise to legitimate reliance where what was 'authorised' amounted to gross injustice. A ban on retrospective punishment, though fundamental, assumes the ordinary context of a broadly just system of criminal law. See J Rivers, 'The Interpretation and Invalidity of Unjust Laws' in D Dyzenhaus (ed), *Recrafting the Rule of Law: The Limits of Legal Order* (Oxford, Hart Publishing, 1999) 40, 53–56.

[58] See G Radbruch, 'Statutory Lawlessness and Supra-Statutory Law' (1946), translated by B Litschewski Paulson and SL Paulson (2006) 26 *OJLS* 1, 7: 'When there is not even an attempt at justice, where equality, the core of justice, is deliberately betrayed in the issuance of positive law, then the statute is not merely "flawed law", it lacks completely the very nature of law'.

Julius Ebbinghaus reached similar conclusions: 'Any subjection of men which is not designed to secure the rights of all is unjust, despotic, and contrary to the law of humanity.' No law exists in the absence of any rightful demand for obedience.[59]

The distinction between law and justice is sharpest when we contemplate legal rules as the legal positivist would typically conceive them. While their validity is ensured by conformity to the 'rule of recognition', which need impose only conditions of manner and form, such rules may have any content whatever, subject only to explicit constitutional constraints.[60] The content of a legal rule, on this view, reflects its author's intentions or purposes, which are to be ascertained from the language employed: the normative rule is a direct reflection of the text that contains it. There is a direct correspondence between text and norm, which consists in an authoritative pronouncement.[61] Law, on this conception, provides only for formal equality: the rules, whatever they permit or require, must be applied to everyone in accordance with their explicit instructions.[62]

On a rival view, the content of a legal rule is derived, instead, from a study of the larger corpus of law to which it contributes. It is not the author's intentions or purposes that count; nor is there automatic correspondence between text and norm. The interpreter revises her understanding of the relevant field of law in the light of the defects or deficiencies to which the enactment has called attention. Respect for democratic deliberation and decision is demonstrated by attention to the failings of the current law, as widely perceived, and analysis of the nature of the remedy proposed or provided. But moral judgement is required, blending old and new, incorporating the statutory scheme within the larger fabric of legal and constitutional principle. The context is critical and extends far beyond ordinary linguistic considerations. A statute is not so much a 'source' of law, supervening on interpretative deliberation, as a pointer to perceived deficiencies in current legal analysis, contributing to such deliberation. Legal equality, on this conception, is deeper than merely formal equality: it means equality before the law as a whole, informed and structured by general principles.

Although statutory rules are often treated, in the positivist manner, as authoritative pronouncements of the legislature, they are better understood according to the rival interpretative view. Statutory rules should be ascertained and applied in a manner more closely akin to our reception of common law rules. We do not normally associate

[59] See J Ebbinghaus. 'The Law of Humanity and the Limits of State Power' (1953) 3 *The Philosophical Quarterly* 14, 17.

[60] For the rule of recognition, see Hart (n 2) 100–10. Hart's 'soft' positivism allows, contingently, for content restrictions in particular jurisdictions.

[61] Compare M Greenberg, 'The Standard Picture and Its Discontents' in L Green and B Leiter (eds), *Oxford Studies in Philosophy of Law*, vol I (Oxford, Oxford University Press, 2011) 39. Greenberg summarises this view in terms of an 'explanatory directness thesis': there are no explanatory intermediaries between the authoritative pronouncement's being made and the norm's obtaining (ibid 44–54).

[62] John Gardner denies that a legal positivist need favour particular methods of interpretation, observing that lawmakers can shape their laws by anticipating familiar modes of judicial interpretation: see J Gardner, *Law as a Leap of Faith* (Oxford, Oxford University Press, 2012) 42–47. But Gardner's commitment to the sources thesis – that a legal rule obtains its validity from its source rather than its merits – is finally inconsistent with the common law approach defended here. Even if a statute is valid in virtue of its mode of enactment, the associated legal rules are 'valid' (ie correctly ascertained and morally binding) only in virtue of their merits as plausible components of the law as a whole.

common law rules with judicial pronouncements. They are rather generalisations from specific decisions, guided not only by judicial reasoning but also by our critical appraisal of such reasoning. Judicial dicta contribute to deliberation and debate, assisting our efforts to refine legal rules by tracing their connections with other rules and principles. There is an interplay between rule and precedent decision, akin to reflective equilibrium between moral precept and specific example. The rule is merely a revisable interpretation of the precedents on which it depends, while the correctness of a precedent itself depends on its conformity to a pattern of similar decisions – a pattern that the rule attempts to discern and crystallise. Legal equality is attained by adherence to a coherent scheme of rules, distinguishing intelligibly between different instances.

When we recognise the ideal of legal equality as a basic constitutional value, we must repudiate the authorial intent view of statutory rules. They are better treated as being analogous to common law rules, sensitive in application to a broad range of legal and constitutional values. There need be no straightforward identity between a normative rule and ordinary textual meaning. If in some cases legal certainty is usefully bolstered by adherence to ordinary meaning, in other cases that desideratum may give way, on due reflection, to wider considerations of justice. Ordinary meaning is, in any case, dependent on the context in which it is sought. The further we cast our gaze, taking in the wider implications of a new rule for the system in which it must operate, the more nuanced our interpretation will become. The legal effect of an enactment, accordingly, is always a matter of judgement, sensitive to all the applicable moral reasons.[63]

Corresponding to these divergent accounts of legal rules and legal equality are contrasting conceptions of democracy. The intentionalist approach finds the connection between law and morality largely in the deliberative process that precedes enactment. Confronted by moral disagreement, we should loyally accept the outcome of fair democratic procedures even when we deplore it. Any challenge on the ground of violation of rights should itself be submitted to the same democratic forum, where our disagreements about the nature and scope of rights must be resolved. Waldron is a well-known advocate for this view, denying the legitimacy of constitutional judicial review, at least under the conditions of a flourishing liberal democracy.[64]

A different view of democracy places greater weight on moral deliberation throughout all stages of interaction between government and governed. If the legal rule is a generalisation, drawing on a range of moral considerations, its application to the particular case cannot be automatic. A prospect of serious injustice on the facts must prompt a reappraisal: the rule, correctly interpreted, may not apply in the ordinary way. Exceptional treatment may be justified in all the circumstances. Democratic equality is

[63] There are in fact many candidates in linguistic theory for the role of 'ordinary' meaning, which extend well beyond bare semantic content. As Greenberg argues, the standard assumption that legislation should be understood on the model of communication is also suspect. It is only on the basis of moral and political considerations that we can choose between the various meanings available. The creation of standards that promote justice and welfare is unlikely to be assisted by treating a statute's contribution to the law as a matter of what is communicated (even if communicative intentions could be plausibly ascertained): see M Greenberg, 'Legislation as Communication? Legal Interpretation and the Study of Linguistic Communication' in A Marmor and S Soames (eds), *Philosophical Foundations of Language in the Law* (Oxford, Oxford University Press, 2011) 217.

[64] See especially J Waldron, 'The Core of the Case Against Judicial Review' (2006) 115 *Yale Law Journal* 1346.

not offended by an adaptation or reinterpretation of rules, recognising the special sacrifice that their inflexible application would impose in particular instances.

A blanket ban on assisted suicide, enforced by reference to a statutory provision making it an offence to provide such assistance, cannot accommodate the needs of someone who wishes to terminate a life of intolerable suffering or indignity but who lacks the physical capacity to do so alone. If satisfactory safeguards can be devised to protect those who may be vulnerable to interference or pressure, an absolute rule violates fundamental equality. An individual's welfare, as he judges it, is cruelly and unconscionably sacrificed for no good purpose.[65] It makes little difference, however, whether we say that the statutory ban must be qualified, as necessary, or instead that it does not apply, on correct interpretation, to wholly exceptional cases. If we reject the conception of rules as authoritative pronouncements, in favour of the alternative view, we also eliminate the difference between qualification (or amendment), on the one hand, and interpretative revision, on the other. We insist that the application of rules is always dependent, in part, on the consequences for those involved; it must honour the basic rights that those circumstances may bring into play.[66]

IV. Constitutional Rights and Judicial Review

I have argued that law and morality are intertwined, legal obligations being those moral obligations that accompany membership of a legitimate political community. Obedience to law is an expression of mutual civility, which requires cooperation with others in pursuit of the public good within the constraints of justice. Justice in this context means respect for the rights, powers, privileges and duties that the law affirms when correctly interpreted, in accordance with constitutional principle. Grounded in a basic commitment to human dignity, constitutional rights honour the fundamental equality of persons. While fundamental rights do not guarantee any particular state of affairs, being sensitive in application to social and political context, they limit the grounds on which government can justify its coercive action. Such rights reinforce the basic ideal of equality, or equal citizenship, by imposing strenuous requirements of justification, obliging public authorities to show good reason for the distinctions they make between persons or groups. Fundamental rights forge an alliance between legal practice and political principle: they give specific content to abstract moral ideals, delineating the boundaries of legitimate governmental authority.[67]

[65] In *Carter v Canada (Attorney General)* 2015 SCC 5, [2015] 1 SCR 331, the Supreme Court of Canada held that a prohibition on assisted suicide was inconsistent with a person's freedom to request palliative sedation, refuse artificial nutrition and hydration, or require the removal of life-sustaining medical equipment. In *R (Nicklinson) v Ministry of Justice* [2014] UKSC 38, [2015] AC 657, the UK Supreme Court majority declined to decide whether or not the equivalent prohibition infringed the European Convention on Human Rights, article 8. However, Lady Hale and Lord Kerr challenged the legitimacy of an absolute ban on assisted suicide, emphasising the acute suffering of the claimants.

[66] For further discussion, see TRS Allan, 'Political Obligation and Public Law' in L Burton Crawford et al (eds), *Law under a Democratic Constitution: Essays in Honour of Jeffrey Goldsworthy* (Oxford, Hart Publishing, 2019) 249, 262–67.

[67] Compare Weinrib (n 52) ch 5.

A legitimate legal order is one that treats its subjects respectfully as independent-minded and morally autonomous agents, whose respect for public authority in turn depends on their critical appraisal of their government's claim to rule. Because obedience to law requires interpretation of the relevant standards, involving moral judgement, restrictions on personal freedom that impinge on the exercise of that judgement are rarely justified. Constitutional rights to freedom of thought, speech, conscience and association are therefore fundamental, reinforcing the moral and intellectual independence of the law's subjects. If the right publicly to criticise governmental action is an essential feature of democracy, the right to challenge its legality is central to the rule of law. These rights are closely allied features of liberal democracy, reflecting the status of the citizen as a person entitled to respect for his rational moral agency.

There is a close alliance between freedoms of conscience and expression, on the one hand, and rights of procedural fairness or due process, on the other. Whether seeking to enforce her legal rights or to defend herself against doubtful claims, a person may appeal to the law as she understands it in the light of the legal and political principles that secure its coherence. She defends an interpretation of the law that has its foundation in the general principles of legitimate governance that underpin her allegiance – her commitment to the rule of law. In invoking the applicable rules and precedents, defending her view of their bearing on the facts of the case, the litigant stands finally on a theory of the law as a whole – an account of the law that makes coherent moral sense of its various rules and requirements. Procedural fairness is not limited to the accurate application of rules to the facts of particular cases; it encompasses the right to argue about the correct interpretation of those rules, preserving the link between law and justice.[68]

Jeremy Waldron makes a similar argument about the contribution of judicial hearings and legal argument to law's intrinsic respect for human agency. In allowing litigants to offer submissions that embrace a vision of the law as a whole, they are treated as thoughtful participants in a unified system of governance: they can draw on 'their own view of the relation between their actions and purposes and the actions and purposes of the state'.[69] The law is a public resource that promotes human dignity by treating its subjects as the bearers of reason and intelligence.

Waldron does not, however, draw the natural conclusion, which is that such institutional and procedural features of law must curtail its power to authorise grave injustice. If we accept that the law must present itself as 'standing in the name of the public and as oriented to the public good', it is not enough, as Waldron suggests, that every rule or ruling must at least *purport* to serve the public good.[70] It is implicit in the status of the citizen as independent moral agent that any such claims may, if appropriate, be challenged. Any genuine legal rule or ruling must be justified by recourse to a plausible account of the public good, consistent with the constitutional rights that basic equality affirms. The argumentative character of legal procedure or process, responsive to the moral independence of the law's subjects, has substantive consequences: implausible official interpretations of law, inimical to basic rights, cannot be maintained.

[68] See further TRS Allan, 'Procedural Fairness and the Duty of Respect' (1998) 18 *OJLS* 497.
[69] J Waldron, 'The Concept and the Rule of Law' (2008) 43 *Georgia Law Review* 1, 35–36.
[70] ibid 31–32.

A larger network of constitutional rights can be readily constructed on the basis of our vision of the law's subject as independent-minded citizen, responsible for an interpretation of the law's requirements capable of withstanding critical moral scrutiny. If rights of due process are closely linked with freedoms of speech and conscience, due process itself depends on the citizen's access to the courts for the vindication of his legal rights. That right of access is in turn supported by rights to legal advice and representation, without which the promise of judicial protection for rights might easily be drained of its practical value.

When, in *Daly*, the House of Lords intervened to protect the right to confidential legal advice against unnecessary state interference, the court adapted the demands of legal principle to the context in point.[71] The practice of routinely excluding prisoners from their cells during searches for contraband risked the unwarranted scrutiny by prison officers of privileged legal correspondence. Statutory powers of prison management, under the Prison Act 1952, could not be construed as permitting such unnecessary interference with important legal rights. Cooperative prisoners should not be treated as if they were threatening or disruptive, endangering their legal rights without good cause.

In stressing that the case was decided at common law, rather than by recourse to the ECHR, the court signalled, in effect, the universal character of its guiding principles.[72] Insofar as the familiar civil and political rights, characteristic of liberal democracy, afford necessary safeguards for human dignity, they translate moral requirements into law. If different jurisdictions apply divergent conceptions of the these rights, they retain legitimate authority only insofar as these various conceptions have internal integrity: they represent plausible interpretations of the rule of law, adapted to the local context. Public law and political morality remain united, the former specifying the practical implications of the latter.[73]

In *Osborn*, Lord Reed offered *Daly* as an example of the overlap between the common law and article 8 of the ECHR, which would support a similar conclusion on the question of legality.[74] Observing that the Convention articles, like other guarantees of human rights in international law, were expressed at a high level of generality, Reed explained that they must be fulfilled at the national level by much more specific arrangements in domestic law. The right to a fair trial, under article 6, for instance, is effectuated through the detailed rules and principles of the law of evidence and procedure, administrative law, and the law relating to legal aid. The Human Rights Act 1998, which gives domestic effect in the United Kingdom to the Convention rights,

[71] *R (Daly) v Secretary of State for the Home Department* [2001] UKHL 26, [2001] 2 AC 532.

[72] Lord Bingham described his method as 'an orthodox application of common law principles'. For further discussion, see Allan (n 5) 243–59.

[73] Compare Lord Cooke observation, in the context of the common law's affirmation of the fundamental right to confidential legal advice, that 'some rights are inherent and fundamental to democratic civilised society'; conventions, constitutions, and bills of rights 'respond by recognising rather than creating them': [2001] UKHL 26, [2001] 2 AC 532 [30].

[74] *Osborn v The Parole Board* [2013] UKSC 61, [2014] AC 1115 [58].

'does not supersede the protection of human rights under the common law or statute or create a discrete body of law based upon the judgments of the European court'.[75]

Constitutional rights, then, have a conceptual core that builds on the central idea of the responsible citizen, whose grasp of the law's requirements reflects his deeper commitment to human dignity as the foundation of all legitimate authority. The familiar civil and political rights, underpinning liberal democracy wherever it flourishes, express those conceptual implications of legitimate governance. The specific content of these rights, as they operate within the domestic legal order, depends, however, on history and practice. Each jurisdiction will develop a systematic understanding, providing a morally coherent structure of rights that reflects legal tradition and local experience. It is only in the light of a theory of the law as a whole, refining principle by recourse to precedent, that we can determine the justice of any specific legal claim or the truth of any given legal proposition.[76]

The doctrine of proportionality, now a central feature of the judicial protection of human rights, is plainly a moral principle, serving the fundamental idea of equality. While the rule of law requires compliance with general rules, even when they dictate undesirable consequences in particular cases, it is threatened by the infliction of serious injury on individuals out of all proportion to any general public advantage. Legal rules must be interpreted, accordingly, in a manner that renders them legitimate, avoiding unjustified discrimination between persons or groups. Insofar as rules confer discretion on public authorities, officials must make proportionate decisions, appropriately sensitive to the constitutional rights that preserve fundamental equality.

It does not follow that public law must degenerate into freewheeling *judicial* discretion, balancing public and private interests on the facts of each case. Constitutional rights retain their peremptory force only if they are resistant to such balancing, operating instead to define the boundaries of legitimate state action. Rights cannot coherently be reduced to a shifting 'calculus of social interests'.[77] Legal rules must retain a degree of independence of their underlying rationale, preserving the distinction between legislation and adjudication; judicial discretion must not be substituted for legal doctrinal analysis. Insofar as the standard account of proportionality supports a case-by-case balancing of interests, in which rights must give way in the face of countervailing interests of sufficient strength, it must be challenged. On that picture, constitutional rights would buckle under the pressure of conflicting public interests and courts would become sole arbiters of public policy, usurping the roles of both legislature and executive government.

George Letsas is rightly wary of doctrinal orthodoxy: 'Proportionality is neither about means-end rationality, nor about cost-benefit calculations, nor about balancing

[75] ibid [57].

[76] There is, accordingly, no good reason to suppose that basic rights at common law are either fewer or weaker than those enumerated in enacted bills of rights. Nor are common law rights limited to those that have already been articulated and applied by courts in previous cases: see T Fairclough, 'The Reach of Common Law Rights' in M Elliott and K Hughes (eds), *Common Law Constitutional Rights* (Oxford, Hart Publishing, 2020) 295.

[77] Simmonds (n 12) 181, quoting Rawls (n 56) 4.

moral rights with other moral considerations.'[78] The judicial test of proportionality is, instead, an inquiry into whether a public authority has contravened a person's status as an equal member of the political community by acting on impermissible grounds. Blanket or indiscriminate measures wrongly exclude morally relevant considerations. And equality forbids reliance on certain dubious grounds, which are usually irrelevant to impartial decision or action. These include not only such 'suspect' grounds as race, religion, and sexual orientation, but many others, including a person's political or philosophical beliefs, traits of character, and genetic or biological makeup.[79]

Letsas focuses on the jurisprudence of the European Court of Human Rights at Strasbourg, contending that its talk of 'balancing' is quite misleading. While a court must sometimes consider the effect of a measure on both applicant and society at large, it does so with a view to discovering what moral rights people have; it must not trade off genuine rights against the collective interest. In particular, the Strasbourg court has upheld a wide range of rights in the teeth of majority preferences, even if in some cases it has wrongly assigned weight to morally irrelevant factors. The court's action often belies its words; we should not mistake diagnostic tools for a constitutive theory of rights.[80] There is no important difference between pursuing legitimate ends by improper means and pursuing illegitimate ends: in each case equal respect is infringed. If the court accepts a government's claim that its end is legitimate, it will condemn reliance on considerations that, judged accordingly, appear irrelevant – 'disproportionate' to the aim in view.[81]

In Letsas's analysis, by denoting the moral value of equality – or 'equal respect and concern' – proportionality plays a constitutive role in determining a person's moral rights against his government. The best reconstruction of legal doctrine must begin outside the legal judgments themselves: we must 'begin with normative arguments about the nature of human rights as moral rights made *independently* of legal practice'.[82] We must begin with our basic moral commitments, as Letsas suggests, because we must interpret legal practice in their light. Our legal interpretation aims to show why practice marks out the boundaries of the legitimate exercise of state coercion. A practice that could not be justified by recourse to the basic idea of equality would be illegitimate – incapable of giving rise to any concrete legal rights at all. If in most cases considerations such as a person's race or religion or sexual orientation are morally irrelevant to governmental decision-making and action, we can identify human rights of universal application. The rule of law requires courts everywhere to uphold these rights, resisting measures marred by such dubious distinctions between persons. Insofar as any state violates these rights, it departs from law, properly understood: it apes the forms of law while flouting its substance.

There is a close affinity, accordingly, between the proportionality doctrine, as deployed in human rights law, and the ordinary principles of legality applied in English

[78] G Letsas, 'Rescuing Proportionality' in R Cruft et al (eds), *Philosophical Foundations of Human Rights* (Oxford University Press, 2015) 316, 340.
[79] ibid 330.
[80] ibid 325–28.
[81] ibid 336–38.
[82] ibid 328.

administrative law. In each case, the issue is whether a person's treatment is the consequence of impermissible reasoning – reasoning corrupted by reliance on morally irrelevant factors or marred by inattention to morally pertinent ones. When irrelevant matters are allowed to play a role, administrative discretion is deployed for an improper purpose. When relevant considerations are ignored, or seriously undervalued, the exercise of discretion is unlawfully fettered: a potentially beneficial discretion is subverted by bureaucratic rigidity, unfair to those involved. If in certain cases an administrative action or decision appears plainly unreasonable – inconsistent with a proper respect for basic equality – we can usually infer a corruption or inadequacy of reasoning. The court's judgment gives objective confirmation to the legitimate outrage of those adversely treated.[83]

Common law doctrine has been developed to support basic rights by curtailing the permissible grounds of justification for administrative action. When impartiality is undermined by the influence of irrelevant considerations, extraneous to the proper exercise of discretionary power, the resulting official actions are *ultra vires* and, in principle, invalid.[84] The failure to distinguish between persons, or groups of persons, on relevant grounds has a similar consequence, vitiating administration action. A policy that requires not only disruptive but also well-behaved prisoners to be excluded from their cells, during searches for prohibited items, discriminates unfairly against the latter group. There is a risk to the privacy of confidential legal materials, held within a prisoner's cell, which it is unnecessary to incur when the prisoner's presence poses no threat to a properly conducted search. The importance of the right to confidential advice, in connection with the possible institution of legal proceedings, makes such a rigid policy hard to justify. Equality of treatment is dependent on attention to context: it forbids the enforcement of blanket rules, insensitive to considerations of legal and constitutional principle.[85]

When proportionality is embraced as a measure of legality, we simply acknowledge the full implications of the familiar test of 'rationality'. To insist that rules or requirements should be suitably directed to legitimate ends, and necessary to achieve such ends in all the circumstances, is merely to limit the scope for arbitrary state action. When these tests are not met, official policy has been misdirected by reliance on flawed criteria, extraneous to any defensible public purposes. Admittedly, it is usually insisted that there is a further stage of assessment: the restriction of rights must be proportionate, overall, to the attainment of legitimate ends (or proportionality *stricto sensu*).[86] A naked balancing of competing interests, however, would risk improper substitution of judicial opinion for that of Parliament or Government: it would amount to judgement

[83] See also Allan (n 5) 112–14.

[84] See for example *R v Secretary of State for the Home Department, ex p Venables* [1998] AC 407 (HL), holding invalid the imposition of a 'tariff' sentence affected by 'public clamour'. Parliament was taken to have conferred the power on the minister 'on the supposition that, like a sentencing judge', he would not act 'contrary to fundamental principles governing the administration of justice' (Lord Steyn, ibid 526).

[85] *R (Daly)* (n 71).

[86] For an outline of the various stages of a proportionality assessment, drawing on the judgment of Dickson CJ in *R v Oakes* [1986] 1 SCR 103, see Lord Reed's judgment in *Bank Mellat v Her Majesty's Treasury (No 2)* [2013] UKSC 39, [2014] AC 700 [74].

on the 'merits', obliterating the line between law and policy. Either the proportionality test mimics the ordinary criteria of rationality, or reasonableness, or its legitimacy is put seriously in doubt.[87]

Although the proportionality test is usually invoked to assess the legality of an 'infringement' of rights, it is better understood as a test of compatibility. There is no *infringement* if, on their correct interpretation, constitutional rights permit the relevant state action in all the circumstances. Only certain kinds of measure, conducive to the furtherance of legitimate public interests, can justify an incursion into individual liberty. A constitutional right is a safeguard against actions or decisions that are not justified, restrictions on freedom that political morality condemns. There is no genuine conflict between rights and countervailing interests when it is understood, in Weinrib's terms, as the clash between a right, on the one hand, and on the other an objective 'integral to the maintenance and refinement of a legal order committed to respecting and protecting the human dignity of all who are subject to its authority'.[88] Recognising that proportionality is itself a moral doctrine, intended to advance the ideal of constitutional justice, Weinrib distinguishes his own analysis from those of theorists, such as Alexy, who defend proportionality as a morally neutral structure for the resolution of conflicting rights and interests.[89]

In *R (Lord Carlile of Berriew QC) v Secretary of State for the Home Department*, Arden LJ (in the Court of Appeal) held that the question of whether an interference with rights of freedom of speech was no more than necessary to achieve the minister's objectives depended on determinations of rationality, legality and procedural propriety: it did not permit 'the substitution by the court of its own judgment on the merits'.[90] In the Supreme Court, however, judicial opinion was divided. Lord Kerr denied that it was a matter of whether the minister had been shown to have made an error of principle: 'We do not ask whether the Secretary of State's view is tenable; we ask whether it is right.'[91] Lord Sumption, in response, objected that Kerr's approach was 'nothing less than a transfer to the courts of the constitutional function of the Home Secretary' in circumstances where, in view of the pertinent issues of national security and public safety, the court was quite incapable of performing it.[92]

[87] See further Allan (n 5) 243–49.

[88] Weinrib (n 52) 222. Weinrib's characterisation of the issue as one of 'constitutional conflict' reflects his adherence to doctrinal orthodoxy, as it is presented, most notably, by the Supreme Court of Canada: ibid 218–23.

[89] Weinrib distinguishes his position from Alexy's Law of Balancing, which must adjudicate between competing principles, standing in opposition to each other rather than as competing determinations of an underlying norm of just governance: *Dimensions of Dignity* (n 52) 234–45. (See Alexy (n 14) ch 3.) Weinrib defends the proportionality *stricto sensu* requirement as necessary, in part, to balance conflicting rights by recourse to their shared foundation in the values of a free and democratic society (ibid 229–34, citing Dickson CJ's majority opinion in *R v Keegstra* [1990] 3 SCR 697 by way of illustration). But this is arguably an interpretative matter pertaining to the nature and scope of the rights in issue, encompassed by ordinary doctrinal analysis.

[90] *R (Lord Carlile of Berriew QC) v Secretary of State for the Home Department* [2013] EWCA Civ 199, [2013] 3 WLUK 536 [93].

[91] *R (Lord Carlile of Berriew QC) v Secretary of State for the Home Department* [2014] UKSC 60, [2015] AC 945 [158].

[92] ibid [49]. Lord Neuberger agreed with Lord Kerr's criticism of the approach of the Court of Appeal but observed that in practice, in this sort of case, the difference in approaches would 'rarely produce different results' (ibid [69]).

Acting on the advice of the Foreign Office, the Home Secretary had decided that it was not conducive to the public good for a dissident Iranian politician, Maryam Rajavi, currently resident in Paris, to enter the United Kingdom. Rajavi had previously supported terrorist violence in Iran. Lord Carlile and other British politicians had asked for the ban to be lifted so that Rajavi could address meetings at Westminster. The Home Secretary responded by observing that there were other means of communicating with Rajavi: she did not need to enter the country. Removal of the ban would, it was explained, endanger relations with Iran, jeopardising British interests and British policy in such areas as nuclear non-proliferation and human rights in the Middle East. Anti-British government rhetoric in Iran might, moreover, provoke a hostile public reaction, putting British nationals and Embassy staff at risk.

Kerr's opinion that the minister had failed to give due weight to the importance of the right of free speech, affirmed by article 10 of the ECHR, was rejected by the Divisional Court, the Court of Appeal, and a majority of the Supreme Court. Sumption observed that the court had no evidential basis or expertise with which to substitute its own assessment of the risks to national security, public safety and the rights of others for that of the Foreign Office. It could only assess whether the Home Secretary had 'set about her task rationally, by reference to relevant matters and on the correct legal principle'.[93] There was no further or distinctive role for a proportionality test to play.

Kerr also argued that the risk of an adverse reaction by the Iranians to Rajavi's admission deserved little weight, in the overall balance of judgement, because it should be condemned as 'unreasoning and unreasonable', 'profoundly anti-democratic' and contrary to British standards and values.[94] As Sumption observed, however, the relevance of that consideration was very doubtful: the issue was simply whether such a reaction was sufficiently likely and injurious to legitimate British interests.[95] A similar issue had arisen in the *Corner House* case, in which the High Court had held it contrary to the rule of law for a prosecutor to discontinue a criminal investigation in response to threats from a foreign state to suspend intelligence co-operation.[96] Rejecting that approach, the House of Lords denied that such a threat, with its implications for the safety of United Kingdom residents, could not in principle be a consideration relevant to a proper exercise of administrative discretion. The issue was simply:

> whether, in deciding that the public interest in pursuing an important investigation into alleged bribery was outweighed by the public interest in protecting the lives of British citizens, the Director [of the Serious Fraud Office] made a decision outside the lawful bounds of the discretion entrusted to him by Parliament.[97]

Carlile and *Corner House* are useful illustrations of the point that the legality of executive action depends on whether or not relevant considerations have been taken into account and irrelevant ones ignored. It may also, admittedly, depend on whether the weights attached to relevant considerations, where they conflict, were plausible – within a range

[93] ibid.
[94] ibid [171]–[172].
[95] Compare Lord Neuberger, ibid [77], to the same effect; see also Lord Clarke [116].
[96] *R (Corner House Research) v Director of the Serious Fraud Office* [2008] EWHC 714 (Admin).
[97] *R (Corner House Research) v Director of the Serious Fraud Office (JUSTICE intervening)* [2008] UKHL 60, [2009] 1 AC 756 [38] (Lord Bingham).

of reasonable judgement, dependent in part on official expertise and experience. That qualification cannot, however, signal any critical difference between rationality and proportionality tests. It would make no sense to insist on attention being paid to pertinent considerations if they could nevertheless be summarily dismissed, ignoring their real importance – or indeed greatly exaggerated, overwhelming other considerations also required to be taken into account. These are undeniably matters of judgement and degree. But it is only if the overall balance of judgement is grossly disproportionate – or wholly unreasonable – that a ministerial discretion is rendered invalid.[98] However regrettable the Director's decision, in *Corner House*, to abandon his investigation, it was nevertheless a proportionate one: his deliberations had neither been deflected by irrelevant considerations nor attributed to the danger contemplated a wholly implausible weight.

As Lord Reed observed, in a prominent case, there must normally be scope for the exercise of judgement by those branches of government that bear democratic responsibility for their decisions: 'The making of government and legislative policy cannot be turned into a judicial process.'[99]

V. Conclusion

I have sought to redeem Peter Cane's understanding of the close connection between law and morality by offering an appropriately expansive account of the rule of law, forging an alliance between legality and legitimacy. The requirements of law are identified by an interpretation of legal practice; and interpretation can proceed, combining fact and value, wherever legal practice can be embraced as a morally appropriate means of collaboration between equal members of the political community. When the equal dignity of persons provides the moral foundation of an interpretative theory of law, focused on legal practice organised around that basic idea, the law is the public face of justice. Political morality dictates obedience to law – the law as construed in the light of the general principles that secure its legitimacy. Injustice is a matter of discordancy between practice and principle, a failure to extend the implications of general principle to circumstances in which they properly apply. While obedience to law is normally a requirement of mutual civility, it does not mean conformity to merely purported rules or rulings, issued in plain violation of the rule of law by breaching legal or constitutional principle. We must be alert to distinguish between genuine obligations and counterfeit ones, inconsistent (as far as we can fairly judge) with the principles that provide the law's unity and moral coherence.

Although that unity of law and morality is conducive, most especially, to a proper understanding of common law reasoning – practical reasoning in the context of a shared tradition, attentive to familiar principles and paradigms – its truth is apparently

[98] Compare *R (Miranda) v Secretary of State for the Home Department (Liberty intervening)* [2014] EWHC 255 (Admin), [2014] 1 WLR 3140 [40] (Laws LJ, requiring, as regards a challenge to the balance of competing interests, demonstration of a 'plain case').

[99] *Bank Mellat v Her Majesty's Treasury (No 2)* [2013] UKSC 39, [2014] AC 700 [93].

neglected or denied by the majority of constitutional theorists today. In their efforts to rescue to rescue democratic politics democratic politics from what they fear is unwarranted encroachment by the judiciary, such theorists emphasise the gulf they perceive between doctrinal legal reasoning, on the one hand, and unfettered parliamentary debate and deliberation, on the other. If, however, law and politics alike must be chiefly focused on matters of justice, developing and enhancing a liberal-democratic tradition, it is futile to erect artificial barriers between these complementary domains. Confronted by the threat of serious damage to constitutional equality, courts can readily adapt their statutory instructions to the context in point, averting such damage when necessary to preserve legitimacy. The moral conscience, critical to interpretative truth, comes into play immediately, guiding the interpretation of law, rather than waiting to resolve – as a purely private judgement – a supposed conflict between law and morality.

Constitutional rights are accordingly resistant to illegitimate infringements, while their relative flexibility – adaptability to context – renders them fully compatible with political freedom, fostering the pursuit of public goods. Such rights hold public authorities to appropriate standards of reasoning, prohibiting measures that cannot be justified in the light of legal and constitutional principle but preserving, nonetheless, a broad sphere of unfettered policy choice. Determinations of proportionality leave space, on correct analysis, for political judgement and official expertise and experience. A proportionate decision is one that is rationally defensible in the light of legitimate purposes, giving due weight to all relevant considerations. The moral ideal of equality, or equal dignity, supports a complex structure of rights, translating universal requirements of political morality into more concrete entitlements, attuned to the history and experience of the domestic legal order. Legal judgement is irreducibly moral judgement, seeking coherence within the body of rules and principles that regulate the relationship between citizen and state.

It is hard to square Waldron's well-known scepticism about judicial review, as regards primary legislation, with his recognition of the ways in which judicial hearings and legal argument affirm the citizen's dignity.[100] If the rule of law honours the citizen's moral and intellectual independence by encouraging him to seek a defensible reconciliation between public and private interests – one that can withstand the test of independent judicial scrutiny – he must be free to challenge official claims about the law's demands. Recourse to judicial review transforms the idea of equal human dignity into a justiciable legal norm, making the exercise of public authority accountable to each person's right to just governance.[101] Even if the courts are denied strike-down powers to invalidate a statute, they can interpret it in the light of legal principle: they can read the statute in a manner that limits its capacity to authorise injustice. In that way the rule of law

[100] It is not so easy to distinguish between 'strong' review of primary legislation, on the one hand, and 'weak' review, permitting interpretation sensitive to rights, or judicial review of administrative action, on the other. Acceptance of a human rights tradition or culture, of the kind Waldron does envisage, has powerful implications for all interactions between the different branches of state: see D Dyzenhaus, 'The Incoherence of Constitutional Positivism' in G Huscroft (ed), *Expounding the Constitution. Essays in Constitutional Theory* (Cambridge, Cambridge University Press, 2008) 138.

[101] Compare Weinrib (n 52) 171–72.

is preserved: no one's fundamental right to equal respect is infringed.[102] If statutory rules are conceived on the model of common law rules, obtaining their meaning from a theory of the law as a whole, they cannot violate basic rights. They operate within the perimeter these rights provide, drawing only those distinctions between persons and groups that can be justified in view of legitimate public ends.[103]

While an international bill of rights may set out, in highly abstract form, the moral standards to which governments should in principle conform, it cannot dictate concrete consequences in particular cases. Too much depends on local context and domestic legal tradition. Common law constitutional rights, by contrast, can be understood as natural or moral rights, equivalent in principle to international standards but more closely adapted to the immediate context. Combining precedent and principle, common law rights protect fundamental equality by holding public authorities to rigorous standards of justification. Measures that distinguish between persons on impermissible grounds, inconsistent with the rights that give specific content to the idea of equal dignity, have no obligatory force. The law's requirements are always the product of a moral theory of the law as a whole – a theory informed by abstract ideas of equality and dignity but extending, in detail, to encompass all the legal rules derived or inferred from statute and precedent.

As the product of moral argument, the law is ultimately a matter of conscience: each interpreter must try to square her account of the law's demands with the principles that underpin its legitimacy. She need not set her own judgements against those of her community. Her legal judgements reflect her understanding of what political morality, in context, itself prescribes. Practical reasoning operates in a social and political milieu, informed in the case of legal reasoning by precedent and principle. In determining the law's demands, seeking legal and moral coherence, the interpreter serves the law's integrity in a manner that preserves her own.

[102] Weinrib's insistence on strike-down powers, by contrast with what he considers the weaker forms of 'commonwealth constitutionalism', exemplified by the United Kingdom, rests on a failure to appreciate the importance of legal interpretation, adapting valid rules to varied contexts as constitutional principle requires (see ibid 160–66).

[103] See my appraisal of Waldron's position in Allan (n 5) 325–31. Waldron's distrust of judicial analysis in contested rights cases ultimately stems from his refusal to embrace legal reasoning as a genuine form of moral reasoning. See J Waldron, 'Judges as Moral Reasoners' (2009) 7 *International Journal of Constitutional Law* 2, 12–13; and for discussion and critique, see Allan (n 28) 14–19, 26–27.

6

Participation and the Duty to Consult

JANET McLEAN*

I. Introduction

In his 2003 contribution to a festschrift for Carol Harlow, Peter Cane identifies 'participation' as one of the core values of public law. He reprises this theme in a 2010 article analysing the different ways in which citizens participate and assessing the qualities and expectations that attach to the different kinds of participation.[1] In that article he suggests that '[t]he principle that individuals should be heard before decisions are made that affect them personally is more deeply embedded in English legal culture than the principle that citizens should be allowed to participate in public policy formation processes'.[2] The relative absence of Anglo-Commonwealth administrative law doctrines to enforce participation in policy-making also features as an important point of comparison in Cane's study of administrative law in the United Kingdom, Australia and the United States.[3]

In this chapter I take up these themes and investigate the potential for duties to consult to support (or distort) political participation in policy-making. Public authorities regularly engage citizens in numerous different forms of participation. A particular and increasingly juridified category of political engagement is by way of consultation. Is framing a particular form of political engagement as a legal obligation enforceable or desirable?

Duties to consult promise better information, deliberation and participation in policy-making. Too frequently, however, those who have been the subject of consultation processes experience disappointment, frustration or unrealised expectations. The responsiveness of a decision-maker to submissions and the congruence between the decision and the submissions made during a consultation process usually falls far

* Thanks to Paul Rishworth QC, Edward Willis, Elizabeth Fisher, Joanna Bell, Justin Borg-Barthet, Robert Taylor and Adelyn Wilson for their helpful comments on an earlier draft. All errors and views are my own.

[1] P Cane, 'Participation and Constitutionalism' (2010) 38 *Federal Law Review* 319.

[2] P Cane, 'Theory and Values in Public Law' in P Craig and R Rawlings, *Law and Administration in Europe: Essays in Honour of Carol Harlow* (Oxford, Oxford University Press, 2003) 16.

[3] P Cane, *Controlling Administrative Power: An Historical Comparison* (Cambridge, Cambridge University Press, 2016) 291 ff

short of what would be expected in litigation or even mediation. Nevertheless, from the perspective of applicants for judicial review, the adequacy of the consultation process can become a strategic target for legal challenge for the reason that policy proposals are not challengeable as 'decisions', and once policies are set in stone, judicial review is unlikely effectively to be able to reverse them, if it is available at all. Apart from those public agencies which repeatedly run consultation exercises often following detailed guidance,[4] policy makers tend to be uncertain about what processes are required or at worse cynically manipulate timelines to ensure that consultation minimally disrupts a predetermined policy agenda. Legislative drafters worry about what, if any, legal consequences will or should follow if consultation is defective in any way and it is not unknown for drafters to add a caveat to statutory consultation provisions that no legal consequences follow a failure to consult or to consult properly.[5]

The normative question remains whether it is desirable to single out one particular form of political engagement – consultation – and to turn it into a legally supervised and enforced obligation, and if so, what form such legal enforcement should take? Should judicial intervention only occur when something has gone seriously wrong measured against other judicial review standards and grounds? Does treating consultation as a legal obligation risk the privileging of particular forms of political engagement and also particular interests in ways that might distort political and policy making processes?

Taking the United Kingdom and New Zealand case law as my starting point, I begin by considering the common law duty to consult, and its fair process rationale. I turn then to consider how much the statutory duty to consult depends on its common law antecedent and whether and how much the substance of the duty to consult should vary according to its legislative rationale. In section II I offer a preliminary taxonomy of how statutory duties to consult arise and may be enforced depending on their context and rationale and consider some of the factors that ought to be taken into account. In the final section I consider duties to consult indigenous peoples and their distinct rationale.

II. The Rationales for Duties to Consult: Individualised Fairness or Political Participation

A. Generally

Cane is correct to say that the common law has been better at recognising an individual's right to participate in decisions affecting them personally, than it has been at recognising an individual's right to participate in policy formation. That has not always been the case as a matter of British institutional practice. At least as far as landed property interests were concerned, there were numerous opportunities for participation in

[4] eg, the NZ Commerce Commission.

[5] Section 18 of the NZ Electricity Industry Act 2010 sets out elaborate requirements of who must be consulted before regulations can be made, but the same provision states that a failure to consult 'does not affect the validity' of any regulations which are subsequently made.

the government of the United Kingdom up until the early nineteenth century. At the parliamentary level, sponsors of local legislation (the predominant form of legislation at the time) would initiate legislation and be heard along with local objectors in formal hearings.[6] At the local level, the 'amphibious old Justices' who performed both judicial and administrative functions would hold hearings about whether to build a road, where it should go, what materials it should be built with and who should pay for it.[7] Those quasi-judicial processes recognised and gave effect to local self-government. Local property owners were instigators of legislation rather than consultees.

Participation in policy-making decreased after electoral reform and the advent of more centralised government – as indeed nineteenth century critics of the new centralising tendency had feared it would. By the twentieth century a cleavage had been established between the enforceability of rights to participate in decisions affecting persons individually and general policy making. This is nicely illustrated by *Bushell v Secretary of State for the Environment*.[8] The claimants objected to traffic flow projections which formed the basis for the routing decisions about proposed new motorways. They were denied the opportunity to cross-examine the department's witnesses about the reliability of those projections and the methodology on which those projections were based. The majority of the House of Lords distinguished between general government policy – which it said would clearly not be suitable for local discussion and examination – and the more local question of where a new motorway should actually go – which they recognised as possibly amenable to cross-examination in a proper case. The majority's approach represents a restrictive view of the relevance of local knowledge and interests to wider policy-making and demonstrates a twentieth century understanding of the central-local government divide.

The distinction between policy formation and individualised decision-making was only made obvious in the *Bushell* case because the distinction followed the central-local government divide. It will not always be so clear. Once a policy affecting a large class of people has been set in stone an individual directly and adversely affected by it may not be able to bring an individual challenge on the grounds of fair process, so an attack on the policy may well effectively be the best available substitute for an attack on the decision itself and consider similar factors. When a statute confers power on a decision-maker to exempt persons or classes of persons from the usual rules or procedures, the distinction will be blurred in another way. The exercise of such a power may simultaneously involve an individualised decision and policy formation.

The development of a duty to consult has the potential to bridge the cleavage between participation in decisions affecting individuals and participation in public policy. I now turn to consider how common law fair process has recognised the duty to consult.

[6] These highly participatory hearings were vulnerable to corruption and manipulation and rendered the legislative process extremely expensive because of the necessity of employing London agents, see J McLean, *Searching for the State in British Legal Thought* (Cambridge, Cambridge University Press, 2012) 28–29.

[7] FW Maitland, 'The Shallows and Silences of Real Life' in HAL Fisher (ed), *The Collected Papers of Frederic William Maitland* 3 Volumes (Cambridge, Cambridge University Press, 1911) vol I 467, 474.

[8] [1981] AC 75 (HL).

B. A Duty to Consult as an Aspect of Common Law Fair Process

The duty to consult was initially recognised as an aspect of common law fair process. It was triggered by the nature of the interest at stake,[9] and a past practice of consultation[10] or a public authority's promises of consultation.[11] While there are iconic cases in which, for example, a local authority was found to owe a duty to consult existing residents before making a decision to close a residential rest home,[12] cases which uphold a common law duty to consult are relatively rare.[13] In addition to identifying a sufficient interest in the policy,[14] there generally needs to be a *closed* class of people who will be adversely affected (and not just potentially affected in the future) by a change of scheme,[15] and there is a reluctance to find a prior practice of *consultation* (as distinct from other political practices of engagement).[16] A failure to consult does not necessarily give rise to procedural review. It may indicate that there has been a departure from administrative law standards more generally. For example, in one case a minister was found to have *Wednesbury* unreasonably failed to take account of whether there had indeed been a substantial change of policy when deciding whether or not to consult relevant interests.[17] In another case, consulting some interested parties but not others who were similarly situated within a closed class was treated as evidence of an abuse of power.[18] Among the reasons given for courts not to intervene is that to do so would intrude on parliamentary business by delaying the introduction of a Bill to Parliament.[19]

[9] The high water mark being *R v North and East Devon Health Authority, ex p Coughlan* [2001] QB 213 (CA), where there was both a special interest and an explicit promise which formed a substantive and not just a procedural legitimate expectation.

[10] *CCSU v Minister of the Civil Service* [1985] AC 374 (HL).

[11] This is the formulation in *R (Flatley) v Hywel Dda Health Board* [2014] EWHC 2258 (Admin).

[12] *R v Devon CC, ex p Baker* [1995] 1 All ER 73 (CA); *R v Brent LBC, ex p Gunning* (1985) 84 LGR 168 (QB).

[13] See, for successful common law cases enforcing a consultation requirement, *R v Secretary of State for the Home Department, ex p Khan* [1984] 1 WLR 1337 (CA) and *R (Luton Borough Council) v Secretary of State for Education* [2011] EWHC 217 (Admin).

[14] In *R (Niazi) v Secretary of State for the Home Department* [2007] EWHC 1495 (Admin), [2007] ACD 75 [10] this was described as a 'position analogous to that where an authority contemplates depriving someone of a benefit or advantage in which he has an interest'.

[15] See ibid (potential applications for compensation for miscarriages of judgments) and also *R (Bapio) v Secretary of State for the Home Department* [2007] EWCA Civ 1139 where the abolition of a scheme which exempted trainee doctors from needing a work permit would 'bring a host of litigious issues in its train'.

[16] *R (Bapio)* (n 15); *R (on the application of Unison) v Secretary of State for Health* [2010] EWHC 2655 (Admin), [2011] ACD 10 (where the practices of engagement were considered to be a political arrangement not susceptible to judicial review).

[17] *R (on application of C) v Secretary of State for Justice* [2008] EWHC 171 (Admin), [2008] ACD 32.

[18] *R (Luton Borough Council) v Secretary of State for Education* [2011] EWHC 217 (Admin), [2011] ACD 43. Selective consultation between rival interests has been treated by the common law (at least in the absence of a statutory duty or implied statutory duty to consult) as '[translating] what would otherwise just be desirable or sound practice into a formal obligation, particularly as here where the changes are significant, and there was an easily accessible body to consult': ibid [63]. In *Lower North Island Red Deer v Minister of Conservation* [2017] NZHC 1346 [78] Simon France J in the New Zealand High Court treated the party who had been overlooked in the consultation process as having a legitimate expectation of consultation, and their interests as constituting a mandatory relevant consideration. Discretionary relief was not exercised to quash the decision in that case in part because of all of the other decisions it would unravel and its effects on other interests.

[19] *R (on the application of Unison) v Secretary of State* [2010] EWHC 2655 (Admin), [2011] ACD 10. The New Zealand Supreme Court has criticised the 'creep' of claims to parliamentary privilege in order to protect ordinary policy making processes: see *Ngati Whatua Orakei Trust v Attorney General* [2018] NZSC 84, [2019] 1 NZLR 116.

One view of the common law duty to consult is that it should give individuals likely to be the most adversely affected by a proposal for change of a regulatory scheme an opportunity for input before the policy is set in stone. Such an understanding of the common law duty would have the effect of conferring special political participation privileges only on those individuals or legal entities most likely to be directly and seriously impacted by a policy, and contribute to the design of transitionary provisions or alternative policies. The cases often fall short of even that vision.[20] It is no exaggeration to say that the United Kingdom and New Zealand case law does not represent any resounding support by the judiciary for political participation of this kind. The common law has developed the duty to consult as an aspect of fairness and has consciously or unconsciously resisted the development of a distinct political participation rationale. As the New Zealand Court of Appeal put it, 'while it might be said there was a common law duty to act fairly, this does not go as far as to posit that consultation will be required wherever it would be fairer'.[21]

The cases discussed so far all involve plaintiffs' attempts to supplement the statute with common law consultation processes or to infer duties to consult from the context of the statute.[22] There are sometimes hints from the judges, however, that unsuccessful arguments based solely on the common law may have had greater traction if there had been a statutory provision requiring consultation.

C. Statutory Duties to Consult

(i) In Principle

A priori, what difference should the presence of a statutory duty to consult make to this analysis? In many cases the statute will do little more than codify the obligations of consultation at common law as when statutes refer to a closed list of narrowly identified interests which must be consulted. More commonly, statutory provisions mention specific classes of interest and also add an open-ended provision which refers to 'any other affected interests'. The effect could be taken as expanding the range of interests traditionally recognised by the common law for fair process purposes and thus the classes of people who can expect special consultation privileges.[23] This raises the prospect of a very large number of individuals or entities able to claim consultation rights against a public decision-maker. Sometimes statutes grant a discretion to public authorities about whether and how to consult, but when statutory consultation provisions use mandatory language, they represent an unequivocal commitment to consultation.

[20] eg *R (Bapio)* (n 15) which involved immigration changes to introduce visas for foreign doctors training in the UK.

[21] *Wellington City Council v Minotaur Custodians Ltd* [2017] NZCA 302, [2017] 3NZLR 464 [44].

[22] *Nicholls v Health and Disability Commissioner* [1997] NZAR 351 (HC).

[23] The courts increasingly take an expansive view of actionable interests in any event. As Varuhas suggests, while legitimate expectations may once have effectively expanded the scope of procedural fairness and standing to non-legal interests and losses of benefit, legitimate expectations are no longer required to perform this role: J Varuhas, 'Mapping the Law of Legitimate Expectations' in M Groves and G Weeks (eds), *Legitimate Expectations in the Common Law World* (Oxford, Hart Publishing, 2017) 36–37.

Prima facie then, statutory provisions recognise which interests attract special consultation processes – often expanding the interests beyond the closed class recognised by the common law – and often go beyond a 'promise' or 'practice' and express a *legislative* commitment to consultation. Prima facie then, one would expect more by way of legal consequences *automatically* to follow a *statutory* obligation to consult as a question of legality.

Already we ought to be able to anticipate some of the problems likely to be associated with statutory duties to consult. Statutes sometimes effectively codify situations where the common law would recognise a duty to consult anyway for reasons of fairness. But they also often extend the interests attracting a duty to consult beyond those recognised in the common law: the common catch-all 'any other affected interests' could sometimes include just about everybody. The rationale for consultation may not necessarily be about fairness and may be more about encouraging – or appearing to encourage – political participation. The reasons to consult different groups will likely be mixed. This opens up the class of people who might possibly have legally enforceable rights against public authorities.

(ii) In Practice

For these reasons, the practical effect of such provisions has not been either uniform or clear. Some judges have suggested that common law understandings act as a gloss on statutory duties to consult – effectively to confine them or at least to differentiate what a duty to consult requires depending on the interests at stake measured by existing fair process doctrines. Other judges seek to define and confine the duty in another way – emphasising that what should be expected by way of consultation depends on the context and meaning of the statute and the purpose and rationale for the consultation. The leading United Kingdom Supreme Court case of *R (Moseley) v Haringey London Borough Council*[24] introduces some of the nuanced differences between these two approaches.

Having lost central government funding for council tax benefits, Haringey Council was proposing a scheme to pass on the shortfall by removing council tax exemptions for some of its poorest and most vulnerable residents. It had a statutory obligation to consult with 'such … persons as it considers are likely to have an interest in the operation of the scheme'. Its consultation materials did not suggest any alternatives such as raising existing council tax rates or reducing local services. The Court found the Council had 'presented the proposed reduction in council tax support as if it were an inevitable consequence of the Government's funding cuts, and thereby disguised the choice made by Haringey itself'.[25] The Court granted a declaration that the consultation was unlawful (though it did not require the consultation to be undertaken again).

The Judges agreed on the result, but differed on how much the substance of a statutory duty to consult depends on its common law antecedents. Lord Wilson (with whom Lord Kerr agreed) argued that 'irrespective of how the duty to consult has been

[24] [2014] UKSC 56, [2014] 1 WLR 3947.
[25] ibid [42].

generated, that same common law duty of procedural fairness will inform the manner in which the consultation should be conducted' and that the 'consultation should be fair'.[26] While Lord Wilson recognised it was 'arguable' that all other residents had a financial interest in the scheme and thus may be owed a duty, he went on to focus exclusively on what consultation obligations were owed as a matter of fairness to the litigants who were vulnerable beneficiaries currently entitled to council tax benefits who were being threatened with having to pay some or all of their council tax in the future. He seemed to draw a direct analogy between the fairness cases involving the loss or withdrawal of a benefit and the situation of the beneficiaries in this case. This approach would adjust the expectations of consultation depending on what interests are at stake. So long as they qualified as a closed class, their individual interests in the potential loss of benefit would likely have been recognised by common law fairness.

Lord Reed, by contrast, framed the issue much more as a matter of political participation emphasising that '[*a*]*ll* residents of the local authority's area could reasonably be regarded as likely to have an interest in the operation of the scheme' (emphasis added).[27] The implication is that the duty to consult in this case applied regardless of the strength of the interests of the claimants – and the unstated corollary is that the duty to consult ought therefore not to be too onerous. He deliberately gave 'less emphasis to the common law duty to act fairly' and focused on 'the statutory context and purpose of the particular duty of consultation with which we are concerned'.[28] He went on to state that:

> [t]he common law imposes a general duty of procedural fairness upon public authorities exercising a wide range of functions which affect the interests of individuals, but the content of that duty varies almost infinitely depending on the circumstances. *There is however no general common law duty to consult persons who may be affected by a measure before it has been adopted.*[29] (emphasis added)

Statutory duties of consultation, according to Lord Reed, 'vary greatly depending on the particular provision in question, the particular context, and the purpose for which the consultation is to be carried out'.[30]

Lord Reed implicitly recognised the polycentric nature of the contested policy decision and that it is not the fairness of the consultation which is at issue but rather whether it is meaningful in sufficiently informing all of the consultees of 'what the proposal is and exactly why it is under positive consideration, telling them enough (which may be a great deal) to enable them to make an intelligent response'.[31] Lord Reed decoupled what constitutes good consultation for the purposes of political participation from what constitutes good consultation understood in terms of fair process. Though he never discussed it in these terms in this particular context of extremely vulnerable litigants, his reasoning is sensitive to the potentially harmful consequences that the endowment effect could have in a future case. Conferring special consultation rights on those potentially most affected by a new policy and with the greatest predisposition to fight change could unduly hamper a public authority's ability to make changes in public

[26] ibid [23].
[27] ibid [37].
[28] ibid [34].
[29] ibid [35].
[30] ibid [36].
[31] ibid [39], quoting *Coughlan* (n 9).

policy and distort the wider political process. Such an approach is potentially limiting of judicial intervention because it seeks to define *minimum* standards of consultation which could potentially apply to every affected person, and not only to those with the most to lose by change.

Later courts have demonstrated a reluctance to judicially define and supervise processes for political engagement or to enter into the identification of interests affected by the decision. The New Zealand Court of Appeal in *Minotaur v Wellington City Council*[32] was, for example, singularly reluctant to find a legal *duty* to consult a certain group of interests in a particular manner. In doing so the Court appears to adopt both Lord Wilson's approach which requires the assessment of the interests which trigger the consultation process and also purports to follow Lord Reed's approach. The provisions of the NZ Local Government Act 2002 gave local councils a discretion to decide whether and how to engage with the public. The Council having decided to consult, the Court in *Minotaur* said it would only intervene if there was evidence indicating that something had gone seriously wrong in an administrative law sense.

At first instance, the High Court had found that the Council had irrationally decided to consult tenants and to ignore owners of properties affected by proposed new parking permit rules. Taking a much more deferential approach, the Court of Appeal, in the absence of reasons from the Council, went so far as to infer that a good reason for differentiating between owners and tenants was that landlords were not *directly* affected. (Landlords claimed that the proposals would negatively affect the desirability of their properties to car-owning professionals and attract lower value tenants such as the student market.)

The Court of Appeal in *Minotaur* was clearly concerned about juridifying the terms of political engagement. Landlords had been informed and engaged by general public notices and websites but not by individualised formal notices. The Court could have simply confined their reasoning on the basis that the decision to consult was discretionary under the Local Government Act 2002. Instead it chose to go further and to characterise the earlier statutory duty to consult cases as requiring serious administrative wrongdoing before statutory rights to consultation will be enforceable. An earlier New Zealand High Court case was distinguished as giving rise to a legitimate expectation.[33] The wrongdoing in *Haringey* was characterised as artificially narrowing the policy choices available.

The cases, then, leave us with the idea that statutory duties of consultation 'vary greatly depending on the particular provision in question, the particular context, and the purpose for which the consultation is to be carried out',[34] with the possibility that some independent wrongdoing has to be involved before the matter will be actionable and with the concern that a court should not do too much to intervene in what are fundamentally political processes, lest they privilege particular interests too much and distort the political process more generally. Alternatively, or as well, a common law gloss may apply to statutory duties to consult so as to adjust what is required by consultation according to the interests at stake.

[32] *Minotaur* (n 21).
[33] ibid [46]. The case distinguished was *Pascoe Properties v Nelson City Council* [2012] NZRMA 232.
[34] *Pascoe Properties v Nelson City Council* [2012] NZRMA 232 [36].

Having briefly surveyed the case law on common law and statutory duties to consult I now turn in the next section to consider factors which law-makers and judges should consider when enacting or interpreting statutory duties to consult.

III. What Difference should a Participatory Purpose Make? The Beginnings of a Taxonomy

Sometimes a statutory duty to consult may go little further than to codify or extend a fairness expectation already recognised by the common law. But often statutory duties to consult have the distinct rationale of enhancing political participation broadly understood. In either case there is a need for principles to confine the application of such duties so as not to render policy making processes a litigious muddle or to privilege particular interests to too great a degree. In the section that follows, my focus is on the political participation rationale for consultation for the reason that it has the greater potential to extend obligations to consult beyond what is currently recognised in the common law.

Most people would agree that political participation is desirable. There are numerous ways to give effect to it. What we need to identify is what particular elements should create a legally enforceable obligation to politically engage in a particular way.

A. The Nature of the Decision-Maker

The first important element to consider is the nature of the decision-maker. The classic Westminster view of the executive tends not to differentiate between political and bureaucratic actors. Despite the significant changes to the way in which the executive has been internally reorganised since the 1980s, the classical view remains that executive responsibility is always channelled through public agencies back up the bureaucratic chain to the individual minister. According to this view, bureaucratic units bear no direct or independent accountability relationship to the public. In practice, however, different units of the bureaucracy enjoy varying degrees of operational and policy independence from ministers and complex relationships with the executive branch as a whole. Sometimes their distance from ministers is mitigated by their direct engagement with the public. Whether the authority involved in consultation is an elected representative or an independent public authority will be an important point of distinction.

Consultation can complicate relationships between civil servants, ministers and the public. Civil servants running a consultation process may be nervous about participants leapfrogging the process by making their representations directly to ministers, fearing it will interrupt their advisory role and the comprehensiveness of the process. There is the potential for civil servants and ministers to become rival representatives of the public interest. It is difficult to argue that consultation processes run by civil servants should *supplant* other forms of interest representation in a representative democracy.

We might share Joseph Williams J's implicit concern in *Minotaur* not to supplant Burkean representative democracy altogether or to privilege one form of political engagement with the public over the range of ways in which the public engages with politicians. Nevertheless, consultation processes arguably *can*, if performed meaningfully, enhance the representation of an electorate's interests, create feedback loops to representatives, elicit information not normally available to policy and decision-makers and reveal likely unintended effects of policy and legislative changes. In other words, participation can enhance deliberation.

When the decision belongs to an elected representative, a central question will be whether the consultation potentially is able to enhance political representation and deliberation. The difficulty with the way that consultation was conducted in both the *Haringey* and *Pascoe* cases was that it could not possibly have enhanced political representation. In the case of *Haringey* this was because the officials who came up with the scheme appeared not to have put up alternatives either to residents *or to the elected representatives*.[35] The political process went wrong at an early stage, rendering any subsequent consultation meaningless. The problem in *Pascoe* was also that the consultation could not enhance political representation but for the different reason that there was no feedback loop from the officials running the consultation to the elected decision-makers. Lacking any sufficient connection between the consultation exercise and political deliberation, in both cases consultation amounted to meaningless window-dressing.

If political representation enhancement is the rationale for the particular consultation then a light touch judicial review is warranted in most cases in which the decision-maker is an elected representative. Only if something has gone seriously wrong, rendering consultation meaningless, will judicial intervention be appropriate. In such cases even a failure to consult similarly situated persons should not necessarily be actionable so long as the interests are truly similar and have already been fed back into the political process. In the *Minotaur* case, the interests of tenants with cars pretty much coincided with the interests of landlords in maintaining higher value 'professional' and 'car-driving' tenants.

B. Duties to Consult and Legislative Bargains

Even when the decision makers are electoral representatives there will still be special cases in which greater supervision is warranted. In many fraught areas of public policy, modern legislation does not set out a policy direction itself but rather settles how policy will be made and by whom. In such cases, a statutory duty on ministers to consult certain parties can be the price of the legislative agreement or the sine qua non for the legislative bargain. A striking example of such a bargain is to be found in the New Zealand Gambling Act 2003. It includes a very detailed list of stakeholders with conflicting interests whom the minister must consult when developing the government's problem gambling strategy (gambling operators, casinos, the TAB, Lotteries Commission,

[35] It was a council official who was the author of the proposal for the Haringey cabinet, and it can be inferred from the Supreme Court's judgment that, had alternatives been put, at least one councillor would have been sympathetic to them.

problem gambling services, and others likely to be substantially affected).[36] Similar consultation obligations arise before the minister can make regulations under the Act.[37]

This is squarely an example where the rationale for consultation is political participation rather than fairness. Gambling and casino officers and the TAB, and perhaps even the Lotteries Commission which is funded out of the proceeds of gambling, may well have a property interest in the gambling rules which would be recognisable at common law. But the other half of the legislative bargain – those public health and mental health practitioners associated with problem gambling services – would not. What if the government were to consult the commercial operators and beneficiaries of gambling and ignore the other side of the legislative bargain? That really would be to distort the political agreement recognised by the legislature and the safeguards set in place by Parliament on the content of gambling policies and regulations. Much of the real work of the statute is left for later decision through interest group representation.

It may be tempting for the government to argue that such a duty to consult on policy is non-justiciable, that it is all part of an unenforceable legislative bargain, or acts merely as an aide memoire for the minister. But in terms of a political participation rationale, ignoring such interests is the equivalent of failing to take account of relevant considerations. A proper remedy would be to quash the policy or invalidate the regulation.

C. Statutory Duties to Consult as Internal Coordinating Rules: Intergovernmental Consultation

Another role that statutory duties to consult play in modern bureaucracy is to enhance the internal coordination between the various units of the executive.

By far the most frequent use of statutory duties to consult in New Zealand is not for the purpose of recognising individual interests or providing for fair processes or political participation at all but is rather for improving the internal coordination of the executive branch of government. Internal-facing rules of these kinds are addressed to the different organs that make up the executive rather than to the citizen. So, for example, ministers or public authorities are required to 'consult' with other ministers or agencies before exercising certain powers. Requiring consultation is simply one mechanism which attempts to mitigate the difficulties of organising 'whole of government' responses to policy challenges. Long a problem, difficulties of coordination have been exacerbated by a proliferation of independent or quasi-independent agencies.

The use of duties to consult in this way should not be so surprising. As with my earlier example of legislative bargains which do not put policy into legislative form but set out the who and how of policy-making, modern legislation is not so much about giving effect to rules or policies, but rather is more concerned with allocating resources, creating agencies, granting jurisdiction and broadly delineating the relationships

[36] Section 318(1)(h).
[37] Section 372.

between agencies and ministers.[38] This represents a change from the direct 'transitive' resolution of policy problems by the legislative rules of earlier times, to more indirect 'intransitive' resolution through the empowerment of agents who are allocated the task of resolving policy problems.

It is tempting to treat all intergovernmental duties to consult as non-justiciable – leaving their enforcement to politics and to the internal mechanisms of the public service such as employment performance appraisals, and key performance indicators. In most cases the public are likely to be none the wiser that any breach has even occurred. Should we treat the failure to observe these kinds of duties to consult as attracting any legal consequences?

In most cases it is hard to see what legal consequences should follow a failure to consult in these circumstances. There are examples, however, which suggest the desirability of at least *some* external supervision of such processes in certain cases. Sometimes the requirements to consult are suggestive of the mandatory relevant considerations that ought to be taken into account when making certain decisions, or operate as important constraints on agency power for the protection of individual rights.

Two examples are illustrative. Ideally, ministers should consult each other on matters where their portfolios overlap. But what if a statute designates consultation between specified ministers before the decision reaches Cabinet, for example, if the lead minister, the Minister of Energy, is required to consult the Minister for the Environment before taking a particular decision? Such a duty to consult is indicative of the matters relevant to the decision. In this type of case, failure to consult may prima facie indicate a failure to take account of the environmental consequences, or, more likely, *support* an independent argument brought by a citizen that environmental matters have not been weighed as a factor in the policy decision.

Even more problematic is the type of case in which the requirement to consult is for the indirect purpose of protecting the citizen's rights when there may not be other legal avenues available for redress. A striking example from New Zealand legislation is the requirement for the Director-General of Customs to consult the Privacy Commissioner before entering agreements with chief executives of government departments allowing them to access personal information on databases for the purposes of counter-terrorism and national security.[39] In most of those cases, individuals would never even know that their information has been accessed. In such cases, and especially if the failures to consult the Privacy Commissioner are repeated or systemic, it may be possible and appropriate for successful judicial review action in the form of mandamus to be available. Both of these examples illustrate that a failure to a consult may not necessarily form an independent cause of action but rather support another action available in judicial review.

[38] E Rubin, 'Law and Legislation in the Modern Administrative State' (1989) 89 *Columbia Law Review* 369.
[39] Intelligence and Security Act 2017, s 280M(6).

D. Independent Public Agencies

Duties to consult perform a different role when they are conferred by statute on independent regulatory agencies. Rather than enhancing political representation or deliberation, they partially serve a legitimating role, as a substitute for political representation, and help to regulate competing interests. Duties to consult in these contexts may serve to compensate for the ministerial accountability and responsibility deficits associated with public entities operating at arm's length from ministers and with minimal statutory or ministerial direction. They may operate to create a direct relationship between the regulatory agency and the public or proxies for the public which is independent of ministerial responsibility. Accordingly it seems to be quite appropriate that the relationships generally between such bodies and stake-holders and the public or their proxies should be highly regulated and subject to relatively high degrees of judicial supervision. The formality of such arrangements may be necessary to avoid regulatory capture or favouritism and to advance transparency. There is an important caveat, however. We need to maintain a degree of scepticism about how well independent agencies and stakeholders respectively are placed to act as proxies for the public interest when assessing whether and how much to regulate such relationships. This is difficult to assess in the abstract.

E. Consultation about Fees and Levies with Industry Players

Within the broader category of independent public agencies are those public authorities which are required by statute to consult with industry participants when pricing business access to essential facilities (access pricing) and placing limits on the maximum revenue or profit that a monopoly business can earn (price control regulation). Prior to the privatisations of the 1980s, access pricing was an inter-governmental decision and statutory tariffs regulated the terms and price paid by consumers.[40] Now these functions are undertaken by public agencies at arm's length from ministers.

Perhaps because the market is undergoing re-regulation after almost complete deregulation, in New Zealand access pricing and price control has been a target for a great deal of litigation. Consultation processes have been used by consultees to advance a litigation strategy rather than necessarily to reach the 'right decision'. Rightly or wrongly, the relationship between the public authorities and those consulted in these settings tends to be more competitive than deliberative, and there is a greater expectation that the public authority will act as an impartial administrative adjudicator rather than as a participant or facilitator.

Consultation by agencies involved in access pricing has been acknowledged in the New Zealand case law as having the purposes of providing at least some protection against abuses of monopoly power and as an avenue for creating a degree of

[40] In New Zealand consumer owned electricity companies are not subject to price control on the basis that they are more transparent, and because they are owned by their customers there is no incentive to set monopoly prices.

transparency. The case law acknowledges that there will be winners and losers of any proposed changes to pricing formulae and that industry participants serve as proxies for the general public. Not so openly acknowledged is that consultation also serves as an opportunity to *inform* the fee setting agency about the consequences of the proposed formulae on the market and of factual errors in its own calculations.[41]

While the leading case of *Wellington Airport* acknowledges that the 'obligation to consult can be seen as providing some protection to the [industry participants] and the public against an abuse of monopoly power',[42] it finds consultation to fall short of 'negotiation based upon information transparency which involves the [monopoly] making available all information which it is necessary for the [users] reasonably to satisfy themselves that the [monopoly's] position is not being abused'.[43] Something short of agreement and more than mere prior notification is required. Industry parties must be given sufficient information to be adequately informed so as to make intelligent and useful responses; sufficient time must be given; and it cannot be merely a charade. The discussion must be meaningful, and a final decision must not yet have been made.[44] The fee-setting authority is entitled to have a working plan already in mind, but must keep its mind open and even be prepared to start afresh. Notably, there is no requirement that the degree of consultation be proportionate to the interests potentially affected.[45]

These guidelines, deriving from *Wellington Airport* about what is required by consultation, have been adopted by other agencies which set access prices, including the Electricity Authority. Given the billions of dollars at stake, it is unsurprising that what is required by meaningful consultation has been further tested in the courts. One unsuccessful High Court claim was to the effect that the consultation about complex new pricing formulae for the transmission price of electricity to electricity supply companies was 'meaningless, being limited, insufficient and inadequate'.[46] The context was a significant geographical redistribution of the costs of electricity. The claimants were arguing that the standard for consultation set by *Wellington Airport*[47] was inadequate because the propensity for a decision-maker's 'confirmation bias' meant it was unlikely to be prepared to start again or to view submissions with an open mind but rather to use submissions to confirm its original hypothesis. A decision-maker's 'consultation fatigue' creating a desire to bring consultation to an end was another psychological factor weighing against genuine and meaningful consultation. The court, however, declined to intervene at 'such an early stage in the consultation process'.[48]

No doubt that particular litigation served broader strategic purposes but it does raise important questions about how best to ensure that consultation is meaningful

[41] *R (Royal Brompton and Harefield NHS Trust) v Joint Committee of Primary Care* [2012] EWCA Civ 472.
[42] *Wellington International Airport Ltd v Air New Zealand* [1993] 1 NZLR 671 (CA) 676.
[43] ibid.
[44] ibid 675, citing *Port Louis Corporation v A-G of Mauritius* [1965] AC 1111 (PC).
[45] This is not surprising given the slow reception of proportionality into New Zealand law. The requirement for proportionality has been removed from the current UK Government consultation guidelines but was included in earlier versions.
[46] *Trustpower v Electricity Authority* [2016] NZHC 2914, [2017] 2 NZLR 253.
[47] *Wellington Airport* (n 42).
[48] *Trustpower* (n 46) [60]–[64], [103].

in such settings, particularly given that the public authority will also have strategic targets and deadlines to meet. One possible way to balance the power in favour of the market participants and to make the consultation more meaningful would be to require the public authority to give reasons for its adoption of a particular pricing formula (explaining how it would best serve the public interest) even with a risk that that might prolong the process even further and encourage disputes about what counts as an adequate reason or a proper form of reason-giving (would duties be owed to the industry participants individually, for example, or would a general report be sufficient?).

Price control regulation raises some different issues. When one considers the extensive United States statute and case law on public utility rate fixing,[49] a mere duty to consult seems a pretty small measure to take in addressing the relationships between the various actors. This is the reason why some jurisdictions give the utility regulator the power to access the company's financial records to guard against fictitious capitalisation or enact other disclosure requirements.[50] The duty to consult is only the tip of the iceberg so far as setting fair rates of return is concerned.

In this section, I have outlined a very preliminary taxonomy of some of the elements which will be relevant to a determination of whether and how duties to consult should be judicially enforced. In the next section I deal with the duty to consult with indigenous people, which has a distinct rationale and derivation.

IV. Duties to Consult with Indigenous People

In New Zealand, the duty to consult with Maori is not derived from the common law duty of fairness or exclusively from statute (though sometimes statutory provisions codify the duty) but has been recognised by the courts as deriving from judge-made 'principles' which have their source in the Treaty of Waitangi between the Crown and Maori chiefs in 1840. In Canada, a similar duty is said to be 'grounded in the assertion of Crown sovereignty which predates the Union'.[51] As Chief Justice McLachlin explained in *Haida Nation*: 'the controlling question in all situations is what is required to maintain the honour of the Crown and to effect reconciliation between the Crown and the Aboriginal peoples with respect to the interests at stake'.[52]

The narrow common law natural justice as fair process frame has sometimes constrained or obscured the development of a distinct duty to consult indigenous peoples. Judges tend to undertake sometimes convoluted reasoning. In *Haida Nation*, the Supreme Court stated that the degree of consultation required continues to depend on the judge's assessment of the strength of the aboriginal claim (in advance of or in substitution for actually considering that claim), and the seriousness of the

[49] See, eg, W Pond, 'The Law Governing the Fixing of Public Utility Rates: A Response to Recent Judicial and Academic Misconceptions' (1989) 41 *Admin Law Review* 1.

[50] New Zealand has recently brought into effect disclosure requirements which enhance regulatory control.

[51] *Haida Nation v BC (Minister of Forests)* [2004] 3 SCR 511 [59].

[52] ibid [13].

potential impact on the right.[53] In that case the Haida Nation had claimed title for at least 100 years. The cases refer to asserted as opposed to proven aboriginal rights and title.[54] Property is undoubtedly at stake in such cases but so also is political authority. Property and political interests are entangled but in ways it may be too uncomfortable for the Courts fully to unravel.

Richard Stacey has compellingly argued that the rationale for imposing duties on the Crown to consult indigenous peoples should be regarded, not as a particular version of fair process, but as serving the distinct function of ameliorating the sovereignty and democratic deficits affecting the political participation of indigenous peoples.[55] He regards the duty to consult as creating opportunities for indigenous expressions of sovereignty and as tempering the Crown's exercise of sovereignty.[56] This is very different from ordinary processes of political engagement and at its best it aspires to enable shared deliberation and reconciliation. The Crown, in such consultations, should act as a facilitator or participant rather than an impartial arbiter.

V. Conclusion

No one thinks consultation is a bad thing. It can improve public decision-making, contribute to and correct the factual bases on which policy is made, alert decision-makers of unintended consequences to individuals or more widely, improve feedback loops, enhance political representation and promote fairness. Legal enforcement of duties to consult (arising either by statute or the common law), however, has the potential to exaggerate the endowment effect, privileging particular interests against changes which may benefit others and create a strait-jacket for how public authorities engage with their various publics.

Perhaps for these reasons, the judges have placed numerous restrictions on the common law duty to consult. Meanwhile, in New Zealand and the United Kingdom, provisions creating statutory duties to consult have proliferated, commonly expressed in a way which appears significantly to extend who is owed a duty. This is an interesting example of how ideas flow not only from politics to law but also from law to politics.[57] But it has left the judges with a dilemma of whether and how to enforce such statutory duties. Should they read them with a common law fairness gloss, or through a political participation lens?

This paper suggests that there are many and various different rationales for statutory duties to consult which go beyond common law fairness: they can enhance political

[53] ibid [39], [43]–[45].

[54] Ibid [26]–[38].

[55] R Stacey, 'Honour In Sovereignty: Can Crown Consultation with Indigenous Peoples Erase Canada's Sovereignty Deficit?' (2018) 68 *University of Toronto Law Journal* 405.

[56] ibid 417.

[57] Cane (n 2) 19: 'law can absorb political values, so the political system can absorb legal values'.

engagement, can give effect to a political bargain, can perform a coordinating function between different parts of the executive, can lend public legitimacy and accountability to independent agencies, can mitigate against abuses of monopoly power, and can even sometimes aim to ameliorate a sovereignty and democratic deficit. What consultation means varies in these different settings – sometimes warranting only minimal judicial supervision, and at others strict regulation. At times consultation will enhance deliberation, at others the public authority will find itself much more in the role of an independent arbiter.

There is no doubt that participation is a core value of public law. The varieties of modes of participation lend strength to its practice and need to be preserved.

7

Controlling Administration: The Rise of Unilateral Executive Power in the United States

JERRY L MASHAW

I. Introduction

In his magisterial work on comparative systems of administrative control, Peter Cane argues that 'significant differences between control regimes' that check and channel administration in the three countries that he studied 'may be partly explicable in terms of differences between the systems of government' of those countries.[1] The systems of government that Cane examined are distinguished at the very general level by their tendency to concentrate or diffuse political power. The distinction between diffusion and concentration was explained in the following way:

> A fundamental difference between diffusion and concentration is that under diffusion, the various empowered institutions are separately and distinctly authorized to exercise whatever powers they have been given and are in that sense 'coordinate'. By contrast under concentration, authority is ultimately derived from a single 'sovereign' institution to which all other institutions are in some sense subordinate.[2]

Thus, in a diffusion system, like the separation of powers system in the United States, administrative control is parcelled out to three coordinate control institutions: Congress; the President; and the Judiciary. In a concentrated system, like the Westminster Parliamentary system, the control of administration is at least formally lodged in Parliament.

Administrative control regimes are indeed crucial to understanding how contemporary governments work. We live in administrative states. Most law making in the United States, for example, is done by administrative agencies, not Congress. And the US system of separated powers presumably yields a control regime in which coordinate

[1] P Cane, *Controlling Administrative Power: An Historical Perspective* (Cambridge, Cambridge University Press, 2016) 11.

[2] ibid 5.

branches of the government, in differing ways, check and channel the authority of the bureaucracy. And, because this checking function is diffused, these separated institutions also check each other's control of administration.

In a broad sense, Cane's analysis is surely correct. The authority that administrators exercise is based almost exclusively on congressional statutes and the resources that they rely upon in the exercise of those powers is also provided by congressional appropriations and staffing limits. In theory, at least, Congress can call any administrator or agency to account through powers of investigation, public hearing and ultimately authorising appropriations legislation.

Similarly, the President has significant authority to mould the path of administrative action by appointing officials sympathetic to administration policy and removing them for failure to faithfully execute their offices or, in many cases, for merely failing to implement administration policies. And, while congressional statutes establish the powers and procedures by which administrators develop and implement policy, administrative agendas are often set by presidential direction. To the extent that administrators have broad discretion both about whether and how to act, and they do, both policy development and enforcement at the administrative level can vary significantly from one presidential administration to the next.[3]

Finally, American courts have been authorised under the Federal Administrative Procedure Act to exercise broad powers of review over the legality of administrative action. And, in the American context, legality has an expansive meaning. American courts are authorised to review administrative action not just for consistency with the Constitution and relevant statutory requirements, but also for reasonableness or non-arbitrariness. Because 'reasonableness' is a quite elastic standard, American courts, in some sense, share the policy space provided to administrators by congressional legislation.

On this broad overall description, the American system of separated powers seems to feature quite diffuse modes of authority with their own separate techniques for sharing the channelling and checking functions that Cane examined. My suggestion in this brief essay is that the American system of separated powers has become much more concentrated in the control of administrative action than the formal powers of the three branches of government might suggest. In many ways, the control of administration has shifted to the presidency. This has been the result both of practice, the ways in which modern congresses have delegated authority, and the ways presidents have developed to control administration.[4] Perhaps equally importantly, these developments have been

[3] The way these policy changes are achieved is developed in some detail in JL Mashaw and D Berke, 'Presidential Administration in a Regime of Separated Powers: An Analysis of Recent American Experience' (2018) 35 *Yale Journal on Regulation* 549.

[4] There are a large number of political science and historical studies documenting this trend. See, eg, M Belco and B Rottinghaus, *The Dual Executive: Unilateral Orders in a Separated and Shared Power System* (Stanford, Stanford University Press, 2017); DP Gitterman, *Calling the Shots: The President, Executive Orders, and Public Policy* (Washington, DC, Brookings Institution Press, 2017); KR Mayer, *With the Stroke of a Pen: Executive Orders and Presidential Power* (Princeton, Princeton University Press, 2001); EA Posner and A Vermeule, *The Executive Unbound: After the Madisonian Republic* (New York, Oxford University Press, 2010); A Rudalevige, *The New Imperial Presidency: Renewing Presidential Power After Watergate* (Ann Arbor, University of Michigan Press, 2005).

embedded in law by Supreme Court constitutional doctrines that empower presidents and diminish the control authority of both Congress and the courts themselves.

In this brief essay I cannot pursue the many interconnected developments that have given rise to a regime of administrative control that is sometimes characterised as 'presidentialism'. I will instead look briefly at three principal topics: first, the techniques of congressional control over administrative lawmaking and the limitations on those controls imposed by Supreme Court doctrine. Second, I will briefly trace the rise of presidentialism in practice and the ways in which Supreme Court doctrine facilitates presidential control. That account will include a brief normative critique of these developments. Finally, I will look at a counter-tendency: the demand for reasons, as courts police administrative actions for arbitrariness. A brief conclusion follows.

II. Congressional Control of Administrative Law Making

It is an open secret that most lawmaking at the federal level occurs in administrative agencies. Whereas congresses pass, at most, a few hundred statutes per session, agencies issue thousands of regulations, guidance documents, memoranda and the like in the same period. This is often seen as a regrettable feature of the modern American governance. Commentators and members of the general public rail against 'unelected bureaucrats' and decry the loss of democratic government that the growth of the administrative state purportedly represents. But while berating federal administrators may be the favourite indoor sport of congressional oversight committees, Congress has not really fought against this trend. Although the signal legislative accomplishments of the Obama administration, the Affordable Care Act[5] and the Dodd-Frank financial services legislation,[6] went on for hundreds of pages, those statutes required, indeed demanded, hundreds of regulations by various administrative agencies in order to be implemented. The only major legislation passed during the Trump administration other than the 'Cares Act',[7] the pandemic stimulus legislation, was a tax 'reform' statute.[8] It too is a complex piece of legislation, but requires hundreds of IRS or treasury regulations and guidance documents to make it operational. The simple truth is that Congress cannot legislate at a level of detail that avoids substantial discretionary policymaking by administrative implementers. Even if it were inclined to do so, it has neither the time nor the information necessary to do a competent job.

It is, of course, a bedrock constitutional principle that Congress cannot delegate away the legislative power. But, other than a few cases during the New Deal period, by a Supreme Court that viewed the Roosevelt administration as getting out of control, courts have been unable to make the so-called non-delegation doctrine operational. This is not surprising. When passing legislation Congress must make tradeoffs among

[5] The Patient Protection and Affordable Care Act, Pub L No 111-148, 124 Stat 119 (2010).
[6] Dodd-Frank Wall Street Reform and Consumer Protection Act, Pub L No 111-203, 124 Stat 1376 (2010).
[7] Coronavirus Aid, Relief, and Economic Security (CARES) Act, Pub L No 116-136 (2020).
[8] Tax Cuts and Jobs Act of 2017, Pub L No 115-97, 131 Stat 2054 (2017).

various sorts of costs: One is the procedural and information costs that Congress would need to bear in order to legislate in detail concerning matters that are often complex, technical and bedeviled by uncertainties. Second, there is the problem of error costs should Congress fail to anticipate what the future holds or guess correctly about currently contested issues of fact. As some wag once said (it is often customary to attribute such quotations to Yogi Berra): 'It is difficult to make predictions, particularly about the future'. Finally, the Congress must consider so-called agency costs, that is, the possibility that administrators in carrying out or implementing the legislation will in fact deviate from what the Congress intended. When a Congress delegates broad discretionary authority to administrators, presumably concluding that the agency costs risks are the lesser of the evils that it confronts, where is a court to stand, constitutionally, to say that Congress lacks the authority to make that judgement? Such a decision smacks of 'substantive due process', an approach to judicial review which the Supreme Court has forsworn save in cases of invasion of individual liberties.[9]

To some degree, of course, the flabbiness of the non-delegation doctrine – all that it requires is that the statute state an 'intelligible principle' to guide the agency[10] – empowers Congress to act in circumstances where it might otherwise feel itself too ignorant to risk making definitive judgements on uncertain and contestable matters. But this empowerment also empowers the administrative state. And, to the extent that administrators are guided importantly by presidential directives or allegiance to presidential policy preferences, these broad statutory provisions empower presidents as well. Given the lopsided locus of lawmaking in the modern administrative state, the lack of a significant non-delegation constraint empowers presidents more than it empowers congresses.

Congresses have hardly been insensitive to this problem, but their attempts to devise remedies short of detailed legislative prescriptions have been largely unsuccessful when tested in court. When Congress believes that an agency has acted in a fashion that is imprudent or inconsistent with the true intent of its governing legislation, it can, of course, amend the statute; or, perhaps, attach riders to appropriations legislation forbidding the use of any funds for the implementation of the offending policy choice. But presidents have a veto power over legislation and in that sense constitute almost a third house of the legislature. In over 200 years of American constitutional history, presidential vetoes have been overridden by two-thirds majorities in both houses of Congress less than 200 times. And, when Congress attempted to give itself a veto not subject to annulment by the President, either through a concurrent resolution or a resolution by one house of congress, the Supreme Court declared that technique unconstitutional.[11] Congress can of course engage in investigations and hold hearings to berate administrators for their policy choices. But these are rather weak constraints given the vast number of choices left to administrative agencies and the limitations on congressional

[9] The literature on substantive due process is extensive. On the rise of substantive process and its abandonment concerning economic and social legislation see, eg, GE White, *The Constitution and the New Deal* (Cambridge, Mass, Harvard University Press, 2000).

[10] See, eg, *Whitman v American Trucking Association, Inc*, 531 US 457 (2001).

[11] *Immigration and Naturalization Service v Chadha*, 462 US 919 (1983).

attention and meeting time. Congress has developed a special fast-track procedure for overturning late-term regulations adopted by an outgoing administration.[12] But this approach works only in circumstances in which there is a change in party control of the presidency and both houses of Congress are controlled by the President's party.

Congressional control of inaction by administrators is perhaps even less effective than is control over their actions. Where Congress in some way mandates the substance of required agency action, it is prone to error. For example, Congress mandated that the Occupational Safety and Health administration adopt, within one year of the passage of its statute, all national consensus standards concerning workplace safety. This resulted in the adoption of a host of nitpicking requirements, such as the height of toilet seats or the colour of ladders, that held the agency up to ridicule and destroyed much of its political support. Where Congress mandates that some regulation on some topic be adopted within a prescribed time period, those mandates have turned out to unenforceable. The Environmental Protection Agency (EPA) has missed most of the hundreds of deadlines in its statutes. When sued, as it sometimes is, for failure to meet these deadlines, courts have little remedial power. They cannot turn back the clock. They can force the agency to propose a schedule upon which it will act, but if it fails to do so a subsequent attempt to enforce the deadline is simply a reprise of the first.[13] For example, when the Supreme Court found[14] that the Clean Air Act mandated EPA action concerning pollutants contributing to climate change, the George W Bush administration managed to delay action until Bush's term expired. And, an agency ultimately forced to act where it prefers not to do so is unlikely to take energetic enforcement action.

Courts are themselves quite sceptical about setting agency agendas save pursuant to extremely specific requirements in an agency's governing statute. No agency can get to all the matters within its jurisdiction; courts are radically uninformed about where the priorities should be; and courts are seldom in a position to determine whether there is sufficient information upon which an agency could adopt sensible policies. As a consequence, some agencies operating in administrations unsympathetic to their mandates have basically gone out of the regulatory business. The Trump administration is perhaps an extreme case in point. According to the Office of Management and Budget (OMB), during President Trump's first three years in office, federal regulatory agencies have added not a single dollar in regulatory costs to the American economy.[15]

To be sure, there are instances of congressional effectiveness in controlling and motivating administrators. But the barriers to effective action are substantial. Of course, where the President and both houses of Congress are controlled by the same political party, Congress is likely to have more influence on administrative policy.

[12] For an analysis of the so-called Congressional Review Act, see D Cohen and PL Strauss, 'Congressional Reviews of Agency Regulations' (1997) 49 *Administrative Law Review* 95.

[13] See, eg, *NRDC v Train*, 510 F 2d 692 (DC Cir 1974) (requiring that the EPA make a 'good faith' effort to meet its deadlines).

[14] *Massachusetts v Environmental Protection Agency*, 549 US 497 (2007).

[15] Indeed, the Office of Information and Regulatory Affairs had OMB reports that administrative agencies have since 2017 eliminated $50.9 billion in overall regulatory costs across the government and anticipated saving 51.6 billion additional dollars in regulatory costs during fiscal year 2020: *Regulatory Reform Results for Fiscal Year 2019*, Office of Information & Regulatory Affairs, www.reginfo.gov/public/do/eAgendaEO13771, accessed 5 July 2021.

Peter Cane is correct that American presidents have less control over Congress, even when both houses have a majority of Representatives and Senators from the President's own party, than British Prime Ministers have with respect to Parliament. In general, even with unified government, presidents will have to negotiate, and they will not get everything that they want. On the other hand, this degree of diffusion may also be breaking down. In the 2020 presidential campaign the Republican Party provided no legislative platform. Apparently its position was that congressional Republicans would support whatever a re-elected President Trump wanted to do.

III. The Rise and Rise of Presidential Control

A. The Role of Practice

If the fact that much federal law is administrative rather than legislative represents a democratic deficit, modern presidents, at least since Ronald Regan, have thought that they could provide a democratic cure – presidential direction of administrative action.[16] Presidents, after all, have the broadest constituency of any elected official. Presidential elections are contested on broad issues of national policy, not on who can bring home the bacon for the local congressional district. Presidential administration may thus provide an important democratic check on the administrative state.

This potentially democracy-reinforcing character of 'presidentialism' was given an elaborate justification by Supreme Court Justice Elena Kagan. Fresh from a stint in the Clinton White House, then-Professor Kagan wrote an article for the Harvard Law Review titled 'Presidential Administration'.[17] Praising President Clinton's practice of appropriating agency action as his own, Kagan extolled the transparency and accountability advantages of presidential direction of administrative action. And Clinton's successors have, if anything, increased the influence of the Executive Office of the President, now itself a sprawling bureaucracy, and the President himself, in policymaking at the administrative level. Presidentialism seems to be a one-way ratchet. The more presidents do, the more we expect them to do. Failure to flex executive muscles in pursuit of political promises is seen by a President's supporters as a betrayal. And, if a sclerotic or oppositional Congress cannot be convinced to go along with the President's plan, then modern presidents have increasingly used unilateral executive action to achieve both domestic and international policy objectives.

Recent actions by the Trump administration make this pattern pretty obvious. President Trump and his appointees have set about the systematic dismantling of most of Barack Obama's major accomplishments. Unable to repeal the Affordable Care Act, the Trump administration has done much to undermine its implementation. Unable to get Congress to reign in the Consumer Finance Protection Bureau, the Trump-appointed

[16] On the development of White House regulatory oversight from the Nixon to the Trump administrations, see JL Mashaw et al, *Administrative Law: The American Public Law System* (St Paul, West Academic Publishing, 2019) 271–92.

[17] E Kagan, 'Presidential Administration' (2001) 114 *Harvard Law Review* 2245.

head of the agency has drastically reduced its enforcement activity. If the EPA can defend its actions in court, an open question, President Obama's Clean Power Plan will be history. The Paris Climate Change Agreement and the Iran Nuclear Deal already are. The elimination of the program of Deferred Action for Childhood Arrivals (DACA) is on judicial hold, as I will discuss below, but the incompetent explanation for its withdrawal is remediable if the administration is willing to provide a sensible explanation.

These actions, combined with President Trump's lawyers' (and the tweeter-in-chief's) recent claims to unchecked power to control all prosecutions by the Justice Department and to the authority of the President to pardon himself if necessary, may suggest that Trump is an anomaly – a President mistaking his constitutional duty to 'see that the laws are faithfully executed' for royal prerogative.

Perhaps. But the problem is deeper. The Trump administration's undoing of the Obama legacy has been made possible by the way the Obama administration constructed that legacy – through presidential administration and unilateral presidential action.[18] After claiming that he could do nothing for the so-called 'dreamers' unless Congress acted, Obama, or more properly the Department of Homeland Security, created the DACA program by an administrative enforcement guideline. Certain that Congress would not approve a climate change treaty, the Paris Climate Accord was articulated in a way that committed the United States to nothing substantive. It could therefore be structured as an executive agreement rather than as a treaty requiring Senate approval, or as an executive-congressional agreement requiring the assent of both Houses. The Iran Nuclear Deal was, from a legal perspective, even more creatively drafted to fit into the President's authority to consent to executive agreements. A reluctant Congress was again bypassed. Unable to get climate change regulation by statute, the Clean Power Plan was implemented by a series of administrative actions involving multiple agencies. In short, Trump's aggressive assertions of executive power to obliterate all things Obamaesque was made possible by Obama's similar assertions of executive power.

B. A Normative Critique

Putting aside the general policy question of whether such dramatic swings in national policy are a good thing in terms of the national welfare, or enhance America's international standing, is this what American democracy was meant to be about? Should we imagine that every presidential election is an occasion for the newly elected occupant of the White House to shout, 'The people have spoken', and set about the independent pursuit of whatever policies he or she thinks contributed to electoral success? Surely not, and for a host of reasons.

For originalists, those who justify or criticise our governing institutions on the basis of what they take to be the Founders' vision, this is (to borrow the title of Peter Shane's book) Madison's Nightmare.[19] The Founders were no friends of plebiscitary democracy.

[18] See Mashaw and Berke (n 3).

[19] PM Shane, *Madison's Nightmare: How Executive Power Threatens American Democracy* (Chicago, University of Chicago Press, 2009).

The national government was constructed precisely to avoid the tyranny of temporary majorities. The Constitution's drafters did not envision a democracy of the sort that was once described to me by a Peruvian friend. 'We have a democracy,' he said, 'We elect our dictators'.

But putting aside the Founders' visions, many of which have been consigned to the dustbin of history, presidentialism as a dominant form of governance is antithetical to democracy in two distinct ways.[20] First, presidentialism, to the extent that it involves the avoidance of congressional action, side-steps a second and important aspect of electoral democracy. Congressman and Senators are also elected, and they represent widely divergent parochial interests. Assembly government must accommodate those divergent interests in order to hammer out national policies. Those accommodations, including accommodating the views of a President whose veto power makes him or her a virtual third house of Congress, demands argument, deliberation and compromise. The separation of powers under the American Constitution is not just an institutional design for the avoidance of tyranny; it combines electoral democracy with an additional vision of democratic governance – deliberative democracy. As democratic citizens, we want more from our government by way of justification for its actions than the simple statement 'we won the election'. We want reasons for government action, an explanation of why this or that policy is good for the country, even if it is not good for some of us individually. And we want our voices to be heard not just through presidential elections but through our representatives as well. Muscular presidentialism that avoids congressional involvement in national policy making undercuts democratic governance at least as much as it supports it.

Finally, the justification offered for aggressive presidentialism, that it infuses democratic governance into the administrative state, ignores the degree to which administrative policy making has its own democratic pedigree. From the perspective of electoral democracy, policy-making administrators get their authority from statutes passed by elected officials and their positions from presidential appointments consented to by a Senate majority. They do not get their authority or offices from presidents acting independently. When challenged to justify their actions in court, administrators must point to statutory authority not presidential direction.

Perhaps even more fundamentally, the anti-democratic reputation of administrative action is misguided because it ignores the fundamentally democratic character of administrative rulemaking when analysed from the perspective of deliberative democracy. Administrators adopting regulations must make proposals published in the Federal Register. They must permit any party to make comments on those proposals. They may, and often do, hold public hearings in various parts of the country to solicit the oral views of those who support and oppose the proposed action. And when they take an action, they must justify it by giving the reasons. Those reasons must not only demonstrate that the agency has statutory authority to act and that it has an adequate factual and scientific predicate for its action, but also that it has taken account of the commentary

[20] For a more extended discussion of administrative process and democratic theory, see JL Mashaw, *Reasoned Administration and Democratic Legitimacy: How Administrative Law Supports Democratic Government* (Cambridge, Cambridge University Press, 2018) 163–79.

that it received on its proposal. Any failure to respond to a material suggestion or objection by outside commentators is a ground for judicial invalidation of the regulation for failure to provide a sufficient rationale. Nor may the agency rely on anything in justifying its regulation that is not in the record of the rulemaking proceeding, a record that is open to all and, in the digital age, easily accessible by anyone with a smartphone. Administrative rulemaking is perhaps the most open, transparent and deliberative process in all of American government. Tight presidential control of administration, control that centralises decision making in the opaque processes of the Executive Office of the President and that attempts to make all the administrative decision making a function of presidential will rather than reasoned deliberation, diminishes the democratic legitimacy of administrative governance. To add a normative perspective to Peter Cane's essentially descriptive analysis, diffusion in the American system supports democratic governance.

To be sure, as Justice Kagan argued, presidential administration *can* promote democratic governance. National presidential elections often provide evidence of a shift in majoritarian policy preferences – a shift in the majority's view of the proper agenda for national action. And some of those actions are appropriately carried out through administrative rather than legislative means. Presidents should not be faulted for responding to voters' apparent preferences by issuing directions concerning agency agendas and the appointment of officials sympathetic to the agenda that has been specified. And the requirements of administrative law, working through the medium of judicial review, can to some degree curb the excesses of presidentialism, as President Obama and President Trump have both learned. The excesses of presidentialism are always a matter of degree. Presidential administration can be democracy reinforcing if basic democratic and rule-of-law norms are respected, norms that reinforce a coordinate regime of administrative control. Without that respect we lurch toward authoritarian government.

C. Judicial Reinforcement

Given the dangers implicit in presidentialism understood as strong control of administrative action by the sitting President, one might have thought that presidential exercises of control might be met with judicial scepticism. The dominant understanding of the legitimacy of administrative action in the United States was for many years premised on some combination of delegated authority from Congress, the expertise and independence of administrators, and the representation of multiple interests in the administrative process.[21] However, in 1984 in *Chevron USA Inc v Natural Resources Defense Council, Inc*,[22] the Supreme Court imported political control by the President directly into administrative law doctrine. The question before the Court was how much deference should be paid to an agency's interpretation of its own statute. The Court's response was that unless Congress had spoken directly to the issue that the agency had to decide, the

[21] RB Stewart, 'The Reformation of American Administrative Law' (1975) 88 *Harvard Law Review* 1667.
[22] *Chevron, USA, Inc v Natural Resources Defense Council, Inc*, 467 US 837 (1984).

agency's interpretation of its own authority and of the appropriate policy choice to be made under the statute should be affirmed provided that choice was a reasonable one, whether or not a court thought that the choice was the best choice available. The Court premised this apparently strong form of deference both on agency expertise and on political control. In the Court's words

> [A]n agency to which Congress has delegated policymaking responsibilities may, within the limits of that delegation properly rely upon the incumbent administration's views of wise policy to inform its judgments. While agencies are not directly accountable to the people, the Chief Executive is, and it is entirely appropriate for this political branch of government to make such policy choices ….[23]

Certainly, there are good arguments for preferring political policy choice to judicial policy choice. And there are also reasonable arguments for preferring that interpretation of technical statutes be informed by the understanding of those who have lived with them and have the responsibility for implementing them.

However, other developments have tended to marginalise expert judgement in favour of political control. A thick layer of political appointees now sits atop most agencies and bureaus. And the polarisation of politics in the United States, leading to much more rigidly defined political parties, has made political control through presidential appointment a much more potent force in agency decisionmaking. While presidents continue to review agency policy choice through the Office of Management and Budget and issue directives designed to set and channel agency agendas, control can now be exercised implicitly through the appointment of ideologically aligned agency personnel.

The Supreme Court's approach to these developments has been to double down on presidential control. First, the Court has made clear that Congress may not insert itself into either the appointment or removal of administrative personnel save through the constitutionally-specified mechanisms of Senate advice and approval of the heads of departments and agencies and Congress's constitutional power over removal by impeachment. In addition, the Court has recently whittled away at congressional authority to provide some independence to agency decision makers through 'for-cause' removal provisions. These removal cases are particularly important for understanding the degree to which administrative law doctrine now supports a vision of the 'unitary executive' that both centralises and politicises administrative action.

It is fair to say that the courts' jurisprudence on the removal power has always been something of a mess. The issue of congressional restrictions on the removal of officers did not reach the Supreme Court until 1926 in *Myers v United States*.[24] This was a suit for back pay by the estate of a postmaster of the second class who was removed from office in violation of the Tenure of Office Act. That statute required that officers appointed by the President and confirmed by the Senate be removed only with the Senate's approval.

[23] ibid 865.
[24] *Myers v United States*, 272 US 52 (1926).

In opinions that stretched over 243 pages of the original US Reports, ex-President Taft, then Chief Justice of the US for the majority, and Justices Brandeis and Holmes in dissent, examined the debates in the First Congress, the ratification debates in the states and subsequent early discussions and practices. In the end, the majority found that the Tenure of Office Act unconstitutionally interfered with the President's power of removal by giving the Senate a role in the removal process that was not authorised by the text of the Constitution. Of course, the President's removal power is nowhere specified under the Constitution either, but dicta in the majority opinion strongly suggested that the Constitution's lodging of 'the executive power' in the President, demanded that the President have unfettered authority to remove executive officers.

Those dicta seemed to have been rejected only ten years later in *Humphrey's Executor v United States*.[25] The problem in *Humphrey's* was that President Roosevelt, when removing Humphrey from the Federal Trade Commission (FTC), had failed to specify any cause for his removal, as the Federal Trade Commission Act required. In a somewhat tortured majority opinion the Court decided that the FTC did not exercise executive power and therefore did not run afoul of *Myers*' broad dicta. On the majority's view the FTC was 'quasi-legislative' and 'quasi-judicial' rather than executive. What does that mean? Apparently, because the FTC decides cases it is quasi-judicial and because it has authority to adopt the rules it is quasi-legislative. The FTC's investigative powers were also classified as quasi-legislative.

The opinion in *Humphrey's Executor* did not make much sense. FTC commissioners are not judges and they are not legislators. Their task is to implement a federal statute and that is an executive function. These officers are executive officers and the Court's distinction of the postmaster in *Myers* as exercising purely 'executive' function hardly bears examination. The Post Office makes rules about what can be carried in the mail and postmasters make judgements about whether things that are presented for carriage satisfy those rules. The Court provided no explanation for why these functions are not quasi-legislative and quasi-judicial.

The general understanding of how to harmonise *Humphrey's* with *Myers* settled on a simple explanation: The *Myers* case involved Congress inserting itself into the removal process. In *Humphrey's* there was no such 'aggrandisement' of congressional power and therefore separation of powers was not really implicated. This understanding of the fountainhead cases on the removal powers seems to be confirmed 50 years later in *Bowsher v Synar*,[26] which held that statutory provisions allowing Congress to remove the Controller General by statute were unconstitutional. But *Bowsher v Synar* was a confusing a case in which only a plurality of the Court believed that the Controller General was an executive officer who could not have tenure dependent upon congressional action. Other members of the Court reached the same result by classifying the Controller General as a legislative officer who had been authorised to adopt legislation without going through the process of bicameralism and presentment.

And the next case involving for-cause removal provisions seemed to drive a stake into the heart of the *Myers* opinion. *Morrison v Olson*[27] involved a challenge to the

[25] *Humphrey's Executor v United States*, 295 US 602 (1935).
[26] *Bowsher v Synar*, 478 US 714 (1986).
[27] *Morrison v Olson*, 487 US 654 (1988).

independent counsel provisions of the Ethics and Government Act of 1978. This so-called 'independent counsel' statute gave a specially appointed prosecutor the authority to investigate allegations of criminal conduct against high federal officials. The statute granted the independent counsel 'full power and independent authority to exercise all investigative and prosecutorial functions and the powers of the Department of Justice, the Attorney General, and any other officer or employee of the Department of Justice' other than functions relating to wiretap applications.[28] The Act further provided:

> An independent counsel appointed by this chapter may be removed from office, other than by impeachment and conviction, only by the personal action of the Attorney General and only for good cause, physical disability, mental incapacity, or any other condition that substantially impairs the performance of such independent councils' duties.[29]

Here was surely an executive officer exercising purely executive functions. If the *Myers* dicta represented sound constitutional doctrine these provisions should have been unconstitutional. Not so, said the Supreme Court. The Supreme Court skated its way around *Myers* and *Humphrey's Executor* and offered an entirely new test for constitutionality of restrictions on the President's removal power in the following terms:

> Appellees contend that *Humphrey's Executor* … [is] distinguishable from this case because [it] did not involve officials who performed a 'core executive function'. They argued that the decision in *Humphrey's Executor* rests on a distinction between 'purely executive' officials and officials who exercise 'quasi-legislative' and 'quasi-judicial' powers. In their view when a 'purely executive' official is involved, the governing precedent is *Myers* not *Humphrey's Executor* ….
>
> We undoubtedly did rely on the terms 'quasi-executive' and 'quasi-judicial' to distinguish the officials in *Humphrey's Executor* from those in *Myers*, but our present considered view is that the determination of whether the Constitution allows Congress to impose a 'good cause'-type restriction on the President's power to remove an official cannot be made to turn on whether or not that official is classified as 'purely executive' ….
>
> Considering for the moment the 'good cause' removal provision in isolation from the other parts of the Act …, we cannot say that the imposition of a 'good cause' standard for removal by itself unduly trammels on executive authority ….
>
> Nor do we think that the 'good cause' removal provision at issue here impermissibly burdens the President's power to control or supervise the independent counsel, as an executive official, in the execution of her duties under the Act …. [B]ecause the independent counsel may be terminated for 'good cause' the executive through the Attorney General retains ample authority to assure that the council is competently performing her statutory responsibilities in a manner that comports with the provisions of the Act.[30]

The majority opinion in *Morrison* comes very close to establishing a principled basis for determining whether for-cause removal restrictions in fact invade any legitimate power that the President holds under the Constitution. At least implicitly, the majority opinion views the President's constitutional authority to oversee executive officers as limited to the authority to ensure 'faithful execution' of the laws. That, of course,

[28] ibid 662.
[29] ibid 663.
[30] ibid 689–93.

is the principal domestic responsibility that the Constitution gives the President. Because the majority opinion also seems to view the 'causes' embedded in a good cause removal requirement as encompassing any conduct that would interfere with faithful execution, requiring that the President state a cause creates no improper interference with the President's constitutional responsibilities.

However, the *Morrison* majority opinion does not quite articulate this straightforward principle. Instead it adopts a vague standard of whether a provision 'unduly trammels' the President's executive authority. Moreover, the majority fails to ground its conclusions in a clear statement that would distinguish between administrative powers derived from legislation and powers that the President holds independently under the Constitution, but may delegate to others. Where administrators' competences come from Congress, the President's directive authority would seem properly limited to ensuring faithful execution, but not necessarily so with respect to independent powers that the President holds based on the Constitution alone. And because the Court suggested that there might be some yet unspecified group of officers for whom for-cause removal would be improper, the door was left open for further developments that might muddy the waters.

Free Enterprise Fund v Public Company Accounting Oversight Board[31] (PCAOB) stirred up this silt and breathed new life into *Myers*. The *PCAOB* case involved an objection to the for-cause removal provisions included in that Board's statute because the Board members were removable by the Securities and Exchange Commission (SEC), a Commission whose members were (by stipulation of the parties, not by statute) also subject only to removal for-cause. In finding this double for-cause provision unconstitutional, the majority began by resuscitating *Myers* as the fountainhead of removal jurisprudence. It treated its subsequent decisions in *Humphrey's* and *Morrison* as limited exceptions to the *Myers* principal that presidents, as an inherent aspect of the executive power, must be able to hold officers accountable by removing them. Because *PCAOB* presented a novel question, the Court viewed *PCAOB* as asking whether this too fell within previously established exceptions. The answer was no, although it is not clear from the opinion why. The opinion simply concludes that double for-cause protection 'contravenes the President's constitutional obligation to ensure the faithful execution of the laws'.[32]

Presumably the constitutional infirmity was that the President could not remove SEC commissioners who failed to remove PCAOB board members who in the President's view were not faithfully executing the law. But there is no explanation of why this is a problem. SEC commissioners who failed to remove faithless PCAOB members are failing to exercise their responsibility under the law and should be therefore removable. Moreover, as Justice Breyer pointed out in his dissent, invalidating the for-cause removal provisions in the PCAOB statute did nothing to further the President's power to remove PCAOB members. That authority is still lodged with the SEC and its commissioners are subject to removal only for cause. Indeed, that for-cause removal provision prevents a president from keeping a PCAOB member that the President would prefer to keep but the SEC wishes to remove.

[31] *Free Enterprise Fund v Public Company Accounting Oversight Board*, 561 US 477 (2010).
[32] ibid 484.

The other shoe cementing a constitutional presumption of unfettered presidential removal authority dropped in *Seila Law v Consumer Finance Protection Bureau*[33] *(CFPB)*, in the Court's 2019 term. The CFPB is an agency established by the Dodd-Frank financial reform legislation. It is headed by a single administrator who is removable only for cause. And, as the majority opinion put the question in the case, it was whether presidential power to remove principal officers, that is, those required by the Constitution to be appointed by the President and confirmed by the Senate, is a necessary feature of the President having been 'vested' with 'the executive power' by article 2. The majority answered 'Yes'. Indeed it went further when it interpreted the *Myers* case as establishing a general rule of unencumbered presidential removal for all executive officers. Cases permitting for-cause removal since *Myers* were distinguished as either involving multi-member commissions (*Humphrey's Executor*) or as involving inferior officers (*Morrison v Olson*). *Free Enterprise v PCAOB* was interpreted as reaffirming *Myers* and as refusing to extend the *Humphrey's* exception beyond the facts of that case.

There are many puzzles about the potential reach of *Seila Law v CFPB*. Principal among them is whether the exceptions for multi-member agencies (*Humphrey's*) or inferior officers (*Morrison v Olson*) remain relevant. It is surely easier to remove one officer in a single-headed agency than to remove several if a president wants to change the direction of a multi-member commission. And if *Myers* is the landmark decision that establishes the general rule, it is a decision that relates to inferior officers, a postmaster of the second class. But these and other puzzles need not detain us.

The important point for current purposes is that a Supreme Court majority now seems to view the Vesting Clause in article 2 as providing a broad and inherent set of implied powers, including the power to remove executive officers at will, entirely divorced from the President's principal responsibility under article II to see that the laws are faithfully executed. This is tantamount to the conclusion that any authority given to any executive officer by congressional legislation is by constitutional implication given to the President. The President can direct how that authority is to be used and remove any officer who fails to follow the President's direction.

Article I of the Constitution, which gives Congress the authority to make all laws necessary and proper for the carrying out of the responsibilities of any branch of the government and any of its departments, simply does not figure in the analysis. This is a very strong form of concentration of the power to control administration. It places a heavy thumb on the scales that balance presidential and congressional power in favour of the executive. The remaining question is whether judicial review of administrative action tends to redress the balance.

IV. Judicial Review, Congressional Control and the Demand for Reasons

Judicial review of administrative action in some form has been a feature of American public law since the founding of the Republic. Throughout the nineteenth century,

[33] *Seila Law v Consumer Finance Protection Bureau*, 140 S Ct 2183 (2020).

however, review was limited to common law actions against officials and to very truncated forms of mandamus and injunction.[34] In essence, review in these latter forms was unavailable if statutes gave an officer any discretion in implementing the law. The reasonableness of official action was not justiciable. Indeed, federal courts viewed any attempt to provided broader substantive review of executive actions as a violation of separation of powers – as thrusting the courts into administration. In short, for the first hundred years of the Republic, control of administration, to the extent that administrative discretion was involved, was left to the political branches of the government.

These limitations began to break down in the early twentieth century. By the mid-twentieth century a focus on the reasoning provided for administrative decisions, particularly in rulemaking, was emerging as an important strain in the so-called 'hard look' approach to judicial review of administrative action. In succeeding decades, particularly following the iconic decision in the *State Farm*[35] case, it became clear that the demand for reasoned decision-making had multiple sources.

Constitutional due process requires that reasons be given for administrative adjudications whenever private parties have rights to some form of adjudicatory hearing.[36] The Administrative Procedure Act[37] and other more specific statutes demand reason-giving in connection with a host of agency functions, including virtually any agency action that has either individual or general legal effect. Many of these requirements were premised on either the need to facilitate appropriate judicial review in a system of separated powers or to protect rights of participation in agency proceedings. In most cases reason giving supported both purposes.

Over time, these requirements for reason-giving became increasingly demanding. On judicial review, agencies may not rely on facts or arguments not previously ventilated in the administrative record.[38] Agency processes must give adequate notice of the issues to be decided[39] and agency decisions must explain their consideration and acceptance or rejection of the facts or arguments offered by participants in their proceedings. In rulemaking proceedings, any interested person may participate, and agencies must respond to petitions for the adoption, amendment, or rescission of a rule.

Many of these requirements emanate from judicial decisions, but both statutes and executive orders have broadened the topics about which administrators must reason when making decisions.[40] The demand that agencies consider environmental effects, cost effectiveness, the balance of costs and benefits, effects of agency action on small entities and vulnerable populations, the distributional effects of governmental

[34] On judicial review of administrative action in the early republic, see JL Mashaw, *Creating the Administrative Constitution: The Lost 100 Years of American Administrative Law* (New Haven, Yale University Press, 2012) 65–80.

[35] *Motor Vehicle Mfr Ass'n of US, Inc v State Farm Mutual Automobile Ins Co*, 463 US 29 (1983).

[36] The basic requirements for administrative due process are elaborated in *Goldberg v Kelly*, 97 US 254 (1970).

[37] The Federal Administrative Procedure Act is at 5 USC §551 ff.

[38] *Securities and Exchange Comm'n v Chenery, Corp*, 332 US 194 (1947).

[39] See, eg, *United States v Nova Scotia Food Products Corp*, 568 F 2d 240 (2nd Cir 1977).

[40] These requirements are embodied in a number of statutes and executive orders. See, eg, the National Environmental Policy Act, Pub L No 91 190, 83 Stat 852 91970) (codified at 42 USC §4321 ff. The Regulatory Flexibility Act, Pub L No 96-354, 94 Stat 1164 (1980) (codified as amended at 5 USC §601 ff); and Executive Order No 13,563, Improving Regulation and Regulatory Review, 76 Fed Reg 3, 821 (2011).

action, or effects on the balance of authority between state and federal government, all broaden the range of topics that mission-specific agencies must reason about and, simultaneously, the individual and group interests that they must take into account. In a broad sense these anti-tunnel-vision requirements are focused on making administrative action that might be instrumentally rational from the perspective of an agency's particular mission more substantively reasonable when viewed from the broader perspective of competing public goals and values.

This description paints with a broad brush, and we will shortly take up some of the limitations on the power of judicial review to diffuse power concerning the control of administrative action. But, taken together, administrative law's contemporary reasonableness demands aspire to construct a system of administrative governance that is well-informed, highly participatory, complexly interconnected with political and legal monitors and insulated against – although surely not immune from – the seizure of public power for private or partisan gain. And, as I have argued at length elsewhere,[41] these requirements construct a regime of administrative governance that, whatever its faults, yields forms of public action that are democratically legitimate viewed from the perspective of either theories of electoral or aggregate democracy or theories that focus more on the availability of participatory and deliberative processes. They also make the control regime more diffuse.

Reasoned administration thus challenges presidentialism and the concentration of authority that presidentialism represents. At one level this competition is obvious. Absent those cases in which the President has either constitutional or statutory authority to act unilaterally, administrators cannot simply say 'the President made me do it' as a justification for administrative action. For example, President Clinton famously proclaimed in the Rose Garden that he had authorised the Food and Drug Administration (FDA) to regulate tobacco pursuant to the Food, Drug and Cosmetic Act.[42] In the litigation following the FDA's efforts to do so, the President's purported 'authorisation' was not mentioned. The FDA was required to approach the question of regulating tobacco within the parameters of the relevant statutes. And, notwithstanding the capaciousness of the definition of 'drug' under the Food, Drug and Cosmetic Act, the Supreme Court was quite clear that Congress had not intended to include tobacco products in that definition.[43] Judicial review thus reinforces congressional control as established by statute, at least to the extent that congressional purposes seem clear to the reviewing court. To that degree judicial review preserves the diffusion of powers of control over administrative action, the control of prior congresses expressed in legislation.

This limitation on political direction should not be over-read, however. In an important decision, the late Judge Patricia Wald of the District of Columbia Court of Appeals made clear that political judgement, including the basic policies of a contemporary presidential administration, would inevitably colour the decisions made by administrative agencies faced with conflicting statutory demands and uncertain factual or scientific predicates.[44] But that is quite different from saying that political considerations

[41] Mashaw (n 20) 163–79.
[42] See Kagan (n 17) 2282–84.
[43] *FDA v Brown & Williamson Tobacco Corp*, 529 US 120 (2000).
[44] *Public Citizen v Young*, 831 F 2d 1108 (DC Cir 1987).

themselves are justificatory. And, while courts are reluctant to probe whether decisions that are otherwise appropriately reasoned are in fact based on different and illicit or irrelevant political motives, the Supreme Court has recently been hospitable to claims that agency action taken to align with presidential preferences may be investigated to determine whether the reasons given are a mere pretext for illicit political motivations not made relevant by an agency's statutory mandates.

In *Trump v Hawaii*,[45] for example, the Supreme Court was willing, over strenuous objection, to entertain the question whether the Trump administration's ban on travel from six predominately Muslim countries was predicated on an illicit religious animus, a propensity that President Trump had exhibited throughout his campaign for President. The travel ban, in its third and much more restricted form, was approved, but on the basis of a lengthy multi-agency study of the national security implications of allowing travel from nations with large numbers of potential terrorists and inadequate systems for vetting travelers to the United States.

Department of Commerce v New York[46] carried this hospitality toward claims of pretextual justifications one step further when it invalidated the Department of Commerce's attempt to add a citizenship question to the 2020 census. The complaining parties were allowed to demonstrate that the purported justification for adding the citizenship question simply had no basis in fact. As Chief Justice John Roberts wrote, in a sentence that surely understated the clarity with which the facts demonstrated that the government's rationale was false, 'We are presented, in other words, with an explanation for agency action that is incongruent with what the record reveals about the agency's priorities and decision-making process.'[47]

Finally, in *Department of Homeland Security v Regents of the University of California*,[48] the Supreme Court invalidated the government's attempt to rescind the Obama administration's DACA program. The Court, again via an opinion by the Chief Justice, relied almost exclusively on the failure of the Department to provide adequate reasons for its rescission. Not only was the rescission predicated on an inadequate legal conclusion, the agency had failed to consider a number of other matters that the Court viewed as essential to reasoned decision-making.

The transparency of the Trump administration's attempts to take actions that align with the President's view of immigrants and immigration policy surely contributed to the Supreme Court's willingness to enter the troubled waters of uncovering pretextual political reasons. But these cases illustrate the general idea that reason-giving has now become fundamental to the legitimacy of administrative action. As the Chief Justice put it in the census case, 'The reasoned explanation required by administrative law is meant to ensure that agencies offer genuine justifications for important decisions.… Accepting contrived reasons would defeat the purpose of the enterprise.'[49]

Judicial review demanding that administrators use the appropriate procedures under the Administrative Procedure Act for changing existing regulations and defects

[45] *Trump v Hawaii*, 138 S Ct 2392 (2018).
[46] *Department of Commerce v New York*, 139 S Ct 2551 (2019).
[47] ibid 2575.
[48] *Department of Homeland Security v Regents of the University of California*, 140 S Ct 1891 (2020).
[49] *Department of Commerce*, 139 S Ct, 2551, 2575–76 (2019).

in the reasons given for those changes have derailed a fair number of deregulatory actions in the Trump administration. The Institute for Policy Integrity at New York University School of Law has calculated that only 14 per cent of the Trump administration's regulatory actions have been upheld against challenge in the lower federal courts.[50] Trump's recent predecessors, by contrast, won about 60 per cent of the time. But, again, one should not over interpret these results. These cases largely involve remands for reconsideration. The Trump administration's actions have been hasty and often incompetent, but most have not been permanently blocked. If administrators repair the defects in their procedures and explanations, they are likely to be sustained. Some initiatives, like adding a citizenship question to the census, have been abandoned, presumably because the administration simply had no legitimate reason for this change. Moreover, there was abundant evidence that as a way of providing an accurate enumeration of persons resident in the United States, this was a bad idea. In many other situations, however, the administration simply has to do its homework and it will likely prevail on some version of its original proposal.

The reason for the limited impact of judicial invalidation is not hard to find. As the Supreme Court noted in the *Chevron* case, there are solid grounds for judicial deference to agency policy choice. Hence, while the Administrative Procedure Act authorises substantive judicial review for arbitrariness or lack of substantial evidence, courts have largely proceduralised these apparently substantive provisions. The courts look to see whether an agency has given reasons, whether those reasons track the criteria that are made relevant by the authorising statute, and whether the agency has indulged considerations that are foreclosed by a reasonable interpretation of the agency's statutory authority. They also look to see whether the agency's factual determinations are plausibly supported by the evidence in the administrative record. But, courts do not substitute their substantive policy judgements for administrators, nor do they require that administrators who are changing prior policies demonstrate that their new policies are better than the old ones. By demanding that administrators reason within the confines of their statutory authority, courts reinforce the separation and diffusion of powers between the political branches of the US government. By deferring on substantive matters to agency judgements, the courts support the separation of powers understanding that an independent and unelected judiciary is not meant to make government policy. And they simultaneously reinforce presidential powers of control and direction.

Finally, we should recognise that there is a large domain of presidential and administrative decision-making that is scarcely subject to judicial review at all. Over a hundred statutes provide for extraordinary administrative powers whenever a president declares 'an emergency'.[51] Actions taken under these emergency powers may be reviewable if a plaintiff can be found who can satisfy rigorous standing requirements. But the President is not subject to review under the Administrative Procedure Act and, even if she were, statutes providing for emergency declarations seldom provide any standards for

[50] *Roundup: Trump-Era Agency Policy in the Courts*, Institute for Policy Integrity (2020), https://policyintegrity.org/trump-court-roundup, accessed 5 July 2021.

[51] A list of statutes providing emergency powers as of 2019 can be found at *A Guide to Emergency Powers and Their Use*, Brennan Center for Justice, https://www.brennancenter.org/our-work/research-reports/guide-emergency-powers-and-their-use.

determining whether the emergency was properly declared. Such declarations are essentially nonjusticiable. Congress has the power of the purse, supposedly, but presidential administrations have vast authority to determine how money is spent. And, it is black letter law that administrative inaction, absent some clear statutory requirement that action be taken is rarely subject to judicial review.[52] No agency can do all that it is authorised to do, and courts feel that they have no capacity to determine, again save in rare instances, how an agency should set its agenda. An administration promising deregulation, like the Trump administration, can achieve many of its goals simply by not adopting any new regulation and by failing to enforce those already in place.

In the end, judicial review is a brake on hasty and incompetent administration, or simple law breaking by an aggressive presidential administration, but there are very large gaps in the degree to which judicial review can maintain diffuse centres of control over administration in the face of determined presidential control.

V. Conclusion

The control regime with respect to administrative action established by American constitutional and administrative law is indeed diffuse in relation to regimes more nearly approximating the Westminster parliamentary system. And, I have not here emphasised the many informal ways in which that diffusion is reinforced by internal processes and legal controls within administration, or norms of comity that lead agencies and the Executive Office of the President to consult with Congress through its relevant committee before taking actions that the administration believes will be controversial.[53]

Nevertheless, as the title of this chapter suggests, I believe that there has been over the last several decades a fairly steady erosion of congressional controls over administration and a significant concentration of control in the presidency and the substantial bureaucracy that is now the Executive Office of the President. There have been, of course, ebbs and flows affecting the balance of powers between the executive and legislative branches over the course of US constitutional history. Federalism also complicates the degree to which governmental power can be concentrated in either political branch within the federal government. Whether the current trend toward concentration of power in the executive will be reversed is anyone's guess. History suggests that it can be. Perhaps that is the critical lesson that we should take away from Peter Cane's comparative analysis of administrative control regimes. A regime of diffused powers leaves unsettled in many circumstances who should be in control of administration as well as well as who will be.

[52] *Heckler v Chaney*, 470 US 821 (1985).

[53] See generally J Goldsmith, *Power and Constraint: The Accountable Presidency After 9/11* (New York, WW Norton & Co, 2012).

PART III

Intersections

8

Administrative Compensation: Bypass or Dead End?

CAROL HARLOW

I. The 'Fundamental Tenet'

A noteworthy feature of the common law systems of the United Kingdom and Commonwealth is the absence of any fixed boundary between what is public and what is private. Officially, they operate under the principle that:

> The state and its officers are subject to the ordinary processes of law in much the same manner as all other persons are governed by law. Public authorities, therefore, hold no special status in the legal ordering of our society and there is nothing peculiar in the application of legal method to disputes involving public bodies. Our [United Kingdom] constitution is a product of the ordinary law of the land and the position of the state and its emanations is determined by general principles of private law.[1]

Cane, in an article discussing the relationship between the civil law remedy of damages and the public law concept of illegality, has called this 'the fundamental tenet' of the English public law system.[2]

The 'fundamental tenet' has its uses. It reflects an egalitarian attitude to officialdom; it helps, as Aronson once remarked, 'to put government on a level playing field with the rest of us'.[3] But the sense of equality that it purports to embody is essentially misleading. According to Cane, 'English courts are disinclined to apply the (private) law of tort in unmodified form to organs of government'[4] and, as generations of judges and academics have noted, public authorities possess, and their officials act under, powers that are not available to the general public or to private corporations.[5] The state has many

[1] M Loughlin, *Public Law and Political Theory* (Oxford, Clarendon Press, 1992) 1.

[2] P Cane, 'Damages in Public Law' (1999) 9 *Otago Law Review* 489.

[3] M Aronson, 'Government Liability in Negligence' (2008) 32 *Melbourne University Law Review* 44.

[4] P Cane, 'Accountability and the Public/Private Distinction' in N Bamforth and P Leyland (eds), *Public Law in a Multi-Layered Constitution* (Oxford, Hart Publishing, 2003) 247.

[5] WI Jennings, *The Law and the Constitution*, 5th edn (London, University of London Press, 1959) 312; ECS Wade, 'Introduction' in AV Dicey, *Introduction to the Study of the Law of the Constitution*, 10th edn (London, MacMillan, 1959) cxx–cxxvi.

obligations that do not fall on private shoulders. Human rights law does not apply to private parties and can be claimed only against emanations of the state. The application for judicial review in England and Wales (with which Cane's paper dealt) is a specialised public law procedure dispensed by a specialised branch of the High Court and is not available against private parties. A specialised procedure governs public procurement – admittedly at the behest of the European Union – while misfeasance in public office is a nominate tort and sometimes a criminal offence and misfeasance in private office is not.[6] Should we then continue to insist that the state or government or public authorities and bodies – I use these terms loosely – be aligned with private parties for purposes of civil liability as, with modifications, they continue to be in common law legal systems? Or should we go for special principles or even a separate system of liability?

The 'fundamental tenet' has created many doctrinal problems for the law of torts, for which many solutions have been suggested – the most comprehensive being to sweep the existing system away and install, as French-style systems do, a separate system of administrative liability,[7] a solution that I for one have always rejected.[8] In section II of this paper, I look briefly at the fate of some of the efforts at reform. My main objective is, however, to look at ways in which problems of government liability might be bypassed or at least alleviated without recourse to the tort system. In section III, I consider Cane's solution, suggested many years ago in his innovative article on damages as a public law remedy.[9]

In section IV I consider the tradition of administrative compensation and ex gratia payments, distinguishing 'damages' from 'compensation', terms that many lawyers see as interchangeable. In tort law, 'compensatory damages' are considered the norm. Lord Bingham, contrasting tort law and human rights, once described the role of tort law as being 'to provide monetary compensation for those who have suffered material damage rather than to vindicate the rights of those who have not'.[10] In this paper, however, I reserve the term 'compensation' for monetary payments to address loss or damage suffered, made by government (using this term inclusively) without legal liability. Such damage may be caused by fault or illegality but compensatory payments may also be made in the absence of fault. I shall look for an umbrella concept sufficiently robust to act as a general principle of compensation. I shall touch on the questions whether administrative compensation schemes need parliamentary authorisation and whether they can be sufficiently systematic and fair to engender public confidence.

[6] M Aronson, 'Misfeasance in Public Office: a Very Peculiar Tort' (2011) 35 *Melbourne University Law Review* 1; M Aronson, 'Misfeasance in Public Office: Some Unfinished Business' (2016) 132 *LQR* 426.

[7] See, eg, T Cornford, *Towards a Public Law of Torts* (Aldershot, Ashgate Publishing, 2008) and for a comparison of the two systems, D Fairgrieve, *State Liability in Tort* (Oxford, Oxford University Press, 2003).

[8] C Harlow, '"Public" and "Private" Law: Definition Without Distinction' (1980) 43 *Melbourne Law Review* 241; C Harlow, *Compensation and Government Torts* (London, Sweet & Maxwell, 1982); C Harlow, 'Public and Private Law: A Redundant Divide' in J Varuhas and S Wilson Stark (eds), *The Frontiers of Public Law* (Oxford, Hart Publishing, 2019).

[9] Cane (n 2).

[10] *Watkins v Secretary of State for the Home Department* [2006] UKHL 17, [2006] AC 395 [9]. And see Lord Bingham, 'Tort and Human Rights' in P Cane and J Stapleton (eds), *The Law of Obligations, Essays in Celebration of John Fleming* (Oxford, Clarendon Press, 1998).

II. Damages in Public Law

Historically in English administrative law, judicial review was not the main avenue of redress for those seeking monetary compensation from a public body and damages were not among the public law remedies for unlawful administrative action. There were many reasons for this, not the least being that the application for judicial review was a twentieth century innovation; traditionally, public law redress came in the shape of named prerogative orders of habeas corpus, certiorari, prohibition and mandamus, etc, each affording a single specific form of redress: certiorari was, for example, a quashing order, while mandamus issued orders to the administration. Towards the end of the nineteenth century and start of the twentieth century, the equitable remedies of injunction and declaratory judgment came to be added to the toolkit of public law.[11] Before the Crown Proceedings Act 1947, it was not possible to sue the Crown for damages, although other public bodies could be held liable in tort.

In 1969, shortly after the Law Commission for England and Wales was created, it set its sights on a wide-ranging reform of administrative law. It asked for a Royal Commission to conduct a comprehensive inquiry in which the question 'How far should remedies in respect of administrative acts and omissions include the right to damages?' would be included.[12] The idea was rejected by the Lord Chancellor. The Government did not then allow and has never since allowed this or a similar question to be included in a Law Commission programme.

The Law Commission was left with only a narrow mandate to review the form and procedure of the prerogative orders; substantive issues, including the question of damages, were excluded. The unified application for judicial review that resulted from the Law Commission's report[13] combined access to the prerogative orders in a single application for judicial review but retained the private law character of damages.[14] The power to award damages in an application for judicial review is today statutory and retains the restrictive formula that a court in awarding damages must be 'satisfied that such an award would have been made if the claim had been made in an action begun by the applicant at the time of making the application'.[15] In other words, it adopts the 'fundamental tenet' approach by retaining a link between damages and civil liability.

The JUSTICE/All Souls Committee (an unofficial Royal Commission that took over the Law Commission's wider remit)[16] devoted a whole chapter to

[11] See the early editions of SA de Smith's *Judicial Review of Administrative Action* (first ed London: Stevens & Co, 1959). The use of the declaration as a public law remedy is generally dated to the case of *Dyson v Attorney-General* [1911] 1 KB 410 and [1912] 1 Ch 158 (CA): see SA de Smith, *Judicial Review of Administrative Action*, 3rd edn (London, Sweet & Maxwell, 1973) 428–31.

[12] Law Commission, *Administrative Law* (Cmnd 4059, 1969).

[13] Law Commission, *Remedies in Administrative Law* (Law Com No 73, 1976).

[14] Order 53 of the Rules of the Supreme Court 1977/1955, later ss 31(4)(a) and (b) of the Supreme Court Act 1981 (UK), now renamed the Senior Courts Act 1981 (UK). In addition to damages, the Act now authorises 'restitution or the recovery of a sum due'.

[15] Senior Courts Act 1981 (UK), s 31(4)(b), inserted by SI 2004/1033.

[16] As its name suggests, the Committee was a joint academic initiative of JUSTICE, a branch of the International Commission of Jurists, and All Souls College, Oxford. It was chaired by the Warden of All Souls and funded by the Leverhulme Trust and other private donors: see JUSTICE /All Souls Review, *Administrative Justice – Some Necessary Reforms* (Oxford, Clarendon Press, 1988) App 2, 369.

administrative compensation. The Committee noted that 'the law takes no account of the fact that the administration is capable of inflicting damage in ways which a private person cannot' and that, in contrast to continental legal systems, courts in the United Kingdom had no power to award 'damages' for the 'many types of wrongful administrative conduct that do not fit into the recognized common law categories'.[17] It pronounced that reform was clearly needed and recommended legislation to provide for compensation for 'material injury caused either by wrongful acts or omissions or by unreasonable or excessive delay'. The Committee had brought the question of compensation on to the agenda, but in the form of a legal right to 'compensation', enforceable in the courts. It goes without saying that no such legislation found its way on to the legislative agenda.

A. Human Rights

By the turn of the century, the Human Rights Act 1998 was in force and the Law Commission, at the request of the Government, published a report on damages in human rights cases. The Commission spoke in terms of compensation rather than liability and thought that implementation of the Human Rights Act would not require major changes to the law on damages:

> The Strasbourg Court seeks to compensate applicants under the Convention fully for any loss which they can prove resulted from a violation of the Convention. Where courts in this country have established appropriate levels of compensation for particular types of loss in relation to claims in tort or delict, it would seem appropriate for the same rules to be used in relation to a claim under the Human Rights Act 1998.[18]

In fact, the formulation of the Human Rights Act 1998 is confusing and leaves many unresolved problems for the courts to deal with. The Act empowers a court which finds the act of a public authority unlawful to grant redress in the form of 'such relief or remedy within its powers as it considers just and appropriate' (section 8(1)), while limiting the award of damages to cases where, taking account of all the circumstances of the case including alternative remedies, 'the court is satisfied that the award is necessary to afford just satisfaction to the person in whose favour it is made' (section 8(3)). This is to treat damages as a form of public law redress and as a subsidiary tool in the toolkit of judicial remedies. Yet an implicit link with existing civil law is retained, as the Act restricts the courts entitled to award human rights damages to those competent 'to award damages, or to order the payment of compensation, in civil proceedings' (section 8(2)).[19] On the other hand, section 8(4) obliges the court to 'take into account the principles applied by the Strasbourg Court of Human Rights (ECtHR) in relation to the award of compensation under Article 41 of the Convention'. Article 41 makes no specific mention of damages or of compensation but simply empowers the Court of

[17] ibid ch 11, 331 and 364.

[18] Law Commission, *Damages Under the Human Rights Act 1998* (Law Com No 266, 2000) iv.

[19] The subsection was intended to prevent the award of damages as compensation by criminal courts and to inhibit the spread of compensation by tribunals that would not otherwise be empowered to award compensation.

Human Rights in limited circumstances to 'afford just satisfaction to the injured party'. The overall effect of section 8 is therefore to move damages in human rights cases away from the civil law, and, indeed, outside the common law altogether, though preserving a tenuous link with tort law.

This thread the English courts proceeded to snap with two restrictive rulings based on the proposition that the Human Rights Act 1998 is not a tort statute but has different and broader objectives. The primary remedy for a violation of human rights is the finding of violation, which is a central part of the 'just satisfaction' to which the complainant is entitled. In this, the House of Lords in the leading case of *Greenfield*[20] was duly following the practice of the ECtHR, which habitually treats the finding of the violation as *in itself* just satisfaction under article 41. Consequently, and in line with the probable intention of the UK legislature, damages would not be patterned on tort law damages but on the 'just satisfaction' awards made by the Court of Human Rights. This choice, which also reflects a traditional judicial prudence with public funds, was a net loss to victims of human rights violations, since Strasbourg awards are relatively ungenerous and only exceptionally substantial.[21]

The early *Bernard* decision[22] shows, however, how the Human Rights Act 1998 can be used creatively as a basis for compensating human rights violations. Enfield Council, the local housing authority, had for several years housed the disabled claimant and her family in accommodation manifestly unsuited to her disablement and likened by the court to a pigsty. When, after a long struggle, the family succeeded in showing in a judicial review application a violation of the claimant's rights to private and family life under article 8 of the European Convention on Human Rights, the authority complied by allocating the family appropriate new accommodation with financial security as to rent. In reply to a further claim for damages, the Council argued that this amounted to 'just satisfaction'. Sullivan J was unconvinced. In addition to the intolerable living conditions, the claimant had been threatened with eviction, there had been no admission of error, no explanation, no apology, and nothing to indicate that the defendant's procedures had been improved so that the same kind of mistake would not occur in the future. Sidestepping judicial guidelines from Lord Woolf in *Anufrijeva*[23] that the courts should not award exemplary or aggravated damages in human rights cases, Sullivan J awarded financial compensation to members of the family, patterning his awards on the hardship awards made by the local government ombudsman.

B. Damages and Compensation

So far we have been confining the term 'damages' to civil liability. Damages are not normally available for a violation of human rights, and under the Human Rights Act 1998, 'compensation' takes the form of 'just satisfaction' according to principles established by

[20] *R v Home Secretary, ex p Greenfield* [2005] UKHL 14, [2005] 1 WLR 673 [19]–[20] (Lord Bingham).

[21] See, for further discussion of damages in human rights cases, R Clayton, 'Damage Limitation: The Courts and Human Rights Act Damages' (2005) *PL* 429; J Steele, 'Damages in Tort and Under the Human Rights Act: Remedial or Functional Separation?' (2008) 67 *CLJ* 606.

[22] *R (Bernard) v Enfield LBC* [2002] EWHC 2282 (Admin).

[23] *Anufrijeva v Southwark London Borough Council* [2003] EWCA Civ 1406, [2004] QB 1124 [52]–[53] (Lord Woolf MR).

the ECtHR. Cane, discussing damages as a public law remedy, would break the link between civil law liability and public law illegality, but he does not draw a distinction for this purpose between damages and compensation. Indeed, his definition of damages as 'monetary payments which address loss suffered, or gains made, or resource-shifts, or reprehensible conduct'[24] is wide enough to encompass both civil law actions and the public law action for judicial review, the subject of his article. But damages for Cane denotes the outcome of a legal process, a usage that I follow. In contrast, compensation does not depend on legal process (except in human rights cases). The term refers to payments made voluntarily by government, which is not always authorised by statute and is not always the consequence of fault. Compensation is, in other words, primarily an administrative rather than a legal concept.

III. Damages for Illegality

In 2004, the Law Commission returned to the subject of government liability with a discussion paper on monetary remedies in public law.[25] The spur was a lecture given by Michael Fordham to a Government Legal Service Conference. The Administrative Court had power to award 'damages' on an application for judicial review, provided always that they could have been awarded in a civil claim, and Fordham was arguing for greater use of this power by the judiciary. This could be institutionalised in a new power to award a 'reparation order' when, 'in all the circumstances of the case, it would be just and convenient for the order to be made'.[26] There was no need, Fordham argued, for damages as a reparation remedy to be driven by civil law notions of compensatory damages, still less full reparation; the liability of the state did not lie in tort but as 'a claim in public law for compensation'. The link with civil law liability would be broken and new principles of compensation established.

The Law Commission seized on the idea, publishing a consultation paper on remedies against public bodies.[27] They hoped for a government mandate to undertake a full investigation of monetary remedies in public law, but instead met widespread criticism. There was some support for the judge-made distinction between liability based on a duty owed to a private individual and a public duty 'owed to the world at large', which carries no right to damages.[28] The Government, concerned mainly with cost, was particularly hostile. There was anxiety at the prospect of the increased financial burden on public bodies that would result from the imposition of compensation, the Law Commission proposals 'risked creating the impression of a "general right to financial redress" which would over-emphasise the rights of individuals to the detriment

[24] Cane (n 2) 491–92.

[25] Law Commission, *Monetary Remedies in Public Law: A Discussion Paper* (11 October 2004, https://s3-eu-west-2.amazonaws.com/lawcom-prod-storage-11jsxou24uy7q/uploads/2015/04/Monetary_Remedies_Paper.pdf).

[26] M Fordham, 'Reparation for Maladministration: Public Law's Final Frontier' (2003) *Judicial Review* 104 [18], citing s 31(2) of the (then) Supreme Court Act 1981 (UK).

[27] Law Commission, *Administrative Redress: Public Bodies and the Citizen, A Consultation Paper* (Law Com CP No 187, 2008) *(Administrative Redress)*. And see Law Commission, *Administrative Redress: Public Bodies and the Citizen* (Law Com No 322, 2010).

[28] Law Commission (2008) (n 27) [29] and ch 2 generally.

of society as a whole', and it was important to avoid the creation of a 'compensation culture'.[29] While maintaining grumpily that the criticisms were not insurmountable and would not create an undue burden on public bodies, the Law Commission drew back from their project, substituting an inquiry into redress through the ombudsmen. Fordham's proposal fell by the wayside.

Cane's 1999 article contributed a fresh way of looking at the problem and moved the debate on to a higher intellectual plane. Hitherto the core of the debate centred on government *liability*, the key question being whether this should be governed by private or public law. Cane's take off point was the 'fundamental tenet', for which he sought legal justification, concluding that there are no good reasons of principle why government should not be subject to liabilities different to those imposed on citizens or enjoy defences to liability not also enjoyed by citizens. The 'fundamental tenet', in short, is not soundly rooted in legal policy and practice.

At this point, however, Cane leaves the customary pathway of arguments over liability and duty of care to proceed by a novel route. Adopting a public law perspective, Cane focuses on damages as a remedy for 'illegality' in its public law sense of breaches of public law principle on the part of government.[30] By dealing with damages as one of the set of public law remedies normally available in an action for judicial review, Cane forges the direct link between illegality and damages that the judiciary has either been disabled by the 'fundamental tenet' from making or perhaps been unwilling to make.[31]

Cane sees damages as serving four main functions:

(1) *compensatory damages* make up for injury, harm, damage, loss, etc suffered by someone as a result of the conduct of another;
(2) *restorative damages* require resources obtained from another to be returned;
(3) *disgorgement damages* require gains made 'at the expense of another' to be disgorged;
(4) *punitive damages* punish a person for their conduct towards another.[32]

Whether or not Cane's classification is a necessary component of his argument, it is sufficient to extend the ambit of damages beyond the compensatory function with which tort law damages are so strongly associated. With hindsight, his categories may need to be extended. Damages are often said to be deterrent, although Cane categorically rejects this function.[33] There are too differences of opinion over the precise relationship between punitive, aggravated and exemplary damages.[34] Again, a strong case has been made for a vindicatory public law function for damages, especially in human rights cases. The verdict of a court after public proceedings affords a form of accountability that no award

[29] ibid [2.23].

[30] While Cane includes payments made 'without admission of, or even in the admitted absence of, legal liability' within his definition of compensatory damages, he explicitly excludes damages in cases caused by legal government activity from his consideration: Cane (n 2) 491–92.

[31] See the speech of Lord Diplock in *Home Office v Dorset Yacht* [1970] AC 1004 (HL), which is founded on the public law notions of ultra vires and *Wednesbury* unreasonableness and reads almost like a dissent.

[32] Cane (n 2) 491.

[33] ibid 499. Contrast P Schuck, *Suing Government: Citizen Remedies for Official Wrongs* (New Haven, Yale University Press, 1983), who bases his theory of government liability largely on deterrence, without providing empirical evidence.

[34] See Law Commission, *Aggravated, Exemplary and Restitutionary Damages* (Law Com 247, 1997) pt II.

of compensation as 'a tangible recognition of society's sympathy and concern' can ever offer.[35] In the notorious recent case of the 'taxicab rapist', the victims sued for a violation of their entitlement to an appropriate investigation in terms of article 3 of the European Convention on Human Rights despite the fact that they had obtained compensation from the criminal injuries compensation scheme and payments from the Metropolitan Police and the perpetrator's insurers.[36] In *Ashley v Chief Constable of Sussex Police*,[37] where a member of the force shot dead an unarmed person but was acquitted of murder, the Chief Constable, in an effort to suppress publicity, admitted negligence and offered full compensation. Yet he failed in an attempt to have civil claims in assault and battery struck out. The deceased's relatives, who had previously fought unsuccessfully for a public inquiry, refused to withdraw nor would the House of Lords compel them. Varuhas argues convincingly for vindicatory damages 'to mark the sense of public outrage' at the grave violation of an important human right.[38] Steele suggests that vindicatory damages 'protect the benefit of the right for society as a whole, not just the value of the right to the claimant'; in other words, vindicatory damages mark the 'public law' element of human rights.[39] So perhaps we should add:

(5) *vindicatory damages* emphasise the importance of a violated right.

Cane goes on to ask three main questions concerning the use of damages in public law proceedings: What is the role of damages in remedying public law wrongs? Why were damages seen as less suitable for use in public law than in the private law of obligations? Are there any sound reasons of legal or social policy why damages should play a lesser role in redressing breaches of public law than in redressing breaches of private law? He sets up three rather abstract reasons why damages might be thought an unsuitable remedy for public law wrongs. First, damages are 'intrusive', thus marking a departure – by permitting the judiciary to tell the executive what to do – from the tradition of self-restraint or 'deference' that denotes the English style of judicial review.[40] Second, an award of damages involves shifting financial resources, which is a breach of the fundamental constitutional principle that resource-allocation is an executive function. A third, less lofty objection is that an award of damages enriches individuals at the expense of the collectivity.

Effectively, these are straw men that Cane is able easily to dispose of. Other public law remedies possess the same or similar characteristics; injunctions and mandatory orders are (more) intrusive, a mere declaration of invalidity may have a substantial effect on resources as indeed may a finding of civil liability.[41] Indeed, the case both for liability

[35] C Harlow, 'A Punitive Role for Tort Law?' in L Pearson et al (eds), *Law in a Changing State: Essays in Honour of Mark Aronson* (Oxford, Hart Publishing, 2008).

[36] *Commissioner of Metropolitan Police v DSD* [2018] UKSC 11, [2019] AC 196. Compare *Doe v Metropolitan Toronto Board of Commissioners of Police* (1998) 160 DLR (4th) 697.

[37] *Ashley v Chief Constable of Sussex Police* [2008] UKHL 25, [2008] 1 AC 962.

[38] J Varuhas, *Damages and Human Rights* (Oxford, Hart Publishing, 2016) 125–29.

[39] Steele (n 21) 619.

[40] J King 'Institutional Approaches to Judicial Restraint' (2008) 28 *OJLS* 409.

[41] This was indeed the rationale for the Ipp Review in which Peter Cane participated: see Commonwealth of Australia, *Review of the Law of Negligence* (Final Report, September 2002). Around this time, the finding of liability in *R v Transport Secretary, ex p Factortame (No 5)* [2000] 1 AC 524 (HL), reportedly cost the state in the region of £55 million.

in tort and for public law remedies is frequently evaluated by courts against the likely effect on departmental budgets, the purposes of welfare or the possible 'freezing effect' on official behaviour. Thus Cane is free to conclude that damages should be available as a remedy against the state in all cases of illegal government action provided that substantial damages would be an appropriate response to the applicant's claim given the four functions of awards of damages.[42] His conclusion fails, however, to meet the government objection to creating an expectation of a 'general right to financial redress'.

Cane sets two important limits to his proposed remedy: the award of damages must be 'substantial' and entitlement limited to those made worse off through illegality ('exogenous losers'). This awkward term he defines generously as 'the operation of an illegitimate feature of a government programme (even though in the way it was designed to operate) or by the operation of a legitimate government programme in an illegitimate way'.[43] He expressly excludes liability for those who suffer loss through the 'legitimate operation of legitimate government programmes in the way they were designed to operate' (endogenous losers), as he believes this would be 'self-defeating';[44] it would tend to undercut the legitimate purpose of statute or government policy. Cane has to admit that 'we do pay damages to some endogenous losers' and that 'all governments adopt more or less formalized schemes for payments of damages without admission of liability',[45] but he treats this as an anomaly and does not follow the point further. He slips back into 'fundamental tenet' mode, asserting that 'public law damages liability ought to be thought of as supplementing existing heads of damages liability where this is thought appropriate to remedy breaches of public law which do not fall within existing causes of action'.[46]

Where does this leave his innovative concept of damages as a public law remedy? As a largely residual remedy, capable of resolving cases of *individual* hardship; for a *general* principle of compensation we need to look elsewhere.

IV. Rationalising Administrative Compensation

In his seminal study of judicial review, Stanley de Smith observed that English law was 'strong on compensation (as distinct from damages)', referencing a long historical tradition of compensation in English law.[47] Even the very limited remnants of prerogative power to expropriate private property in time of war carry a right to compensation at common law. Again, during the eighteenth and nineteenth century, statutory compensation was provided when land was compulsorily purchased for infrastructure development by private Act of Parliament, a practice generalised by the Land Clauses Consolidation Act 1845. And ex gratia payments were for many years the accepted way

[42] Cane (n 2) 505.
[43] ibid 497.
[44] ibid.
[45] ibid 515.
[46] ibid.
[47] SA de Smith, *Judicial Review of Administrative Action*, 3rd edn (London, Sweet & Maxwell, 1973) 21–22, n 79.

to make up for Crown immunity in tort. de Smith also noted, however, that a 'coherent body of general principle' to regulate the subject was lacking.[48]

In contemporary governance, administrative compensation serves several functions. Ex gratia payments are used routinely to settle potential legal liability or redress losses where the administration does not dispute or does not wish openly to acknowledge that it has acted unlawfully, unreasonably or has just got things wrong. Treasury Guidance on managing public money is pragmatic. Civil servants are advised that it may be appropriate to consider making a financial payment where public sector organisations 'fail to meet their standards', or where they fall short of 'reasonable behaviour'. Any such payments should 'follow good practice.' They should not, however, be offered routinely and decision-makers should take account of the impact on the [public body's] future business as well as the legal rights of the other party or parties. 'Schemes of financial redress' should be cleared with the Treasury before commitments are made.[49] No formal authorisation is necessary for such payments, but the Treasury Guidance advises that:

> where a pattern develops, and a number of cases raising similar points need to be dealt with, it may make sense to develop an extra statutory scheme … If any such scheme seems likely to persist, the [public body] concerned should consider whether to bring forward legislation to set it on a statutory footing[50]

Systematisation has gone a little further where an ombudsman is involved. Ex gratia payments are used routinely as a remedy for maladministration without specific statutory authorisation, but, in 1994, a parliamentary select committee, concerned at the haphazard way in which the practice was evolving, asked for a study of redress from the Parliamentary Commissioner for Administration. The Commissioner recommended that compensation should be made to the victims of maladministration in all cases of 'abnormal hardship' and 'exceptional worry and distress'.[51] Today, the Principles for Remedy on the website of the Parliamentary Commissioner and Health Services Ombudsman (PHSO) call for pecuniary redress where 'maladministration or poor service has led to injustice or hardship and it is not possible to put the complainant back into the same position as they would have been in had things gone right in the first place'. Payments should also be made where appropriate to 'others who have suffered injustice or hardship as a result of the same maladministration or poor service'.[52]

This principle of equal treatment is not without problems. Habitually respected by administrators, it may have the effect of transforming a single ex gratia payment into an unauthorised compensation scheme. When, for example, the Jobseeker's Allowance (Employment, Skills and Enterprise Scheme (ESE)) Regulations 2011 were ruled *ultra vires* by the Court of Appeal, the cost of meeting claims for back payments in pending

[48] ibid.

[49] HM Treasury, *Managing Public Money* (2013, updated 2019) 28 [4.11.4]–[4.11.5].

[50] ibid Annex 4.14.6. A local authority needs ministerial approval for ex gratia payments.

[51] See Select Committee on the Parliamentary Commissioner for Administration, *Maladministration and Redress* (HC 1994–95, 112).

[52] Parliamentary Commissioner and Health Services Ombudsman, 'Principles for Remedy', 10 (https://www.ombudsman.org.uk/about-us/our-principles/principles-remedy).

cases was estimated by the Department to be in the region of £130 million.[53] Far from 'developing an extra statutory scheme', the Government felt it appropriate to introduce fast track retrospective legislation to obliterate these claims.[54]

A. Statutory Authorisation

Neither ex gratia payments nor administrative compensation technically require statutory authorisation although, as already indicated, statutory compensation is a practice dating back many centuries and there seems to be an expectation that compensation schemes should have a statutory base. When the Criminal Injuries Compensation Scheme (CICS) was first set up in 1964 for victims of criminal violence, it was on an ex gratia basis, using (presumed) prerogative powers. The case advanced for this extra-statutory structure was that it was the first scheme of its kind in the world and the Government wished to see how it worked out and to retain the ability to make adjustments; moreover, the cost was uncertain.

Pressure mounted over the years for a statute, largely because this would create rights and entrench entitlement – besides allowing Parliament a say in the way awards were to be calculated. Finally, against the wishes of the Government, the CICS reached the statute book via a Lords amendment to the Criminal Justice Act 1988, which never came into force. The CICS continued to operate as an administrative compensation scheme until the Criminal Injuries Compensation Act 1995, the present basis for the scheme, passed into law. It then lost its informal ex gratia character but remains stylistically an administrative compensation scheme. The Act gave the relevant minister wide discretionary powers to 'make arrangements for the payment of compensation' and authorised him to draw up a 'tariff' standardising the amount of compensation and regulating how it was to be calculated. There are today 25 bands covering payments between £1,000 and £250,000 in respect of 400 listed injuries.

Serious hardship may be caused where statute omits to mention compensation. In *Trent Strategic Health Authority v Jain*,[55] the authority, using statutory powers, had applied for a care home to be closed for public health reasons without giving notice to the proprietors or affording them an opportunity to comment. The proprietors were subsequently exonerated by an appeal tribunal, which was scathing about the authority's conduct, but it was too late to save the business. No statutory compensation was available. With some regret, the House of Lords ruled that the closure power involved a public law duty owed to the public at large and was not a duty owed to homeowners. There was no statutory compensation for the Jains and they were owed no duty of care,

[53] *R (Reilly) v Work and Pensions Secretary* [2012] EWHC 2292 (Admin); [2013] EWCA Civ 66, [2013] 1 WLR 2239; [2013] UKSC 68, [2014] AC 453.

[54] See HC Deb 19 March 2013, vol 560, cols 826–831. Subsequently, in *Reilly v Work and Pensions Secretary* [2016] EWCA Civ 413, [2017] QB 657, the Court of Appeal validated the Jobseekers (Back to Work Schemes) Act 2013 except in respect of hearings for claimants who had an appeal of a sanction decision in the tribunal system when the Act came into force. For these the Court issued a declaration of incompatibility with art 6 of the ECHR. This judgment was implemented by the Draft Jobseekers (Back to Work Schemes) Act 2013 (Remedial) Order 2019.

[55] *Trent Strategic Health Authority v Jain* [2009] UKHL 4, [2009] 1 AC 853.

while the Human Rights Act 1998, which could have underwritten a 'just satisfaction' award, was not in force at the time. The claim was ultimately resolved by a friendly settlement of the *Jain* case in the ECtHR, where the UK Government undertook to make an ex gratia payment to the proprietors of £733,500 to cover any pecuniary and non-pecuniary damage as well as costs and expenses.[56]

There are constitutional reasons why it is problematic for courts to order reparation for loss that flows from legislation. It is, as Cane foresaw, likely to undercut the purpose of the legislation;[57] moreover, resource-allocation is considered an executive prerogative. For judges to order financial remedies in the absence of specific legislative authority may be seen as a usurpation both of the lawmaking function of the legislature and also of the resource-allocation function of the executive, a point illustrated when the Government tried to introduce 'tariff-based' awards of criminal injuries compensation in the face of contrary legislative provision.[58] Unfortunately, it is seldom the case that the legislator makes the position clear or even thinks about it. The Law Commission once suggested a general presumption in favour of potential liability unless there was an express statutory provision against liability.[59] Peter Hogg, the Canadian constitutional lawyer, suggested that compensation issues were sufficiently important to be 'benchmarked' when new regulation or legislation was under consideration.[60] This result could be achieved by making compensation a mandatory element in the pre-legislative impact assessments routinely required today.

B. The Search for Principle

Based on tort law, government liability is generally fault-based.[61] For administrative compensation the position is more complex. A 'hardship' or 'exceptional hardship' rule is accepted within government as a ground for compensation, although these concepts are nowhere elucidated or defined. As suggested by the Treasury Guidance, this extends to situations outside liability where a service 'fails to meet its standards' or 'falls short of reasonable behaviour'. Ombudsmen expect that redress will be made for 'maladministration causing injustice', though these concepts too remain undefined. It is, however, acceptable to construe fault so as to bring illegality, maladministration and unreasonable behaviour within its framework alongside the tort law concept of negligence. Otherwise, the position is, as Cane realised, inherently more problematic.

There are three plausible explanations for compensation without fault. The first is the risk principle according to which the risk of all losses or exceptional losses that

[56] *Jain and Jain v The United Kingdom* [2010] ECHR 411.

[57] Cane (n 2) 493–94.

[58] See *R v Home Secretary, ex p Fire Brigades Union* [1995] 2 AC 513 (HL).

[59] Law Commission, *The Interpretation of Statute* (Law Com No 21, 1969).

[60] P Hogg, 'Compensation for Damage Caused by Government' (1995) 6 *National Journal of Constitutional Law* 7, 12.

[61] The strict liability of the trespass torts is both exceptional and problematic: see notably *R v Governor of Brockhill Prison, ex p Evans (No 2)* [2001] 2 AC 19 (HL); *Lumba v Secretary of State for the Home Department* [2011] UKSC 12, [2012] 1 AC 245.

spring from the activity of public administration should be borne by the state. The second is the welfare principle, rooted in a concept of the state as provider of welfare and protector of those in financial and social need that developed during the nineteenth century. The third is a principle of social solidarity whereby exceptional losses are not left to lie on individuals but are shouldered by the community as a whole. This last finds legal expression in the French principle of 'equality before public charges' on which Street based his proposal for no-fault liability in 'a new code of administrative liability'[62] and, more recently, in a Council of Europe Recommendation on Public Liability. This requires Member States to ensure reparation flowing from action taken in the general interest if it would be 'manifestly unjust' to allow the injured person alone to bear the damage, only one person or a limited number of persons have suffered damage and the act was 'exceptional' or the damage was an 'exceptional result of the act'.[63]

C. Welfare and Social Solidarity

Criminal injuries compensation involves payments from public funds for injuries caused by third parties without government fault – unless one accepts that the state is at fault for somehow failing to prevent the crime,[64] or is responsible for the social conditions that produced the criminal. When an advisory Home Office Working Party was asked to provide justification for criminal injuries compensation, it professed itself unable to find any reason of constitutional or social principle as a basis for compensation other than welfare.[65] But it added that 'considerations of sympathy for the innocent victim' were 'more likely to appeal to the public than any more abstruse principles that might be formulated'. It seems that the 'shaky intellectual foundations' of the British scheme are not unique; all criminal injuries compensation schemes suffer from the difficulty of finding any rationale other than public sympathy.[66] Duff, however, proffers four classes of theoretical justification, including the insurance-type rationale that the costs of crime should be borne by all citizens as an unavoidable feature of modern life and the highly abstract theoretical idea that the state accepts responsibility as part of the 'social contract' between the citizen and society. Miers favours a social solidarity principle, though he also suggests (improbably) that a compensation scheme promotes trust in the criminal justice system.[67]

[62] H Street, *Governmental Liability* (Cambridge, Cambridge University Press, 1953) 79. For a short explanation of the concept, see R Errara, 'The Scope and Meaning of No-Fault Liability in French Administrative Law' (1986) *Current Legal Problems* 157; D Fairgrieve, *State Liability in Tort* (Oxford, Oxford University Press, 2003) 144–53.

[63] Council of Europe, 'Recommendation No R (84) 15 of Committee of Ministers to Member States Relating to Public Liability' (18 September 1984) pt II.

[64] As suggested by *Jane Doe v Toronto (Metropolitan) Commissioners of Police* (1989) 58 DLR (4th) 396 (SCC).

[65] Home Office, *Compensation for Victims of Crimes of Violence* (Cmnd 1406, 1961) [18].

[66] P Duff, 'Criminal Injuries Compensation. The Symbolic Dimension' (1995) 40 *Juridical Review* 102, 106.

[67] D Miers, 'State Compensation for Victims of Violent Crime' in I Vanfraechem et al (eds), *Justice for Victims: Perspectives on Rights, Transition and Reconciliation* (Abingdon, Routledge, 2014) 111–14.

The Working Party chose welfare, stating somewhat inconsequentially that, 'although the Welfare State helps the victims of many kinds of misfortune, it does nothing for the victims of crimes of violence *as such*, notwithstanding that they are largely deprived of the means of self-protection and in most cases have no effective remedy at law'.[68] 'As such?', Atiyah remarked derisively, 'What are the grounds for singling out victims of violent crime as a "special class outside the normal processes of the welfare state"'? If the Working Party believed that the benefits provided by the welfare system were inadequate, the right solution was to increase them.[69] Atiyah here highlights the way that welfare and social solidarity explanations of compensation privilege one class of victim at the expense of another and may not always provide justification for the choice.

D. Equal Treatment

When government was contemplating vaccine damage compensation, a no-fault scheme was proposed for 'that minority of tragic victims who are adversely affected by vaccinations, on the basis that vaccination is carried out as a matter of public policy in the general interest'.[70] By limiting compensation to children, the Government called on public sympathy in the shadow of the thalidomide tragedy, but by limiting the scheme to children who were at least 80 per cent disabled, it opened the thorny question of why the class of less disabled children had been excluded. It came under pressure to extend compensation first to the less severely disabled, then to other categories of vaccine victims, finally to the disabled at large, while demands to increase the benefits were founded on the more generous provision for thalidomide victims, some of which was funded in reality from voluntary public donations. MPs fighting to increase government contributions to compensation for thalidomide victims were told by the Minister of Health that:

> despite the understandable tide of emotion about thalidomide children they are not the only very severely congenitally disabled people. We have to keep a balance in our minds, which are filled with those who are limbless because of the thalidomide drug. There are other children suffering from very severe congenital disabilities also, with great strain on their parents.[71]

When Margaret Thatcher came into power, she was able to justify refusal to extend the scheme with reference to equality: her government 'planned to improve life for all disabled people and was not willing to give more special treatment to a group that already benefited hugely over other equally disabled people'.[72]

Many years later, a similar point was made in a debate on the Riot Compensation Bill, designed as a replacement for the Riot (Damages) Act 1886, which had placed an

[68] Council of Europe, 'Recommendation No R (84) 15 (n 63).

[69] P Cane, *Atiyah's Accidents, Compensation and the Law*, 4th edn (Weidenfeld and Nicolson, 1987) 29–34.

[70] See HC Deb 9 May 1978, vol 949, col 973.

[71] HC Deb 29 November 1972, vol 847, col 439 (Sir Keith Joseph). Over the years, further state compensation has been conceded.

[72] G Millward, 'A Disability Act? The Vaccine Damage Payments Act 1979 and the British Government's Response to the Pertussis Vaccine Scare' (2017) 30 *Social History of Medicine* 429.

obligation to compensate for riot damage on local police services. Perhaps surprisingly, the 1886 Act was based overtly on the concept of social contract. It was said to be:

> the legal expression of what has been called the 'implied contract' between the public and the police. This requires that the public respect the leadership of the police when required and that the police maintain law and order. If law and order breaks down in a riot situation the police become liable to compensate those affected.[73]

When, following widespread London rioting in 2011, the Government agreed in 2016, under considerable pressure from the Association of Insurers, to take over the responsibility, the House of Lords was told only that 'the Government should *of course* provide a safety net to ensure that the victims of riots are adequately compensated'.[74] Lord Pannick asked why?

> The Bill perpetuates an anomaly, because there is no statutory right to compensation in the event of a natural disaster, such as flooding, or in the event of an epidemic. Other public bodies, such as hospitals, have a liability only if negligence can be proved. Under the riot compensation law, the police are liable to pay large sums of compensation whether or not they are at fault. That is particularly striking because the general common-law rule … is that the police generally owe no liability in negligence for failing to prevent serious crime, even if they are at fault.[75]

The conflicting forms of equality implicit in these arguments emerge more clearly in the ombudsman investigation into the 'Debt of Honour' affair.

When the Blair Government decided hastily and unexpectedly to make a single ex gratia payment of £10,000 to each of the surviving members of British groups held prisoner by the Japanese during World War II, the Minister announced to the House of Commons a non-statutory ex gratia compensation scheme 'in recognition of the unique circumstances of their collective captivity'.[76] The beneficiaries would be former members of the armed forces and Merchant Navy and 'British civilians who were interned', the implication being that all 'surviving British civilians who were interned by the Japanese in the Far East during the Second World War' would be eligible. In fact, neither the criteria for eligibility nor the meaning of 'British' had been finally decided.

It emerged later that some British nationals living overseas who would otherwise have been eligible were to be excluded by 'birth link' and 'blood link' requirements that applicants must be British subjects born in the United Kingdom or with a parent or grandparent born there. An action group representing British civilians in the Far East applied for judicial review. The Court of Appeal dismissed the appeal; although the introduction of the scheme had not been well handled by the Government, they could not see the scheme as unlawful.[77] A second, successful legal challenge followed, based

[73] T Edmonds and P Strickland, *Riot (Compensation) Bill*, House of Commons Briefing Paper 07239 (1 December 2015) 3. See also N Kinghan, *Independent Review of the Riot (Damages) Act 1886: Report of the Review* (2013 https://assets.publishing.service.gov.uk/government/uploads/system/uploads/attachment_data/file/255990/riot_damages_act_review.pdf).

[74] Riot Compensation Bill HC Deb 26 February 2016, vol 769, col 538 (Lord Trefgarne).

[75] ibid, 26 February 2016, vol 769, col 540 (Lord Pannick). And see *Michael v Chief Constable of South Wales Police* [2015] UKSC 2, [2015] AC 1732; S Tofaris and S Steel, 'Negligence Liability for Omissions and the Police' (2016) 75 *CLJ* 128.

[76] HC Deb 7 November 2000, vol 356, col 159 (Dr Lewis Moonie).

[77] *Abcifer v Defence Secretary* [2003] EWCA Civ 493, [2003] STC 669.

on the anti-discrimination provisions of the Race Relations Acts 1976 and 2000. The Court of Appeal thought the scheme discriminatory and awarded in addition to the statutory sum of £10,000 a further sum in respect of indirect discrimination for hurt feelings (£3,000) based on an award of damages in tort.[78]

Meanwhile, a complaint had been submitted to the Parliamentary and Health Service Ombudsman, Ann Abraham, who found maladministration causing injustice. The scheme had been introduced too quickly; the eligibility criteria were unclear and were explained confusingly; and the Government had been unable to show why early payments under the scheme had been made.[79] The Ombudsman set out criteria for the administration of administrative compensation schemes:

> [159] Good administration of extra-statutory schemes requires clearly articulated entitlement criteria to ensure that those potentially covered by the scheme are not put to unnecessary distress or inconvenience by uncertainty or conflicting information. Such a need is all the more essential when the relevant issues are sensitive, as is clearly the case here.
>
> [186] I would expect a system designed in accordance with principles of good administration to be transparent, to produce consistent outcomes and not to be designed in such a way as to produce inconsistent outcomes. That this is the case should also be demonstrable.[80]

There has until recently been a natural tendency to treat compensation as an administrative function and to leave it largely in the hands of politicians and civil servants. There are a number of reasons why the time may have come to reshape this practice. This is not what we expect of modern administration. Public administration operates today in the framework of widely accepted good governance principles of accountability, transparency and public participation to which governance is expected to conform.[81] For purposes of consistency, administration also functions in a framework of rules and of administrative procedures, which help to structure administrative discretion and to which again compensation schemes like all administration should conform.[82] As Anne Abraham suggests, schemes should be based on 'clearly articulated criteria'; designed to ensure consistency and fairness; published, easily accessible and comprehensible to claimants; and simple to use. Second, there are in place statutory principles that govern the way government is expected to behave. Section 6(1) of the Human Rights Act 1998 makes it unlawful for a public authority to act in a way which is incompatible with a Convention right, while section 1(1) of the Equality Act 2010 lays on all public authorities a public sector equality duty to bear in mind when making decisions of a strategic nature how those protected by the Act may be affected. This too should apply to compensation.

[78] *R (Elias) v Defence Secretary* [2005] EWHC 1435 (Admin); [2006] EWCA Civ 1293, [2006] 1 WLR 3213.

[79] Parliamentary and Health Service Ombudsman, *A Debt of Honour* (HC 2005–6, 324) a report under s 10(3) of the Parliamentary Commissioner Act 1967 to Parliament: see Public Administration Select Committee, *A Debt of Honour* (HC 2005–6, 735).

[80] Parliamentary and Health Service Ombudsman (n 79) [159] and [186].

[81] Notably in the UK, the so-called Nolan standards (Committee on the Standards in Public Life, *Standards in Public Life* (Cm 2850, 1995).

[82] As exemplified in *R (Gallaher Group Ltd) v The Competition and Markets Authority* [2018] UKSC 25, [2019] AC 96.

A 'coherent body of general principle' to cover payments from public funds in compensation is easily within our grasp. A binary system is emerging in which courts should retain three important functions. They would hear actions for damages against public authorities, based so far as possible on private law liability principles. They would retain their power to award payments for 'just satisfaction' in cases of violations of human rights law. They would preferably gain an enhanced power to award damages in respect of illegality in an action for judicial review; whether the loss suffered or the illegality should be exceptional is a matter for debate.[83] And whether a new reparation order would be sufficient to change the judicial mindset is questionable. Speaking from judicial experience, Sedley LJ once said: 'it may well be that – despite the presence for some years in the rules of a power to award damages on an application for judicial review – a legal entitlement to them cannot now come into being without legislation'.[84]

Administrative compensation needs to be systematised: it should be fair, consistent, transparent and clear. At an abstract theoretical level, administrative compensation derives legitimacy from two main sources: either it is authorised by the legislature or it is based on the same ethic of social solidarity that underpins all welfare and social assistance. But regard must also be paid to the important administrative value of equal treatment. Ex gratia compensation recommended by ombudsmen as a remedy for maladministration seems to have gained a measure of public confidence and ombudsman principles for redress form a useful template both for ex gratia payments and for the operation of administrative compensation schemes. Transparency, consistency, accountability and equal treatment are standard requirements today of administrative law and public administration. The time has come to apply them across the board.

[83] This would effectively mirror the rule in C-6, 9/90 *Francovich and Bonifaci v Republic of Italy* [1991] ECR I-5357.

[84] *R v Commissioners of Customs and Excise, ex p F & I Services Ltd* [2001] EWCA Civ 762, [2001] STC 939 [73].

9

Tort and Regulation

DONAL NOLAN

I. Introduction

The multiple connections between tort and public law are complex and important, and as a leading scholar in both disciplines Peter Cane has been ideally placed to explore those interactions in his writings. A characteristically insightful article in which he draws upon that dual expertise is entitled 'Tort Law as Regulation'.[1] My chapter in this collection also considers tort and regulation, but whereas Peter's article was centrally concerned with the potential of tort law *as* a regulatory mechanism, my interest lies in the relationship between the two. There is of course already a substantial body of literature on this question in a common law context, but most of it is written by American scholars, and I shall argue that there are features of the legal landscape in the United States which make the dynamic between tort and regulation there quite distinctive. Elsewhere the commentary is more limited, with almost all of it focused on one of two particular areas of tort law, namely nuisance and product liability.[2] By contrast, my aim in this chapter is to provide a holistic account of the inter-relationship between tort and regulation. Furthermore, whereas much of the existing literature treats tort and regulation as competing and 'mutually exclusive legal forms',[3] I follow Ben Pontin's example by envisioning them as complementary rationalities capable of operating in parallel and of interacting in mutually beneficial ways.[4]

As a private lawyer, my main concern is with the tort side of the picture, and the basic message of the chapter is that as a matter of general principle tort law should not automatically defer to regulatory norms and outcomes but should instead incorporate them into its own analytical frameworks. At first blush, that argument may not seem very controversial to a reader on this side of the Atlantic. After all, the most obvious example of automatic deference is a regulatory compliance defence, and thus far these

[1] P Cane, 'Tort Law as Regulation' (2002) 31 *Common Law World Review* 305.

[2] An exception is B Pontin, 'Tort Interacting with Regulatory Law' (2000) 51 *Northern Ireland Legal Quarterly* 597. See also M Lee, 'Safety, Regulation and Tort: Fault in Context' (2011) 74 *MLR* 555, focusing on negligence claims for personal injury.

[3] Pontin (n 2) 601.

[4] ibid.

have not made much headway in English tort law. But there is no room for complacency in this respect. Producer interests have, for example, argued for such a defence to be recognised in the European strict product liability regime transposed into UK law by the Consumer Protection Act 1987.[5] Furthermore, two first instance decisions effectively sought to import planning and regulatory norms into the English law of nuisance,[6] and while these decisions were later overturned by appellate courts (albeit only after 20 years in the case of planning controls),[7] the debate is far from over, with some commentators arguing for at least a degree of deference to public law in that context,[8] and others championing the independence of common law norms.[9] Furthermore, my argument extends to regulatory *non*-compliance, and so challenges the assumption of many tort lawyers that it is appropriate to treat the breach of a public law norm as automatically actionable in private law in certain circumstances.

Four observations about the scope of the chapter are in order. First, as will already be clear, I am not concerned with the choice between tort law and regulation, but with the relationship between them when they operate side-by-side. (It follows that nothing I say in favour of tort law should be interpreted as an argument *against* regulation.) Second, because my underlying interest is in the relationship between tort and public law, the scope of my enquiry is limited to governmental regulation, and does not extend to voluntary codes of conduct, self-regulation, industry standards, clinical guidelines and the like (though many of the arguments that will be made may be equally applicable to these 'softer' forms of regulation). Third, I am interested in the normative influence[10] of regulatory rules and outcomes on tort law and its operation. Other interactions between tort and regulation – such as the tort liability of regulators,[11] or the ways in

[5] See, eg, D Fairgrieve and R Goldberg, *Product Liability*, 3rd edn (Oxford, Oxford University Press, 2020) para 10.97.

[6] *Gillingham Borough Council v Medway (Chatham) Dock Co Ltd* [1993] QB 343 (QBD); *Barr v Biffa Waste Services Ltd* [2011] EWHC 1003 (TCC), [2011] 4 All ER 1065.

[7] *Barr v Biffa Waste Services Ltd* [2012] EWCA Civ 312, [2013] QB 455; *Coventry v Lawrence* [2014] UKSC 13, [2014] AC 822. I return to the regulatory compliance issue in nuisance below (text following n 26). On the relationship between nuisance law and planning controls, see D Nolan, 'Nuisance, Planning and Regulation: The Limits of Statutory Authority' in A Dyson et al (eds), *Defences in Tort* (Oxford, Hart Publishing, 2015) 187–96.

[8] See especially the writings of Maria Lee, to which reference will be made throughout this chapter.

[9] See especially the writings of Ben Pontin (again referred to throughout this chapter), who describes this question as 'arguably the most contentious issue in nuisance law': B Pontin, *Nuisance Law and Environmental Protection: A Study of Nuisance Injunctions in Practice* (Witney, Lawtext Publishing Ltd, 2013) 182.

[10] These words are intended to exclude instances where regulation simply forms part of the factual matrix of a tort case, as where the effect of an EU regulation concerning drinking water was to make the supply from a polluted borehole unsuitable for domestic use: *Cambridge Water Co v Eastern Counties Leather plc* [1994] 2 AC 264 (HL). Other examples would be cases where the presence of regulatory controls at the time a defendant acted enables a court to conclude that the defendant should have known of a particular risk, or conversely where their absence militates in the defendant's favour on the question of fault: see, eg, *Thompson v Smiths Shiprepairers (North Shields) Ltd* [1984] QB 405 (QBD) 419–20 (absence of regulations concerning industrial noise).

[11] Hence I am not concerned with what Cane calls 'indirect enforcement' of regulatory norms via the law of tort, meaning measures taken against regulators to incentivise their acting against regulated parties: P Cane, 'Using Tort Law to Enforce Environmental Regulations' (2002) 41 *Washburn Law Journal* 427, 449. This is not to assume, however, that that question is irrelevant to the issues under discussion (for a link, see ibid 463–64).

which regulatory mechanisms draw upon tort law[12] – fall outside my purview. And finally, my primary focus is on English law, though reference will be made to authorities from the rest of the Commonwealth and the US as well.

Three further preliminary points should be made. The first is that for the most part my arguments are intended to hold true for all forms of regulation.[13] Hence, for example, I do not distinguish at a general level between prior authorisation of the regulated activity and regulation by way of standard-setting for activities that do not require such authorisation.[14] While it is no doubt true that these two forms of regulation tend to interact with tort law in different settings (prior authorisation in product liability and nuisance, and standard-setting in negligence and breach of statutory duty), for present purposes the distinction is not of great import at a general level. Nor do I distinguish between cases where regulation imposes 'minimum standards' and those where its aim is to optimise the conduct of a given activity.

The second preliminary point is that I do not see the law of tort as primarily an instrument of deterrence.[15] It follows that I do not share the assumption underlying much of the US scholarship in this area, namely that tort law and regulation serve similar functions, an assumption with potentially significant implications for the relationship between the two. Having said that, however, I am perfectly happy to admit that tort law may have deterrent *effects* – and indeed over-deterrent effects, whereby it discourages beneficial activity, such as the development of useful new drugs – and to the extent that there are concrete historical examples of tort law having such effects, these may have implications for some of the arguments that are made.

And the final preliminary point is that it can be taken as read throughout the chapter that the regulation in question is aimed at preventing the type of harm that has been suffered (or the type of accident that has produced it) and at protecting the class of persons of which the tort claimant is a member. These are preconditions both of the imposition of tort liability for regulatory non-compliance (whether styled as 'breach of statutory duty'[16] or 'negligence per se'[17]) and also of the non-conclusive effect of regulatory violations via the application of ordinary tort principles in, for example, negligence.[18]

The structure of the chapter is straightforward. I first discuss how tort and regulation do in fact interact, before turning to how they should interact.[19] I then add

[12] A classic example being the way in which the law of statutory nuisance relies on the common law of nuisance to determine whether specified forms of interference are unlawful: Environmental Protection Act 1990 (UK), Pt III.

[13] For a typology of different forms of social regulation, see A Ogus, *Regulation: Legal Form and Economic Theory* (Oxford, Oxford University Press, 1994), pt III.

[14] For an exception, see text to nn 154–57 below.

[15] For a thorough debunking of justifications of tort liability in deterrence terms, see C Hodges, *Law and Corporate Behaviour: Integrating Theories of Regulation, Enforcement, Compliance and Ethics* (Oxford, Hart Publishing, 2015) 145–57.

[16] See, eg, *Gorris v Scott* (1874) LR 9 Ex 125 (regulation governing sea carriage of livestock designed to protect against the spread of contagious disease and not perils of the sea).

[17] *Restatement (Third) of Torts: Liability for Physical and Emotional Harm* (2010) §14.

[18] In negligence, this conclusion would rest on orthodox remoteness reasoning, limiting recovery to the materialisation of the risks that made the defendant's conduct negligent in the first place: see J Goudkamp and D Nolan, *Winfield & Jolowicz on Tort*, 20th edn (London, Sweet & Maxwell, 2020) para 7-071ff.

[19] Pontin (n 2) 617: 'All this opens up a number of issues concerning the "is" and "ought" of the theme [of interaction between tort and regulation], which would benefit from further research'.

some possible caveats and consider some counter-arguments, before drawing some conclusions.

II. Forms of Interaction

In this part of the chapter I set out the various ways in which governmental regulation exerts normative influence on the law of tort. A central distinction drawn is between conclusive and non-conclusive effect. By conclusive effect, I mean that the regulatory rule or outcome is dispositive in its own right. By non-conclusive effect, I mean that the regulatory rule or outcome is just one factor to be taken into account in the tort analysis. Suppose, for example, that a factory worker is injured because a piece of machinery is not fenced off, in breach of a regulatory rule. In a claim for breach of statutory duty, the violation of the regulation has conclusive effect, because it in itself determines the outcome of a key stage of the tort analysis (namely, the requirement of a statutory breach). By contrast, in a negligence claim the same regulatory breach has non-conclusive effect, because although it is a relevant consideration in the fault enquiry it does not automatically determine its outcome.

When it comes to the conclusive effect of regulatory norms, it will be helpful to split the discussion along another fault line, namely that between compliance and non-compliance. By contrast, that distinction – though of course still vitally important in practice – is less useful as an organising tool as regards non-conclusive effect, and so that form of interaction will be addressed in the round. Finally, while all regulatory influence on tort law must ultimately be either conclusive or non-conclusive, there are some forms of interaction between regulation and tort which do not fit neatly into the three categories already identified, and which it will therefore be helpful to consider separately. The end result is that the discussion that follows is divided into four parts: (A) conclusive compliance; (B) conclusive non-compliance; (C) non-conclusive effect; and (D) other forms of interaction.

A. Conclusive Compliance

When compliance with a regulatory norm in itself determines the outcome of a tort case, we are dealing with what is in effect a defence of regulatory compliance.[20] A good example of this defence is the legislation in various Canadian provinces immunising businesses from liability for odour nuisance provided they comply with planning laws and applicable regulations.[21] That immunity is, however, legislative in origin, and the common law of tort has set its face against regulatory compliance defences at the level of general principle, though there are isolated exceptions. The general principle can be illustrated by the position in negligence, where it is well established that

[20] I say 'in effect' because theoretically non-compliance could be made an element of the relevant cause of action, so that the claimant would bear the relevant burdens of pleading and proof, but in practice it is clearly more common for the defendant to have to show that she has complied with the regulatory norm in question.

[21] AM Linden and B Feldthusen, *Canadian Tort Law*, 9th edn (Toronto, LexisNexis, 2011) 600–601.

compliance with applicable regulations is not conclusive of whether the defendant exercised reasonable care. In *Bux v Slough Metals Ltd*,[22] an employers' liability case, Stephenson LJ said:

> There is, in my judgment, no presumption that a statutory obligation abrogates or supersedes the employer's common law duty or that it defines or measures his common law duty either by clarifying it or by cutting it down … It is not necessarily exhaustive of that duty or co-extensive with it … The statutory obligation may exceed the duty at common law or it may fall short of it or it may equal it.[23]

Similarly, in *Baker v Quantum Clothing Group Ltd*,[24] Lord Dyson denied that there was a rule of law that a regulatory instrument 'necessarily sets the standard of care for the purpose of the tort of negligence'.[25] Compliance with such an instrument would 'often afford a defence to a claim in negligence', but there were circumstances where it would not.[26]

Another context in which the courts have rejected a regulatory compliance defence is nuisance. The leading case is *Barr v Biffa Waste Services Ltd*,[27] where local residents brought claims in respect of the smells emanating from the defendant's landfill site. A waste management permit granted by the Environment Agency allowed the defendant to deposit controlled waste on the site subject to a number of conditions, one of which was that it prevented or otherwise controlled, minimised and monitored odour at the site by taking measures described in the permit 'or as otherwise agreed in writing' with the agency. It was conceded that the defendant had not been in breach of the permit, nor negligent, and at first instance Coulson J held that it followed that the nuisance action must fail, saying that 'it would be unsatisfactory, to say the least, if the common law did not generally march in step' with the detailed legislation regulating waste management,[28] and that conducting tipping activities in conformity with the permit should afford the defendant 'a complete defence to a claim in nuisance'.[29] That decision was however overturned by the Court of Appeal, which reasserted the independence of the common law principles governing private nuisance from regulatory norms. According to Carnwath LJ:

> The common law of nuisance has co-existed with statutory controls … since the 19th century. There is no principle that the common law should 'march with' a statutory scheme covering similar subject matter. Short of express or implied statutory authority to commit a nuisance … there is no basis, in principle or authority, for using such a statutory scheme to cut down private law rights.'[30]

That statement was approved by Lord Neuberger in *Coventry v Lawrence*,[31] and encapsulates the orthodox position that regulatory compliance is not generally a defence to

[22] *Bux v Slough Metals Ltd* [1973] 1 WLR 1358 (CA).
[23] ibid 1369–70. See also ibid 1364–65 (Edmund Davies LJ).
[24] *Baker v Quantum Clothing Group Ltd* [2011] UKSC 17, [2011] 1 WLR 1003.
[25] ibid [101].
[26] ibid. See also *Matuszczyk v National Coal Board* 1953 SC 8 (OH) 19.
[27] *Barr* (n 7).
[28] *Barr* (n 6) [304].
[29] ibid [346].
[30] *Barr* (n 7) [46].
[31] *Coventry* (n 7) [92].

a nuisance claim. The same is true when it comes to product liability claims brought under the strict liability regime laid down in the Consumer Protection Act 1987.[32]

Nevertheless, Coulson J's departure from orthodoxy in *Barr v Biffa Waste Services* was not a one-off, and there are other examples of English judges effectively treating regulatory compliance as conclusive against tort liability. In *Hughes v Welsh Water plc*,[33] for example, which involved the discharge of effluent by a sewage works, a county court judge held that the defendant's compliance with the terms of its discharge consent meant that it could not be liable in nuisance for damage caused by phosphate in the effluent.[34] And in *Budden v BP Oil Ltd*,[35] the Court of Appeal held that because the defendant petrol producers had complied with regulations governing the maximum amount of lead in petrol, negligence actions brought against them by children who claimed to have suffered injury through ingesting lead in the atmosphere must fail. Imposing liability, Megaw LJ said, would amount to the courts 'laying down a permissible limit … inconsistent with, the permissible limit prescribed by the authority of Parliament', which would result in a 'constitutional anomaly'.[36] *Budden* is an unusual case, because the generalised nature of the breach allegation did seem to give rise to an obvious tension with the regulatory norm – the more usual scenario involves the interaction between a general regulation (such as a speed limit) and a one-off fact-sensitive enquiry into the defendant's conduct (was the defendant driving too fast, in the particular circumstances?). But nevertheless, insofar as the court ruled out even the *possibility* that conduct in compliance with the regulation could be negligent, it was seemingly contrary to principle.[37]

Regulatory compliance is distinguishable from the well-established defence of statutory authority, which is available to a defendant whose activity has been authorised by Parliament, and who has taken all reasonable steps to minimise the interference it is causing. This defence requires a direct expression of Parliamentary will, and does not extend to decisions of administrative agencies acting under legislative powers.[38] A compliance defence is also distinguishable from regulatory 'pre-emption', which is to say the complete exclusion of tort liability in situations falling within the scope of the relevant regulatory scheme. In such a case the defendant's regulatory compliance is irrelevant, as no tort claim can be brought regardless.

Two final points should be made about conclusive compliance. One is that a regulatory compliance defence can of course be limited to particular modes of regulation, such as prior authorisation. And the other is that we need to distinguish between regulatory compliance and regulatory approval. Suppose, for example, that a regulator decides that a new drug complies with the relevant regulatory norms and approves its use, or that

[32] *Wilkes v DePuy International Ltd* [2016] EWHC 3096 (QB), [2018] QB 627 [101]; *Gee v DePuy International Ltd* [2018] EWHC 1208 (QB) [175].

[33] *Hughes v Welsh Water plc*, Llangefni County Court, 21 June 1995.

[34] Compare *Cook v South West Water plc*, Exeter County Court, 15 April 1992 (holding the opposite).

[35] *Budden v BP Oil Ltd* (1980) 124 SJ 376 (CA).

[36] ibid 376.

[37] Compare Lee (n 2) 565, arguing that *Budden* can be analysed as a case of non-conclusive compliance, but that it 'comes very close' to a regulatory compliance defence.

[38] In theory, the grant of statutory authority could be contingent on prior regulatory authorisation of the activity, or the conduct of the activity in compliance with regulatory norms. In such a scenario the distinction between the statutory authority and regulatory compliance defences would largely collapse.

a regulator declares that a power plant is being operated in compliance with pollution controls. In either scenario the regulator may have made a mistake (perhaps because crucial information has been withheld). It follows that where a regulatory *compliance* defence is recognised, a tort claimant can seek to overcome it by attacking the regulator's decision. By contrast, a regulatory *approval* defence cannot be circumvented in this way.[39]

B. Conclusive Non-Compliance

The most prominent example of conclusive non-compliance in English law is the tort of breach of statutory duty, whereby the violation of a regulatory norm is made actionable at the suit of a person who suffers loss or damage as a result of it. Here we can observe complete deference to the standards set by the regulatory regime in question, the normative content of which is imported wholesale into tort law.

Breach of statutory duty is formally reconciled with tort orthodoxy by the principle that liability is imposed only if Parliament intended the violation of the regulatory norm to give rise to a private right of action. After all, if legislation expressly confers a right of action on individuals for breach of a regulatory norm[40] the courts must obviously carry out Parliament's will, and it is not much of a stretch to extend this to the implicit conferment of such a right. The difficulty is, however, that generally Parliament had no such 'intention' either way or, if it did, there is no evidence of it, with the result that the tort of breach of statutory duty has essentially been constructed on a fictional foundation. Nevertheless, the courts developed a complex set of principles governing the search for the chimera.[41] In recent years, however, the courts have tended to conclude that Parliament did not intend regulatory breaches to be privately actionable, and while there was a presumption to the contrary when it came to breaches of workplace safety legislation,[42] in 2013 Parliament reversed that presumption, and made it rebuttable only by express provision, thereby robbing the tort of most of its remaining significance.[43] In any case, there is not a great deal to say about the normative influence of the statutory norm in breach of statutory duty, as it is total. But it is worth noting that, although the relevant rule will often be stricter than the default negligence duty of reasonable care, this is not inevitably the case, and that even where it is not – and the regulatory norm is less strict than, or co-terminous with, the common law duty – suing in breach of statutory duty may offer a claimant advantages. In general it is likely to be

[39] For insightful discussion of this distinction in the context of prior approval of pharmaceuticals, see MD Green, 'Statutory Compliance and Tort Liability: Examining the Strongest Case' (1997) 30 *University of Michigan Journal of Law Reform* 461. I return to the distinction below, text to nn 148–52.

[40] See, eg, Environmental Protection Act 1990 (UK), s 73(6). Sometimes statutes do the opposite, and state that their provisions do not give rise to a private right of action: see, eg, Guard Dogs Act 1975 (UK).

[41] See Goudkamp and Nolan (n 18) paras 8-005–8-015.

[42] This dates back to *Groves v Wimborne* [1898] 2 QB 402 (CA). It is no coincidence that at the time that case was decided, negligence claims by employees were hamstrung by the doctrine of common employment, which did not apply to claims for breach of statutory duty.

[43] Enterprise and Regulatory Reform Act 2013 (UK), s 69 (amending the Health and Safety at Work, etc Act 1974 (UK), s 47(2), which had given statutory effect to the judicial presumption).

simpler to show that a specific regulatory standard has been breached, while in some cases the burden of proof as to fault may be reversed in the claim on the statute.[44]

Notwithstanding the long, slow demise of breach of statutory duty as a cause of action in English law – and its abolition as a common law cause of action in Canada in the 1980s[45] – the idea of tort law giving conclusive (or near-conclusive) effect to non-compliance with regulatory norms is a pervasive one across both the common law and the civil law. Although in most European jurisdictions the breach of a statutory rule has only non-conclusive effect, in a minority it automatically amounts to 'fault' for the purposes of extra-contractual liability,[46] while in others it gives rise to a presumption of fault.[47] A similar idea can be seen in American tort law, where regulatory violations are accorded special status within negligence law, by virtue of the doctrine of 'negligence per se'.[48] According to the stricter version of this doctrine, adopted in most states, the unexcused breach of an applicable statute or administrative regulation is negligence as a matter of law, with the result that the issue of breach of duty is removed from the jury.[49]

There are important differences between breach of statutory duty and negligence per se.[50] One is that the latter can be excused, for example by proof that violation of the statute was clearly safer than compliance.[51] This means that, strictly speaking, negligence per se is a form of non-conclusive effect,[52] though in practice the strictest and most common variant of it is closer to breach of statutory duty than it is to the 'evidence of negligence' approach discussed under the heading of non-conclusive effect below.[53] Another difference is that while negligence per se typically applies only when a common law negligence action already exists, breach of statutory duty is not so constrained, and can be used to claim, for example, for pure economic loss, where there is a general 'no-duty' rule in negligence.[54] A third difference is that the theoretical foundation of negligence per se is not statutory interpretation (viz, the notion that the statute was intended to give rise to a private right of action), but a purely common law analysis according to which breach of the regulatory norm is simply determinative of negligence.[55]

[44] See, eg, *Baker* (n 24) [125]. There is also a reversal of the burden of proof as to fault in one of the few remaining contexts where the breach of statutory duty tort has real bite, namely claims against highway authorities for failure to maintain the highway: Highways Act 1980 (UK), ss 41, 58.

[45] *R v Saskatchewan Wheat Pool* [1983] 1 SCR 205 (SCC).

[46] See, eg, B Winiger et al (eds), *Digest of European Tort Law, Volume 3: Essential Cases on Misconduct* (Berlin, De Gruyter, 2018) ch 4 (conclusive non-compliance rule in Belgium, France and Italy).

[47] ibid 653 (Portugal), 670 (Finland), 689 (Slovenia).

[48] *Restatement (Third) of Torts: Liability for Physical and Emotional Harm* (2010) §14.

[49] The weaker version renders the regulatory breach only evidence of negligence, which replicates the English approach as far as negligence is concerned (see below, text to nn 59–64). According to another variation, regulatory breach gives rise to a rebuttable presumption of negligence. The distinctions between the three variants can be subtle.

[50] For an assessment of the two techniques, see K Stanton et al, *Statutory Torts* (London, Sweet & Maxwell, 2003) para 1.013.

[51] *Restatement (Third) of Torts: Liability for Physical and Emotional Harm* (2010) §15.

[52] See, eg, WP Keeton et al, *Prosser and Keeton on Torts* (St Paul, West Publishing, 1984) 228.

[53] See text to nn 59–64.

[54] See, eg, *Monk v Warbey* [1935] 1 KB 75 (CA). This point is emphasised by K Stanton, 'New Forms of the Tort of Breach of Statutory Duty' (2004) 120 *LQR* 324, 333–34.

[55] KS Abraham, 'The Relation between Civil Liability and Environmental Regulation: An Analytical Overview' (2002) 41 *Washburn Law Journal* 379, 394.

And a fourth is that negligence per se cuts both ways, so that the *plaintiff's* breach of a regulatory norm can be argued to be conclusive of the existence of contributory negligence.[56]

Two further points should be made about the American approach to conclusive non-compliance. First, the use of negligence per se is closely bound up with jury trial: the choice of variant of the doctrine determines how much leeway is given to the jury, with adoption of the strictest described as evidencing 'distrust of the jury's ability to determine the "appropriate" weight of the statutory violation in deciding whether liability should be imposed'.[57] And second, the conclusive effect of regulatory breach is not limited to negligence, but extends to strict product liability, where in cases concerning alleged design or marketing defects non-compliance with an applicable product safety statute or administrative regulation renders a product 'defective with respect to the risks sought to be reduced by the statute or regulation'.[58]

C. Non-Conclusive Effect

In general, English tort law gives regulatory norms non-conclusive effect, so that while they may influence the liability analysis they are not in and of themselves determinative of the outcome. This is equally true of compliance and non-compliance, and can be seen in three main areas: negligence, nuisance and strict product liability. For the most part the non-conclusive effect of regulations is simply assumed by the courts, though occasionally Parliament spells it out in the relevant legislation.[59]

The non-conclusive effect of regulatory norms is a routine feature of negligence litigation. For example, if it is alleged in a road accident case that the defendant was driving too fast at the relevant time, then the applicable speed limit will inevitably be the court's starting point. However, it is not the only guide, and a court may conclude that a speed under the limit was nevertheless excessive in the circumstances,[60] or conversely that driving a little in excess of it was not unreasonable. The important point is that the regulatory norm is always incorporated into the fault analysis rather than supplanting it. This has been the consistent approach of the courts since the early days of negligence. In *Blamires v Lancashire & Yorkshire Railway Co*,[61] for example, where a victim of a train derailment argued that the accident could have been avoided if the statutory requirement of a means of communication between passengers and driver had been complied with, Brett J said that it was right 'to use the Act as *some evidence of* what is due and ordinary care under the circumstances of this case' (emphasis added).[62]

[56] See, eg, *Tedla v Ellman*, 19 NE 2d 987 (NY 1939).

[57] C Forell, 'Statutes and Torts: Comparing the United States to Australia, Canada, and England' (2000) 36 *Willamette Law Review* 865, 871. One of the rationales for negligence per se provided in the *Restatement (Third) of Torts: Liability for Physical and Emotional Harm* (2010) is closely bound up with jury trial: see §14, cmt c.

[58] *Restatement (Third) of Torts: Products Liability* (1997) §4(a).

[59] See, eg, Road Traffic Act 1988 (UK), s 38(7) (breach of the Highway Code).

[60] See, eg, *Jackson v Murray* [2015] UKSC 5, [2015] 2 All ER 805 (driving past a stationary school bus at dusk).

[61] *Blamires v Lancashire & Yorkshire Railway Co* (1873) LR 8 Ex 283 (Court of Exchequer).

[62] ibid 289.

There are many subsequent decisions to similar effect, concerning both compliance and non-compliance.[63] It follows that while regulatory norms potentially carry great weight in the negligence analysis, nevertheless 'violators [may be] reasonable' in some cases, and 'compliers may be negligent' in others.[64]

A similar picture emerges if we switch our focus to other areas of tort law. We have already seen that in nuisance there is no defence of regulatory compliance, but at the same time there is no denying the profound impact which the non-conclusive effect of regulatory norms can have in nuisance cases, most obviously when it comes to assessing whether the interference with the use and enjoyment of the claimant's land was unreasonable. A good example is *Hirose Electrical UK Ltd v Peak Ingredients Ltd*,[65] where the question was whether odours emanating from a factory making food additives on an industrial estate were a nuisance to the unit next door. According to Mummery LJ, that the factory's operations were carried out in compliance with planning controls and 'without objection or intervention' by the relevant statutory enforcement authorities were 'relevant indicators of the levels of discomfort and inconvenience caused by the smell'.[66]

The same approach is adopted when it comes to strict product liability.[67] In *Wilkes v Depuy International Ltd*,[68] Hickinbottom J reiterated that a product's compliance or non-compliance with applicable regulatory standards is a relevant consideration when deciding whether it has a defect for the purposes of the Consumer Protection Act 1987.[69] And while he confirmed that the 'simple fact of regulatory approval' was not a defence under the legislation,[70] he made it clear that in some cases it might carry a great deal of weight:

> [W]here every aspect of the product's design, manufacture and marketing has been the subject of [substantial scrutiny], by a regulatory body comprised of individuals selected for their experience and expertise in the product including its safety, on the basis of full information, and that body has assessed that the level of safety is acceptable, then it may be challenging for a claimant to prove that the level of safety that persons generally are entitled to expect is at a higher level ....[71]

As that statement makes clear, the weight to be attached to a non-conclusive regulatory norm 'is a matter of fact and degree in the individual case'.[72] Less weight will be ascribed to it if the regulatory instrument is compromised as a result of political pressure by interested parties or because it 'covers a field in which apathy and fatalism has prevailed'.[73] Similarly, a regulation will lose much of its normative force if it is out-of-date, perhaps

[63] See, eg, *Franklin v Gramophone Co Ltd* [1948] 1 KB 542 (CA); *Bux* (n 22).

[64] C Morris, 'The Role of Criminal Statutes in Negligence Actions' (1949) 49 *Columbia Law Review* 21, 44.

[65] *Hirose Electrical UK Ltd v Peak Ingredients Ltd* [2011] EWCA Civ 987, [2011] Env LR 34.

[66] ibid [40].

[67] Fairgrieve and Goldberg (n 5) paras 10.93–10.97.

[68] *Wilkes* (n 32).

[69] ibid [99]–[101].

[70] ibid [101].

[71] ibid [100]. See also [124], applying this approach on the facts. The position adopted in *Wilkes* mirrors that in the *Restatement (Third) of Torts: Products Liability* (1997) as far as regulatory compliance is concerned, although non-compliance is conclusive of defectiveness: see §4.

[72] *Gee* (n 32) [175] (Andrews J) (strict product liability). See also *Bux* (n 22) 1369 (negligence).

[73] *Baker* (n 24) [101] (Lord Dyson).

by reason of evolving knowledge,[74] or if it has become customary to take more stringent precautions.[75] Conversely, the more detailed, comprehensive, rigorous and recent the regulation, and the more pertinent it is on the facts,[76] the more weight it will carry in the tort enquiry.

An important general point about the non-conclusive effect of regulatory norms is that they are internalised into the tort analysis rather than operating as an external force which is applied to it. This process of normative assimilation is facilitated by the open-ended nature of the tort standards in question, which eliminates any tension to which the interaction between regulatory law and tort law might otherwise give rise and which enables tort law to take the regulatory context into account without compromising its normative autonomy. In negligence, for example, the test of 'reasonable care' amounts in effect to one of prevailing community standards and expectations, and these are of course profoundly affected by the regulatory environment, with speed limits being a classic case in point.[77] Similarly, the nuisance standard of unreasonable interference boils down to the question of whether the claimant can reasonably be expected to put up with the consequences of the defendant's activity,[78] and again it is entirely appropriate that the regulatory context be factored into that assessment; if, for example, legislation sets maximum noise limits for industrial premises, then in general residents near a noisy factory should not be expected to put up with noise above those levels. It is also worth noting that the ease with which legislative standards are factored into these assessments is replicated in the case of other external norms, such as codes of practice and clinical guidelines. And since all types of external norm are dealt with in the same manner, there is no need for tort law to draw sharp distinctions between them, or to concern itself with technicalities which may not have much bearing on the norm's significance for the tort analysis, such as whether the originating statute was validly enacted.[79] It also follows that (unlike in the case of conclusive effect) the non-conclusive effect of a regulatory norm may extend beyond the precise circumstances governed by it.[80]

That brings me to my final observation about the non-conclusive effect of regulatory norms, which is that I am not seeking in any way to downplay its importance in the law of tort. For a start, without those norms the task of the courts would be much harder, as in each case the judge would have to decide from scratch what was generally acceptable in terms of driving speed in a built-up area, occupational noise exposure, industrial

[74] Lee (n 2) 565.

[75] See, eg, *Wintle v Bristol Tramways and Carriage Co* (1917) 117 LT 238 (CA) (failure of lorry to display two lights on a dark night negligent where that was customary in the area, even though the relevant regulation required only one).

[76] See, eg, *Gee* (n 32), where the absence of specific safety standards addressing the allegedly defective features of a hip prosthesis meant that the fact of regulatory approval was 'of limited assistance in the overall evaluation' of the defectiveness question ([489]).

[77] See, eg, Lee (n 2) 580, arguing that 'regulation can be an expression of collective values' (and, I would add, can also shape those values).

[78] *Coventry* (n 7) [179].

[79] See, eg, Morris (n 64) 31.

[80] See, eg, ER Alexander, 'Legislation and the Standard of Care in Negligence' (1964) 42 *Canadian Bar Review* 243, 269–71. A good example is *Thomas Stone Shipping Ltd v Admiralty* [1953] P 117 (CA) (regulations inapplicable to ships belonging to the Crown relevant when assessing standard of care to be expected of such a vessel).

pollution and so on.[81] Furthermore, I would readily accept that the regulatory context is frequently decisive in all three of the settings which have been considered here. The point is simply that in the case of non-conclusive effect (unlike conclusive effect) tort law interacts with regulation on its own terms, thereby maintaining its normative independence. And this remains true no matter how much weight is placed on the regulatory norm in a particular case, and no matter how often the result of the tort analysis happens to coincide with that of the regulatory process.

D. Other Forms of Interaction

We have already come across another form of interaction between tort and regulation, namely regulatory pre-emption, whereby tort liability is completely excluded in situations falling within the parameters of a given regulatory scheme. Regulatory pre-emption by legislative fiat is uncommon in English law, though there are examples: one can be found in the Nuclear Installations Act 1965, where common law liability is excluded for injury or damage caused by a nuclear incident connected to an installation covered by a nuclear site licence.[82] Turning to the common law, the lines become more blurred. Suppose for example that a court in a negligence case were to decide that because the situation in question was covered by a comprehensive regulatory scheme, it was not appropriate to recognise a duty of care. Would that amount to regulatory pre-emption of negligence liability?[83] If such a decision were to be grounded simply on the fact of the scheme's existence then it would be hard to deny that it was. By contrast, were the decision to be based on a range of considerations, only one of which was the presence of the regulatory scheme, then the description would be less apposite; the better view then might be that, rather than the regulatory scheme displacing negligence altogether, it was instead being factored into the negligence analysis, albeit at the duty stage rather than (as is more usual) at the breach stage.

That brings us to *Marcic v Thames Water Utilities Ltd*,[84] which has been described as an example of regulatory pre-emption in the common law of nuisance.[85] The claimant in *Marcic* brought an action in private nuisance against the local sewerage undertaker because the sewerage system occasionally overflowed, causing the external flooding of his home. The House of Lords dismissed the claim on the ground that imposing liability would be inconsistent with the limitations on the enforcement of sewerage undertakers'

[81] See, eg, *Coventry* (n 7), where Lord Carnwath pointed out the difficulties in noise nuisance cases of establishing 'objective and verifiable criteria by which to judge either the existence of a nuisance or the limits of any injunction' ([224]) and said that a detailed framework of conditions governing noise levels accompanying a grant of planning permission 'may provide a useful starting point or benchmark' for the court's consideration of these issues ([218]). On the facts, however, 'the conditions of the planning permissions, such as they were, were of little help to the judge' ([227]).

[82] Nuclear Installations Act 1965 (UK), s 12(1)(b). The Act creates a strict liability in place of the common law: see K Oliphant (ed), *The Law of Tort*, 3rd edn (London, LexisNexis Butterworths, 2015) paras 23.51–23.52.

[83] This scenario is perhaps unlikely, since (at least in recent times) the courts have tended to eschew this kind of argument from 'alternative remedies' in the negligence context: see ibid para 17.20.

[84] *Marcic v Thames Water Utilities Ltd* [2003] UKHL 66, [2004] 2 AC 42.

[85] M Lee, 'Occupying the Field: Tort and the Pre-emptive Statute' in TT Arvind and J Steele (eds), *Tort Law and the Legislature: Common Law, Statute and the Dynamics of Legal Change* (Oxford, Hart Publishing, 2013).

drainage obligations set out in the relevant regulatory legislation, the Water Industry Act 1991 (UK). It is important to note that this decision did not rest on the defendant's *compliance* with the regulatory scheme: the argument was rather that the scheme left 'no room in this case for a common law cause of action in nuisance'.[86] That certainly looks like the language of pre-emption, but matters were complicated by the peculiarities of the law on sewers.[87] Before *Marcic* there was a clear rule that nuisance liability could not attach to a sewerage undertaker for not building new sewers when its existing system was rendered inadequate by housing developments,[88] which was precisely the problem in the case. The Court of Appeal in *Marcic* considered that this rule had been superseded by later cases imposing liability on occupiers for failing to take reasonable steps to prevent hazards arising on their land from causing a nuisance to their neighbours.[89] However, the House of Lords held that the rule relating to sewers remained good law, and it was in so holding that the House attached significance to the existence of the parallel regulatory regime under the 1991 Act,[90] which in its view showed a clear legislative intention to entrust to the regulator rather than the courts the complex question of whether more or better sewers should be constructed. It follows that in *Marcic* regulatory pre-emption was deployed not to cut down existing rights, but as an argument against expanding liability, and in a setting with its own unique history and dynamic. The case is, therefore, of very limited general significance and there is little reason to suppose that it is a harbinger of a trend in English law towards immunity from tort liability for activities conducted under regulatory oversight.

Such a trend towards regulatory pre-emption has however been observable in American tort law for some time, with the primary driver being the supremacy clause of the US Constitution, which states that in conflicts between federal and state law, the former prevails. That clause can be interpreted to mean that where the defendant's activity is governed by a comprehensive regulatory scheme of federal origin, claims in state tort law are pre-empted by that scheme. The federal pre-emption doctrine is controversial and the case law and commentary voluminous,[91] but its origins in a unique constitutional and institutional context limit its significance for other common law systems. Furthermore, the US Supreme Court's jurisprudence on pre-emption focuses on express or implicit Congressional intent, with the result that 'by definition the analysis never reaches the level that really seems to matter from a policy perspective: comparative analysis of institutional competence'.[92] Two observations are worth making, however. One is that the assumption that there can be a clash between state tort law and federal risk regulation seems in part to reflect a peculiarly American vision

[86] *Marcic* (n 84) [36] (Lord Nicholls).

[87] ibid [59], where Lord Hoffmann emphasised that the relevant authorities were concerned with sewers and not 'general principles of the law of nuisance'.

[88] See, eg, *Smeaton v Ilford Corpn* [1954] Ch 450 (Ch D).

[89] See especially *Leakey v National Trust* [1978] QB 849 (QBD).

[90] See, eg, *Marcic* (n 84) [30], where Lord Nicholls pointed out that the defendant was only responsible for the sewers in question because they were vested in it by the regulatory legislation.

[91] For a helpful summary, see JCP Goldberg and BC Zipursky, *The Oxford Introductions to US Law: Torts* (New York, Oxford University Press, 2010) 389–94.

[92] RL Rabin, 'Reassessing Regulatory Compliance' (2000) 88 *Georgetown Law Journal* 2049, 2058.

of tort law as pre-eminently a regulatory mechanism.[93] And the other is that the US experience shows how fuzzy the boundary is between regulatory pre-emption and regulatory compliance, since in some cases the conclusion that state tort law is pre-empted by the federal regulatory framework is contingent on the defendant having complied with that regulatory regime, so that what looks like regulatory 'pre-emption' is in fact regulatory 'compliance'.

One particular category of pre-emption recognised in the American context is 'impossibility' pre-emption, which arises where the tort norm and the regulatory norm are irreconcilable, so that it is impossible to comply with one without violating the other. In the UK, the statutory product liability regime recognises a defence along these lines, which is applicable when the defect in a product 'is attributable to compliance with any requirement imposed by or under any enactment or with any retained EU obligation',[94] with the result that it was not possible to comply with the provision without rendering the product defective. When it comes to negligence, matters are more complex. Clearly the existence of a given regulatory provision may be relevant to the question of whether the defendant acted reasonably, as we saw above. And in some cases, the norm will in effect foreclose the analysis. So if there is legislation requiring that airbags be installed in all new cars, a claimant will obviously be unable to establish that it was negligent of a car manufacturer to install airbags, since it had no choice in the matter.[95] However, it is possible to imagine an emergency situation, in which it would be unreasonable to comply with a strict regulatory norm. Suppose for example that the only way for a driver to avoid hitting a child who suddenly runs into the road in front of her is to swerve and mount the pavement. Even if there is an absolute rule against driving on the pavement, it would clearly be unreasonable not to do so. In this scenario, then, the driver cannot discharge her tort duty of care while also complying with the regulatory norm.[96]

Although pre-emption is arguably the most important of the forms of interaction between tort and regulation which do not fit neatly into the three categories discussed above, it is not the only one. Another possibility is the use of presumptions, such that conduct not in compliance with a regulatory scheme is presumed to be negligent/unreasonable etc, or conversely that compliant conduct is presumed not to be.[97]

[93] Lee (n 85) 397: '[t]he assumption in most US Supreme Court cases [on pre-emption] is that tort is regulation … so that relatively little attention is paid to what we might call private law goals … [this] makes pre-emption easier …'.

[94] Consumer Protection Act 1987 (UK), s 4(1)(a). 'Enactment' here means any primary or secondary domestic legislation.

[95] See *Restatement (Third) of Torts: Liability for Physical and Emotional Harm* (2010) §16(b). A Scots case that comes close to this is *Wyngrove's Curator Bonis v Scottish Omnibuses Ltd* 1966 SC (HL) 47, where the pursuer contended that a bus operator should have installed a central pillar on the rear platform of its buses. The defenders argued that fitting such a pillar would have contravened a regulation governing the minimum width of the entrance opening. In the view of the Second Division of the Court of Session, the regulation would not have been breached by installation of a pillar, but Lord Walker said (at 69) that if it would have been then he would 'not have been able to hold' that the defenders were obliged to install one. The issue did not fall to be determined by the House of Lords, since in its view regardless of the regulation the courts below had been wrong to hold that the failure to install a pillar had been negligent.

[96] For discussion, see *Restatement (Third) of Torts: Liability for Physical and Emotional Harm* (2010) §16, cmt g. As that comment makes clear, it may be possible to read an implied exception into the statutory norm, but that will not always be the case.

[97] See, eg, *Sterling Trusts Corpn v Postma* [1965] SCR 324 (SCC) (non-compliance).

While strictly speaking this is just a variation on the standard approach whereby the regulatory norm or outcome influences the tort analysis in a non-conclusive manner, the formal weighting of the regulatory compliance or non-compliance in this way accords it special status in the tort analysis, so that, for example, non-compliance operates in a similar manner to *res ipsa loquitur*.[98]

Yet another technique is to take the regulatory framework into account at the remedies stage.[99] The decision whether to grant an injunction in an ongoing nuisance case illustrates the possibilities. It was suggested in *Coventry v Lawrence*[100] that the fact that the defendant's activity was being carried out following a prior grant of planning permission would weigh against the issuing of an injunction,[101] with Lord Sumption going so far as to suggest that it might be appropriate to hold that as a matter of principle injunctions should not be granted in such a case.[102] A similar approach could be taken to regulatory compliance more generally, and there were hints in *Barr v Biffa Waste Services* that additional flexibility at the remedies stage might be an appropriate trade-off for the refusal of the courts to recognise such compliance as a defence in the law of nuisance.[103] Indeed, the law could even go further, and prohibit injunctive relief in cases of regulatory compliance. In the 1950s Parliament rejected a legislative proposal which would have done precisely that in cases where the discharge of pollutants into rivers was compliant with a discharge consent, and which would therefore have confined those whose common law riparian rights were violated by the discharge to a remedy in damages.[104]

III. Arguments against Conclusive Effect

In this part of the chapter I show why tort law generally should not defer to regulatory norms and outcomes, but should instead process them by means of its own particular modes of analysis. This leads me to conclude that tort law should in general not recognise defences of regulatory compliance or make regulatory breaches automatically actionable.

The discussion that follows is organised around some fundamental distinctions between regulation and tort liability as instruments of legal intervention. As well as giving more structure to the analysis, this will highlight the extent to which the arguments

[98] See, eg, Alexander (n 80) 271–72.

[99] See, eg, M Lee, 'Tort Law and Regulation: Planning and Nuisance' (2011) 8 *Journal of Planning & Environment Law* 986, 990: '[t]he continued strength of private nuisance in a regulatory state probably depends on a more flexible approach to remedies'. See also Abraham (n 55) 388, for the suggestion of a link between the limiting of injunctive relief in American nuisance law and the growth of environmental regulation.

[100] *Coventry* (n 7).

[101] ibid [125] (Lord Neuberger), [169] (Lord Clarke).

[102] ibid [161]. But see [167]–[168] (Lord Mance), [246]–[247] (Lord Carnwath), arguing that this went too far, and that there should not even be a presumption against injunctive relief in a case where planning permission had been given. See further, D Nolan, 'Injunctions' in W Day and S Worthington (eds), *Challenging Private Law: Lord Sumption on the Supreme Court* (Oxford, Hart Publishing, 2020).

[103] *Barr* (n 7) [124].

[104] See B Pontin, 'Defending "Fundamental" Riparian Rights from Proposed Regulatory Law Limitations: Lessons from Parliamentary History' (2006) 17 *Water Law* 3, 10.

in favour of the general principle against deference pertain to particular features of regulation and tort, which may help us to identify the circumstances in which the case for the application of that principle is either particularly strong or relatively weak. The distinctions are as follows: (A) public interest/private interest; (B) public enforcement/private enforcement; (C) specific rules/general standards; (D) ex ante intervention/ex post intervention; and (E) administrative decision-making/judicial decision-making. These dualities are all to a greater or lesser extent paradigms, and some important qualifications of them will be flagged as we go along. One general point to note about them relates to the distinction between tort's standard-setting and enforcement roles,[105] the point being that the importance of the duality in question may relate primarily to one or other of those roles (most obviously standard-setting for the third, and enforcement for the second).

Before I turn to consider the first of those dualities, though, I should make one further observation. No serious evaluation of the interaction between tort and regulation could be conducted without reference to the extensive literature on the issue in the US. However, it must be emphasised that there are several characteristics of the legal and institutional context in the US which have had a considerable influence on the debate there, and which are not replicated in the rest of the common law world. The first is the use of juries in tort cases. This is critically important for the fifth of our dualities, because in the situations with which we are concerned, the choice of decision-maker in the US is generally between administrator and jury, whereas in most of the rest of the common law world it is between administrator and judge. Contemporary scepticism about the functioning of the tort system in the US has been said to focus on the role of the jury,[106] and this is indeed evident in arguments for the superiority of regulation over tort and in favour of a regulatory compliance defence.[107] A second distinctive feature of the American legal landscape pertaining to the fifth duality is the alleged poor quality and partisanship of the experts who appear in tort cases.[108] These criticisms have not been made with the same force elsewhere. Other distinctive features of the American tort system which should be borne in mind are: (1) that each state is an independent jurisdiction, which means, for example, that in the product liability context the same product can be the subject of multiple trials in different states, often yielding different outcomes;[109] (2) the prevalence of punitive damages awards, which, in the eyes of many, add to the unpredictability and arbitrariness of the system; and (3) the absence of a 'loser pays' costs regime, which accentuates over-deterrence concerns. Finally, turning to the regulation side of the equation, it has been said that 'American regulatory institutions, processes and styles are often very different from their British counterparts',[110]

[105] See Cane (n 11) 449.

[106] Rabin (n 92) 2061.

[107] See, eg, RB Stewart, 'Regulatory Compliance Preclusion of Tort Liability: Limiting the Dual-Track System' (2000) 88 *Georgetown Law Journal* 2167, 2177ff.

[108] See, eg, the scathing assessment of M Angell, *Science on Trial: The Clash of Medical Evidence and the Law in the Breast Implant Case* (New York, WW Norton, 1996) 109–32.

[109] See Stewart (n 107) 2169, who argues that as a result 'the tort system cannot ensure desirable consistency and coordination in legal requirements'.

[110] Ogus (n 13) v. See, for example, the contrast Ogus draws between the 'typical American regulatory agency' and its British counterpart (ibid, 104).

while ideological aversion to 'big government' manifests itself in deep scepticism in the US about the merits of top-down regulation. For all these reasons, great care must be taken when seeking to extrapolate from the American learning on tort and regulation lessons for other legal systems.

A. Public Interest/Private Interest

An obvious objection to tort deferring to regulation is that while the former is primarily concerned with the protection of private interests, the latter may be primarily concerned with the broader public interest. So while, for example, a regulatory decision on industrial pollution levels may be based on an overall assessment of the costs and benefits of the polluting activity, in the tort of private nuisance the focus will be on its impact on individual properties. The fact that the two systems are approaching the problem in such different ways, and for such different purposes, is a powerful argument against one of those systems deferring to the other.[111] This ties in with an important process concern about a regulatory compliance defence, which is that the effect of such a defence is to deprive claimants of their private law rights without their necessarily having standing to challenge the regulatory decision which has had this effect.[112] That concern in turn underlies the well-established principle that decisions taken in the public interest curtail private rights only if they amount to a direct expression of legislative will, a principle given effect in tort through the defence of statutory authority.[113] An additional defence of regulatory compliance threatens to upset the careful balance which this defence strikes between private and public interests, most obviously in nuisance cases.[114]

It could be objected that not all regulation is primarily concerned with the public interest, rather than private interests.[115] Even in the nuisance context, for example, planning authorities and regulators obviously do consider the interests of those living in close proximity to the relevant activity, and when it comes to workplace safety and product safety the private interests of workers and consumers are clearly central to the regulatory task. But it would be absurd to suggest that regulatory decision-making is always driven by private interests, or that, where it is, they necessarily coincide with the interests protected by the law of tort. Besides, even where it is, and they do, the process concern remains.

[111] See *Coventry* (n 7) [95] (Lord Neuberger), [194] (Lord Carnwath) ('planning controls and the law of nuisance may pull in opposite directions').

[112] See *Wheeler v JJ Saunders Ltd* [1996] Ch 19 (CA) 28; *Coventry* (n 7) [90]–[99]; *Burr* (n 7) [102]; Nolan (n 7) 201–202.

[113] See *Coventry* (n 7) [90], where Lord Neuberger objects as a matter of principle to the idea that the decision of a planning authority could deprive a person of a claim in nuisance where no suggestion to this effect is made in the planning legislation.

[114] See generally Nolan (n 7). This principle is elevated to constitutional status by Pontin (n 9) 186–87.

[115] See H Dagan and R Kreitner, 'The Other Half of Regulatory Theory' (2020) 52 *Connecticut Law Review* 605, arguing that while, for example, environmental protection agencies focus on aggregative cost/benefit, a significant subset of regulatory practice is more concerned with delineating the terms of our interpersonal transactions.

B. Public Enforcement/Private Enforcement

Let us suppose that the public/private interest distinction did not exist (as indeed seems to be assumed in much of the law and economics literature). Would there still be advantages to having tort law as a private enforcement mechanism operating in parallel with public enforcement by regulatory authorities? Clearly there would (though whether a private enforcement rationale is sufficient *on its own* to justify tort liability is a more difficult question, to which I will return[116]). The case for private enforcement is largely based on the possibility of regulatory failure. There are numerous instances of such failure exposed by tort litigation, especially in the contexts of industrial pollution and product safety.[117] Frequently these failures are the result of incompetence or inadequate resources. But sometimes the problem is 'regulatory capture', the phenomenon whereby the regulator becomes subservient to the regulated, with the result that the regulatory process loses much of its bite.[118] Although the problem of regulatory capture may have been exaggerated,[119] it stands to reason that, for example, a local authority regulator may be reluctant to take tough enforcement measures against a company which is the biggest single employer in its area and which contributes significant sums to the authority's coffers through business rates.[120] Furthermore, the highly specialised nature of many regulatory activities means that regulators may be heavily influenced by industry norms and knowledge when setting standards, and that there may be considerable interchange of employees between the regulatory agency and the regulated sector, which may militate against robust intervention and enforcement. The possibility of regulatory failure provides an additional justification for a parallel system of tort remedies, which can fill the public enforcement gap, while also enabling 'bottom-up' citizen participation in, for example, environmental protection, by contrast with the 'top-down' public enforcement model.[121]

C. Specific Rules/General Standards

The third duality contrasts the precision of regulatory norms with the generality of tort standards, most obviously those used in negligence ('reasonable care') and nuisance

[116] See below, text to nn 163–69.

[117] For examples concerning industrial pollution, see Pontin (n 9) 127; M Wilde, 'Nuisance Law in Industrial Wales – Local and National Conflicts (Part 2): Oil Refining, the Common Law and Regulation' in P Bishop and M Stallworthy (eds), *Environmental Law and Policy in Wales: Responding to Local and Global Challenges* (Cardiff, University of Wales Press, 2013). For examples concerning drug safety, see R Goldberg, *Medicinal Product Liability and Regulation* (Oxford, Hart Publishing, 2013) 162.

[118] Ogus (n 13) 57–58.

[119] ibid 94–95.

[120] That regulatory capture hampered past efforts to tackle industrial pollution in the UK is a persistent theme of Ben Pontin's work. And he points out that in the post-war period parliamentary opposition to a regulatory compliance defence in river pollution cases was in part driven by the fear that the exercise of regulatory powers would be unduly influenced by 'sectional interests': Pontin (n 104) 9–10.

[121] See J Steele, 'Private Law and the Environment: Nuisance in Context' (1995) 15 *LS* 236, 239–40. But see too Cane (n 11) 455–56, who points out that this can also be achieved by other means, such as the use of citizen suits for regulatory violations.

('unreasonable interference'). As far as regulatory norms are concerned, the duality is itself a generalisation, for the specificity of these varies enormously, and over time there has been a move away from highly particularised rules to more general standards expressed in terms of 'best available techniques' and the like.[122] Nevertheless, there are still many contexts in which exact regulatory standards are necessary and appropriate, not least because they are generally much easier and cheaper to enforce,[123] and because it is often its precision which gives the regulatory command the power to affect behaviour.[124] (Just imagine the impact on road safety if we replaced speed limits with a general instruction to drive at a 'safe' or 'reasonable' speed.) In any case, there is no doubt that the distinction is critically important when it comes to the interplay between tort and regulation, and it points to another quite fundamental objection to tort deference to regulatory norms. That objection is that whether the defendant has complied with a precisely expressed regulatory standard can *never* be automatically dispositive of the question of whether a broadly expressed tort standard has been breached, since while the former is relatively fact-*in*sensitive the latter is by its very nature highly fact-sensitive.[125] It is, for example, a well-established principle of negligence law that the breach of duty enquiry cannot as a matter of principle be reduced to the simple application of a pre-existing rule, such as that a pedestrian should always look both ways before crossing a road.[126] And the fact that the pre-existing rule is a regulatory norm does nothing to change that fact, since (as we have already seen) there are bound to be situations in which it is reasonable to violate such a norm, and indeed unreasonable to comply with it. This is a point which is frequently missed in discussions of private actions for breach of statutory duty and negligence per se, where it is common to see claims such as 'violation of a statute is by definition unreasonable',[127] a statement which is palpably false as a matter of negligence law.[128]

Two further points should be made about this duality between precision and generality. One is that the over-inclusiveness of regulatory norms is of course well understood by the regulators themselves, who can respond to it by exercising discretion when it comes to enforcement action.[129] By contrast, if, for example, we make regulatory breaches privately actionable via the tort of breach of statutory duty, there is

[122] On the different types of regulatory standards, see Ogus (n 13) ch 8.

[123] See R Baldwin et al (eds), *A Reader on Regulation* (Oxford, Oxford University Press, 1998) 15.

[124] On the 'optimal specificity' of regulatory standards, see Ogus (n 13) 168–70.

[125] For a compelling expression of this objection, see *Grand Trunk Railway of Canada v Ives* 144 US 408 (1892) 427.

[126] *Qualcast (Wolverhampton) Ltd v Haynes* [1959] AC 743 (HL) is the leading authority.

[127] See, eg, ER Thayer, 'Public Wrong and Private Action' (1914) 27 *Harvard Law Review* 317, 322–23 (Thayer calls the view that regulatory breach is merely evidence of negligence 'perplexing and difficult of comprehension', a description surely better suited to his position, especially as regards its incomprehensible reliance on proximate cause); G Williams, 'The Effect of Penal Legislation in the Law of Tort' (1960) 23 *MLR* 233, 252.

[128] See GL Fricke, 'The Juridical Nature of the Action Upon the Statute' (1960) 76 *LQR* 240, 242–51. In addition to the problem of fact-insensitivity, there are others. Suppose, for example, that a child claimant is faced with a plea of contributory negligence per se for violating the traffic code in a jurisdiction where (as is usual) the negligence standard of care is lowered for children. If the regulatory breach is automatically negligent then no such adjustment is possible (though in practice this is a situation where it seems the breach will be excused for these purposes: see *Restatement (Third) of Torts: Liability for Physical and Emotional Harm* (2010) §15(a)).

[129] See Hodges (n 15) 165.

nothing to stop a claimant from suing in a case of over-inclusiveness, and indeed every incentive for them to do so if it will bring forth compensatory damages. The result can be that a defendant is held liable for breaching an absolute regulatory standard when it had no real choice but to do so,[130] an outcome which is not easy to justify, and which may undermine the more nuanced process of regulatory enforcement. And the other point is that the generality of tort's standards means not only that they can be applied in a flexible manner to the facts of individual cases, but also that they tend to provide more comprehensive coverage than specific regulatory standards which are limited to particular activities, processes, etc. This gives tort an important interstitial role, enabling it to make up for the presence of gaps in the relevant regulatory regime, or indeed for the absence of any such regime at all.[131]

D. Ex Ante Intervention/Ex Post Intervention

The distinction between specific rules and general standards is connected to the next duality, which is that 'regulators look forward', either by giving prior approval to a future activity, or by setting precise standards for its conduct, whereas 'tort cases look backward', applying general standards to the way in which an activity was conducted in the past.[132] Again, this distinction rests on paradigms, and where regulation itself employs broad standards (such as 'best available techniques') it starts to collapse. But in the many instances where the distinction can be drawn, it points to yet further reasons why tort law should not defer to regulation. It is helpful when considering these to distinguish three distinct problems.

The first problem is that an ex ante regulatory regime may not be put in place until well after the inception of a given activity. In such a case, tort's backstop role may come to the fore, and there are many historical examples illustrating this.[133]

The second problem is the time gap between ex ante regulatory action and the defendant's conduct. Here the advantages of ex post tort intervention are obvious. New techniques and information, along with other changes of circumstances, may require a reasonable actor to go beyond the measures stipulated by the regulator, and failure to do should be capable of attracting tort liability. A regulatory compliance defence may enable regulated parties to just sit back and do nothing until the regulators catch up.[134] And note that this phenomenon is an argument not only

[130] See, eg, *John Summers & Sons Ltd v Frost* [1955] AC 740 (HL) (liability for failure to fence grindstone even though this would have made it unusable).

[131] Tort can play this role even in very heavily regulated areas: see, eg, Rabin (n 92) 2082 (arguing that prescription drug injury claims frequently arise in circumstances falling outside the scope of the 'comprehensive' regulatory scheme).

[132] DB Dobbs et al, *Hornbook on Torts*, 2nd edn (St Paul, West Academic, 2016) 10.

[133] See, eg, AWB Simpson, *Leading Cases in the Common Law* (Oxford, Oxford University Press, 1995) ch 7 (regulation of copper smelting came only after the decision in *St Helen's Smelting Co v Tipping* (1865) 11 HLC 642; 11 ER 1483).

[134] This issue may be exacerbated by the problem of 'regulatory lag', whereby regulatory standards do not keep up with developments in the regulated sector: see TM Schwartz, 'Regulatory Standards and Products Liability: Striking the Right Balance Between the Two' (1997) 30 *University of Michigan Journal of Law Reform* 431, 444–45, 451.

against conclusive compliance, but also against conclusive non-compliance, since one reason why non-compliance with a regulatory rule may be reasonable is that the rule is obsolete.[135] (The way in which tort responds to this problem points to a more general advantage which it has over regulation, namely that the latter tends to rely on intervention by the regulator, whereas tort law keeps potential defendants on their toes by subjecting them to a general, and therefore, dynamic standard. Suppose, for example, that a pharmaceutical company is considering whether actively to research adverse side effects of its drugs. In a regulation only environment, it has no incentive to do so unless and until the regulator requires it to, whereas the threat of tort liability may force it to adopt a more proactive stance.)

The third problem is the time gap between the defendant's conduct and the trial. This is not significant where the tort analysis rests on fault, since an assessment of the blameworthiness of conduct must of course be made in the light of the information available to the actor at the time of the conduct itself. However, it is potentially important when it comes to strict tort liability, so that for example a court tasked with assessing whether a product fails a risk/utility test of defectiveness may wish to rely on evidence of adverse effects which has only come to light since the product was marketed.[136] And to the extent that that is the case, a regulatory compliance defence is again problematic, since by definition that after-acquired knowledge cannot have informed the ex ante regulatory decision, with the result that the defence may soften the strictness of the liability and thereby frustrate the purposes for which it was imposed.[137]

E. Administrative Decision-Making/Judicial Decision-Making

The final duality contrasts regulatory decisions made by executive agencies and tort decisions made by judges. This issue of relative institutional competence has a much blunter edge outside the US, where key decisions in tort cases are made by a jury. Nevertheless, it still raises some important questions which should briefly be considered. In addressing them it must be emphasised that I am not asking whether tort or regulation is 'better' but instead whether in this context administrative and judicial decision-making can profitably operate in parallel, as opposed to one being subservient to the other. It should also be noted that this issue is more relevant to conclusive compliance than to conclusive non-compliance, where typically there is no parallel decision of a regulator, just a regulatory enactment to be given conclusive effect by the judge in the tort litigation.

As regards conclusive compliance, a typical scenario might involve a judge being asked to decide whether a waste treatment plant which a regulator has decided is being

[135] Keeton et al (n 52) 229. In *Conrad v Springfield Consolidated Ry Co* 88 NE 180 (Ill 1909), an old ordinance required guard wires to be put on certain electric cables. The defendant suggested that these were 'a menace rather than a protection' and that their use had largely been discontinued in recent years, but applying a negligence per se analysis the court refused to investigate this possibility.

[136] Oliphant (n 82) para 19.57.

[137] M Mildred, 'Pharmaceutical Products: The Relationship Between Regulatory Approval and the Existence of a Defect' [2007] *European Business Law Review* 1267, 1278.

operated in compliance with regulatory controls is causing a nuisance.[138] What are the relative merits of the agency and the judge as decision-makers in this case? It should readily be apparent (though it seems not to be to many lawyer economists) that that question cannot be isolated from the other distinctions identified above. After all, the point of many of those distinctions is that the questions posed of regulators and judges are not the same, and it stands to reason that different types of decision may be better suited to different decision-makers: judges may be better placed to decide ex post if the interference in a nuisance case was intolerable, for example, while a regulatory agency may be better placed to decide ex ante what measures should be taken to reduce pollution, and so on.[139] To that extent the final duality is really parasitic on the others.

But it is possible to identify contexts where the decisions to be made by the administrator and the judge are substantially the same. Suppose, for example, that a medical device approved by a regulator is said to be defective for the purposes of strict product liability.[140] In such a scenario, both the regulator and the judge are faced with the same basic question, namely whether the benefits of the device as designed outweigh the risks it poses.[141] Here it could be argued that all things being equal (ie, in the absence of new information, etc), the judge should not be allowed to second-guess the agency's decision, since the latter has superior expertise and knowledge. Clearly there is some force in this argument, but perhaps not as much as one might at first think. After all, judges second-guess the decisions of experts all the time, and a case of this kind is not that far removed from, say, an application for judicial review of an agency decision. This is because of the non-conclusive effect of the regulatory determination, which in such a scenario is bound to be highly significant, so much so that the case is likely to revolve around possible flaws in it. Furthermore, in assessing whether there were such flaws, the judge will be assisted by expert witnesses, whose evidence will be tested by rigorous cross-examination, as well as by vast amounts of data and analysis gathered by the parties. While the chances are that the judge will end up agreeing with the regulator anyway, the process of adversarial litigation may throw up clear evidence of regulatory failure, justifying a converse conclusion. Finally, it is as well to recall that regulators rely on outside expertise just as courts do; that judges may be able to carry out a more thorough evaluation of the evidence than a regulator struggling to perform a multitude of tasks with limited resources; that regulators may be unduly influenced by sectoral interests; and so on.[142] When it comes to institutional competence, therefore, an elite and well-resourced judiciary serviced by high-quality lawyers and experts may be more than a match for a regulator.

[138] See, eg, *Barr* (n 7).

[139] Cane (n 1) 314–15. As Lee says (n 85, 397), when asking institutional competence questions we need to consider 'what we want an institution to be competent at'.

[140] See, eg, *Wilkes* (n 32).

[141] The appropriate test for defectiveness in such a scenario is controversial, but a risk/utility approach is consistent with the UK case law: see Goudkamp and Nolan (n 18) para 11-031ff.

[142] One American study concluded that 'the case for administrative superiority [over the courts] rests in large part on selective idealization': CP Gillette and JE Krier, 'Risk, Courts and Agencies' (1990) 138 *University of Pennsylvania Law Review* 1027, 1100.

F. Additional Complications of Conclusive Compliance Rules

Finally, we should note some additional complications which may arise from the use of conclusive compliance rules in particular, and which are likely to mean that, rather than preventing litigation, a regulatory compliance defence simply shifts its focus. The issue is itself complex, and only a brief overview can be given here.[143] The first complication is what counts as 'regulation' for the purposes of a regulatory compliance defence. Ideally, this would be limited to legislative enactments and their progeny, but the line between this kind of public regulation and private regulation such as industry codes of practice is notoriously difficult to draw, while self-regulation adds further complexity to the picture.[144] Second, what does an operative regulatory norm or determination encompass? Would a compliance defence extend, for example, to 'off-label' use of a prescription drug which has been granted regulatory approval?[145] And if a regulation stipulates for one precaution to be taken against a given risk, to what extent would a compliance defence preclude a claimant from arguing in a negligence case that another precaution should have been taken against the same risk?[146] Third, which causes of action would such a defence encompass? Deceit as well as negligence? *Rylands v Fletcher* as well as nuisance? Fourth, what if there are inconsistent standards governing the same activity?[147] And fifth, would a regulatory compliance defence extend to target standards requiring 'best available techniques' and the like? (If so, the task of the court in applying it may be at least as involved as an enquiry into whether the defendant was negligent, etc.)

Some of these questions may be resolvable by unambiguous legislative provisions setting out the precise circumstances in which a regulatory compliance defence will apply, and indeed they point to the conclusion that such defences should be the preserve of Parliament rather than the courts. But another complication remains, which is the extent to which a claimant is free to contest the deployment of the defence on the ground that a relevant regulatory determination was flawed, for example because it was based on misleading or inadequate information, the regulator was swayed by industry pressure, and so forth.[148] Not allowing claimants to do this in effect transforms the defence from one of regulatory compliance into one of regulatory approval,[149] which can serve as a 'shield for industry misfeasance' in the form of deliberate withholding of information from regulators and such like.[150] Conversely, however, opening the door to such

[143] For a much more thorough exploration of these issues, focused in particular on pharmaceutical product liability, see Green (n 39), who concludes (507–508) that in that context a regulatory compliance defence 'is not nearly as neat nor as clean a reform' as many of its advocates may imagine.

[144] Lee (n 2) 561.

[145] Meaning uses the approval does not cover. See further on this complication, Rabin (n 92) 2077–79.

[146] See, eg, *Croston v Vaughan* [1938] 1 KB 540 (CA), where a regulation required vehicles to be fitted with brake lights, but it was argued that it had been negligent not to also give a hand signal when stopping suddenly.

[147] Lee (n 2) 571.

[148] See, eg, the list of preconditions for reliance on regulatory compliance as conclusively establishing non-defectiveness set out in the *Restatement (Third) of Torts: Products Liability* (1997) §4, cmt e.

[149] See above, text to n 39.

[150] Green (n 39) 488–89.

arguments may generate much complex litigation on satellite issues[151] and raises the question of whether recognition of the defence is really worth the candle.[152]

It should be noted that none of these complications attach to the non-conclusive effect of regulatory norms, where the norm is simply accommodated into the tort enquiry alongside custom, codes of practice and the like, and in such a way that no bright lines need be drawn.

IV. Potential Caveats and Counter-Arguments

There are some potential caveats to the argument in the previous section that generally tort law should not automatically defer to regulatory norms and outcomes but should instead incorporate them into its own analytical frameworks. There are also some counter-arguments which should be addressed. It makes sense to consider the caveats first.

A. Potential Caveats

The first potential caveat concerns remedies. Suppose that an activity which is causing an ongoing nuisance is one for which planning permission has been granted and which is being carried out in conformity with any applicable regulatory regime. As we have seen,[153] it has been suggested that even if the compliance should not serve as a defence to liability, it should at least be taken into account when deciding whether to grant an injunction, and one possibility would be to make it dispositive of that issue. While many of the arguments against making compliance conclusive still apply here, it is less invidious than at the liability stage, as the claimant will still receive compensation for the violation of her tort rights, in the form of damages in lieu of an injunction. It follows that there is a stronger case for making regulatory compliance conclusive at the remedies stage of the tort enquiry, although my own view remains that even here non-conclusive effect is to be preferred.

The second caveat is that the case for a regulatory compliance defence is stronger where it is argued that a product which has been given prior regulatory approval has a design defect for the purposes of strict product liability. In this scenario, the question of defectiveness boils down to a risk/utility analysis, with the result that the judge's task is very similar to the task of the regulator who approved the product in the first place, and the closing up of the normative space between the regulatory and liability regimes removes some of the arguments against the latter deferring to the former. There are also two further considerations which militate in favour of the defence in this context. One is that prior approval is typically required for new drugs and medical devices, where

[151] These might include potentially difficult causation questions, such as whether any missing information would have affected the regulatory decision: ibid, 491–492.

[152] See Schwartz (n 134) 456, arguing that a court may prefer simply to weigh the compliance heavily rather than engaging in a detailed exploration of the regulatory process.

[153] See above, text to nn 99–104.

there is often thought to be a particularly high risk of over-deterrence, which a regulatory compliance defence might serve to counteract.[154] And the other is that the defence could be limited to strict liability, and not applied to negligence, thereby preserving what we might think of as a claimant's core common law rights.[155] Even here, though, there are strong arguments the other way, most obviously the ability to factor into an ex post judicial assessment information that has come to light since prior approval was given,[156] and the likelihood that a regulatory compliance defence would merely shift the focus of litigation.[157] Again, therefore, on balance non-conclusive effect remains in my view the preferable approach, at least in the UK.

The third caveat picks up on the point made in the previous paragraph about the preservation of the claimant's core common law rights. Regulatory compliance or pre-emption is more justifiable in cases that do not involve these, for example where the court is considering whether to impose strict liability rather than fault liability,[158] or liability for an omission as opposed to positive conduct.[159] When it comes to strict liability in particular, this is arguably best left to legislation in any case, while the greater risk of over-deterrence again weighs in favour of a regulatory compliance defence.[160]

The fourth caveat is that there is clearly a need in any legal system for a public policy override, whereby tort liability can be excluded where doing so is essential for the furtherance of compelling public interests. In English law, that override takes the form of legislative authorisation of the defendant's activity, which gives the defendant a defence of statutory authority provided all reasonable steps are taken to minimise the disruption which the activity causes.[161] In addition, there is of course nothing to stop Parliament from expressly pre-empting common law liability altogether if it wishes.[162]

Finally, we come to the possibility that conclusive non-compliance rules such as the tort of breach of statutory duty are best understood as private enforcement mechanisms for public law norms. On this analysis, there is no need to justify liability in private law terms; rather, its justification lies in the reinforcement which a private right of action gives to the regulatory regime itself. Hence it has been argued that the American 'negligence per se' rule furthers the aims of the regulatory system by providing an additional incentive for compliance with government standards, and that this may be particularly important when the agencies charged with enforcement are often under-resourced and overstretched.[163] I have argued elsewhere that there is a degree of overlap between tort

[154] For this and other reasons, there is often thought to be a particularly strong case for a regulatory compliance defence in the case of medicinal products: see, eg, Schwartz (n 134) 440; Goldberg (n 117) 159–60.

[155] It is also worth noting that if over-deterrence is a concern, there are other ways of addressing it, such as a narrow test of defectiveness and a broad development risk defence.

[156] See especially Green (n 39) 495–96; Fairgrieve and Goldberg (n 5) para 10.97.

[157] See text to nn 143–52 above. The article by Green which is relied upon in that discussion relates specifically to prior approval and strict product liability.

[158] See D Howarth, 'Pecunia Non Olet' (2011) 70 *CLJ* 499, 501 ('restraining common law development [by reference to regulation] is entirely different from cutting back common law rights'). See also *Barr* (n 7) [95].

[159] See the discussion of the *Marcic* case, text following n 84 above.

[160] Cane (n 1) 325.

[161] The defence is most often observed in the nuisance context: Goudkamp and Nolan (n 18) paras 15-056–15-059.

[162] See text to n 82 above.

[163] Schwartz (n 134) 449–50.

and public law as legal categories,[164] and if this analysis of breach of statutory duty is correct then it is just another example of this phenomenon. But while a private enforcement rationale may indeed have underlain the early development of the action on the statute, at a time when public enforcement was relatively weak, and memories of the 'common informers' of the early modern era fresher, there is little evidence for such a rationale in the modern case law. Furthermore, it is difficult to reconcile such a rationale with the remoteness-type limits on liability that were identified at the outset of this chapter,[165] and also with the recognition of a defence of contributory negligence.[166] At a more fundamental level, any system of private enforcement tends to be patchy because of its reliance on those entitled to redress choosing to seek it,[167] and is open to the objection that, by bypassing regulatory agencies, it precludes the possibility of giving de facto flexibility to uniform standards by the use of discretion at the enforcement stage, a valuable regulatory technique.[168] Finally, even if these objections to private enforcement can be overcome, arguably something along the lines of the American 'citizen suit' is a preferable mechanism to employ for this purpose than the use of conclusory non-compliance rules in the law of tort.[169]

B. Counter-Arguments

I now wish to consider some possible counter-arguments against a general principle that tort law should not automatically defer to regulatory norms and outcomes. The first is that such deference may simplify the law and make the adjudicative task easier.[170] Hence, for example, a court in a product liability case could avoid the challenges of deciding ab initio whether a new drug was defective by simply deferring to the decision of the agency which approved its use. Similarly, conclusive non-compliance rules may simplify the court's task in, say, a workplace injury case, by enabling the judge to bypass the potentially difficult question of whether the employer was at fault. I am sceptical about this simplification claim in the case of conclusive compliance, because we have already seen that a regulatory compliance defence is unlikely to simplify the law at all.[171] The claim does however provide a possible justification for conclusive non-compliance rules. Ultimately, the question boils down to the advantages of a simpler adjudicative enquiry as compared with the disadvantages of applying an over-inclusive regulatory standard to determine questions of tortious compensation. And while the balance may be different in a system based on trial by jury, it seems to me that when it comes to judicial decision-making the costs outweigh the benefits, particularly when one bears in

[164] D Nolan, 'Tort and Public Law: Overlapping Categories?' (2019) 135 *LQR* 272.

[165] Text to nn 16–18 above. See on this point Fricke (n 128) 253.

[166] *Caswell v Powell Duffryn Associated Collieries Ltd* [1940] AC 152 (HL).

[167] See further J McLaren, 'Nuisance Law and the Industrial Revolution: Some Lessons from Social History' (1983) 3 *OJLS* 155.

[168] Ogus (n 13) 171.

[169] Cane (n 1) 312.

[170] See, eg, *Restatement (Third) of Torts: Liability for Physical and Emotional Harm* (2010) §14, cmt e (negligence per se).

[171] See text to nn 143–52 above.

mind the non-conclusive effect of the regulatory norm in the tort analysis and the knots that common law courts have tied themselves into when it comes to the application of conclusive non-compliance rules.[172]

A second counter-argument is an institutional comity concern, which is to say that by not deferring to regulatory standards in tort cases the courts are failing to show appropriate respect to the legislative branch.[173] Clearly, there is no question that courts must defer when Parliament expressly tells them to, but that is not in any doubt. Beyond that scenario, however, comity concerns are rooted in the misconception that by not deferring to the regulatory norm the court is somehow second-guessing it, a misconception itself based on the false assumption that the purposes of the regulatory and tort regimes are the same. It is simply a non-sequitur to argue, for example, that because Parliament imposed criminal liability for certain conduct, it necessarily intended there to be civil liability for loss caused by it as well,[174] or indeed vice versa.[175] Furthermore, there is a powerful counter to the comity objection as regards conclusive compliance, which is that it seems strange to argue that respect for Parliament requires us to conclude that when it enacts regulatory legislation to protect certain groups (workers, consumers, etc) the effect of the protective measure is to cut down their common law rights.[176]

The third counter-argument is that the relationship between tort and regulation should not be reduced to a single formula either for or against deference, but should instead be based on close scrutiny of the process by which the regulatory decision was reached. This is the view of Maria Lee, and is epitomised by her claim that the authority of regulatory norms in the negligence standard of care enquiry 'is best assessed via engagement with the process by which those norms were reached'.[177] This position may be best interpreted as a variation on the non-conclusive effect idea, since ultimately it is still the court in the tort litigation which decides to what extent it should follow the regulatory lead.[178] To that extent it seems to me to be formally reconcilable with the general principle for which I have been arguing, but at a substantive level it remains concerning, since (depending on the scope of the judicial enquiry into the regulatory process) this position may address only some of the objections to deference which I have identified, such as the possibility of regulatory failure, and not others, such as the mismatch between specific rules and general standards, and the advantages of

[172] Williams (n 127) 239–40, observes that sometimes courts in breach of statutory duty cases respond to the over-inclusivity problem by reading down the scope of the regulation, thereby complicating the law and adding to the difficulty of stating it.

[173] Thayer (n 127) 324; *Restatement (Third) of Torts: Liability for Physical and Emotional Harm* (2010) §14, cmt c.

[174] Dobbs et al (n 132) 250–51.

[175] On the dangers of reading too much into legislative inaction, see DA Farber and PP Frickey, 'In the Shadow of the Legislature: The Common Law in the Age of the New Public Law' (1991) 89 *Michigan Law Review* 875, 892.

[176] The same paradox arises in the case of environmental regulation and nuisance law: ibid 892–93 (by applying federal pre-emption doctrine to state nuisance law the US Supreme Court 'took a legislative endorsement of environmentalism as a message for judges to withdraw common law restrictions on pollution').

[177] Lee (n 2) 556. See also Lee (n 99) 987 (making the same argument in respect of the role of planning permission in nuisance law).

[178] As Lee herself makes clear: see, eg, Lee (n 2) 572 ('we would never expect the courts to give up their authority … to generate private law norms').

combining ex ante and ex post interventions.[179] It is also questionable how practicable it is for a judge in a private law case to be required to enquire into matters such as 'the ways in which interests were weighed' in the planning process,[180] and the likely complexity of such enquiries threatens to undercut any advantage deference might otherwise offer in terms of simplification of the adjudicative task.[181]

Finally, it could be argued that giving conclusive effect to regulatory norms will act as an incentive to comply with those norms, and that conclusive compliance rules reduce the risk of over-deterrence. As these are both empirically based arguments, the onus is on those who deploy them to produce evidence in support. It seems plausible to suppose that conclusive effect may help to ensure compliance, but I suspect its impact is very limited, and contingent on a host of other factors, such as the rigour of the public enforcement regime and the frequency of tort litigation in the relevant field. As for justifying regulatory compliance defences by reference to the risk of over-deterrence, the evidence that this is a serious problem in the contexts (such as product liability) where the concern is most commonly raised has not been forthcoming.[182] It should also be emphasised that the likelihood of over-deterrence depends on cultural and institutional factors, and while my intuition is that the danger may be real enough in the US, as regards the rest of the common law world I remain unpersuaded.

V. Conclusion

The overall message of this chapter is twofold. First, that the relationship between tort and regulation is complex and multifaceted. And second, that tort and regulation should be seen as complementary rather than competitive. Despite the complexity of the relationship between these two areas of law, I have sought to show that from a private law perspective it should be governed by a single general principle, namely that tort law should not automatically defer to regulatory norms and outcomes but should instead incorporate them into its own analytical frameworks. The principle can of course admit of exceptions, and I have flagged some potential caveats in the final part of the chapter. Nor does it entail that tort law ignore regulation: far from it. The point is rather that

[179] This does though depend both on the type of regulatory decision in play and on what Lee means by engagement with the regulatory process. For example, when it comes to grants of planning permission the specific/general distinction is irrelevant (as the planning inspector comes to an 'all things considered' determination in the unique circumstances of the case), whereas the ex ante/ex post distinction remains highly pertinent. Then again, Lee's approach seems to extend beyond matters of process to include things like the age of the planning permission (ibid 989), a nod to the ex ante/ex post duality. The more the enquiry into the regulatory determination encompasses, the more the enquiry collapses into a non-conclusive effect analysis, where these sorts of factors go to the weight to be attached to the regulatory norm or decision. My overall feeling is that if Lee's approach is not sensitive to all of the arguments I have made for a general principle of non-deference then it is flawed for that very reason, and if it is so sensitive then in substance it is the standard non-conclusive effect approach for which I am arguing.

[180] ibid 989.

[181] The complications are similar to those arising from a regulatory *compliance* defence (as opposed to a regulatory *approval* defence): see text to nn 151–52 above.

[182] Goldberg (n 117) 159–60.

tort law must retain its own normative integrity, by giving non-conclusive, rather than conclusive, effect to regulatory standards and determinations. As Lee says:

> [S]ometimes the distinction between deferring to external norms and their pragmatic but non-hierarchical use will be a fine one. But it is nonetheless important ... The approach of the courts to external norms means that the courts maintain their own authority and responsibility to set standards, but are able also to acknowledge and rely on the authority of other actors. Courts neither hand over their authority to external sources, nor ignore the authority and relevance of those sources.[183]

Although I have distinguished throughout between conclusive compliance rules and conclusive non-compliance rules, and at times identified arguments against deference applicable to only one of these, it must be emphasised that the case against conclusive effect cuts both ways. Hence while some commentators have argued against a regulatory compliance defence while defending conclusive non-compliance principles,[184] in my view the two essentially stand or fall together.[185] It follows that not only should English law continue to set its face against regulatory compliance defences, but also that the tort of breach of statutory duty should be limited to cases where Parliament has expressly enacted that violation of a legislative provision is to be privately actionable.

The argument for tort deferring to regulation tends to be rooted in the assumption that they serve the same basic purposes, an assumption which clearly I do not share. But even if we adopt that assumption, more sophisticated instrumentalist analysis demonstrates that tort and regulation are capable of working effectively as parallel systems of norm generation. In particular, a tort liability regime based on general standards of reasonableness and the like provides a failsafe mechanism for regulatory systems, thereby reducing the pressure on those systems to ramp up intervention in a way that may stifle innovation.[186] This benefit of tort law is not merely theoretical, but can be illustrated by reference to the nineteenth century British experience.[187] Furthermore, in tort's absence, regulatory systems might be required to adapt their standards and processes to take more account of the private interests no longer protected by civil liability.[188] And tort litigation may also serve to improve existing regulatory systems by

[183] M Lee, 'The Sources and Challenges of Norm Generation in Tort Law' (2018) 9 *European Journal of Risk Regulation* 34, 46.

[184] See, eg, Rabin (n 92) 2051. The justification Rabin gives for the asymmetry is the usual one, namely that regulatory standards set only a 'minimum standard of safety'. See also *Restatement (Third) of Torts: Products Liability* (1997) §4, cmt e. However, this explanation is question-begging, while the characterisation of regulation in terms of 'minimum standards' flies in the face of modern regulatory methods.

[185] The case for a symmetrical principle against conclusive effect has also been made on economic grounds: S Shavell, 'Liability for Harm versus Regulation of Safety' (1984) 13 *Journal of Legal Studies* 357, 365–66.

[186] See Rabin (n 92) 2076; Abraham (n 55) 398. For an economic analysis demonstrating that the optimal level of regulation would be stricter without tort liability, see CD Kolstad et al, '*Ex Post* Liability for Harm vs *Ex Ante* Safety Regulation: Substitutes or Complements' (1990) 80 *American Economic Review* 888.

[187] B Pontin, 'Tort Law and Victorian Government Growth: The Historiographical Significance of Tort in the Shadow of Chemical Pollution and Factory Safety Regulation' (1998) 18 *OJLS* 661, 674–75 (tort law relieved 'pressures towards ever more detailed and prescriptive bureaucratization' in factory safety regulation), 679 (without civil redress alkali inspectors were concerned that they would need to introduce stricter preventative measures).

[188] See, eg, Pontin (n 104) 6, pointing out that nuisance liability has helped government to resist pressure for third party merits appeal in planning cases.

bringing to light regulatory violations, regulatory gaps and regulatory failures,[189] as well as triggering beneficial technological developments which can subsequently be rolled out by the regulatory regime.[190] Nor are the benefits of a parallel system one-way traffic. As we saw earlier,[191] the existence of regulatory standards governing so many aspects of social life is invaluable to courts tasked with applying tort's general standards to the facts of particular cases. And the existence of a rigorous regulatory regime may also enable tort law to adopt a relatively minimalist approach, based on its core concepts of fault and causation, rather than developing stricter forms of liability or watering down causation rules in response to threats posed by especially dangerous or harmful activities.[192]

Painstaking historical analysis of the relationship between nuisance and regulation has led Pontin to highlight the advantages of the two operating in tandem as complementary forms in a pluralistic legal landscape.[193] According to him, '[r]egulatory law and common law are inter-dependent, rather than substitutable', with the result that limitations on the latter can have a detrimental effect on the design and enforcement of the former.[194] As his scholarship demonstrates, the past history of tort and regulation is a story of private and public law combining to perform mutually complementary functions in response to new technologies and other threats to individual and communal well-being. And while advocates of tort's subjugation to regulatory law may frame their case as a necessary adaptation to modern conditions, close consideration of the complex relationship between tort and regulation shows that the former continues to play an indispensable role governing interpersonal relationships in the shadow of the regulatory state.

[189] ML Lyndon, 'Tort Law and Technology' (1995) 12 *Yale Journal on Regulation* 137 ('an important social learning mechanism'). See also Rabin (n 92) 2069–70; Abraham (n 55) 391; Goldberg (n 117) 165 (arguing that for this reason the structural connections between drug regulators and the tort system should be enhanced). For an example of nuisance litigation performing this function, see *Marcic* (n 84) [26]–[28].

[190] The existence of this phenomenon is a key finding of Pontin's study of nuisance injunctions: Pontin (n 9).

[191] Text to nn 59–81 above.

[192] As to strict liability, see *Cambridge Water* (n 10) 305 (extensive environmental regulation a reason not to extend common law strict liability in pollution cases). Regarding causation, departures from causation orthodoxy are sometimes driven by deterrence concerns which would be heightened by the absence of other incentives to act with due care: see D Nolan, 'Causation and the Goals of Tort Law' in A Robertson and H Tang (eds), *The Goals of Private Law* (Oxford, Hart Publishing, 2009).

[193] See especially Pontin (n 9).

[194] ibid 130.

10

Regulating Relationships: The Regulatory Potential of Tort Law Revisited

JENNY STEELE

I. Introduction

This chapter revisits the question of tort law's regulatory potential. At the same time, it reconceptualises what kind of regulatory potential this might be. In his article, 'Tort Law as Regulation',[1] Peter Cane acknowledged that tort's regulatory potential was of legitimate interest, but also concluded that it was inherently limited. It was limited because it did not match tort's key concern, which Cane identified as 'rules and principles of inter-personal responsibility for harm'.[2] While it was, he argued, certainly fair to assess the extent to which tort may be used to achieve regulatory goals, it would not be fair to criticise it for failing to achieve something with which it is not centrally concerned. Viewing tort through a regulatory lens, he concluded, would always lead to a distorted image.

The approach in this chapter is different, in that it does not equate tort's regulatory potential with its ability to achieve adjustments in behaviour defined in advance as desirable from an external perspective. Rather, it seeks to identify the possible regulatory character of tort, in a way that takes account of its internal structure, institutions, and concerns. Attending to these features, what sort of regulation might tort, as it stands, already be? I am seeking a regulatory lens which will sharpen, rather than distort, our perception of tort. I find this in its responsive structuring of duties and liabilities within relationships. Responsiveness is a key theme of the discussion in this chapter, and it is important to note that it has a range of meanings.[3] Tort is described here as 'responsive' both because it responds to the claims and concerns of the regulated community (in which I include both claimants and defendants); and to the extent that it is open to consideration of surrounding values and context, including the impact on

[1] P Cane, 'Tort Law as Regulation' (2002) 31 *Common Law World Review* 305.
[2] ibid 306. See also P Cane, *The Anatomy of Tort Law* (Oxford, Hart Publishing, 1997).
[3] 'Responsiveness' is an important theme of contemporary regulation scholarship (see section II) and, in a different form, it has also featured in some influential socio-legal analysis: P Nonet and P Selznick, *Law and Society in Transition: Toward Responsive Law* (New York, Harper and Row, 1978).

other relationships and the connection with other aspects of law. As with any branch of law, 'responsiveness' brings with it certain risks and tensions; but is increasingly understood to be essential to effective legal institutions.

Cane's article expressly limited its analysis of tort's 'regulatory potential' to consideration of its capacity to change behaviour (through standards, monitoring, and compliance) in line with regulatory goals.[4] Since tort law utilises both standards and sanctions, and since it is hard to deny that the courts – and sometimes legislators and litigants – have at least some ambition to affect behaviour and discourage breaches of tort's duties, this is an understandable starting point. It is also a starting point which has been addressed in existing literature on the regulatory capacity of tort, sometimes with more positive conclusions.[5] But as Cane argued, this approach focuses primarily on one aspect of the law of tort, namely controlling the behaviour of defendants, and thus it is a poor fit with tort's internal structure, which does not consider this question on its own. It is fair to say that tort is concerned with 'behaviour' only where additional criteria justifying responsibility for interference or harm are satisfied.[6]

As I have said, this chapter takes a different direction in searching for the regulatory potential of tort, asking how we might consider tort law to be 'regulatory', while addressing the conceptual structure of tort. Could tort law's principles of responsibility be the very key to understanding the distinctive regulatory nature of tort, as a branch of private law? For tort scholarship, if we can understand tort as regulatory, this will affect the understanding of some of its principles, the reasoning processes applied in developing these principles, and the way that these reasoning processes are evaluated. It would mean, for example, that familiar questions about the capacity of tort to operate where there are public law systems in place would be questions, not about regulation versus common law principle, but about different regulatory systems interacting. It will also shed light on the way we might understand the relationship between tort and contract as aspects of private law's regulation of (predominantly) private actors. Perhaps most immediately, it will help us to address the tension between rival styles of reasoning that can be observed in the most significant tort decisions. For regulation scholarship, such an analysis would suggest that the regulatory contribution of private law, but most particularly of tort, has been neglected, despite its fit with some of the core interests of recent theories of regulation. I argue that law which responds to disputes and seeks to adjust or improve the nature of interaction within relationships may justly be viewed as regulatory, and that it will have distinctive strengths and weaknesses. This, of course, requires adoption of a less narrow definition of regulation than has typically been adopted when assessing tort's regulatory potential, as explored in section II.

The illuminating effect of analysing tort as regulatory can be seen by placing tort law within the well-known 'regulatory trilemma'.[7] The 'trilemma' holds that law may fail in

[4] Cane (n 1) 312: '[f]rom a regulatory perspective, tort law is analogous to traditional command-and-control regulation'.

[5] Cane (ibid), gives the example of 'citizen suits' in the USA, which have gained some support. See also S Rose-Ackerman, 'Tort Law in the Regulatory State' in P Schuck (ed), *Tort Law and the Public Interest: Competition, Innovation and Consumer Welfare* (New York, Norton, 1991).

[6] Even 'maliciously causing harm' has not developed as a general justification for responsibility: see further, section V.

[7] G Teubner, 'Juridification Concepts, Aspects, Limits, Solutions' in G Teubner (ed), *Juridification of Social Spheres: A Comparative Analysis in the Areas of Labor, Corporate, Antitrust and Social Welfare Law*

its regulatory objectives in three different ways. It may remain internally coherent yet fail to have any impact on the practices it seeks to influence (we may refer to this as ineffectiveness). It may be effective in such a way that subverts social practices (inappropriateness, or lack of responsiveness). Or, it may become so open and responsive to social practices and external perspectives that it subverts its own coherence (lack of coherence, leading – we may add – to loss of authority). In each of these three ways, regulatory law may be vulnerable to instability. I argue that the analysis applies comfortably to the law of tort; and that its application is capable of being enlightening, rather than distorting. It reflects real tensions surrounding tort's degree of openness and aspiration to influence. We can certainly frame doctrinal struggles within the law of tort in terms of efforts to maintain the law's own coherence, while responding to external perspectives and weighing a range of interests and considerations.

The chapter therefore proposes a perspective on tort as a form of regulation which places it within much broader assessments of the challenges facing legal systems, but without losing sight of the particular structural and conceptual nature of the subject. Indeed, these must be incorporated into any assessment of its regulatory character. In order to introduce this way of addressing tort, the chapter is structured as follows. In section II, I consider how an expanded notion of 'regulation' beyond 'command and control', consistent with some of the recent concerns of regulatory scholarship, is needed in order to encompass private law. In section III, I highlight two important insights from 'Tort Law as Regulation' which I believe help us to understand the regulatory character of tort, and the significance of acknowledging it. One directs our attention to the importance of both parties and their relationship. It cautions against the perception of tort simply in terms of an event – in which one party is active and the other suffers harm – rather than in terms of the relationships within which legal claims occur. The other invites us to consider tort as something broader than its substantive principles. In section IV, I ask what we can learn from the example of contract scholarship, which has been considerably more ready to approach private law in terms of regulation. It is suggested that there is no stark distinction between tort and contract which would explain or justify the lack of attention to tort's regulatory role and character in similarly responsive terms. The readiest explanation for the lack of attention to tort in this sense lies in the diversity of the relationships to which it applies.

Section V turns to the critical question of how tort constructs and regulates various relationships. It does this 'responsively' in more than one sense. It is responsive in that its regulatory functions respond to demand and are designed to be sensitive to the needs of the regulated community, which includes both claimants and defendants. In this respect, it has the capacity (not always realised, of course) to develop some of the features of 'really responsive' regulation,[8] replicating some of the same understanding and reasoning processes as regulated parties. It will be best able to do this in respect of relationships whose internal values and discourses are comprehensible to private law (and where it can help to build these values and discourses). Lack of responsiveness,

(Berlin, W de Gruyter, 1987). See also C Parker and J Braithwaite, 'Regulation' in P Cane and M Tushnet (eds), *Oxford Handbook of Legal Studies* (Oxford, Oxford University Press, 2003).

[8] R Baldwin and J Black, 'Really Responsive Regulation' (2008) 71 *MLR* 59–94.

or a perception of it, may lead directly to pressure for political reform, demonstrating a loss of authority.[9] Or, the courts themselves may respond to criticism or their own uncertainty by seeking more coherence,[10] or more restraint.[11] Tort law is also responsive in the different sense, set out by Nonet and Selznick, that courts will adopt varied reasoning styles and as part of this, will consider a wide array of interests and potential outcomes of their decisions. There is a tension between the appeal to specifically legal arguments framed in terms of rights and duties, and to more local and contextual understandings of the likely influence of liability decisions. The concluding section of the chapter (section VI) draws together the threads and asks how we might begin to judge tort's regulatory potential, adjusting the approach to its regulatory character as presented here.

II. 'Regulation'

As explained, this chapter begins its exploration of tort's regulatory potential with a prior question: can we identify the regulatory character of tort (in such a way as to take seriously its structure and tools of analysis)? A necessary change in asking this revised question is greater sensitivity in defining what counts as 'regulatory'.

Defining regulation is recognised to be problematic. Regulation has often been associated with the work of specific regulatory agencies, whose role is to influence behaviour and to achieve social welfare goals. Morgan and Yeung note, for example, that a dominant strand in regulation scholarship regards regulatory law as an institution used by the state to achieve chosen collective (community) goals.[12] This is broadly the notion of regulation adopted by Cane, as we saw in section I, since it appeared to him to map onto tort's concern with standards and behaviour. But available notions of regulation are much broader than this definition. As Morgan and Yeung go on to note, at its broadest, 'regulation' encompasses all forms of social control, whether intentional or not, and whether imposed by the state or other social institutions.[13] Similarly, Parker and Braithwaite have noted the growing interest in 'regulatory pluralism': in their words, 'the state is not, and never has been, the sole font of regulation',[14] and the broadest reading of regulation is 'influencing the flow of events'.[15] Parker, Scott, Lacey and Braithwaite

[9] The rise of 'compensation culture' rhetoric in the United Kingdom, and of 'tort reform' movements in the United States and Australia, rest on claimed failures to fit the needs and values of the regulated community.

[10] See, eg, *Poole BC v GN* [2019] UKSC 25, [2020] AC 780. See also related cases considered in section V.

[11] See, eg, *White v Chief Constable of South Yorkshire* [1999] 2 AC 455 (HL) (where public opinion would not have responded well to police officers claiming successfully for psychiatric damage where relatives of deceased members of the public could not) and *Tomlinson v Congleton* [2003] UKHL 47, [2004] 1 AC 46 (at a time when 'compensation culture' rhetoric was emanating from government and the press). That coherence was not the key concern in *White* is illustrated by open discussion of the number of anomalies that exist within the law of tort.

[12] B Morgan and K Yeung, *An Introduction to Law and Regulation: Text and Materials* (Cambridge, Cambridge University Press, 2007) ch 1.

[13] ibid 3–4.

[14] Parker and Braithwaite (n 7) 129.

[15] ibid 119. This broadest definition is linked by Parker and Braithwaite to 'governance' and Foucauldian governmentality. It is far removed from the perception that regulation must involve the adoption of a clearly defined welfare goal.

propose a definition of regulation as 'the intentional activity of attempting to control, order or influence the behaviour of others'.[16] Plainly, law is not essential to regulation understood in these broader senses; and the issuing of commands is not the sole form that regulation can take. While some forms of regulation require intentional ordering, others do not; and 'ordering' need not be aimed at a specific and clearly defined welfare goal. There is certainly no reason why only a certain form of law should be analysed as regulatory; nor is it inevitable that a regulatory analysis will involve measuring an area of law against achievement of a set welfare goal.

At the same time, regulation scholars have shown growing interest in exploring diverse forms and sites of regulation, in response to shortcomings in the traditional model of 'public' regulation, and in response to changing notions of the role of the state. As Parker and Braithwaite put it:

> In the new regulatory state, policy-makers and researchers have lost confidence in the ability of traditional regulation via 'command-and-control' to adequately govern conduct, especially business conduct.[17]

They go on to explain that attention has shifted to processes of monitoring and enforcement. The inner workings of private law do not fit well with this particular new centre of attention. Liabilities do not lend themselves so well to analysis in terms of negotiated compliance.[18] Yet private law is an alternative, and in its own way decentred site of regulation, which is potentially responsive both to party demand (arising especially from market activity), and to the interaction between private law, and other regulatory frameworks.[19] There has been greater readiness to identify some of the new directions in regulation with the law of contract, than with the law of tort, partly because the 'new regulatory state' has expressly adopted contractual principles as a (proposed) alternative to state regulation. It has been pointed out that a similar move to prioritise tort principles has not been part of the agenda.[20] Indeed tort has been rhetorically undermined rather than strengthened, and subjected to reform movements during the same era. While contract might appear to be associated with a 'deregulation' agenda, tort is seen as imposing sometimes inappropriate liabilities. Both sides of the dichotomy are misleading, and I will argue in sections IV and V that tort and contract cannot be entirely separated in relation to their mode of regulation. The regulatory role of tort is harder to identify partly because tort covers a wide range of relationships. That does not mean that it is divorced from relationships.

[16] J Black, 'Critical Reflections on Regulation' (2002) 27 *Australian Journal of Legal Philosophy* 1. See also C Parker et al (eds), *Regulating Law* (Oxford, Oxford University Press, 2004); J Stapleton, 'Regulating Torts' in Parker et al, ibid, 122.

[17] Parker and Braithwaite (n 7) 127.

[18] Yet there has been analysis of private negotiation in the light of injunctive remedies. See, eg, B Pontin, 'The Common Law Clean Up of the "Workshop of the World": More Realism about Nuisance Law's Historic Environmental Achievements' (2013) 40 *Journal of Law and Society* 173, with a particular emphasis on enforcement. More generally, it could be argued that the practice of settlement is in substance a pattern of negotiation.

[19] A Corbett, 'The (Self) Regulation of Law: A Synergistic Model of Tort Law and Regulation' (2002) 25 *University of New South Wales Law Journal* 616.

[20] Stapleton (n 16).

Responding to the weakened confidence in 'command and control', broader notions of regulation have emerged which abandon the primacy of governmental activity, leaving space for varied mechanisms of social ordering. These developments have often skipped over private law, yet they can be understood to open the door to studies of private law, including tort, as regulation.[21] To achieve this for tort, not just for contract, we need to prise apart the link between tort law and standard setting, and approach it instead as a means of guiding the ordering of relationships. For example, Morgan and Yeung have responded to the broadening notion of regulation by seeking to identify the potential roles of law within it, proposing that law may have 'facilitative' or 'expressive' roles that in turn cast the law in the role of 'threat' or of 'umpire'. Law, on their analysis, 'forms part of the infrastructure that links the state to the market, to the community, and to individuals'. This way of identifying the core of the legal role in 'decentered' regulation[22] clearly opens the door to exploring the potential and pitfalls of private law as regulation.

In 'Tort Law as Regulation', Cane referred to the emergence of new directions in legal scholarship but, as we have seen, he expressly took the view that command and control was the variety of regulation that had the best fit with the 'standard-setting and sanctions' aspect of the law of tort.[23] I suggest, however, that if we are genuinely to understand the regulatory character of tort, the choice of a 'command and control' lens represents a missed opportunity. The association of a regulatory lens with command and control is tempting given the availability of standards and sanctions within the law of tort. There is an obvious space in which the 'core' understanding of regulatory law, as setting and enforcing standards might fit within the law of tort; and it is easy enough to see why litigants might be seen as potential 'enforcers' of public standards. But the parallel is inevitably open to Cane's riposte that it is a poor match for the internal structure of tort. The association with command and control and instrumental behaviour modification is flawed as an interpretation of tort's regulatory character; and inevitably leads to the conclusion that its potential is limited.

If we are to move on from this, we might consider how tort can be related to 'responsive regulation'.[24] 'Responsive regulation' has been championed not only because it fits political trends to decentre the state, but on the basis that regulation which is in tune with and responsive to the thought processes and priorities of regulated parties is able to avoid some of the obstacles faced by traditional models of regulation. A pertinent aspect of responsive (or 'really responsive'[25]) regulation

[21] S Halliday and C Scott, 'Liability as Regulation' (2006) Compensation Culture Project Working Paper No 1, https://scholar.google.com/scholar?oi=bibs&hl=en&cluster=1015540747452904577, accessed 6 July 2021. The authors' particular concern was with the impact of liability on public authorities, and with the regulatory network of parties which exists around the imposition of liability.

[22] J Black, 'Decentring Regulation: Understanding the Role of Regulation and Self-Regulation in a '"Post-Regulatory" World' (2001) 54 *Current Legal Problems* 103.

[23] Cane (n 1).

[24] I Ayres and J Braithwaite, *Responsive Regulation Transcending the Deregulation Debate* (New York, Oxford University Press, 1992). Responsive regulation is discussed by Cane, but not taken up as the standard to measure tort's regulatory potential.

[25] Baldwin and Black (n 8): where regulation is 'really' responsive, more elements of the culture of the regulated parties – encompassing interests, values, mechanisms and reasoning – is considered pertinent.

is a greater proposed integration of private and public concerns and values, as well as private and public 'regulatory' actions. To the extent that tort law's functions centrally include the structuring of rights and responsibilities within relationships, it can be seen as having a 'regulatory' function, amounting to a responsive – and decentered – form of intervention into these relationships. Even the well-known regulatory weakness of private law, that it reaches its decisions reactively, is a characteristic that can be understood in terms of 'decentering': private law's interventions arise from demand, in the form of legal disputes, and in this sense it is responsive to the regulated community.[26] That community generates questions which will lead to the refinement of rights and liabilities. It is not only claimants and their advisors who frame these questions – 'repeat' defendants choose which claims to settle and which to resist, thus seeking authoritative resolution. Rather than approaching tort in terms of 'command and control', I think it more promising to consider tort as providing tools of responsive regulation, in need of better understanding.

The law of tort can be approached and assessed as seeking to be responsive to the needs of the parties whose relationships it regulates; to the character of those relationships; and to their context. Although it necessarily subjects the parties to governing ideals and values, exercising authority by reference to these ideals, it plainly seeks to do so through attention to the specific contexts with which it deals.[27] That is not, of course, to say that it does this equally well in different contexts.[28] But much debate in tort cases can be seen as reflecting this attempt, as can its structure. Before the rise of interest in responsive regulation, factors of the same type were recognised as among the potential attributes of private law. For example, private law's responsiveness was described as allowing it to help manage social transitions, developing new forms of reasoning while also drawing on established intellectual resources.[29] In section V, I will suggest that judicial reasoning in the law of tort is in many cases a good fit with this model; and that some of the 'open textured' standards which attract the most criticism are in fact examples of this.

Borrowing the 'responsive regulation' lens, which understands that regulation can take place in multiple sites and through the actions of different actors, there is room for an understanding of tort law as regulatory while integrating – in fact treating as essential – its concern with responsibility. In seeking such an understanding, I suggest that what tort law regulates is not behaviour in a narrow sense, but relationships. This is linked to Collins' argument that private law (not just the law of contract) 'is an instrument of the state for controlling and shaping private ordering'.[30] The range of 'relationships' governed by tort is however wide, and this makes it hard to generalise about tort's regulatory nature. The need to develop responsively across this wide range

[26] I am treating both parties to a biparty dispute as the regulated community, and not just the defendant: see further section III.

[27] There is no doubt it does this better in some contexts than others. The point here is that new contexts pose new challenges for the law – tort, for example, does not simply extend its 'principles' to new contexts without consideration of whether they fit and what the consequences might be.

[28] It is likely that the courts are much more comfortable with assessing the context of some relationships, particularly those that are routinely governed by private law, than others.

[29] P Selznick, *Law, Society, and Industrial Justice* (New York, Russell Sage Foundation, 1969) ch 2.

[30] H Collins, *Regulating Contracts* (Oxford, Oxford University Press, 1999) 58.

also contributes to an apparent incoherence – or 'disintegration'[31] – in some of its working principles, and highlights the risks in attempting to reason away the existence of this disintegration.

III. Two Important Observations from 'Tort Law as Regulation'

Having said that there is a missed opportunity in 'Tort Law as Regulation', linked to the decision to approach tort in terms of command and control, it should also be said that there are features of the original article which have helped to inspire the current attempt. I would like to identify two powerful observations in Cane's essay which not only point in the right direction, but also give some sense of purpose to trying to identify the regulatory character of tort.

First, Cane argued that there has been a narrow focus, within tort scholarship, on tort as defined in terms of 'the doing and suffering of harm'. The insistence that this defines the essential character of the law of tort makes the connection between tort parties appear to be about just this. Cane associated this particularly with Weinrib's work,[32] and thought it a good reflection of the internal structure of tort, but not so good when it comes to understanding how the subject operates. I would go further, and argue that it is misleading to suggest that tort – internally – treats parties as connected just by the doing and suffering of harm. Tort law is concerned with relationships, but does not abstract their relationship from its context in this way. There is no major disjunction in this respect between the structure of tort and the way it operates. In fact tort takes account of far more than the doing and suffering of harm, in understanding whether there are relevant duties which connect the parties.[33] It is the legal rights and duties, not the damage or harm, that connects the parties for the purposes of the law of tort, and these rights and duties are determined with reference to the nature and context of the parties' interaction and the relationship within which this takes place.[34] This is fundamental to the analysis of what tort is regulating, if it is a form of regulation. It will be regulating the relationship between parties, their respective rights and duties, and not simply the harmful or sanctioned behaviour of the defendant. This is not some peripheral instrumental purpose, but the central concern of the courts in responding to the parties' claims.

Second, Cane remarked, in my view importantly, that there has been much more focus on tort law in terms of rules and principles – elements of the doctrinal 'substance' of the law – than on institutional action.[35] Of course, a shift in focus in this respect would be necessary if we were seeking an instrumental account of tort of a classic

[31] ibid ch 4: discusses '[p]roductive disintegration' in responsive contract law.

[32] E Weinrib, *The Idea of Private Law* (London, Harvard University Press, 1995); Cane (n 1) 310.

[33] I use 'duties' here in a broad sense, not referring solely or specifically to the 'duty of care' in negligence.

[34] See further section V.

[35] This too is linked by Cane with Weinrib's 'formalistic' approach: Cane (n 1) 310. But I would suggest it is a broader phenomenon.

behaviour-change type. But a focus on institutional action may also be used to unveil other features of tort law in operation. For example, a focus on institutional action might ask, what are courts, legislatures, litigants, and others *doing* and *achieving*, and maybe trying to achieve, when they develop, operate, and use the law of tort? Is it right to say that tort law 'is' a collection of principles and rules? Or is it a set of responses to certain problems and disputes, which utilises and develops such principles and rules? These perspectives need not be 'external' to the conceptual structure of tort as Cane suggests.[36] In seeking to define the potential nature of tort law as regulating relationships (the exercise in hand here), those problems would be generated by and in response to the interactions between parties and their claims for legal remedies, not envisaged by some extrinsic social programme. Considerations which are broader than the immediate parties, and the interaction with other sources of regulation (legal or not), will inevitably be injected into these responses, as they develop over time.

If the law of tort is not only a set of rules and principles, but also a series of institutional actions seeking to raise and resolve claims and to regulate the relationships between parties by recognising and defining legal rights and duties, it can readily be analysed as a regulatory response. This will remain the case, even if the rules and principles are not perceived as being set to achieve some 'extrinsic' goal. In other words, while all regulation is no doubt rightly described as 'instrumental' on some level, the very outcomes it seeks may themselves be derived through responsive development. Private law solves problems that are the product of party interactions and disputes. At the same time, courts (among the key decision-makers in tort law) are potentially responsive not only to what we are used to thinking of as the 'internal' values and principles of tort, but also to other social and legislative norms and principles.[37] They remain attentive to multiple aspects of the impact of their decisions. Just as no tort case is solely about the doing and suffering of harm between the parties, but also about their relationship, so also tort problems are not resolved solely by focus on the specific parties before the court, but on features of the relationship that are likely to arise again. It is apparent to courts and litigants that the answers provided will have the effect of subjecting further relationships to regulation through private law.

IV. Can Contract Scholarship Show the Way?

Can scholarship of contract law help us find our way to a 'regulatory' understanding of tort? Collins' approach to regulation of and through contract is referred to by Cane, but ultimately does not affect his conclusions for the reasons we have seen: tort, he suggested, is similar to command and control. From the perspective offered by this chapter, however, the example of contract offers considerable assistance. It is more

[36] ibid 311: '[v]iewing tort law and the tort system through a regulatory lens involves an essentially similar instrumentalist methodological manoeuvre to that adopted by welfarist critics'.

[37] On openness to influence from legislation, see, eg, A Burrows, *Thinking About Statutes: Interpretation, Interaction, Improvement* (Cambridge, Cambridge University Press, 2018).

tempting to address tort law in terms of command and control, because tort imposes standards where contract is at least classically perceived as adopting the standards agreed by the parties. Equally, contract has been associated with deregulatory politics, while tort has been sometimes regarded from the perspective of deregulatory politics as too demanding and ill-fitting (a failure of responsiveness).

On the other hand, I think it is recognised that tort and contract cannot in all cases be easily and starkly contrasted. Both may operate together in very similar ways, often on the same set of facts, providing very similar remedies and applying similar or identical standards – for example, the standard of reasonable care within professional contracts. The analysis of contract in terms of regulation should certainly be relevant to thinking about the law of tort. As suggested in section II, it will be important to prise tort away from the 'command and control' model, if we are to understand its potential regulatory character in parallel to contract.

While there has been resistance to reading contract in terms of regulation, at least some areas (such as consumer law) have undeniably absorbed welfare standards. The key issue has been whether contract as a whole can be called regulatory, and in what sense. It might be tempting to conclude that only a modified version of contract law, which incorporates external standards, can be regarded as regulatory, and that this is a departure from 'classical' contract law, which merely supports self-regulation by parties. This, however, would be overly simplistic. As we have seen, Collins described private law as 'an instrument of the state for controlling and shaping private ordering'.[38] This can be readily applied to tort: what it resolves is not just harm, but harm caused within diverse relationships with attendant rights and responsibilities. Although Collins' representation of contract contrasts with a traditional understanding of contract principles as 'pre-political', it is not limited to a small range of interventions which can be said to be based on welfare goals. Brownsword's model of 'static' and 'dynamic' individualism, meanwhile, does not specifically label the law of contract as 'regulatory', but does ask how contract should respond when its rules appear to be detrimental to the interests of the community.[39] Together with TT Arvind, the present author has explored the connections between contract doctrine, and different perceptions of markets, arguing that a broadening of perspective in this way – in which a perception of the market as essentially comprised of autonomous individuals contracting on symmetrical terms is only one perception among many, and can be more or less close to the truth of a particular market – can reveal much more clearly that the law of contract is an exercise in regulation of contracting activity.[40] All of these approaches emphasise that there is no simple dichotomy between 'core' contract and 'welfarist' contract, and both can be seen as regulating according to the needs of different market conditions and perceptions. It is suggested that even to the extent that it supports self-regulation and protects the parties

[38] Collins (n 30) 58. Collins adds that this will be done 'according to a variety of competing policy objectives'. The term 'policy objective' has I think become rather over-burdened with rival meanings, and is not essential to the argument here.

[39] R Brownsword, 'Static and Dynamic Market Individualism' in R Halson (ed), *Exploring the Boundaries of Contract* (Aldershot, Dartmouth, 1996).

[40] TT Arvind and J Steele, 'Remapping Contract Law: Four Perceptions of Markets' in TT Arvind and J Steele (eds), *Contract Law and the Legislature* (Oxford, Hart Publishing, 2020).

from factors such as fraud, providing appropriate remedies for breach (key components of 'classical' contract law), contract inevitably operates to regulate market activity.[41]

This being the case, significant for present purposes is Collins' discussion of the *regulatory potential* of private law in terms of its 'reflexive' nature.[42] Despite the shortcomings of private law, Collins argues that it has advantages to do with its adaptability to the needs of the parties, seeking its own solutions to the 'regulatory trilemma' and particularly its third element – how law can preserve its own coherence, and thus authority, while remaining effective and sufficiently open.[43] This analysis too is readily applicable to tort. The language, concepts, and principles of private law are adapted to the context in which it operates; a key challenge is to achieve effective outcomes without losing coherence. Collins' argument is that the reflexive capacity of private law can be combined with more collective policy orientation, in order to develop more productive regulation.

All of this is applicable to private law much more broadly than the law of contract. Nevertheless, it remains true that we have a harder time identifying the regulatory role of tort law in 'responsive' terms. When it has been attempted, it has been considered lacking in promise, on the basis that tort is not like contract, and on the basis that tort simply provides a few exceptional limits to what the defendant is free to do.[44] While the law of contract concerns itself with a particular type of relationship, identified as 'contractual', what does tort law regulate, if it is not just 'behaviour'? (The route we agreed with Cane was of limited analytical promise.)[45]

Tort is wider than contract, but it is suggested that it is not sharply different. It covers relationships which are similar to contract, and it also overlaps with contract by recognising concurrent liability. But it also covers relationships and interactions which are far removed from contract. In the following section, I argue that tort does not simply provide minimal constraints on 'unilateral actions' of potential defendants, based in the doing of harm, but helps to order rights and duties within relationships. For tort to develop guiding principles which are sufficiently open to context yet with a sufficient appearance of coherence to survive faced with the 'regulatory trilemma', and particularly its third prong, is a difficult task. The existence of a tension, however, does not prove that the law must in fact simply be doing something else. In the next section, I suggest there are clear signs of this sort of tension, and that these can be productively understood in terms of its regulatory nature.

[41] Note also Ellis' argument that even within the domain of commercial contracting – in this instance particularly the construction industry – 'the main source of regulation is contract law'. Here, legislation had been required to deal with regulation of inequality between contracting parties, which had created a dysfunctional market. Though a legislative solution was required, this was not a case of foisting external values onto the law of contract. C Ellis, 'Regulating Commercial Contracts: What Can We Learn from Part II of the Housing Grants, Construction and Regeneration Act 1996?' in Arvind and Steele (n 40).

[42] Collins (n 30) ch 4: Collins chooses to use the notion of 'reflexivity' rather than 'responsiveness'.

[43] ibid 68–69. On the 'trilemma', see section I of this chapter.

[44] Stapleton (n 16).

[45] Collins (n 30) 45: it seems worth noting Collins' brief references to 'tort regulation', as an alternative to 'contract regulation', when addressing the problem of classification within private law. The point is about the classification of a dispute as raising issues of contract or of tort, and Collins draws attention to the potential for losing the regulatory potential of tort by addressing a situation in terms of contract. In other words he does not regard the regulation of private ordering as confined to the law of contract.

V. Tort Law as Regulating Relationships

In this section, I will begin to expand the idea that tort regulates relationships of various types, by recognising and adjusting rights, duties and remedies between the relevant parties. In this way, the relationships are recognised and adjusted by private law. While they cover a wide range (a factor returned to below), the relationships with which tort concerns itself remain analogous to contract rather than to, say, family or social relationships. The relationships that are the subject of tort regulation are bounded and relatively precise (not open-ended) – which is to say, they present some of the features that Selznick associated with contract.[46] When we think about what amounts to a tortious 'wrong' and what merits repair, courts (and scholars) are at least implicitly thinking about these relationships – their definition as subject to tort remedies, and the appropriate balance of rights and duties given their context – than simply about two parties connected by 'doing and suffering harm'. This is not a hidden, extraneous process, but an important component feature of tort doctrine and practice. That it does not feature so strongly in tort theory impedes understanding of the continuities between tort and contract, and of the regulatory character of tort.

The breadth of relationships covered by the law of tort is one of the deepest challenges for analysis of tort as regulatory. But I suggest that this challenge merely reflects a difficulty that pervades the development of tort doctrine. Asking whether and how tort is regulatory is a route to fresh understanding of some of the deeper tensions of the subject, as courts seek to negotiate the regulatory trilemma. A good amount of tort 'doctrine', and some of its more contested argumentative devices (or principles) are concerned with identifying the relevant relationships to which tort regulation is appropriate. Are tort duties and remedies appropriate in this particular relationship? If so, which duties? Such questions do not focus uniquely on the defendant and their behaviour, nor uniquely on the harm that they have done.

Part of the difficulty is that while contract deals with relationships which are identified as 'contractual', tort deals with relationships on a broader spectrum.[47] At one end of this spectrum there is limited interaction between the parties, which may be unintentional, or intended by one party but not the other. Interactions between economic rivals invite their own particularly minimal regulatory framework, for example, where not even intentional harm is considered sufficient in the absence of other factors, such as unlawful means.[48] A competitive, antagonistic, or arms' length relationship is nevertheless a relationship, and awareness of its nature is a component of tort reasoning. Along the continuum are relationships akin to or overlapping with

[46] Selznick (n 29) 53–62. See also Collins (n 30) 14. The characteristics are: voluntarism; limited commitment; mutuality; and boundedness.

[47] Contractual relationships also lie along a spectrum. Much debated is a continuum between 'discrete' and 'relational' contracts, which has some parallel with the range of tort relationships explored here.

[48] Hence the doctrinally confusing limitations in the area referred to as 'the economic torts'. Decisions of the House of Lords and Supreme Court have consistently preferred 'restraint' over coherence in this area. Presumably this indicates that restraint (a contextual idea) is more important than coherence in maintaining the law's responsiveness here: *OBG Ltd v Allan* [2007] UKHL 21, [2008] 1 AC 1; *JSC BTA Bank v Khrapunov* [2018] UKSC 19, [2020] AC 727.

contract, where the parties may have taken on bounded duties to one another, or one party has more or less expressly taken on such a duty. Overlapping with the latter are duties which are associated with particular roles, such as solicitor and client, occupier and visitor or trespasser, employer and employee, or doctor and patient. Even here, it is possible to define these with more or less specificity. For example, is a particular professional relationship one of information-giving, or is it one of advice?[49] Ultimately, there are also relationships which appear further from contract, not because the parties are strangers, but for the very different reason that they concern relationships of great dependency: local authorities and children in their care are one example;[50] it seems that schools and pupils are another, at least where provision of the core curriculum is concerned.[51]

Why is it not more evident that tort deals with and regulates relationships, rather than generating responses to events where one party (of an unidentified type) has caused another party harm, as though only these components (harm, causation, and behaviour) were pertinent to the question of whether there is a tort? If parties were simply approached as connected by doing harm, approaching tort in terms of regulatory potential would indeed look 'blurred', as responsibility would simply appear in the guise of a retrospective response to the causation of damage. Tort would qualify or restrict a background system of autonomy and self-regulation only by intervening to correct harm, according to abstract principles. The notion that tort is structured around the doing and suffering of harm is its equivalent, in this respect, to classical contract doctrine.[52]

I will explore three possible reasons for the neglect of tort's role in regulating relationships. In responding to these reasons, I will try to explore a little further its regulatory nature. The three reasons are: the conceptual dominance of (atypical and misunderstood) 'stranger danger' cases; the temptation of generalised concepts (and at the same time, their key role in combating the regulatory trilemma); and the persistent notion of the passivity of one party in a tort case.

A. Stranger Danger

One reason why tort's regulation of relationships is underestimated is the perception that what I will call 'stranger danger' cases are central to the law of tort. The majority of tort claims for personal injury are road traffic claims. But the reason that road traffic claims can thrive is that tort is supported by a range of other legal and other arrangements, notably the duty to insure, without which the law of tort could not sustain this

[49] This distinction was made by Lord Hoffmann in *South Australia Asset Management Corpn v York Montague Ltd* [1997] AC 191 (HL). It has become a key feature of damages for loss of chance in the context of professional services.

[50] *Barrett v Enfield LBC* [2001] 2 AC 550 (HL), as interpreted and approved by the Supreme Court in *Poole* (n 10).

[51] *Woodland v Swimming Teachers Association* [2013] UKSC 66, [2014] AC 537.

[52] See also Stapleton (n 16): she broadly makes this point, though she draws from it the conclusion that tort cannot be seen as regulatory even to the extent that contract can, because it makes minimal demands on defendants in respect of their freedom of action. As explained throughout, the focus of this chapter is on tort's role in defining rights and liabilities within relationships.

'central' example.[53] Typically, injured parties have no prior knowledge of the person who causes harm through their negligence on the roads. It is tempting to see them as symptomatic of the entire law of tort because such claims are so numerous. At the same time, they appear, quite misleadingly, to be simple in their structure, illustrating the 'bilateral' nature of the law of tort. I would reject the argument that because the connection between the specific parties is an event – the collision – this is not about relationships; and equally reject the implication that for this reason, it is not regulatory. For the law to structure a relationship does not require that the parties have had prior communication. At the same time, the law of tort in relation to road traffic is at the centre of a regulatory web. Without surrounding regulatory devices such as compulsory insurance and licensing, tort could not operate in the road traffic context in the way that it does.[54] Liability for harm done by autonomous vehicles will cast into stronger relief the regulatory character of tort law here, as the law grapples with the choice between operator/owner liability, and manufacturer liability, for injuries done by autonomous vehicles.[55] But this represents just one in a long line of interventions into the structuring of relationships between road users (including pedestrians and cyclists, as well as drivers and passengers). The regulatory context suggests that this is a more realistic approach than to see tort liabilities as imposing limited restraint on the freedom of individuals per se. Road users are defined for this purpose in terms of their activity and relationship with others.

The general point is that 'stranger danger' occurs in categories and these cases too can be seen in terms of relationship. A relationship involving no prior contact may nevertheless be categorised as raising particular issues associated with the type of relationship it is. The parties too may have expectations and understandings, despite the lack of contractual agreement. This is the case, for example, with manufacturer and consumer cases. The law's reasoning distracts from this when it casts itself in very wide, almost universal terms. These wide terms can be misleading. *Donoghue v Stevenson*,[56] for example, can be seen as a move in the law's process of developing regulation of relationships, in which it was determined that the relationship between manufacturer and consumer was susceptible to tort regulation. It was not an escape from this process of development: if anything, it laid the groundwork for its continuation. The relationship itself, and its connection to surrounding aspects of legal regulation (notably contract), were considered within the judgments, and were used in order to generate broader theories of liability. Broad though they are, the inevitable lack of universality in these broader statements, and the significance of the specific type of relationship considered if tort regulation is to extend to new relationships, has become increasingly clear.[57]

[53] R Lewis, 'Insurance and the Tort System' (2005) 25 *LS* 85: in particular, damages would be too high for most defendants if there was no supporting system of insurance, which in the UK and many other jurisdictions is compulsory.

[54] See also R Merkin and J Steele, *Insurance and the Law of Obligations* (Oxford, Oxford University Press, 2013) ch 9.

[55] Automated and Electric Vehicles Act 2018, Part I of which is now in force (April 2021).

[56] *Donoghue v Stevenson* [1932] AC 562 (HL).

[57] Evidenced by the fact that 'incremental development' has been championed by the Supreme Court as *the* essential feature of development in the law of negligence. The attempt to rely on a few general concepts at the same time is explored below.

This leads us to a second reason why 'relationships' are often overlooked in understanding the law of tort, in favour of a sense that the parties are linked by the doing and suffering of harm.

B. The Temptation to Speak in Terms of Generalised Concepts

It is well known that English jurisprudence rowed back from seeing the duty of care, or any 'test' for it, in general or universal terms, with the reversal of Lord Wilberforce's attempt to state a universal test in *Anns v Merton LBC*.[58] That attempt exemplified the dangers highlighted by the regulatory trilemma. It laid bare, through inclusion of a second 'stage', the need for openness. Its universality, in other words, was too clearly undermined by the chance of an overriding consideration derived from the context of the claim in hand. The possibility that there might be relevant considerations was expressed in an entirely open fashion, and relevant factors – it seemed – could be entirely divorced from the relationship in hand. The replacement for this approach, set out in *Caparo Industries plc v Dickman*,[59] tried to escape this problem. In doing this, *Caparo* can be understood as preoccupied with the regulatory trilemma. Its response to the third prong of the trilemma – the potential for loss of coherence or collapse into other forms of reasoning – was to integrate a range of factors directly into the appraisal of the parties' relationship.

Though *Caparo* has been reimagined, we can see this close contextual and responsive concern with relationships equally clearly in the more recent decision in *Poole BC v GN*.[60] This decision culminates a series of cases in which the Supreme Court is generally understood to have set the law of negligence on a more 'principled', and less policy-dependent footing.[61] *Poole* makes clear that the correct approach to 'novel' duties of care is to be located chiefly in terms of 'incremental development' – the law should proceed from the starting point of currently recognised duties. The existence of a 'duty of care' may be seen as a proxy for the question whether tort will regulate a relationship according to negligence principles, and tort law must continue to move in a highly contextual fashion when determining which relationships are to be subject to its regulation. The rejection of a 'three-stage test' for structuring such discussion makes the basis for further development all the more opaque. The Supreme Court has simultaneously identified incrementalism (a contextual idea) as the foundation of law's response; and tried to give the appearance of greater simplicity. The differentiation between actions causing harm and 'failures to benefit',[62] and the identification of 'assumptions of responsibility' as a guiding idea for exceptional cases, are designed to be the focus of future deliberation and to give a sense of 'coherence'. While the first of these appears to be simplifying –

[58] *Anns v Merton London Borough Council* [1978] AC 728 (HL).
[59] *Caparo Industries plc v Dickman* [1990] 2 AC 605 (HL).
[60] *Poole* (n 10).
[61] *Michael v Chief Constable of South Wales* [2015] UKSC 2, [2015] AC 1732; *Robinson v Chief Constable of West Yorkshire Police* [2018] UKSC 4, [2018] AC 736.
[62] See especially *Robinson* (n 61) and *Poole* (n 10). The latter decision sought to elevate this distinction to a defining role in public authority liability cases. The identification of 'exceptions' from this general position with assumptions of responsibility places a heavy burden on this very uncertain concept.

carving out some 'easy' cases which lie either side of the line – the second remains a deeply evasive notion. Some of the reasons for this are related to the wide range of the relationships which are dealt with by the law of tort. 'Assumption of responsibility' is a fragile notion, but it draws consideration to the relationship in hand. In terms of the current discussion, it may be seen as attractive for its ability to help the courts avoid the implications of the trilemma, lending apparent coherence and distinctiveness to what is in reality an open and contextual consideration.

Here we may borrow once again from contract theory. It has been suggested that increasingly 'reflexive regulation', in which private law seeks to be responsive to the needs and values of the parties and the context of their disputes, is likely to provoke some sort of 'productive disintegration' in legal principles, as private law adapts to deal with problems that it can, internally, recognise.[63] The overloading of the concept of 'assumption of responsibility' is symptomatic of this sort of process. It allows contextual reasons for departing from the clear and 'longstanding' principles[64] connected with acts and omissions, to be presented in a coded fashion. There is a sense in which this concept has been identified as marking out the key to 'exceptional' duties because it can be presented as an abstract principle, on the same footing as a distinction between acts and omissions, or between causation of physical harm and other things, and not a contextual means of regulating relationships. But this abstraction means glossing over some very wide divergences in what the concept could possibly mean in different contexts within the law of tort. Linked to this are clues about the role of tort in comprehending or constructing, and regulating relationships.

The growing significance of 'assumption of responsibility', and particularly its operation in the guise of a generalised concept that can justify responsibility, obscures some radically different types of relationship being addressed by the concept. We can present some of these in terms of 'bounded relationships', somewhat akin to contract.[65] Law attaches particular consequences to decisions to enter relationships which involve responsibility, in a particular form, to the other party. Thus, tort duties in this context (and others by analogy) have an 'extent'.[66] The distinction between information cases and advice cases referred to earlier can be usefully analysed here. Providing '*information*' has been defined as implying a narrower assumption of responsibility than offering advice, because the provider of information is conceived as doing nothing to sway the autonomous decision of the recipient, other than by providing the basis for the decision to be made. Offering '*advice*' however, places the two parties in a different relationship, in which there is much greater dependence on the professional opinion and guidance of the advisor. This distinction can make an enormous difference to the scale of the damages that might be awarded, when an error is made and the other party acts in

[63] Collins (n 30) ch 4. Responsiveness is always qualified and there will always be communication problems, but this is true of all forms of regulation.

[64] The terminology used by Lord Reed, with a clear intention to secure law's authority and coherence.

[65] 'Akin to contract' is one of the forms of language adopted to justify liability – on the basis of a 'special relationship' – in *Hedley Byrne & Co Ltd v Heller & Partners Ltd* [1964] AC 465 (HL), which is also the foundation of the notion of 'assumption of responsibility'.

[66] This was set out in *South Australia Asset Management Corpn* (n 49), and is an idea used in many subsequent cases. That tort duties might have an 'extent' is a function of the concern with relationships. Doubts about the possibility that tort duties might have an extent are explicable on the basis that tort duties are thought about as universal and owed to the world (freedom/conduct focused).

reliance. 'Reliance', indeed, has a different connotation, depending what form of relationship is thought to be involved.[67] The nature and extent of reliance draws attention to the conceptualisation of both parties, not just the defendant, within the relationship in question.

But also operating, apparently in precisely the same way according to the Supreme Court, are assumptions of responsibility in a very different and much broader sense, where parties enter into a relationship of dependence. For example, where children are in care, or when schools provide education to children. In respect of the former, the Supreme Court has recognised that the binary distinction between acts and failures to benefit does not apply.[68] In the latter, and particularly controversially, it has been recognised that non-delegable duties may arise. 'Non-delegable duties' are a particularly strong indication that tort law recognises the significance of dependence in these sorts of relationships.[69]

As already noted, the Supreme Court in *Poole* presented assumption of responsibility as an abstract legal principle, portraying the law as resting on 'long-standing principles'. There was a concern to avoid resting liability on 'policy' considerations which in some areas had become increasingly unsatisfactory. This result of earlier cases could, however, be seen in terms of a failure of responsiveness or reflexivity: the reasons given by the courts were ill-fitting and lacking in basis, rather than of a wrong category. Drawing on the terms employed by Nonet and Selznick, we could suggest that the new direction tries to cure the initial weakness using the authority strategies of 'autonomous law', in retreat from the potential vulnerabilities of 'responsive law' reasoning. Those vulnerabilities are akin to the 'loss of coherence' linked to the third prong of the trilemma, and are associated with its very openness to context and a range of interests and outcomes.

The developments in the Supreme Court in cases such as *Poole* could be read as an exercise in rescuing the authority of law. If it was also an exercise in simplification, it is likely to run into difficulties, given tort's role in the regulation of diverse relationships. Not surprisingly, lower courts have found it difficult to determine how this criterion should apply to cases that have followed *Poole*, with claims proceeding to trial for determination of just this issue.[70] The Supreme Court's attempt to simplify the analysis to be applied to public authority cases, and to make this analysis much more a case of legal principle, could be seen as a reaction to 'disintegration', but that disintegration may have been present for substantial reasons.[71] The deep ambiguity of assumption of

[67] In its recent decision in *Manchester Building Society v Grant Thornton UK LLP* [2021] UKSC 20, [2021] 3 WLR 81, the Supreme Court has described the distinction between 'advice' and 'information' in terms of a continuum, rather than a dichotomy. It is therefore unwise, according to the Supreme Court, to begin by trying to categorise a relationship in terms of one or the other. Rather, the focus is on identifying the purpose of the duty, and categorisation in terms of information or advice may be the outcome of this process. The idea of a continuum of relationships, and the need to scrutinise the relationship in hand, is consistent with the general argument here.

[68] See, eg, *Barrett* (n 50); *Poole* (n 10).

[69] *Woodland* (n 51). Non-delegable duties were initially devised to deal with cases arising within the employment relationship – an area where there is a large overlap between tort and contract duties.

[70] See, eg, *AA v CC* (CC, 22 September 2020).

[71] The bigger problem may have been that it was clumsily done, and was a risk to confidence in legal standards. Thus the response may have been to resolve the issues caused by often attacked decisions such as *Hill v Chief Constable of West Yorkshire* [1989] AC 53 (HL). The reasoning in this case – whatever the value of the decision itself – can certainly be seen as conservative and protective.

responsibility does not by itself invalidate the notion. But to resist its ambiguous nature could be counter-productive: the very different instantiations of 'assumption of responsibility' in different types of relationship may eventually need to be admitted in order to avoid further distortion. There is work to be done that relates directly to the question of what relationships are regulated by tort, and how concepts may suffer if an attempt is made to stretch them too thinly.

C. The Apparent Passivity of One Party to a Tort Case

A pervasive lack of focus on 'relationship' in tort's regulatory nature is also connected to a perception that one party is merely passive, in a way that is not true of contract. This perception holds that tort protects claimants in a particular way by imposing minimal restraints on those who might injure them. In contract, there is understood to be some degree of mutuality and reciprocity, at least in the intention to enter into a contractual relationship, even if this mutuality can be exaggerated.[72] But tort has an equivalent stage. The question that has to be answered in the law of tort, if it is to regulate a particular dispute, is not 'is there a contractual relationship', but the inherently more complex question, 'is there a relationship importing responsibility'. Questions about setting standards that modify behaviour are not relevant unless we also ask this. Though it might intuitively be thought that behaviour that is bad enough, and which causes harm of some sort, will mean we can dispense with the examination of the relationship and its context, even here, it is not the case. The economic torts are illustrative, as is the fate of the 'action in *Wilkinson v Downton*'.[73] The detailed requirements of the action for malicious prosecution, including 'prosecution' and absence of reasonable and probable cause in addition to malice, provide a further example.[74]

There are many components to an investigation into the relevant relationship. But one common and significant feature of negligence claims in particular (though not solely of relevance to such claims) will be mentioned here. In negligence claims, the question can sometimes legitimately be asked, why did the tort claimant not provide their own protection against this risk? Or if they did, why should this be overridden? As Lord Hoffmann memorably put it, why me?[75] While this was said in relation to a case of 'pure' omission, a similar question also arises where there are multiple connected parties, perhaps where tort claims are attempted within a contractual chain or matrix. In terms of the focus of analysis, the initial breach of duty pales into insignificance as a risk that could easily be anticipated, and probably was anticipated at some point in the

[72] Particularly where there is a significant inequality between the parties.

[73] *O (A Child) v Rhodes and another (English PEN and others intervening)* [2015] UKSC 32, [2016] AC 219.

[74] See, eg, *Mosley v Associated Newspapers Ltd* [2020] EWHC 3545 (QB), [2021] 4 WLR 29; *CXZ v ZXC* [2020] EWHC 1684 (QB): actions were refused where claimants sought damages for maliciously instigating damaging investigations.

[75] This question was posed in relation to 'omissions' or failure to benefit in *Stovin v Wise* [1996] AC 923 (HL). Given the discussion of security that follows, it is worth underlining that an insurer in this case was trying to identify an alternative resting place for some of the cost of liability, in an action for contribution against a public authority.

chain; and the question is whose role it is to provide security. Again, illustrating that this is not solely a question that is of importance in relation to omissions, there are questions about the extent of liability, within particular relationships, where a risk that could be anticipated is amplified by other factors (such as falls in market value). Here, the idea of 'scope of duty' fits the idea of a regulatory concept that is responsive to context, better than it fits the notion of an abstract and universal legal principle. Its utility to courts is not matched by its fit with the way that tort scholars typically think about the subject.

A slightly different example which nevertheless highlights the significance of the claimant's role, other than as a person who has suffered harm, concerns relationships importing particular vulnerability or, short of this, reliance. In other words, vulnerability – like reliance – is not generally a quality of claimants alone, but a feature of the claimant's relationship with the defendant. The relationship is one of vulnerability where the claimant is particularly dependent on the defendant. Again, the law of tort does not approach such claims as though they incorporated two parties whose only connection is the doing and suffering of harm. The quality of the relationship is relevant to the rights and duties that are recognised by tort.

In all of these examples, the identity of the claimant is not a neutral factor, which would allow us to divert away from the conceptualisation of the relationship and focus instead on the defendant's behaviour and its effects. Indeed, analysis of the relevant relationship is a major component in the job that faces the courts. On both sides of the acts-omissions dichotomy there are cases which can be approached in terms of a claimed duty to provide security. If that is the case then, at a minimum, it becomes easier to conceptualise tort as dealing with prospective, rather than retrospective, questions, while the questions can still be defined in terms of 'responsibility'. But equally, if tort is ordering the rights and duties of parties in this way, and identifying the appropriate location of responsibility, this may ease our task in explaining how and in what way tort law can be approached as 'regulatory'. This is, precisely, how tort regulates. The application of 'corrective justice' mechanisms is itself a regulatory exercise.[76]

D. Returning to the 'Blurred Lens' Problem

Having visited these examples, does it still appear that adopting a regulatory approach will always lead us to use a 'blurred lens' to perceive a subject which is inherently concerned with principles of personal responsibility?

I argue that in fact, the regulatory lens (as modified in section II) can help us to see tort law more sharply, and to understand some of its inner workings and problems more clearly, than can be managed without such a lens. The regulatory perspective allows us to ask what participants are doing when they argue in relation to responsibility. The question of responsibility is, in part, a prospective one. In form of course, the court decides that a party was responsible. But in substance, the court also determines where responsibility lies – or how this may be decided – in future cases, leading parties to

[76] There is a connection here with the argument of J Gardner, 'What is Tort Law For? Part 2. The Place of Distributive Justice' in J Oberdiek (ed), *Philosophical Foundations of Tort Law* (Oxford, Oxford University Press, 2014), that the distribution of corrective justice is an inevitable element in the law of tort.

rethink and in many cases to reorder their relationships.[77] Rather than assessing the value and coherence of tort law principles and doctrines in the abstract, this regulatory lens enables us to understand the root of the complications that have arisen in these doctrines, and to some extent the *need for* these complications. We should not of course celebrate complication where it can be avoided, but there are sometimes positive reasons for the kind of hesitant, incomplete, and open-textured concepts that the law of tort has habitually created. Some of these concepts work quite effectively, and come to organise significant areas of private interaction, while remaining open to critique from a logical and analytical point of view.[78] Responsive standards are often open-textured, but should not be too quickly dismissed as unsatisfactory. Where the key concern is with authority, rather than with responsiveness – the tension illuminated by the third limb of the trilemma – there will be pressure to redefine or even veil the nature of these standards. This may be provoked by over-expansion (*Anns*[79]); or by over-conservatism or protectionism (*Hill*[80]). This is indicative of the nature of the trilemma.

I suggest that tort law sets and adjusts expectations within certain relationships; it develops and refines concepts in response to issues that arise within these relationships, and it often faces its biggest challenges in relation to the question of which these relationships are going to be. Courts determine the ambit of tort law – the range of relationships in which its analysis is appropriate – and also the content of that analysis. The nature of the dominant remedy – repair – undoubtedly affects the particular question of responsibility that is asked. Tort law does not ask or answer an open-ended question about responsibility. It generally asks the question whether there is a responsibility to prevent or avoid harm and to make that harm good if it is suffered. That does not mean that tort dissolves into something else, like 'command and control'. The ambition to set expectations within relationships, including the question of when repair is the right response, *and* to define the relationships within which its various theories are appropriately applicable, is inherent to the institutional action involved in tort, and fits with its doctrinal moves. But those questions – including when the analysis is 'appropriately applicable' – are conducted *with awareness* of the social context of tort, and the fact that damages awards have effects – affecting behaviour; avoiding losses; acting as the gateway for distribution via insurance; affecting contractual relationships – is a part of tort reasoning.

VI. Conclusion: Assessing Tort's Regulatory Potential

I have argued that tort's regulatory character is best appreciated by refining the regulatory lens. With a focus on the regulation of relationships, rather than on the achievement

[77] For example, insurance arrangements may change; new guidance and information may be mandated (eg in the medical context); subcontracts may involve new terms; employers may adopt new safety regimes or employment checks.

[78] See, for example, the evolving distinction between advice and information cases in relation to loss of chance damages (n 67). Another example is the idea that tort duties have a 'scope' or extent (see further, n 66).

[79] *Anns* (n 58).

[80] *Hill* (n 71).

of specified goals (such as avoidance of pollution, or achievement of compensation), we can see evidence that tort is regulatory, and that some features of its reasoning are illuminated by considering it this way. It remains to ask, however, does tort regulation serve an important purpose in responding to disputes and structuring relationships?

I would suggest that tort regulation can be seen to serve social purposes consistently with its structure and institutional resources, though it can of course be assessed as doing this more or less effectively. The struggle with ineffectiveness is endemic to law. Although the law of tort has grown by responding to claims, and not according to a blueprint or masterplan, this does not make it impossible to describe it as regulatory. Nudging and responding are themselves regulatory strategies, requiring a series of judgements as to what is appropriate or desirable, but not necessarily requiring a single formal welfare objective. These processes are useful: it is helpful to have a way of determining responsibility within relationships of various kinds, that does not need a new regulator or new body of rules for every relationship. If we did not have a law of tort, therefore, it is likely there would be demand for its creation, and that it would serve social purposes to do so. Such a creation would need a basis for its claims to authority; but would also need to be sensitive to the needs of the regulated parties, and to know when to give way to social welfare goals wielded by other authorities, and when to absorb elements of those goals and associated values into its decision-making. Further, it would need to adapt to deal with social change, and may find itself challenged by new types of claim, where it must seek to extend its jurisdiction to new types of relationship. Nobody would choose to create the law of tort exactly as it stands today. But over time, it is quite likely that boundaries and tensions would begin to arise in some of the same places.

As a way of regulating relationships, tort rarely manages on its own, has limits to what it can achieve, and sometimes gets in the way. It has also been thoroughly exposed, when approached in terms of a goal of compensation for personal injury, as expensive and fickle. The courts know that tort suffers the perils of potential ineffectiveness, inappropriateness, and loss of authority associated with the regulatory trilemma, and they understand that multiple systems of regulation coexist. Perhaps tort could be said to have been too responsive – vested interests have not often been shaken by the law of tort, and 'sensitivity to context' can often spell conservatism.[81] However, the law of tort is able to respond to new situations, with its own legitimacy arguments, and it is adaptable and reflexive. It can be, and has been, adapted and channelled, supported or undermined, from within as well as by statute, according to decisions about its regulatory impact.

[81] See, eg, *Hill* (n 71), which has led to later correction (possibly over-correction) in the law. See also *Alcock v Chief Constable of South Yorkshire Police* [1992] 1 AC 310 (HL); *Chagos Islanders v Attorney General* [2004] EWCA Civ 997; *Jalla v Shell International Trading and Shipping Co* [2021] EWCA Civ 63 (limitation period for a nuisance caused by an oil spill runs from the time the spill is addressed, not from the occurrence of further damage). But see *Vedanta Resources plc v Lungowe* [2019] UKSC 20, [2020] AC 1045; *Okpabi v Royal Dutch Shell plc* [2021] UKSC 3, [2021] 1 WLR 1294.

PART IV

The Nature and Role of Legal Scholarship

11

Thinking about Doctrine in Administrative Law

LEIGHTON McDONALD*

I. Introduction

Despite (or, perhaps, because of) the diversity and depth of his scholarship, Peter Cane's engagement with law has been characterised by mastery of its doctrine. A persistent commitment of his work is that a careful study of legal norms and concepts can do more than educate us about the law's content in a specific area. It can also enrich our understanding of the social world beyond.[1] Cane's commitment to taking doctrine seriously is, however, nuanced because he also holds the view that the prescriptive work of doctrinal scholars – at least in common law systems – is of limited normative force.

Cane's work in administrative law has always been mainly directed to explanation (rather than exposition or prescription) but his scholarship has become increasingly interested in underlying questions of method. In his path-breaking comparison of the legal control of administrative power in England, the United States, and Australia, Cane crafted and applied an historically grounded institutionalism to explain the 'control regimes' within which administrative power is exercised.[2] Control regimes – the institutions, practices and norms of administrative law – include but are not limited to the legal norms applied as 'grounds' of judicial review of administrative decision-making. Control regimes thus include the stuff of legal doctrine. The hypothesis of the book is that our understanding of the shape and content of administrative law's doctrine (along with its institutions and practices) is enriched by situating it in the

* Thanks to Will Bateman, Liz Fisher, Mark Lunney, Joshua Neoh, and Tom Poole for very helpful criticisms and suggestions.

[1] By illuminating, for example: the nature of the values that underpin law in particular areas (P Cane, 'Theory and Values in Public Law' in P Craig and R Rawlings (eds), *Law and Administration in Europe: Essays in Honour of Carol Harlow* (Oxford, Oxford University Press, 2003)); how we should conceptualise the nature of law itself (eg P Cane, 'Public Law in *The Concept of Law*' (2013) 33 *OJLS* 649); and how we understand our other normative concepts and practices (P Cane, *Responsibility in Law and Morality* (Oxford, Hart Publishing, 2002)).

[2] P Cane, *Controlling Administrative Power: An Historical Comparison* (Cambridge, Cambridge University Press, 2016).

broader habitat of 'systems of government'.[3] Laying aside the separation of powers idea for a fresh lens, Cane characterises the divergences in broader systems of government in England, the United States, and Australia by reference to the extent that they diffuse or concentrate public power. His conclusion is that the doctrine (along with other features of administrative law's control regimes) is, by and large, given structure and sense by these configurations of government. Understanding doctrine in this structural way decentres (without necessarily discounting) interpretations or accounts of the law that assume divergences can be explained by the value preferences of law-makers in different jurisdictions.[4] The contours of administrative law doctrine are better understood insofar as broader structures of government can help to explain them.

Cane's scholarly ambition and achievement in *Controlling Administrative Power* was to provide a 'fresh, plausible and suggestive'[5] *explanatory* account of the legal terrain he navigates. The analysis – which makes liberal use of historical and comparative sources, along with the empirical and theoretical literatures in political science – cannot be cabined within the methods ordinarily associated with traditional 'doctrinal scholarship'.[6] Thus, in this book we see a scholar with unimpeachable doctrinal credentials reaching beyond conventional 'internal' approaches to legal scholarship.[7] Careful attention is directed towards the expert explication of the positive law in each jurisdiction but doctrine is explained as an outgrowth of institutional behaviour and design rather than through an interpretation of its own data points – judicial decisions, and primary and secondary legislation. Cane's purpose is not to offer an interpretation of the law as a normatively coherent body of principle; nor is his analysis directed at judicial readers with prescriptive intent.

Of course, there is no single way to take doctrine seriously; nor, I will suggest, is there a single way to understand the idea of doctrine itself. And Cane's structural turn should not be read as scepticism about the dividends of doctrinal scholarship *en masse*.[8] Nevertheless, the methodology and thesis explored in *Controlling Administrative Power* challenges us to think harder about the sort of illumination the study of doctrine in administrative law is liable to project. This chapter takes up that challenge, albeit through

[3] ibid 11.

[4] ibid 1.

[5] ibid 511.

[6] There are different modalities of doctrinal scholarship (see further section IV) but perhaps the generic element of most such modes is that they employ, in one way or another, 'the sort of language and arguments that a judge might be convinced to adopt': SA Smith, 'Taking Law Seriously' (2000) 50 *UTLJ* 241, 247. Such scholarship tends to take the perspective of an insider of the system and rely on sources that are 'predominantly those that are thrown up by the legal process' itself: C McCrudden, 'Legal Research and the Social Sciences' (2006) 122 *LQR* 632, 633, quoting D Ibbetson, 'Historical Research in Law' in P Cane and M Tushnet (eds), *Oxford Handbook of Legal Studies* (Oxford, Oxford University Press, 2003) 864.

[7] On the 'common', though 'incomplete', distinction between internal and external approaches to legal scholarship, see E Fisher, 'Through 'Thick' and 'Thin': Comparison in Administrative Law and Regulatory Studies Scholarship' in P Cane et al (eds), *The Oxford Handbook of Comparative Administrative Law* (Oxford, Oxford University Press, 2020). Fisher argues that a distinction between thin and thick research projects is a better way to categorise administrative law and regulatory studies scholarship.

[8] After all, Cane's instincts are pluralistic. The theory of controlling administrative power developed in the book is not presented as the definitive account but rather as an account with significant explanatory power.

the adoption of something of an exploratory tone. My primary goal is to open up questions rather than to provide definitive answers.

Although the chapter is ultimately about how legal scholars think and write about doctrine in administrative law it begins with a discussion of the concept of doctrine itself – in general and then in the particular context of administrative law. It is something of a common law puzzle that talk of 'doctrine' is pervasive in the law and legal scholarship yet the concept of legal doctrine appears to have eluded sustained analysis. Two broad usages of doctrine can, however, be identified: doctrine as compendium (of positive law sources) versus a coherentist conception. Drawing on Cane's work on the history of tort law scholarship, I argue that both judges and jurists encounter serious limitations in their respective attempts to fill out the more interesting (coherentist) conception of doctrine with concrete content – that is, in a way which extends beyond the accepted positive sources of law to generate systemic properties. Next, I explain why a systemic conception of administrative law doctrine has always been a fraught project. The idea of administrative law doctrine in this sense developed later in English law (and Commonwealth jurisdictions) than it did in other legal domains. When it did emerge it coincided with the twentieth century consolidation of the administrative state. An irony of the delayed emergence of administrative law conceived as a coherent system of legal norms to regulate and legitimate administrative power is thus that it was born around the same time that the administrative state's breadth of coverage and the variability of its schemes became impossible to deny. I argue that the particularity and statutory complexity which characterises the practical exercise of much administrative power in an administrative state has worked to compound the difficulties of fashioning a systemic concept of doctrine. Put differently, the ongoing juridification of the functions of government associated with the administrative state compresses and complicates the legal space within which general norms of administrative law – reflecting its systemic properties – can claim to be dispositive. The compendium usage of doctrine is uninteresting, while in the context of administrative law the coherentist enterprise appears overly ambitious, if not illusory.

Given the difficulties that beset the development of the concept of doctrine generally and the conception of doctrine in administrative law in particular, the final section of the chapter asks how, if at all, doctrinal scholarship might contribute to the search for 'fresh, plausible and suggestive' explanatory accounts of the subject. To facilitate this inquiry, I distinguish three broad modes of doctrinally-oriented academic writing within administrative law. The first continues 'the textbook tradition',[9] the second builds theories of administrative law norms which claim to be based on a close reading of the cases, and the third involves a form of 'meta' or 'structural' analysis of the case law. Although none of these modes should be dismissed as a fool's errand, I suggest that the third mode of doctrinal analysis is most likely to shine illumination on the nature of doctrinal discourse and disputes within a particular jurisdiction. Its focus is explanatory insofar as it enables scholars to reveal the general ways in which judges think about how to specify and articulate the norms of administrative law in the context

[9] D Sugarman, 'Legal Theory, the Common Law Mind and the Making of the Textbook Tradition' in W Twining (ed), *Legal Theory and Common Law* (Oxford, Blackwell, 1986).

of the administrative state. As general approaches to thinking about administrative law's norms reflect or respond to different underlying questions about the legitimacy of administrative law and the administrative state, structural readings of case law help illuminate what is at stake in what are normally described as doctrinal debates. In this way doctrinal scholarship promises to add a further layer of explanatory depth to predominantly external accounts of administrative law, such as Cane's historical institutionalism.

II. The Elusive Idea of Doctrine in the Common Law Tradition

Doctrinal scholarship has long been under general attack[10] but it is not, in fact, disappearing – in administrative law or elsewhere.[11] Of course, one consequence of the legal realism movement was to spur a continuing debate about the extent to which legal doctrine *causes* judicial decisions.[12] And scepticism on that score has been especially pronounced in the United States, where it has been suggested that legal realism played a role in the decline of the legal treatise.[13] Nevertheless, references to legal doctrine remain pervasive in legal practice, education, and scholarship.[14] Tenaciously, doctrine remains 'the currency of the law'.[15] It continues to be argued in courts, invoked by judges, taught in law schools, and dissected and evaluated in much legal scholarship.

Yet the tenacity of doctrinal discourse in contemporary legal thought is matched by the elusiveness of the underlying idea or concept of doctrine. To be sure, legal scholars have questioned the role of doctrine in the adjudicative process and some have considered how new (individuated) doctrines are created.[16] But the underlying idea of doctrine has been the subject of relatively little independent investigation.[17]

[10] As Dan Priel suggests, the relationship between legal realism and doctrinal analysis is more complex than the common narrative of outright hostility from the former towards the latter: 'Legal Realism and Legal Doctrine' in P Chiassoni and B Spaić (eds), *Judges and Adjudication in Constitutional Democracies: A View from Legal Realism* (Springer, 2021).

[11] *cf* J Varuhas, 'Taxonomy and Public Law' in M Elliott et al (eds) *The Unity of Public Law? Doctrinal, Theoretical and Comparative Perspectives* (Oxford, Hart Publishing, 2018) 45.

[12] E Tiller and F Cross, 'What is Legal Doctrine?' (2006) 100 *Northwestern University Law Review* 517 consider the different perspective brought to bear on this question by legal scholars and social scientists and, also, how their respective approaches may be tested. The jurisprudential questions raised by realist doubts as to whether doctrine is the primary determinant of judicial decisions are considered in L Green, 'Positivism, Realism, and Sources of Law' in T Spaak and P Mindus (eds), *The Cambridge Companion to Legal Positivism* (Cambridge, Cambridge University Press, 2021).

[13] AWB Simpson, 'The Rise and Fall of the Legal Treatise: Legal Principles and the Forms of Legal Literature' (1981) 48 *University of Chicago Law Review* 632.

[14] That is certainly so in Australia and the UK. On the persistence of doctrinal legal scholarship in the United States, see R Ellickson, 'Trends in Legal Scholarship: A Statistical Study' (2000) 29 *Journal of Legal Studies* 517.

[15] Tiller and Cross (n 12). This tenacity of doctrine talk has obviously not crowded out other modes of thinking about law.

[16] eg E Rubin and M Feeley, 'Creating Legal Doctrine' (1996) 69 *Southern California Law Review* 1989.

[17] As noted by NE Simmonds, 'Protestant Jurisprudence and Modern Doctrinal Scholarship' (2001) 60 *CLJ* 271. See also, Priel (n 10) (on the lack of interest shown by legal philosophers) and JM Smits, 'What is Legal Doctrine? On the Aims and Methods of Legal-Dogmatic Research' in R van Gestel, H-W Micklitz, and

There are exceptions but the concept of doctrine underpinning scholarship about its content, (ir)relevance to legal adjudication, or its creation is typically assumed rather than analysed.

One reason for the inattentiveness to the concept of legal doctrine may be that the idea of doctrine is simply uninteresting. On one common usage, 'doctrine' is cast as a proxy for the compendium of legal orders, rules, and principles that comprise a particular legal domain (such as contract, tort, or constitutional law).[18] If doctrine merely refers to 'positive law', then independent questions into its nature can be set aside without analytical or conceptual loss. Doctrine, thus understood, is simply the conventional term used by lawyers, judges and legal scholars to refer to positive law in a particular legal domain. Within this usage, 'doctrine' can be and is invoked to refer to the entire normative heap in a particular area of law or to individual norms buried within it. There are many instances of the specification of individual 'doctrines' which pick out an individuated rule or an inter-related set of norms. Examples of this locution drawn from administrative law include, the '*Chevron* doctrine' (United States), the '*Carltona* doctrine' (England), and the 'jurisdictional fact doctrine' (Australia).

There is nothing mysterious in this usage. But it seems to miss something important which is also carried within the ordinary meaning of doctrine. The meanings of doctrine recorded in the *Oxford English Dictionary* include the idea of a taught 'body of instruction' – something like a coherent or unified set of principles. Without some underlying values or principles to sweep an area of law into discernible order, doctrinal analysis would be doomed to repetition or amount to little more than an 'indexing' exercise.[19] Moreover, without some sort of discernible shape, the notion that there are distinct areas of law – a feature of legal life which seems endemic to legal systems – is unlikely to crystallise. Put differently, absent this systemic idea of doctrine it would be difficult to make sense of the social practice that allows lawyers and scholars to identify distinct areas of law.

It is, therefore, unsurprising that a systemic or integrative conception of doctrine has also emerged in the context of law and legal scholarship. Doctrine, on this usage, signals the 'systematisation of a whole area of the law'.[20] The raw materials of the law may initially appear as just one damn norm after the next. Doctrine demonstrates otherwise. The purpose of doctrinal writing, on this usage, is the identification of systemically

E Rubin et al (eds), *Rethinking Legal Scholarship: A Transatlantic Dialogue* (Cambridge, Cambridge University Press, 2017) (on legal scholarship generally).

[18] eg H Dagan, 'The Real Legacy of American Legal Realism' (2018) 38 *OJLS* 123, 124 and M Eisenberg, *The Nature of the Common Law* (Cambridge, Mass, Harvard University Press, 1988), who use 'doctrine' to refer to legislative enactments, judicial decisions and other pedigreed sources of law to draw a distinction between doctrinal reasons or propositions and other normative reasons or propositions that play a role in judicial decisions.

[19] *cf* L Fuller, 'Legal Realism' (1934) 82 *University of Pennsylvania Law Review* 429, 432. Cane has noted that the 'most common forms of legal literature in the early modern [common law] period were "abridgements" and "digests" of primary materials, organised without analytical system, often alphabetically': P Cane, 'Law, Fact and Process in Common Law Tort Scholarship' in J Goudkamp and D Nolan (eds), *Scholars of Tort Law* (Oxford, Hart Publishing, 2019) 369. Modern legal writing with such characteristics would be unlikely to attract the label of 'scholarship'. see D Feldman, 'The Nature of Legal Scholarship' (1989) 52 *MLR* 498, 503.

[20] Simmonds (n 17) 271.

integrated principles that can knit together doctrine's data – the rules, principles, orders, concepts and so on that can be found in law's 'documentary record'.[21] These underlying systemic principles can then be deployed to resolve controversies about the meaning of legal norms or to suggest how cases should be resolved where the relevant legal norms provide insufficient guidance.[22] In this way, legal doctrine is revealed to be something more than the sum of its positive law parts. This also explains why so much legal scholarship is normative in its orientation, extending beyond descriptive and explanatory objectives.

The concept of doctrine in this systemic or coherentist sense may turn out to be illusory but it cannot be accused of banality. Even the most limited conception of coherence – consistency, in the thin sense of the absence of incompatible obligations – can be related to basic rule of law requirements and preconditions of political legitimacy. The difficulty, however, is that the idea of doctrine as the outworking of systemic principles has not proved easy to pin down and develop. That is certainly so if one accepts that the 'grubby, disorderly world' of law[23] can be interpreted to (more or less) cohere in a variety of plausible ways. Given law is produced over time by multiple legal actors who work in different institutions and have conflicting interests, that prospect should hardly surprise. If alternative interpretations are genuinely available (and for argument's sake I assume they are), how is the doctrinal (systemic) content of the law to be determined, let alone authoritatively settled? A coherentist conception of doctrine is clear enough in outline but its application inevitably takes the judge or jurist beyond the exposition of the law.[24]

Consider first the position of the judges. Can judges settle debates about how to specify and articulate the law's 'systemic properties'? As Cane has reminded us, common law courts have the power to 'legalise norms' but their primary function remains the adjudication of disputes.[25] Judge-made law is a by-product of resolving disputes with at least a modicum of consistency and can, he suggests, be justified on that basis.[26] When making law the courts are obliged to 'ensure, as far as it is possible and desirable, that the body of legal norms is internally consistent and coherent'.[27] To this extent, the judiciary is collectively responsible for the development of the underlying principles of the system.

[21] P Cane, 'Taking Disagreement Seriously: Courts, Legislatures and the Reform of Tort Law' (2005) 25 *OJLS* 393, 407.

[22] Edward Rubin labels this the 'coherentist approach to scholarship': E Rubin, 'From Coherence to Effectiveness: A Legal Methodology for the Modern World' in R van Gestel et al (eds), *Rethinking Legal Scholarship: A Transatlantic Dialogue* (Cambridge, Cambridge University Press, 2017).

[23] Sugarman (n 9) 29.

[24] For an argument that positivist jurisprudence, insofar as it embraces gaps and penumbra within the law, has diverted generations of legal theorists from a proper engagement with the nature of legal doctrine and doctrinal writing, see Simmonds (n 17). However, even if the law is conceived of as gapless because apparent gaps can be closed by reference to systemic principles, the fact remains that those systemic principles may themselves be the subject of disagreement amongst judges and jurists alike. *cf* J Waldron, *Law and Disagreement* (Oxford, Oxford University Press, 1999) ch 8.

[25] Cane prefers to refer to law-making powers as the power to legalise norms, to emphasise the reality that typically 'legal norms do not come from nowhere': Cane (n 21) 401–402.

[26] ibid.

[27] ibid 407.

Nevertheless, as Cane has also argued, it remains the case that the common law is developed through the adjudication of disputes which are tied to particular fact situations. 'The common law' is not 'identifiable separately from and prior to a consideration of the facts of the case' and, for this reason, its rules and norms are products directly extracted from the judicial process.[28] The law-making role for the common law judge is complicated by this duality. Although judges make the law (legalise norms) in individual cases, the responsibility for the articulation of legal doctrine – in its systemic sense – is a job for the judiciary considered as a whole. Individual judges must keep an eye on the consistency and coherence of the system but it remains a subsidiary social function of courts and one for which judges ultimately must bear collective responsibility.

Cane contrasts the position of a common law judge with that of judges working under the 'civil law model'.[29] Civil law procedure, he explains, is primarily designed to prepare the factual background of a case so that the law developed independently of those facts can be applied. Under this model, it is the *jurists* who are the driving force in the systematisation of the law. He writes:[30]

> This is not to say, on the one side, that civilian judges do not contribute to the development of the law by exercising discretion in its application to individual cases. Nevertheless, their contributions do not 'make' the law in individual cases; instead, they provide grist for the juristic mill. Nor is it to say, on the other side, that jurists have law-making authority in their own right. Under the civil law model (at least in its modern manifestations), the legislature alone has law-making 'authority'. Indeed, it is the very absence of judicial authority to make law that provides space for both judges and jurists to contribute to the development of the law, which is as it were, a joint enterprise between Bench and Academy.

The contrast with doctrinal creation under the civil law model helps us see why it is doubtful that systemic properties will be adequately articulated through the processes of the common law which allocates the task subsidiary status. Doctrine as 'systemic properties' needs to be discovered, discerned or developed in some sort of comprehensive fashion, a result that seems unlikely when the judicial focus is on deciding individual cases. Put differently, the logic of the common law decision-making process is tilted towards the situational rather than the systemic.[31]

[28] Cane (n 19) 372.

[29] Although 'historically based' Cane does not claim that this model accurately states the law in a particular jurisdiction at a particular time. The purpose of the contrast between common law and civil law models is to 'interpret and explain': ibid 360.

[30] ibid 373. See also S Taekema, 'Methodologies of Rule of Law Research: Why Legal Philosophy Needs Empirical and Doctrinal Scholarship' (2021) 40 *Law and Philosophy* 33, who explains that in some legal systems, the common law distinction between primary sources of law and doctrine written by scholars is not clear-cut as the writings of jurists can form an important supplementary source of law.

[31] The point has been made by many but for a recent engaging discussion, see S Swaminathan, 'What the Centipede Knows: Polycentricity and "Theory" for Common Lawyers' (2020) 40 *OJLS* 265. According to Swaminathan (290), what common law judges do is shot through with mutual adjustment, tacit knowledge, and teleological opacity. As such, he argues that it is highly resistant to 'any grand systematic theory'. Even though Dworkin argued in favour of right answers in legal adjudication, his 'protestant' theory of interpretation is inconsistent with the *authoritative* statement of doctrine. See G Postema, '"Protestant" Interpretation and Social Practices' (1987) 6 *Law and Philosophy* 283.

The position of the 'jurist' in the common law tradition also warrants consideration. The label 'jurist' is often used as a rough synonym for 'legal academic' writer, but in the common law it most often designates an eminent legal writer – one who is, as it is sometimes grandly put, 'learned in the law'. The leading authors of the textbook tradition in common law systems are routinely described in this way. But within the common law tradition of thought 'jurist' is also a label that has been applied to eminent judges, in particular appellate judges who are credited as having made profound or lasting contributions in framing or developing legal doctrine. To this extent we can see that judges and legal academics can both be jurists, and what defines them as such is their contribution to the systematisation of areas of the common law through the formulation and articulation of underlying principles. Here, however, my use of jurist will focus on academic jurists (accepting that this category might be extended to include the extra-curial writings of judges).

Doctrinal writings of jurists – scholarship that, on the systemic usage of doctrine, by definition goes beyond the mere exposition of positive law sources – lack authority. But to what extent do and should judges treat the necessarily creative academic adventures in doctrinal systematisation as *persuasive* sources of law?[32]

The authors of the early legal treatises (textbooks, in modern parlance) purported to order areas of law by reference to a systemic conception of doctrine. In outline, the authors of the seminal texts began with attempts to define a discrete subject matter before proceeding to offer an overall framework where discernible legal principles were presented as being 'deducible from' a 'large multitude of cases'.[33] This mode of analysis was very different from two precursor forms of legal literature: abridgments (more or less disorderly reportage and sporadic analysis of primary materials) and the elaboration of legal 'maxims' thought to derive from universal principles yet which were expected, naturally, to find reflection in common law reasoning.[34] As Brian Simpson explained, the existence of abridgments provided the raw material enabling the work product of the courts to be seen, more ambitiously, as the authority for generally applicable legal propositions. And whereas the assumption underlying the juristic accumulation of 'maxims' had been a unity embedded within the common law considered as a whole, the treatise writers, less ambitiously, sought out system in discrete areas of law. The historical process was ornate[35] but by the early twentieth century the emergent purpose of a law professor was, for Dicey, clear enough: 'to set forth the law as a coherent whole – to analyse and define legal conceptions – to reduce the mass of legal rules to an orderly series of principles and to aid, stimulate and guide the reform or renovation of legal literature'.[36]

Thus, the trick for the textbook writer became to present an inevitably creative rendering of the law as the elucidation of *existing* legal doctrine. The inability of jurists to claim legal authority on their own account resulted in a declared commitment to an

[32] As opposed, that is, to binding or permissive sources of law. On the distinction between authoritative and permissive sources of law, see Green (n 12).

[33] TFT Plucknett, *Early English Legal Literature* (Cambridge, Cambridge University Press, 1958) 19.

[34] Simpson (n 13).

[35] ibid.

[36] AV Dicey, *Can English Law be Taught at the Universities?* (London, Macmillan & Co, 1883) 18, quoted in Sugarman (n 9) 30.

'expository orthodoxy' but this did not prevent a burst of intellectual creativity spurred by the parallel assumption that coherence would emerge from the proper analysis of the existing law. Indeed, the timing for the authors of the early treatises was auspicious: '[t]he collapse of the forms of action, the fusion of law and equity and the unprecedented freedom this afforded textbook writers to reconstitute the common law was freely admitted by jurists and practitioners alike.' The practical result, Sugarman suggests, was 'unparalleled opportunity for juristic legislation'.[37]

Although the influence of jurists on judges is difficult to track and trace, there is some evidence that particular doctrines in the form of common law rules and principles have been co-produced.[38] For this reason we need to read Cane's conclusion that 'under the common law model, "jurists" have no distinctive niche in the legal ecosystem' carefully.[39] Jurists do not, as he explains, possess anything even approaching a formal role in the process of norm legalisation (in contrast to the civil law tradition). However, insofar as jurists are (institutionally speaking) better placed than the judges to undertake the necessarily creative task of norm systematisation, they can carve out something of a niche if judges are willing to listen.

Having said that, it should also be recognised that the ossification of the basic legal categories of established common law areas of law has narrowed the scope for genuinely creative juristic input into doctrinal development. To the extent contemporary legal scholars in the textbook tradition have a niche, it has been aptly characterised as an increasingly 'narrow ledge'.[40] Yes, judges have sometimes been and continue to be influenced by scholarly critiques and exhortations about the development of legal norms. We can also accept that scholars arguably played a pivotal role in embedding the notion that the domains of doctrine within the common law could and should be viewed as a coherent (albeit imperfectly realised) whole. But if doctrinal creativity – at the level of arguing how the messy reality of the law should best be brought into coherent view – can be characterised as 'meddling with the *content* of the law'[41] it will likely fall on deaf judicial ears.[42] If doctrinal scholars want to be heard by judges, the small target strategy they typically adopt makes a lot of sense. Bluntly put, scholarly efforts to smooth over the raw materials of the law with a doctrinal veneer are only likely to have influence if they are mindful of judicial tastes.[43]

Two broader social changes have served to reinforce that position: the increasing sway of democratic ideals and the corrosive effect which open acknowledgement of reasonable disagreement has had on the idea that the common law is the outgrowth of common reason. When cases cannot be resolved by reference to the law's documentary materials considered in light of the judiciary's collective (ill-defined) responsibility to achieve coherence, judicial appeals to social norms or common sense are scuppered

[37] Sugarman (n 9) 33.
[38] N Duxbury, *Jurists and Judges: An Essay on Influence* (Oxford, Hart Publishing, 2001). See also, P Mitchell, 'Patterns of Legal Change' (2012) 65 *Current Legal Problems* 177.
[39] Cane (n 19) 382.
[40] Sugarman (n 9) 33.
[41] ibid 34.
[42] Cane (n 19) 375.
[43] See also R Unger, *What Should Legal Analysis Become?* (London, Verso, 1996) 46–52.

by the existence of pervasive, good faith disagreement.[44] This problem has dogged Herculean judicial pretensions and ambitious prescriptive doctrinal writings of scholars alike.

The massive expansion of the profession of legal scholars in the twentieth century has certainly increased juristic resources but has also worked to aggravate the precarity of life on the 'narrow ledge' of conventional doctrinal scholarship as scholars vie for judicial attention.[45] On the one hand, genuine originality may render doctrinal writings, practically speaking, irrelevant. On the other hand, scholarly consensus about systemic principles in a given area of law or what particular doctrines of the law require may rest on nothing more robust than shared biases. It is true that some judges have openly encouraged assistance from academics who share the judicial 'concern with the correct and coherent development of the law'.[46] But the dialogue remains judge-directed and even if judges were willing to take a doctrinal backseat, grinding judicial workloads limit the amount of relevant scholarship that can realistically be read, raising legitimate questions about whose scholarly voices will register.

To illustrate the circumscribed nature of any dialogue between the bench and academy, consider the contemporary development of the new private law theory[47] – scholarship that in older jargon might have been referred to as 'particular' jurisprudence. This mode of scholarship is doctrinal insofar as most of its proponents claim to give an account of a domain of law by reference to two overarching criteria. The first is a criterion of 'fit'. A theory articulating doctrine's systemic properties must fit (in a Goldilocks sense) the primary documentary legal materials. For some theorists this requirement fades into the background of their normative agenda but it is rarely consciously jettisoned. The price of doing so would be to make explicit the slippage from legal to political or moral discourse, from explaining what doctrine does require to what it should require.

The second criterion is coherence. Many assume that this criterion requires moral commitment on the part of the theorist – that the principle or set of principles invoked to explain the law must be accepted. Less ambitiously, others assume that coherence need only be demonstrated by reference to principles that are intelligible to insiders of system, regardless of the theorist's own normative preferences.[48] My purpose is not to enter the debate about the nature of 'particular jurisprudence' (ie theories of domains of law).[49] The point is merely to note that such theories are sophisticated efforts to systematise the law in a particular area – to give an explanation of that law which also prescribes how the law in the area should be developed by reference to intelligible or

[44] See Cane (n 21); *cf* Eisenberg (n 18).

[45] For a time the problem was managed (though not overcome) by the irrational judicial norm that allowed the citation of only deceased doctrinal writers.

[46] S Kiefel, 'The Academy and the Courts: what do they mean to each other today' (2021) 44 *Melbourne University Law Review* 447, 448.

[47] See generally, A Gold et al (eds), *The Oxford Handbook of the New Private Law* (New York, Oxford University Press, 2020).

[48] See generally, S Smith, *A Theory of Contract Law* (Oxford, Oxford University Press, 2004) ch 1.

[49] For an illuminating discussion, see T Khaitan and S Steel, 'Theorising Areas of Law' (draft manuscript on file with author).

justifiable principles that already explain its significant features. Modern day textbook writers are less ambitious than their theoretically inclined colleagues, but there is an obvious sense in which any attempt to describe an area of law will be organised in a way which reflects value choices.[50]

What, then, explains the (impressionistically established) fact that well-regarded textbooks tend to be cited more frequently than well-regarded monographs containing more theoretically ambitious interpretations of a domain of law (or significant part of one)? Particular jurisprudence is certainly a richer source of ideas about how legal doctrine can meaningfully be understood as a coherent body of intelligible principles. But doctrinal exposition which ramps up the dial of normative coherence is unlikely to capture or persuade individual judges who understand, perhaps better than some private law theorists, that the judiciary is a 'they' not an 'it' and that doctrinal creation is an institutionally embedded endeavour.

To summarise: there are two common general usages of 'doctrine' in contemporary legal literature. The first usage (doctrine as positive law) is not interesting enough to warrant independent study. The second usage (doctrine as systemic properties) in common law systems is likely to be underdeveloped by judge jurists working their day jobs for institutional reasons or lacking authority and inevitably controversial if developed by academic jurists. This insight helps to explain why a rich or thick concept of doctrine which carries normative force has remained elusive.

III. Judicial Review Doctrine in The Administrative State

Having sought to clarify the general usages of 'legal doctrine', I turn to consider the development of a systematised approach to thinking about doctrine in administrative law in particular. Here my argument will be that the development of a general principles approach to administrative law was part of an effort to secure the conditions for legitimate administrative government but that legal features of the administrative state compound the generic difficulties (discussed in section II) associated with efforts to articulate and apply a systemic sense of doctrine.

As noted above, although the early textbook writers played a key role in the crystallisation of doctrine in particular legal domains, their self-image was that of expositor. As Dicey put it, the task of the scholar jurist was to show the various elements of the law as a 'coherent whole' thereby ordering *extant* principles. Administrative law norms, conceived as a (somewhat) coherent set of principles of judicial review, were latecomers to the common law's systematisation party. Whereas as the seminal textbooks in private law appeared in the nineteenth century, the seminal English administrative law texts were creatures of the mid-twentieth century. The reasons for this are connected to the delayed demise of the formulary system in the context of public law.[51] But when

[50] Smith (n 48) 6. This point is discussed further below. See text at nn 86–88.

[51] For a brief explanation, see P Cane and L McDonald, *Principles of Administrative Law: Legal Regulation of Governance* (Melbourne, Oxford University Press, 2008) 23–25.

the time arrived for administrative law's transition from a law focused on forms to one directed towards substance judges and jurists both played a role.

The key intellectual move was away from a law focused on the satisfaction of the formulae for the issue of a particular prerogative writ to a law focused on general norms that constrain government decision-makers. As Janet McLean suggests, the work of the early textbook writers in Britain was significant. In the work of de Smith and Wade in particular, she discerns a self-conscious effort to 'extract and construct a new set of general principles gleaned from the common law and designed for the judicial control of the administration by way of special rules'.[52] These principles came to be expressed through the language of 'grounds of review'.

In this way jurists played a creative role in the *framing* of administrative law's norms (aka the grounds of review) even as the courts remained responsible for the development of 'a body of general principles to govern the relationship between citizen and State' in its contemporary form.[53] According to Paul Daly, the courts' creative legalisation of administrative norms (in a number of Commonwealth jurisdictions) was stimulated by reform of the prerogative writs, allowing these ancient remedies to be 'retrofitted to the rising administrative state'. Reforms that swept away technicalities associated with the writs 'had the unintended effect of permitting judges to develop a body of general principles of administrative law'.[54]

This 'remarkable' post World War II 'period of expansion and new articulation of the grounds of judicial review'[55] can plausibly be thought to have taken advantage of intellectual space prised open by jurists such as de Smith.[56] Yet, even if it is accepted that the textbook writers played a role in setting the courts' doctrinal agenda, they made less progress in demonstrating how the set of judicially crafted aspects of judicial review do or might cohere. As Galligan observed in 1982, judges rarely make the effort to 'construct a pattern of interlocking rules' underpinning their decisions and the textbook writers had – to that point, at least – not provided much assistance in suggesting an adequate theoretical basis to bundle the enterprise into a coherent whole.[57] Having provided intellectual impetus for doctrinal creativity by the courts, jurists' efforts to identify systemic principles to regulate the relationship between citizen and State were – for the remaining decades of the twentieth century – relatively modest. In particular, the textbook writers tended to focus on smaller scale interventions about how an individualised doctrines might be developed.[58] The broader legal context of the administrative state, I suggest, helps explain why a clear conception of doctrine in the systemic sense has struggled to take hold and to be filled with stable content in administrative law, in particular.

[52] J McLean, *Searching for the State in British Legal Thought: Competing Conceptions of the Public Sphere* (Cambridge, Cambridge University Press, 2012) 166; referring to SA de Smith, *Judicial Review of Administrative Action* (London, Stevens & Sons Ltd, 1959) and HWR Wade, *Administrative Law* (Oxford, Clarendon Press, 1961).

[53] DJ Galligan, 'Judicial Review and the Textbook Writers' (1982) 2 *OJLS* 257, 258.

[54] P Daly, 'The Inexorable Rise of Judicial Review' *Prospect Magazine* (28 September 2020).

[55] T Endicott, *Administrative Law*, 3rd edn (Oxford, Oxford University Press, 2015) 62.

[56] See also P Daly, 'Leading Works in Public Law: de Smith's Judicial Review of Administrative Action (Stevens & Sons, London, 1959)' in P O'Brien and B Yong (eds), *Leading Works in Public Law* (forthcoming).

[57] Galligan (n 53) 268–69.

[58] See further discussion at nn 85–88.

If de Smith's text on judicial review of administrative action played a transformative role in the doctrinal coming of age of judicial review, it should be remembered that he acknowledged from the get-go that the elucidation of the systemic properties and principles of administrative law was (and would remain) a fraught undertaking. Indeed, his introductory chapter concluded with something of a *mea culpa*:

> [I]t must be said that exposition of the scope of judicial review primarily in terms of the existing case-law presents peculiar difficulties. They arise above all because of the heterogeneity of the subject-matter on which judicial review operates and the variety of conditions under which it is invoked. There are obvious dangers in hopping from one branch of administrative law to another with an over-zealous determination to elicit general principles of judicial review, and it may well be that the law can be stated most accurately (though at very great length) by a succession of commentaries on the interpretation of individual statutes and statutory instruments. Nevertheless, it is the present writer's opinion that the degree of unity in the principles traceable in the law of judicial review has been somewhat underestimated, and the scheme of presentation followed … will reflect that opinion.[59]

That administrative law could fruitfully be understood as a generally applicable set of judge-made principles was thus not assumed to be self-evident. Indeed, the earliest English texts on administrative law were structured around 'an exploration of different kinds of administrative scheme' and paid particular attention to the extent to which those particular schemes relied upon rule-making or adjudication to achieve their purposes.[60] Nevertheless, de Smith's focus upon the identification of presumptively applicable principles of judicial review has become the conventional way of thinking about the subject of administrative law.

This conventional approach to defining administrative law – at least where the focus is on legal techniques used by courts – conceives the core of the subject as a generally applicable 'set of judicially-created legal doctrines'.[61] The associated legal rules and principles may be displaced by statutory interventions. But the approach remains general insofar as these principles mark out 'default' requirements for lawful administrative action.[62] A common and helpful way of understanding the default standards which emerged to comprise the grounds of review is as a judicial response to the perceived prevalence of discretionary administrative power and the consequent risk of arbitrariness in government decision-making. The grounds of review immersed discretionary power in a body of legal principles designed to diminish the threat of legal arbitrariness.[63] In addition to doctrines designed to structure discretionary powers the generally applicable norms of administrative law also appeared in the guise of methodologies

[59] de Smith (n 52) 25. See also P Cane, *An Introduction to Administrative Law* (Oxford, Clarendon Press, 1985) 9–10.

[60] J Bell, 'Rethinking the Story of *Cart v Upper Tribunal* and Its Implications for Administrative Law' (2019) 39 *OJLS* 74, 97 discussing FJ Port, *Administrative Law* (London, Longmans Green & Co, 1929) and J Griffith and H Street, *Principles of Administrative Law* (London, Pitman & Sons, 1952). Notably, the second of these volumes was published in the same decade as de Smith's own text.

[61] J Bell, *The Anatomy of Administrative Law* (Oxford, Hart Publishing, 2020) 1.

[62] *Minister for Immigration and Citizenship v Li* (2013) 249 CLR 332 [92] (Gageler J).

[63] See generally DJ Galligan, *Discretionary Powers: A Legal Study of Official Discretion* (Oxford, Oxford University Press, 1990) and KC Davis, *Discretionary Justice: A Preliminary Inquiry* (Urbana, Louisiana State University Press, 1969).

(often styled as 'standards of review') to scaffold the interpretation of the specific requirements of statutory regimes.[64]

An interesting facet of this now conventional way of thinking about administrative law is that it emerged at a point in time when the twentieth century proliferation of administrative and regulatory schemes was well underway and continuing apace. By the mid-twentieth century doctrinal coming-of-age of administrative law two fundamental features of the administrative state were unmissable. First, government decision-making extended across the breadth of economic and social life (including but not limited to schemes associated with the welfare state). The range of administrative government far outstripped the sorts of concerns and legal interests traditionally recognised and protected by the common law. Second, the way in which individual and collective interests attained legal relevance within administrative government was not uniform. The burgeoning administrative state was built with statutory blocks that 'varied considerably in terms of aim and structure'.[65]

Joanna Bell has helpfully identified three distinct examples of legislative frameworks that underpinned the emergent administrative state in England: first, schemes to regulate the making of individualised decisions to impose burdens or confer benefits; second, schemes to regulate decision-making where individual applications affect third-party interests; and, third, schemes to protect collective or public interests.[66] Some administrative schemes confer legal entitlements, whereas others repose discretionary powers on officials. Some protect the interests of individuals, whereas others protect collective interests. And within each category of statutory schemes some are sparse, whereas others are densely populated with detailed rules and requirements (details which have increasingly been shunted into delegated legislation). The application of general norms of administrative law must, therefore, contend with at least two vectors of diversity: a staggeringly wide range of policy domains and variety in the legal architecture of administrative schemes.

These features of administrative government prompt an obvious question: Why did the idea of systemic general principles take root in the inhospitable ground of an increasingly differentiated and complex administrative state? One plausible hypothesis is that this approach holds out the promise that administrative law can meaningfully contribute to the legitimation of administrative power.[67] The administrative state and its modalities of governance have always been a greater source of constitutional anxiety in the United States than in Australia and England. But even in the Anglo-Australian context vast delegations of rule-making and discretionary powers have butted up against constitutional values such as the rule of law and parliamentary supremacy.[68] Judicially

[64] eg doctrines of implicit deference pursued through the analytic framework of the fact/law distinction.

[65] Bell (n 61) 48. See also W Friedmann, *Law and Social Change in Contemporary Britain* (London, Stevens & Sons, 1951).

[66] Bell (n 61) 68–72.

[67] T Poole, 'Legitimacy, Rights and Judicial Review' (2005) 25 *OJLS* 697.

[68] G Hewart, *The New Despotism* (London, Ernest Benn, 1929). Despite the polemical nature of this tract, it 'set the agenda for academic administrative lawyers and their defence of the administrative state for decades': McLean (n 52) 174. In Australia, the long-term existence of what is now called the Senate Committee for Delegated Legislation and the more recent growth of so-called integrity branch institutions directed to the control of discretionary powers can be explained in this context.

generated general principles which confine and structure the exercise of discretionary power[69] can also be explained as a partial response to claims, prevalent in the first half of the twentieth century, that the administrative state is systematically incompatible with basal constitutional values. My claim, however, is not that the development of a general principles approach to administrative law has wholly succeeded in legitimating administrative government but, rather, that their creation can be understood as an attempt to contribute to that project.

Can, however, the project of legitimating administrative government underwrite a meaningful systemic sense of doctrine in the context of the administrative state? Some administrative lawyers appear to be losing faith with approaches that place general principles at the core of their subject, or at least give them too great an emphasis. Bell, for instance, argues that the ever-present and changeable policy/legal complexity of the administrative state confounds conventional understandings of administrative law.[70] Unpacking the subject's layers of statutory complexity reveals a diversity of administrative structures, protected values and interests, and legal relationships. This diagnosis is at once arresting and familiar. It is arresting because unpicking the complex 'anatomy of administrative law' has significant implications for how the subject ought to be imagined. Bell's case studies of English and Welsh law suggest that judges are keenly attentive to legal particulars and complexity in administrative law adjudications; the grounds of review, it turns out, are tools that are relatively rarely required. Indeed, clear understandings of administrative law are confounded, she goes on to argue, by juristic efforts to *unify* administrative law's general norms under the banner of any overarching or master principle.[71]

Yet scepticism about the limits of systemic doctrine also resonates within mainstream understandings of administrative law. It is commonplace for textbook writers to observe that administrative power is overwhelmingly statutory power and that the grounds must therefore be applied in their statutory habitat. Indeed, some of the grounds – like the consideration grounds – operate like traffic signs, directing the legal inquiry to particular aspects of the legislative scheme but doing little independent normative work. Even the fair hearing rule, which is in principle capable of independent operation, has a chameleon-like content that is sensitive to particular statutory contexts.[72] For these reasons, the interaction between general doctrine and statutory context has long been understood as an important reason why administrative law's norms are difficult to expound and apply, and why a precedent case may carry little legal force outside of its own statutory context.[73]

What implications should the interaction between judicially generated principles and statutory specifics have for *how we think* about administrative law doctrine? One possible response is to emphasise that generality and specificity exist in perennial

[69] *cf* Davis (n 63).
[70] Bell (n 61).
[71] ibid ch 7.
[72] Eg *Kioa v West* (1985) 159 CLR 550 (HCA) 584.
[73] See, eg, P Cane et al, *Principles of Administrative Law*, 3rd edn (Melbourne, Oxford University Press, 2018) 125–29.

tension within administrative law, something (we have seen) that was acknowledged by de Smith. Another more challenging response is to acknowledge that the purposes of administrative law may change as the legal architecture of the administrative state changes. For example, the architectural variety within the administrative state's myriad legislative schemes suggests that the legal control of discretionary power is not the only legal problem for which general administrative law norms may be part of the solution. Indeed, a perusal of the modern day statute book (in Australia, at least) highlights the fact that many administrative schemes are groaning with legislative detail[74] (detail which is often multiplied at the level of delegated legislation) and which is sometimes designed to squeeze as much discretion out of decision-making as is possible. As Bell points out, the situation the court confronted in *Cooper v Wandworth Board of Works* – where the statute was entirely silent on procedural requirements – is rare in the context of contemporary legislation.[75] An apt example is the Australian Migration Act, which has evolved from a sparse to sprawling piece of legislation. Of course, many legislative schemes, including some of the most wordy, maintain express[76] or implicit discretionary elements.[77] Scholars of regulation have taught that the appropriate balance between rules (and rigidity) and standards (and flexibility) must be calibrated differently according to regulatory purposes and context.[78] Nevertheless, one might expect that the sheer increase in the volume of legislation (measured both by number of statutes and overall pages)[79] would diminish the space within which the default norms of administrative law can meaningfully operate. That, at any rate, is a plausible hypothesis.

The complex and amorphous trend toward juridified administrative decision-making also provides a context within which Sarah Nason's recent empirical study of first instance judicial review cases in England and Wales can be read. Nason found that 'judges largely do not apply doctrinal concepts of justification' but, rather, 'apply ordinary common law principles of statutory interpretation'.[80] On her interpretation of the data, most cases are resolved on the basis of 'whether there was reasoning of adequate quality in the challenged decision', assessed against criteria drawn from the particular statute under consideration.[81] Although Nason's methodology is very different to Bell's, the overall message is similar: the textbook writers' emphasis on grounds of review and generally applicable concepts obscures the reality of administrative law adjudication.

[74] LB Crawford, 'The Rule of Law in the Age of Statutes' (2020) 48 *Federal Law Review* 159.

[75] Bell (n 61) 102–103, citing C Harlow and R Rawlings, 'Proceduralism and Automation: Challenges to the Values of Administrative Law' in E Fisher et al (eds), *The Foundations and Future of Public Law (in Honour of Paul Craig)* (Oxford, Oxford University Press, 2020).

[76] That is certainly so with respect to the Migration Act 1958. See K Rundle, 'Non-Compellable Powers: A Relational Analysis' (2019) 30 *Public Law Review* 300.

[77] Attempts at 'codification' within parts of the Migration Act 1958 have also failed to squeeze all discretionary elements out of the system. See G Hooper, 'Three Decades of Tension: From the Codification of Migration Decision Making to An Overarching Framework for Judicial Review' (2020) 48 *Federal Law Review* 401.

[78] J Braithwaite, 'Rules and Principles: A Theory of Legal Certainty' (2002) 27 *Australian Journal of Legal Philosophy* 47.

[79] For some statistics, see Crawford (n 74).

[80] S Nason, *Reconstructing Judicial Review* (Oxford, Hart Publishing, 2016) 24.

[81] ibid 24–25.

Of course, a tension between generality and diversity also arises in the context of private law. Should, for example, contract law be conceived by reference to general principles or particular species of contracts? Private law adjudication also often involves the interaction between judge-created norms and statutory provisions. Private law theorists (who seek coherent interpretations of a body of law) can and have been called to task for failing to be sufficiently attentive to statute in their efforts to show that their theories fit the legal materials and thus fall within the realm of interpretation rather than invention.[82] However, whereas in the private law context the purpose of statutory intervention is typically to directly modify common law rules and principles, in the administrative law context statutory interventions are typically directed to achieve particular regulatory or administrative purposes. This helps explain why administrative lawyers often explicitly separate out 'general administrative law doctrine' (which is typically power limiting) from doctrine specific to a particular domain of administration (where the legislative purposes are typically to confer powers to achieve particular goals and purposes).[83] For this reason, perhaps, the tension between variability and generality in administrative law is especially difficult to manage: the overarching purpose of specific statutory powers and schemes is to confer power and enable government action whereas the general norms tend to impose requirements that limit power or otherwise temper its exercise.[84]

The development of judge generated norms of administrative law can be understood as a response to persistent concerns about the legitimacy of administrative governance. These developments have no doubt had successes in this regard but, nevertheless, the project of unifying legal doctrines in administrative law by reference to a systemic sense of doctrine has always been ambitious given the ongoing compression of common law space wrought by an age of statutes which foregrounds statutory particulars and purposes or other forms of contextualism.

IV. 'Fresh, Plausible and Suggestive' Doctrinal Scholarship

The idea of doctrine (generally) and administrative law doctrine (in particular) is difficult to pin down. In this context it is hardly surprising to find that there are different modalities of doctrinal scholarship in administrative law. What, then, can be said about doctrinal scholarship or its productive modalities in the absence of an accepted underlying conception of doctrine itself?

In this final section of the chapter I distinguish three broad modes of doctrinally-oriented academic writing within administrative law: the first continues the textbook tradition; the second involves a turn to theory that attempts to keep the cases front and centre; and the third adopts a 'meta' or 'structural' orientation to the analysis of the cases. Without discounting the value and purposes of the first two (more familiar)

[82] J Goudkamp and J Murphy, 'Tort Statutes and Tort Theories' (2015) 131 *LQR* 133.

[83] Such as planning law. See, for example, E Fisher, 'Law and Energy Transitions: Wind Turbines and Planning Law in the UK' (2018) 38 *OJLS* 528, 545.

[84] Of course, specific statutory provisions may impose conditions and limits on the exercise of powers.

modes of doctrinal scholarship, I will suggest that the third approach has the best prospects to contribute to the development of fresh, plausible and suggestive *explanatory* accounts of administrative law. The focus in structural doctrinal scholarship is not on the development of a coherentist account of the law. Rather, a meta or structural approach to doctrine aims to reveal how judges think about the specification and articulation of the norms of administrative law, without assuming a uniform or static judicial approach. In doing so it enables consideration of the question: what is at stake when we observe different methodologies – developed within the cases – for the legalisation and articulation of administrative law norms?

The textbook tradition of legal writing continues to attract the energies of notable scholars in administrative law. Administrative law textbooks come in various shapes and sizes. Some aim to comprehensively deal with the law. More commonly, others aim to provide an introductory account serving primarily pedagogical purposes. Comprehensive textbooks order a vast amount of legal information. And such work undoubtedly assists judges. For example, the identification of tensions between existing cases, rules or principles can stimulate and prompt judicial reasoning in difficult cases. Textbook-style analysis is also a helpful precursor to thought about law reform and legislative change.[85] As valuable as these contributions are, however, this mode of writing fits within the more general thesis (explained in section II) that doctrinal scholarship is relegated to an increasingly narrow ledge, a ledge from which the building of systemic doctrine is a precarious endeavour. Textbooks contribute to building a shared (although not fixed) sense of what marks out the boundaries of administrative law, and provide a helpful entry point into the law's details. In so doing many loose ends are identified and discussed in a sophisticated way. But text writers understandably shy away from tying loose ends together with systemic principles which would draw them into controversial normative assessments about what those principles are and how to best interpret them.

Consider, for example, the sophisticated acknowledgement in the leading Australian comprehensive text on judicial review law that 'there is inevitably a creative component to any synthesis' of the law and that this 'involves making some normative assumptions or choices'.[86] Nevertheless, the authors maintain that '[p]recedents must and do count for something, and our tasks as textbook writers must be to discern patterns, to generalise, to predict, and occasionally to urge'.[87] This work enjoys an unparalleled reputation and is by far the most cited scholarly source on the law of judicial review in Australian courts. The judicial citations, however, typically relate to the book's granular insights or to relatively non-controversial interpretations of the case law rather than to propositions about systemic properties which knit together rules and principles and thereby guide legal reasoning. Within this tradition of doctrinal writing there is a clear tension between its expository orientation and the task of *explaining* its contours by reference to a broader coherent normative order. Thus, we should not be surprised that texts which

[85] See, eg, the reliance on the work of textbook authors in the last major report published by the Administrative Review Council in Australia: *Federal Judicial Review in Australia* (No 50, 2012).

[86] M Aronson et al, *Judicial Review of Administrative Action and Government Liability*, 6th edn (Pyrmont, Thomson Reuters, 2017) 2.

[87] ibid 3.

are highly regarded by the practicing profession and the judiciary tend to manage that tension by loosening the working conception of coherence.

A great deal of administrative law scholarship that appears within the pages of law journals also adopts the basic orientation, forged by the textbook tradition, to the task of the scholar which prizes accuracy of exposition and internal consistency. Such scholarship accepts that the dialogue between jurists and judges is anchored more firmly by the judges' work product than accounts of normative coherence. And the modesty of doctrinal urgings demonstrate acceptance that critique should be circumspect and interstitial. Through a dialogue with the bench and bar, scholars are able to contribute to the evolution and refinement of legal norms and concepts. But this dialogue remains rooted in the internal point of view – with the scholar implicitly (or explicitly) addressing the judiciary – and this limits its broader explanatory value. To the extent some doctrinally-oriented administrative law scholars have engaged in theoretically more ambitious attempts to explain the case law by revealing richer accounts of normative coherence, those accounts have tended to focus on particular doctrines rather than proffering theories of administrative law as a whole.[88]

It may be, however, that doctrinally-oriented administrative law scholarship is on the cusp of a theoretically oriented turn, inspired by the new private law theory (briefly discussed in section II) and set to be propelled by thicker and more encompassing understandings of coherence. This sort of work is not unknown in the literature, and the scholarship of TRS Allan serves as a prominent example.[89] But other scholars have recently joined the fray, developing a variety of philosophically sophisticated theories of administrative law. For example, Adam Perry has suggested that the grounds of judicial review in English law prescribe the circumstances where 'it is rational for an official to reconsider, retain, suspend, or apply a plan'.[90] The legitimacy of judicial review as an enterprise can be understood by reference to an account which shows how it is explicable by reference to this foundational principle. But, as this example demonstrates, such theories need not rely heavily on existing tropes of legal argument. Ideas related to planning agency and law conceived of as plans have not figured in the published reasons of judges.

One benefit of big picture, doctrinally-focused administrative law theory is its capacity to suggest fruitful new ways of understanding the purpose of particular norms and, also, its capacity to suggest 'new connections and new directions for research'.[91] Such theories also clearly provide a way to think about law reform. They are presented not only as an account of what the law is but also purport to show how the law fits into an intelligible and attractive normative system. Doctrinally informed theories of

[88] As observed by A Perry, 'Plan B: A Theory of Judicial Review' (Research Paper No 66/2017, Faculty of Law, University of Oxford, 22 November 2017) https://ssrn.com/abstract=3075886. For engaging examples of theoretical doctrinally oriented scholarship on particular administrative law doctrines, see A Perry, 'The Flexibility Rule in Administrative Law' (2017) 76 *CLJ* 375 and A Perry and F Ahmed, 'Standing and Civic Virtue' (2018) 134 *LQR* 239.

[89] Eg TRS Allan, *The Sovereignty of Law: Freedom, Constitution, and Common Law* (Oxford, Oxford University Press, 2013).

[90] Perry, 'A Theory of Judicial Review' (n 88).

[91] ibid.

administrative law can thus provide impetus for productive lines of critique through suggestive accounts of what the function of the law should be or how value trade-offs can be managed. They can also function as a foil to root and branch critiques of the legitimacy of administrative law. But such theories share the general risks and pitfalls of scholarly efforts to formulate a coherentist conception of doctrine in a thorough-going way. To recap, chief amongst these is epistemic overreach – the necessarily reconstructive nature of interpretive theories means that they go beyond the evidence generated by the institutionally complex processes of legal reasoning and adjudication. Put differently, theoretically rich accounts of doctrine assume that the reasons why judges resolve cases will map onto the reasons that underpin the justificatory account considered to best explain (most of) the legal materials. Doctrinally-oriented theories which emphasise coherence can thus quickly morph into first order normative theories if legal actors in fact act on the basis of different reasons or motivations.

Another difficulty is that theoretical accounts of the law which dial up unity of principle or coherence of purpose necessarily gloss over the institutional realities of doctrinal development. The collective task of the judiciary in its law-making guise is to make legal norms. But judges, as Cane has emphasised, 'are under no obligation to specify the purposes and goals of the rules they make, and they typically do not do so, at least not clearly, comprehensively, or with analytical rigour'.[92] In these circumstances, philosophically rich theories of administrative law risk being insufficiently attentive to real world messiness, a mess which may reflect cross-cutting interests that have been imperfectly accommodated by law makers in the construction of administrative schemes and, also, diversity in judicial points of view. Aspects of doctrinally-oriented theory may, of course, be picked up here and there, but the slim prospects of doctrine in a systematic sense being downloaded holus-bolus provokes sharp questions about the normative force such theories are able to carry. And, if one's scholarly purpose is explanatory, doctrinally-oriented theoretical accounts of administrative law appear ill-equipped to deal with the actuality of diversity and divergence of thought within the judicial reasoning (especially evident in appellate courts).

Yet thorough-going scepticism also faces problems as a basis for explanatory accounts of administrative law. A singular emphasis on the complexity and diversity of administrative law, in preference to unifying or 'monistic' scholarly accounts of administrative law, raises the question of how administrative law can sustain itself as an area of law. Absent a threshold degree of orderliness it would not make sense to describe any collection or norms and institutions an area or field of law at all. In response to this worry, Bell contends that it is possible to continue the study of *generalist* administrative law which does not rely on monistic analysis. 'The central point,' she suggests, is 'that, even if administrative law lacks an "organising concept", it is important to maintain a body of scholarship which looks at how the courts oversee public administration across

[92] P Cane, 'Administrative Law as Regulation' in J Braithwaite et al (eds), *Regulating Law* (Oxford, Oxford University Press, 2004) 216.

different areas'.[93] Were that focus lost, we 'would lose the ability to identify important patterns in how the courts approach review, as well as the potential to identify outliers'.[94]

On one level, a defence to administrative law scholarship which continues to be attentive to generally applicable principles or 'patterns' while also emphasising complexity and plurality of values might be characterised as an attempt to have one's cake and eat it too. On another level, such responses illustrate the point made earlier (in section III) that the tension between variability and generality is especially vivid in administrative law. The tsunami of statutory activity over the course of the life of modern administrative law has worked to foreground the variability in the legal norms that guide and constrain administrators. But it continues to be the case that judges apply legal norms which have dubious legislative or constitutional provenance in an attempt to bring order and consistency and to render the administrative state acceptable by reference to ideas about government legitimacy.[95] If the tension between variability and generality is perennial then a key question for doctrinally-oriented legal scholarship is to describe how judges go about *managing* what is an unavoidable tension – to describe, that is, the methodology they apply to specify and articulate the norms that guide and constrain administrators. Putting the point this way directs us to a third mode in generalist doctrinal scholarship in administrative law, a mode of generalist analysis which proceeds without presupposing the existence of normative coherence or the stability of overarching organising concepts.

Focusing on how judges think about the identification and articulation of administrative law norms signals something of a methodological turn in doctrinal scholarship in administrative law. An illuminating example of this mode of scholarship is to be found in Dean Knight's stimulating study of judicial review in Australia, New Zealand, England and Canada.[96] Knight argues that administrative law necessarily needs to provide judges with a methodology to vary the depth of scrutiny of their judicial review function to modulate between vigilance and restraint in the supervision of administrative power. His analysis is revealing, as it indicates that the doctrinal tools used to determine the intensity of judicial review varies over time (in particular jurisdictions) and between jurisdictions. The first variation is demonstrated through a careful examination of the changing emphasis in the presentation of English law across seven editions of de Smith's textbook. From that analysis, Knight extracts four distinct methodologies which are dubbed 'schemata' of review.[97] The second line of variability is illustrated by matching particular schemata more or less closely with the contemporary law in the Commonwealth jurisdictions investigated in the study.[98] Importantly, Knight recognises that within any legal system there are likely to be multiple methodologies

[93] Bell (n 61) 245.

[94] ibid 245.

[95] *cf* A Vermeule, 'Rules, Commands and Principles in the Administrative State' (2020) *Yale Law Journal Forum* 356.

[96] D Knight, *Vigilance and Restraint in the Common Law of Judicial Review* (Cambridge, Cambridge University Press, 2018).

[97] ibid 5–7.

[98] Though one of the schemata, labelled 'contextual review', did not figure prominently in any jurisdiction, finding reflection only in public law scholarship: ibid ch 5.

or *ways of thinking* about how the norms in a particular area of law are identified and articulated.[99] So 'while each method can be seen in a number of jurisdictions at different times, some associations of varying strength are identified'.[100] This recognition contemplates doctrinal changes driven by movements within the ways of thinking internal to the judiciary in a particular jurisdiction (eg the replacement of a predominant schemata with another over time). Put differently, although Knight's analytical framework is 'more-or-less synchronic',[101] the 'doctrinal manifestations' of the schemata he identifies are acknowledged to be contestable and changeable.

Knight describes his study as 'meta-level' doctrinal analysis. That is a helpful descriptor as the focus is not directly on the content of the norms of administrative law but on how judges think about articulating those norms. This mode of analysis can also, however, be helpfully explained as an effort to understand how thinking about the identification and articulation of norms is *structured* according to different patterns of thought.

The ultimate purpose of Knight's study appears to be the identification of 'the strengths and weaknesses of the different schemata', an evaluation which he suggests can be facilitated by considering how well each fares according to Lon Fuller's well-known criteria of legality (generality, accessibility, prospectivity and so on).[102] Meta-level or structural doctrinal analysis need not, however, have evaluation as its primary or ultimate purpose. For one thing, without linking vying ways of thinking about norms to the institutional objectives of law makers in a particular jurisdiction, evaluative conclusions are free-floating.[103] Structural doctrinal analysis can, however, add explanatory value to the extent that it illuminates what is at stake in different approaches to norm legalisation (ie different structures of argument about the recognition and content of legal norms) evident in administrative law cases. More particularly, doctrinal analysis which reveals general ways of thinking about the specification and articulation of administrative law norms can provide insight into how those approaches to thinking about doctrine within a particular jurisdiction have been developed in response to institutional objectives and legitimacy narratives. This possibility is best illustrated with an example.

Based on an analysis of judicial review cases in the High Court of Australia, I have argued (with Will Bateman) that the way in which the legal limits of administrative powers are articulated has moved from a 'grounds' approach to a 'statutory' approach.[104] The 'grounds' (of review) way of thinking about administrative law norms was developed by the judges from the middle decades of the twentieth century and informed the

[99] Unger (n 43) 41 puts this point this way: '[n]o style of discourse, however powerful its influence, occupies the whole of a legal culture or penetrates all of a legal mind'.

[100] Knight (n 96) 2.

[101] P Cane, 'Book Review: *Vigilance and Restraint in the Common Law of Judicial Review*' (2019) 82 *Melbourne Law Review* 200, 202.

[102] Knight (n 96) 4, 249–57.

[103] For this reason the stated aim of Knight's comparative analysis is not to explain or justify the dominant schemata in each jurisdiction by reference to its own 'legal and political culture, history or infrastructure': ibid 20.

[104] See W Bateman and L McDonald, 'The Normative Structure of Australian Administrative Law' (2017) 45 *Federal Law Review* 153. See also, L McDonald, 'Jurisdictional Error as Conceptual Totem' (2019) 42 *University of New South Wales Law Journal* 1019.

categorised grounds listed in the Administrative Decisions (Judicial Review) Act 1977 (Cth) – a statutory scheme for judicial review in federal law. The statutory approach – which developed within the doctrinal trappings of 'jurisdictional error', the concept used to give content to a constitutionally entrenched provision of judicial review – has promoted an overall framing of the applicable norms by reference to statutory purpose. The core interpretive claim of this structural analysis is that, within this frame, there has developed a discernible emphasis on statutory purpose and particulars, and a corresponding reluctance to identify and articulate *ex ante* administrative law norms and requirements.[105]

In this Australian example, the mixed empirical and interpretive question of whether or not there has been a discernible shift in how judges conceive of and specify administrative law norms is not susceptible of a straightforward answer, involving as it does a deep dive into a complex body of law. Distinguishing between broad ways of thinking about how to manage the tension between generality and variability in administrative law norms should not, however, be expected to find reflection in clear-cut rules. Moreover, the contending structures of thought have points of overlap. For these reasons, the ascendency of a 'schemata' or 'way of thinking' is, as Knight insists, best understood as a matter of emphasis and degree. Nevertheless, this sort of analysis contributes explanatory insight to the extent that alternative ways of thinking about how administrative law norms are recognised and applied correspond with alternative institutional values. Thus, the ascendency of the statutory approach in Australia can be understood as a judicial response to the (real or perceived) legitimacy problem posed by the counter-majoritarian nature of judicial review, whereas the grounds approach can be understood as a response to calls for the legitimation of administrative government given (real or perceived) threats posed by arbitrary decision-making.

Again, drawing links between a schemata of review and an associated set of institutional and social values is likely to generate contention and debate.[106] The point of the Australian example, then, is merely to illustrate how analyses of this structural sort can explain 'doctrinal' disputes and developments by reference to broader institutional concerns. The purpose of doctrinal scholarship on this model is not to claim doctrinal force for a particular interpretation of the law (in an attempt to show that interpretation as a necessary outworking of systemic principles) but rather to show how different ways of thinking evident in the case law are calibrated by alternative sets of institutional and social values. Such analyses help explain what is at stake for the legitimacy of our institutional arrangements when the norms of administrative law are contested. Yet the analysis remains 'doctrinal' to the extent that it drills deeply into the cases to identify general ways of specifying the norms of administrative law. Such scholarship starts with the language and arguments used by judges before thinking about how these connect with broader questions about the legitimacy of administrative law and administrative power.

[105] Broadly speaking, this conclusion is consistent with the recent studies (considered in section III) of English and Welsh administrative law which suggest that the traditional grounds of review are less important than commonly imagined by the textbook writers.

[106] For an alternative, insightful interpretation of the Australian cases, see LB Crawford, 'Immaterial Errors, Jurisdictional Errors and the Presumptive Limits of Executive Power' (2020) 30 *Public Law Review* 281.

V. Conclusion

Cane's work in administrative law has always taken doctrine seriously, not merely by seeking accurately to chart its content but also through a commitment to explain its broader shape and development. In the conclusion to *Controlling Government Power*, Cane describes his purpose as 'straightforwardly explanatory', to 'explore and illuminate continuities and similarities [in the control of administrative power in three jurisdictions] on the one hand, and discontinuities and differences on the other' by understanding their development over time.[107] His historical and comparative approach is designed to aid understanding 'from both sides of the comparison' and his institutionalism to situate 'administrative law in the context of a larger system of institutions, norms and practices concerned with the allocation and control of public power'.[108]

How can doctrinal writing in the common law tradition contribute, if at all, to the *explanation* of administrative law? This chapter has explored some reasons why thinking about doctrine in administrative law is a fraught undertaking. Some of these reason relate to the difficulty of pinning the general idea of doctrine down and others relate to the difficulty of managing the tension between variability and generality in the particular context of administrative law. My argument has not been that the textbook tradition and more theoretically inclined coherentist writings have nothing to offer, but rather that they face limitations and problems that should lead us to doubt their power to explain the body of legal doctrine and doctrinal disputes in particular jurisdictions. Those questions may be better illuminated by scholarship which attempts to reveal structures of thought within judicial approaches to the specification and articulation of administrative norms and which asks how those approaches correspond to particular social values and institutional objectives. That mode of doctrinal analysis seems to me to run parallel to Cane's historical and comparative institutionalism. To this extent, structural approaches to reading administrative law cases have the potential to add a further layer of depth to explanations which give primary emphasis to broader structures of government in explaining the content of administrative law 'doctrine'.

[107] Cane (n 2) 510.
[108] ibid 520.

12

Administrative Tribunals: An Essay about the Legal Imagination of Administrative Law Scholars

ELIZABETH FISHER*

Now here is an experiment for administrative law scholars. Picture an administrative tribunal and its contributions to administrative law. Chances are it is not a very legal or very crisp picture. There are exceptions, but as a general rule, administrative tribunals do not loom large in the *legal* imagination of administrative law scholars.[1] It is not that they are completely out of the frame.[2] Rather, tribunals are sidelined. In being so, they tend to be characterised as pragmatic institutions delivering administrative justice rather than legal entities that are both constructed by, and contributing to, administrative law. The end result is an inaccurate picture of administrative law.[3] This is not just because administrative law scholars overlook the legal significance of tribunals. It also means they do not fully grasp the institutional nature of 'law' in administrative law either.[4]

This chapter is an exploration of how tribunals figure in the administrative law imagination that draws primarily on examples from the United Kingdom (UK) and Australia. First, I provide a brief overview of administrative tribunals. Second, I show how the heuristics legal scholars use often make the legal nature of tribunals invisible. Third, I explore more generally how tribunals do not figure significantly in the imagination of administrative law scholars. In the fourth section I show how this means that the legal significance of administrative tribunals as both legal objects constituted by law

* Thank you to Mark Aronson, Joanna Bell, Robert Carnwath, Leighton McDonald, Brian Preston, Ceri Warnock, and Nick Wikeley for thoughtful comments on an earlier draft. Any errors or omissions remain my own.

[1] P Cane, *Administrative Tribunals and Adjudication* (Oxford, Hart Publishing, 2009) 274.

[2] ibid and R Thomas, *Administrative Justice and Asylum Appeals: A Study of Tribunal Adjudication* (Oxford, Hart Publishing, 2011). Also note nearly all administrative law textbooks have chapters on tribunals, albeit usually at the back of the book.

[3] Cane (n 1).

[4] An argument made by HW Arthurs, *'Without the Law': Administrative Justice and Legal Pluralism in Nineteenth Century England* (Toronto, University of Toronto Press, 1985) 133.

and legal subjects contributing to law is overlooked. In the final section I consider the implications of my analysis for understanding administrative law.

There are three points to make before I start. First, this work is very much inspired by Peter Cane's work exploring both the architecture and substance of administrative law. That work spans more than 40 years.[5] A contribution of this chapter is to show how Cane's important work on administrative tribunals is part and parcel of his broader intellectual commitment to make sense of the actual structural realities of administrative law.[6]

Second, my focus is on administrative law scholarship. How scholars teach and write about administrative law has a significant influence on administrative law imagination and on what are understood to be the practices and possibilities of the subject.[7] The legal significance of administrative tribunals is well recognised by many in administrative law practice.[8] While there are exceptions, scholarship is a different matter. Here I focus on mainstream Commonwealth administrative law scholarship that takes a primarily 'internal' view of the law.[9]

I. Tribunals: A Primer

As Cane notes, '[a] common feature of contributions to the literature on "tribunals" is an initial, somewhat despairing observation that the term "tribunal" is used to refer to many different types of institutions, followed by a discussion that fails to realise the implicit promise of definitional sensitivity'.[10] The legal significance of this irony will be explored below. Here, however, let me provide a sketch of tribunals.

Generally speaking, the term 'administrative tribunal' refers to a body that engages in adjudication and/or dispute resolution in carrying out external review of a primary administrative decision.[11] The growth of administrative tribunals is also understood as part of the growth of an 'accountability' sector.[12] The work of tribunals is usually only triggered when a particular act of a public body is 'appealed' to a tribunal.[13]

[5] Examples of Peter's early administrative law work include P Cane, 'A Fresh Look at Punton's Case' (1980) 43 *MLR* 266; P Cane, 'Natural Justice and Legitimate Expectation' (1980) 54 *ALJ* 546; and P Cane, 'Standing, Legality and the Limits of Public Law' [1981] *PL* 322. A recent example of Cane's structural analysis can be found in P Cane, *Controlling Administrative Power: An Historical Comparison* (Cambridge, Cambridge University Press, 2016).

[6] P Cane, 'Public Law in *The Concept of Law*' (2013) 33 *OJLS* 649; and P Cane, 'Theory and Values in Public Law' in P Craig and R Rawlings (eds), *Law and Administration in Europe: Essays in Honour of Carol Harlow* (Oxford, Oxford University Press, 2003); and Peter Cane, 'Imagining Public Law' (2006) 31 *Aust J Legal Philosophy* 153.

[7] Forsyth as quoted in Dame S Elias, 'Administrative Law for "Living People"' (2009) 68 *CLJ* 47, 51. See also E Fisher and S Shapiro, *Administrative Competence: Reimagining Administrative Law* (Cambridge, Cambridge University Press, 2020).

[8] It is interesting to note in this regard L Neville Brown's critique of P Cane, *Introduction to Administrative Law* (Oxford, Clarendon Press, 1986) for its only having 11 pages on tribunals. See L Neville Brown, 'Review: Introduction to Administrative Law' (1987) 6 *CJQ* 288, 289.

[9] Noting that the line between internal and external approaches is a blurred one. See C McCrudden, 'Legal Research and the Social Sciences' (2006) 122 *LQR* 632.

[10] Cane (n 1) 2.

[11] For a detailed discussion of adjudication and review, see ibid ch 1.

[12] ibid ch 7.

[13] On the limits of this as an accountability mechanism, see ibid 185–86.

Most tribunals hear 'appeals' from individual decisions but, in some instances, tribunals have explicit policy making roles.[14] An important feature of tribunals is their triadic structure in which a 'neutral third party' adjudicates the case.[15] That neutral third party will normally have the power to assess a decision on its merits and to remake a decision. What exactly it can do varies from context to context.[16]

Tribunals are created by legislation and their power comes from legislation. Tribunals have a long history although the nature of that history varies.[17] Tribunals have been created both as ad hoc legal responses to particular accountability needs and/or as proactive acts of creating and rationalising accountability/dispute resolution structures. An example of the former was the creation of the Data Protection Tribunal in the UK to hear appeals from the Data Protection Registrar who administered the Data Protection Act 1984 (UK).[18] With the passing of the Freedom of Information Act 2000 and other legislative reforms, the Tribunal became the Information Tribunal. In 2010 it was integrated into the consolidated tribunal structure created by the Tribunals, Courts and Enforcement Act 2007 (TCEA 2007). The TCEA 2007 is an example of the latter type of more proactive tribunal reform.[19] It created a two-tier chambered structure for many of the administrative tribunals that already existed in the UK.[20] Its Upper Tribunal (UT) can also hear judicial review cases.[21] But the TCEA's rationalised structure has limits. As Lady Hale noted of the TCEA 2007: 'The new structure may look neat but the diversity of jurisdictions accommodated means that it is not as neat as it looks'.[22]

The creation of the Federal Administrative Appeals Tribunal in Australia in 1975 is a different example of proactive reform. A new tribunal structure was created as part of a larger set of administrative law reforms.[23] These processes of reactive and proactive reform do overlap and there have also been ongoing amalgamation initiatives.[24]

Administrative lawyers tend to be taught two facts about tribunals. First, that they do a lot of work, far more than superior courts.[25] As Elliott and Thomas put it, they are 'big business'.[26] For example, the First Tier Tribunal (FTT) and UT in the

[14] For example, the powers of the New Zealand Environmental Court under ss 85(3) and 293(8) of the Resource Management Act 1991 (NZ) in relation to plans.

[15] Cane (n 1) 10.

[16] E Fisher, 'Administrative Law, Pluralism and the Legal Construction of Merits Review in Australian Environmental Courts and Tribunals' in L Pearson et al (eds), *Administrative Law in a Changing State: Essays in Honour of Mark Aronson* (Oxford, Hart Publishing, 2008).

[17] C Stebbings, *Legal Foundations of Tribunals in Nineteenth Century England* (Cambridge, Cambridge University Press, 2006) and Arthurs (n 4).

[18] Data Protection Act 1984 (UK), ss 3, 13, and Sch 2.

[19] Stebbings (n 17) 5 noting how tribunals were not just created in reactive processes.

[20] For an overview of the developments behind it see R Carnwath, 'Tribunal Justice – a New Start' [2009] *PL* 48.

[21] TCEA 2007, ss 15–19.

[22] *Cart v The Upper Tribunal* [2011] UKSC 28, [2012] 1 AC 663 [23].

[23] R Creyke and J McMillan, 'Administrative Law Assumptions … Then and Now' in R Creyke and J McMillan (eds), *The Kerr Vision of Administrative Law at the 25 Year Mark* (Canberra, Centre for International and Public Law, 1998).

[24] Tribunals Amalgamation Act 2015 (Cth) and R Creyke, 'Australian Tribunals: Impact of Amalgamation' (2020) 26 *Australian Journal of Administrative Law* 206.

[25] C Harlow and R Rawlings, *Law and Administration*, 3rd edn (Cambridge, Cambridge University Press, 2009) 487 and T Endicott, *Administrative Law*, 4th edn (Oxford, Oxford University Press, 2018) 448.

[26] M Elliott and R Thomas, 'Tribunal Justice and Proportionate Dispute Resolution' (2012) 71 *CLJ* 297, 298.

UK hear around 400,000 cases a year[27] compared to 3400 judicial review applications filed in England and Wales in 2019.[28] The UT also receives considerably more judicial review applications than the Administrative Court – 5679 in 2019/20.[29] In Australia, between July 2019 and May 2020, over 50,000 cases were lodged with the Australian Federal Administrative Appeals Tribunal (AAT)[30] compared to 286 filings with the Australian Federal Court from July 2018 to June 2019 in relation to administrative law, constitutional law, and human rights law.[31]

Citing statistics from these centralised tribunal structures only gives a partial picture, however. While UK tribunal architecture is relatively amalgamated there still exist other tribunal and tribunal-like structures not integrated into the main structure. In 2017/18 the Traffic Penalty Tribunal considered 28,669 appeals from over 9 million penalty charge notices issued in England and Wales.[32] The Planning Inspectorate had over 96,000 appeals to it from planning-related decisions between April 2015 and March 2020.[33] In Australia, states also have their own administrative tribunals that are often integrated with civil dispute tribunals.[34] Nearly 85,850 cases were lodged with the Victorian Civil and Administrative Tribunal in 2018–19, with 18,407 of them in the Administrative, Planning and Environment, or Human Rights Divisions.[35] There also exist other specialist tribunal structures at both the state and Federal levels, such as those state courts and tribunals pertaining to environmental and planning law.[36] For example in 2018 the New South Wales Land and Environment Court (NSWLEC) had 1486 cases registered before it.[37]

The 'big business' nature of administrative tribunals underscores the need for accountability and dispute resolution in regard to public administration.[38] Administrative lawyers, both scholars and practitioners, understand tribunals to be a necessary, inevitable, and more efficacious method of meeting that need.[39] Take for example,

[27] Senior President of Tribunals, *Senior President of Tribunals' Annual Report 2019* (2019) 7. Statistics can be found at https://www.gov.uk/government/collections/tribunals-statistics, accessed 8 July 2021. Note that these include statistics from the employment tribunal which is not an administrative tribunal. Also note the lack of ease of comparison between comparing the statistics from different adjudicative bodies.

[28] Ministry of Justice, *Civil Justice Statistics Quarterly, England and Wales, January to March 2020 (provisional)* (June 2020) 12.

[29] Ministry of Justice, *Tribunal Statistics Quarterly*, https://www.gov.uk/government/collections/tribunals-statistics, accessed 8 July 2021.

[30] Administrative Appeals Tribunal, *AAT Caseload Report for the period 1 July 2019 to 31 May 2020* (2020), https://www.aat.gov.au/about-the-aat/corporate-information/statistics, accessed 8 July 2021.

[31] Federal Court of Australia, *Annual Report 2018–19* (2019) 142.

[32] Traffic Penalty Tribunal England and Wales, *Annual Statistics Report 2017/8* (2020) 4.

[33] Planning Inspectorate – Appeals Data – 01 April 2015 to 31 March 2020 (2020), https://www.gov.uk/government/statistics/planning-inspectorate-appeals-database, accessed 8 July 2021.

[34] Creyke (n 24).

[35] Victorian Civil and Administrative Tribunal, *Annual Report 2018–2019* (2019) 9.

[36] Fisher (n 16).

[37] The Land and Environment Court of New South Wales, *Annual Review 2018* (2019) 30.

[38] Cane (n 1) chs 6 and 7.

[39] An excellent overview of these considerations in the leadup to the passing of the TCEA can be found in M Adler, 'Tribunal Reform: Proportionate Dispute Resolution and the Pursuit of Administrative Justice' (2006) 69 *MLR* 958.

section 2A of the Administrative Appeals Tribunal Act 1975 (Cth) which governs the Australian AAT:

> In carrying out its functions, the Tribunal must pursue the objective of providing a mechanism of review that:
>
> (a) is accessible; and
> (b) is fair, just, economical, informal and quick; and
> (c) is proportionate to the importance and complexity of the matter; and
> (d) promotes public trust and confidence in the decision-making of the Tribunal.

The existence of tribunals also highlights the way in which 'superior' courts have rarely had an 'adjudicative monopoly' in regard to disputes concerning public administration.[40]

The second fact that administrative lawyers are taught about tribunals is that they are separation of powers 'misfits'. As Stebbings states, tribunals are a 'hybrid species of dispute resolution body hovering somewhat uncertainly between the judicature and the executive'.[41] She argues that, UK tribunals emerged in the nineteenth century as part of administrative regimes, but in the twentieth century became far more an adjunct of the courts.[42] But where any particular tribunal 'hovers' will depend on its specific legislative framework. It is also the case that some tribunal structures such as that of the FTT/UT and the NSWLEC combine tribunals with forms of superior court power.[43]

Administrative lawyers use different forms of shorthand to signify the misfitting nature of tribunals, the prefix 'quasi',[44] and the phrase 'administrative justice'[45] being two examples. While both these terms embrace the hybrid nature of administrative tribunals, they do not necessarily illuminate it. Emphasising the specialised nature of tribunals is another way of explaining why tribunals do not fit neatly into a separation of powers framework, as well as a justification for understanding them in more instrumental terms.[46]

As a practical matter, the misfitting nature of tribunals manifests itself in a number of ways. Tribunals can be thought of as 'court substitutes',[47] but tribunals in conducting review on the merits do not generally formally produce common law precedents. With that said, tribunal decisions do bind the parties, and in many cases are perceived to lay down standards for future action.[48] Tribunals are often said to 'stand in the shoes of the primary decision-maker' but are also carrying out a form of review.[49] Tribunals are valued because they are not courts, but are often assessed by how 'judicialised' they are.[50]

[40] H Arthurs, 'Rethinking Administrative Law: A Slightly Dicey Business.' (1979) 17 *Osgoode Hall LJ* 1, 11 and Arthurs (n 4). See also Warnock's discussion of Swanimotes from the 13th century: C Warnock, 'Reconceptualising Specialist Environment Courts and Tribunals' (2017) 37 *LS* 391, 405–406.

[41] Stebbings (n 17) 273.

[42] ibid 334.

[43] On the FTT/UT see ss 11–12 and ss 15–20 of the TCEA 2007. On the NSWLEC compare s 17 and 20 of the Land and Environment Court Act 1979 (NSW).

[44] HWR Wade, 'Quasi-Judicial' and its Background' (1949) 10 *CLJ* 216 and Cane (n 1) 140.

[45] Cane (n 1) 209–20.

[46] See Warnock (n 40) for a critique of this.

[47] As Cane notes, this is particularly in the UK. See Cane (n 1) 69.

[48] ibid 182–88 and GDS Taylor, 'The New Administrative Law' (1977) *ALJ* 804, 805.

[49] Noting this can mean many different things. See Fisher (n 16).

[50] M Groves, 'The Power of an Administrative Tribunal to Inform Itself' (2015) 22 *Australian Journal of Administrative Law* 235, 236–40.

Tribunals are normally described as adjudicative,[51] but they can engage in a variety of different forms of dispute resolution (as can courts).[52] Tribunals are not bound by the rules of evidence and procedure,[53] and are understood often to be more inquisitorial, but civil procedure and the rules of evidence provide important sources of inspiration.[54] There are different ways in which tribunals are related to superior courts[55] and different routes of appeal from administrative decisions.[56] Furthermore, there will exist different views over exactly what type of adjudicative process any particular tribunal is engaged in.[57]

II. Tribunals and Scholarly Heuristics

What is clear from the last section is that tribunals are not only separation of powers misfits, but also the significant variation between tribunal structures amplifies their misfitting nature. Trying to bring them into legal view suffers not only from the problem that they do not fit into conventional assumptions about law and administration, but also that tribunals give rise to the problems of 'definitional sensitivity' that Cane has flagged. Overall tribunals are hard for legal scholars to *legally* picture. As Edward Santow comments:

> Aside from a few pictures in the books of my childhood (presumably of dubious zoological reliability), I have never seen an elephant, and yet I am confident that I would recognise one immediately if I encountered it in the hulking, grey flesh. And yet, even for those of us who work in administrative law, there remain difficulties in determining whether a certain adjudicative body is a tribunal, a court or something else.[58]

Santow is not posing an abstract question. What an adjudicative body actually is, and what is its legal powers are, are often questions that have consequential legal significance.[59]

Consider the differences of opinion between the Administrative Court[60] and the Court of Appeal[61] about the legal nature of the UT in the *Cart* litigation. The TCEA 2007 declares the UT is 'to be a superior court of record'.[62] The question of legal nature was initially relevant to the question of whether the UT could be subject to a common

[51] Cane (n 1) 8.
[52] B Preston, 'The Use of Alternative Dispute Resolution in Administrative Disputes' (2011) 22 *Australasian Dispute Resolution Journal* 144, 148–54.
[53] eg the Tribunal Procedure (Upper Tribunal) Rules 2008 (UK), SI 2008/2698, r 15.
[54] Groves (n 50) and D Wallace, 'The Victorian Civil and Administrative Tribunal and the Rules of Evidence' (2018) 25 *Australian Journal of Administrative Law* 171.
[55] Some UK examples: an administrative tribunal with appeals on question of law to a superior court (Town and Country Planning Act 1990 (UK), s 288 for the Planning Inspectorate); a two-tier tribunal structure with appeals to the upper structure on 'any point of law' and then appeals on questions of law to a generalist Court of Appeal (TCEA 2007, ss 11 and 13); a specialist tribunal with a ouster clause (the now repealed Regulation of Investigatory Powers Act 2000 (UK), s 67(8) in relation to the Investigatory Powers Tribunal.
[56] See for example the range of appeal routers to the NSWLEC under Part 8 of the Environmental Planning Act 1979 (NSW).
[57] E Fisher, *Risk Regulation and Administrative Constitutionalism* (Oxford, Hart Publishing, 2007) 136–40.
[58] E Santow, 'Review: Administrative Tribunals and Adjudication' (2010) 21 *PLR* 44, 45.
[59] eg *RR v Secretary of State for Work and Pensions* [2019] UKSC 52, [2019] 1 WLR 6430 and *Burns v Corbett* [2018] HCA 15, [2018] 265 CLR 304.
[60] *R (on the application of Cart) v The Upper Tribunal* [2009] EWHC 3052 (Admin), [2010] 2 WLR 1012.
[61] *R (on the application of Cart) v The Upper Tribunal* [2010] EWCA Civ 859, [2011] QB 120.
[62] TCEA 2007, s 3(5).

law judicial review action for refusing permission to appeal to it from the FTT.[63] Laws LJ in the Divisional Court after lengthy historical analysis concluded that the UT was 'for relevant purposes, an *alter ego* of the High Court'.[64] This did not oust judicial review, although review would be limited to 'jurisdictional' and 'exceptional' legal errors.[65]

On appeal, the Court of Appeal concluded that 'that the UT is not an avatar of the High Court at all: far from standing in the High Court's shoes … the shoes the UT stands in are those of the tribunals it has replaced'.[66] But more importantly, the 'scope of judicial review available in relation to any amenable decision-making body is necessarily a matter of law'.[67] Review would be limited, in light of the tribunal structure under the TCEA 2007 which 'is designed to be so far as possible a self-sufficient structure, dealing internally with errors of law made at first instance and resorting to higher appellate authority only where a legal issue of difficulty or of principle requires it'.[68]

In the Supreme Court, given these rulings, the focus was on what the actual test should be for judicial review of the UT. Lady Hale (with whom the other Justices agreed), concluded that the second tier appeal test should be the standard, a standard rejected by the Court of Appeal as they took a different view on the structure of the tribunal.[69] In all cases, however, the legal nature of the UT was the focus of legal analysis – but in being so its legal nature was not a forgone conclusion. It required substantive legal inquiry.

Another example of the importance of such legal analysis can be seen in the New South Wales Court of Appeal decision of *Ku-ring-gai Council v Bunnings Properties Pty Ltd*.[70] The case concerned a NSWLEC Commissioner hearing a merits appeal against a refusal of consent to a development application. At the first hearing, the Commissioner concluded that the proposed development was not acceptable but allowed the developer to amend their design to address the deficiencies identified.[71] This has been a common practice in the NSWLEC since its creation. After giving leave to the developer to rely on the amended plans, there was a second hearing, after which consent was granted.[72] The Council appealed on a question of law against the consent on the basis that a Commissioner was acting 'judicially' and as that was the case 'reliance could be placed on the "principle of finality" and the prohibition on giving "advisory opinions", as grounds for challenging the impugned procedure'.[73] They also argued that the Commissioner had deployed an 'amber light approach', an approach they argued was impermissible.[74] As described in one case:

> This approach means that the Court not only considers the question of whether the proposal should be approved in the form that is before the Court but also [asks] whether the proposal

[63] Under the TCEA 2007, s 11(4). Note in the Divisional Court cases there was also a separate legal issue to do with the Special Immigration Appeals Commission.
[64] *Cart* (AC) (n 60) [94].
[65] ibid, [94], [99].
[66] *Cart* (CA) (n 61) [19].
[67] ibid [28].
[68] ibid [30].
[69] *Cart* (SC) (n 22) [52]–[56].
[70] *Ku-ring-gai Council v Bunnings Properties Pty Ltd* [2019] NSWCA 28 (2019) 236 LGERA 35.
[71] *Bunnings Properties Pty Ltd v Ku-ring-gai Council* [2016] NSWLEC 1658.
[72] *Bunnings Properties Pty Ltd v Ku-ring-gai Council (No 4)* [2017] NSWLEC 1238.
[73] *Ku-ring-gai Council v Bunnings Properties Pty Ltd* (n 70) [21].
[74] Note they made a similar argument before the Commissioner (n 72) [17] but he never described his approach this way. It was framed that way by the judge in the case that the NSWCA was hearing the appeal from *Ku-ring-gai Council v Bunnings Properties Pty Ltd (No 2)* [2018] NSWLEC 19 [60].

> is capable of approval, with specified modifications imposed by the Court, within the scope of the present proceedings.[75]

Submissions before the Court by the Council framed the issue in terms of whether the power exercised by the Commissioner was judicial or administrative.[76] All judges in the CA recognised that the question was one not about that distinction but about the construction of the relevant statutory regimes.[77] As such, consideration needed to be had to the powers of Commissioners, powers of Councils, as well as to the actual legal effect of a development application. The legal analysis in the case required engagement with a dense legal landscape of intersecting legal concepts.

Preston CJ of the NSWLEC (with whom Beazley P agreed) framed his legal analysis in terms of the legal powers of review the Commissioner had. For him, the important feature of review by a Commissioner was its 'external' nature.[78] While such review was closer to the judicial paradigm, what that signified was the need to act with 'judicial detachment and fairness'.[79] For Preston CJ, both the allowing of the amendment and the final determination were in 'furtherance' of the 'merits review jurisdiction which the Commissioner exercised on the appeal'.[80] That analysis placed the statutory regimes front and centre.

Preston CJ went on to note the limits of thinking in terms of the judicial paradigm. A determination of an appeal 'does not involve adjudication of a dispute about the existing rights and obligations of the parties to the appeal (the applicant for consent and the consent authority)'.[81] He also noted that the appeal procedure is a flexible one in which conciliation is allowed.[82] He concluded that the Commissioner in this case did not undertake an amber light approach.[83] But he did express concerns over that approach, particularly because it diverted focus away from what any particular statutory framework actually allowed.[84]

Basten JA dissented. For him, the Commissioner was effectively a passive receptor of an 'appeal' on a specific decision.[85] He distinguished the Court proceedings from the procedure before the Council.[86] For him, on a reading of the legislation, the power of amendment was 'not readily amenable to application in adversary proceedings before the Court'.[87] Thus, he concluded that the amber light approach 'is not consistent with maintenance of the independent and impartial authority of the Court'.[88] While Basten JA

[75] *The Benevolent Society v Waverley Council* [2010] NSWLEC 1082 [66] per Moore SC.
[76] *Ku-ring-gai Council v Bunnings Properties Pty Ltd* (n 70) [21].
[77] ibid [2] per Beazley P, [22], [71] per Basten JA, [140] Preston CJ.
[78] ibid [160].
[79] *Ku-ring-gai Council v Bunnings Properties Pty Ltd* (n 70) [160]–[161] quoting from P Cane, 'Merits Review and Judicial Review – The AAT as Trojan Horse' (2000) 28 *Federal Law Review* 213. See also [183].
[80] ibid [173].
[81] ibid [179].
[82] ibid [181].
[83] ibid [210].
[84] ibid [200]–[209].
[85] ibid [43].
[86] ibid [47]–[48].
[87] ibid [50].
[88] ibid [73].

recognised that the question was not whether a Commissioner was acting judicially, his analysis does effectively treat them as acting that way.[89]

Overall, as with *Cart*, what can be seen in this case is a court engaging in an institutional analysis of a tribunal. In that analysis the judicial/administrative dichotomy has limited utility, but it remains a powerful influence on legal thinking. It is a heuristic – an intellectual shortcut.[90] The problem is that it is not a very good one. Thus, as Spigelman CJ has noted in relation to the rule for costs in the NSWLEC:

> The longstanding debate amongst judges of the Land and Environment Court in this respect has proceeded on the basis of analogy. Are proceedings like merits review proceedings in an administrative tribunal or are they like adversarial litigation in a court? Such analogical reasoning, in my opinion, diverts attention from the power conferred by the statute and the rule. It is not the analogy that matters. The focus should be on the principles that underlie the practice in, respectively, administrative tribunals and courts.[91]

As the case law above shows, those principles are legal principles. The misfitting nature of tribunals is not just a misfit with a certain principle. It runs deeper than that – it a misfit with the assumptions used to navigate the administrative law landscape.

III. Tribunals and Legal Imagination

In the first couple of lines of this chapter I asked administrative law scholars to engage their imaginations. I was not merely being playful. Imagination is not just for children. It is how we make sense of the world. Take the case law examples in the last section. The judges were required to answer a legal question. How they answered depended upon how they imagined the administrative tribunals that the legal questions related to.

These acts of imagining were not about exercising untrammelled creativity. To talk of imagination is to highlight how within the discipline of law is a set of collective mental constructs that lawyers and legal scholars use in thinking about law and how it applies.[92] It is what is used to navigate a legal problem in applying the 'law' to the facts. It is what is used to determine the quality of legal reasoning. It is what is taught, and it is what scholars focus their writing on.[93] Legal imagination should start from legal, social, and physical facts and return to them.[94]

[89] ibid [45]–[47].

[90] A Tversky and D Kahneman, 'Judgment under Uncertainty: Heuristics and Biases' (1974) 185 *Science* 1174.

[91] *Port Stephens Council v Jeffrey Sansom* [2007] NSWCA 299, 156 LGERA 125 [47]. See also [67], [77].

[92] Consider for example Cane's discussion of Montesquieu's hold on the legal imagination in P Cane, 'Executive Primacy, Populism, and Public Law' (2019) 28 *Washington International LJ* 527, 578.

[93] As all disciplines are underpinned by imagination. See J Beckert, *Imagined Futures: Fictional Expectations and Capitalist Dynamics* (Cambridge, MA, Harvard University Press, 2016); A Levy and P Godfrey-Smith (eds), *The Scientific Imagination: Philosophical and Psychological Perspectives* (Oxford, Oxford University Press, 2020).

[94] E Fisher, 'Legal Imagination and Teaching International Environmental Law' in L Rajamani and J Peel (eds), *Oxford Handbook of International Environmental Law*, 2nd edn (Oxford, Oxford University Press, 2021).

Legal imagination is necessary because the abstract language of legal concepts needs to be applied to specific circumstances. That is part of a process of inquiry, individual or collective, in which any particular interpretation or understanding of a law needs to be tested to see how appropriate it is.[95] Legal imagination can involve an active process of thinking,[96] but it is also constraining.[97] It informs our understanding of what is relevant and irrelevant as we read and write about law. It is what disciplines us in the discipline of law.

As already noted, ideally the constraints that legal imagination provides should map onto legal realities.[98] As Harry Arthurs noted over four decades ago, 'language and ideas in administrative law should be given a concrete and specific form which responds to their actual social, political and economic context'.[99] Let me add to that list, and put at the top of it, legal context. What *Cart* and *Ku-ring-gai Council* highlight is that the 'concrete and specific form' of an adjudicative body requires in-depth and multi-faceted *legal* inquiry of complex legislative and institutional frameworks. That inquiry can also be open to honest legal disagreement.

Unearthing that legal analysis and those disagreements highlights that the problem of 'definitional sensitivity' is legally significant. It also highlights how heuristics such as the separation of powers can make that legal significance invisible. As Warnock has noted in regard to the legal work of environmental courts and assumptions about a 'pure separation of powers':

> there is too much blurring of the traditional delineations [involved in the work of environmental courts] that a pure approach to the separation of powers relies upon – between law, policy and fact, and between qualitatively different types of decision (the legal and the political) and forms of decision making.[100]

This blurring is the actual legal reality. As *Cart* and *Ku-ring-gai Council* also show, that blurring does not lead to the irrelevance of law, but rather to a different type of legal inquiry: an analysis that focuses on what type of adjudicative institution has been created by law.

Neither this fact nor the larger legal life of tribunals is given much attention by legal scholars, however. In the last section, I pointed out the two facts that administrative law scholars tend to know about tribunals – they do a lot of work and they are separation of powers misfits. Textbooks chart far more than that of course. They provide an overview of the tribunal system. The focus is on describing the legislative and institutional framework and to consider what the purposes of tribunals are.[101] But on the whole, tribunals

[95] M Del Mar, *Artefacts of Legal Inquiry: The Value of Imagination in Adjudication* (Oxford, Hart Publishing, 2020) ch 1. Note at the heart of Del Mar's thesis is the interaction between language and imagination, 437.

[96] A Kind, 'Imagining Under Constraints' in A Kind and P Kung (eds), *Knowledge Through Imagination* (Oxford, Oxford University Press, 2016) 147.

[97] S Stern, 'The Legal Imagination in Historical Perspective' in A Amaya and M Del Mar (eds), *Virtue, Emotion, and Imagination in Law and Legal Reasoning* (Oxford, Hart Publishing, 2020) 219.

[98] To see the importance that Cane places on grounded analysis in reality see Cane, 'Imagining Public Law' (n 6) 168 and Cane, 'Public Law in *The Concept of Law*' (n 6) 652.

[99] H Arthurs, 'Rethinking Administrative Law: A Slightly Dicey Business' (1979) 17 *Osgoode Hall Law Journal* 1, 3, 11.

[100] Warnock (n 40) 412.

[101] See as an example, T Endicott, *Administrative Law*, 4th edn (Oxford, Oxford University Press, 2018) ch 12.

are not seen as mainstream features of *doctrinal* administrative law. The chapters on tribunals generally come at the end of textbooks.[102] Any doctrinal issues raised, for example concerning the judicial review of tribunal decisions, tend be seen as isolated questions or as exceptions to general principles.[103]

These chapters, as well as much of the academic literature, often presume that tribunals should be largely understood through engaging in functional and/or socio-legal analysis.[104] The question is whether tribunals are 'effective adjudicators'.[105] The emphasis is on 'proportionate dispute resolution'.[106] Indeed, for many this is their merit and their 'judicalisation' is not something to welcome.[107] In terms of mainstream administrative law scholarship, tribunals are not the focus of sustained doctrinal discussion in the way that particular grounds of review are.[108] The general approach is that tribunals stand outside the norms of legal inquiry.

I am not the first to point out of the lack of doctrinal scholarly focus on tribunals (or legal scholarly focus of tribunals for that matter).[109] Such a statement about scholarly inattention needs to be made with care. There are always exceptions.[110] Assumptions about what scholarship focuses on can be a self-fulfilling prophecy.[111] They can also be out of date,[112] and they can be misleading. Doctrinal lawyers might think of tribunals in functionalist terms, but the 'misfitting' nature of tribunals means that those who take a more 'green light' or 'functionalist' approach to administrative law often view tribunals as 'judicial' in nature.[113] But let me provide two brief examples of how the sidelining of tribunals in the administrative law imagination manifests itself.

[102] eg ibid ch 12 out of 15; HWR Wade and C Forsyth, *Administrative Law*, 11th edn (Oxford, Oxford University Press, 2014) ch 23 out of 24; M Elliott and J Varuhas, *Administrative Law: Text and Materials*, 5th edn (Oxford, Oxford University Press, 2016) ch 18 out of 19; ch 7 out of 10. An exception is P Craig, *Administrative Law*, 8th edn (London, Sweet and Maxwell, 2016) ch 9 out of 30.

[103] eg Elliott and Varuhas (n 102) 748–52, discussing *Cart*.

[104] An exception is P Cane et al, *Principles of Administrative Law*, 3rd edn (Melbourne, Oxford University Press, 2018) 278–92.

[105] R Creyke, 'Tribunals and Merits Review' in M Groves (ed), *Modern Administrative Law in Australia: Concepts and Context* (Melbourne, Cambridge University Press, 2014) 414.

[106] Elliott and Varuhas (n 102) 751.

[107] JA Farmer, *Tribunals and Government* (London, Weidenfeld and Nicolson, 1974) 4 and D Mullan, 'Tribunals Imitating Courts – Foolish Flattery or Sound Policy' (2005) 28 *Dalhousie Law Journal* 1.

[108] Take for example the edited collection from the three high profile and broad thinking Public Law conferences which touch on tribunals but do not linger on them: J Bell et al (eds), *Public Law Adjudication in Common Law Systems: Process and Substance* (Oxford, Hart Publishing, 2016); M Elliott et al (eds), *The Unity of Public Law? Doctrinal, Theoretical and Comparative Perspectives* (Oxford, Hart Publishing, 2018); J Varuhas and S Wilson Stark (eds), *The Frontiers of Public Law* (Oxford, Hart Publishing, 2020).

[109] G Richardson and H Genn, 'Tribunals in Transition: Resolution or Adjudication?' [2007] *PL* 116, 118; Cane (n 1) 274; and Arthurs (n 4).

[110] See the references in n 109 and Thomas (n 2).

[111] J Mashaw, *Greed, Chaos, and Governance: Using Public Choice to Improve Public Law* (New Haven, Yale University Press, 1999) 1.

[112] For some recent doctrinal engagements see S Daly, 'Public Law in the Tax Tribunals and the Case for Reform' [2018] *British Tax Rev* 94; E Laurie, 'Assessing the Upper Tribunal's Potential to Deliver Administrative Justice' [2012] *PL* 288; R Creyke, 'Judicial Review and Merits Review: Are the Boundaries Being Eroded?' (2017) 45 *Federal Law Review* 628; and M Groves and G Weeks, 'Editorial: Tribunals – Their Continued Evolution and Reform' (2020) 26 *Australian Journal of Administrative Law* 189.

[113] This is particularly so in the UK: M Loughlin, *Public Law and Political Theory* (Oxford, Oxford University Press, 1992) 179 and see the discussion on tribunals in the 1st edition of C Harlow and R Rawlings, *Law and Administration* (London, Weidenfeld and Nicolson, 1984) ch 3.

The first is some of the scholarly response to Cane's work on tribunals. In 2000 Cane published an article that examined 'the relationship between so-called "merits review" of administrative decision-making, and "judicial review" of administrative action'.[114] His 'provocative', even 'heretical',[115] argument was that the distinction between merits review as exercised by the Federal AAT and judicial review as exercised by the Federal courts was not 'as stark as they are often portrayed'.[116] That argument was unorthodox in the Australian Federal setting because the Australian Constitution provides a very distinct definition of 'judicial power'. Furthermore, 'a dense thicket of case law about the meaning of the term "judicial power" encases the federal Parliament in a straight-jacket that significantly limits its room for manoeuvre in creating adjudicatory institutions'.[117]

In his later work Cane reiterated his thesis, but his attention was far more on the legal and normative interrelationship between judicial review and merits review.[118] As he noted in one article:

> Judicial review should be understood not only in terms of the relationship between the judicial branch of government on the one hand and the legislative and executive branches on the other, but also in terms of the relationship between the various components of what we might call the 'adjudicatory' branch – that is to say, courts and tribunals.[119]

His 2009 book on the topic was a comparative analysis of that relationship as part of a wider exploration of the form, function, and purpose of tribunals. He described it as 'a constitutionally-based theoretical account of the nature and role of tribunals' so as to counteract a lack of focus on their 'position in the constitutional structure or the juridical nature of their functions'.[120]

Whatever one may think of Cane's argument, what is striking is how scholarly responses to it underscore how tribunals are sidelined in legal argument. Thus, Australian administrative lawyers and scholars, in disagreeing with it, asserted the importance and actuality of the merits/judicial review distinction (including on politically pragmatic grounds)[121] while also recognising the problematic nature of the distinction and the legal complexity of both forms of review.[122]

Other scholars found Cane's doctrinal focus problematic. Adler argued that Cane should have taken a more 'law-in-context' approach[123] and Thomas noted that Cane made 'surprisingly little use of the large body of sociolegal research'.[124] The overall impression was that administrative law scholars found it perplexing to try and fit the

[114] Cane (n 79) 213.
[115] Cane (n 1) 179.
[116] Cane (n 79) 213.
[117] Cane (n 1) 286.
[118] ibid 179–88. See also Cane et al (n 104) 278–92.
[119] P Cane, 'Judicial Review in the Age of Tribunals' [2009] *PL* 479, 480.
[120] Cane (n 1) 274.
[121] A Mason, 'Administrative Law Reform: The Vision and the Reality' (2001) 8 *Australian Journal of Administrative Law* 135, 139 and A Mason, 'Judicial Review: Constitutional and Other Perspectives' (2000) *Federal Law Review* 333.
[122] Creyke (n 112) and M Allars, 'The Nature of Merits Review: A Bold Vision Realised in the Administrative Appeals Tribunal' (2013) 41 *Federal Law Review* 627.
[123] M Adler, 'Review: *Administrative Tribunals and Adjudication* by Peter Cane' (2010) 37 *JLS* 526, 527.
[124] R Thomas, 'Review: *Administrative Tribunals and Adjudication*' (2011) 70 *CLJ* 274, 275.

book into the pre-existing intellectual landscape. The misfitting nature of tribunals also pertains to modes of intellectual thought.

Another example of how tribunals do not easily register in the legal imagination can be seen in relation to the academic response to *Cart*.[125] Elliott and Thomas, two very thoughtful administrative law scholars, have argued that 'the Supreme Court's reasoning was primarily influenced not by doctrinal considerations, but by concerns of proportionate dispute resolution'.[126] Indeed, Boughey and Crawford criticise the case on this basis, arguing that the Court is using the wrong criteria for 'filtering' cases. They state:

> the distinction between jurisdictional and non-jurisdictional errors of law is a method for recognising the power of a supreme parliament to confer limited authority on administrative bodies, and to define the scope of that authority. We argue that therefore, the distinction cannot be replaced by a different filtering tool, which does not retain this core function, without answering far more difficult questions about the constitutional relationship between the judiciary and the parliament: questions which *Cart* did not profess to answer.[127]

In other words, they do not recognise that the legal reasoning of the Supreme Court was particularly 'legal'. But as Bell notes, and as seen in the last section:

> The court in this case did not reason by reaching beyond the legal sources to draw on ideas from some extra-legal dimension on no other basis than that the judges thought them to be normatively desirable. The considerations on which the courts drew were, rather, carefully extracted from the legal materials that were at play in the litigation, including, importantly, the legislative framework in the background.[128]

At all levels this material included precedent, legislation, and legal history.

IV. Tribunals as Legal Objects and Legal Subjects

The legal question in *Cart*, raising as it did the scope of judicial review in relation to a new legal regime, was novel. But the type of legal analysis the judges engaged in was not. Courts, in assessing other legal questions that arise in the course of judicial review or judicial supervision of tribunals, are having to carry out a similar type of analysis. This is because tribunals are legal objects. They may conduct merits review, they may be separation of powers misfits, they may be seen as dispensing administrative justice, but they are also legal entities. And complex ones at that.

What types of tribunals exists in any jurisdiction, and what powers they have will be shaped by legal culture.[129] As seen above, at the Australian Federal level, the nature and structure of the Administrative Appeals Tribunal is directly shaped by understandings

[125] See J Bell, 'Rethinking the Story of Cart v Upper Tribunal and Its Implications for Administrative Law' (2019) 39 *OJLS* 74 for an excellent in-depth survey of these responses.

[126] Elliott and Thomas (n 26) 314. Although note the interesting legal question posed in Elliott and Varuhas (n 102) 753.

[127] J Boughey and L Burton Crawford, 'Reconsidering *R(on the application of Cart) v Upper Tribunal* and the Rationale for Jurisdictional Error' [2017] *PL* 592, 593.

[128] Bell (n 125) 84.

[129] Cane (n 1).

of the separation of powers as set out in the Australian Constitution. As Cane puts it, 'the meaning of the statement, that a tribunal is not a court' means something more significant in Australia than in the UK.[130] In the UK context, Thomas has no problem describing tribunals as 'independent judicial bodies' because there is no strict separation of powers in operation.[131] Likewise, the Senior President of Tribunals in UK described the relationship between courts and tribunals as 'one judiciary, one system and better outcomes'.[132]

Legal culture is also relevant to how the powers of tribunals are legally defined. Merits review as a legal concept can come into legal vision far more at the Australian Federal level because of the constitutional importance of distinguishing it from judicial review. In contrast, the review powers of the FTTs and UT attract less attention because there is not the same legal significance in making that distinction. In this regard, it is important to remember just how 'thick' legal culture is.[133]

Furthermore, tribunals are directly constituted and limited through legislation and forms of delegated legislation that govern their jurisdiction, who can staff them, and what types of questions they can consider. Legislation can be silent, vague, or quite specific in setting out the architecture of tribunals.[134] But the role of legislation does not end there. Consideration is also required of the legislation under which the primary decision-maker is making a decision. As Kirby J stated in *Shi v Migration Agents Registration Authority*, in deliberating on whether in carrying out merits review the AAT could consider evidence that emerged after the primary decision was made:

> It is undesirable to attempt universal or unqualified propositions. Here, the issue is how to define the jurisdiction and powers of the Tribunal in conducting a review of a decision of the Authority, having regard both to the general provisions of the AAT Act, affording the power of review, and to the more specific provisions of the Migration Act, defining the characteristics of the decision that is subject to review. Only when all of the relevant features of the two inter-related statutes are understood can a correct decision be arrived at as to the ambit of the review in question and the manner in which it should be conducted.[135]

This need to consider interlocking legislation can also be seen in *Ku-ring-gai Council*.[136]

These cases also highlight that judicial review doctrine will also shape tribunals as legal constructs.[137] In determining the scope of judicial review of any particular tribunal, assumptions will need to be made about the nature of such tribunals. *Cart* is another

[130] ibid 4.

[131] R Thomas, 'Administrative Justice and Tribunals in the United Kingdom: Developments; Procedures; and Reform' (2020) 26 *Australian Journal of Administrative Law* 255, 256. What makes them distinct is their limited jurisdiction.

[132] Senior President of Tribunals (n 27) 4.

[133] E Fisher, 'Through "Thick" and "Thin": Comparison in Administrative Law and Regulatory Studies Scholarship' in P Cane et al (eds), *The Oxford Handbook of Comparative Administrative Law* (Oxford, Oxford University Press, 2020).

[134] Fisher (n 16) and S Li, 'Merits Review of Regulatory Determinations in the Economic Regulation of Energy Utility Infrastructure' (2016) 83 *AIAL Forum* 56.

[135] *Shi v Migration Agents Registration Authority* [2008] HCA 31, (2008) 235 CLR 286 [25]. See also [92]–[93] per Hayne and Heydon JJ. See also *Frugtniet v Australian Securities and Investments Commission* [2019] HCA 16, (2019) 266 CLR 250 [14]–[15], [51].

[136] *Ku-ring-gai Council v Bunnings Properties Pty Ltd* (n 70).

[137] This is made particularly clear in Allars (n 122) and Creyke (n 112).

illustration of this. Or take, for example, Justice Kirby's often-quoted statement about how a court should review a Commissioner's decision of the NSWLEC:

> Here, the parliament has specifically envisaged a tribunal which included lay assessors [Commissioners]. It would be quite wrong, in my opinion, for this Court to examine their decisions as if they were written by a lawyer. I am not, by these comments, suggesting double standards; simply that the Court should take into proper account the composition of the tribunal, as it has been created by the parliament.[138]

The grounds of review are thus shaped by understandings of the nature of a tribunal.[139] So much so, that what is deemed an error of law depends on an assessment on a tribunal's legal nature.[140] Case law concerning how tribunals must consider policy is another example of how review by a superior court legally constructs an understanding of a tribunal,[141] for example, the Federal Court of Australia's case law concerning the 'open intellectual process' the AAT should engage in to be satisfied by a certain state of affairs.[142] Key to understanding that process is understanding the legal and institutional nature of the AAT itself.[143] Superior courts will also construct understandings of a tribunal in the process of interpreting legislation that governs a primary decision-maker.[144]

As already seen with *Cart* and *Ku-ring-gai Council*, there can be honest disagreement about a tribunal's nature. *R (on the application of Privacy International) v Investigatory Powers Tribunal*[145] involved the interpretation of an ouster clause that operated in relation to the Investigatory Powers Tribunal (IPT), which is staffed by judges who review decisions made by government, particularly the security services. The question of interpretation required engagement with the statutory text, precedent, and the nature of the IPT itself.[146] Differences of opinion between the justices over the exact legal meaning of the ouster clause can be partly explained by how they understood the IPT. Lord Carnwath (with whom Lady Hale and Lord Kerr agreed), in concluding that the clause 'applie[d] only to a legally valid decision relating to jurisdiction',[147] noted arguments that the IPT did not just consider national security issues,[148] and that decisions of the IPT 'also ha[d] possible implications for legal rights and remedies going beyond the

[138] *Brimbella Pty Ltd v Mosman Municipal Council* (1985) 79 LGERA 367, 368.

[139] For another example of this see the case law discussed in N Lieven and A Byass, 'Challenges to Decisions of the Upper Tribunal' (2012) 17 *Judicial Review* 297.

[140] See also *Jones v First Tier Tribunal* [2013] UKSC 19, [2013] 2 AC 48 [35]–[36] and *Gillies v Secretary of State for Work and Pensions* [2006] UKHL 2, [2006] 1 WLR 781 [40]–[45].

[141] *Drake v Minister for Immigration and Ethnic Affairs* (1979) 24 ALR 577.

[142] *SZSLA v Minister for Immigration, Citizenship, Migrant Services and Multicultural Affairs* [2020] FCA 944, [37]–[44].

[143] ibid [39]; *SZQPY v Minister for Immigration and Border Protection* [2018] FCA 359 [24] and [27].

[144] eg the New Zealand's Supreme Court interpretation of s 5 of the Resource Management Act 1991 (NZ) in *Environmental Defence Society Inc v New Zealand King Salmon Co* [2014] NZSC 38, [2014] 1 NZLR 593. See the discussion in C Warnock, 'Reconceptualising the Role of the New Zealand Environment Court' (2014) 26 *JEL* 507.

[145] *R (on the application of Privacy International) v Investigatory Powers Tribunal* [2019] UKSC 22, [2020] AC 491.

[146] M Elliott and AL Young, '*Privacy International* in the Supreme Court: Jurisdiction, the Rule of Law and Parliamentary Sovereignty' (2019) 78 *CLJ* 490, 493. Although note that, while they flagged this, it did not feature in the title of their case note.

[147] *R (on the application of Privacy International) v Investigatory Powers Tribunal* (n 145) [109].

[148] ibid [25].

scope of the IPT's remit'.[149] In this regard, he raised concerns about 'local law'.[150] Lord Lloyd-Jones, agreeing with Lord Carnwath on the interpretative issue,[151] noted the institutional arguments, but saw the resolution of the interpretative question as turning on the need for clearer wording. He stated:

> Similarly, the IPT's rules and procedures create a 'bespoke' system particularly well suited to the adjudication of controversial issues in the context of national security and directed to protecting the public interest. Furthermore, there can be no doubt as to the outstanding judicial quality of the members of the IPT. However, the exclusion of the review jurisdiction of the High Court in cases of error of law, if achievable at all, would require a provision of much greater clarity making abundantly clear that that was what it sought to achieve.[152]

Lord Wilson, in dissent, stressed how much the IPT was like a court.[153] Lord Sumption (with whom Lord Reed agreed), also dissenting, concluded that as well,[154] and also placed emphasised that tribunal procedure reflected 'the importance of ensuring the confidentiality of secret material'.[155]

Tribunals are thus part of a tailored and complex legal architecture. That architecture also evolves both in regard to the legislation governing tribunals and legislation governing a primary decision-maker.[156] *Cart* is an example of the former, and there are many examples of the latter. As Preston CJ has noted in the NSW planning context:

> A development consent granted under the EPA [Environmental Planning and Assessment] Act is to be construed having regard to the statutory provisions governing its grant. Care needs to be taken not to substitute for the primacy of the statutory provisions governing the grant of a development consent, "principles" built up from judicial decisions on the construction of consents under former planning legislation (the Local Government Act 1919) and applied to current planning legislation (the EPA Act).[157]

These two forms of legislative evolution also interact with each other.

But tribunals are not just passive actors in administrative law. There are not just objects to be governed. They are also active subjects in the process of making and evolving administrative law and the law in their specific area of operation. Given the heuristics used by administrative law scholars, this is a lot harder for them to see. But the active role of tribunals can be seen in a range of different ways.

Most obviously, they produce their own forms of expository justice in regard to the substantive areas they are adjudicating in. The creation of the UT is a case in point. Cane has described this as the 'normative function' of merits review.[158] As Bygrave and McCallum note:

> The relatively few public decisions made by the NDIS [National Disability Insurance Scheme] Division of the AAT to date has critical relevance for persons with disability and

[149] ibid [139].
[150] ibid [112], [139].
[151] ibid [147].
[152] ibid [167].
[153] ibid [247]–[250].
[154] ibid [197].
[155] ibid [196].
[156] Groves and Weeks (n 112) 190.
[157] *Hunter Industrial Rental Equipment Pty Ltd v Dungog Shire Council* [2019] NSWCA 147, (2019) 101 NSWLR 1 [268].
[158] Cane (n 1).

> people working in the disability sector who look to published AAT decisions as examples of interpreting the statute, good practice, and whether the NDIS is achieving its objectives.[159]

The specialisation of tribunals is thus not only subject matter specialisation but also legal specialisation – with a dynamic interrelationship between the two.[160]

For example, the NSWLEC has explicitly developed a body of influential reasoning in relation to planning principles. As the Court's website explains:

> A planning principle is a statement of a desirable outcome from a chain of reasoning aimed at reaching, or a list of appropriate matters to be considered in making, a planning decision.
>
> While planning principles are stated in general terms, they may be applied to particular cases to promote consistency. Planning principles are not legally binding and they do not prevail over councils' plans and policies.[161]

Alongside this, the Court's merit review decisions have been legally influential in regard to environmental principles,[162] and the assessment of large scale natural resource projects.[163]

The influence of tribunal decision-making can also be internal to a tribunal structure. For example, a logic behind creating the UT was that it provided an 'unprecedented opportunity to work towards a more coherent and distinctive system of tribunal justice, drawing together the strands of the principles developed for the various jurisdictions'.[164] Specific regimes that produce such norms have also been created, for example the process by which the Immigration and Asylum Chamber of the UT issue Country Guidance determinations.[165] In many areas of legal and regulatory practice tribunals stabilise thinking.[166]

Thus, tribunals, Groves and Weeks argue, 'influence and respond to the world in which they operate, including the legislation that fashions and refashions them'.[167] They evolve institutionally to meet their adjudicatory needs, for example in terms of dispute resolution processes or case load management.[168] They have also developed their

[159] LP Bygrave and R McCallum, 'The National Disability Insurance Scheme and Administrative Decision-Making: Unique Challenges and Opportunities' (2020) 26 *Australian Journal of Administrative Law* 191, 198.

[160] C Warnock, 'Environment and the Law: The Normative Force of Context and Constitutional Challenge' (2020) 32 *JEL* 365.

[161] Available at https://lec.nsw.gov.au/lec/practice-and-procedure/principles/planning-principals.html accessed 12 July 2021.

[162] B Preston, 'The Australian Experience on Environmental Law' (2018) 35 *EPLJ* 637, 655–56 and E Scotford, *Environmental Principles and the Evolution of Environmental Law* (Oxford, Hart Publishing, 2017) ch 5.

[163] *Bulga Milbrodale Progress Association Inc v Minister for Planning and Infrastructure and Warkworth Mining Ltd* [2013] NSWLEC 48, 194 LGERA 347 and *Gloucester Resources Ltd v Minister for Planning* [2019] NSWLEC, (2019) 234 LGERA 257

[164] Carnwath (n 20) 56. See also Laurie (n 112).

[165] F Vogelaar, 'A Legal Analysis of a Crucial Element in Country Guidance Determinations: Country of Origin Information' (2019) 31 *International Journal of Refugee Law* 492. See https://www.judiciary.uk/about-the-judiciary/who-are-the-judiciary/judicial-roles/tribunals/tribunal-decisions/immigration-asylum-chamber/, accessed 8 July 2021.

[166] E Fisher, 'Law and Energy Transitions: Wind Turbines and Planning Law in the UK' (2018) 38 *OJLS* 528, 552–55 and N Pain and G Pick, 'The Murray-Darling Basin in Court: Administering Water Policy in the Eastern States of Australia – Administrative and Other Challenges' (2019) 37 *EPLJ* 301, 306–12.

[167] Groves and Weeks (n 112) 190.

[168] B Preston, 'Operating An Environment Court: The Experience of the Land and Environment Court of New South Wales' (2008) 25 *EPLJ* 385 and Warnock (n 160).

own ways of assessing the arguments before them[169] and novel legal practices such as concurrent evidence procedures.[170]

More significantly, tribunals interact with the case law that governs them.[171] Take, for example, *Ku-ring-gai Council* above. While only decided in early 2019, it is already influencing how NSWLEC Commissioners see their role.[172] In some cases it is reinforcing certain practices of amendment.[173] In others, Commissioners distance themselves from the amber light approach and thus articulate with greater precision the legal basis for their action.[174] In other cases, it is authority for a general understanding of merits review.[175] In being so, it is relevant to other legal questions.[176] Thus, for example, in *Benmill Pty Ltd v North Sydney Council (No 2)*[177] on the basis of Preston CJ's description of Class 1 merits review, the judge concluded that merits review could not give rise to issue estoppel.[178]

This process of interaction is not just about one fixed institutional body influencing a fixed idea of law. It is far more fluid than that. Some of this is to do with the issue of 'definitional sensitivity' flagged in section I. How a tribunal and merits review are constructed in any legal culture will shape what type of norms they produce. Thus, I have shown how interpretations of the precautionary principle, an environmental principle, are directly linked to assumptions that operate in relation to an environmental court's understanding of merits review.[179] But it also runs deeper than that. I have also shown how the state-sponsored legal pluralism of planning adjudication interacts with the legal formalism of judicial review to produce tensions in the development of the jurisdictional fact doctrine.[180]

V. Reimagining Administrative Law

The two pieces of work cited at the end of the last section would not have been possible without Cane's work.[181] Nor would this chapter. All pieces start with the insights from

[169] P Ky, 'Qualifications, Weight of Opinion, Peer Review and Methodology: A Framework for Understanding the Evaluation of Science in Merits Review' (2012) 24 *JEL* 207.

[170] G Edmond, 'Secrets of the "Hot Tub": Expert Witnesses, Concurrent Evidence and Judge-led law Reform in Australia' (2008) 27 *CJQ* 51, noting developments in a range of Australian administrative tribunals.

[171] A very obvious example is *Re Drake and Minister for Immigration and Ethnic Affairs (No 2)* (1979) 2 ALD 634.

[172] Note, there has been further judicial consideration of the amber light approach and how it cannot give rise to a legitimate expectation or arguments about procedural fairness. See *RebelMH Neutral Bay Pty Ltd v North Sydney Council* [2019] NSWCA 130 [107]–[111] and *Saffioti v Kiama Municipal Council* [2019] NSWLEC 57 [25].

[173] *The Next Generation Pty Ltd v Independent Planning Commission* [2020] NSWLEC 13 [17]; *Eastern Suburbs Leagues Club Ltd v Waverley Council* [2019] NSWLEC 130 [150].

[174] *Haiek v City of Parramatta Council* [2020] NSWLEC 1061 [79]–[80] eschewing the amber light approach but allowing a specific condition.

[175] *Charara v Ku-ring-gai Council* [2019] NSWLEC 183 [38].

[176] *Blacktown City Council v Satmell Holdings Pty Ltd* [2019] NSWLEC 93, [32]–[37].

[177] [2020] NSWLEC 44.

[178] ibid [65].

[179] Fisher (n 57) ch 4.

[180] E Fisher, '"Jurisdictional" Facts and "Hot" Facts: Legal Formalism, Legal Pluralism, and the Nature of Australian Administrative Law' (2015) 38 *Melbourne University Law Review* 968.

[181] I am not the only one inspired by his work. See Warnock (n 40).

his work on tribunals and Australian administrative law.[182] That work opens up legal and scholarly imagination. It provides a set of analytical constructs with which to explore and examine legal realities about tribunals and to move beyond heuristics. While recognising the misfitting nature of tribunals, he does not eschew law, or even the separation of powers for that matter.[183] Rather, he is encouraging scholars to see a legal reality.

That is not just significant for thinking about tribunals. As Arthurs has argued, 'By viewing law as a more complex and highly differentiated phenomenon than we have tended to do, it may be possible to identify its existence, and promote its presence, in places and by procedures which differ from those of conventional legal analysis and prescription'.[184] Or to put the matter slightly differently, it may be that a legal study of the legal nature and legal work of tribunals underscores the need for legal scholars to reimagine the *law* in administrative law. Or to be more precise, reimagine how they think about such law.

As Cane notes about public law theory, 'to my mind, legal theory can afford neither to have its head in the conceptual clouds nor its feet stuck in the mud of everyday legal life'.[185] Elsewhere he has emphasised the importance of a 'non essentialist' approach to theorising about law which maps 'pervasive, common (even if not commonly known or appreciated) features of actual legal systems that are plausibly considered to be significant'.[186] While these are comments more about jurisprudence than administrative law, they are directly relevant to the legal significance of tribunals. Tribunals may be an underappreciated feature of administrative law, but they are pervasive, common, and significant. As complex legal objects and subjects, they should attract scholarly attention, and in turn catalyse scholarly reflection.

In particular, tribunals highlight the institutional nature of administrative law – something that is often overlooked in conventional legal analysis.[187] As Cane has noted in discussing the focus on rules in Hart's *The Concept of Law*:

> …. a significant proportion of legislative provisions in modern states do not lay down rules in the sense of general standards of conduct but rather create particular legal institutions, allocate specific resources to them, confer on them specific powers and duties, and give them more or less situation-specific instructions about the way such powers and duties are to be exercised.[188]

That is a good description of administrative law – a body of law concerned with constituting, limiting and holding public institutions to account.[189] Much of the doctrinal analysis discussed above is about both the institutional powers and structures of a particular tribunal as well as those of the decision-makers they are reviewing. What a study of tribunals highlights is that the institutional dimension of administrative law

[182] See also P Cane, 'The Making of Australian Administrative Law' in P Cane (ed), *Centenary Essays for the High Court of Australia* (Chatswood, NSW, LexisNexis Butterworths 2004).
[183] Cane (n 1) 14–15.
[184] Arthurs (n 40) 43.
[185] Cane, 'Imagining Public Law' (n 6) 169.
[186] Cane, 'Public Law in *The Concept of Law*' (n 6) 651–52.
[187] Fisher and Shapiro (n 7).
[188] Cane, 'Public Law in *The Concept of Law*' (n 6) 659.
[189] Fisher and Shapiro (n 7).

is not just about empowering and limiting public administration, but also about the legal nature of the adjudicative bodies that hold public administration to account.

Furthermore, these adjudicative institutions are not just instrumental legal objects that deliver 'cheap and cheerful'[190] administrative justice. They are active legal subjects interacting with courts, public administration, and judicial review doctrine. As adjudicative sites of dispute resolution and accountability they are also stabilising forces that can address and manage both the dynamism and particularity of administrative law. They are also producing legal norms. Tribunals illustrate the importance of dispute resolution in relation to what Cane describes as 'individuated directives' (as opposed to standards),[191] and also how the resolution of disputes needs to be coordinated, both between each dispute and with primary decision-making structures. Indeed, tribunals show how regimes addressing collective action problems also need to encompass dispute resolution.[192]

Asking administrative law scholars to see what has been sidelined in administrative law thinking is a big intellectual ask. That is because it is not just an exercise in shifting scholarly attention: it is an exercise in recalibrating the mental constructs that frame and guide the subject. Let me flag three particular examples of this.

The first is the separation of powers – a legal concept that has haunted this chapter, just as it haunts administrative law thinking. As they are separation of powers 'misfits', recognising the legal significance of tribunals would appear to be in opposition of that doctrine, or at least a 'pure' version of it.[193] But, really, what such recognition requires is to look behind the concept when it is used as a heuristic to the values it expresses.[194] As Warnock notes:

> the aim of the separation of powers is to prevent the abuse of governmental power and despotism. As Rubin says, a conceptual metaphor alone will not protect us: we need to place rather greater weight on practical measures, ensuring that institutions operate with integrity and are appropriately constrained.[195]

The separation of powers in many ways is the easiest mental construct to address. As seen above in cases such as *Cart* and *Ku-ring-gai Council*, it masks legal realities. Recognising the importance of integrity and accountability of institutions over strict divisions of powers thus yields important intellectual insights.[196] In cases such as these we can see judges engaged in a deeper form of legal analysis.

A trickier mental construct to recalibrate is that administrative law scholarship has tended to assume that 'law' is a relatively fixed concept. I say 'assume' because there has not been as much reflection on the issue as one might expect.[197] That is not to say there

[190] Thomas (n 131) 256.
[191] Cane, 'Public Law in *The Concept of Law*' (n 6) 654.
[192] Fisher (n 166).
[193] Cane (n 1) 32.
[194] ibid 14–15.
[195] Warnock (n 160).
[196] EL Rubin, *Beyond Camelot: Rethinking Politics and Law for the Modern State* (Princeton, NJ, Princeton University Press, 2005) and J Tomlinson and R Thomas, 'A Different Tale of Judicial Power: Administrative Review as a Problematic Response to the Judicialisation of Tribunals' [2019] *PL* 537, 559.
[197] *cf* J Bell, *The Anatomy of Administrative Law* (Oxford, Hart Publishing, 2020).

are not points of disagreement about administrative law – the constitutional justifications for judicial review,[198] how to taxonomise the grounds of review,[199] and how to map the scope and nature of judicial review.[200] But there is an assumption that law, and in particular the grounds of review, is a set of rules derived directly from the common law and that it should be as universal and stable as possible.

The irony of course is how frustrating this vision of law is in practice. The law/fact divide is perceived as important but does not operate with analytical precision.[201] While many scholars who have an astute eye on the doctrine point to the importance of context,[202] others worry that 'context' is used by judges to act in a way that is seemingly arbitrary.[203] Perry has gone searching for a theory of judicial review due to his 'private law envy'.[204] What a study of tribunals is doing is highlighting that this might not be the place to look. As Cane has suggested, 'the background values of the law are to be found in [the] complex interaction between legislation and judicial activity'.[205] In that mix are tribunals. By studying them as legal objects and legal subjects, more sense may be made of the things that do not make sense in legal doctrine. Thus, for example, it might be shown how 'fact finding' is not just one thing, but a product of particular institutional structures.[206]

Indeed, a study of tribunals highlights the need to take the institutional nature of administrative law seriously. There is often a presumption that law and public administration are separate[207] – a separation carefully described by Harlow and Rawlings in their red light/green light theory description.[208] This assumption has led not only to a sidelining of tribunals and administration. It has led to a focus on how law is shaped by different strands of political and ideological thought outside law. 'Behind every theory of administrative law there lies a theory of the state'[209] is somewhat accurate but, as Cane himself has argued, 'English debate about a relationship between public law and political theory has diverted attention away from legal values'[210] embedded in the law. A study of tribunals requires far more attention to be paid not only to those values but also to the dynamism and 'definitional sensitivity' of specific legal arrangements. These things are not just irritations for legal scholars. They are legal realities and as such must figure in legal imagination.

[198] C Forsyth (ed), *Judicial Review and the Constitution* (Oxford, Hart Publishing, 2000).

[199] J Varuhas, 'Taxonomy and Public Law' in M Elliott et al (eds), *The Unity of Public Law? Doctrinal, Theoretical and Comparative Perspectives* (Oxford, Hart Publishing, 2018).

[200] D Knight, 'Contextual Review: The Instinctive Impulse and Unstructured Normativism in Judicial Review' (2020) 40 *LS* 1.

[201] eg Creyke (n 112).

[202] eg P Craig, 'Taxonomy and Public Law: A Response' [2019] *PL* 281 and Bell (n 197).

[203] eg Knight (n 200).

[204] A Perry, 'Plan B: A Theory of Judicial Review' (Oxford Legal Studies Research Paper No 66/2017), https://ssrn.com/abstract=3075886, accessed 8 July 2021.

[205] Cane, 'Theory and Values in Public Law' (n 6) 6.

[206] Fisher (n 57).

[207] E Fisher, 'The Open Road?: Navigating Public Administration and the Failed Promise of Administrative Law' in E Fisher et al (eds), *The Foundations and Future of Public Law: Essays in Honour of Paul Craig* (Oxford, Oxford University Press, 2020).

[208] Harlow and Rawlings (n 25) ch 1.

[209] ibid, 1.

[210] Cane, 'Theory and Values in Public Law' (n 6) 14.

VI. Conclusion

This reflective essay is inspired by Cane's ongoing intellectual commitment to unearth and make visible the actual architecture of administrative law. With that said, unlike much of his work, I have not engaged in a methodical mapping of the legal nature of administrative tribunals. Rather, through exploring a range of examples, I have highlighted the current limits of the scholarly imagination when it comes to administrative law.

Legal scholarship should illuminate.[211] The problem has been that much administrative law scholarship does not do that when it comes to administrative tribunals. Administrative tribunals, despite their legal significance, are not in the main field of scholarly vision. The legal understanding of them remains hazy. Santow has suggested that tribunals suffer from 'lawyerly snobbery … To put it bluntly: many lawyers find judicial review more complex, and so more interesting and worthy of close attention, than merits review by tribunals'.[212] The irony, as can be seen from the discussion in this chapter, is that administrative tribunals are profoundly legally complex. They are multifaceted legal constructs that actively contribute to administrative law in a range of ways.

Seeing this irony shows that the inattention to administrative tribunals is not just a product of scholarly snootiness. Rather, it is far more about how we as scholars imagine law and how our mental constructs sideline the legal complexity of tribunals. As already noted, the mind experiment I asked readers to engage in at the start of this chapter was not just playfulness on my part. In essence, it was an invitation to think about how assumptions about the legal world frame administrative law thinking. It was also an invitation, in the spirit of Cane's work, to take the 'law' in administrative law seriously.

[211] D Feldman, 'The Nature of Legal Scholarship' (1989) 52 *MLR* 498, 503.
[212] Santow (n 58) 44.

13

Cane as Law Reformer: *Götterdämerung* or House of Cards?

MARK LUNNEY

In the Anglo-Australian common law legal tradition, academics have played a relatively minor role as law reformers. This is no slight on academics: there has been no unwillingness to serve on law reform bodies and the like and academics are frequent consultees to consultation documents produced by such bodies as well as by those from government. The problem is that the formal law reform bodies to which academics contribute frequently have no control over the fate of their reform recommendations so that ultimate influence depends on the good will of government to pass the necessary reforming legislation.[1] Similar problems beset engagement with government with the additional problem that the process through which government engages with academic contributions may be opaque. Moreover, while the picture has changed somewhat in modern times, it is still the case that academics without expertise in the practising profession are rarely appointed to judicial office so have little opportunity to infuse their insights into judicial law-making. While it may no longer be true to say that academic writings are rarely cited,[2] given the volume of cases references across the spectrum of judicial decisions to such writings remain statistically rare albeit more frequent in appellate decisions where changes in the common law are usually made. Even where academic writings are cited, however, explicit judicial admissions that the basis of a decision is academic writing are rare. This does not mean that academic opinion is irrelevant; as Paul Mitchell has argued, academics have played their part in conversations about law

[1] In the case of the English Law Commission, the success rate of having recommendations implemented in statute has fallen since the Commission was established in 1965: D Lloyd-Jones, 'The Law Commission and the Implementation of Law Reform' (2013) 15 *European Journal of Law Reform* 333, 338. More broadly, see G Hammond, 'The Challenge of Implementation: Getting Law Reform Reports onto the Statute Book' (2013) 13 *Oxford University Commonwealth Law Journal* 239; G Hammond, 'The Legislative Implementation of Law Reform Proposals' in M Dyson et al, *Fifty Years of the Law Commissions: The Dynamics of Law Reform* (Oxford, Hart Publishing, 2016) 175.

[2] In the Australian context see (among many others by the same author) R Smyth, 'Academic Writing and the Courts: A Quantitative Study of the Influence of Legal and Non-Legal Periodicals in the High Court' (1998) 17 *University of Tasmania Law Review* 164; R Smyth, 'Citing Outside the Law Reports: Citations of Secondary Authorities on the Australian State Supreme Courts Over the Twentieth Century' (2009) 18 *Griffith Law Review* 692; R Smyth and I Neilsen, 'The Citation Practices of the High Court of Australia 1905–2015' (2019) 47 *Federal Law Review* 655.

that have formed the backbone of many statutory reforms.[3] But, absent a formal role as a commissioner of a law reform commission or similar body, academics have been more outside the tent of law reform than inside it.

For most of his academic career, Peter Cane's relationship to law reform has been that of a traditional academic. Despite his long and distinguished career as a scholar of tort law, however, many practising lawyers, and professionals more generally, know Cane for his involvement in one of the more controversial experiments in the reform of private law in Australia, the Ipp Panel. This chapter considers briefly the background to the Ipp Panel and the critics of its findings. It then explores the notion of 'principles-based' reform of the law of negligence as understood by two of the leading judicial figures in the reform movement, James Spigelman, Chief Justice of the Supreme Court of New South Wales and David Ipp, a judge on the New South Wales Court of Appeal. Cane's own writings, both on his involvement with the Ipp Panel and his wider scholarship on private law, are evaluated to consider how his involvement in the Ipp Panel fitted with that scholarship. In light of this analysis, can it be said that Cane was a 'traitor' to tort law and its scholarship by taking part in the Ipp Panel review, or was it simply a case of putting your money where your mouth is?

I. The Background to the Ipp Panel

The Ipp Panel, or more correctly the Panel of Eminent Persons chosen to review the law of negligence in accordance with the mandate of the ministerial meeting of May 2002, was an important part of the response of Australian governments to what was widely believed to be an insurance crisis of the early 2000s. It is certainly true that the largest public liability insurer in Australia, HIH Insurance, collapsed into insolvency during 2001 and one of Australia's largest providers of medical indemnity insurance, United Medical Protection/AMIL, only survived through a support package from government. As part of the fallout from these failures, tort litigation, primarily negligence, was identified as a contributing factor to the failures in the insurance market which had made third-party liability insurance increasingly expensive or in some cases unobtainable.

It is not necessary for the purposes of this chapter to attempt to evaluate the strength of the arguments of the critics who advocated for change. At one level, there is no doubt that the specific causes of the failure of the two large insurers had nothing to do with levels of tort litigation. As the HIH Royal Commission highlighted, the failure of HIH Insurance lay as much with corporate mismanagement as with any surge of personal injury litigation.[4] But from government circles the line was consistently taken that the legal system was part of the problem. As Senator Helen Coonan, Federal Minister for Revenue and Assistant Treasurer, put it, '[t]here is a widely held view that the current problems in the insurance market are due in large part to the operation of the legal system'.[5]

[3] P Mitchell, 'Patterns of Legal Change' (2012) 65 *Current Legal Problems* 177.

[4] Parliament of Australia, *Report of HIH Royal Commission into the Failure of HIH Insurance* (2003) xvii.

[5] H Coonan, 'Insurance Premiums and Law Reform – Affordable Cover and the Role of Government' (2002) 25 *University of New South Wales Law Journal* 819.

As part of a multi-pronged response to the crisis,[6] Commonwealth and state and territory governments commissioned a panel to conduct a review of the law of negligence. While a panel had been recommended by the Trowbridge Report, an influential study by a consultancy firm tasked with ascertaining the reasons for the crisis, the panel that was chosen did not reflect the recommendations in its report. A four-person panel was chosen, two of whom (the chair, Justice Ipp, and Cane) were lawyers with the other two places going to representatives of the medical profession and local government.

There were considerable limits placed on the Ipp Panel in drafting its report. First, the timescale in which the report had to be drafted was extremely limited: 12 weeks from commencement to final report, with an interim report to be drafted after eight weeks on a number of areas thought to require urgent attention. Second, the Terms of Reference significantly limited the nature of the recommendations that the panel could make. As Cane has noted, this was not 'lawyers' law reform'. It bore few of the hallmarks of traditional judicial and academic involvement in law reform by serving on formal law reform commissions or responding to consultation documents issued by those bodies. In particular, it was not the panel's role to evaluate whether, and in what way, the law of negligence was responsible for the crisis. The prelude to the Terms of Reference made this clear:

> The award of damages for personal injury has become unaffordable and unsustainable as the principal source of compensation for those injured through the fault of another. It is desirable to examine a method for the reform of the common law with the objective of limiting liability and quantum of damages arising from personal injury and death.[7]

Apart from this broad remit, specific areas of law were flagged for reform: the liability of public authorities, the use of the assumption of risk defence, contributory negligence, the standard of care in negligence, and the liability of not-for-profit organisations for damages for negligently-inflicted death or personal injury. The panel was also told to develop proposals to replace joint and several liability with proportionate liability for personal injury and death, a proposal that had been previously rejected in a detailed report by Professor Jim Davis of the Australian National University.[8]

[6] In 2002, the Commonwealth Government commissioned two reports from the Australian Competition and Consumer Commission (*Insurance Industry Market Pricing Review*, March 2002; *Second Insurance Industry Market Pricing Review*, September 2002). It also commissioned Trowbridge Consulting to write a report on the difficulties surrounding public liability insurance: both the report to the intergovernmental meeting of Ministers in March (*Public Liability Insurance: Analysis for Meeting of Ministers*, 26 March 2002) and the recommendations for action (*Public Liability Insurance: Practical Proposals for Reform*) to the Insurance Issues Working Group of Heads of Treasuries of 30 May 2002 were very influential in determining governmental responses. The scale of political interest is evident from the 'Public liability insurance' page on the Parliament of Australia website which lists over 30 documents either from or prepared for Commonwealth and State governments relating to reform of public liability insurance, available at https://www.aph.gov.au/About_Parliament/Parliamentary_Departments/Parliamentary_Library/Publications Archive/archive/publicliability.

[7] Parliament of Australia, *Review of the Law of Negligence Final Report* (September 2002), available at https://treasury.gov.au/sites/default/files/2019-03/R2002-001_Law_Neg_Final.pdf ('The Ipp Report').

[8] New South Wales Attorney General's Department, *Inquiry into the Law of Joint and Several Liability: Report of Stage 1* (Australian Government Publishing Service, 1994); New South Wales Attorney General's Department, *Inquiry into the Law of Joint and Several Liability: Report of Stage 2* (Australian Government Publishing Service, 1995). The Inquiry was commissioned by the Commonwealth and New South Wales Attorneys-General.

For all the controversy that the final report engendered, it is worth pointing out that, far from willingly acquiescing in all the directions given in the Terms of Reference, the Ipp Panel in some cases rejected the direction to produce proposals for reform. One area where this was done was proportionate liability. The report noted that, while the Terms of Reference could be read as requiring reform proposals to implement proportionate liability, the panel's task was to review and evaluate options for reform. Its 'firm view' was that claims for negligently-caused personal injury and death should not be reformed by introducing proportionate liability.[9] Similarly, the panel did not recommend that not-for-profit organisations receive protection from liability in negligence for personal injury.[10] Public authorities were given only a limited policy defence rather than any immunity.[11] More generally, in many areas the panel recommended legislative restatement of the common law, sometimes with modifications that would limit liability[12] but in other areas that could potentially expand liability.[13] Viewed with 20 years' hindsight, the Ipp Report seems much more of a lawyer's proposal for reform than was portrayed as at the time of its release. Given the huge knowledge imbalance (of the law) between the legal and non-legal members it was in one sense inevitable that this would be the case. However, there was another, more structural feature of the reform that made the character of the recommendations inevitable.

II. 'Principles-Based Reform' of the Law of Negligence

One of the criticisms of legislative tort law reform of the early twenty-first century is that it was driven instrumentally by the insurance industry. However, there was also a strand of judicial criticism of the law of negligence as it was operating in practice which raised similar concerns, albeit not expressly grounded solely in fears about the availability of liability insurance. The most prominent critic was the Chief Justice of New South Wales, James Spigelman. Writing in 2002, Spigelman argued that judicial attitudes to claims for compensation for personal injury resulting from negligence were cyclical.[14] When negligence emerged as an independent tort in the second half of the nineteenth century, judges had been suspicious and developed a number of liability-restricting devices to limit the success of claims for personal injury. Many of these devices were abolished or reined in by legislative change. Throughout the twentieth century, however, judges became imbued with the welfare state mentality that dominated post-World War II Anglo-Australian society. The high watermark of this change was the abolition in New Zealand in 1973 of much of the law of tort that provided compensation for accident victims and its replacement by a general administrative no-fault accident compensation scheme. The author of that report, Justice Woodhouse, was subsequently commissioned by the Whitlam Labor

[9] The Ipp Report (n 7) 178 (Recommendation 44).
[10] ibid 61 (Recommendation 10).
[11] ibid 158 (Recommendation 39).
[12] ibid 106–07 (Recommendation 28) (breach of duty).
[13] ibid 117–18 (Recommendation 29) (causation).
[14] JJ Spigelman, 'Negligence: The Last Outpost of the Welfare State' (2002) 76 *Australian Law Journal* 432.

Government to produce a similar report for Australia which resulted in recommendations for a similar, more extensive scheme.[15] By 'stretching' both the law and the facts to ensure that injured plaintiffs recovered compensation, judges created a *de facto* extension of the welfare state where liability insurance allowed for losses to accident victims to be spread among the class of injurers broadly responsible for creating the risks of those injuries or, in the case of the public bodies, the general public. The high point of this trend was seen as *Nagle v Rottnest Island Authority*,[16] a decision of the High Court of Australia allowing a plaintiff to recover when injured by voluntarily diving into a lake under the control of the defendant authority and hitting his head on the bottom with catastrophic consequences.[17]

For Spigelman, none of this suggested that seismic legislative change was needed in the law relating to negligently-inflicted personal injury.[18] Pointing to the wide variations in legislative regimes for motor vehicle and workplace accidents between and within states and territories, the result of this kind of 'underwriter driven reform' was contrasted with 'principle-driven reform' which proceeded in accord with the application of 'universally applicable principles'. This latter reform was largely in the hands of lawyers: not only could such a review be carried out by law reform bodies but also a 'useful source' of such principles were minority or overruled judgments that would have restricted recovery in particular situations.[19]

Over the next five years, Spigelman repeated this message in a number of articles and speeches based on this original piece.[20] To the extent that legislative reform mirrored the Ipp Report recommendations in respect of general principles – such as the restatements of the law on breach of duty and causation – it seems Spigelman approved. However, he disliked the introduction of caps and thresholds, or at least some of them.[21] However, by 2006, Spigelman was commenting that 'in many respects' the statutory changes were unprincipled and that '[a] number of persons, including myself, have indicated that in various respects the statutory changes have gone too far'.[22] While some of these criticisms related to the lack of uniformity among Australian jurisdictions these changes created – and the Ipp Panel did recommend uniform

[15] Political opposition from a variety of groups, including some lawyers' organisations, delayed the progress of the legislation implementing the scheme and it did not survive the fall of the Whitlam government: H Luntz, 'Looking Back at Accident Compensation: An Australian Perspective' (2003) 34 *Victoria University of Wellington Law Review* 279.

[16] *Nagle v Rottnest Island Authority* (1993) 177 CLR 423.

[17] Compare *Tomlinson v Congleton Borough Council* [2003] UKHL 47, [2004] 1 AC 46.

[18] Compare Luntz, who argued that the law was already recalibrating in favour of defendants by the time the reforms were advocated: H Luntz, 'Torts Turnaround Downunder' (2001) 1 *Oxford University Commonwealth Law Journal* 95.

[19] Spigelman (n 14) 441.

[20] JJ Spigelman, 'Tort Law Reform in Australia' (2004) 112 *British Insurance Law Association Journal* 1; JJ Spigelman 'Tort Law Reform: An Overview' (2005) 104 *Australian Construction Law Newsletter* 6; JJ Spigelman, 'Tort Law Reform in Australia: An Overview' (2006) 14 *Tort Law Review* 5.

[21] In his 2002 article, he thought there was 'no' principle on caps and thresholds for non-pecuniary loss but did approve of a cap on claims for loss of earning capacity: Spigelman (n 14) 448. *cf* N Mullaney, 'Tort Reform and the Damages Dilemma' (2002) 25 *University of New South Wales Law Journal* 876, who argued that caps on earning capacity claims were equally unprincipled.

[22] Spigelman (2006) (n 20) 13–14.

legislation[23] – the unavoidable conclusion is that Spigelman disagreed with some of the key changes recommended in the Ipp Report.

Spigelman's critique of the reform process, however, did not stem from any objection to factors external to the law being used as drivers for law reform. His principles-based reform was not founded on a philosophical commitment to a formal theory of law such as corrective justice or to a belief that reform interfered with a plaintiff's vested rights. In fact, Spigelman's reasons for thinking reform was necessary were polycentric. There was an economic component. Judges could not be indifferent to the economic consequences of their decisions and this included the increased costs of third-party liability insurance premiums consequent on particular decisions.[24] But the place of personal responsibility also played a prominent role:

> There is a distinct retreat in Australian jurisprudence, as in a broad range of social policies, from the hitherto dominant relativism by which misconduct is to be explained and, generally, excused, on the basis of the difficulties experienced by a person in his or her upbringing or other social interaction.[25]

This too was no trump card; it had to be balanced with compassion, the understanding of personal failings and the social need to maintain mutual community responsibility, particularly for the seriously injured. No one balance was immutable: it would be made differently 'in different societies and at different times within a society'.[26]

Seen from this perspective, there are similarities between Spigelman's views and those of David Ipp, the chair of the panel. Writing in 2003, Ipp framed the boundaries of the law of negligence as a series of compromises between competing values. Short shrift was given to arguments that it was a 'basic human right to recover full compensation for negligence according to the rules of the common law': this ignored 'the consequences of such a lack of constraint for the wider community'.[27] Social attitudes, 'a general public sentiment of moral wrongdoing', where sentiment was a reflection of deep-seated moral, political, social and economic values, a reflection of the values of the society itself, were central to the boundaries of the law of negligence.[28] Four years later, when statutory reform had been enacted in all Australian jurisdictions, Ipp was less enthusiastic about what had been enacted but remained unwavering in his view that the reform was ultimately a balancing exercise between competing interests.[29] Lawyers were not the 'saints' in this process: while recognising the legitimate concerns expressed by lawyers' representative bodies, '[l]awyers are not to be under-estimated in the politics of negligence'.[30]

[23] The Ipp Report (n 7) 26 (para 1.9).

[24] Spigelman (n 14) 435.

[25] Spigelman (2006) (n 20) 8.

[26] ibid.

[27] DA Ipp, 'Negligence – Where Lies the Future?' (2003) 23 *Australian Bar Review* 158, 158.

[28] DA Ipp, 'Policy and the Swing of the Negligence Pendulum' (2003) 77 *Australian Law Journal* 732, 734.

[29] DA Ipp, 'Themes in the Law of Torts' (2007) 81 *Australian Law Journal* 609 (apart from legislation that specifically implemented the recommendations of the report).

[30] DA Ipp, 'The Politics, Purpose and Reform of the Law of Negligence' (2007) 81 *Australian Law Journal* 456, 457.

And while disparate groups were involved in the politics of negligence, Ipp remained an optimist about consensus:

> There is a clear clash of values and interests between the different participants in the politics of negligence. The clash, however, although clear, need not necessarily result in blindness to what is at stake. Clarity of vision, restraint, leadership, and wisdom are capable of leading to a fair, and reasonably harmonious, set of laws of negligence that will enable all to get on with the ordinary business of life.[31]

Earlier in the year Ipp had made a wry reference to empathising with the comments of an Israeli UN representative from the 1960s who observed that the Israelis were sooner or later blamed for everything.[32] The heated debate at the end of 2002 indicates both the fraught task the Ipp Panel had in creating a reasonably harmonious set of laws of negligence and the thankless task in which those who attempted to do so were engaged. The disparate groups in the politics of the reform of the law of negligence were represented in microcosm in a special edition of the *University of New South Wales Law Journal* published at the end of 2002, after the Ipp Panel had released its recommendations. The anti-reformers spanned those who saw any change as an unwarranted infraction of victims' rights to those who saw the proposed reforms as a lost opportunity to highlight the flaws of tort law as a compensation system. Some argued there was no evidence of the connection between costs of the tort system and the insurance crisis.[33] Rob Davis from the Australian Plaintiff Lawyers Association thought the Ipp Panel was 'stacked with persons ideologically committed to tort reform regardless of the true causes for premium increases', a claim not supported by any analysis in the remainder of the piece.[34] On the other side, Helen Coonan, Commonwealth Assistant Treasurer, Robert Debus, Attorney-General for New South Wales, and Alan Mason, Executive Director of the Insurance Council of Australia, argued in favour of tort law reform while recognising other factors were also at play in the insurance crisis.[35] Comparative voices were also heard, detailing the process of tort reform in the United States and Canada and its replacement in New Zealand.[36] A sitting High Court judge defended jury trial[37] and Peter Handford from the University of Western Australia, uniquely among the academic contributors, found something to praise in the recommendations dealing with limitations of action.[38] And in one of the most interesting contributions Vines

[31] ibid 464.

[32] DA Ipp, 'The Metamorphosis of Slip and Fall' (2007) 29 *Australian Bar Review* 150, 150–51.

[33] R Graycar, 'Public Liability: A Plea for Facts' (2002) 25 *University of New South Wales Law Journal* 810.

[34] R Davis, 'The Tort Reform Crisis' (2002) 25 *University of New South Wales Law Journal* 865.

[35] Coonan (n 5); R Debus, 'Tort Law Reform in New South Wales: State and Federal Interactions' (2002) 25 *University of New South Wales Law Journal* 825; A Mason, 'Reform of the Law of Negligence: Balancing Costs and Community Expectations' (2002) *University of New South Wales Law Journal* 831.

[36] S Sugarman, 'United States Tort Reform Wars' (2002) 25 *University of New South Wales Law Journal* 849; B Feldthusen, 'Posturing, Tinkering and Reforming the Law of Negligence – A Canadian Perspective?' (2002) 25 *University of New South Wales Law Journal* 854; S Todd, 'Negligence Liability for Personal Injury: A Perspective from New Zealand' (2002) 25 *University of New South Wales Law Journal* 895.

[37] I Callinan, 'Problems in Insurance Law' (2002) 25 *University of New South Wales Law Journal* 859.

[38] P Handford, 'Limitation of Actions and Tort Reform' (2002) 25 *University of New South Wales Law Journal* 871.

recognised the historically contingent nature of 'personal responsibility' but argued for more express consideration of the notions of responsibility that underlay a system based on fault *and* compulsory liability insurance.[39]

Before turning to what contribution Cane could make to this smorgasbord of reform options, two points should be made. Despite the avowedly pluralist nature of the special issue, none of the contributors was a legal theorist. While some authors used the language of rights, none argued that the rules and structure of tort law should conform to some sort of strict correlative Hohfeldian rights-duty analysis. More understandably, there was nothing from corrective justice theorists. Corrective justice theorists generally think that factors external to the interpersonal relationship of the parties in a tort claim should not be taken into account in determining liability. Moreover, they are indifferent as to the legitimacy of what kind of system should (say) provide compensation to injured victims of accidents or how that should relate to how that system is funded. Accepting that the popularity of corrective justice as the philosophical foundation of tort law may have increased since 2002, it is nonetheless striking how little impact it had on debates.[40] As Hedley has noted, the absolutism of these theorists makes their work particularly unsuitable to a legislative process in which the balancing of competing interests is a necessity.[41] A second, related, point is that, despite the absence of theoretical support for the position, it was asserted by some critics of the reform process that any reform should have been left to the courts rather than the legislature. Notable in this respect was the contribution of Peter Underwood, Senior Puisne Judge of the Supreme Court of Tasmania.[42] While many of his criticisms of the reform process mirror those mentioned above, an important component of Underwood's critique rests on a preference for common law (judicial) development of the law rather than by legislation:

> There will develop two regimes, side-by-side, judge-made law and sporadic, unprincipled legislation, each fighting against each other. This of course, is bad enough, but some might say that it is scandalous that the remedy for financial difficulties in the insurance industry is an attack on common law principle rather than government revenue raising, especially as there are nothing but untested perceptions to justify such legislative incursions.[43]

It was not that all legislative change was objectionable – 'ameliorative' statutory alteration was acceptable – but 'wide-ranging changes to the principles that have been gradually and carefully worked out by courts over time' gave rise to the risk of 'judicial development being subject to the unnecessary and instantaneous editing of the legislature'. This is not quite the common law as the 'artificial perfection of reason'[44] but the virtue of the autonomy of common law principle from external drivers of reform is clear. Yet by the time of the Ipp Panel significant legislative changes had already been made to common law principles in the context of motor vehicle accidents and

[39] PE Vines, 'Tort Reform, Insurance and Responsibility' (2002) 25 *University of New South Wales Law Journal* 842.

[40] P Cane, *The Political Economy of Personal Injury Law* (Brisbane, University of Queensland Press, 2007) 63–64.

[41] S Hedley, 'The Rise and Fall of Private Law Theory' (2018) 134 *LQR* 214.

[42] P Underwood, 'Is Ms Donoghue's Snail in Mortal Peril?' (2004) 12 *Torts Law Journal* 39.

[43] ibid 59.

[44] E Coke, *Commentary upon Littleton* (Co Litt, first published 1628) 97b. For the context of the statement see M Lobban, 'The Common Law Mind in the Age of Sir Edward Coke' (2001) 33 *Amicus Curiae* 18.

accidents at work, numerically the two most important areas for fault-based liability. Either directly (as operators of fault-based compensation schemes) or indirectly (as regulators of an insurance market for the compulsory provision of third party liability policies) government had important interests in how the tort system *in practice* operated. While the legislative variety gave rise to merited criticism that a victim's entitlement to compensation unjustifiably varied according to the location of the accident, there was already a track record of restrictive legislative reform in those contexts well before the insurance crisis of 2002. The availability and affordability of liability insurance were not issues that newly arose in 2002. They had driven tort reform in the 1980s and 1990s and it is no surprise that some of the Ipp Panel recommendations, and later legislative changes, find their roots in these earlier reforms. And, more generally, Underwood makes no reference to the legislative abolition of negligence liability in workplace or motor vehicle accidents that had periodically been tried in Australian jurisdictions before 2002, or the radical replacement of fault-based accident liability in New Zealand in 1973.[45] Underwood's critique is very different from, say, Harold Luntz, the long-time advocate for an Australian no-fault accident compensation scheme. While Luntz had no truck with liability-insurer reform of negligence law, he also had no time for doctrinal reform of negligence law which contributed to a flawed system of accident compensation.[46] Only wholesale statutory abolition of much of tort law and its replacement with a statutory no-fault scheme could improve the situation, a solution that saw little merit in retaining the 'gradually and carefully worked out' common law regime.[47]

III. Cane and the Ipp Panel

In 2003, Cane published an article, 'Reforming Tort Law in Australia: A Personal Perspective', in an issue of the *Melbourne University Law Review* part dedicated to the retirement of Harold Luntz.[48] Given Luntz's criticisms of the entire reform process, this might seem an odd choice but Cane's ultimate message was tailored as advice to those, like Luntz, who favoured the abolition of fault-based liability for personal injury and the introduction of no-fault compensation schemes. In the course of the article – which is largely descriptive of both the background to the reforms and the process by which the Ipp Panel reached its conclusions – Cane makes a number of observations that are important for ascertaining his views both on the process and on his reasons for participating.

The first is his analysis of the insurance crises. As noted above, pro and anti-reformers traded blows over whether the liability costs were a trigger of the crisis. Like Ipp,[49] Cane accepted that, while there was obviously a link between the costs of liability and the costs of premiums for liability insurance, it was unlikely that increasing liability

[45] Luntz (n 15).

[46] H Luntz, 'Reform of the Law of Negligence: Wrong Questions – Wrong Answers' (2002) 25 *University of New South Wales Law Journal* 836.

[47] H Luntz, 'The Australian Picture' (2004) 35 *Victoria University of Wellington Law Review* 879.

[48] P Cane, 'Reforming Tort Law in Australia: A Personal Perspective' (2003) 27 *Melbourne University Law Review* 649.

[49] Ipp (n 27) 159.

costs were the sole trigger for the insurance crises.[50] But in a sophisticated analysis of the nature of insurance and its costing, Cane pointed out how insurance was viewed differently by the different participants in liability insurance. For insurers the provision of insurance is a commercial business. Viewed from the perspective of insureds and victims, insurance is a kind of public good:

> [M]any people do believe, I think, that insurers have some sort of moral obligation to ensure that the social functions of liability insurance – risk spreading and compensation – are performed. In this sense, insurance is viewed rather like an essential service.[51]

Crises in insurance were thus about expectation gaps: the expectation that insurance as an essential service would be readily available at a relatively stable price and the reality that the provision of insurance was not akin to the provision of a public utility. If a recalibration of tort law was necessary to allow these expectations to continue, reform had a social dimension not captured by doctrinal legal analysis.

Having framed the problem in this way, the second feature of Cane's article on the Ipp Panel and its recommendations is its rejection of the idea that reform of personal injury law to deal with this problem should necessarily be lawyer-driven. Some observations were merely factual: the task of the panel was not to conduct a review of personal injury law in the way an established law commission might do so; the reforms were driven by Treasury ministers and not Attorneys General; and the prime audience for the report was politicians, not lawyers or academics.[52] In other places, however, Cane implicitly responds to criticism of these features. Reform of personal injury law was not exclusively 'lawyers' business' so criticism of the composition of the panel (with half its membership being non-lawyers) was not accepted.[53] More importantly for this chapter, Cane also expresses a preference for political and legislative, as opposed to judicial, change to the principles of tort law.[54] He partly explained his view earlier in the article: '[l]aw reform is a means to an end – namely, the reallocation of resources away from the tort system to other valued activities – but not an end in itself'.[55] Anyone familiar with Cane's work would not have found these sentiments a surprise because they are consistent with views he had expressed in the lead-up to the Ipp Report. Questions of responsibility, and allocation of risk and resource around personal injury compensation, had been at the heart of his most recent scholarship on the law of tort.

IV. Correlativity and Corrective Justice: The Importance of Weinrib

It would be claiming too much to say that Cane's views on the matters he later considered in the Ipp Report arose in response to Weinrib but it is certainly true that Weinrib's

[50] Cane (n 48) 660.
[51] ibid 659.
[52] ibid 666–67, 669–70.
[53] ibid 669.
[54] ibid 671.
[55] ibid 664.

The Idea of Private Law, published in 1995,[56] provided a vehicle for Cane to both critique more formal theories of tort law and to articulate more of his own thoughts. The genesis of this response can be seen in Cane's review article on Weinrib's book in 1996, 'Corrective Justice and Correlativity in Private Law'.[57] He clearly thought it was an important piece and in later writing referred to it as expressing his reasons for rejecting Weinribian corrective justice as an adequate analysis, both normatively and descriptively, of tort law. There are a number of important components of Cane's thinking that can be identified in this piece. The first is that he agreed with Weinrib that correlativity was an inescapable structural feature of private law (including tort law). For that reason, he saw the primary merit in Weinrib's book as showing 'clearly why certain theories about the functions of and justifications for private law are inadequate …'.[58] The second was the failure of corrective justice, as explained by Weinrib, to explain the structure of tort law as it operated in practice. Weinrib's disinterest in the application of his theory to concrete cases, and his insistence that corrective justice and distributive justice 'covered the field', meant that distributive choices had to be made when the guidance from corrective justice was exhausted.[59] It was also the case, according to Cane, that distributional criteria could apply within a corrective justice framework. While Weinrib focused on the fault requirement, Cane went to the duty of care element in negligence. Decisions on duty of care were consistent with corrective justice because, by and large, they concerned the relative positions of the two parties before the court. But they were also inherently distributional, because a decision on whether a duty of care was owed in a particular setting applied beyond the facts of the individual case. Denying a duty of care preferred injurers as a class in the type of case under consideration and finding a duty of care favoured victims as a class in that same situation.[60] Moreover, a finding that a duty of care existed where it was previously thought there was no such duty was distributional: legal rights were transferred from injurers to victims (albeit on condition that fault was established). Thus to say that the 'the meaning of private law is corrective justice is to give an incomplete account of the structure of private law'.[61]

Nowhere in the article does Cane himself refer to the distributional function of negligence law as political: he cites Weinrib's correlation of 'distributive justice' and 'political' rather than making this point. Nothing should be read into this failure because it was not necessary for the article for Cane to go this far. Weinrib had argued that distributional criteria were political and could not by definition form part of the structure of private law and Cane's task was to show this was incorrect. The classification of the distributive criteria was beside the point. But what was implicit in the review of *The Idea of Private Law* was made explicit in Cane's *Anatomy of Tort Law*, published the following year.[62] Other contributions to this volume deal with the substance of Cane's reimagining of tort law but the premise of the book is that the best way of understanding

[56] E Weinrib, *The Idea of Private Law* (Cambridge Mass, Harvard University Press, 1995).
[57] P Cane, 'Corrective Justice and Correlativity in Private Law' (1996) 16 *OJLS* 471.
[58] ibid 487.
[59] ibid 479.
[60] ibid 480–81.
[61] ibid 482–83.
[62] P Cane, *The Anatomy of Tort Law* (Oxford, Hart Publishing, 1997).

tort law was as a series of ethical rules and principles of personal responsibility. While correlativity was a structural feature of tort law, this did not inculcate any particular theory of moral philosophy by virtue of that structure (as corrective justice explanations of tort law largely do). Equally, mono-theory instrumental explanations of tort, such as the maximisation of wealth or welfare, were equally unattractive. For Cane, notions of responsibility were foundational to tort law so appealing to another standard was normatively unattractive. It was also descriptively inaccurate, as many of the structural features of tort law, such as its correlativity, were ill-suited to achieve the instrumental ends suggested for tort law. Cane did not deny that tort law could have indirect extrinsic effects, but these operated within the correlativity framework and were largely subservient to ethical rules and principles of responsibility that underpinned tort law. While one direct effect of the operation of the tort system was its prophylactic role in allowing people to arrange their lives so as to comply with the law, this was different from its indirect effects on compensation for injury and economic efficiency claimed by some as the justification for tort law.

What were the ethical rules and principles of responsibility that underlay tort law? It is difficult to discern a pattern of such principles, separated from Cane's dissection of tort law into protected interests, sanctioned conduct, and sanctions, in *The Anatomy of Tort Law*. But this was not an oversight; it stemmed from Cane's fundamental disagreement with the mono-theorists. Cane's view of tort law was that it was underpinned by a diverse menu of ethics and principles of responsibility that defied explanation through adherence to a single theory.[63] As *The Anatomy of Tort Law* shows, this did not make Cane a tort law anarchist: it was possible to dissect tort law in more meaningful ways than the remedial structure left to modern law from the forms of action. But tort law was a human artefact and Cane understood tort law through this prism:

> The reason why my explanatory account of tort law is not based on a single principle, and the reason why I have not attempted to propound a normative vision of tort law is partly that I take a certain view of human nature and of human morality which is different from that which I believe underlies theories such as those of Weinrib and the economic analysts … This approach seems to me to be based on an unrealistic view of human nature. It is typical of human beings that they pursue in their lives a large number of different goals, at least some of which conflict among themselves. Faced with such conflicts, people must choose to prefer one of the conflicting goals over the others … Tort law is infected with the same tendency to pursue multifarious and potentially conflicting goals as are other forms of human purposive activity. But it is even less likely than in the case of individuals that the life of a society will be informed by a unifying principle which could be brought to bear to resolve conflicts of goals within tort law. Here, as in the lives of individuals, conflicts of goals tend to be resolved by giving priority to one goal over another (or others) in the circumstances of individual cases according to value judgements which may themselves, in different circumstances, conflict with other social goals.[64]

[63] Compare T Weir, 'Review of The Damages Lottery and The Anatomy of Tort Law' (1998) 57 *CLJ* 204, 205, who in a review of the book thought he paid 'almost no attention to the relation between plaintiff and defendant, which must surely be both a factor in the correlation and relevant to the matter of ethical responsibility'.

[64] Cane (n 62) 224–25.

Far from being a hindrance, this plurality and indeterminacy was the very soul of what it meant to be human, to explore the 'diversity, variety and infinite possibilities' which gave human life value.[65]

While the balancing of competing ethical rules and principles of responsibility was not constrained by mono-theories, there is little in *The Anatomy of Tort Law* that explicitly evaluated tort law's institutional mechanisms for doing this. In the introductory chapter Cane notes that tort law was made by both judicial decision as well as legislative processes and that a judge could exercise deference if it was thought the kind of decision she was being asked to make was more suited to a legislature (the question of 'institutional competence').[66] Understandably, as these were framing comments in an introductory chapter, no examples are given of where the balance should lie in individual cases. In fact, *The Anatomy of Tort Law* says little about when the magnitude of the proposed disjuncture with the previous balance drawn between competing goals is such that institutional competence requires legislative rather than judicial action. The exception is important. In the final section of the book, Cane considers arguments for the abolition of tort law. In fact, as he notes, this argument had only been seriously raised in the context of claims for personal injury and death by victims of accidents. Here the limitations of tort's law structure – a correlative system based on ethical rules and principles of responsibility – came up against (in his view) a more compassionate societal view that was primarily concerned with ensuring the needs of accident victims. Here Cane was unequivocal; the choice was 'at bottom, a political one'.[67] As the later analysis shows, this was not necessarily an equating of political with legislative but it did involve understanding that the wider political context had a role in determining where the balance was to be drawn: welfare state politics supported a resolution of the competing interests more in favour of social welfare than did the individualistic philosophies that underpinned the politics of Thatcher and Reagan.[68]

The Anatomy of Tort Law is fundamental to understanding Cane's involvement in and approach to the task of the Ipp Report. Tort law was the result of a series of compromises between competing normative positions. It required choices to be made, choices that needed to respond to a variety of social and political contexts. But the fact that there was no unifying moral principle did not mean tort law was unconcerned with moral values. While some components of tort law might be abolished and replaced – this was the politics of personal injury law – *The Anatomy of Tort Law* was ultimately about the relationship between coherence on the one hand and moral pluralism on the other.

V. Distributive Justice and Responsibility

Cane returned to these issues in two important publications in the shadows of the Ipp Report. In 'Distributive Justice and Tort Law',[69] Cane's critique of corrective justice

[65] ibid 225.
[66] ibid 19–20.
[67] ibid 235.
[68] ibid 235–36.
[69] P Cane, 'Distributive Justice and Tort Law' [2001] *New Zealand Law Review* 401.

approaches to tort law repeats many of his earlier arguments but hones his own explanation of the relationship between correlativity, corrective justice and distributive justice. Corrective justice provided the structure within which distributive justice operated, an inevitable consequence of correlativity. But distributive justice in tort law did not necessarily mean distributive justice in a global sense. Rather, distributive justice in tort law looked to the allocation of liability as between classes of victims and injurers (such as consumers and manufacturers). In other words, the focus of distributive justice in tort law was on the fairness of the rights and obligations '*as between doers and sufferers of harm*'.[70] It was this choice that was protected through corrective justice. This relative evaluation of what would be distributively just at the local level did not automatically equate to a globally fair distribution. But for Cane that argument missed the point: whether tort law distributed risks of harm fairly, viewed globally, was a different question from whether tort law distributed risks at all. If the manner in which tort law distributed risks of harm and obligations of repair was unfair, 'so much the worse for tort law'.[71]

While there is little new in 'Distributive Justice and Tort Law', the explicit recognition that tort law's allocation of risk/obligation of repair was not, or not necessarily, based in any normative framework created the bridge through which tort law could be seen as political. Again, Cane does not explicitly state that the choices made in the risk/obligation allocation is political. 'Political' is discussed in the critique of Weinrib's view that distributive concerns were necessarily political and, while Cane makes the argument that tort law is distributive, what implications this had for (say) law reform is not explored. But the conclusion of the article gets us much closer to Cane's views on the place of political change in tort law. The recognition that tort had distributional effects raised a constitutional challenge: who was to decide the distributive questions? There were only two ways of dealing with the problem: courts must be disqualified (by their own actions or through some other mechanism, presumably political) from dealing with cases 'that raise distributive issues that are thought more appropriately dealt with by another branch of government', or the democratic deficit of courts had to be addressed.[72] Cane's conclusion – that as courts would continue to play a role in making tort law tort scholars should aim to offer courts a sound theoretical framework for considering distributive issues – does not really address the questions he earlier raised. In the preceding paragraph he did 'not underestimate the difficulty' of asking tort lawyers to engage with the 'huge and complex' literature on distributive justice, much of it 'pitched at a level of abstraction too high to be of much direct use to lawyers'.[73] If tort scholars would find the task Herculean, there can have been no expectation that judges deciding cases within the evidentiary and procedural constraints of correlativity would achieve the task. Yet courts would continue to decide cases, however imperfect their understanding of distributive justice. Perhaps Cane had to accept that questions of distributive justice were within the operational, rather than constitutional, competence of courts as to deny this went some way to accepting Weinrib's views that distributive justice was not a matter for courts. There was a difference between courts 'doing' distributive justice badly and not doing it at all. But the place for the other branch of government – the overtly political – was left tantalisingly vague.

[70] ibid 413.
[71] ibid 418.
[72] ibid 420.
[73] ibid 419.

Some but not all of these themes were taken up in a wider narrative on responsibility that formed the basis of Cane's 2002 monograph, *Responsibility in Law and Morality*.[74] As in his earlier work, the focus of the book is not about the nature of any political choices that had to be made in the formulation and application of legal rules but its broad themes had important implications for that question. Cane's interest in writing *Responsibility in Law and Morality* was not to arrive at some kind of 'absolute' truth about the nature of responsibility. Rather, he was interested in responsibility practices in general and responsibility practices in law in particular. While Cane made it clear he was agnostic as to the possibility of such an evaluation, the Cane that had written about responsibility as a constructed human artefact was unlikely to be attracted to the idea of an immutable and acontextual holy grail of this nature. But neither did Cane think that law and morality were separate or even hierarchical systems; they were symbiotic and mutually informing. Thus, another of Cane's themes in the book was to argue that insights for moral philosophy could be gained from looking at law's actual responsibility practices (using, as he had argued in *The Anatomy of Tort Law*, a menu of sanctioned conduct, protected interests, and sanctions). By looking at those practices, Cane takes aim at perhaps his main target of the book: agent-based views of the nature of responsibility in moral philosophy. Although he accepted that the responsibility practices of various areas of law – particularly the criminal law – could be explained consistently with agent-focused accounts of responsibility, private law – including tort law – could not. Time and again throughout the book Cane notes the dissonance between what an agent-focused view of responsibility might entail and what the responsibility practices in law actually entailed. In his view, this was because the interest in freedom of action, which in his view also underpinned Weinrib's interpersonal justice, was not the only factor that determined responsibility practices in law. Interests of victims as victims, and interests of victims as part of a wider social community, also contributed to the identification of what responsibility required in concrete cases. Whether someone could be responsible said nothing about what that responsibility meant on the ground.

While unpacking responsibility practices in law required engagement with concrete legal rules, *Responsibility in Law and Morality* is primarily not about the merits of the combinations that had been chosen for those responsibility practices. To that end there is nothing that can be taken as prophesising Cane as a law reformer. More broadly, however, it is hard to read *Responsibility in Law and Morality* without sensing a certain frustration at the unworldliness of some of the philosophical literature Cane was critiquing.[75] In a review of the book, Watkins noted that on one philosophical view of responsibility, '[w]hether a person's actions reflect back on them as agents isn't something

[74] P Cane, *Responsibility in Law and Morality* (Oxford, Hart Publishing, 2002). Some of the arguments of the book are raised in a shorter form in P Cane, 'Responsibility and Fault: A Relational and Functional Approach to Responsibility' in P Cane and J Gardner (eds), *Relating to Responsibility: Essays in Honour of Tony Honoré on his 80th Birthday* (Oxford, Hart Publishing, 2001).

[75] See also P Cane, 'The Anatomy of Private Law Theory: A 25th Anniversary Essay' (2005) 25 *OJLS* 203, 210: '[i]t is only by ignoring the dialectical nature of the common law that austerely formalistic, conceptual accounts of private law (of which Weinrib's is the leading example) can be made to appear at all plausible. What other understanding of the nature of the common law could possibly support the idea that "the only purpose of private law is to be private law"'.

that can be decided by the fiat of legislators, judges, or the community but needs to be uncovered, like all normative facts, through perception and careful reasoning'.[76] As Cane noted throughout the book, however, while philosophy could have two-bob each-way (my term), law needed to come to a conclusion on questions of responsibility. It is probably true, as some reviewers noted,[77] that Cane overplayed the interconnectedness of legal and moral philosophy but Cane's point was that philosophical indifference to the realities of law's responsibility practices deprived philosophy of a vast corpus of potentially relevant material. While this provoked, unsurprisingly, a backlash from those who thought Cane had misunderstood agent-focused accounts of responsibility,[78] legal philosophers generally found it an important insight, one going as far as saying that Cane was 'too defensive' in pushing the value of legal notions of responsibility to the philosophical: '… his stance on this matter is clearly correct and is not in need of such persistent underscoring'.[79] But even reviewers sympathetic to this project revealed a potential shortcoming. One of Cane's seven suggestions for thinking about responsibility was to think of it distributionally, a means of allocating a resource that people could use to protect their interests. The way that resource was allocated was an important part of any account of responsibility.[80] Cane's point, as it was in 'Distributive Justice and Tort Law', was to reject accounts of responsibility that either ignored or rejected this phenomenon but there is little about how law distributed these resources. This led William Lucy to argue that Cane's failure to distinguish between rules distributive in intent and distributive in consequence was a flaw in the book.[81] It also led to a certain unease in another reviewer that Cane's relatively deferential approach to law in general, and common law decision making in particular, gave too much weight to the moral compromises reached in law.[82] In different ways, these were criticisms that Cane had been insufficiently critical of the substance of the law both in its distributive consequences and its moral underpinnings.

Whatever the strength of these arguments – and in his participation in the Ipp Panel he certainly showed himself willing to address these issues pragmatically – the suggestion that Cane's view mirrored, even if unintentionally, those of an earlier generation of lawyers who extolled the genius of the common law and feared legislative codification,[83] was not borne out by his participation in the Ipp Panel. Another of Cane's seven suggestions for thinking about responsibility was that it should be thought about contextually, meaning no more than 'that much can be gained by thinking about responsibility

[76] J Watkins, 'Responsibility in Context' (2006) 26 *OJLS* 593, 601.

[77] ibid. See also N Levy, 'The Responsibility of Lawyers and the Responsibility of Philosophers' (2004) 9 *Australian Journal of Legal Philosophy* 172.

[78] R Brownsword, 'Review of Responsibility in Law and Morality' (2003) 23 *LS* 177, 181–82; A Beever, 'Perspectives of Responsibility in Law and Morality' (2003) 27 *Melbourne University Law Review* 905; J Evans, 'Cane on Responsibility' (2004) 29 *Australian Journal of Legal Philosophy* 164.

[79] M Kramer, 'Review of Responsibility in Law and Morality' (2004) 113 *The Philosophical Review* 133. See also B Bix, 'Review of Responsibility in Law and Morality' (2006) 114 *Ethics* 124.

[80] Cane (n 74) 283.

[81] W Lucy, 'Review of Responsibility in Law and Morality' (2003) 66 *MLR* 658, 660–61.

[82] Bix (n 79) 125.

[83] ibid 125–26.

in relation to a particular society and a particular time, and in relation to particular social activities and problems, and particular value systems'.[84] While Cane clearly saw institutional features of judicial law-making as conducive to creating forms of responsibility practices consistent with morality, there is nothing to suggest that the kind of re-evaluation a contextual approach might require was antipathetic to a legislative process. In fact, his explicit recognition of the lack of democratic legitimacy in judicial decision-making might suggest a preference for legislative rebalancing although the suggestion that legislative law-making 'is not expected to conform to the rigorous standards of rationality and reason-giving that apply in the judicial law-making process' does not sound like an endorsement.[85] But this latter comment was made in the context of explaining why judicial law-making was of more interest to his project than legislative. There is really nothing in *Responsibility in Law and Morality* that addresses whether thinking about responsibility in the way Cane posits necessarily required substantive law reform to take a particular form.

VI. Off the Fence?

The discussion so far repudiates any suggestion that Cane entered the Ipp Panel deliberations with any reforming zeal. Nor does it suggest that he was in any sense 'hostile' to the position reached through the common law: in *Responsibility in Law and Morality* he had just extolled the virtues of such a system to inculcate principles of applied morality that had counterparts in more abstract conceptions of morality. But it is perfectly possible to explain Cane's involvement in the Ipp Panel as entirely consistent with his more abstract views on responsibility and distributive justice.[86] If responsibility was viewed socially, contextually and relationally, the legislature was clearly a not inappropriate body to decide how these factors would interact in concrete rules. Moreover, if Cane's analysis was ambivalent about the distributive consequences of the patterns of liability rules, the Ipp Panel's Terms of Reference took away any need to address the issue. Taking the Spigelman line, the politicians told the panel that (in Cane's language) the balance between sanctioned conduct, protected interests and sanctions needed to be altered: '[t]he award of damages for personal injury has become unaffordable and unsustainable as the principal source of compensation for those injured through the fault of another'.[87] As Cane's view of responsibility did not embody any particular commitment as to how the elements of responsibility he identified could be blended, this was less of an issue

[84] Cane (n 74) 282–83.
[85] ibid 9–10.
[86] It is a quite different point to argue that this was the reason for Cane's appointment. More likely was his prominence as a co-author of a leading text of the law of torts in Australia or, perhaps, his inheritance of Atiyah's *Accidents of Compensation and the Law*, a text which highlighted the failure of (especially) negligence law as a means of compensating those injured through accidents and the 6th edition of which, authored by Cane, had recently (in 1999) been published (thanks to Professor James Goudkamp for the latter suggestion). More prosaically, as the holder of a research chair (as head of the Department of Law at the Research School for Social Sciences at the Australian National University), Cane was also known in Canberra.
[87] The Ipp Report (n 7) ix.

for him than for other tort scholars who defended a particular balance represented by the status quo. Equally the failure to recommend abolition and replacement by broad-based compensation schemes in the Terms of Reference was not objectionable because correlativity was an essential feature of law's responsibility practices. This was not to say that no-fault accident compensation might not be a better way to treat accident victims – indeed Cane admitted that this was his personal preference[88] – but this was not the only way to deal with the question. Put simply, the responsibility practices involved in the law relating to the recovery of damages for personal injury were an attempt to seek a reflective equilibrium about complex concepts.[89] Cane had never denied a place for the legislature to contribute to this process and had made compelling arguments about the limits of the courts in this regard.[90] His expertise was needed on the panel to elaborate in more detail, in his terms if not in terms of those who appointed him, 'what are the responsibility practices' in this equilibrium and what options there might be to change them in light of the Terms of Reference. Given this role, there could hardly have been anyone more suited to the task.

As discussed earlier, one of the most strident critics of the process of reform of which the Ipp Panel formed part was Justice Peter Underwood. Cane responded to his criticisms the following year by challenging the assertion that judicial reform was to be preferred to legislative reform in cases of disagreement over complex issues. While the article, 'Taking Disagreement Seriously: Courts, Legislatures and the Reform of Tort Law'[91] was about more than the tort reform process, there is no doubt (as it is mentioned) that Underwood's article was a key driver to its being written.[92] In a sophisticated analysis, Cane pointed out that both courts and legislatures were in the business of legalising norms, most of which existed outside the legal system. The processes by which courts did this (through triadic – two disputants and a neutral third party – processes) and legislatures did this (pluralistic, multi-polar) were different. Moreover, there was good reason to limit the ability of courts to legalise norms because this was done at the point of application and changes at that point gave rise to concerns over fairness and predictability. For this reason, coherence and consistency were themselves legal norms that applied to court norm-legalisation that did not apply to legislative norm-legalisation. For Cane, however, this did not mean that coherence and consistency were irrelevant in the legislative context, simply that 'legislatures are freer than courts to promote other values at the expense of coherence and consistency'.[93]

These general arguments were given teeth when Cane turned to discuss their application to the reform process (and, by implication, his involvement in that process). If the pluralistic nature of legislative norm-legalisation did not render it preferable to the

[88] Cane (n 48) 651.
[89] Cane (n 74) 17.
[90] ibid 6–10, 17.
[91] P Cane, 'Taking Disagreement Seriously: Courts, Legislatures and the Reform of Tort Law' (2005) 25 *OJLS* 393.
[92] ibid 395–96.
[93] ibid 407.

more closed court process, why not? His response was to trot out some elementary legal realism:

> The first argument [that judicial norm-legalisation was preferable] apparently rests on the idea that whereas political processes are apt to produce partisan outcomes, judicial processes produce neutral and impartial outcomes. It is only necessary to state this proposition in order to appreciate its falsity. Whatever judicial impartiality might mean, it cannot protect judges from having to make choices between competing normative propositions.[94]

While Cane accepted that judges typically did not make decisions on the basis of crude self-interest, 'the assumption that participants in political processes are typically or frequently motivated by self-interest is contestable and contested'.[95] Returning to his earlier work, he pointed out that the process of adjudicative norm-legalisation also involved preferring the interests of one social group to the interests of others, an exercise in balancing the interests of personal and financial security against freedom of action. But the legacy of the Ipp Report gave the analysis a distinctly pointed edge. Accusations that legislative modification of the common law were arbitrary and unprincipled 'typically rest on a normative objection to the particular balance the legislature has struck between competing interests'.[96] In his 2003 article in the *Melbourne University Law Review* Cane had expressly said this balance was a political question but here he went further: the question was whether genuine, reasonable and intractable disagreement over where the balance should be struck should be managed by judicial or political processes? Directly challenging the Underhill line, Cane argued for political processes: '[u]nless we think that judicial processes are likely to do a better job than political processes can of managing disagreements about tort law, there is no reason to prefer judicial to legislative development of the law, and good reason to prefer the latter'.[97]

Nowhere in Cane's previous writings had a justification for contributing to the tort reform process through membership of Ipp Panel been so clearly made. There was nothing fundamentally new in his reasoning but the conclusions he now drew made explicit why legislative reform of tort law of the scale required in the Terms of Reference of the Ipp Report was legitimate. Accepting that the very short time scale for Ipp Report made construction of 'anything approaching an internally coherent and consistent regime of personal injury law'[98] impossible, he nonetheless asserted that, on the whole, 'there is little reason to think that the statute book is significantly more internally incoherent than the common law'.[99] However, by the time of the article Cane was aware that, whatever the general position regarding the comparative coherence of common law and statutory regimes, the tort reform legislation that was the result of the Ipp Report had been subjected to piercing criticism for (among other things) its lack of

[94] ibid 413.
[95] ibid 413–14.
[96] ibid 414.
[97] ibid.
[98] ibid 415.
[99] ibid.

consistency and coherence.[100] But even if this was a slightly defensive attempt to divert attention from the weaknesses of the legislation implementing the Ipp Report, he was unrepentant in critiquing those who argued for the purity of the common law and the sinfulness of the legislative process:

> The image of powerful governments acting on a whim and manipulating the political process to promote personal and sectional interests is as much an over-simplification as that of totally disinterested judges resolving interpersonal disputes by applying normatively neutral principles.[101]

The powerful undercurrent of this argument is that critics of the legislative process were naïve at best and, perhaps, disingenuous at worst. It also provides a justification for Cane's involvement in the Ipp Panel and for the integration of legal expertise in legislative law reform in a more direct way than the traditional recommendations of law reform bodies. And while it was not a necessary progression from his earlier work, there was also no legitimate reason for the sense of betrayal that some critics, while explicitly exonerating the members of the Ipp Panel, implicitly reserved for its legal members. From Cane's perspective, there must have been some irony in the critics of the legislative tort reform process advocating that its aims could have been achieved instead by judicial realignment. If this was so, the disagreement was as much about means rather than ends, and 'Taking Disagreement Seriously' justified the means through which Cane had participated.

'Taking Disagreement Seriously' in many ways marked a turning point in Cane's scholarship and not just in private law. Doctrinally, Cane's interests moved from private to public law, and methodologically to comparative and historical analysis, but the opportunity to deliver three lectures in the McPherson Lecture Series in March 2007 allowed him an opportunity to reflect on the past ten years of his tort scholarship and its interrelationship with his work on the Ipp Panel. Parts of the lectures, 'The Political Economy of Personal Injury Law',[102] contain familiar descriptions of Cane's views on monistic theories of private law and the shortcomings of the regulatory justification that economic analysis suggested for tort law, but there are at least two things worth noting about Cane's approach to the topic. The first is that politics was at the forefront of a global assessment of personal injury law. In line with the topic, the lectures began with one on politics, concluding with sections on the politics of regulation, compensation, responsibility and law-making. Incremental reform was defended as a political reality;[103] applying negligence law was as much a political exercise as *making* it;[104]

[100] Apart from examples cited earlier, see B McDonald, 'Legislative Intervention in the Law of Negligence: The Common Law, Statutory Interpretation and Tort Reform in Australia' (2005) 27 *Sydney Law Review* 443; Legislative Council General Purpose Standing Committee No. 1, *Inquiry into Personal Injury Compensation Legislation* (December 2005); B McDonald, 'The Impact of the Civil Liability Legislation on Fundamental Policies and Principles of the Common Law of Negligence' (2006) 14 *Torts Law Journal* 268; J Keeler, 'Personal Responsibility and the Reforms Recommended by the Ipp Report: "Time Future Contained in Time Past"' (2006) 14 *Torts Law Journal* 48 (original lecture 25th February 2005).

[101] Cane (n 91) 416.

[102] Cane (n 40).

[103] ibid 4–5.

[104] ibid 28.

tort law was doubly distributive, doubly political because it distributed risks *and* resources.[105] And if the impetus for the creation of the Ipp Panel was dissatisfaction with the judiciary's politics of responsibility in applying the law, this was simply part of Cane's wider point that 'debates about the role of courts in making and developing personal injury law are political debates about the distribution of government power'.[106] In describing the changing nature of this balance Cane recognised the pragmatic advantage courts had in getting their way: it was difficult to use legislation to influence judicial application of general principles in individual cases. He indicated dissatisfaction with the legislation that incorporated the Ipp Panel's suggestion for subtle reform of those principles.[107] Whatever the operational difficulties, however, there is no sense in which legislative reform, even if radical and broad brush, was in some sense improper. In their time legislative changes that made it easier for plaintiffs to recover – such as the abolition of the defence of common employment and the abrogation of contributory negligence[108] – also represented significant changes to the allocation of risks and resources between injured and injurers but this fitted with the allocation thought politically desirable by the judiciary. There could be no doubt after *The Political Economy of Personal Injury Law* that Cane had little time for what he saw as prioritising one form of distributive allocation over another by making it appear apolitical.

The second point to take from *The Political Economy of Personal Injury Law* is that Cane gives some indication that he thought there was an irreducible minimum of the tort-law base for recovery of damages for personal injury. These were monetary compensation for monetary loss and correlative causation.[109] It might be that other balances between risk and resources outside the tort system would be preferable to that achievable within the tort limitations, but such a scheme would not be tort law. The Ipp Panel's Terms of Reference fell well within this irreducible minimum. This is not to say that these necessarily formed the baseline for recommendations for reform – Cane's politics of law reform was far more nuanced than that – but it does suggest that the human artefact that was tort law could be crafted in very many ways and remain tort law.[110]

Viewing tort law politically also had potential benefits beyond defining the boundaries of principles-based statutory reform of the law of negligence. In his 2003 *Melbourne University Law Review* article, Cane had argued that the best chance for those who supported the *replacement* of the fault-based tort system (radicals) as the basis of compensation for personal injury with a broad-based accident compensation scheme

[105] ibid 26.
[106] ibid 33.
[107] ibid 30.
[108] Whether apportionment for contributory negligence assisted plaintiffs globally is difficult to test empirically because of the inscrutability of the jury verdicts that determined most tort actions until well into the twentieth century. Juries may well have applied apportionment *de facto* by refusing to formally find a plaintiff guilty of contributory negligence – and thus defeat the claim – but took it into account by reducing the amount of damages awarded. See also EGD Van Dongen and H Verdam, 'The Development of the Concept of Contributory Negligence in English Common Law' (2016) 12 *Utrecht Law Review* 61; W Cornish et al, *Law and Society in England 1750–1950*, 2nd edn (Oxford, Hart Publishing, 2019) 468–69.
[109] Cane (n 40) 93.
[110] ibid.

lay in getting its advocates to engage politically to achieve it.[111] Political salience was the key and taking part in reform debates could provide an opportunity to highlight the case for abolition. As the Terms of Reference for the Ipp Panel were not construed as covering abolition, Cane's point was not specific to it but was the wider one that the more people believed that 'the tort system is as bad as the radicals believe' the more likely it was that abolition would return to the political stage.[112] Four years later, with reform of tort law now off the political mainstream, Cane made the same point with pointed pithiness:

> The stark choice confronting people who are suspicious of the political process is between letting go of their suspicion and abandoning hope of radical change to tort law, however strong the arguments for such change.[113]

This was not simply advice for others to follow: Cane, the self-confessed radical,[114] had put his money where his mouth was and engaged in the political process.

VII. Conclusion

The tort reforms that came out of the Ipp Panel remain controversial and continue to attract opprobrium.[115] Yet almost 20 years after their enactment, it is striking that not one jurisdiction has pulled back, in any meaningful way, from the statutory reforms passed a generation earlier.[116] Rather than admit them as a mistake, an increasingly

[111] Cane (n 48) 676.

[112] ibid.

[113] Cane (n 40) 104.

[114] Cane (n 48) 651.

[115] A Field, '"There must be a Better Way": Personal Injuries Compensation Since the "Crisis in Insurance"' (2008) 13 *Deakin Law Review* 67; J Bell-James and K Barker, 'Public Authority Liability for Negligence in the Post-Ipp Era: Sceptical Reflections on the "Policy Defence"' (2016) 40 *Melbourne University Law Review* 1. A persistent critic has been Professor James Goudkamp: see, eg, J Goudkamp, 'A Revival of the Doctrine of Attainder? The Statutory Illegality Defences to Liability in Tort' (2007) 29 *Sydney Law Review* 445; J Goudkamp, 'Self-Defence and Illegality under the Civil Liability Act 2002 (NSW)' (2010) 18 *Torts Law Journal* 61; J Goudkamp, 'The Young Report: An Australian Perspective on the Latest Response to Britain's "Compensation Culture"' (2012) 28 *Journal of Professional Negligence* 4; J Goudkamp, 'Reforming English Tort Law: Lessons from Australia' in E Quill and RJ Friel (eds), *Damages and Compensation Culture: Comparative Perspectives* (Oxford, Hart Publishing, 2016) ch 4.

[116] Perhaps prompted, at least initially, by federal government reports after the tort reform legislation had passed noting the success of the legislation in stabilising in the insurance market: see Commonwealth of Australia, *Reform of Liability Insurance Law in Australia* (Commonwealth Treasury, Canberra, 2004) 12 ('[t]he comprehensive programme of law reform has been a major contributor to this stabilisation and governments firmly believe that these reforms create a platform for a more stable and predictable insurance environment in the long term'). See also the slightly more equivocal Commonwealth of Australia, *Available and Affordable: Improvements in Liability Insurance following Tort Reform in Australia* (Commonwealth Treasury, Canberra, 2006) 75. Less surprisingly, the reforms received considerable support from the insurance industry, including interest in the United States. See, eg, 'Defence News – Tort Law Reform Steaming in Australia' (2002) 69 *Defence Counsel Journal* 406; S Stuart-Clark and R McInnes, '2002: Australia's Year Zero of Tort Reform: But the Federal Government's Response is Crucial' (2003) 70 *Defence Counsel Journal* 341; S Stuart-Clark and C Harris, 'Tort Law Reform in Australia: Fundamental and Potentially Far-Reaching Change' (2005) 72 *Defence Counsel Journal* 16; Insurance Council of Australia, *Industry in Focus: Tort Law Reforms a Success Five Years On* (October 2009). For a different view of the effect of reforms on litigation rates see E Wright, 'National Trends in in Personal Injury Litigation: Before and After "Ipp"' (2006) 14 *Torts Law Journal* 233.

prevalent theme in tort law academic writing in Australia has focused on attempting to theorise the relationship between statute and common law in private law.[117] This may signify grudging acceptance rather than enthusiastic approval of the changes but it maintains the centrality of tort law in discussions about compensation for personal injury. The prospect of the abolition of tort law for personal injury claims and its replacement with a no-fault scheme is, in the post-pandemic world, as unlikely as it has ever been. Cane would not be surprised. Perhaps for different reasons, he would agree with Partlett that '[g]narly tort law will continue to exist'[118] precisely because it is a product of a wider world that requires compromise and balance between a host of competing values. Tort reform was about a recalibration of these balances, and, although approaching it differently, Cane shared this understanding of what reform entailed with both James Spigelman and David Ipp, two of leading judicial figures in the reform process. For Cane, 'principles-based' reform left considerable discretion in how the building blocks of tort – protected interests, sanctioned conduct and sanctions – could be put together whilst still remaining tort law.

Whilst Cane's interests have more recently moved away from private law, he has continued to critique formal theories of law, highlighting their incompleteness and arguing that they advocate the theorist's preferred normative theory of private law rather than being based on past or present understandings of the subject.[119] In his last foray into tort law scholarship, the overview text *Key Ideas in Tort Law*,[120] two of his 'key ideas' of tort law are that tort law is political and that tort law 'is here to stay – live with it!'[121] He observed that in the 1970s political debates about personal injury law focused on how to replace tort law but 'now they focus on how to live with it while solving what are considered its most significant problems'.[122] As his writings indicate, for Cane the answers to these problems were no less political in nature than abolition, and law reform through legislation was clearly one, if not the only, appropriate way to reach the kind of pragmatic social consensus on responsibility he saw as being at the heart of tort law. In this way, his contribution to the process of legislative reform through being a member of the Ipp Panel was no more (or less) than a show of fidelity to his long-held academic views.

[117] For recent examples see M Leeming, *The Statutory Foundations of Negligence* (Alexandria, Federation Press, 2019); P Vines and MS Donald (eds), *Statutory Interpretation in Private Law* (Alexandria, Federation Press, 2019).

[118] D Partlett, 'Of Law Reform Lions and the Limits of Tort Reform' (2005) 27 *Sydney Law Review* 417, 442. Compare the similar sentiments of Lord Sumption in relation to the United Kingdom: J Sumption, 'Abolishing Personal Injuries Law: A Project' [2018] *Journal of Personal Injury Law* 1.

[119] P Cane, 'Rights in Private Law' in D Nolan and A Robertson (eds), *Rights and Private Law* (Oxford, Hart Publishing, 2012) ch 2.

[120] P Cane, *Key Ideas in Tort Law* (Oxford, Hart Publishing, 2017). For a detailed discussion of this work see Sugarman (chapter 4).

[121] ibid chs 8, 10.

[122] ibid 106.

14

Philosophical and Judicial Thinking about Moral Concepts: Cane's Critique of Philosophical Method 20 Years On

ANTHONY J CONNOLLY

I. Introduction

In the opening sentence of his 2002 book, *Responsibility in Law and Morality*, Peter Cane states that 'like "right", "duty" and "property", "responsibility" is a fundamental legal concept, a basic building block of legal thought and reasoning'.[1] In the rest of the book he sets out to offer a sustained account of the concept of responsibility from this 'distinctively legal point of view'.[2] The work as a whole comprises an account of that concept of responsibility collectively articulated and utilised by judges in the world's common law – or, in Cane's terms, 'Anglian' – jurisdictions in the course of their judicial practice over centuries.[3] By virtue of the dependency of lawyers and doctrinal legal scholars (including Cane himself) upon such judges for much of their own conceptual vocabulary and theoretical infrastructure, the book is also an account of the concept of responsibility utilised by these other classes of legal thinker. Cane designates the concept in question here as 'the legal concept of responsibility'[4] and spends the greater part of the book unpacking its *content* – that is, what the term 'responsibility' *means*, what the phenomenon of responsibility *is* – for judges, lawyers, and legal scholars within common law jurisdictions.[5]

[1] P Cane, *Responsibility in Law and Morality* (Oxford, Hart Publishing, 2002) 1.

[2] ibid 2.

[3] Cane says, ibid 7, 'The analysis in this book is based on the legal literature of what might be called "Anglian" legal systems – that is, legal systems the conceptual structure of which is derived from that of English law'.

[4] ibid 3.

[5] I don't intend to engage in any detail in this chapter with Cane's account of what this legal concept actually involves, other than to say that it bears a number of important differences from the concept of responsibility posited by analytic moral philosophers. I will have more to say about these differences below. Put very simply, Cane emphasises the *social systemic* nature of responsibility, whilst the philosophers emphasise its nature as a moral quality possessed by *individuals*. See N Levy, 'The Responsibility of Lawyers and the Responsibility of Philosophers' (2004) 29 *Australian Journal of Legal Philosophy* 172, 173.

In addition to engaging in this analytic and descriptive project, Cane also argues in the book that the legal concept of responsibility offers important *general* insights into responsibility – insights which are of theoretical and practical value beyond the legal sphere, beyond the specific adjudicative practice of judges and beyond the legal systems they operate within.

> The conviction that provoked this book was that careful study of the legal concept of responsibility and of the legal practices associated with it could tell us a good deal not only about legal responsibility, but also about responsibility more generally.[6]

This is to say that the legal concept of responsibility, although developed within a legal context, is of *extra-legal* import and usefulness. It has a broader societal role, interacting with – both influencing and being influenced by – concepts of responsibility used within discursive and practical contexts other than law. One such context is the day-to-day moral discourse and practice of ordinary people within those societies Cane speaks to.[7] Responsibility is not just a legal concept; it is also a moral concept used by people to make sense of and regulate their everyday interactions with each other. Cane says,

> I have argued that the relationship between law and morality … is symbiotic. I have suggested that essentially similar criteria of sound reasoning about complex concepts apply in both the moral and the legal domains. By virtue of its institutional resources, law makes a distinctive and important contribution to the development of the rich tapestry of our responsibility concepts and practices. Consequently, the study of responsibility in law is just as indispensable for a thorough understanding of responsibility as is study of moral responsibility. By focusing on responsibility in law, this book offers a contribution to our understanding of responsibility, full stop.[8]

Thus, in the course of pursuing his core legally oriented project, Cane has cause to reflect upon the nature and importance of the concept of responsibility articulated and utilised across a range of *non-legal* discursive and normative contexts within a society such as his, including the context of ordinary everyday moral discourse and practice. More importantly, for my purposes here, one of the non-legal contexts Cane is drawn to discuss in the book is that of contemporary analytic moral philosophy.[9]

This is because a key element of Cane rendering the concept of responsibility he is interested in 'distinctively legal' involves distinguishing it from what he takes to be the *philosophical* concept of responsibility – the concept which operates within the discursive field of analytic moral philosophy. Moral philosophy within the modern academy, like philosophy at large, is made up of numerous strands or schools reflecting different assumptions, methods and traditions. In his engagement with moral philosophy,

[6] Cane (n 1) 3.

[7] That is, those societies in which 'Anglian' law operates. Throughout the book, Cane terms this context 'morality'. Within analytic philosophy it is also referred to as 'folk morality'. Both terms are intended to connote those people within a society who are enculturated into and maintain the dominant worldview or conceptual scheme of that society, moral or otherwise. In this chapter, I will use either term as appropriate. As we shall see below, within pluralistic societies and across societies globally, the existence and criterial nature of a conceptually and cognitively homogenous 'folk' is problematic.

[8] Cane (n 1) 28.

[9] Which, as we shall see, claims to serve as the authoritative interpreter and systematiser of all moral concepts.

Cane's primary focus is the school of Anglophonic, analytic philosophy. This is the school which has come to dominate the philosophy faculties of many, if not most, of the leading universities of the English-speaking world. It is also the school of philosophy which has most influenced the course of Anglian jurisprudence over the course of the twentieth century.[10] An important feature of this school – at least at the time Cane was writing about it in his book – is that philosophers in this school regard their own methodologically distinctive reflections on the nature of responsibility as conceptually and theoretically *authoritative*. Further, philosophers of this school have inferred from this self-regard that the accounts of responsibility offered by non-philosophers – including judges and legal scholars – are conceptually and theoretically *deficient*.[11]

Cane's particular interest in Anglophonic analytic moral philosophy may be explained, then, not merely by its institutional and theoretical proximity to – and, hence, influence upon – his own field of Anglophonic academic legal scholarship, but also by its controversial and highly provocative claim to methodological and, hence, epistemic *primacy* over all other discursive enterprises which purport to know and theorise the content of the concept of responsibility – judicial practice and legal scholarship, included. Cane is provoked to engage with it because it calls into question the very legitimacy of the legal concept of responsibility he sets out to champion in the book.[12]

Cane believes that analytic moral philosophy holds a very dim view of the legal concept of responsibility and of the conceptual engineering practice of judges and other legal thinkers. In this belief, he is not without justification. The analytic moral philosopher, Neil Levy, for example, has said,

> Legal responsibility, the notion(s) of responsibility enshrined in legislation and enforced and interpreted by courts, is regarded by philosophers as a watered-down version of moral responsibility … It is, at best, an attenuated version of responsibility full-blown, diminished by the compromises forced upon it by the practical necessity of assigning blame and imposing sanctions, in a world of imperfect information. At worst, it is downright confused or even immoral, reflecting sectional interests at the expense of morality or forcing together incompatible elements.[13]

Levy went on,

> from [a philosophical] perspective, the responsibility concept of the law is seriously deficient, [and] in multiple ways … Legal responsibility, we might say, is compromised responsibility: whether its failings are avoidable or not, it *falls short* of the highest standards of morality.[14]

Again, Cane is concerned with this particular branch of philosophy because his project in the book is *not merely* to analyse out the content of the legal concept of responsibility as an exercise in doctrinal exegesis, but to argue for the wider value of that concept to his society at large – including, as an element of that society, the academic discipline of

[10] Witness its influence on HLA Hart, for example: HLA Hart, *The Concept of Law* (Oxford, Clarendon Press, 1994).

[11] I term this intellectual self-regard the hegemonic conceptual claim of analytic moral philosophy.

[12] Levy (n 5) 172 says 'one of Cane's central aims is to oppose what he (rightly, in my view) sees as the traditional philosopher's attitude toward legal notions of responsibility'.

[13] ibid.

[14] ibid 173.

philosophy.[15] Such argument demands of him, he thinks, a rebuttal of any serious claim that denies this wider value.

It is important to note that Cane's aim is not to argue for the theoretical *supremacy* of the legal concept of responsibility over that maintained by ordinary people or philosophers – that would be to fall prey to an intellectual hubris akin to that of the philosophers he critiques. He says,

> I expressly reject the idea that if law and morality conflict, law should be considered superior to morality. Given my focus on social practices and the institutional accounts I offer of both law and morality, it would make no sense for me to treat law as the benchmark of responsibility any more than I am inclined to accept that morality fills this role.[16]

Rather, his aim is to argue for an open mind on the question of the legitimacy – the theoretical and practical value – of the conceptual engineering activity of different discursive communities within a society and to recognise, where appropriate, the value of the conceptual output of those communities – not as an article of faith but on the basis of widely acknowledged good reasons for doing so.[17]

And, of course, Cane believes that there *are* good reasons to acknowledge the value of the legal concept of responsibility. Law, Cane says,

> possesses *institutional resources* that enable it to supplement extra-legal responsibility norms and practices, to influence thinking about responsibility outside the law, and to provide a way of managing, if not resolving, extra-legal disagreements about responsibility … By virtue of its institutional characteristics, law makes a distinctive contribution to our responsibility practices; and … for this reason, it deserves careful attention in its own right, and should not be viewed as a distorted reflection of morality.[18]

In arguing that there is no good reason to believe that analytic philosophy should maintain a monopoly over the proper understanding of responsibility or of any other moral phenomenon, Cane reveals himself to be a pluralist about the legitimacy of various of the concepts of responsibility circulating in societies such as his.[19] But he is not a radical relativist about this. Whilst he holds that different concepts of responsibility – that is, concepts operating in different discursive and practical contexts – may meet all reasonable and relevant criteria for coherence, utility and authority within those contexts (and potentially beyond them),[20] he does not believe that every concept of responsibility is as good as any other in any context. He maintains (rightly, in my view) the existence of socially embedded but, nonetheless, legitimate (dare we say, objective?) standards of conceptual suitability for or effectiveness within – and even across – contexts of use.

[15] Cane (n 1) 3: 'The idea is that by starting with a body of legal materials and with the legal version of the complex concept of responsibility, we can add to and enrich analyses of responsibility that more or less ignore the law'.

[16] P Cane, 'Author's Response to the Commentators' (2004) 29 *Australian Journal of Legal Philosophy* 185, 189.

[17] Cane (n 1) 25 says, 'I am suggesting that responsibility might be a heterogeneous, context-specific practice and concept; and that if this is indeed the case, context-specific study of legal responsibility will enrich our understanding of responsibility more generally'.

[18] ibid 3.

[19] ibid 2, 'Responsibility is a term that is used in many different senses, and it is no part of my project to stipulate how it should be used'.

[20] Potentially including, across the whole of a society.

Cane's advocacy of the value of legal concepts and of judicial concept-making involves him over a small but important part of the book in a sustained critique of the indifference – and in some cases, hostility – which he believes analytic philosophy maintains towards such concepts and such practice. This critique takes the dual form of a critique of the very assumptions and methodology which ground the hegemonic claims of analytic moral philosophy, coupled with a largely independent argument for the moral value in general of legal concepts and legal concept-making.

It is the first of these limbs of Cane's critique which serves as my focus in this chapter. My aim in this chapter is to outline and explore the cogency of Cane's critique of the claim of analytic moral philosophy to intellectual primacy in relation to the concept of responsibility – and, by extension, to any moral concept or phenomenon. I do not intend to engage in a detailed evaluation of the plausibility of the legal concept of responsibility articulated by Cane in the book or of the wider value he ascribes to that concept – though I am content to acknowledge here the cogency of Cane's thesis that judicial concept-making on this topic and many others is of theoretical and practical value beyond the bounds of legal practice, broadly construed, extending even to the field of academic philosophy.

More specifically, my focus is Cane's critique of the assumptions and methodology which ground the hegemonic claims of analytic moral philosophy. I want to explore the degree to which his critique of nearly 20 years ago foreshadowed important aspects of the critique of the methodology of analytic philosophy which later emerged within that very school, through the rise of the so-called 'experimental philosophy' movement. Twenty years on, I want to consider whether Cane's relatively circumscribed critique of analytic moral philosophy, offered by him in aid of making room for the legal concept of responsibility, might be supplemented and strengthened by means of newer theoretical resources provided (ironically) by analytic philosophy itself.

A final introductory comment. Notwithstanding this circumscription of my project, I believe that what is at stake in it (and in the original work of Cane which motivates it) is not merely a narrow intellectual 'boundary dispute' between the academic disciplines of philosophy and law, of interest only to a few within those disciplines. It is in part that, admittedly. But it goes beyond that to engage with and illuminate a number of other more general and important issues, such as the nature and sources of a society's shared knowledge of moral phenomena such as responsibility; the identity of legitimate authorities on or guides to such knowledge; and the epistemic and broader cultural roles of agents and institutions such as academic scholars and the judiciary within the kind of society Cane situates himself.

II. Moral Philosophy and Moral Concepts

A. The Hegemonic Conceptual Claim of Science

The starting point for making sense of the claim of analytic moral philosophy to hegemony over the content of moral concepts is the analogous claim of the natural sciences to hegemony over the content of natural world concepts – concepts such as electron, gravity, carbohydrate, respiration, and climate change, for example. Science claims *and is widely admitted to possess* an authority or hegemony in relation to knowledge of and theorising about the phenomena comprising the natural world. It is on this basis that it also claims and is widely admitted to possess an authority or hegemony in relation to knowledge of and theorising about the *content of our concepts* of those natural world phenomena.[21] Let me unpack this a little.

At the heart of science's claim to epistemic hegemony over our concepts of the phenomena of the natural world lie three core and individually necessary assumptions. The first is a *metaphysical* assumption that those phenomena comprising the classes of natural phenomena identified, conceptualised and theorised by science *exist* and have a nature (or set of properties) both individually and as a class, independently of human knowledge of them.[22] This is to say that they exist as a universal matter of fact and that their nature (what they are made of, how they are structured, how they interact with other phenomena) is a universal matter of fact, independent of any human perspective on such facts, including any ethnic, gender-based or other intra-human identity-based perspective.[23]

Further – and very importantly for our later discussion – the categories of phenomena identified by science exist within the lives of all human beings everywhere and have the potential to impact upon those lives, independently of any human identity variables. From the laboratories of MIT to the barrios of La Paz, oxygen, for example, exists and plays the same characteristic physical, chemical, and physiological role in the lives of all people, whether they are aware of it or not.

The second assumption of the natural sciences here is that its agents (scientists) maintain an epistemic status as effective inquirers into the natural world. This status, which is assumed to be based on what science maintains are largely universal human perceptive and cognitive capacities,[24] permits scientists to progressively know and articulate the nature of the things of the natural world. An important corollary of this second assumption is that because scientists and other human agents have the capacity to know of the existence and nature of these things, there are true concepts of these things available to be possessed and potentially known[25] by all cognitively competent human agents.[26]

[21] See K Popper, *The Logic of Scientific Discovery* (London, Hutchinson Press, 1959); G Hempel, *Aspects of Scientific Explanation* (New York, Free Press, 1965); T Kuhn, *The Structure of Scientific Revolutions*, 2nd edn (Chicago, University of Chicago Press, 1970); P Kitcher, *The Advancement of Science* (Oxford, Oxford University Press, 1993).

[22] A realist view of the natural world is the dominant view within the natural sciences. See BC van Frassen, *The Scientific Image* (Oxford, Oxford University Press, 1980); M Devitt, *Realism and Truth* (Oxford, Blackwell, 1991); S Psillos, *Scientific Realism: How Science Tracks Truth* (London, Routledge, 1999).

[23] ibid.

[24] Which are refined by appropriate socialisation into a largely universal folk-science or 'common sense' community, as well as into the universally applicable worldview and methods of the natural sciences themselves.

[25] I am making a distinction here between tacit possession of a concept, on the one hand, and conscious and reflective possession, on the other. It is the latter which is of primary concern in this chapter. One may possess a concept which informs one's actions appropriately without being able to call that concept to mind and articulate its content. Consider, for example, the vast conceptual repertoire tacitly possessed by children, despite their limited ability to explicitly define those concepts, if asked. See, for example, A Gopnik and H Wellman, 'Why the Child's Theory of Mind Really is a Theory' (1992) 7 *Mind and Language* 145.

[26] 'As Joseph Raz puts it [in relation to legal concepts] "Our aim is to understand society and it institutions." Conceptual analysis is simply the primary tool that the Hartian Positivist employs to this end': B Leiter, *Naturalizing Jurisprudence: Essays on American Legal Realism and Naturalism in Legal Philosophy* (Oxford, Oxford University Press, 2007) 66.

Finally, natural science assumes that it exclusively possesses a distinctive and uniquely effective methodology for coming to know the true and comprehensive nature of the phenomena of the natural world and, therefore, the true and comprehensive content of the concepts of natural world phenomena. This methodology works for everyone suitably trained in it. It is effective independently of the cultural identity, gender, or language of its practitioners and it generates knowledge, concepts and theories of the natural world which are universally true or objective.[27] I will term this set of propositions the methodological assumption of natural science.

Very simply, scientific methodology is one in which hypotheses about the way the natural world might be are subject to actual, real world, empirical and experimental testing of their truth or falsity, all against the background of an accumulated commonsense and scientific worldview. Conclusions about the way the world is are generated by this process through a process of reasoning within this worldview. These conclusions may have the effect of generating changes to the scientific understanding of – its concepts and theories of – the natural world and its myriad phenomena.

A conclusion which natural science draws from this third claim is that by virtue of the exclusive epistemic effectiveness of scientific method, as well as inherent epistemic flaws in other (non-scientific) methodologies that seek to know the natural world, these other methodologies and any concepts or theories derived from them are not epistemically legitimate methods, concepts or theories of the natural world. They will not provide humans with optimal knowledge of the things of the natural world. Only science can do that. Consequently, their *concepts* of the things of the natural world will not be as true – or as near the truth – as the concepts of science.

Science justifies its claim to hegemony – and the folk largely admit that hegemony – because the empirical methodology of hypothesising and experimentation which science relies upon has been *seen to work*. It has been acknowledged as a successful methodology for understanding, explaining and guiding intervention in the natural world by the relevant standards of epistemic success maintained by reasonable human agents everywhere, no matter their gender, ethnicity or other non-universal features. This is not to say that science or the general population believe that science presently knows all that there is to know about the natural world or that everything that it presently claims to know is absolutely certain. It is to say that there is nothing *better* than science and its methodology for gaining knowledge of the natural world.

I stated above that because scientists and other human agents have the capacity to know of the existence and nature of the phenomena and classes of phenomena of the natural world, there are true concepts of these things available to be possessed (or known) by all cognitively competent human agents. Because I should not presume the familiarity of readers with relevant philosophical and psychological literature and because it is central to understanding both the claims of analytic moral philosophy and those of Cane himself, let me elaborate a little here on this relationship between our knowledge of things and our concepts of things.

[27] Popper (n 21); A Chalmers, *What is This Thing Called Science?* (Brisbane, University of Queensland Press, 1976); S Gimbel, *Exploring the Scientific Method* (Chicago, University of Chicago Press, 2011).

According to our most credible current theories of how the human mind works,[28] knowledge of a phenomenon entails possession of a concept of that phenomenon. Concepts are among the building blocks of human mental states, including our states of knowing about the world.[29] Natural world concepts serve as the mental basis of all our knowledge of and capacity to practically engage with the things of the natural world.[30] A concept of some particular phenomenon may be conceived of as encapsulating an agent's (or, collectively, an institution's) knowledge of that phenomenon.[31] To possess a concept of a phenomenon is to know something about that phenomenon and to know something about a phenomenon is to possess a concept of that phenomenon.

This 'something about' a phenomenon which a concept encapsulates is termed the *content* of that concept. To possess a simple concept of apple is to know, for example, that an apple is a spherical, edible, red/yellow/green fruit. This set of properties – rendered explicit by a definition of the term apple or theory of the category apples – comprises the content of this simple concept of apple.[32] And so, to possess a concept of a thing is to know either explicitly or tacitly the content of that concept (the propositions and component concepts which make up that concept) and to be able to explicate that content by means of something like a definition or theory.[33] For *theoretical* discourses such as the natural sciences, concept possession *entails* explicit and communicable knowledge of the content of that concept.[34]

Of course, whether the content of a given concept of a thing truly or completely describes the nature of that thing is a contingent matter. People, groups of people, and even scientists as a cohort have possessed and may presently possess concepts that although meeting acceptable standards of theoretical and practical legitimacy, only *partially* describe relevant phenomena or contain relatively circumscribed elements of error or falsehood.[35]

[28] Here I draw on the work of contemporary philosophers, psychologists, and cognitive scientists such as Susan Carey, Eric Margolis, Jesse Prinz, and Edouard Machery. See S Carey, *The Origin of Concepts* (Oxford, Oxford University Press, 2009); JJ Prinz, *Furnishing the Mind: Concepts and Their Perceptual Basis* (Cambridge, MIT Press, 2004); E Machery, *Doing Without Concepts* (Oxford, Oxford University Press, 2009); and the excellent papers, including by Margolis, in E Margolis and S Laurence (eds), *Concepts: Core Readings* (Cambridge, MIT Press, 1999).

[29] Carey (n 28) 5; Margolis and Laurence (n 28) ch 1; D Braddon-Mitchell and F Jackson, *Philosophy of Mind and Cognition* (Oxford, Blackwell Publishers, 1996), chs 11 and 14.

[30] ibid.

[31] This is the so-called 'theory-theory' of concepts. See Margolis and Laurence (n 28) ch 1; G Botterill and P Carruthers, *The Philosophy of Psychology* (Cambridge, Cambridge University Press, 1999) ch 4.

[32] As is evident here, the content of a concept is made up of other concepts, with their own contents. This reflects the complex, aggregative and holistically interrelated nature of concepts, conceptual schemes and worldviews – something we do not have to engage with here, thankfully. See Carey (n 28); J Fodor and E Lepore, *Holism: A Shopper's Guide* (Oxford, Blackwell Publisher, 1992).

[33] Susan Carey argues that concepts can best be understood as theories (Carey (n 28) chs 12 and 13). See also Margolis and Laurence, *Concepts* (n 28) 43–47. Though I rely on a theory-based account of concepts here, it is important to note that it is not without its critics within the philosophical and scientific literature. See Margolis and Laurence (n 28) for an overview of alternative approaches to concepts on offer at present.

[34] Scientists are charged not merely to *understand* the natural world but to *communicate* that understanding to each other and to their wider society.

[35] Too much of which would justify a finding that the person or persons in question don't actually possess the concept in question at all.

B. The Hegemonic Conceptual Claim of Analytic Moral Philosophy

By virtue of its claim to know the natural world and possess the best concepts of that world presently available to humans, science claims and is widely admitted to maintain an exclusive authority in relation to the contents of *natural world* concepts. Analytic moral philosophy justifies its claim to hegemony over the content of *moral* concepts such as responsibility on the grounds that its systematic, dialectic and reason-based engagement with and inquiry into the moral sphere (including into the phenomenon of responsibility) resembles in epistemically sufficient respects the engagement and inquiry of science into the natural world. Because the moral sphere of things does not exist in the same way that natural phenomena exist – its ontological status is different from that of, say, chemical or biological phenomena[36] – it is not knowable in exactly the same way as the natural sphere is knowable by natural science.[37] It is knowable by an introspective and non-empirical means whose differences from empirical enquiry reflect the metaphysical differences between moral and natural phenomena.[38]

Like the natural sciences, the claim of analytic moral philosophy to epistemic hegemony over our moral concepts may be understood as resting upon three assumptions analogous to those relied upon by science. The first is a *metaphysical* assumption that moral phenomena such as responsibility *exist* in some ontologically legitimate sense and have a nature (a set of properties) both individually and as a class, independently of human knowledge of them.[39] This is to say that they *exist* – somehow, somewhere – as a universal matter of fact and that their *nature* is a universal matter of fact, independent of the perspective on that nature held by any ethnic, gender-based or other intra-human identity-based human sub-group.[40] For example, many contemporary naturalistic moral philosophers seek to explain the existence of moral phenomena by identifying some constellation of social practice, performed by concrete human beings, upon which moral phenomena supervene or otherwise find embodiment in the world.[41]

Likewise – and here things get more controversial – some significant portion of analytic moral philosophers and the ones Cane is most centrally engaged with in the book – maintain that the categories of at least some of the moral phenomena identified

[36] Crucially here, unlike chemical phenomena, for example, whose existence does not depend on human thought and action to be instantiated in the world, moral phenomena such as responsibility arguably *do* so depend.

[37] This explains the historical resistance of the natural sciences to make moral phenomena their subject matter – although this has been changing over the past few decades. See R Joyce, *The Evolution of Morality* (Cambridge, MIT Press, 2006); W Sinnott-Armstrong (ed), *Moral Psychology, Volume 3 The Neuroscience of Morality: Emotion, Brain Disorders, and Development* (Cambridge, MIT Press, 2008).

[38] This is so, no matter which metaphysics of morality a philosopher commits to. No contemporary moral philosopher – whether supernaturalist or naturalist – conceives of moral phenomena as metaphysically *identical* to the natural phenomena studied by the natural sciences.

[39] Hart (n 10); DO Brink, *Moral Realism and the Foundations of Ethics* (Cambridge, Cambridge University Press, 1989).

[40] G Harman, *Moral Relativism and Moral Objectivity* (Oxford, Blackwell Publishers, 1996).

[41] See, for example, Hart's naturalistic attempt to ground the ontology of both morality and law in social rules: Hart (n 10). See also, E Ullmann-Margalit, *The Emergence of Norms* (Oxford, Clarendon Press, 1977); G Brennan et al, *Explaining Norms* (Oxford, Oxford University Press, 2013).

by analytic moral philosophy not only *exist* as a general matter of fact within the lives of *some or other* group of people but, in fact, hold sway within the societies and individual moral lives of *all people everywhere*. Responsibility is one of these moral categories. Responsibility – like moral goodness, for many – informs human morality *universally* in the same way that oxygen 'informs' the *physical* being of humans universally. According to this view, it is not the case that one kind of moral responsibility operates within society A and an entirely different kind of moral responsibility operates within society B. The analytic moral philosophers in question are neither moral relativists *nor* moral pluralists in this regard. There is a single class of phenomena termed 'responsibility' which universally applies to the lives of all people. That class of things comprises the subject matter analytic moral philosophy seeks to understand and theorise.[42]

This meta-consensus obtains despite some disagreement between schools of moral philosophy as to the precise *mode* of existence of these phenomena. Views here range from relatively marginal supernaturalist accounts which argue that moral phenomena – the good, justice, responsibility, and so on – exist within a radically different ontological space than that with which science is concerned, to more widely held naturalistic accounts which argue that moral phenomena are ultimately rooted in phenomena – universal aspects of the thought and practice of concrete human beings, for example – which are not independent of the natural world science is concerned with and which can be understood and *ultimately* explained with reference to that world as theorised by science.[43]

As with natural phenomena, because analytic moral philosophers and other human agents possess a capacity to know of the existence and nature of moral phenomena, there are true *concepts* of such phenomena available to be possessed and potentially known by all cognitively competent human agents. The contents of these true concepts describe the properties of those phenomena referred to by those concepts. As mentioned above, the content of a true concept of a thing comprises a kind of theory of the nature of that thing. Building on this, the *second* assumption of analytic moral philosophy is that its agents – in this case, philosophers – maintain an *epistemic status* which, in turn, grounds their status as effective inquirers into the phenomena and concepts of the moral world. In this case, this status is assumed to be based not on largely universal human *perceptive* capacities but on largely universal human *introspective* capacities to come to know the true content of the concepts of moral phenomena.[44] Analytic moral philosophers hold themselves out to be as universally representative of human enquirers as the practitioners of the natural sciences are.

[42] This view is expressed in Levy's statement on behalf of analytic moral philosophy that 'philosophers want to discover the *truth* about responsibility: what it is and whether we have it'. Truth is, by its very nature, universal in application for these philosophers. The 'we' here is everyone: Levy (n 5) 173.

[43] The Catholic legal philosopher, J Finnis, *Natural Law and Natural Rights* (Oxford, Clarendon Press, 1980) and the Kantian moral philosopher Christine Korsgaard, *The Sources of Normativity* (Cambridge, Cambridge University Press, 1996) tend towards this non-naturalist end of the spectrum. Hart (n 10) and F Jackson, *From Metaphysics to Ethics: A Defence of Conceptual Analysis* (Oxford, Oxford University Press, 1998) are examples of a more naturalistic approach.

[44] Again, this universal conceptual capacity is refined in practice by socialisation into a largely universal folk-moral community. See fn 24 above.

In pursuing a critique of HLA Hart's similarly analytic approach to the concept of law, the legal philosopher Ian P Farrell calls out this assumption, saying that,

> in developing his theory of the concept of law, Hart makes numerous assertions regarding the intuitions of the educated man. In doing so, he appears to simply assume that all educated persons share his intuitions. And not just all well-educated, English men: Hart's assertion of the generality of the concept of law entails that all members of any society with a modem legal system must share Hart's relevant linguistic intuitions.[45]

Third, analytic moral philosophy holds to a *methodological* assumption that it exclusively possesses a distinctive and uniquely effective methodology for coming to know the true and comprehensive nature of moral phenomena and the true and comprehensive content of moral concepts.[46] This methodology is *conceptual analysis*. This method is said to be effective for any person of basic cognitive competence who is suitably trained in it – again, independently of the cultural identity, gender, or language of its practitioners. Like scientific method, the method applied by analytic moral philosophy is alleged to generate concepts and associated theories of moral phenomena which are universally true or objective matters of fact.[47] It proceeds on the basis of the assumption referred to above that a true concept of a thing truly describes that thing and that in coming to know the content of such a concept through its analysis, one comes to obtain a true understanding and theory of that thing.[48]

Put simply, the methodology of conceptual analysis comprises four phases. The first phase is the introspective calling to mind of the concept in question – say, the concept of responsibility – as the analyst in question conceives it. This operative concept may be a 'raw' folk concept or a previously analysed version of a folk concept (philosophers have been analysing folk concepts for a very long time). This preliminary stage is based

[45] I Farrell, 'HLA Hart and the Methodology of Jurisprudence' (2006) 84 *Texas Law Review* 983, 1008. Farrell goes on, prophetically, adding 'If Hart's views prove not to be representative to this extent, his generality claim would be directly rebutted': ibid.

[46] Jackson (n 43) 42, calls this immodest conceptual analysis in recognition of its epistemic ambitions. Leiter and Langolais say 'that it aims to deliver knowledge about the actual nature of its subject-matter by consulting intuitions about how the concept extends to possible cases (the contrast is with conceptual analysis that aims to determine to what the concept refers, while allowing that the sciences will answer the question about the actual character of the referent, if there is one)': B Leiter and A Langlinais, 'The Methodology of Legal Philosophy' (University of Chicago Public Law & Legal Theory Working Paper No 407, 2012) 8–9.

[47] Farrell (n 45) 997. In discussing the content of the concept of law (understood in this context in terms of a definition), Hart said 'In searching for and finding such definitions we are looking not merely at words … but also at the realities we use words to talk about. We are using a sharpened awareness of words to sharpen our perception of the phenomena': Hart (n 10) 14. On this, Leiter and Langlinais say in 'Methodology' (n 46) 4–5, '[Hart's] method does reflect the overall *spirit* of ordinary language philosophy: that we can gain philosophical insight about some phenomenon by attending to the conceptual distinctions we use to talk and think about it … Hart was convinced that it is especially true of social phenomena like law that we can employ *linguistic analysis* to understand their nature'. They go on at 9 'it is still the case that on Hart's theory we can derive knowledge about the actual nature of law by analyzing our shared concept of it as manifest in ordinary language'.

[48] Farrell (n 45) 998. Cane says 'the assumption underlying philosophical appeals to common sense [the philosophers calling up of folk concepts] is that widely-held ideas about responsibility, for instance, are likely to contain more than a grain of "truth" about the nature of responsibility': Cane (n 16) 18.

on an assumption that the philosopher analyst in question *is able* to call to mind some satisfactory version of the concept in question by virtue of their own enculturation into the conceptual scheme of the folk or analytic philosophy. Here the epistemic capacity assumption referred to above comes into play.

The second phase of conceptual analysis involves the introspective positing of an hypothetical scenario relating to or involving the concept in question (a so-called thought experiment).[49] Such scenarios are intended and designed to challenge the coherence or credibility of the content ascribed to the concept in question in a manner akin to the way scientific experiments are intended and designed to challenge the coherence or credibility of a prevailing scientific concept or theory.

The third phase involves the introspective drawing of conclusions about the content of the concept in question on the basis of *intuitions* arising out of the application of the concept within such scenarios.[50] Intuitions are thought to play a role similar to that played by theoretically informed *perceptions* within certain (simple) scientific experimental contexts. Like the perceptions of scientists, the intuitions of a philosopher are assumed to reflect those *all* reasonable and otherwise competent persons would maintain in relation to the thought experiment in question.[51] Farrell describes this phase as follows,

> by examining our intuitions about clear cases, the underlying structure of the concept is revealed: by making explicit what is tacit in ordinary usage of the term, conceptual analysts create a theory of X … we are then able to apply this theory to attain answers in cases which were previously uncertain.[52]

Finally, if justified by the preceding three steps, what follows is the introspective refining of the content of the concept in question, with attendant improvement of our knowledge and theory of the phenomenon referred to by the concept.[53] The result of this process is, it is claimed, the generation of truer and more comprehensive moral concepts than those which informed the start of the process and which were possessed previously by the folk and other philosophers. This phase of the analysis resembles the way science generates truer and more comprehensive natural world concepts than those possessed by the folk and earlier science. Just as scientific method can generate conceptual content – and even concepts the folk or earlier science do not possess – so too, analytic moral philosophy claims to be able to generate not just refined content for existing moral concepts but new moral concepts the folk may not yet possess.

A brief account of the most notorious modern example of the application of conceptual analysis – the so-called Gettier problem – will serve us well in making quick sense of it.[54] This case involved the conceptual analysis of the concept of 'knowledge' by

[49] Jackson (n 43) ch 2.

[50] Leiter defines conceptual analysis as the 'analysis of concepts via appeals to intuitions … about possible cases to determine the extension [content] of those concepts': Leiter (n 26) 183. In Jackson's terms, conceptual analysis comprises 'the method of possible cases' which produces 'an account of the concept that squares with our clear intuitions about the concept': Jackson (n 43) 28.

[51] Levy (n 5) 175 says, 'both law and moral philosophy take as their point of departure the common-sense intuitions which *we all share*, and attempt to systematize them, throwing out those which cannot fit into a reasonably coherent whole'.

[52] Farrell (n 45) 998–99.

[53] Jackson (n 43) ch 2.

[54] EL Gettier, 'Is Justified True Belief Knowledge?' (1963) 23 *Analysis* 121.

the American philosopher Edmund Gettier in 1963. Prior to Gettier's analysis, it was widely thought by analytic philosophers that the content of the concept 'knowledge' was adequately described by the definition 'justified true belief'. Calling to mind this version of the concept and subjecting it to conceptual analysis, Gettier devised two hypothetical scenarios (involving a putative human knower and a surrounding set of facts) in which the ascription of justified true belief to the agent in question clearly obtained but to whom the ascription of 'knowledge' *intuitively* did not. That is, although it was clear in Gettier's scenarios that the agents had justified true belief about the facts in question, Gettier's intuition (and that of many analytic philosophers, subsequently) was that the agents in those scenarios could not properly be said to *know* those facts. The concept of knowledge just did not seem to apply to the imaginary agents in question. Consequently, a definition more complex and comprehensive than mere justified true belief was needed to render a more correct concept of 'knowledge': a concept which would not only cover existing accepted cases of knowledge but also the hypothetical case imagined here. This was something Gettier and others subsequently sought to provide.[55] The outcome of this process was, for many analytic philosophers, a modified and, arguably, better concept of knowledge, one which continues to inform debates in epistemology today.

It is important to note that although the process of conceptual analysis bears *some* resemblance to that of scientific method – for example, both involve the devising of hypotheticals and the subsequent testing of these by reference to some standard – the *nature* of that testing (sensory cum empirical engagement in the case of science, introspective intuition in the case of analytic philosophy) differs markedly. Nonetheless, analytic moral philosophers claim that their testing and their results are as universally acceptable to any human thinker who might turn their attention to these things as the testing and results of science.

It is on this basis that analytic moral philosophy also mimics the scientific claim that its own distinctive method is *exclusively* effective in coming to know the true nature and concepts of its subject matter, morality. Consequently, attempts by other disciplines of inquiry to know these things by non-analytic methods – judicial practice included – cannot and will not be as effective in this regard as analytic moral philosophy. These other disciplines, their methods, and any concepts or theories that flow from the application of those methods are not epistemically legitimate. Non-analytic methods cannot and will not provide humans with optimal knowledge of and concepts of moral phenomena. Only analytic moral philosophy can do that.[56]

In an article written by Cane shortly after the publication of the book, he reflected on the objects of analytic moral philosophy, saying that the basic position of analytic moral philosophers such as Levy,

> is that the 'pure', 'actual' truth about responsibility is available to be discovered; that such truth is not to be found in the law; that philosophers are concerned to find such truth, and that the methods of philosophy … will lead us to the truth about responsibility.[57]

[55] See Q Smith (ed), *Epistemology: New Essays* (Oxford: Oxford University Press, 2008).
[56] T Williamson, *The Philosophy of Philosophy* (Oxford, Blackwell Publishing, 2007).
[57] Cane (n 16) 189.

Levy in his published reply to Cane's charge, agreed with Cane's characterisation of the analytic project, saying 'To [the] compromised legal version of responsibility, philosophers oppose their own, purified, notion: responsibility as it actually is, its truth revealed'.[58]

One last point here to keep in mind before we move on to explore the critique of the claim of analytic moral philosophy to authority in the moral realm, is that an important component of science's justification of its hegemonic epistemic and conceptual claims is that these claims are widely and patently accepted by and deferred to by experts and by the folk. An important indicator of the acceptance by ordinary people of science's conceptual authority is the demonstrable influence which advances in scientific knowledge have had, historically, on folk concepts of the natural world – witness, for example, the historical development of the folk concept of water to include what was originally specialised scientific content, such as that relating to its molecular structure, H_2O. The folk's deference to science is demonstrated by the folk's appropriation of elements of scientific concepts for the folk's own purposes and projects.

As should be apparent to readers, this is not the case with the moral concepts of analytic moral philosophy.[59] Its authority in the wider realms of moral thought and practice – including within the legal realm – is nowhere near that of science. Its influence on folk morality and its concepts appears just as limited. In justifying its hegemonic claims, then, analytic philosophy appears to lack an important ground. One reason for this may be a congenital weakness in the integrity of the method and assumptions upon which its claim to epistemic supremacy in this sphere is founded – a weakness Cane is alert to in his book. Let me explore this now.

III. The Critique of the Hegemonic Conceptual Claim of Analytic Moral Philosophy

A. Cane's Critique

In order to identify and 'call out' its weakness and thereby rebuff the condescension it displays towards legal thought, Cane engages in a relatively circumscribed critique of the aforementioned assumptions of analytic moral philosophy. To reiterate, calling that philosophy's assumptions into question puts pressure on the hegemonic claim built on those assumptions. And to the extent that the hegemonic claim of that philosophy are weakened, Cane's epistemic legitimacy claim on behalf of judicial thought in the moral sphere is offered more opportunity to prevail.

Of course, taking advantage of that opportunity requires the intrinsic value of judicial thought about responsibility and other moral matters to be independently

[58] Levy (n 5) 173.

[59] The legal philosopher Brian Leiter said in a 2007 interview, 'Moral philosophy is almost wholly irrelevant to how people conduct their lives': B Leiter, 'Interview About Legal Philosophy (The University of Texas School of Law Public Law and Legal Theory Research Paper No 120 May 2007) 6.

argued for. Weaknesses in philosophy's claim do not *entail* any correlative strength in law's claim. As I mentioned, earlier, however, that part of Cane's project – the positive part – is not my concern here.[60] I am concerned in this chapter with the negative part of Cane's project – with his critique of the assumptions of analytic philosophy and with the resonances that exist between his critique and that of experimental philosophy.

i. Cane on the Metaphysics of Moral Phenomena and Concepts

Like the analytic philosophers he is concerned with, Cane holds that moral phenomena such as responsibility *exist* in some ontologically legitimate sense. Throughout the book he refers to a phenomenon known as 'responsibility' and speaks of the important role it plays within Anglian legal systems and within their surrounding societies. For Cane, this thing we refer to as responsibility *makes a difference* in the world and in the lives of individuals. Its concrete influence is one useful indicator of its ontological status.[61] On the question of *how* moral phenomena exist – their *mode* of existence[62] – Cane tends toward a social practice account along lines argued by theorists such as HLA Hart and John Searle.[63] 'My main concern', he says early on in the book, 'is with responsibility understood as a set of social practices'.[64] Because a social practice account of morality is maintained by many of the philosophers Cane engages with, however, no significant ground of disagreement on this particular point between Cane and those philosophers arises.[65]

Where there *is* disagreement, though, is in relation to the philosophical claim that the *one same* version and concept of responsibility (and, by inference, of other moral phenomena) holds a place in and informs the moral lives of all people *universally*. Cane's view is that this should not be assumed. Rather, whether and to what extent a particular version or concept of a moral phenomenon obtains in any or all societies or within any or all genders, ethnicities, classes and so on within the one society, is a question that needs to be determined by proper sociological enquiry. It should not be taken as a given on philosophical cum ideological grounds, as some analytic moral philosophers take it.[66]

Cane is quite comfortable with the idea that moral phenomena such as responsibility can manifest in different varieties within different social contexts, social groups, and societies.[67] These varieties can apply and be recognised in different circumstances.

[60] As has been mentioned, Cane's positive case for the legitimacy of the legal concept of responsibility is, in fact, well made in the book.

[61] J Poland, *Physicalism: The Philosophical Foundations* (Oxford, Clarendon Press, 1994) 263–64.

[62] Platonically supernatural or socially natural, for example.

[63] Hart (n 10); J Searle, *The Construction of Social Reality* (New York, The Free Press, 1995). Cane makes reference to Searle in *Responsibility* (n 1) 10, 101.

[64] Cane (n 1) 6.

[65] Though Cane in the book does appear to accuse analytic moral philosophers in general of Kantian supernaturalism, see ibid 23.

[66] Cane (n 16) 189–90.

[67] '[L]egal responsibility can fruitfully be understood as a set of social practices serving a number of social functions': Cane (n 1) 3. Later he says 'much can be gained by thinking about responsibility in relation to a particular society and a particular time, and in relation to particular social activities and problems, and particular value systems': Cane (n 1) 280.

They can demand different things from people in the different circumstances they apply in. He says,

> We should allow of the possibility that the language of 'responsibility' does not mark a homogeneous practice and concept best illuminated by context-indeterminate reflection, but rather that it marks a variegated and heterogeneous set of practices and concepts which can only be fully understood by context-determinate analyses.[68]
>
> I recommend thinking about responsibility *functionally*. Both within the law and outside it, concepts and principles of responsibility do not exist (purely) for their own sake but as part of a complex set of practices of taking responsibility and holding responsible.[69]

As has been mentioned, Cane is a moral pluralist – or, at the very least, a responsibility pluralist – not as an a priori matter but as a contingent empirical cum interpretive matter, resulting from his own research. Contrary to the abovementioned assumption of the analytic moral philosophers, Cane holds that it *may be* the case that one kind or notion of moral responsibility operates within society A and a different kind or notion of moral responsibility operates within society B. In such cases, both phenomena may properly be conceived of as instances of responsibility, not by virtue of them possessing identical sets of necessary and sufficient properties (as analytic philosophers would have it) but by possessing sufficient overlapping similarities or some other features which would ground a reasonable categorisation of them as *varieties of the same thing*:[70]

> much philosophical analysis purports to provide a general or abstract account of a concept such as responsibility without reference to any particular social group, any particular point in time, or any particular set of human values or purposes. The temporal, human and social context of much philosophical analysis is left more or less indeterminate.[71]

Like common law judges – and like the experimental philosophers who were to emerge later – Cane is a bottom-up concept-builder who starts with generally acknowledged actual instances of the thing referred to and constructs its concept from there, with attention to any significant overlaps of properties, for example, amongst those various actual instances. He is not an analytic essentialist who starts with a putative truth and seeks to merely refine it in a top-down manner.[72]

> we should be wary of claims to general validity made for analyses of complex concepts that are the result of *acontextual reflection*. The concept of responsibility, for instance, is used in various social contexts. It may be that there are some characteristics common to all of these usages which, in that sense, might be called 'acontextual'. But in order to identify such common characteristics, it would first be necessary to reflect on responsibility in its various contexts.

[68] Cane (n 1) 25. Levy agrees with this characterisation of Cane's metaphysics, saying that for Cane, 'responsibility is a human concept, and as such reflects the untidy soil out of which it grows. It is born out of responsibility practices, a heterogeneous and variegated lot, and therefore the complexity, the internal tensions, which philosophers deride in the legal version, are native to it': Levy (n 5) 172.

[69] Cane (n 1) 281.

[70] On this point further resonances between Cane's work and experimental philosophy start to come into focus.

[71] Cane (n 1) 22.

[72] J Dickson, *Evaluation and Legal Theory* (Oxford, Hart Publishers, 2001) 17–18; SJ Shapiro, *Legality* (Cambridge, Belknap Press, 2011) ch 1.

> And, of course, it is only by contextual reflection on a concept such as responsibility that we could identify context-specific usages and practices.[73] (emphasis added)

Cane admits that *both* the individual agency-based concept of responsibility maintained by analytic moral philosophers and the social systemic and relational concept of responsibility maintained by Anglian judges are recognisably concepts of the one category, *responsibility*. They differ in referring to and describing responsibility as it arises or is applied in different contexts – the philosophical and the legal, for instance.

Philosophical thinking about responsibility, Cane says,

> implies that if we look hard and long enough, we will discover 'the truth' about what it means to be responsible and about what our responsibilities are. The recommendation to think about responsibility socially does not involve a rejection of this view, or an assertion that study of social practice can tell us all there is to know about responsibility. I am agnostic about this. My view is simply that in the absence of agreement as to what the truth about responsibility is, social practice provides us with an extensive and extremely rich data set about responsibility. By observing social responsibility practices, we are able to explore aspects of responsibility (such as sanctions) which rarely, if ever, receive detailed consideration in the methodologically [analytic] literature.[74]

Both the philosophical and the legal concepts are recognisably concepts of responsibility. Cane's beef with the philosophers is that they deny this and claim that their version of it is the only proper version:

> It is not part of my argument that there are no ultimate responsibility values, no 'truth' about what it means to be responsible and about what our responsibilities are. Nor is it part of my argument that morality does not embody such truths. Rather, my argument is that in the absence of agreement about what moral responsibility is and what our moral responsibilities are, it is not sensible to treat the relationship between morality and law as that of critical standard to conventional practice, or to assume that when the law clashes with moral views about responsibility, the truth must lie in the moral [philosophical] as opposed to the legal position.[75]

To the extent that Cane thinks the judicial concept of responsibility is of relevance to thought and practice beyond that operative within Anglian law, it is only to the wider society or societies within which Anglian legal systems operate that this relevance extends. Cane makes no claim to universality in relation to the application or relevance of the legal concept of responsibility he articulates. He says,

> In contrast to the modernist [analytic] approach to responsibility, my analysis is both contextual and concrete. It is rooted in and based on a specific body of literature, and that literature is the product of an identified set of social practices. These practices have an identifiable cultural and temporal context, and they perform social functions the general identity of which is a matter of wide agreement, even if the details are contested.[76]

[73] Cane (n 1) 24.

[74] ibid 279. Cane has an unfortunate though occasional tendency in the book to use the term 'naturalistic' to refer to what is properly termed rationalistic or a priorist. The paragraph quoted here is a case in point. It is Cane's methodology which is naturalistic, not that of his philosophical adversaries.

[75] Cane (n 1) 281.

[76] ibid 24.

ii. Cane on the Methodology of Analytic Moral Philosophy

Having committed himself to a naturalistic[77] account of responsibility and other elements of morality, Cane pursues his critique of conceptual analysis within the overarching frame of a relatively standard naturalistic suspicion of non-naturalistic, non-empirical methods for knowing these things. Like many empiricists and naturalists before him, Cane is instinctively wary of the introspective, a priorist and 'armchair' quality of conceptual analysis, echoing, on occasion, classic empiricist and naturalist dismissals of the epistemic pretensions of philosophical rationalists such as Kant, for example.[78] Echoing the Canadian legal philosopher Stefan Sciaraffa's worries in relation to the Hartian analysis of the concept of law, Cane worries that moral philosophy's theoretical ambition outstrips its methodological warrant.[79] More specifically, however, Cane offers reasons to suspect the epistemic effectiveness of each of the four phases of conceptual analysis discussed earlier.

It is because Cane conceives of the nature of moral phenomena such as responsibility in the way he does – socially, functionally, multiply – that he is led to an initial scepticism about the epistemic integrity of any theoretic methodology founded on a conception of such phenomena as singular, monolithic, and universally operative. Unlike the categories of natural phenomena identified by science which *do* have this latter quality – electrons, for example, are a singular natural kind which obtains everywhere and at all times in the singular way science conceptualises them – the categories of moral phenomena *do not* and are not, therefore, available to being known by an epistemic method which (like that of science) assumes that they do. Methodology maps onto metaphysics.[80]

In relation, then, to the *concept positing phase* of analysis, Cane challenges *the very idea* of there being a single and universally applicable concept of responsibility (or potentially, of any other kind of moral phenomenon) to be called up and subject to analysis by an analyst. Certainly, an analyst would be able to call up one or more of the *various* responsibility concepts that are maintained by people within the analyst's own conceptual or linguistic community – there is nothing problematic in this, for Cane. Indeed, the common law judges he discusses do it all the time. But to think that any such concept will serve as the ground of a *universally true* theory of responsibility per se is unjustified – at least on Cane's metaphysics of moral phenomena and moral concepts. Likewise, it is not credible to imagine that any given analyst will have introspective access to other socially embedded concepts of responsibility which lie outside their own experience or knowledge.

It is at this point that Cane's position on the second (epistemic status) assumption of analytic moral philosophy becomes apparent. He does not deny that philosophers

[77] Though recall the point I made in fn 74.

[78] In addition to using the language of *a priorist* rationalism to describe his adversaries, Cane also makes occasional, mildly pejorative mention of Kant in the book and in his later response piece. See Cane (n 1) 23 and Cane (n 16) 190, for example.

[79] S Sciaraffa, 'Hermeneutic Concepts and Immodest Conceptual Analysis of the Law' (2010) 10 *Newsletter of the American Philosophical Association* 18, 19–20.

[80] See my argument for this proposition in AJ Connolly, *Cultural Difference on Trial: The Nature and Limits of Judicial Understanding* (Abingdon, Routledge, 2010) ch 1.

possess a universally human capacity to introspectively call concepts to mind and come to know their contents – including concepts of responsibility. But he does deny that any concept they might call to mind as generic introspectors is necessarily universal in its possession or application and that, as a result, those analysts constitute universally representative enquirers into morality and moral concepts. The truth about responsibility in all contexts and at all times is not to be found through the analysis of any one (and necessarily) *context-dependent* concept of responsibility.

In a similar fashion, Cane queries the epistemic integrity of the *hypothetical scenario* phase of conceptual analysis on the basis of his alternative and pluralistic metaphysics of morality and its concepts. He says,

> much philosophical analysis purports to provide a general or abstract account of a concept such as responsibility without reference to any particular social group, any particular point in time, or any particular set of human values or purposes. The temporal, human and social context of much philosophical analysis is left more or less indeterminate.[81]
>
> This characteristic of philosophical analysis finds its most dramatic expression in the so-called 'thought experiment'. Thought experiments are the philosophical analogue of controlled scientific laboratory experiments. They are hypothetical fact situations stripped of any extraneous features that might get in the way of or confuse the analysis of the particular point the philosopher is seeking to establish. For this reason, the situations imagined in thought experiments are often deliberately bizarre and unreal; and like the economists' assumption of perfect rationality, this may raise questions about the validity, outside the precise frame of the analysis itself, of any conclusions drawn by the analyst.[82]

It is because conceptual analysis does not attend to the extraneous contextual features of responsibility and other moral phenomena – a crucial part of Cane's metaphysical picture of morality – that thought experiments stripped of attention to these things are likely to founder.

Likewise, with his criticism of the *intuition application phase* of analysis. In his debate with the analytic moral philosopher Neil Levy on Levy's querying of the extent to which philosophical or legal concepts of responsibility better capture 'our intuitions' on responsibility, Cane queried whether analytic philosophers had an adequate grasp of what they actually meant by the term 'intuitions'.[83] He continued,

> More importantly, I do not understand, and Neil does not explain, the relationship between 'our intuitions' and the 'truth' about responsibility. What reason is there to think that the procedure (which Neil recommends) of getting our 'intuitions' about responsibility into 'wide reflective equilibrium' [via the process of analysis] will show us the pure and actual truth about responsibility as opposed, for instance, to a normatively attractive account of responsibility?[84]

The key weakness of Cane's critique of conceptual analysis as a legitimate epistemic method in the moral sphere is that it rests upon a pluralistic metaphysics of morality and its concepts which his adversaries would reject. Though clearly and repeatedly

[81] Cane (n 1) 22.
[82] ibid.
[83] Cane (n 16) 190.
[84] ibid.

articulated, a satisfactory and detailed *justification* of that metaphysics is not provided by Cane in the book – and why should it be, given his overarching legal exegetical aims? In any event, the justification of any metaphysics is notoriously difficult, no matter how much space one devotes to it. The result, though, is that the strength of Cane's critique of conceptual analysis remains provisional and incompletely persuasive. If one does not buy into Cane's pluralistic metaphysics of morality, one is unlikely to be persuaded by his particular critique of analytic philosophy's method – and, by extension, unlikely to be persuaded by his attempt to rebut that philosophy's claim to hegemony.

Cane's critique of analytic moral philosophy is significant but spare. It calls for further support and supplementation. Quite fortuitously, experimental philosophy has emerged and provides just that. Let me turn to it now.

B. The Critique of Experimental Philosophy

i. *What is Experimental Philosophy?*[85]

According to philosophical naturalism, the world – all that exists, as a matter of fact – is ultimately comprised of (or, in philosophical terms, *realised by*) natural phenomena, those phenomena which find a place in the generally accepted theories of the natural sciences – the most basic of which is physics.[86] This is not to say that the higher-order phenomena of mind, society, law (and responsibility) do not exist. Rather, it is to say that their existence flows from their being in a (philosophically) suitable ontological relationship with the lower-order, natural base of the world – with the stuff of physics, chemistry, biology, and so on. As the philosopher John Haugeland puts it, 'if you took away all the atoms, nothing would be left behind'.[87] If no physical stuff, then no minds, no societies, no laws, and no responsibility. It is a simple but existentially challenging view of things.[88]

Following on from this ontological stance, philosophical naturalism holds as an epistemic and methodological matter that the best way to come to know about and theorise reality and its myriad phenomena is by means akin to or consistent with the methods which have been found theoretically fruitful in the natural sciences.[89] Quoting one of the most influential figures in the history of philosophical naturalism, WVO Quine, Leiter characterises the naturalistic school of philosophy as that school that recognises 'that it is within science itself, and *not in some prior philosophy*, that reality

[85] Readers looking for an accessible overview of this school of philosophy should find useful J Alexander, *Experimental Philosophy: An Introduction* (Cambridge, Polity Press, 2012).

[86] Poland (n 61) 14–19; D Papineau, *Philosophical Naturalism* (Oxford, Blackwell Publishers, 1993) ch 1; Connolly (n 80) ch 1.

[87] J Haugeland, 'Weak Supervenience' (1982) 19 *American Philosophical Quarterly* 96. Poland (n 61) 15 describes naturalism as the view that 'nothing can exist in the absence of physical things'.

[88] Although, naturalism has the potential to be a highly reductivist view of the world, many of its proponents have sought to mitigate that aspect of it. See, eg, J Kim, *Mind in a Physical World: An Essay on the Mind-Body Problem and Mental Causation* (Cambridge, MIT Press, 1998) 2.

[89] 'With respect to questions about what there is and what we can know, we have nothing better to go on than successful scientific theory': Leiter (n 26) 180.

is to be identified and described'.[90] A properly naturalistic inquiry must repudiate any philosophical approach which 'proceeds entirely a priori, that is, without the benefit of empirical evidence'.[91]

Over the course of the twentieth century, Anglophonic analytic philosophy became more and more 'naturalised' in this sense.[92] Experimental philosophy (or Xphi, as it is commonly referred to these days), which emerged into prominence as a discrete branch of analytic philosophy in the first few years of the twenty-first century, is the culmination of this trend.[93] It is characterised by its attempt to subject the very practice of analytic philosophy itself to a more scientific form of scrutiny.[94]

> Experimental philosophers apply the methods of the social and cognitive sciences to the study of philosophical cognition since these methods are better suited than introspective methods to the study of what people, especially other people, actually think ... In this way, experimental philosophy can both complement more traditional approaches to philosophical questions and help identify ways in which these approaches should be reformed.[95]

By virtue of its reformist agenda, a significant part of Xphi's mission involves the critique of the traditional practices of analytic philosophy.[96] Front and centre as an object of inquiry and critique since the inception of Xphi has been that most non-empirical of analytic philosophy's practices, conceptual analysis. Indeed, the paper generally recognised as originating the Xphi school in 2001 was an inquiry into the nature and alleged universality of philosophical intuitions, one of the core elements of conceptual analysis.[97] For many experimental philosophers this task remains the core task of the school.[98]

Shaun Nichols, one of the authors of the 2001 article said in 2008,

> many of the deepest questions of philosophy can only be properly addressed by immersing oneself in the messy, contingent, highly variable truths about how human beings really are ... Experimental philosophers proceed by conducting experimental investigations of the psychological processes underlying people's intuitions about central philosophical issues. Again and again, these investigations have challenged familiar assumptions, showing that people do not actually think about these issues in anything like the way philosophers had assumed.[99]

[90] Leiter (n 26) 183; WVO Quine, *Theories and Things* (Cambridge, Harvard University Press, 1981) 21.

[91] B Leiter and MX Etchemendy, 'Naturalism in Legal Philosophy' in EN Zalta (ed), *The Stanford Encyclopedia of Philosophy*, (Summer edn, 2017), https://plato.stanford.edu/archives/sum2017/entries/lawphil-naturalism/.

[92] S Soames, *Philosophical Analysis in the Twentieth Century, Volume 1: The Dawn of Analysis* (Princeton, Princeton University Press, 2003); S Soames, *Philosophical Analysis in the Twentieth Century, Volume 2: The Age of Meaning* (Princeton, Princeton University Press, 2003); RD Vitzthum, *Materialism: An Affirmative History and Definition* (New York, Prometheus Books, 1995).

[93] Alexander (n 85); J Knobe and S Nichols (eds) *Experimental Philosophy* (Oxford, Oxford University Press, 2008).

[94] Knobe and Nichols (n 93) ch 1. This aim has called into question whether Xphi is actually a mode of philosophy or a mode of cognitive science: T Sorell, 'Experimental Philosophy and the History of Philosophy' (2018) 26 *British Journal for the History of Philosophy* 829; Knobe and Nichols (n 93) 12–14.

[95] Alexander (n 85) 2.

[96] The so-called 'negative program' in experimental philosophy: Knobe and Nichols (n 93) ch 1.

[97] J Weinberg et al, 'Normativity and Epistemic Intuitions' (2001) 29 *Philosophical Topic* 429.

[98] Its very name, *experimental* philosophy, reveals both its methodological orientation and its adversarial stance towards the methodological orientation similarly revealed in the term *analytic* philosophy.

[99] Knobe and Nichols (n 93) 3.

Already in this comment, the reader may detect traces of Cane's context-based approach to moral phenomena and his critique of any non-contextual 'purist' method of knowing about those phenomena. Yet researching his book in the 1990s for its publication in 2002, Cane did not have the advantage of being able to access Weinberg's 2001 paper on intuitions, let alone the vast body of Xphi literature critical of analytic moral philosophy's method which followed that paper. Cane was arguing a *pre*-Xphi naturalistic case about morality and method. In this respect he comprised part of the philosophical and social scientific tradition Xphi was built upon.[100]

Significant elements of Cane's critique of conceptual analysis, though not themselves empirically grounded, foreshadowed the empirical findings of Xphi. What the findings of Xphi have done for Cane's project of rebutting the hegemonic claim of analytic moral philosophy and legitimating the legal concept of responsibility, is not merely reinforce some of his conclusions but do so in a manner which calls into play the authority of *science* and its method. This is not only an authority of widespread social force but one which no naturalistically minded analytic moral philosopher can argue against effectively, other than by mounting a scientific counterargument of their own.[101]

ii. Xphi on the Metaphysical and Epistemic Capacity Assumptions of Analytic Moral Philosophy

Xphi's project – in its development up to now, at least – has *not* been to engage in a positive naturalistic enquiry into the nature of any moral *phenomena* that might populate the world, à la Cane and the analytic moral philosophers. As mentioned above, its primary brief since its inception has been to bring scientifically legitimate methods to bear on the way in which philosophers and others conceptualise, think about, and come to know such phenomena. It is a theoretical program which combines philosophy with the *sciences* of such concepts, thought, and knowledge, namely, the psychological and cognitive sciences.[102] To the extent that these latter raise issues of gender, class, cultural and ethnic differences in the way people conceptualise and think about the world, Xphi also engages with a range of social sciences.[103]

Consequently, Xphi does not offer *direct* support to Cane's pluralistic metaphysics of responsibility and morality nor to his critique of moral philosophy's monist metaphysics. What it does do, though, is offer *indirect* support to Cane's metaphysical position by virtue of its findings on the pluralistic nature of moral concept possession amongst humans. These findings support Cane's own position on conceptual pluralism within the moral sphere – a position which, we have seen, is deeply entwined with his pluralist metaphysics of moral phenomena.

[100] Sorell (n 94).

[101] Which is, ironically, what some defenders of traditional conceptual analysis have sought to do in response to Xphi's critique. See below on this.

[102] See n 95.

[103] Brian Leiter has commented that if the future of naturalised legal philosophy – or naturalised moral philosophy, for that matter – lies in the direction suggested by experimental philosophers (and he believes it does), then that philosophy may be rendered no more than 'an exercise in sophisticated conceptual ethnography': Leiter (n 26) 6.

One of key findings of Xphi, achieved by means of sound and extensive social scientific testing of actual human thinkers over the past two decades is that there is far more diversity in the content of the moral concepts people hold than analytic philosophers have ever supposed.[104] Most relevantly for our purposes, the evidence suggests that, contrary to the core conceptual theory of analytic moral philosophy, there is *not* one single and universally held concept of responsibility.[105] And this is also the case for a raft of other moral concepts.[106]

Not only has it been shown that across a range of national and sub-national contexts around the world notable differences exist in the contents of ordinary people's moral concepts, but these differences have been shown to track differences in the cultural and ethnic backgrounds and gender of those people. This is to say that different categories of people appear to maintain different concepts of the same moral phenomena – people of different ethnicities, genders, social class, and personality type. Commenting on folk notions of moral character, Alexander says that

> due to the influence of empirical work in moral psychology … it turns out that people behave quite differently in different contexts and that even minor contextual differences can influence our moral and ethical behaviour.[107]

For Cane, analytic moral philosophy's assumption of a single universal content to moral concepts such as responsibility is untenable because Cane holds to a metaphysics of what moral phenomena actually are which is different from and incompatible with that held by those philosophers. As I pointed out above, however, proving to any significant extent the superiority of his metaphysics over theirs was not something Cane sought to do in the book. Consequently, his pluralist metaphysics of moral phenomena and associated pluralistic theory of moral concepts is vulnerable to dismissal by those philosophers, on the grounds that it lacks adequate justification. And because so much of his broader critique of analytic moral philosophy flows from these two positions, that broader critique and its associated defence of judge-made moral concepts are also rendered vulnerable.

Again, what is significant about the research outcomes of the Xphi program in this regard, is that they offer *empirical evidence* for the untenability of the moral philosophers' fundamental assumption of a unified conceptual scheme within the moral realm. They cannot help but contribute to Cane's overall critique of those philosophers' hegemonic claim in this field. They proceed from a metaphysics and set of assumptions – that

[104] This is the point made by Knobe and Nichols (n 93) 3. See also E Nahmias et al, 'Surveying Freedom: Folk Intuitions About Free Will and Moral Responsibility' (2005) 18 *Philosophical Psychology* 561; S Nichols and J Knobe, 'Moral Responsibility and Determinism: The Cognitive Science of Folk Intuitions' (2007) 41 *Noûs* 663.

[105] ibid. See also A Felz and E Cokely, 'An Anomaly in Intentional Action Ascription: More Evidence of Folk Diversity' in D McNamara and J Trafton (eds), *Proceedings of the 29th Annual Cognitive Science Society* (Austin, Cognitive Science Society, 2007).

[106] For example, character traits such as courage, honesty, generosity, and cooperativeness. For a brief overview of the vast literature on this see M Alfano et al, 'Experimental Moral Philosophy' in EN Zalta (ed), *The Stanford Encyclopedia of Philosophy* (Winter edn, 2018), https://plato.stanford.edu/archives/win2018/entries/experimental-moral/.

[107] Alexander (n 85) 5, referring to the research of John Doris, Joel Kupperman, and Edouard Machery, amongst others.

of the natural and empirically rigorous social sciences – which those philosophers are not in a position to deny. Why? Because the core assumptions and methodology of Xphi are more like those of science than those of analytic philosophy.

Additionally, as members of the folk, with their own ethnicities and genders, it follows that moral philosophers themselves are also vulnerable to cultural or gender-based biases in their own moral thinking. And indeed, the empirical engagement of Xphi researchers with diverse sample groups of *philosophers* confirms this to be the case.[108] The results of this particular body of research call into question the credibility of the second of analytic moral philosophy's assumptions identified above – the epistemic status assumption – which claims that analytic philosophers can and do epistemically access those moral and other concepts maintained by all human agents. Not only is there no universal concept of responsibility to be analysed, but even if there were, the evidence shows that there is no universal mental capacity to do any such analysis.

All of this also calls into question the rationale for the first phase of *conceptual analysis* – the calling to mind of globally maintained concepts in order to generate a globally true analysis of them. All that philosophers can reasonably hope to achieve by calling up a concept of responsibility and analysing it out is to improve that version of the concept which they and their own specific conceptual community possess. Any improvement to the content of that concept they might be able to achieve by means of subsequent thought experiments and the application of their intuitions (and even the the objectivity of these comes under pressure from Xphi) will only be of local import or will otherwise be limited. By this research, analytic moral philosophers are denied, then, a substantial degree of justification for thinking that their moral concepts – including their concept of responsibility – are distinctively true and, by virtue of that, *superior* to those utilised by other cohorts of thinkers and theorists (such as judges).

iii. Xphi on the Methodological Assumption of Analytic Moral Philosophy

The critique of the first two assumptions grounding analytic moral philosophy's claim to truth and disciplinary hegemony occasioned by Xphi's findings of a pervasive conceptual pluralism in the moral realm generates, as we have just seen, an associated critique of the rationale and effectiveness of the initial concept-positing phase of that philosophy's method. But it does not stop there. In addition to calling into question the epistemic legitimacy of this first phase, Xphi has, through other credible research, cast doubt on the integrity of the other phases of conceptual analysis.

As mentioned, a significant amount of effort has been expended by Xphi in its experimental inquiries into the nature and epistemic value of human – and specifically, philosophical – *intuitions*. Two key sets of findings have emerged from this research.

[108] See, for example, W Buckwalter, and S Stich, 'Gender and Philosophical Intuition' in J Knobe and S Nichols (eds), *Experimental Philosophy: Volume 2* (Oxford, Oxford University Press, 2014); E Machery et al, 'Semantics, Cross-cultural Style' (2004) 92 *Cognition* 1; J Haidt, and C Joseph, 'Intuitive Ethics: How Innately Prepared Intuitions Generate Culturally Variable Virtues' (2004) *Daedalus* 55 (Special Issue on Human Nature).

The first has provided evidence that certain *personality traits* of those human agents exercising their intuition (including philosophers exercising their intuition in processes of conceptual analysis) regularly and systematically influence the outcomes of that exercise. For example, Feltz and Cokely in their work on whether and how personality differences influence intuitions about free will and moral responsibility found that subjects shown by credible and independent psychological tests to be *extroverts* maintained, as a statistical matter, similar intuitions about these things and that these intuitions differed collectively and statistically from intuitions about these things maintained by subjects shown to be of *introverted* personality.[109]

The second type of finding Xphi has produced in its research into intuitions, relevant to our purposes, is that moral intuitions may be subject not merely to internal personality-based influences but also to external *situational* influences, including the way in which the hypothetical scenario under consideration has been designed by the analyst.[110] Research by Joshua Greene and others in 2008 established that test-subjects' intuitions about whether it was morally wrong to redirect a speeding trolley car from a path on which it would hit five innocent people to a path on which it would hit only one (the infamous 'Trolley Problem'), differed depending on the details of the scenario presented to them. Subjects were more likely to intuit that redirecting the trolley car by pulling a *lever* was morally acceptable than redirecting it by pushing another *person* into the path of the trolley car to derail it – even though in both scenarios fewer people were hurt or killed by the redirection method in question.[111]

One explanation for this difference of intuitions was offered by Greene with reference to MRI brain scans he took of the subjects as they participated in the test. The evidence showed that in the person-pushing scenario a range of powerful emotional responses were activated in subjects' brains which were not activated in response to the lever-based scenario. These emotional responses influenced the relevant subjects' intuitions about moral wrongness in that particular scenario.[112] This evidence had the effect of introducing an additional contingent and potentially non-universal psychological factor into the process of conceptual analysis, thus further undermining its claim to scientific objectivity and effectiveness – *emotion*.

The bottom line here is that an analytic moral philosopher setting out to refine the concept of moral wrongness who idiosyncratically designs their hypothetical testing scenario by including the lever option may have a different intuition and come to a different conclusion about the content of that concept than a philosopher

[109] A Feltz and E Cokely, 'Do Judgments About Freedom and Responsibility Depend on Who You Are? Personality Differences in Intuitions About Compatibilism and Incompatibilism' (2009) 18 *Consciousness and Cognition* 342.

[110] P Singer, 'Ethics and Intuitions' (2005) 9 *Journal of Ethics* 331; W Sinnott-Armstrong, 'Framing Moral Intuitions' in W Sinnott-Armstrong (ed), *Moral Psychology, Volume 2: The Cognitive Science of Morality* (Cambridge, MIT Press, 2008); E Schwitzgebel and F Cushman, 'Expertise in Moral Reasoning? Order Effects on Moral Judgment in Professional Philosophers and Non-philosophers' (2012) 27 *Mind and Language* 135.

[111] J Greene et al, 'An fMRI Investigation of Emotional Engagement in Moral Judgment' (2001) 293 *Science* 2105.

[112] An issue that plays out in moral philosophy as a contest between moral consequentialists and moral deontologists. See S Scheffler, *The Rejection of Consequentialism: A Philosophical Investigation of the Considerations Underlying Rival Moral Conceptions* (Oxford, Clarendon Press, 1993).

(including the same philosopher at a different time) who designs their scenario with the person-pushing option. There are countless ways the basic dilemma the trolley problem seeks to illustrate can be set up, each of them liable to skew in different ways the resultant intuitions of their subjects and any conceptual conclusions reached from those intuitions.

This is all to say that the second and third phases of conceptual analysis are even more interrelated than analytic philosophers have thought up until now and that this interrelatedness only *compounds* the potential for counter-universalist factors to subvert the whole enterprise. And, of course, it also compounds the difficulties advocates of this method face in claiming that it resembles scientific method.

If this line of research holds up then it would appear that when moral philosophers apply their intuitions to hypothetical scenarios within a process of conceptual analysis, it is *not* necessarily the case that they all intuit similarly, let alone in a globally representative manner. Rather, it is possible that by virtue of them possessing different psychological or ethnic profiles or designing their thought experiments differently in some *apparently* insignificant detail, they will intuit differently and conclude quite idiosyncratically their analysis of the concept in question. Either way, the effect of this research is to undermine the objectivity and scientific credibility of the intuition-based phase of analysis and, by extension, any analytic conclusions about the concept in question which rely on that phase.

One final word here on the experimental philosophical program. It is not unchallenged. Not only some scientists but – inevitably – a number of analytic moral philosophers have sought to identify methodological or theoretical flaws in Xphi research and results. Some of these challenges have been successful, leading to the suspension of relevant claims made by Xphi and a return to the drawing board for better designed experiments.[113] Such challenges are not peculiar to the findings of Xphi, however. Since the inception of modern science challenges (even widespread challenges) to novel modes of research and findings – particularly those that call into question deep or long accepted propositions or theories – have been part and parcel of the discipline. For most scientists such challenges are a welcome feature. They keep science honest.[114]

Overall, the Xphi program remains on track, however. Because it is truer to the naturalistic and scientistic urges of contemporary philosophy than that strange hybrid, analytic moral philosophy, Xphi is likely, in my view, to win out ultimately and to revolutionise the discipline of philosophy – moral and otherwise – this century. Of course, the good scientists amongst us should be *appropriately* sceptical about its claims – though perhaps not as sceptical as we should be towards those of analytic moral philosophy.

[113] A Kauppinen, 'The Rise and Fall of Experimental Philosophy' (2007) 10 *Philosophical Explorations* 95; E Sosa, 'Experimental Philosophy and Philosophical Intuition' (2007) 132 *Philosophical Studies* 99; H Kornblith, 'Is There Room for Armchair Theorizing in Epistemology?' in MC Haug (ed), *Philosophical Methodology: The Armchair or the Laboratory*?' (New York, Routledge, 2013) 195–216.

[114] See, for example, Karl Popper's views on this: Popper (n 21).

IV. Conclusion

When Cane wrote *Responsibility in Law and Morality*, he did not have access to those resources in support of his case which experimental philosophy subsequently provided. Despite this, the case he *was* able to argue in the book remains a good one – in its dialectical quality, in its philosophical literacy, and in its rationale. I take that rationale to be the enrichment of the moral discourse and moral lives of experts and ordinary people alike, by identifying and clarifying for them a previously unknown or unfairly disregarded body of ideas and applications. It is ironic that, of all things, it should be analytic philosophy, in the guise of its subversive young offspring Xphi, which offers Cane's original project not only retrospective support but a basis for its renewed pursuit into the future.

LIST OF PETER CANE'S PUBLICATIONS

Books

F Trindade and P Cane, *The Law of Torts in Australia* (Melbourne, Oxford University Press, 1985)

P Cane, *An Introduction to Administrative Law* (Oxford, Clarendon Press, 1986)

P Cane, *Atiyah's Accidents, Compensation and the Law*, 4th edn (London, Weidenfeld and Nicolson, 1987)

P Cane, *Tort Law and Economic Interests* (Oxford, Clarendon Press, 1991)

P Cane, *An Introduction to Administrative Law*, 2nd edn (Oxford, Clarendon Press, 1992)

P Cane, *Atiyah's Accidents, Compensation and the Law*, 5th edn (London, Butterworths, 1993)

F Trindade and P Cane, *The Law of Torts in Australia*, 2nd edn (Melbourne, Oxford University Press, 1993)

P Cane, *An Introduction to Administrative Law*, 3rd edn (Oxford, Clarendon Press, 1996)

P Cane, *Tort Law and Economic Interests*, 2nd edn (Oxford, Clarendon Press 1996)

P Cane, *The Anatomy of Tort Law* (Oxford, Hart Publishing, 1997)

P Cane, *Atiyah's Accidents, Compensation and the Law*, 6th edn (Cambridge, Cambridge University Press, 1999)

F Trindade and P Cane, *The Law of Torts in Australia*, 3rd edn (Melbourne, Oxford University Press, 1999)

P Cane, *Responsibility in Law and Morality* (Oxford, Hart Publishing, 2002)

P Cane, *An Introduction to Administrative Law*, 4th edn (Oxford, Clarendon Press, 2004)

P Cane, *Atiyah's Accidents, Compensation and the Law*, 7th edn (Cambridge, Cambridge University Press, 2006)

P Cane, *The Political Economy of Personal Injury Law* (Brisbane, University of Queensland Press, 2007)

F Trindade, P Cane and M Lunney, *The Law of Torts in Australia*, 4th edn (Melbourne, Oxford University Press, 2007)

P Cane and L McDonald, *Principles of Administrative Law: Legal Regulation of Governance* (Melbourne, Oxford University Press, 2008)

P Cane, *Administrative Tribunals and Adjudication* (Oxford, Hart Publishing, 2009)

P Cane and L McDonald, *Cases and Materials for Principles of Administrative Law: Legal Regulation of Governance* (Melbourne, Oxford University Press, 2009)

P Cane, *Administrative Law*, 5th edn, (Oxford, Oxford University Press, 2011)

K Barker, P Cane, M Lunney and F Trindade, *The Law of Torts in Australia*, 5th edn (Melbourne, Oxford University Press, 2012)
P Cane and L McDonald, *Principles of Administrative Law: Legal Regulation of Governance*, 2nd edn (Melbourne, Oxford University Press, 2012)
P Cane, *Atiyah's Accidents, Compensation and the Law*, 8th edn (Cambridge, Cambridge University Press, 2013)
P Cane and L McDonald, *Cases and Materials for Principles of Administrative Law: Legal Regulation of Governance*, 2nd edn (Melbourne, Oxford University Press, 2013)
P Cane, *Controlling Administrative Power: An Historical Comparison* (Cambridge, Cambridge University Press, 2016)
P Cane, *Key Ideas in Tort Law* (Oxford, Hart Publishing, 2017)
P Cane and J Goudkamp, *Atiyah's Accidents, Compensation and the Law*, 9th edn (Cambridge, Cambridge University Press, 2018)
P Cane, L McDonald and K Rundle, *Cases for Principles of Administrative Law*, 3rd edn (Melbourne, Oxford University Press, 2018)
P Cane, L McDonald and K Rundle, *Principles of Administrative Law*, 3rd edn (Melbourne, Oxford University Press, 2018)

Edited Books

P Cane and J Stapleton (eds), *Essays for Patrick Atiyah* (Oxford, Oxford University Press, 1991)
P Cane and J Stapleton (eds), *The Law of Obligations: Essays in Celebration of John Fleming* (Oxford, Oxford University Press, 1998)
P Cane and J Gardner (eds), *Relating to Responsibility: Essays in Honour of Tony Honoré on his 80th Birthday* (Oxford, Hart Publishing, 2001)
P Cane (ed), *Administrative Law* (Aldershot, Ashgate Dartmouth, 2002)
P Cane and M Tushnet (eds), *The Oxford Handbook of Legal Studies* (Oxford, Oxford University Press, 2003)
P Cane (ed), *Centenary Essays for the High Court of Australia* (Sydney, LexisNexis Butterworths, 2004)
P Cane and J Conaghan (eds), *The New Oxford Companion to Law* (Oxford, Oxford University Press, 2008)
P Cane, C Evans and Z Robinson (eds), *Law and Religion in Theoretical and Historical Perspective* (Cambridge, Cambridge University Press, 2008)
P Cane (ed), *The Hart-Fuller Debate in the Twenty-First Century* (Oxford, Hart Publishing, 2010)
P Cane and H Kritzer (eds), *The Oxford Handbook of Empirical Legal Research* (Oxford, Oxford University Press, 2010)
P Cane, H Hoffmann, E Ip and P Lindseth (eds), *The Oxford Handbook of Comparative Administrative Law* (Oxford, Oxford University Press, 2020)
P Cane, L Ford and M McMillan (eds), *The Cambridge Legal History of Australia* (Cambridge, Cambridge University Press, 2022)
P Cane and H Kumarasingham (eds), *The Cambridge Constitutional History of the United Kingdom* (Cambridge, Cambridge University Press, 2022)

Articles

P Cane, 'Injuries to Unborn Children' (1977) 51 *Australian Law Journal* 704
P Cane, 'Recovery for Purely Economic Loss in the High Court' [1977] *University of Western Australia Law Review* 243
P Cane, 'Physical Loss, Economic Loss and Products Liability' (1979) 95 *LQR* 117
P Cane, 'Economic Loss and the Tort of Negligence' (1980) 12 *Melbourne University Law Review* 408
P Cane, 'A Fresh Look at Punton's Case' (1980) 43 *MLR* 266
P Cane, 'The Function of Standing Rules in Administrative Law' [1980] *PL* 303
P Cane, 'Prerogative Acts, Acts of State Justiciability' (1980) 29 *International and Comparative Law Quarterly* 680
P Cane, 'The Metes and Bounds of Hedley Byrne' (1981) 55 *Australian Law Journal* 862
P Cane, 'Standing, Legality and the Limits of Public Law' [1981] *PL* 322
P Cane, 'Standing to Protect the Environment' (1981) 1 *OJLS* 142
P Cane, 'Justice and Justifications for Tort Liability' (1982) 2 *OJLS* 30
P Cane and DR Harris, 'Administration of Justice Act 1982, Section 4(2): A Lesson in how not to Reform the Law' (1983) 46 *MLR* 478
P Cane, 'Negligence, Economic Interests and the Assessment of Damages' (1984) 10 *Monash University Law Review* 17
P Cane, 'Self Regulation and Judicial Review' [1987] *Civil Justice Quarterly* 324
P Cane, 'Economic Loss in Tort: Is the Pendulum out of Control?' (1989) 52 *MLR* 200
P Cane, 'Liability Rules and the Cost of Professional Indemnity Insurance' (1989) 14 *Geneva Papers on Risk and Insurance* 347
P Cane, 'The Law Commission on Judicial Review' (1993) 56 *MLR* 887
P Cane, 'Economic Loss in Contract and Tort' (1994) 58 *Rabels Zeitschrift* 430
P Cane, 'The Liability of Classification Societies' [1994] *Lloyd's Maritime and Commercial Law Quarterly* 363
P Cane, 'Standing Up for the Public' [1995] *PL* 276
P Cane, 'Fleming on Torts: A Short Intellectual History' (1998) 6 *Torts Law Journal* 216
P Cane, 'Damages in Public Law' (1999) 3 *Otago Law Review* 489
P Cane, 'Multiple Torts, Contribution and the Dynamics of the Settlement Process' (1999) 7 *Torts Law Journal* 137
P Cane, 'Open Standing and the Role of Courts in a Democratic Society' (1999) 20 *Singapore Law Review* 23
P Cane, 'The Blight of Economic Loss: Is There Life after *Perre v Apand*?' (2000) 8 *Torts Law Journal* 246
P Cane, 'Fleeting Mental States' (2000) 59 *CLJ* 273
P Cane, 'Indemnizacion por danos medioambientales' (2000) 3 *Anuario de Derecho Civil* 825
P Cane, 'Mens Rea in Tort Law' (2000) 20 *OJLS* 533
P Cane, 'Merits Review and Judicial Review: The AAT as Trojan Horse' (2000) 28 *Federal Law Review* 213
P Cane, 'Are Environmental Harms Special?' (2001) 13 *Journal of Environmental Law* 3
P Cane, 'Distributive Justice and Tort Law' [2001] *New Zealand Law Review* 401

P Cane, 'Tort Law as Regulation' (2002) 31 *Common Law World Review* 305
P Cane, 'Using Tort Law to Enforce Environmental Regulations?' (2002) 41 *Washburn Law Journal* 427
P Cane, 'The Making of Australian Administrative Law' (2003) 24 *Australian Bar Review* 114
P Cane, 'Reforming Tort Law in Australia: A Personal Perspective' (2003) 27 *Melbourne University Law Review* 649
P Cane, 'The Anatomy of Private Law Theory: A 25th Anniversary Essay' (2005) 25 *OJLS* 203
P Cane, 'On the Division of Law-Making Labour' (2005) 8 *The Judicial Review* 211
P Cane, 'Taking Disagreement Seriously: Courts, Legislatures and the Reform of Tort Law' (2005) 25 *OJLS* 393
P Cane, 'Imagining Public Law' (2006) 31 *Australian Journal of Legal Philosophy* 153
P Cane, 'Taking Law Seriously: Starting Points of the Hart/Devlin Debate' (2006) 10 *Journal of Ethics* 21
P Cane, 'The General/Special Distinction in Criminal Law, Tort Law and Legal Theory' (2007) 26 *Law and Philosophy* 465
P Cane, 'Two Understandings of Morality and their Relationship to Politics' (2008) *Criminal Justice Ethics* 34
P Cane, 'Judicial Review in the Age of Tribunals' [2009] *PL* 479
P Cane, 'Participation and Constitutionalism' (2010) 38 *Federal Law Review* 319
P Cane, 'Searching for United States Tort Law in the Antipodes' (2011) 38 *Pepperdine Law Review* 101
P Cane, 'Morality, Law and Conflicting Reasons for Action' (2012) 71 *CLJ* 59
P Cane, 'Public Law in The Concept of Law' (2013) 33 *OJLS* 649
P Cane, 'Reconceptualising Separation of Powers' (2015) 101 *Amicus Curiae* 2
P Cane, 'Records, Reasons and Rationality in Judicial Control of Administrative Power: England, the US and Australia' (2015) 48 *Israel Law Review* 1
P Cane, 'Two Conceptions of Constitutional Rights' (2015) 8 *Insights* 1
P Cane, 'Role Responsibility' (2016) 20 *The Journal of Ethics* 279
P Cane, 'Executive Primacy, Populism, and Public Law' (2019) 28 *Washington International Law Journal* 527
P Cane, 'The Resurgence of Executive Primacy in the Age of Populism: Introduction to the Symposium' (2019) 28 *Washington International Law Journal* 311

Book Chapters

P Cane, 'Contract, Tort and Economic Loss' in M Furmston (ed), *The Law of Tort: Policy and Trends in Liability for Damage to Property and Economic Loss* (London, Duckworth, 1986)
P Cane, 'Economic Loss and Products Liability' in CJ Miller (ed), *Comparative Product Liability* (London, British Institute of International and Comparative Law, 1986)
P Cane, 'Public Law and Private Law: A Study of the Analysis and Use of a Legal Concept' in J Bell and J Eekelaar (eds), *Oxford Essays in Jurisprudence, Third Series* (Oxford, Clarendon Press, 1987)

P Cane, 'The Basis of Tortious Liability' in P Cane and J Stapleton (eds), *Essays for Patrick Atiyah* (Oxford, Clarendon Press, 1991)
P Cane, 'The Limits of Judicial Review' in P Birks and J Beatson (eds), *The Frontiers of Liability*, vol 1 (Oxford, Oxford University Press, 1994)
P Cane, 'Standing, Representation and the Environment' in I Loveland (ed), *A Special Relationship? American Influences on Public Law in the UK* (Oxford, Clarendon Press, 1995)
P Cane, 'Contract, Tort and the Lloyd's Debacle' in F Rose (ed), *Consensus ad Idem: Essays on the Law of Contract in Honour of Guenter Treitel* (London, Sweet & Maxwell, 1996)
P Cane, 'Exceptional Measures of Damages: A Search for Principles' in P Birks (ed), *Wrongs and Remedies in the 21st Century* (Oxford, Clarendon Press, 1996)
P Cane, 'The Constitutional Basis of Judicial Remedies in Public Law' in P Leyland and T Woods (eds), *Administrative Law Facing the Future: Old Constraints and New Horizons* (London, Blackstone, 1997)
P Cane, 'The Constitutional and Legal Framework of Policy-Making' in C Forsyth and I Hare (eds), *The Golden Metwand and the Crooked Cord: Essays on Public Law in Honour of Sir William Wade* (Oxford, Oxford University Press, 1998)
P Cane, 'Retribution, Proportionality and Moral Luck in Tort Law' in P Cane and J Stapleton (eds), *The Law of Obligations: Essays in Celebration of John Fleming* (Oxford, Clarendon Press, 1998)
P Cane, 'Fault and Strict Liability for Harm in Tort Law' in W Swadling (ed), *The Search for Principle: Essays for Lord Goff of Chieveley* (Oxford, Oxford University Press, 1999)
P Cane, 'Consequences in Judicial Reasoning' in J Horder (ed), *Oxford Essays in Jurisprudence, Fourth Series* (Oxford, Oxford University Press, 2000)
P Cane, 'Mens Rea in Tort Law' in N Naffine, R Owens and J Williams (eds), *Intention in Law and Philosophy* (Aldershot, Ashgate, 2001)
P Cane, 'Proximity' in T Blackshield, M Coper and G Williams (eds), *The Oxford Companion to the High Court of Australia* (Melbourne, Oxford University Press, 2001) 570
P Cane, 'Responsibility and Fault: A Relational and Functional Approach to Responsibility' in P Cane and J Gardner (eds), *Relating to Responsibility: Essays in Honour of Tony Honoré on his 80th Birthday* (Oxford, Hart Publishing, 2001)
P Cane, 'Introduction' in P Cane (ed), *Administrative Law* (Aldershot, Ashgate Dartmouth, 2002)
P Cane, 'Accountability and the Public/Private Distinction' in N Bamforth and P Leyland (eds), *Public Law in a Multi-Layered Constitution* (Oxford, Hart Publishing 2003)
P Cane, 'Review of Executive Action' in P Cane and M Tushnet (eds), *The Oxford Handbook of Legal Studies* (Oxford, Oxford University Press, 2003)
P Cane, 'Theory and Values in Public Law' in P Craig and R Rawlings (eds), *Law and Administration in Europe: Essays in Honour of Carol Harlow* (Oxford, Oxford University Press, 2003)
P Cane, 'Administrative Law as Regulation' in J Braithwaite, N Lacey, C Parker and C Scott (eds), *Regulating Law* (Oxford, Oxford University Press, 2004)

P Cane, 'The Making of Australian Administrative Law' in P Cane (ed), *Centenary Essays for the High Court of Australia* (Sydney, LexisNexis Butterworths, 2004)
P Cane, 'Understanding Judicial Review and its Impact' in M Hertogh and S Halliday (eds), *Judicial Review and its Bureaucratic Impact: International and Interdisciplinary Dimensions* (Cambridge, Cambridge University Press, 2004)
P Cane, 'Autonomy of Law' and 'Morality and Law' in DS Clark (ed), *Encyclopedia of Law and Society: American and Global Perspectives* (Los Angeles, Sage Publications, 2007)
P Cane, 'General and Special Tort Law: Uses (and Abuses) of Theory' in JW Neyers, E Chamberlain and SGA Pitel (eds), *Emerging Issues in Tort Law* (Oxford, Hart Publishing, 2007)
P Cane, 'Taking Disagreement Seriously: Courts, Legislatures and the Reform of Tort Law' in M Bryan (ed), *Private Law in Theory and Practice* (London, Routledge-Cavendish, 2007)
P Cane, 'Fault-based Civil Liability', 'NHS Litigation Authority', 'Strict Civil Liability', 'Natural Justice', 'Responsibility', 'Administrative Law', 'Negligence in Civil Law', 'Westminster System' in P Cane and J Conaghan (eds), *The New Oxford Companion to Law* (Oxford, Oxford University Press, 2008)
P Cane, 'Understanding Administrative Adjudication' in L Pearson, C Harlow and M Taggart (eds), *Administrative Law in a Changing State: Essays in Honour of Mark Aronson* (Oxford, Hart Publishing, 2008)
P Cane, 'Judicial Review in the Age of Tribunals' in C Forsyth et al (eds), *Effective Judicial Review: A Cornerstone of Good Governance* (Oxford, Oxford University Press, 2010)
P Cane, 'Judicial Review and Merits Review: Comparing Administrative Adjudication by Courts and Tribunals' in S Rose-Ackerman and PL Lindseth, *Comparative Administrative Law* (Cheltenham, Edward Elgar, 2010)
P Cane, 'Participation and Constitutionalism' in C Charters and D Knight (eds), *We The People(s)* (Wellington, Victoria University Press, 2011)
P Cane, 'Rights in Private Law' in D Nolan and A Robertson (eds), *Rights and Private Law* (Oxford, Hart Publishing, 2011)
P Cane, 'Tort Law and Public Functions' in J Oberdiek (ed), *Philosophical Foundations of the Law of Torts* (Oxford, Oxford University Press, 2014)
P Cane, 'Judicial Control of Administrative Interpretation in Australia and the United States' in H Wilberg and M Elliott (eds), *The Scope and Intensity of Substantive Review: Traversing Taggart's Rainbow* (Oxford, Hart Publishing, 2015)
P Cane, 'The Tort Liability of Public Authorities: A Comparative Analysis' in A Robertson and M Tilbury (eds), *The Common Law of Obligations: Divergence and Unity* (Oxford, Hart Publishing, 2016)
P Cane, 'A Framework for Historical Comparison of Control of National, Supranational and Transnational Public Power' in S Rose-Ackerman, PL Lindseth and B Emerson (eds), *Comparative Administrative Law*, 2nd edn (Cheltenham, Edward Elgar, 2017)
P Cane, 'Tort Law and Government Liability in the Administrative State' in K Barker et al (eds), *Private Law and Power* (Oxford, Hart Publishing, 2017)

P Cane, 'The Common Law, the High Court of Australia and the United States Supreme Court' in P Daly (ed), *Apex Courts and the Common Law* (Toronto, University of Toronto Press, 2019)
P Cane, 'Law, Fact and Process in Common Law Tort Scholarship' in J Goudkamp and D Nolan (eds), *Scholars of Tort Law* (Oxford, Hart Publishing, 2019)

Notes

P Cane, 'The Liability of Builders and Surveyors for Negligence' (1974) 7 *Sydney Law Review* 284
P Cane, 'Contracts of Carriage and Exemption Clauses' (1977) 51 *Australian Law Journal* 841
P Cane, 'Recovery for Purely Economic Loss in Australia' (1977) 93 *LQR* 333
P Cane, 'Civil Liability Under the Consumer Safety Act (UK)' (1979) 3 *Journal of Products Liability* 215
P Cane, 'Deterrence and Strict Liability for Defective Products' (1979) 3 *Journal of Products Liability* 135
P Cane, 'Unsafe Products and the State of the Art' (1979) 3 *Journal of Products Liability* 239
P Cane, 'The Fleet Street Casuals' (1980) 96 *LQR* 355
P Cane, 'Natural Justice and Legitimate Expectations' (1980) 54 *Australian Law Journal* 546
P Cane, 'Negligent Solicitors and Disappointed Beneficiaries' (1980) 96 *LQR* 182
P Cane, 'Ultra Vires Breach of Statutory Duty' [1981] *PL* 11
P Cane, 'Valuation of Shares in the Law of Torts' [1982] *Journal of Business Law* 79
P Cane, 'Negligent Solicitors and Doubly Disappointed Beneficiaries' (1983) 99 *LQR* 346
P Cane, 'Public Law and Private Law: Some Thoughts Prompted by *Page Motors Ltd v Epsom & Ewell BC*' [1983] *PL* 202
P Cane, 'Public Law and Private Law Again: *Davy* v *Spelthorne BC*' [1984] *PL* 16
P Cane, 'Statutes, Standing and Representation' [1990] *PL* 307
P Cane, 'Negligent Solicitor Escapes Liability' (1992) 108 *LQR* 539
P Cane, 'Private Rights and Public Procedure' [1992] *PL* 193
P Cane, 'The Scope and Justification for Exemplary Damages' (1993) 5 *Journal of Environmental Law* 163
P Cane, 'Do Banks Dare Lend to Local Authorities?' (1994) 110 *LQR* 514
P Cane, 'The Changing Fortunes of *Rylands* v. *Fletcher*' (1994) 24 *Western Australia University Law Review* 237
P Cane, 'Classification Societies, Cargo Owners and the Basis of Tort Liability' [1995] *Lloyd's Maritime and Commercial Law Quarterly* 433
P Cane, 'The Inexorable Advance of Negligence' (1995) 3 *Torts Law Journal* 205
P Cane, 'Tortious Interference with Contractual Remedies' (1995) 111 *LQR* 400
P Cane, 'Suing Public Authorities in Tort' (1996) 112 *LQR* 13

P Cane, 'What a Nuisance!' (1997) 113 *LQR* 515
P Cane, 'A Warning About Causation' (1999) 115 *LQR* 21
P Cane, 'The Scope of Malicious Prosecution' (2000) 116 *LQR* 346
P Cane, 'Vicarious Liability for Sexual Abuse' (2000) 116 *LQR* 21
P Cane, 'The Temporal Element in Law' (2001) 117 *LQR* 5
P Cane, 'Causing Conversion' (2002) 118 *LQR* 544
P Cane, 'Another Failed Sterilisation' (2004) 120 *LQR* 189
P Cane, 'Author's Introduction in Book Symposium: Peter Cane Responsibility in Law and Morality' (2004) 29 *Australian Journal of Legal Philosophy* 160
P Cane, 'Author's Response to the Commentators in Book Symposium: Peter Cane Responsibility in Law and Morality' (2004) 29 *Australian Journal of Legal Philosophy* 185
P Cane, 'Church, State and Human Rights: Are Parish Councils Public Authorities?' (2004) 120 *LQR* 41
P Cane, 'The Doctor, the Stork and the Court: A Modern Morality Play' (2004) 120 *LQR* 23
P Cane, 'The New Face of Advocates' Immunity' (2005) 13 *Torts Law Journal* 93
P Cane, 'Outsourcing Administrative Adjudication' (2010) 126 *LQR* 343

Reviews

P Cane, 'The Constitutional Case Law of Japan' [1979] *PL* 100
P Cane, 'Compensation and Government Torts' [1983] *PL* 499
P Cane, 'The Attorney General, Politics and the Public Interest' (1985) 36 *Northern Ireland Legal Quarterly* 175
P Cane, 'Commonwealth Administrative Law' (1986) 45 *Australian Journal of Public Administration* 181
P Cane, 'Administrative Law' (1987) 38 *Northern Ireland Legal Quarterly* 370
P Cane, 'Governmental Liability: A Comparative Study' (1992) 108 *LQR* 509
P Cane, 'European Administrative Law' (1993) 109 *LQR* 143
P Cane, 'Markets and Morals in Contract and Tort' (1993) 13 *LS* 396
P Cane, 'Tort Liability for Psychiatric Damage' (1993) 23 *Western Australia University Law Review* 378
P Cane, 'The Wrongs of Tort' (1993) 7 *Society of Public Teachers of Law Reporter* 30
P Cane, 'Corrective Justice and Correlativity in Private Law' (1996) 16 *OJLS* 471
P Cane, 'Economic Loss' [1999] *Professional Negligence* 131
P Cane, 'State Liability in Tort: A Comparative Law Study' (2003) 23 *LS* 711
P Cane, 'Philosophy and the Law of Torts' (2004) 114 *Ethics* 368
P Cane, 'Consent in the Law' [2007] *Law and Politics Book Review* 577
P Cane, 'Torts, Egalitarianism and Distributive Justice' (2008) 16 *Torts Law Journal* 75
P Cane, 'Torts and Rights' (2008) 71 *MLR* 641

P Cane, 'Faith, Reason and Consent: Legislating Morality in Early American States' [2009] *Law and Politics Book Review* 50

P Cane, 'A Simple Common Lawyer: Essays in Honour of Michael Taggart' (2009) 37 *Federal Law Review* 159

P Cane, 'The Ombudsman Enterprise and Administrative Justice' (2011) 70 *Australian Journal of Public Administration* 332

P Cane, 'What is Private Law?' [2011] *Law and Politics Book Review* 581

P Cane, 'Informal Carers and Private Law' [2014] *Law and Politics Book Review* 34

P Cane, 'Judicialization of Politics: The Interplay of Institutional Structure, Legal Doctrine, and Politics on the High Court of Australia' [2014] *Law and Politics Law Review* 110

P Cane, 'Law in Politics, Politics in Law' [2016] *PL* 348

P Cane, 'Constitutional Recognition of First Peoples in Australia: Theories and Comparative Perspectives' (2017) 41 *Aboriginal History* 221

P Cane, 'Indigenous Australians, Social Justice and Legal Reform: Honouring Elliott Johnson' (2017) 41 *Aboriginal History* 221

P Cane, 'Treaty and Statehood: Aboriginal Self-Determination' (2017) 41 *Aboriginal History* 221

P Cane, 'The Liability of Public Authorities in Comparative Perspective' (2018) 9 *Journal of European Tort Law* 236

P Cane, 'Vigilance and Restraint in the Common Law of Judicial Review' (2019) 82 *MLR* 200

P Cane, 'Context, Context Everywhere' (2020) 16 *International Journal of Law in Context* 459

Government Reports

D Ipp, P Cane, I Macintosh and D Sheldon, *Review of the Law of Negligence* (Commonwealth of Australia, Canberra, 2002)

INDEX

Lightning Source UK Ltd.
Milton Keynes UK
UKHW020402140622
404395UK00003B/47

9 781509 940721